The Whole Word Catalogue 2

edited by
Bill Zavatsky
Ron Padgett

Published in association with Teachers & Writers Collaborative

McGraw-Hill Paperbacks

New York	St. Louis	San Francisco	Auckland	Bogotá
Düsseldorf	Johannesburg	London	Madrid	Mexico
Montreal	New Delhi	Panama	Paris	São Paulo
Singapore	Sydney	Tokyo	Toronto	

Teachers & Writers Collaborative is grateful for assistance in the preparation of materials for this book to the National Endowment for the Arts and to the New York State Council on the Arts.

First McGraw-Hill Paperback Edition, 1977

123456789 BABA 7987

Library of Congress Cataloging in Publication Data

Teachers & Writers Collaborative.
  Whole word catalogue 2.

  1. Creative writing (Elementary education)
I.   Padgett, Ron.   II.   Zavatsky, Bill   III. Title
LB1576.T37 1977   372.6'23   76-56387
ISBN 0-07-063239-1

ISBN 0-07-063239-1

Contents

Introduction

by Bill Zavatsky

Something is afoot in this collection.

Unlike the materials assembled in *The Whole Word Catalogue* that preceded this volume, lines are now being drawn between the "quickie" or "gimmick" assignment and a more philosophical outlook about the role of imaginative doing in education. That is, writers who have been working in the schools are moving away, to some extent, from neatly packaged formulas and towards wider-ranging ideas that often take weeks of work to execute.

This development could have been predicted because it is exactly that, a development of the evolutionary sort, a movement by natural processes of thought from one-celled organisms (the self-contained writing idea) into experiments that demand essay scope. This evolution, I would also say, is the peculiar bailiwick of the Teachers & Writers Collaborative. From the beginning the group has made it possible for a writer or artist to stay in one school, often working with the same students and teachers for a period of years. In this rooted but never static situation, an artist has the growing space to try out new ideas, and to deal with experiences that defy capture in an hour, an hour that is more properly the habitat of the formula. The "artist-in-residence" position furnished by Teachers & Writers and the welcoming school also moves the poet or painter closer to the actual circumstances of the classroom teacher—an arrangement time has proven to be mutually beneficial.

But not so fast. What we term "gimmicks" in this book—those read - it - before - class - then - do - it assignments—haven't outlived their usefulness. While many of them can be picked up and never returned to, the "quickies" bear a relation to the larger events in the imaginative landscape of this collection that is continually made evident. (The "I remember" assignment, for example, can be brought to bear on the entire concept of memory in general, to the nature of the mental image itself, and thus to the examination of the fantasy or dream.)

Another new development in arts education is also made manifest in these pages, though it is nothing new to the artists themselves, who are notorious boundary-crossers. The ability to stay in one school for an extended period of time has made writers curious about filmmaking, filmmakers interested in writing, and for the past few years pens have been exchanged for video cameras, paintbrushes for typewriters. All of the talk about "integrated arts curriculums" and hothouse forcings via educational conferences are put to shame by the experiments of Teachers & Writers workers. It "just happens." And the reason it happens is because the students want it to happen.

In this collection, the heart of the Teachers & Writers Collaborative enterprise is laid bare. Its essense consists in the desire and in the ability to listen, and having listened with complete attention, to act. The non-TWC artists who have contributed to the making of this book work from similar impulses. The more personal education becomes, the more likely it is to produce persons.

How to Use This Book

Leaf through it, by all means! Read it on the bus, the subway, before you go to bed at night. Begin at the beginning and read it through to the end. Begin at the last page and work back to this Introduction. Find topics that interest you, and use them as you will. Feel free to disagree, get angry, be overwhelmed at the brilliant insight of, astounded at the lack of understanding exhibited in, pleased with the practical, tantalized by the theoretical, laughing crazy at the whimsical.

Discard whatever seems useless or wrongheaded. Use what seems sound. Write us and tell us what you like and what didn't work at all. Suggest improvements, rearrangements, additions, subtractions. We're not perfect, God, Mammon, the Secretary of Health, Education and Welfare, Aristotle, Skeezix, Steve McQueen, or Greta Garbo. How will we ever know if you don't tell us?

Actually, this book is a masterpiece. There is nothing like it in educational literature. Never have the ruminations, methods, and opinions of artists and writers working in the schools been gathered into such a compendium. If used in conjunction with the first *Whole Word Catalogue*, *The Whole Word Catalogue 2* is Son of Kong!

To tell the truth, it's as good as the use you make of it!

I and my co-editor would like to thank the following people whose brains, diligence, and persistence made this book a reality:

Steve Schrader, boss and *mensch* and yea-sayer; the staff of Teachers and Writers Collaborative: Nancy Larson, whose eyes, suggestions, and index are sharp as a tack; Neil Colbert, for reading proofs; Laura Gilpin, for outlining us out of madness; Miguel Ortiz, who put it all together so beautifully; Adalberto Ortiz, of the stellar pencils; Sue Willis, who helped organize it; Mary Graves; Phillip Lopate; the contributors who gave their hard-won knowledge generously; Joanne Dolinar of McGraw-Hill, for her enthusiastic reception; and Leonard Randolph, director of the Literature Program of the National Endowment for the Arts, for his continuing support of projects of this kind.

1. Teaching Writing

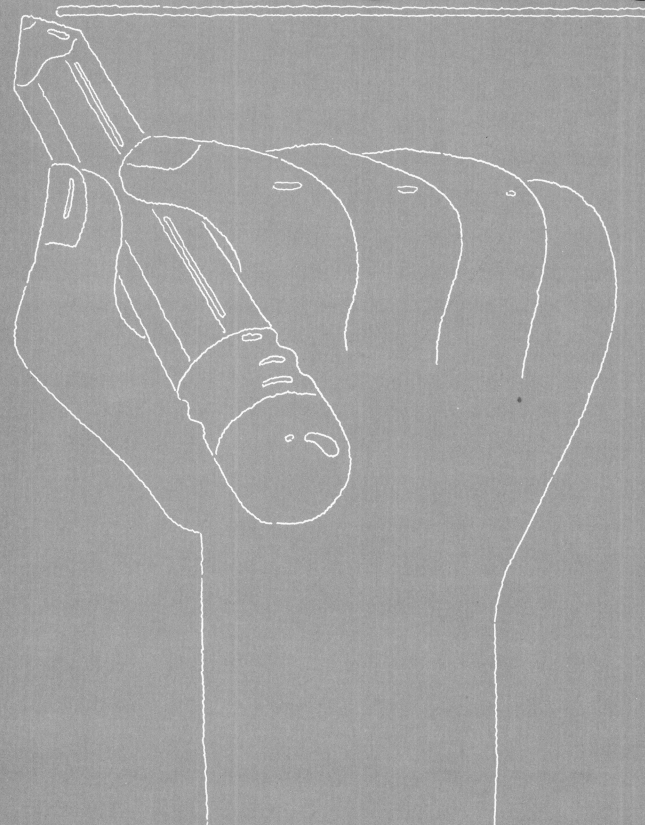

Everything You Always Wanted to Know About Poetry

by Bill Zavatsky

I

Perhaps the last time you really came into close contact with poetry was for a college or graduate school term paper. You haven't had the time or the inclination to "keep up" with poetry since then, and have found yourself avoiding the teaching of it, if you can, or gritting your teeth through the "poetry unit" when it rolls around each year. Most teachers I've met and worked with are in the same boat. Oh, they like poetry well enough, but their raids into twentieth century verse inevitably send them back to those few dependable poems neatly compartmentalized in the school textbooks.

That the art of poetry has become little more than "filler" in school texts—like those odd items wedged in the daily paper that report hailstones the size of cannonballs in Missoula—is such a truism that it's boring to discuss. For most teachers (and for nearly all students) The Poem has become a sideshow item, a species of literary anomaly one walks past with eyes half-turned away, muttering "How interesting. . . ."

How this happened to poetry remains a debatable and complicated question, and I don't think anyone has really confronted it in print. Literary critics write for university professors, poets don't really want to acknowledge the situation (and most couldn't talk about it if they wanted to), and the teacher trying to make sense of what went awry between "Oh Captain, My Captain" and *The Waste Land* shakes his or her head and makes a beeline for the Big Top—prose. There, at least, things usually make sense. The aerialists continue to be daring, the elephants charming, the acrobats skillful, and the clowns are permitted their bouts of controlled nonsense. Little resembles the odd and inexplicable world we have thankfully escaped, of giants, transparent ladies, seal-boys, and half-men/half-women. Like the predictable pleasures of the main arena, school anthology prose whisks away those discomfiting freaks of poetry. Reality,

good old sentence-by-sentence reality, assumes its rightful place in the spotlight. What a relief to understand what the writer is talking about, what he *means*! As for poetry, why, we can always take refuge in the classics. What we forget is that Shelley and Byron and Keats were legendary freaks in their own time, generally impaled by critics and deemed incomprehensible. Time, which tames all but the wildest of lions, has tamed them, too. The poetry of all but the very greatest of poets (and I include the three writers I have just mentioned in that company) eventually turns into a kind of prose. Certainly the bad poetry of great poets does. But great poetry is like Blake's tyger—untamable. From its burning eye we flee, and usually our flight is a retreat into meaning.

Contemporary poetry, that is, poetry written by living poets or written in the recent past, is the biggest headache of all. And the biggest complaint about it is: "I can't figure out what this poet is talking about. What does this *mean*?" The Hunt for the Meaning has become institutionalized as "Appreciation of Poetry 101." Year after year this goes on, until finally (somewhere in college) we are confronted with that terror of terrors, that event we always feared would happen: the poem has grown so complicated, so ornery, that we find it impossible to put together what we have so industriously "analyzed." We give up! What a relief, what a fantastically lucky breakdown! Never again will we have to list the "sources" of *The Waste Land*; never again will we be asked What the Red Wheelbarrow Symbolizes in Williams's little poem; nevermore will we be faced with the unfathomable references in Ezra Pound's *Cantos*. It is finished, thank God! We have graduated!

From the poet's end of it, this Hunt for the Symbol means the death of poetry. Would you discuss the movements of a ballerina by taking your students to an anatomy class and have them watch leg muscles being dissected? It might help to understand the twists and turns, but dead parts don't get up and dance. Neither does the poem after autopsy. The poetry-by-autopsy method may be seen in action in any high school English class studying Shakespeare. The Bard is picked clean, and *Hamlet*, the fierce and philosophical dramatic poem, crashes to the stage on a pile of bones, all curiously resembling scansion marks. Shakespeare has died more deaths than any of his bloody characters, either because he wrote in iambic pentameter, a kind of windup ta-BOOM ta-BOOM machine that can be scored, or in spite of it, in which case the Hunt for the Meaning is on, and poetry be damned. In "interpreting" poetry most teachers have forgotten the great Unwritten Law of its mathematics: a good poem is always more than the sum of its parts. It is first and last the document of a human experience.

Let me put it another way. The same sensibility that kicks poems around until they stand up like a man and *mean* also imbeds butterflies in glass and mounts animal heads on den walls. I am not sentimentalizing. I am not being the dreamy, wishy-washy thinker poets are expected to be. When wildness is once and for all nailed, it becomes an ornament. When all the mystery is crushed out of a poem, when its wings are pinned forever, when it no longer makes weird noises in the night, when it has grown harmless in the trophy-book of the school text, the poem will have attained the state of perfect meaning which is death. It becomes another prize in a landscape of stuffed birds. The saddest part of this education, for students and teachers alike, is that it's much easier to trap a stuffed bird than to skin your knees chasing a wild one. We train ourselves by this method of "analysis" to seek out examples of poetry that, because of their museum-piece status, are safe stuffed owls. This accounts for the preponderance of so much bad poetry even in anthologies that seem to be searching for something so much better, collections like *Reflections on a Gift of Watermelon Pickle* and *Some Haystacks Don't Even Have Any Needle*. Most of these books display the same old trophies, leaking sawdust gussied up with a veneer of contemporary typefaces and flashy layout.

My point is that poetry lives now, and *now* can be as confusing to us as this morning's headlines. How does one "interpret" the kidnapping, the indictments of public officials, the extinct bird, the oil well somebody wants to put on a football field, the untimely rains? *Now* is poetry territory—dangerous, infested, infectious, maddening. We'd much prefer to click off Cronkite in midsentence than force ourselves to pull it together. But if a poem does not fully partake of the *now* of its author's life, it will never survive that moment.

Because of his engagement with the *now*, whatever that *now* may mean to him as an individual, the poet has often been typed as a looney, a misfit, a dreamer, or a plain waster-of-time. Poets have certainly been all these things, and more. But no more so than others who have never written a line. Some of the weirdest people I have ever known I met in a factory where I worked in the yard gang and as a janitor when I was eighteen. None of them wrote poetry.

While an Eliot or a Pound drives readers away with his difficulty, other poets find themselves dismissed as "unpoetic." I will never forget the reaction of one teacher during a workshop I was giving at a Brooklyn school. I was trying to stress that many recent poets have worked hard to bring everyday American speech patterns into their work, and read the following poem by William Carlos Williams:

THIS IS JUST TO SAY

I have eaten
the plums
that were in
the icebox

and which
you were probably
saving
for breakfast

Forgive me
they were delicious
so sweet
and so cold[1]

"But that sounds just like my husband!" cried one of the teachers. "You mean to stand there and tell me that *that's* a *poem*?"

Yes I did. In my secret scenario, Williams had eaten the plums, left a note in the empty bowl in the icebox, and had started to climb the stairs to bed when, in a flash of intuition I am willing to call genius, he stopped himself and ran back downstairs to retrieve the poem he knew he had just written. Unlike my upset teacher, Williams saw no line dividing his activities as a poet from his life as a human being. In "This Is Just to Say," he captured one of the million daily experiences that are as liable to poetic treatment as any other, and he knew it. Rescuing this short, scribbled testament to married life and household order, he performed a poetic action of the first magnitude.

Another poet whose preoccupation with everyday life cast his literary career into obscurity was Charles Reznikoff. In poem after poem he captured the essence of city life in language so clear and simple it could be mistaken for prose. Like Williams, Reznikoff is a master of the seemingly insignificant encounter, the anecdotal experiences all of us have but fail to write down:

> The new janitor is a Puerto Rican;
> still a young man and he has four small children.
> He has been hired because he is cheap—
> not because he is the handy man
> a good janitor is supposed to be.
> I doubt if he ever saw any plumbing
> before he came to this country,
> to say nothing of a boiler and radiators.
> Anyway, he was soon overwhelmed by requests
>   from the tenants
> to do this and fix that.
> He does his best and spends hours at simple jobs,
> and seldom does them well—or can do them at all.
> He was in my flat once
> to do something or other and, when he was
>   through
> asked me if he might sit down
> "Of course," I said and offered him a drink,
> but he would not take it.
> "It is so quiet here," he explained.
> And then he began to talk about a man who lived
>   in the house and taught Spanish.
> He talks to me in Spanish," the janitor said,
> "but I do not understand.
> You see, I am not an educated man."
> His eye caught the print of a water-color by
>   Winslow Homer
> which I have hanging: a palm tree in the Bahamas.
> "That is my country," he said,
> and kept looking at the print
> as one might look at a photograph of one's mother
> long dead.[2]

Reznikoff does not spare us the hard facts. After all, he has to live in this apartment house where nothing gets fixed properly. But on the level of human interaction, his poem is full of compassion. He understands the despair of the young Puerto Rican janitor, and in his clarity of approach to the subject, makes us feel it, too.

Williams and Reznikoff wrote hundreds of poems fashioned directly from their daily lives. Williams could have set up his physician's practice in Paris, but chose instead to return to Rutherford, New Jersey, where he was born and where he worked until he died. Reznikoff lived most of his life on the Upper West Side of Manhattan, walked the streets, wrote articles on the law for a living, and published his books himself. Through work like theirs, teachers who are willing to chance the unfamiliar will discover much that they can bring to their students which concerns the human heart.

II

There must be as many reasons why poetry is written as there are poets writing it. Surely the poet means to tell us something about himself and his world, if only in the most oblique ways, by recording what he deems important enough to pluck from his field of vision with a pen point. This field of vision contains both the inner and outer lives of the writer. Some poets prefer to concentrate on the reality that exists independently of themselves—the "real world" we call it, of people, places, and things. By selecting what they do select to present to us, they tell us who they are. Other poets seem to exist completely in their own spiritual interiors. The world "out there" pales in comparison to their inner life, their thoughts and feelings. Trees and people seem to exist only as comments on what is taking place inside them. We can call the first group "extroverts," the second "introverts," if we wish. Whatever the poet's attitude toward the world and himself may be, there is a continual struggle within him to be true to his own vision. This struggle goes on with each word he writes. Teachers and students should be aware of it. To seize his vision in language as accurately as he can, the poet takes chances, stabs in the dark of the world and the self, both of which are finally unknowable. Teachers and students should likewise be aware of this chance-taking so essential to the making of any art. The French poet Paul Valéry claimed that a poem is never finished, only abandoned. The poet, then, can never be positive he has got it down "right" for all time. In this light, how much more careful should those who study poetry be in fixing "final" interpretations to poems. In fact, the virtue of a great poem is that it can be interpreted inexhaustibly, from generation to generation, century to century, and even from culture to culture. No one has stopped writing about the *Odyssey*; the last word on *Hamlet* has yet to be said.

A great work of art, like the figures on Keats's Grecian urn, is an artifact of time, yet timeless. This is exactly why those cut-and-dried interpretations of poems we present to our students turn them away from the life of poetry, a life which is intimately connected to the mysteries of the human soul. Instead of facing the poem as a living document of human experience (Keats studying the urn in the British Museum, Williams looking out the window at the red wheelbarrow), the "symbols" of the poem are served up for memorization and regurgitation. Instead of being an encounter with the human heart, poetry becomes a task like places and dates. As teachers of poetry, and as students of these methods, we have paid dearly. A vehicle of wonderment that should draw us closer has been turned into just another academic job. Is it any wonder that I have seen third and fourth graders, without knowing the first thing about poetry, go ''Uggggh'' when the word was mentioned?

I want to suggest that students be allowed to discover a poem. Rather than having it force-fed to them, there is a way of reading a poetic text that will allow both teacher and student to encounter it as something living. At first I am going to generalize about this method; then I am going to proceed to a specific reading of a poem that I have walked through in classes that have ranged from the third grade to teacher workshops.

As a teacher presenting a poem to students for the first time, one must be humble and curious. The humility comes in the intentional holding back of one's own interpretation of the poem at hand and realizing that the poem can never be completely understood. It is a salutary thing for students to hear their teacher say, ''I don't really know'' when they really *don't*. Some poems can be investigated exhaustively; others, completely or in part, leave us baffled. The first important step in humanizing the study of poetry is to recognize that. We cannot always explain what attracts us—in poetry or in life. ''Why do you love me?'' says the husband to the wife. Beyond what can be put into words, we must be silent.

One must be curious enough to hear the students out, to let them have their say. Humility again comes into play when a student points out something in the poem that the teacher has never noticed. This has happened to me any number of times, and it is always thrilling. (I even admit to hoping that it will happen!) For example, I and a fourth grade class were discussing William Carlos Williams' poem ''The Last Words of My English Grandmother.'' In the poem, Williams (or a character very much like him) is trying to persuade his dying grandmother to go to the hospital; she doesn't want to go. When I asked the students why the old woman didn't want to go to the hospital, I was expecting them to say something like, ''Because she knows that if she goes to the hospital, she'll die.'' (A very sophisticated response, actually; an adult response. Most children experience the hospital as an enforced separation from their homes. They do not go to hospitals to die, but to have their tonsils out.)

A boy raised his hand, and I called on him. ''She doesn't want to go to the hospital,'' he said, ''because in the hospital all the people wear these white robes, and she might wake up and think that angels were all around her.'' I was astounded at his insight. The boy had made an association between whiteness and heaven that I never would have located in a hospital ward. (Unwittingly, he was speaking metaphorically: doctors and nurses in a hospital are like angels in heaven.) I later learned that he had recently been in the hospital himself, and his answer was based on his

"As a teacher presenting a poem to students for the first time, one must be humble and curious. The humility comes in the intentional holding back of one's own interpretation of the poem at hand and realizing that the poem can never be completely understood."

observations—with a crucial dash of intuition thrown in. Later, when I discussed what he had said with several teachers who had been observing the class, one told me that hospitals have actually done extensive psychological research in this area, and as a result many hospital staffs may now be found clothed in green—the color of life and growth—rather than in white (the pallor of death, the color of the angels!).

Virtuously humble and curious, the teacher can now afford to be practical by making sure that each and every student has a copy of the poem or poems to be discussed. As a poet myself, I beg you please, *please* give the poem some breathing space when you reproduce it for class use. Don't crush twelve poems onto one ditto master; and for goodness sakes don't treat the poem as if it was a wilting violet or a new form of disease by fancying it up in Neo-unctial script. Type it up clearly, and credit the author.

Before we proceed to some ideas that will help you talk about poems as if they were recordings of human experience and not terrifying Masterpieces of World Literature, let me lean on one point. Students will at some point usually depart from the text of the poem and begin making up a lot of nonsense about "what the poem is saying." When they slip off the track (unless the new track is of particular interest), direct them back to the poem itself to see if what *they* are saying in any way corresponds to what the *poem* is saying. I find it necessary in the course of a discussion to do this again and again. The "answers" that may exist (if any) to the problems of the poem, the pith of "what the poem means," are either in the poem or we are guessing. Guesswork can be exciting, germane, and is in fact absolutely necessary. But our guesses (call them "intuition" if you prefer) should always be balanced against the data contained in the poem. In entering any poem, we first want to find out what is going on. Meaning ascribed to what is going on has a secondary function. Experience is our objective; the interpretation of experience, a natural and laudable human activity, still comes later.

III

so much depends
upon

a red wheel
barrow

glazed with rain
water

beside the white
chickens. [3]

This famous poem, which so many teachers know and which appears in dozens of school anthologies, first appeared in a book by William Carlos Williams called *Spring & All*, originally published in 1923. The book itself is a meditation, in alternating prose and verse, and sometimes delightfully chaotic, on the nature of poetry. In the book, the poem that has come to be known as "The Red Wheelbarrow" is followed by this short paragraph:

> The fixed categories into which life is divided must always hold. These things are normal— essential to every activity. But they exist—but not as dead dissections.

In the anthologies, however, this neat (and helpfully explanatory) paragraph never accompanies the poem, and we are forced to come to grips with it "on its own terms." How to do that, asks the teacher. The poem presents the reader with a simple, clear picture in words; what is there here to get hold of, to "analyze"?

This quandary is a wonderful beginning toward a reading of the poem, a foot forward that should in no way be weighed down with despair. I believe that this is exactly what Williams intended, this puzzlement on the reader's part. The poem isn't really any more puzzling than the facts in our own lives that confront us from day to day; or, it is just as puzzling, just as inexplicable—like the chaos of newspaper headlines I referred to earlier. What to make of these objects seen through—is it?—a kitchen window? How do they stack up, make sense, order themselves in relation to our own existence, to which they are mysteriously (or not so mysteriously) linked. There they are out in the yard, Williams seems to be suggesting; there it is, right in front of you, and you don't even look at it! They are separate, they are "fixed categories," he tells us, "normal," but "not as dead dissections." First and foremost, they nearly cry out to be seen with the eyes. But here I am, sinning against my own advice, putting the cart of interpretation before the horse of . . . of simply walking into the poem and looking around.

Any poet worth his or her salt *wants* us to enter their work. "But," as Williams wrote in another poem, "you got to try hard." Perhaps the seeming effortlessness of the poem, its cameo quality, fools us into thinking that there isn't much here worth bothering about. And yet we make the same claim about a great photograph: "If only I had my camera with me, I too could have captured this scene for everyone!" The simplicity, the illusive "easiness" of many works of contemporary art lead up that famous blind alley where all of us stand around clapping each other on the backs, exclaiming, "Pshaw, I coulda done it myself!" Amidst these hollow self-congratulations we must pause a moment to wonder why we've never produced a masterpiece, though geniuses we surely are; and remind ourselves that a lifetime of hard work and missed opportunities goes into the making of that one great picture or poem.

There are many other poems by William Carlos Williams that are similar to the "snapshot" quality of "The Red Wheelbarrow" (the poem bears only the roman numeral "XXII" in *Spring & All*). And there are many other great poems by Williams, as there are great photographs by his friend and mentor, Alfred Stieglitz. But each poem, each photograph, has its own moment. That we realize these moments and fail to write them down or click our shutters, or that we fail to see them at all, is what separates us from them, and what ultimately makes us one with them. We become, if you will, artists through their artistic perceptions, their skill. That is what makes them great.

And now, before all hope is lost of ever doing so, let's enter the poem.

The first question I ask my students (here on the doorstep of the poem) is: What *things*, what real things that you could touch or pick up and handle, are in the poem? Make a list of them. So: wheelbarrow, rainwater, chickens. Hmmm. Well then, I say to them, where do you think this poem is taking place—a baseball park, a hospital room? No, no! they shout. It's on a *farm*! Probably so: a farm. And on this perhaps-farm, like Old MacDonald's, we have some chicks, a wheelbarrow and—what is the state of the atmosphere? Of course: it is raining on the wheelbarrow, the chickens, and the perhaps-farm. My next question is: What, if anything, is happening in the poem? What is the action? The action is nil— things have come to a standstill, the wheelbarrow is sitting there (wherever "there" is, the perhaps-yard) being rained on, "glazed with rain/water."

At this juncture I must remind my students that a poem is made of words—"a machine made of words," somebody called it. The word in this poem that calls the most attention to itself, that "exhibits" itself most openly, is of course *glazed*. What is a glaze? The pottery workshop kids know: that shiny covering you put on a pot; made, I think, from powdered glass. So *glazed* derives from *glass*. The red wheelbarrow is "glazed"—made to have a glassy sheen—by the rainwater that is . . . what?—pouring over it? Does that mean that the wheelbarrow is turned over, wheel in the air, the water pouring over its sides? At this stage we usually get into a discussion about the wheelbarrow, whether it is upright or turned over. All of this may strike you as quibbling, but it nevertheless draws us further into the poem and allows us to fix it more clearly in our minds. After all, this poem is a kind of literary still life, and even the two color-words that Williams permits himself to use ("red" and "white") —three, if we count the sheen thrown off by the

"glazed" wheelbarrow—contribute to a firmer pictorial element in the poem.

Good, we have investigated the poem fairly thoroughly; we can "see" the glossy rained-on wheelbarrow and the white chickens next to it. But we haven't touched the first stanza, the only purely abstract element in the poem. (I say *abstract* in opposition to *concrete* in order to draw a distinction between what exists in the realm of *idea* and that which is palpable to the *senses*: we can wheel a barrow and pluck a chicken; we cannot smell an idea or hear it hit the ground.)

Why, I ask the kids, does "so much depend upon" these things? As you might guess, this is where the fun starts; this is where the interpretation begins. We have grounded ourselves in the facts of the poem. We have made like Sherlock Holmeses and Doctor Watsons. The "so much depends upon" cues us to think, to guess, to use our intuitions provided we keep our feet firmly planted in the language that the poem has presented to us.

Before plunging into discussion, I like to recapitulate the situation in the poem. We are, perhaps, looking at a farm, at a farmyard. It is raining hard enough to "glaze" the wheelbarrow, which is probably (but not certainly) sitting upside down on the ground. Or it has just stopped raining, and the "glaze" is still on the barrow. That is all the poem gives us, all we can know or—if the poet has made his poem well enough—all we need to know. The question I pose to my students to initiate discussion is: What is a wheelbarrow used for on a farm?

Everyone knows, or thinks he knows the answer. You carry manure in it. You carry dirt in it. You carry—ah!—feed in it. My next question, admittedly a leading one: What kind of farm might this farm be? What might be raised on this farm, from the information in the poem? Yes, it might be a corn farm; it might be a cattle ranch; it might even be a rain farm! But the one reasonable conclusion we can draw is that it also might be a chicken farm. Then, I suggest to the students, the wheelbarrow might be used to haul (shaking the loose change in my pocket, a pun that nobody seems to understand)—chicken feed!

Okay, I continue; what if it's been raining for two weeks, or a month. What if there's been a tornado or a hurricane? What if it's just been raining like the blazes all day? "The farmer wouldn't be able to go feed the chickens," one bright youngster shouts. What happens if the farmer can't feed the chickens? "They won't lay any eggs." What happens if they don't lay eggs? "The farmer won't make money because he won't have any eggs to sell." And if he doesn't have any money? "He'll have to eat the chickens." And if he eats the chickens? "He won't have a chicken farm any more." What will he do then? "He'll maybe have to sell his farm and go get a job somewhere." And what if he has to work a job he hates; after all, he's a farmer. "He'd be very unhappy; he might get sick; he might die." Ah, I say to the children, that's why

so much depends
upon

a red wheel
barrow

glazed with rain
water

beside the white
chickens.

IV

I submit that this reading of "The Red Wheelbarrow" isn't as farfetched as it may seem. While I am no expert on farm life, isn't it logical to assume that two or three days of storm could seriously disrupt the day-to-day operation? But whether I'm right or not, there exists yet another way to read this poem, a reading based on its structure, on how carefully Williams has distributed the stanzas, lines, and words upon his page.

One declarative sentence has been broken into four stanzas of two lines each. The poet is forcing our eye into discrete units of composition that nevertheless connect to express a complete thought. The poem is perfectly symmetrical: the first line in each stanza contains three words; the second line in each stanza has one word. Why this breaking up into tiny perceptual steps? Williams even breaks apart the words "wheelbarrow" and "rainwater" as if to show us how they are made of components. Further, each second line contains the same number of syllables: *upon, barrow, water, chickens*; and lines one and seven (*so much depends, beside the white*), and lines three and five (*a red wheel, glazed with rain*) do, too.

Without reference to the explanatory little paragaraph in *Spring & All*, we can see by the evidence that in the very shape of the poem, there is a principle of isolation at work that forces us to deal with virtually one word at a time. Yet, threading its way through the clipped lines and broken compound words is the principle of unification which is the sentence, the complete linguistic thought. "Each thing," Williams seems to be telling us, "is separate, and must be seen as distinct from everything else; yet, almost by virtue of this separateness, everything is joined together." The paradoxical nature of a poem that seems to be stating, "All is separate," may be well over the heads of most elementary and high school students, but it is my opinion that one cannot approach these ambiguities of life early enough. To

invoke Williams's *Spring & All* paragraph, these things of the world do not exist as "dead dissections" that achieve a final isolation because, as the study of ecology keeps insisting, all facets of existence are interrelated, the manufactured wheelbarrow and the live chickens and the rain, the words on the page and the intelligence of the reader in front of them. The symmetry of Williams' poem suggests that even the most random collection of objects follows a scheme, if at the very least the order imposed on them by a writer.

Something remains to be said about the diction Williams uses in this little poem. By diction I mean its tone of voice, the kind of language it contains. Does the poem *sound* like it was written by an Elizabethan courtier? No. Does it *sound* like it was written by a nineteenth century Romantic poet? Nope. The truth is, any one of us could have said it. The tone is casual, straightforward, and the only "poetic" or "esthetic" touch Williams permits himself is the word "glazed." The word "glazed" is, in a sense, the very center of the poem, the moment of dazzle, illumination. Without it, all we would have would be a wheelbarrow and some chickens. We might even say that "glazed" puts the glaze on the poem, gives it the finishing touch it deserves and lifts it into poetry.

Visually, "The Red Wheelbarrow" reminds us of a color snapshot, click!: red wheelbarrow, shiny with rainwater, white chickens. Williams had a fine eye for detail, everywhere apparent in his poems. I will not here go into his friendships with the painters Marsden Hartley, Charles Sheeler, and Charles Demuth, nor his relationship with the great American photographer Alfred Stieglitz.[4] Nor can I hope to outline Williams's involvement with the Imagist Movement in poetry that Ezra Pound and others led.[5] That would take us well outside the boundaries of this essay and into thesis-land, where I adamantly do not wish to go. But out of these artistic friendships came his preoccupation with "seeing" and the recording of it that makes his work so highly visual, so concentrated on objects and experiences most of us never register, and which led him in his later years to give American Poetry a piece of advice it has been chewing on for years: "No ideas/but in things. . . ."[6]

NOTES

[1] In *The Selected Poems* of William Carlos Williams (New Directions paperback), p. 55.

[2] In *By the Well of Living & Seeing: New & Selected Poems 1918-1973*, by Charles Reznikoff (Black Sparrow Press paperback), pp. 113-114.

Reznikoff's complete poetry is now being published by the Black Sparrow Press. *Poems 1918-1936:*

Volume I of The Complete Poems of Charles Rezni-koff has just appeared.

[3] See *Spring and All* in *Imaginations*, by William Carlos Williams (New Directions paperback), p. 138. The poem is anthologized as "The Red Wheelbarrow" in *The Collected Earlier Poems*, by William Carlos Williams (New Directions, hardcover), p. 277; and in his *Selected Poems* (New Directions paperback), p. 30.

[4] For this history see *The Hieroglyphics of a New Speech: Cubism, Stieglitz, and the Early Poetry of William Carlos Williams*, by Bram Dijkstra (Princeton University Press, hardcover).

[5] For the history of Imagism and many examples, see *The Imagist Poem: Modern Poetry in Miniature*, edited and with an introduction by William Pratt (Dutton paperback).

[6] Quoted from the poem, "A Sort of Song," in *The Collected Later Poems*, by William Carlos Williams (New Directions, hardcover), p. 7.

A Talk About
Teaching Poems to Kids

by Lewis MacAdams

I thought I'd talk a little bit about what I've been doing. I got hired by the West Virginia Arts Council and the West Virginia Board of Education last November to come and be a poet-in-residence for West Virginia for five months. I don't really know what my qualifications exactly were for being hired. When I signed my contract, I found out that not one person in the state had read one of my poems. It was very strange; I was sitting there and there were people from the Arts Council and the Board of Education and they were saying things like, "Of course you'll be doing a lot of readings in Lions Clubs and things like that," and it started to ring in my head that they just *couldn't* have read my poems if they thought I was going to go over in the Lions Club circuit. And I said, "Has anybody ever read my poems?" And I had the contract already in my hands. And they said, "No." And I said, "Well, how'd you decide I should get this job?" And they said, "Well, we read some of the other people's poems."

When I received a letter last November, I was working for the Public Utility District in the town I live in, in northern California, laying water pipe. And I thought that this would be a somewhat easier job, but it's turned out to be definitely harder than *any* job I've ever had in my life. Really, it's the most exhausting work. . . . My experience teaching poetry in high schools, or actually *being* in high schools, was limited to three days in Texas—so I had to really make it up. I literally didn't know what I was doing. I never actually had tried to get kids to write poetry. . . .

When I started, I went to Fayette County first. And in Fayette County, they sent me to ten different schools. I was there a month, and I was in ten different schools. The point of the program was to "expose people to poetry," I mean in the sense like you might expose somebody to malaria or something. Also, to get them to write poems. It's very hard; those are really two very different activities. I didn't

have enough time in Fayette County. I was usually only in a school for two or three days, and that's not enough time to get anything happening, at least not for me. These were mostly elementary schools. Kids seem to have better imaginations when they're in the first grade than when they're in the tenth grade. That seems to be almost always true, at least in my experience with kids. It's easier to get kids to write poems the younger they are. They're open to the most off-the-wall suggestions that you have. Kids in high schools are much less likely to listen or to be enthusiastic about something. When you say, "Write me a list of ten things that could never happen," people in the 11th grade just slam their books shut and sit there staring at the ceiling for awhile. You've got to come to them with a little more interesting ideas, or ideas that tickle their fancy. Sometimes difficult to find, actually. On the other hand, kids in high schools are at an emotional level where it's easier for them to understand poetry. So, one of the things I do more often when I'm in high schools is to read poems, poems by myself and poems by all the poets that I like. I always carry around a lot of books of poems and read whatever feels appropriate.

Part of my job seems so strange to me. In the first place, I'm the first man that's ever been in a lot of the schools. I haven't seen an elementary school male teacher since I've been in the state. So, I'm in that role sometimes. I could be teaching shoelace experience; I'm just a *man* who's *there*. Also, I'm usually the first person from out of the West Virginia culture that a lot of people have seen. I've been working in very small towns. The role of reading poems is valuable in that case, because kids *can* hear poems. Obviously, you read poems that relate to their experience. There's a poem by Gary Snyder, called "Hay for the Horses," and it's a beautiful poem about a guy who's been baling hay. He's saying, "The first time I baled hay, when I was seventeen years old, I said to myself, 'I'm sure not gonna do this all my life.' And damn it, this is what I've gone and done." Just when I said the title, "Hay for the Horses," when I was in Braxton County in any of the schools, they loved it. They would get to it instantly because it was in language that the kids understood and it dealt with situations that they understood. I've found that there's really no point in reading them poems where the language is alien. By that I mean Shakespeare, say, or Keats, or poets that I particularly love. . . . I don't really see the point in reading those poems to kids at that level. The point of poetry, I think, is like finding out your own personal truth, and you can't do that unless it's in the language that you speak. Trying to teach them what Keats is talking about is a whole other subject, like teaching them another language. . . .

You have the question of what the emotional range of kids is. . . . In high schools, I feel that you can use books like *The New American Poetry*, published by Grove Press, because that's in American English. I think you have to get the poems in their area. When I try to get them to write poems, I try to get them to write about things that they know about. If they're interested in mini-bikes, which amazing numbers of people are, I try to get them to write about that. Or if they're into cars, it's as easy to write a great poem about a car as it is to write a great poem about a love affair. Well, almost as easy, almost as easy.

You have to have this ground where you can meet people. Everybody in schools writes love poems. They always write love poems that say things like, "My boyfriend's so beautiful; everybody's so great; isn't love great." And they're sentimental. I usually try to get them to write poems about their boyfriends or girlfriends that only talk about their love's *worst* qualities. And they really get into it.

In Burnsville, which is a town that is mostly farming, I took this line from a poem by Allen Ginsberg, called "Supermarket in California." The line was "Who killed the porkchops?" This class was mostly from the country, and I wrote the line up on the board and asked them to write a poem with that title. The first time they wrote it, it was like: "Who killed the porkchops? Was it I? Was it they? Who killed the porkchops?" And I said, "No. I mean literally, who *killed* the porkchops?" I asked how many had ever slaughtered animals, I mean killed their own pigs themselves. About seventy-five percent of the kids in the class had done that, and mostly, actually, really enjoyed it. They always looked forward to spring when they could shoot the pig. I asked them, then, to write about the experience. . . . And one boy in the class wrote this amazingly beautiful piece where he said, "I couldn't sleep Friday night because I knew tomorrow I would have to kill my love," about his pet pig. All of them were on that kind of level, really *true*.

I found that a lot of times kids are tracked into these sort of mediocre or low grade levels because they don't have a certain *kind* of vocabulary that fits the school's idea of what vocabulary is. When you can get to what they know, they can talk about it as well as anybody can. Better, because it's what they know. They can write stories just as well as anybody can. Don't worry about spelling, because that's not the point, really. I think the thing that a lot of teachers get hung up on in poetry is that they don't love poetry. They don't love song; they don't love words —in the true sense, of loving rap, of loving to hear people rap, and loving to hear the language as it's spoken. I don't think you can really teach poetry unless you love it, but I guess that's really true for everything. . . .

Basically, I think you have to have the trust of the students. Everybody's very shy at first in expressing themselves, except one or two people, who are usually slightly manic about it. One of the things that I do is that I read their work out loud. And everybody's saying, "Oh, please don't read these works *out loud. Please* don't read these works out loud." Meaning, "Come on, hurry and read the works," you know. I, personally, don't usually read the names of people. I always make some little lame joke like, if you want this personal recognition, stand up when I read your work and bow or courtsy. Kids never will do that. But everybody always knows whose work it is, or almost always.

One of the assignments that I like to do the first time I have any writing in the class is I'll say, "O.K., take out a pencil and paper and start writing and don't stop for seven minutes. Write for seven minutes without stopping. Write down anything you can think, anything you can see, anything you can feel, anything you can say. Make up new words, write in any language you can make up, write in beast language, or dog language, or write like a vegetable, or do anything that you possibly can; just don't stop writing for seven minutes." Then there's usually this totally stunned silence: "What do you mean? Do I put my name at the top or the bottom?" Then, usually everybody will do it, and there's usually an average of three or four good pieces that'll come out of it—people who can think really great right off the top of their heads. I'll read the pieces that come out pretty well. The kids are usually surprised that that's so. They hadn't really had a sense that you could do that. And once you show them it's possible, it starts to get easier from then on.

What kind of assignment I ask them to write depends on where I am. A lot of times I ask them to write about dreams. Dreams tend to give people permission to be far out, to really use their imaginations. In our culture, we have these reality boxes and then we have dream, or imagination, as being

> **"The imagination is like a muscle in a certain way, and it'll atrophy if it isn't used....It goes back to the basic of the curriculum, of our culture...The imagination is not considered as important as the logical rational mind."**

somewhere else. And if you have this framework of dreams, people can really stretch out in a great way that they usually won't do. Also, I noticed in the high schools, even in Braxton County, which is pretty much country, kids really think a lot about acid. In completely, totally screwed up ways acid has become almost like dream in a way. You say, "O.K., write me a story about an LSD trip." Very few of the kids have ever actually taken LSD, but they have these ideas of what an LSD trip is about. What it is, essentially, are these incredible Wizard of Oz, horror show fantasies. Using assignments like this really gives them permission to use their imaginations. . . . I've tried this in several different schools and everytime it worked. Really amazing things, like little gremlins charging out of the light bulbs. . . .

I, personally, have a few pet hates. I can't stand poems about dogs or cats. Sometimes I just say don't write me anything about a dog or a cat because you really get a lot of works like that, especially in junior high schools. You get poems about their pet dog, how cute he is and all that. Aside from that, there are no boundaries. Make it up. One of the things that makes the gig interesting for you, or me, as a poet, or as a teacher, is that you bring something new, something that'll be interesting to you too. There're books that can tell you hundreds of assignments. You can read Kenneth Koch's book, *Wishes, Lies, and Dreams*, or you can get stuff from the Teachers and Writers Collaborative in New York and they'll give you millions of ideas of ways to get kids to write poems, all of which are good. But I think the thing that really makes things vibrate is when it's really new to you too, when you're creating a situation in the class where it's work that's valuable.

That's really all. That's really what I'm doing more or less. I'm not a teacher by profession; it's all really been new to me. I mean, I never taught, probably never will again. It's too hard, too hard.

Question: Can you talk a little more about what happens to kids' imaginations? Like, why are young kids' imaginations better than, say, kids in high school?

MacAdams: Well, I can't criticize any school system, and I definitely can't criticize any teacher. I mean, it's the hardest job I've seen. But I don't think

there's much emphasis at all on using the imagination. The imagination is like a muscle in a certain way, and it'll atrophy if it isn't used. You see it. As you get older, you see it atrophies in people because it isn't used. It goes back to the basic of the curriculum, of our culture. We're involved in the mind as rational, and we have these ideas of what the mind is. The imagination is not considered as important as the logical and rational mind. It's ignored, essentially, in schools except in, like, what I'm doing, and that's beginning to happen around the country. I think the emphasis is really changing, with all the books coming out on teaching poetry in the schools. It's not basically poetry that's being taught; it's the act of the imagination. I mean, I'm here to say that it is changing. But, at this point, not much is happening, really regularly, in any of the schools I've been in.

Question: Why is teaching the hardest job you've ever had?

MacAdams: Because it's so exhausting, mentally. Since I got out of college, I've been into physical labor. I worked on the railroad, on farms, or laying pipe for the water company. I mean, that way, you work hard, but you don't have to use your mind so much. Teachers are just too overworked, at least in elementary and high schools. And they're too restricted as to what they can teach. I was at Huntington East a couple weeks ago, and there's a guy there, a poet, a damn good poet, and they've got him teaching *The Jerry West Story*. That's ridiculous.

Question: What qualities do you feel make an outstanding "kid poem"?

MacAdams: It's those qualities you can't name. You just see that somebody is really a writer, somebody has that extraordinary ability to make images, to make *true* images, that ring all the way up and all the way down. Personally, my own thrill is running into people that can write. That I can deal with on a level that's not like starting at the beginning. . . . That's really a pleasure when you can talk to people that it matters to.

Question: Which poets have you been reading, most-

20

ly, in the schools?

MacAdams: I've mostly been reading the modern American poets. Like Gregory Corso has a great poem, "Marriage," and I bet I've read that poem seventy-five times in the last four months and it never fails to be completely loved by everybody. It's an amazingly popular poem. And a poet my age from New York, Anne Waldman; kids really like her poems a lot. And Gary Snyder. Allen Ginsberg, sometimes, although he tends to go a little fast. It's really a question of language. A poem like "Marriage"—high school kids are already thinking about marriage, what it is, so it's a subject they can all relate to. And Snyder's poems, I read all the poems about being outdoors and living in the country. Kids can deal with them on the terms of the poems themselves and what they say rather than having to worry about not understanding what the poem even said. It would be different for each poet, what he chooses to teach. . . . I don't read any poems that I don't think are really damn good. Guys like Rod McKuen or Lawrence Ferlinghetti, who are probably the most popular American poets, in terms of sales, they're O.K. I mean I never would put down Rod McKuen or Ferlinghetti at all. Honestly I wouldn't because that's the way a lot of people first come into poetry. But when people ask me about them, I just talk about the poems themselves. I wouldn't read those books, personally, because I don't think they're right on, they aren't good enough. But you come to poetry anyway you can. It's too easy to put down guys like Rod McKuen. I mean, they ain't doin' anybody any harm.

Richard Brautigan is another good person I've found, especially in high schools, that people can relate to. His works are easy enough and they hit quick. I'm not trying to pass on any culture—that's one of the basic points. . . . I just read poems that I really like. I don't have any cultural standards, like that, I don't think.

Question: Are there any questions, concerns, that the kids ask you about repeatedly, everywhere you go?

MacAdams: Everybody's very curious about drugs, at every high school. They see that I'm not the same as the teacher who went to the teacher's college down the road and has been in the service for forty years. . . . And I always answer as clearly as I can. Something that I haven't really learned to overcome yet is that sense that what I'm doing is licentious; that I'm just talking about freaking out. That's why I need more time than I've had. It's not too hard to get people to freak out, to just write anything they want to. It's harder to get them to see the sense of discipline that it takes to be a poet. Somehow, everybody has this idea that it's easier to be a poet than to be violinist. And it ain't true. Somehow, because people know how to write their names, or descriptions of apple trees and stuff, they think they're more quickly qualified to be a poet. That's a hard thing to get people to see, to be clear about, without trying to quash them. To get free, but also to realize where that freedom lies. That's hard; that's really hard. . . . The fact is that most kids want to be free and most kids really enjoy writing, if they can write. There are some places I've been where kids literally can't write. They can probably write their names, but they can't *write*. There, you have to do something else; I'm not sure exactly what. But once kids have a certain verbal facility, not even much of one, then they really enjoy it, they really like to write. It gives them a pleasure to write about their boyfriends or girlfriends. It becomes a joy. And it's not hard to teach; it's not hard to get people to do.

This piece is reprinted from *The Trellis Supplement*, summer 1974.

The Transition from Speech to Writing

by Phillip Lopate

There used to be a debate when teachers of writing got together: how long should the discussion go on before asking the kids to write?

Some felt it was necessary to arouse the adrenalin first, to start the juices flowing, the memories rolling, the words bouncing around in the students' heads. Others favored a more poker-faced, neutral style: a brief exposition of the assignment at hand, no more than five minutes, then get down to writing. They maintained that a long, excited discussion might drain the students of their urge to express themselves, or carry their energy to a disruptive level inimical to quiet writing. The first group, the animators, countered that it was worth the risk to generate excitement about literature and ideas. Behind this rather narrow trade-question was a much more serious one: what was the actual causal relationship between speech and writing?

It is usually surmised that talking is a good prelude to writing, though the terms of this conversation, the precise means of setting the scene and controlling it effectively have been left rather vague. Let us say that a teacher wants his students to try their hand at a poetic form, such as a sestina, haiku or list poem; or, at something more thematic, such as writing spooky stories for Halloween. The normal way to go about it—the instinctive, unquestioning way we usually do go about it—is to have a discussion about the characteristics of the form or genre, to give a few examples so that everyone understands, and then to ask the students to try writing one of their own.

I am assuming for purposes of this article that some writing will be taking place in the classroom. Of course, the teacher *could* assign the writing for homework, and spend class time on critiques, as in a college writing workshop. But at the younger grade levels it is often impossible to set up such a seminar atmosphere. The only way many of the children will ever write is if they are asked to write at school. And getting them to try it directly after discussion is as

good a time as any, since the ideas are still fresh.

During the discussion the teacher will probably want to draw out as many students as possible: for instance, with Halloween stories, encouraging different children to tell actual scary things that had happened to them, to give the subject matter an anchoring in personal experience. It is generally assumed that the more interesting the discussion, the better the writing which will follow.

This is not necessarily true. If it were always so, life would be much easier. What I have found is that there is no way of predicting the calibre of writing which will ensue from a particular presentation. Neither a juicy discussion, nor a lazy, neutral or perfunctory presentation gives any guarantee of the creative output in the students' works. The discussion has its own dynamic and its own need which I try to satisfy; the writing is an entirely different activity.

In fact, in recent months I have tried an experiment by acknowledging this separateness and refusing to tie them together: first, by conducting a discussion on any area of life and literature, then, by giving the students the choice of writing whatever they wished —that is, purposely not stipulating a writing assignment. This holding back of an assignment had a perverse character to the children (as well as to myself); it perplexed them. Some children tried to second-guess me by writing stories on the day's discussion topic anyway, supposing that that must be what I really wanted. Others struck off in an independent direction. Still others chose to play around, while a minority kept whining, "What are we supposed to *do*?" I refused to tell them what to write about; I wanted them to answer that question for themselves. In short, more anxiety but also more varied individual response resulted from this tactic than from my providing one uniform topic.

Collaborative Class Poems

Collaborative or group composition is midway

between group discussion and solitary writing; therefore, we may be able to surmise something about both processes by analyzing it.

Let us say the discussion has gone well. Still, something is missing—I can tell by their eyes, they do not look quite ready to write. In order to illustrate the technique of writing poetry, I may decide to do a collaborative poem with the whole class. A collaborative class poem is one in which the students call out ideas and the teacher writes them on the blackboard or on paper. The teacher acts as coordinator/scribe: depending on his personality or his sense of the class's needs, he can either include every suggestion uncritically, or else discard some ideas and ask the group to edit or improve other lines. At the outset he might establish certain rules, such as repeating a verbal formula in every line (using "In the middle of Halloween night. . ." as a recurring refrain, for instance—to stay with our Halloween example). Or he might have the class improvise one continuous, open-ended, fright poem. But however open the form is, it will tend to suggest an ending somewhere along the way: either the class is running out of steam, or a triumphant twist has been hit upon which naturally caps the poem. Two cheers, if the piece is any good, because there is something miraculous about the spontaneous manufacturing of an actual *poem* by a group of students who didn't know they had it in them.

Then the teacher asks his students to try one "on their own."

Here is where he often runs into trouble, just when everything seemed to be going so well. The handing out of paper is greeted with expressions of resistance, as if they were getting a spelling test. "But they were just enjoying poetry so much!" one may think with disappointment. What one fails to take into account is the wide gulf which separates the social excitement of the collective poem from the lonely individual effort.

One of the most important side effects of the collaborative class poem is that it validates the social group. The pride which a child feels at seeing his classmates and himself pull off a successful collaborative poem is the exultation of being part of a winning team and is of different order from the inward satisfaction gained by lone authorship. It may be equally and in some cases more important for the student to experience that sense of group pride, but the two satisfactions should never be confused.

Even aesthetically, the collaborative class-written poem is not just a tooling-up for individual work; it is a sort of invisible genre in its own right. The method of production, with its peculiar demands of blending multiple voices into one stream of verse, enforces certain decisions, compromises and markings which

amount to an identifiable style. Wit,* fast tempo, rapid changes of point of view are the basis of style, which gives some children's collaborative poems a very avant-garde surface. I often wonder what will be the lasting effect of collaborative poems on the writing of individual students. I secretly hope that the collaborative poem, on the blackboard for all to see, will provide a visual model for the appearance of modern verse—the look of a poetic line, the uses of end-stop and enjambment. And some children do pick up these things; but most return to their usual style, rhymed or whatever. Certainly the reckless tempo, linguistic freedom and subject leaps which characterize the collaborative class poem, rarely carry over to the individual student's work. This is probably because the liberties of discontinuity which a thirty-headed intelligence can take, abetted by a sophisticated adult coordinator, are usually greater than a single mind working alone. The burden of *author's responsibility* is eased in a group composition setting, so that a student may feel free to call out "crazy" ideas which he would not want to put down in his own handwriting.

What is lost in one area is gained in another; very often the individually written works are much more convincing and deeply felt than collaborative poems. But without entering into comparisons of quality, one thing is certain: compositions written by a large group are recognizably different in style from those written alone. And the child makes this distinction in his own mind.

The children see the collaborative poem as one kind of activity, a form of fun, and the individual writing as another activity, more related to their daily schoolwork. We teachers may think of the two as one continuous flow, but they don't. No more than does a child when his father takes him swimming, and holds his chest underneath, and then casually removes his hand for a second to let the kid try it by himself. No matter how casually you make that moment of abandoning support (taking the hand away, calling for individual writing), the child is bound to notice it.

Often after I have done a collaborative poem with a class and begun introducing Stage Two, several children will wheedle and beg, "Let's do another one. Come on, that was fun, let's do one more together!" And on those occasions when I have insisted that it was time to write individually, sometimes the coyness and wheedling turned to resentment.

This has happened enough times over the years so the I unconsciously flinch whenever I come to that transitional point. I may try to introduce the writing as unobtrusively as possible—slip it over on them, you

---

* Wit for the simple reason that children would be more apt to expose their humorous side publicly than their somber one.

might say—but already I am bracing for a fight. It's one of the most disagreeable parts of being a writing teacher, this power struggle. For an indecisive moment the tide can turn either way. The anti-writing students know that if they push strongly enough, they can manipulate the situation into a free period. Meanwhile the children who want to write watch silently, and the neutralists are ready to go either way. Often I step into the indecisive moment and impose an austere, silent mood—a tyrant. But even when I tell them that "no one has to write if he doesn't want to," some are still annoyed that the group entertainment is over, annoyed at the drying-up of social interaction.

I have to think of the kid who had so many good lines to contribute to the class poem, but who fidgets in boredom and dismay once paper has been handed out. He stares around him, looks up at the board's instructions as if unable to believe that this is happening to him, tries to engage the eye of another kid with the hope of promoting some merriment, and, finding himself shushed by the teacher, begins to understand that he is absolutely cut off from the consolations of human company. He is drowning without even being able to scream for help.

To write is to have to *go under*, to dive into the deepest part of oneself. It was one thing to call out a few clever lines when everyone else was talking; another, to face the prospect of committing his soul to paper. The panic on the face of someone being made to write when he doesn't feel like it suggests a loathing against a forced invasion of privacy: in short, a rape, against which only those students most in touch with their muscles' desires are capable of defending themselves. Usually those students are called hyper-kinetic, or in simpler language, troublemakers.

I approach the boy.

"Tony, how is it that you, who had so many good ideas to give to the discussion awhile ago, can tell me you have nothing to write about?"

He shrugs: that's just the way it is, boss.

"Why don't you try writing down the thing about the burglar alarm—make it into a story."

He looks at me as if I'm an idiot. He has already delivered that story to the public. Why tell it again? And in a way he's right. I am being dishonestly ingenuous. I wonder why is it necessary to have a handwritten copy of everything for posterity?

In some cases, the student may lack reading and writing skills and be ashamed of having his ignorance exposed. Fine—then his reluctance is understandable, and you can work with him on acquiring the skills. But with other children, there is no lack of technical skills; they simply don't see the necessity of translating spoken words into written form.

I keep circling around that chancy, awkward, difficult moment of the progression from speaking to writing, because in a sense I feel that the ease of transition has been exaggerated. The pedagogy of creative writing in the last ten years has continually stressed the closeness of oral to written expression. And this comparison is valid, especially if it can reduce the fearful attitude of people toward writing as an elitist practice, and connect the student to something he knows how to do much better—talk. But there is the possibility that we may be overstressing the similarities and underestimating the differences between the two modes of expression, as a false gesture toward making everyone who has anxieties about writing weaknesses feel better.

"Don't worry, speech and writing—it amounts to the same thing." On the contrary. One can easily appreciate many people's preference for speech. Speech is sociable. Speech has the tendency to rekindle euphoric faith in a social order: with every exchange it knits and reknits the relationship between people. Speech is improvisational, relatively unpremeditated, impulsive: you open your mouth not knowing exactly what is going to come out or when you are going to stop, but you trust to your adrenalin. The whole body speaks through speech, not only the tongue. Speech rushes on its adrenalized path, it doesn't look back. It is an under-selected tape of messages that almost erases itself in its headlong flight. Speech longs to go on forever, for an infinity. The last thing it wants to do is stand still. Nor can it stand still.

Writing, however, is more intentional. It is secreted from a more underground, ambitious part of the will than that nervous urge that generates speech. People are right to be intimidated by writing. Writing is intimidating and kids know it. To pick up a pen is to seek to force another's thoughts in an extremely controlled, channeled direction. Unlike the speaker, who more charitably allows for a peripheral view of the surroundings, the author cuts off all exits and forces his listener to focus on the narrow page.

Nowhere is the difference in volition between writing and speech more evident than in a comparison between those writers who have purposely striven for a talky style, and the record of a transcribed tape. Fiction writers such as Celine, Ring Lardner, and Raymond Chandler have testified to the stylistic pains it took to give written language the natural, colloquial quality of everyday speech. By contrast, transcripts of tape-recorded conversation (see the Watergate Papers) often have an otherworldly abstractness and lack of *voice* that makes them maddeningly thin.

Finally, good writing, especially good poetry, is able to stand still—and not merely because the words are pinioned typographically to the page. It is the peculiar charm of good poetry that its words can have a visual, totemic power, in addition to, or sometimes even opposed to, their utilitarian meaning, which arrests the reader in his flight. A good line of verse, to use Valery's simile, sends the reader back like a pendulum swing to the beginning of the line again.

It has always been felt that words have a certain power, when placed alongside specifically chosen other ones, to send off resonances between themselves like adjoining tuning forks. And even if most of the writing which our students do never attains that art of vibrating particles, it seems to me that once they embark on the act of writing they are already inheritors of the whole necromancy of literature. They are already practitioners, like it or not; they are already lost to the world. They have begun on an uphill climb which could easily stretch to infinity. Don't you think they suspect this? Some of them seem to be loving it. Others appear to be groaning. . . . Maybe those who resist have good reason to balk at setting out on an activity which is so monstrous in its potential demands.

Imagery and Comprehension

by Rose Ortiz

If I close my eyes and try to hear a voice, mine or someone else's, I notice that I see myself or the person whose voice I'm trying to hear. It's as though for me thinking cannot take place without mental images. Most of the time this happens so quickly that I don't catch myself creating or evoking images for my thoughts, but if I try to do an exercise like closing my eyes and remembering my mother's first name, I see my mother first then her name comes. I know that when I listen to the radio, I have images for the people I hear. I went to a radio station after listening to it for two years and people were walking around talking. I heard the familiar voices, but had a strange sensation seeing the people out of whom these voices were coming. I expected them to look like the people I imagined them to be.

Also, when I listen, whether it be to the radio or to someone talking, I have noticed that I can "see" what they are saying. For example, when someone describes going to a party, if I know the person well and know where the party is, I can "picture" the room or house and the people in it. If I don't know the person too well or don't know the house, I realize that I picture not the house of the party, but a house where I've been for a party, and if that house isn't appropriate, I choose another. I've also noticed that if I don't picture any house, I'm not so much with the person who is speaking as I am when I do.

In a reading class that I teach at Staten Island Community College, I made up the following story: One day I went to the beach. It was very cold and deserted. Suddenly I spotted an old man. He seemed to be carrying a cane and looked very tired and weak. He had holes in his clothing and holes in his hat which was all out of shape. His whiskers were so long that it looked like he hadn't shaved in weeks. As I got closer, he began to look different. He changed somehow into a young, exciting looking, strong, handsome man wearing a football jersey which had a number on

it. What was the number?

All of my students had a number. Going around the room each said a different number. At the part where the old man turned into the young one, everyone smiled including me. I had no idea where the story would go. All I knew when I began was that I wanted to tell a story which would be strong in imagery and might end with a twist. I wanted the twist in hopes of seeing their reactions—smiles, laughter or puzzled looks. They stayed with the story and each provided a number.

These students, most of whom have been labeled as having comprehension problems, didn't have any problems comprehending my story. Afterwards I asked them to report what they had noticed about themselves while listening to my story. Each said that he or she had seen an old man. Some said he was drunk. For some he was black, for others white. When the old man changed into a young one they said that they could drop the old one and replace him with the young one. They replaced him either with someone they knew who played football or with a professional player. Some even described the colors of the uniform. When I asked which beach they had seen there were as many answers as people: South Beach, Jones Beach, Coney Island, Rockaway, Manhattan Beach, no beach—instead a river bank, or a beach at a lake.

I gave this exercise because I know that if people can evoke mental images when listening to a story, they can evoke mental images by turning words on a printed page into speech and evoke images for the "speech" on the page. In fact I followed up this story exercise by asking them to read a short passage about a boy playing on a beach. I hadn't planned it that way, but while telling the story I had remembered that the book of passages we were using contained one about a boy on a beach. I asked them to read the passage to themselves and try to make mental pictures for each sentence they read. (I knew that some might have trouble decoding, or sounding out some of the words, and this also needs to be taken into account because it may affect comprehension.) If they noticed the picture getting fuzzy, or if they lost it entirely, they should stop, reread the sentence and recreate the image.

Afterwards they reported their experiences. For some this was the first time they had read a piece and understood it after the first reading. Others said that doing this made it easier to concentrate on the passage. One said that he'd noticed that when a piece was interesting, he would picture it automatically, but if it wasn't interesting, he wouldn't see it. When I asked whether he found this piece interesting he said, "Well, it was alright, but you told us to picture it so I did. I bet if I tried to picture other stories that weren't interesting, I could remember them too."

The fact is that it doesn't happen automatically. Some people have greater reading facility than others. They do it so well that sensing or picturing a story appears to happen automatically the way walking, after doing it for many years, seems to be automatic. A few moments of self-observation, when beginning a book or article or when you begin to listen to someone talk about something that happened when you weren't there, may yield the awareness of how the first image comes. When the speaker starts, your mind may be somewhere else and then suddenly you realize that you want to listen—so you turn on the "set." If the subject or place talked about is familiar, it is harder to catch that moment, but when it is unfamiliar, take the time to observe!

For me evoking images when I read was not automatic. It wasn't until I noticed that I could retain what people say by creating images that I realized that I might use imagery as a means of retaining stories, articles or novels once I had turned them into speech. If I can do that, why not create three dimensional mental images for things I read about in biology, physics, chemistry or mathematics? Mathematicians and scientists who must retain complicated mathematical abstractions tell me that they need to make up or construct images in order to understand particular concepts. None of this happens automatically. It is and can be worked on deliberately.

Once I noticed this, reading became a very different experience. I could understand when and why I hadn't read with comprehension. It was no longer a hit or miss game which varied according to the material. It wasn't until I studied with Dr. Caleb Gattegno,* to become a teacher of reading, that I understood the inextricable relationship between reading and speaking, and began to focus very closely on what it was that allowed me to retain what people said. Once I realized that it wasn't words I remembered but meanings in the form of images, I was able to transfer this image-making process from my listening to my own reading. Readers with even more skill have learned, with certain material, to go from the text to the image without vocalizing or subvocalizing, and might be less inclined to value the speech-to-image relationship. But even they might concede that sometimes when they read a really interesting novel they feel as though they are watching a movie; they "get so into the story that they can't put it down." I had never had this experience until several years after I had completed college. I never got lost in a book. I was always vividly aware of the separation between myself and the books I read. I had to read and reread almost everything because I hadn't been aware of what I was doing when I did comprehend—when it happened it was accidental, never deliberate. Perhaps if I had made reading a habit when I was a child, I would have discovered it many years ago and would have expected it to come automatically to me too. If I have trouble now with a particular text, I could blame it on the author, who in some cases, of course, is to blame.

It is often stated that people whose parents read to them as children tend to have fewer reading problems than people whose parents didn't. The former experienced literary language orally. In some cases they were encouraged to "look at the pretty pictures" and when there were none, to make up their own. I can still remember books that were read to me as a child; one recollection is of little bears walking around a house. Of course they never left the page, but I can at will think about the bears and see them walking around. I can also "see" Little Red Riding Hood walking through a forest and then talking to a wolf dressed up as her grandmother. Though I've never seen a film or show of Little Red Riding Hood, I carry an animated version in my mind.

Despite many childhood experiences like these, I still had problems reading with comprehension. Why? Perhaps because I didn't look at the words as my mother read, but only at the pictures when she turned the book my way. I didn't notice on my own that words in a book should be read with the melody and intonation of speech and my mother, not being a teacher of reading, hadn't known that this was cru-

---

* Dr. Gattegno is the originator of an approach to literacy called "Words in Color," and the author of many books, among them: *What We Owe Children: The Subordination of Teaching to Learning* (New York, Outerbridge & Dienstfrey, 1970). *In the Begin-* *ning There Were No Words: The Universe of Babies* (New York, Educational Solutions, Inc. 80 Fifth Ave., 10011, 1973), *Towards a Visual Culture* (New York, Outerbridge & Dienstfrey, 1969), and *The Common Sense of Teaching Mathematics* (New York, Educational Solutions, 1974).

"I don't have to teach comprehension. They learned to comprehend if they speak the language."

cial. My teachers in school did not seem to know any better. They did not do the job of communicating the process to me, or they assumed that I understood it. Well I hadn't. And in the few cases when I had, for example, when required to read plays or other dialogue, I was so worried that I might make a mistake that I didn't give my attention to creating images.

When someone speaks to me I turn on the T V set in my mind. If my set is off the imagery stops and so does the comprehension. Either I stay with the image or I drift off. Sometimes one image triggers another and I'm off in my own world. A colleague of mine remembers that when he was in a high school math class, his teacher did the following problem: If a man's barn is 10 yards long and 13 yards wide and he walks around it 5 times how far does he go? The story of the problem was so much more interesting to him that in his mind he was on a farm and not with the mathematics.

If my students heard the beach story and wandered off to the time when they were on the beach, when such and such happened, they wouldn't have been with my story. People call this concentration. I can't remember how many times teachers said to me, you don't comprehend what you read because you don't concentrate. That was not concrete enough. I would try to concentrate, but on what? The number of pages in the book? The size of the print? The spellings of the words on the page? The meaning, when it didn't connect to my own experience and I didn't realize that I'd have to do the connecting, or that sometimes I'd have to work harder than others to evoke an image? Concentrate on the fact that I was dumb and therefore couldn't comprehend? Concentrate on the fact that I was reading too slowly and sometimes meaning came and at other times it didn't?

If teachers can focus on what they do when they read or when they listen to someone speak or read aloud and then transfer this or translate it into approaches to teaching reading, perhaps they would really help students to read with comprehension rather than leave it all to chance.

I once worked with a 16-year-old student who had barely learned to read. More specifically, he had a very limited sight vocabulary and all reading for him was a hit or miss processs. After some preliminary work, he decoded the sentence *Mom and Dad met Tom*. He read this devoid of intonation and unlike his normal speech. He read one word at a time, "Mom—and—Dad—met—Tom." When I asked him to say it

faster, once again devoid of normal speech quality, but a bit faster he said, "Mom-and-Dad-met-Tom."

"Faster."

"Mom - and - Dad - met - Tom." (His face almost expressionless, staring into space.)

"Faster."

(Same, only faster.)

"Even Faster."

(Same.)

"Now like you speak."

"Mom and Dad, Mom and Dad! How did they get here?"

His face lit up, he turned to check the door, it was as if these words were reserved only for when he actually saw his parents. Speaking their names seemed to trigger an image so strong that he checked the door and said, "How did they get here?" The connection was made. Certainly other work needed to be done: decoding, becoming familiar with all the signs (spellings) of English, the conventions of written English and other conventions of reading—but he certainly did not have to wait until after he'd been decoding for some time to work on "reading comprehension." In fact, it would have been harmful and a waste of his time not to have read with comprehension from the start.

Popular methods used by teachers of reading include asking students to act out stories or plays they read, draw diagrams, describe characters, read a text while listening to a recorded version of it, etc. Teachers may do the right things, but often don't know why they work. When I ask them why they assign these exercises, their answers vary: "the kids enjoy it," "it makes reading fun," "it brings it to life." But why does it bring it to life? It does so because it helps students to call upon an ability they have—the power to evoke mental images when listening to speech. But this may not be transferred to reading, because they have not been made aware of what it is that they do. Some people are capable of coping with fiction or general nonfiction but are stumped when confronted with more technical kinds of writing. So one may find people who are very competent readers of fiction but cannot get through a textbook. They have not been able to make the transfer from one kind of material to the other, because they are not fully aware of what they do when they listen or read well.

In some cases the listener or reader may not have the images to evoke. This usually occurs with unfamiliar words or with material which is out of his or her experience, astrophysics for example. This is a problem different from the one I have been describing. In one case the person has the images but has not made the connection. In the other, there are no images to connect with. They must be invented.

Another problem arises when material is presented in a style unfamiliar to the listener or reader. In such cases the grammatical constructions, because they are different from ones habitually used by the person when speaking, interfere with the evocation of images.

In these cases I may need to help students acquire experience either with subject matter, specialized vocabulary or different language styles. I do not have to teach comprehension. They've learned how to comprehend if they speak the language. I don't have to teach them to use their powers of imagery; they use them all the time; for example, when I say draw a picture of a horse, although none is in the room, they can put one on paper. What I can do is create exercises like that of acting out a story or drawing pictures for sentences, or ask them to tune in the TV sets of their minds and help them to transfer, to the task of reading, what they do while listening.

I'm amazed at the number of teachers who create exercises for highlighting the relationship between imagery and writing, but are skeptical about doing the same for the relationship between imagery and reading with comprehension.

Personal Writing

by Anne Martin

There once was a girl
That wanted to be a poemist
But she couldn't think of a poem
But then she said to herself
I will make one up myself
And she did.
But then the girl forgot it
And then she remembered it
And then she forgot it
And it kept on going forever
And that was the end of the girl.
And the girl kept on forgetting
For all of her life.

Debbie, Grade 2

Just a few years ago it seemed necessary to persuade people that primary school children had things to say and could learn to write them, even with minimum technical skills at their disposal. Since then, the work of Kenneth Koch and others has become widely known, and teachers have tried new writing ideas which have had spectacular results with even the youngest children. Koch himself expressed surprise that the methods of releasing children to write could work so easily for teachers who were enthusiastic but not trained as writers. Comparisons, wish poems, color poems, and repetition of line forms have become almost standard fare in many classrooms. If this has freed children to enjoy writing and to learn varied ways of using language, and if it has given teachers a way to open up new approaches to teaching writing, then it has been all to the good.

There is, however, some danger that these methods are becoming a new orthodoxy, that the excitement of the process and the easy excellence of the products are overshadowing some very important purposes of writing: to learn to know what we need to say and how to say it. Even adults who have had some experience in writing may often find it difficult to express themselves clearly in their own way. For children who have barely begun to write and who are still struggling with the physical chore of mechanics, it is all the harder. But I am convinced that primary age children can be helped to find their own voices. To do that, it's not enough to use writing ideas such as Koch's or variations of our own. Teachers' suggestions of this kind certainly widen children's experience with language. But I think the value of introducing these kinds of writing exercises lies not in the products that emerge but in the process through which children learn techniques which they can later use in expressing their own ideas. The essential thing is for teachers to try to help young children write honestly out of their own needs and obsessions, even when this may result in writing that is often quirky, unpredictable, and not necessarily a source of pride on bulletin boards.

The seductive thing about the Koch type exercises is that the products are often so charming. Here are some examples from first and second graders in my classes:

I wish I was a flower
Because people could pick me up.
They would smell me and bring me home.
Maybe they would have other flowers
And I would look pretty.

I wish I was my father.
Then I would go out to eat
Because I like Chinese food.

I wish I had a long dress
Of diamonds on gold strings,
And white silk under the diamonds.
I wish I was a Queen Elizabeth.
I wish I was the prettiest girl.

I wish I didn't have to go to school
I wish it rained cats and rabbits
I wish the whole world was full of bubbles
I wish we could dig the bubbles
And go on a high diving board
And jump on the bubbles.

I used to be a dog
But now I am a cat
I used to be a tiger
But now I'm a mountain lion.
I used to walk
But now I crawl.
I used to be a ant
But now I'm the universe.

I used to like mathematics
But now I love it.

I used to be a mouse
But now I'm a dinosaur.
I used to fall in a bucket of water
But now I push it away from my bed.

It is obvious that the children are playing with language and enjoying it. Maybe they are sometimes even expressing ideas important to them. But most of the time I think they are just complying with a writing assignment, giving the teacher what he is looking for, coming up with the kind of writing that is sure to please adults and other children. When I was reading Koch's books, I began to get very weary as I read through pages of examples of children's writing which should have fascinated me. Finally I realized that there was a sameness in the examples that went beyond the similarity caused by a common form. The children were writing things that sounded like Koch's own ideas. They were doing it with verve and skill, but after too much of it I felt it sounded hollow. Again, let me stress that I think these joyful writing experiences are useful and maybe necessary, but they should be only a preliminary to more individualized writing.

When teachers stop looking for delightful products and encourage children to write in their own way, the process becomes more complicated and sometimes discouraging. In first grade by the middle of the year, I give each child a little writing notebook, or "diary," in which the children write several times a week or whenever they wish. The first entries are laboriously printed one-sentence statements of fact: "I went to the zoo and it was fun." "My sister got a new dress." After some weeks the entries get a little longer and sometimes have more spark to them:

I got a geologist lab and I used too much hydro-chloric acid and it went bubbling.

I got a bloody nose. Was it yucky! My mother wiped it off.

My tooth was a little bit loose but I tugged and tugged and tugged and then! My tooth came out!!!!!

I am going to see the Wizard of Oz. The witch is green and the whole thing is a dream and I have seen it nine times.

Often the children can't think of anything to write, and I try to suggest things they have told me or the class. But many times the diary entries are dull and uninspired—a far cry from the sparkling poems evoked by a teacher-given writing idea.

However, I have found that if I am patient and persistent, if I don't expect too much too soon, some amazing things sometimes start to happen to the children's writing. Some of the children slowly begin to find a style and theme of their own. Missy was a bright but frightened first grader who had so little confidence in herself that she would weep and mope at the slightest challenge. She didn't dare risk less than perfection, and would tear up her papers or sulkily refuse to try anything new. After several months, Missy relaxed more about her own capabilities, and she spent much time in writing her diary. I asked Missy for permission to reproduce her diary for my own pleasure. Here are some of her entries:

April 4
my father drov me to school and I thot Mrs. Martin was already there and I was the first one there and I tride to open the door But it was locked.

April 11
tonihgt I am going to get new shoos and my sister is going to get new shoos to and I am excited.

April 25
I know how to play tennis a little and my father got me and my sister a tennis ball and when I started I kept missing and I got mad and when I learned my sister tried and she got mad too.

April 27
The boys chased me when it was recess and I ran a round a tree and I got tired or running and they cot me.

May 8
I colld up my frend on saturday and my frends mother said on sunday you can come over and when it was sunday I thot I woondt come over But I did. and on saturday nihgt my sister and my father and me went to a fair and we went on three rides and on the first ride I laughed and on the seckind ride I was a

scarde because at first it went a round and it went faster and faster and it went higher and higher.

May 15
on mother day I got my mother some nailpolish Thar was red and I theeck the other was pink. and saturday I had to take a bath and it was my sister's turn to take a bath.

May 18
I played tennis and my tennis rackit is beter then the other one and I gave my sister my sneeckers and I walked home without my sneeckers and my soks got dirty.

Missy's diary, in its unselfconscious detail, revealed a particular child's world in a way I thought was both delightful and touching.

When Sid was in the first grade, he was often dreamy and far away in his thoughts. It was hard to reach him because he had a surface friendliness that firmly drew the line at real contact. Although the children's diaries are their own and may be kept private, Sid was one of the many children who always showed me their entries after they wrote. I noticed that he mostly wrote about New Hampshire where he spent his summers, and I encouraged him to keep writing about it. Over a period of weeks he kept adding to his diary, and he finally decided to collect these entries under the title "New Hampshire Stories." I think that it's significant that each story has the magic name New Hampshire in it. There are place names that evoke pictures in my mind too, and I think that the loving description in Sid's writing catches the reality of a child's attachment to a beautiful place where he has been happy. It also catches the particular flavor of New Hampshire itself. Perhaps some of Sid's preoccupations were his memories of the country and his strong wish to be there again.

NEW HAMPSHIRE STORIES
by Sidney

When I go to New Hampshire, every day when I get up in the morning I look out the window. I see a fox jumping on something.

When I go up to New Hampshire in the spring, I go swimming in the warm water. And I like to swim, so I swim almost the whole afternoon. Then I have to go up to the house for a nap.

I went up to New Hampshire. Our snowman was still up. The next day it was up but littler. The next day it was gone.

I was going to New Hampshire, and I saw a dead skunk. It smelled. It was on the road.

I like to go to New Hampshire in the summer because I can go swimming. At first it's cold, but then it gets warm in the lake.

A bear was walking in the woods. It was in New Hampshire. When it saw me, it ran away. I went home.

One day we went to New Hampshire. Our car broke down. We had to spend the night in our car. I got scared because I heard noises.

As the children move from the first to second grade, I have noticed a real change and development in their diary writing. For one thing, the value of privacy suddenly increases. While most children still show me what they write, they no longer want to read it to the class, though they are sometimes willing to have it "published" in our class magazine. Some of their diary entries are shared with friends but not with me, and some are altogether secret. I am strictly scrupulous about looking at the diaries only by permission, and I never urge a child to show me something that he is unwilling to share. When I was teaching first grade, a colleague expressed some displeasure that some of my former students wanted to continue their diary writing into second grade. She felt this was an immature wish to escape back into a freer world of writing where spelling wasn't important and children weren't expected to learn about paragraphs and "research." I was appalled that personal writing should be valued less than the artificial conventions of paragraphing or the industrious copying from textbooks that is termed research work.

Now that I am teaching second graders to whom I gave writing notebooks during the first week of the year, I am gratified by the varied use they are making of their diaries, and the tremendous progress they have made in their ability to express themselves in writing. My second graders have expanded their writing books to include poems, descriptions, whole books in chapters, science writing, and personal comments. It seems to me that at any age a child should be encouraged to write freely into a personal writing book. Not only is there nothing babyish or escapist about this kind of writing, but it may turn out to be the most genuine and important written expression a child has in school. It is probably no accident that quite a few of my former first grade writers have told me that either they don't write much anymore or they do it only at home. It takes a very determined young writer to insist on continuing personal writing during his small amount of free time at school if it is not encouraged or valued as a major part of the day's regular activities.

In my class this year, the main emphasis is on writing, which the children usually do first thing in the morning. Here are some examples of the variety of styles and forms used by my second graders. Amy, who reads a great deal and has a keen sense of humor, is writing a book named *The World of Harry*. It is about a very human rabbit and his adventures at home and school. She has already completed four chapters. Here is one that I especially liked:

Chapter III   The Shack

A little ways from Harry's house, there was a little shack. Once when Harry was seven years old, Harry went into the shack. And something said, "Get out before I shoot." Harry ran to California and back. When he got home he went to bed. Now remember, that was a long time ago.

One hot summer day his mother said, "Harry, why don't you and your friends go down to the beach?" "Well," Harry said, "Bob can't come. And Danny went to Mexico. But Gloria can come. I'll go call Gloria on the telephone."

But poor Harry. Gloria went to the movies with Big Bill Richie. Little did Harry know that Big Bill Richie and Gloria were getting married. Harry was so mad he put red ants in the wedding cake, and Gloria had to go to the hospital. But Harry didn't care because he didn't like Gloria anymore.

Tony is a brilliant mathematician who has problems with other people because of his aggressive pugnacious attitude. He can argue for hours rather than admit he is mistaken, but he wants to have friends. Although Tony doesn't like writing much, he wrote the following poem which expresses his own troubled feelings about human relations in a clever, half-humorous way. He now says he likes to write poetry best of anything.

Poem with No Name

I think that I think
That I can't think
About what I think
I'm sorry I got it wrong
I'll try again.
I think that I
May be wrong.

I think that I think
About what you think.
I do think I'm wrong
About what you think.
I'm all mixed up
So I'm wrong.

You think that I think
That you think
About what I think.
Sometimes I think
About what you think
When I am wrong.

I have found that reading poetry to the children just before they write in their diaries sometimes leads them to write poems without my asking them to do it. They themselves often define their writing as poems. Misha, who has been read to a great deal at home, considers himself a potential poet. He often insists on rhyme, but sometimes manages it gracefully. He also tries to incorporate his literary heritage into his writing. Here are two of his poems:

I feel like a volcano
Lashing fire against a rock
Blowing up and shooting down
The birds that come in a flock
Pushing up the flames
That come in awful rays
Blowing up the mountains
That show up the evening days.

Once in the middle of winter
I was doth dreaming
A snow fairy came along
And said, "What is thou doing here?
Come along to the castle
And have your feet warm."
So I came along and was presented before the king.
He cried, "To the dungeons with thee!"
Then, I blinked and woke.

Debbie is also a "poemist." Her parents have recently separated, and she is obsessed with family themes. Here is her poem about a butterfly:

I was born in a log cabin
And so was my brother
And he had yellow dots
and black wings.
And my brother did not like me
And my mom liked me better
than my brother.
I am yellow with black wings
And I am sick of telling him
to stop shouting
And I just fly away.

Using the same first line as Misha, Debbie's poem came out distinctively her way:

Once in the middle of winter
A girl went out to fetch some wood.

"I think that a teacher's calm confidence that the child himself will come up with an idea is often more reassuring than tricky ideas invented by teachers."

And when she came home
Her mom yelled at her
Because she was late
And she ran to her room and cried.

In order to encourage children to develop their own themes, I occasionally give them each an individual writing assignment that I think might appeal to them. My student teacher and I spent some time discussing a suggestion for each child, and she typed them up beautifully for each child. For Malcolm who loves map study, she drew a little treasure map and asked him to write his adventures while searching for the treasure. He was entranced and wrote feverishly all morning. I think it is the only time a child in the class ever sustained the present tense for more than a sentence or two, and that device underlines Malcolm's sense of drama (and humor):

I am starting on my search for the hidden treasure. Here we go. Right now I am at the lookout mountain. I think I will go up and see what I can see. I can see a hut. And I am thirsty. So I will go to the hut and get some water. Now I am at the hut and boy is that water delicious. But I better be going now.

Now I am at the deserted ship. There is a closet. I think I will open it. Oh no! A pirate was in it! Oh good, a quicksand trap. I will go around the quicksand. And the pirate goes in it. Boy am I thirsty but I am not at the hut. But I am in a coconut grove. So I can drink coconut milk. Boy is that coconut milk bad. I will be going now.

Oh no! A volcano is smoking. Oh good, it is only doing its daily smoke. Oh boy! Here is the gate. But it is too high so I can't climb it. But I can dig under the gate! I am on the other side of the gate! And here is the treasure!!

Since this year I moved on with some of my last year's first graders into second grade, I was able to observe certain children's progress in developing a definite style of their own. Alyssa is a mature, outgoing child who is geared sensitively towards other people. Last year in first grade her diary entries read like this: "My dog is crazy. He plays with a baby doll that I found outside, and he is a big dog." This year her entries suddenly began to interject little personal comments to the reader, such as "and buleve me it was not, repeat *not*, very fun" or "by the way I forgot to tel you wat my cousin's name is." This is very much the way Alyssa speaks, and she has managed to catch her own converstional tone not only in her diaries but now also in her stories:

Once in the middle of winter I saw a squirrel. She was so cold I brought her in so that she could get warm. And I asked my mom, "Can I keep the squirrel?" and can you imagine, she said yes. Well I was so happy that I almost fainted, but luckily I didn't. So each day I had to feed her, but that was all right. I still love her.

Laura, the youngest child in my class, had a hard time writing anything last year. A good effort for her a year ago was: "I went sledding. My dad pulled the sled. I liked it." Writing still isn't easy for Laura, and her verbal ability is still way ahead of her writing skill, but she is now beginning to find her own way:

When I woke up
I looked out the window.
When I saw the snow
I got dressed quick.
When my mother saw me
She was surprised.

Some of the children are just beginning to put personal touches in their writing now and then. Russell has a quite sophisticated sense of humor, and in his description of the Statue of Liberty he wrote, "The Statue of Liberty has a Bible so she can read it when she has nothing to do." Julia has a judicious air when she speaks and now also often when she writes: "If I was a butterfly I would like it in a way, and in a way I wouldn't because it has such a short life. But for the butterfly it is very long." Adee has shown much curiosity about adult life, and she wrote: "Mom, since you were married, what is it like when you get married? Well anyway, bring me to my wedding." Some personal styles are mysteriously offbeat. Peter, a fluent writer in first grade, became intrigued with writing everything backwards. As he became adept at printing backwards as easily as forwards, I became just as good at reading it, which never ceased to surprise him. There probably wasn't any particular value in allowing Peter to develop this skill, except his obvious enjoyment of it. He was the only child I've ever taught who showed such persistent delight in writing backwards, and I think he appreciated my interest in his individualistic experiment.

Of course there are many first and second graders who are not yet at ease in writing. And even the children who are developing their own style are sometimes not in the mood or just uninspired. When teachers stop worrying too much about the products of writing, they can accept the unevenness of any writer's results, and they can tolerate occasional unresponsiveness to writing assignments. At first I used to worry about children who consistently said they could not think of anything to write. I would suggest things, or remind them of things they had told me, and sometimes that worked for them. But I find now that often the best thing is just to ask them to sit quietly and think for a while. More often than not, something will emerge that is more real to the child than what I would have suggested. I think that a teacher's calm confidence that the child himself will come up with an idea is often more reassuring than tricky writing ideas invented by teachers. And if nothing comes to the child that day, perhaps tomorrow or next week he will come in with shining eyes to announce, "I know what I'll write in my diary today!" and then spend most of the morning recounting an important event in his life.

At the same time that I encourage children to have their own ideas, I also frequently assign topics that may have come out of classroom experiences or discussions. When I brought the children fortune cookies, we read their fortunes and then each child wrote some fortunes of his own and cut them up into strips. The next day the children chose their fortunes and wrote about them. Sarah chose YOU ARE

GOING TO BE FAMOUS and wrote:

If I were famous I could boss everybody around. I could have holidays anytime. I would be rich. And I would live in a palace. And I have two little girls. And I would always tell people to leave me alone when I am reading.

There are some assigned topics that almost always evoke a response from children, such as themes of love and hate, brothers and sisters, and nature writing after direct contact with the outdoors or animals. All these assignments, along with Kenneth Koch type of stimulation, offer a range of writing ideas and approaches to children. But the impetus to write must eventually come from each child himself, and not in response to a teacher's suggestion.

When Anthony was in first grade, he came running in from the playground all excited about an imaginary game he had played, and he begged to be allowed to write it down immediately:

At Greenland there was a green tree and it was big. And it was under the water in a bubble. And our raft was washed on the shore. And there was a big! big!!!! hill. And Ivar and me got attacked.

The urgency of Anthony's need to write things down is what I would eventually hope to see sporadically for all children. I spent my childhood writing skillful compostitions, and later in college writing good perspective papers, earning A's along the way without difficulty. But it is only quite recently that I have begun to find out what I really want to write—many years too late, as far as I'm concerned. Most of us are like the girl in Debbie's poem who alternately forgot and remembered her poem "for all of her life," a process that "kept on going forever." As a teacher, I hope that some of my children can remember what they want to say at least some of the time, and that I can help them in the attempt to stay in touch with themselves and to express their unique view of the world.

Teaching Poetry Writing to Rural Kids

by Ron Padgett and Dick Gallup

Dick Gallup served as Poet-in-Residence in West Virginia for five months in 1974. What follows are his impressions of that residency, with emphasis on teaching poetry writing in rural settings. The interview is followed by a selection of poems written by children (grades 1-12) who worked with him.

GALLUP: People who teach in a rural situation usually come from rural backgrounds. In other words, you don't find too many teachers who grew up in Chicago or Detroit teaching in the wilds of West Virginia or in the mountains of Pennsylvania. Usually it's people who grew up if not in that area, then in a similar area.

PADGETT: Did you find it any easier or harder to teach in those places?

GALLUP: Well, it's easier in that there are fewer demands on you in a certain way. For example, you don't have to be quite the showman that you have to be to get the attention of the kids in the New York City school where you come in and you're just one more excitement in the day. You're the only excitement in a month or a year or the decade.

PADGETT: But if you have a writing idea and you try it with a class in a small school out in the country, do you generally find that the kids there take to it, or is there any difference?

GALLUP: There's some difference. I usually think of things in terms of problems, what problems the kids have in the areas that will affect the way they approach writing assignments. And I guess the biggest problem they have as a group is the problem of self-image, in that in some strange way they consider themselves worthless. In other words, they think that the thoughts that they have as children are absolutely worthless. This is the result of a combination of a few things. One is thinking that the people who live in the suburbs and the cities are sort of like the real people of America and that they, on the other hand, are just hicks, living in the hills. That's an attitude that they

get from the adults. It's an adult's way of looking at it, it's not a child's. The thing with the kids is that—and this is different from area to area, in some areas which are very "traditional," very "backward," —the children seem to be treated at home in some really incredible way, in that they're not allowed to speak. They're told to keep their mouth shut, on all occasions, at the dinner table, and if they want to talk, they go outside. When they're in the house around mom, dad, grandma and grandpa they're supposed to keep their mouth shut. So that they get the idea that anything they might say is worthless because they're not allowed to say it. If you try doing writing assignments with them that deal with power —"If I Ruled the World" or Wish Poems, things like that—often it's very difficult to get any idea of the thing across because they're so far removed from believing that they could rule anything, other than a frog, or a tadpole. Or that they could wish for anything, wish for things to be different than they are: they feel absolutely powerless. I found it very difficult to get them to do this sort of assignment.

PADGETT: What gives you the impression that they don't get to talk at home?

GALLUP: Speaking to the teachers, in some places. There were a couple of places where I taught in West Virginia which were very much this way, so much so that even people from fifteen miles away found it strange. There was one particular little school up in the hills. People who were administrators or who worked from school to school didn't like to eat lunch in this school because it was too strange and weird because the kids didn't say anything. It was quiet, it was unnaturally quiet. And the administrators thought that the school teachers did it, that they somehow had these kids hypnotized into never saying boo. The first few times I came to this school all they said was Yes sir, Mr. Gallup, No sir. That's virtually all they would say. Eventually I got them to open up a little bit by just doing a number on them over and over again, continually trying to bring them out. I talked to the teachers about it. They also had noticed that they were very quiet and some of them tried to get the kids to be more expressive and didn't have too much success. And they told me that these kids are just shut outside the door and that's the way they're dealt with in this particular area. The people had brought up their children like that for the last hundred years in an area which was stable—the families had *stayed there*—so it was a tradition that went back. And it was one valley, really. It was like fifteen miles long and ten miles wide and these kids went to this school and they all lived in this valley and it was its own little society. I found it was often the case in West Virginia. The people would be quite different from the people who lived in the valley just over the mountain. And if you talked to these people about the people who lived over this particular mountain (which wasn't much of a mountain after all and there's a road over it) and you asked "Do you know any of the kids that live over in the other valley?" or, "Well, do you know any kids that go to this other school?" which would be in the next valley, they wouldn't know shit. So there's no communication between these people. The parents didn't know each other, except occasionally as relatives.

PADGETT: Do the kids learn about other people's behavior through television? I know at one school I worked at in West Virginia the kids said they didn't have a television.

GALLUP: Right.

PADGETT: Welfare hill people or something?

GALLUP: It's not a matter of their being on welfare. Some of the people up there have a reasonable amount of money, they're not that poor, but the fact is they can't get the cable in because there aren't enough people.

PADGETT: So these kids' ideas on how to behave come right out of their family and school environments.

GALLUP: They were untouched and that's one of the bonuses of the situation: you had human mentality untouched by television and untouched by radio because "radio" ceased to exist in 1950. I mean, they can hear music, but not as a form of communication (like listening to Jack Benny or something). So they had no media with social keys in it.

PADGETT: And how was this a bonus exactly?

GALLUP: If you got the kids to express themselves it was a sort of pure expression of just what their imaginations could come up with and what was in their background, and it wasn't colored at all by this television business. So that occasionally you would find some kid who would write a nature poem that would resemble something like an ancient Greek lyric or ancient Chinese poetry, but not artificially stimulated. . .

"They were untouched and that's one of the bonuses of the situation: you had a human mentality untouched by television and untouched by radio because 'radio' ceased to exist in 1950."

PADGETT: Not drawn from any secondary sources...

GALLUP: Right. You'd get this real serenity. And that I found to be a real bonus. It's fantastic to be able to work with kids who really haven't had their heads turned around by all these various stimulations of contemporary America. If you can get them to say what they're thinking it's very interesting, because it's not going to be something they got one way or another from some place else, something that you know about too. It comes from looking at a flower in a field or something.

PADGETT: In one class at Grassy Lick Elementary I remember asking a kid what he did after school and he said he milked the cow. I seized upon this and asked, "What kind of a dream do you think a cow would have?" He looked at me as if I were some kind of an idiot. He had a very common sensical attitude. It wasn't unimaginative at all, he was simply common sensical. And I remember it kind of stunned me for a second. He didn't have that kind of sophistication, that intellectual or imaginative sophistication that city kids can have that enables a kid to synthesize these kinds of concepts. He still had a kind of charming, to me, common sense attitude. I never had a kid in an urban area react like that. I just remember the kids at Grassy Lick didn't seem to take to "crazy" ideas very much.

GALLUP: No they don't. And in a way they're absolutely right. If they just live up in the mountains and they're going to live there all their lives and they just deal with things in a very common sensical way ... it's naive but on the other hand it's perfectly sane...

PADGETT: It's perfectly sane in terms of itself. In a larger context it might be a dangerous attitude.

GALLUP: If you leave the mountains, it's a dangerous attitude. It's probably sane in terms of a stable agricultural agrarian traditional culture. The minute you put some other input into it, it doesn't work. But it's a stable sort of thing which I find interesting partly because the idea today is that progress is perhaps a bad idea. We need to have some sort of stability rather than having growth all the time and it's interesting because these people actually have a stable situation. The pluses to it are just placidity, really. And the minuses, if you're associated with it for any period of time, the minuses become absolutely overpowering so that most people who live in that situation and have any creative intelligence feel incredibly stifled. If there's any possibility of any place else to go or anything else to do, you do it. You leave.

Another thing I wanted to talk about was how in a rural situation you get a very clear picture of how the economic system in this country works; and it has to do with how the kids are brought up, and how they're treated in school, and the way the various authorities treat the people, and the way that they're manipulated in order to support the economy in the area and to make money for those who make money, which are only a few really. The poor people are brought up to have a not-too-good opinion of themselves, and sexual repression is encouraged by the people in power and by most of the religious people. They create a sort of frustration and anxiety out of this and then they put people to work and let them make a little money, the idea being that they will express this repressed sexual energy by buying things, by working hard to make money so that they can buy things. It's a vicious system, this system of exploitation. I don't see anything else you could call it. I talked to kids who are in the high schools about what they were doing with their lives, trying to make them a little more conscious about choices they could make, but the way they are exploited in the situation is not simply a surface thing where you can say, "Listen, they're ripping you off by doing this and the other thing, and all you have to do is stop them." It's not that simple. The roots of it go very deep into their personality and the ways that they're molded at a young age to make them dependent on the system which is exploiting them. [1]

PADGETT: So they cannot continue to exist simply as themselves if they're going to wreck the system?

GALLUP: Right, if they wreck the system, they're destroyed.

PADGETT: Well, you've described a people as the prey of oppressors, subject to anxiety and repression, but you've also described them as people who are placid and have serenity.

GALLUP: That's different. That's the people who live in the valleys and are farmers. They're isolated. They live on farms or on top of the mountain, which is a different society also. The people who live on the top of the mountains are entirely different from the people who live "down." In fact they always go back up. They come down into Keyser or some town that's down in the valley and they don't like it and they go back up to the top where they do two things. They either cut wood, take it to the paper mill, or they strip-mine, find a little place that has a little coal, three guys in a truck can strip-mine and make enough money to live on. Or they just drive a truck for somebody. They just stay apart.

PADGETT: I was under the impression that high school kids were bused in to a central school..

GALLUP: Right. And that makes a big difference. At school they're in a more central location and they have a lot more stimulation from the outside world. They show them a lot of movies and bring things in and it adds up, so that they have a lot more connection with the world. The kids that are really backward and that are really just screwed into the

"Anywhere around the country I've found that good teachers were about the same, but that the bad teachers are always bad in a lot of different ways."

hills, they're just kept out there until they get to be 14 or 16 and then they don't have to go to school at all.

But in any case, the high school kids in a rural situation have a certain naiveté which I think is really a product of good health and plenty of exercise. They tend to be very healthy animals, and it gives them a naiveté in their outlook on life, thinking that things are good and they're happy. They are direct and open and if you talked to them about something and they understood you, they would respond to it; and if they didn't understand you, they would be puzzled and ask you to explain it to them. There was no hostility there, no hostility toward someone asking them something or making demands on them. I found that terrific actually, very refreshing.

PADGETT: I wanted to ask you about some of the teachers. The idea I had was that they didn't seem all that different from teachers here in New York except that they were less harried and anxious and exhausted at the end of the day. But as far as their interest in what I was saying or their ability to understand or use it, it seemed that some of them had it and some of them didn't.

GALLUP: The rural schools had some good teachers and the good teachers were the same as good teachers anywhere. They were interested in anything you had to tell them, they were interested in any way they could help the kids. They understood some of the problems that the kids had and were interested in exposing them to things in a good way so that they could handle it when they were further away from their little home ground. And they were very interested in finding if the kids were intelligent enough to go further than high school. The good teachers were like that. Generally, it just seemed to be a matter of intelligence: if they were intelligent they were good because there weren't that many kids per class, and they had the federal money from that Johnson program started a few years ago for depressed areas. So that they had lots of teachers and helpers. Anywhere around the country I've found that the good teachers were about the same, but that the bad teachers are always bad in a lot of different ways. The good ones are always good because they treat the children like human beings, and they're intelligent and they try to figure out things that they can do with and for the kids.

PADGETT: Did you change your way of teaching poetry when you went into a small rural school?
GALLUP: I did change a lot of things. First of all, because of their weak self-image you couldn't start out by having them pretend they have a lot of power or can make the world the way they want it, sort of the ultimate utopia city trip. The utopia idea [2] was like an ultimate carrot to hold out to the city kids to get them to use their imagination in an aggressive sort of way. In the rural situation, that doesn't work because they've got no strong idea of themselves, or of changing the world. Another thing is that a lot of them are nonverbal to a large extent. First of all, they're told to shut up at home, and second, they spend a lot of time wandering around the fields or hunting with a .22 or fishing or doing the chores. So they're very nonverbal, they don't think in words. You can't turn them on by just trying to get words to come out. One of the things I did was to have them do things which were visual, like using map assignments to begin with, because that way they could get into a fantasy world more easily by using the map. Then I would get them to put words into it by naming places on their maps and just get some pin-pricks of words through their craniums and to see that they could enjoy it and that words were fun. Then when I'd come back again, I'd get them to start writing things, actually writing sentences. It's not like the problem you have in a "depressed" city school where you can't get kids to write words because they're allergic to pencils and paper. The rural kids haven't been turned off to pencil and paper, they just haven't ever been turned on.
PADGETT: What were other assignments that you thought worked well?
GALLUP: The "I Remember" poem, because some teachers there tend to relate to their kids on a very "traditional" level. In other words, they instruct the children and they don't talk to them about their own experiences much. So, if I found a class like that, I would often do an "I Remember" assignment, not because I thought they would write terrific poems—because if you do I Remembers with kids in the second and third grades you don't usually get such great poems—but you do get a terrific relationship with the class and they just start telling you things they remember. And you have this session of just talking about things, about their experiences. In a

way the important part of it is oral rather than what they write down, even though you have them write some things down just to get them into the habit of writing so you can do something else the next time. But it's a way of getting the kids to relate to you as a person rather than as a teacher.

PADGETT: What other assignments did you use?

GALLUP: Making up the Creatures.

PADGETT: So you didn't call it "Monsters." [3]

GALLUP: I didn't call it Monsters because I told them it could be nice. I called them Creatures.

PADGETT: Did you have them draw first?

GALLUP: No. I universally had them write it first and draw it second. And usually I began by doing a collaboration with them on the board and putting down a couple of the parts myself and having them give me some other parts and then drawing a picture myself of the creature we created and then having them do their own.

PADGETT: Did you use a standard form like "Eyes of a . . ." or did you tell them they could do it any way they wanted?

GALLUP: Usually I used it as an opening assignment and I told them very specifically how to do it. Write the name of the creature at the top.

PADGETT: A highly structured assignment. . .

GALLUP: Right. Write "He has," put a colon and then say, "Eyes of a" this, "Teeth of a" that. I encouraged them to say what kind of a heart he had, what kind of thoughts he had, what kind of liver, brain, what dreams he had, anything, not just the parts they were going to draw but also things such as how many children he had and if he was married and what he liked to eat.

PADGETT: Do you have any way of knowing whether the kids read comics? Or what kind of reading they did at home? For instance, you go way out to Grassy Lick and you go into the second grade, how many of the kids there would know who Frankenstein is?

GALLUP: I don't know, I didn't ask them, I wish I had.

PADGETT: Or would they know King Kong? I just wonder how many would know those popular culture heroes. More kids know King Kong than Johnny Appleseed. I wonder if they'd know who Hank Aaron is? It would be interesting to know, getting back to the Creatures, what they base their notions on. In New York, they watch Creature Feature or Chiller Theatre. There's a wealth of incredible monstrosities. It seems that out there the kids might create nicer creatures, rather than the Japanese fire-breathing, town-stomping monsters you get in New York.

GALLUP: I also used haiku, as three line poems really. I used them largely the way we did the day you were there. [4]

PADGETT: Right. The two and the one with the socko at the end. That seems to be very effective. It's very mechanical and kind of hokey; it's just one little specialized tiny form but it's something that kids don't forget. What else?

GALLUP: Conceptual poems such as Opening Poems. [5] "I open something and something comes out" and Dreams, [6] they work pretty well. In the Middle Poems worked all the time. Generally I used simple conceptual assignments, such as Opening Poems, for connecting things in a strange way: "I opened a pig and valentines came out." And Like Poems, to try to teach simple association, how to connect things in emotional terms. I told them to connect their images by keeping things in the same mood, or color, or mood-color (and to throw in a couple of ringers to sort of wake people up). And this way to start them at ground-zero, to teach them the way human synapses work and build upon the simple concepts that are programmed into our brain-computer. To teach them how to select a program they already knew, one way of relating things, a simple conceptual or emotional shape.

The fact that they were always happy to see me meant I didn't have to go around the bend to think of great things to get them interested. I did try to come straight on and teach them these things, without talking about them so much as by having the kids just do them. I tried to be as direct and simple as I possibly could and teach them the most basic things I could teach. And it worked pretty well.

PADGETT: Do you know if there's any sort of local story-telling tradition? Local stories about real people that get a legendary quality from elaboration?

GALLUP: I don't know. I didn't run into it. I did use pantoums a lot. Lots of pantoums. [7] And acrostics.

PADGETT: What'd they think of that?

GALLUP: Loved it. They liked acrostics and again they didn't have to make sentences. I also had some kids write plays. I usually divided the class up into committees and had each child in each committee be a character. They sit around and they make the play by having each child be one character and putting in the lines of that character. I gave them various suggestions for titles of plays to write, and I encourage them to put things other than human beings in the plays, animals, talking chairs, glasses. . .

PADGETT: Picasso has a play like that, *Desire Caught by the Tail*. A lot of Dadaist plays have objects as characters. . . . [8]

While I'm thinking of it, you said something about the children's responses toward nature having a kind of purity or naiveté, that. they would write things which reminded you of Greek lyrics or early Chinese poetry. Did you ever actually read them any Greek lyrics?

GALLUP: No. The poem that made me think of this

was written near the end of my stay there. I hadn't really keyed into that before. I tried reading Chinese poetry, [9] some of which was pastoral, and it would tend to put them to sleep. What would really wake them up were Richard Brautigan's poem about everybody gets VD and things like that or poems that had a little twist to them. The most I would do to encourage them to write pastoral poems would be if there were some boy who wouldn't know anything to write about, I'd say, what do you do all the time, do you fish alot? and he'd answer yes, and I'd ask him if he had a rifle, did he hunt squirrels, and he'd say yes he did that or he'd say he didn't fish or hunt, just walked around. I'd say write a poem describing what it's like, what you feel when you're out walking around in the woods, and some of them would actually do it. That's the way I got at the pastoral thing rather than through models. I think I talked to some of the high school kids about the idea of pastoral poetry using nature as a mirror for a human existence and also as stressing continuity of values and the changing of the seasons in terms of change and also in terms of being cyclical. I gave them some examples. It was a special workshop at Hampshire High School. But with the kids in grade school I might try to give them one little idea like that, take one idea, one image and relate it, and say it to them about three times in five minutes, and go on with the hope that eight years later one of the kids would wake up in bed and say Oh!

But a little more about what goes and what doesn't go. In rural areas the more devious thought patterns don't go so well. They don't really understand irony. Here in New York my daughter's classroom is called "Lynn's Paradise," Lynn being the teacher, and by that they mean that it isn't at all paradisical. But out in West Virginia the kids usually don't go around through the back door that way: irony doesn't seem to work at all. This is with kids, say, ten or eleven.

And another thing: surrealistic imagery doesn't work. I mean like cows playing the flute, it doesn't really hit them. You have to come at them frontally, very straight.

The other thing that doesn't go well is Wit. What passes for wit in a rural setting is your local "character" who fires off good ones. Which is fine for "native" wit. But intellectual wit is something else.

I want to say something about what they do appreciate. They have an appreciation of Beauty. In other words you can talk to them about something being beautiful and they have a more straightforward attitude toward it than to something that's witty, and you can get kids to write about things they think are beautiful.

PADGETT: You mean they can appreciate both a beautiful subject and beautiful language?

GALLUP: Both. Most can appreciate a beautiful subject. The ones who can appreciate beautiful language are the ones blessed with an ear.

PADGETT: Sitting here I just thought that it might be good to try doing simple poetry events or happenings with them, nothing complicated by a lot of machinery or anything. It seems the kids, with their sense of directness and literalness, might really dig it. For instance, have each kid get a pencil and paper and go outside and run in different directions, counting to a hundred. When they get to one hundred, stop, write down the first thing they see, turn around and run back to the classroom. Obviously what they wrote down would be of little importance here, but it would be just fun to do that kind of thing. You could even have the teachers running the hundred yard dash!

GALLUP: That's a terrific idea! And you could do it without getting run over by a cab.

PADGETT: I can just see them running over the hills.

GALLUP: It'd be terrific if some of them didn't come back, just run right on home and say, "Boy that poetry teacher sure is stupid. He aimed me right toward home. So I kept running until I crashed right through the front door."

Notes

[1] Interested readers might refer to *Hillbilly Women* (Avon, $1.25), a fascinating collection of interviews, mostly with coal miners' wives and daughters, by Kathy Kahn, and *Pedagogy of the Oppressed.* (Seabury Press, $2.95) by Paulo Freire, the Brazillian who has worked for years to develop ways in which the "oppressed" can deal critically with the world without experiencing what we call "an education."

[2] See *Imaginary Worlds* by Dick Murphy (Teachers and Writers Collaborative publications). "Creating Worlds" by Marvin Hoffman (*Whole Word Catalogue 1*, p. 42).

[3] See *The Whole Word Catalogue 1*, p. 18, "Ghosts and Monsters."

[4] See p. 163.

[5] See pp. 42, 43.

[6] See *Wishes, Lies, and Dreams*, Kenneth Koch, Chelsea House, 1970

[7] See pp. 43, 151.

[8] For example Tristan Tzara's "the gas heart" in *Modern French Theatre*, transl. & ed. Michael Benedikt and George E. Wellwarth (E. P. Dutton, N.Y., 1964).

[9] Mostly Wang Wei, Li Po, Tu Fu.

The sun is sleeping in the sky
The sun is hot
I get sleepy
Soon I am dreaming about a robin flying south
I am dreaming about a river
Running through the valley and flooding the town
The sun is mad at the river
I am mad at the river
I am dreaming about the moon
The moon makes light at night
I am dreaming about the sun
The sun is bright

Kathy
Grassy Lick Elem.

I see people
I hear the wind
I smell food in my lunchbox
I taste my peanutbutter sandwich
I touch my pencil
I think it's going to be a good day.

Alisa Murphy
Keyser Elem.
Mrs. Crowe's Class

I opened a cherry
and found a stone

I opened a stone
And found a bone

I opened the bone
And found a dog

I opened the dog
And out jumped a log

I opened the log
And out came the fog

I opened the fog
And out came the sun

I opened the sun
And out came happiness.

Elizabeth Hicks
Romney Elem.
Miss Wozniak's Class

A   Acrobatic alligators acted at an arena
B   Billy busted big blue bubbles
C   Cooky Carrie cracked coconuts carelessly
D   Donald Duck despises dumb Dutchmen
E   Edward Elephant ate eleven eggplants
F   Frogs feast frozen food
G   Gargoyles grab grinning grannies
H   Heartless Henry had hairy hippies
I   Inky icecream is all over Ivan
J   Janey jumped jingling jumpropes
K   Kicking kangeroos can kill kittens
L   Lighten licked long laundry
M   Mimi married Mike the Macaroni man
N   Nancy knitted nine neckties
O   Oscar Owl overdid an oily omelette
P   Patty peppers peanutbutter patties and pancake
Q   Quick Queens quit quite often
R   Ron relishes raspberries and radishes
S   Seven swans swim southward
T   Tim tapped ten telegrams to Tommy
U   Uncle Ums underwear is unusually ugly
V   St. Valentine's vest is violet
W   Wicked Wanda wanted white window shades
X   Xerxes X-Rayed xylophones
Y   Yellow Yaks ate yummy yoghurt
Z   Zebras zip zestfully through Zebu

Kenny, Wilfong & Sam
Romney Elem.
Mr. Serrian's Class

Romney's closed
and stores went away
Cashregisters are closed,
and money ran away.
Stores are closed,
and food went away.
Parks are closed,
and recreation went away.
Streams are polluted
and fish went away.
Forests burned,
and animals sprang away.
Ponds froze,
and frogs leaped away.
School closed,
and children went away.
Doors slammed,
and people went away.
Books closed,
and words went away.
Eyes closed,
and sight left.

Patricia
John Cornwell Elem.

The Flying Horse

One day I imagined I saw a flying horse.
I think it was a dream.
But I could see it plain as day.
I could hear it make a sound.
I tried to touch his long white mane.
I could feel a warm wind as he flew away.
I could smell and taste the nice clean air.
I wish that horse would come back.
I hope he will some day.
I can sense it.

Lori Evans
Romney Elem.
Mrs. Allen's Class

A girl in my class is absent
She got in trouble
What for I don't know
She was suspended

She got in trouble
She was arrested for disobeying privacy
She was suspended
Now she is in bed

She was arrested for disobeying privacy
Now she is in bed
She is scared
She likes to be with people

She is scared
A girl in my class is absent
She likes to be with people
What for I don't know

Anonymous
Romney Elem.
Miss Crookshank's Class

Monday is like a boulder crushing your head in
Tuesday is like sitting on a wasp nest
Wednesday is like biting your tongue
Thursday is like going into the jaws of death
Friday is like a sunny day
Saturday is even better
Sunday is building a model and it falling apart

Rhonda
Keyser Elem.

I opened a book and poems came out
I opened a poem and meaning came out
I opened meaning and thoughts came out
I opened thoughts and Ideas came out
I opened Ideas and things came out
I opened things and we came out
I opened us and poems came out
I opened poems and books came out

I opened Mr. Colebank and paddles came out
I opened his paddles and nails came out
I opened nails and Iron came out
I opened Iron and Cobalt came out
I opened cobalt and Colebank came out

Elizabeth Anderson
Romney Elem.
Miss Crookshank's Class

The horse was dead in Denmark. Meanwhile, Hank
the Sloppy Farmer wanted another, but he had no
money. Hank sat down where the horse had died.
Boo Hoo. Now I don't want to live, if the horse gave
milk and meat. Ah! Who cares? At last the Farmer
fell asleep! Eternal sleep!

Ray Ault
Ft. Ashby HS
Grade 11

I have a bike
and I zoom zoom zoom on my bike
down the road
and zoom up the road

and I spin my wheels
and I spin and spin
but I start zooming up the road
because my tire has a flat

and I zoom all around the road
and I zoom zoom zoom all around
the road
and I hit a stump and zoom

and zoom back up the hill
and went down the
road and I went home and I hit
my car and I zoom zoom zoom all the way
home again

Smokey Longerbean
Wiley Ford Elem.

Like pretty girls with pretty hearts
Like fresh air
Like clean water
Like peace and quiet
Like doing nothing
Like the sound of a jutterbug on a clear night
Like the fight of bass on a line
Like being all alone
Like the sound of water and rocks
Like days without tests
Like the sound of a chainsaw in the distance
But most of all I like days without school

Richard
Piedmont HS
Grade 9

Like kicking a pebble with bare feet
Like waking on a super sunny day
Like talking to yourself when no one's around
Like singing out of key   just for the heck of it
Like being the only one right
Like telling the world a secret
Like saying your own special prayer
Like being completely satisfied with a day
Like not being afraid to be yourself
Like being your own friend.

Anon.
Keyser HS
Grade 12

Honorably ridding himself of the troublesome boys
When the parrot began to whistle
He had very little feeling for animals that day
The boys learned they were too late
And the old staring simpleton had hot meat for his supper

Anon.
Hampshire HS
Grade 10

School

Here I sit in this damn class
I think of nothing but your sweet ass
Looking out the window at the birds
If I can't get seconds I'll take thirds
As I think about it all
I wish this building soon would fall
I've taken this trash for 12 long years
While I could have been at Kemps soakin up a few beers
I hate this place and I always will
I wish they'd turn it to an oil spill
For all my life I'll hold a grudge

Anon.
Keyser HS
Grade 12

Starting slowly
    Creeping:
I wasn't aware
I was captured by the thought
Am I here?
    Or am I taken over
Yes someone wrote this.
    I know I didn't

Who has brought me to this?

Rhetta
Hampshire HS

44

What is real?
    Take away sight
    images appear for I create
Naked legless baby scream showing your descendants.
    Wind creates a fantasy with my hair
I vomit nectar of the sweet, sweet earth.
        One blue eye understands me
        Two gray eyes fight me
        Five red eyes rape me.
Kind face of the underyears suck my blood
    But my heart is for the animals to devour
        Take away sight
Dark, vicious animal rips my legs apart
    Drains all my energy by forked tongue
I vomit poisonous nectar of the coloptop flower
        One blue eye understands me
        Two grey eyes fight me
        Five red eyes rape me
Sucking my blood shall not destroy me.
    I shall live in you—Naked legless baby.

Rhetta
Hampshire HS

Genius

I am retarded.
Miss Nancy said so.

I am a beautiful person.
Mommy said that.

I love people, but people hurt
Mommy loves me, but mommy
doesn't hurt.
Mommy feels good.
I am mixed up.
Why does Mommy feel good and
people hurt?

People are dumb.
People lie.
They never talk to the flowers
or the animals.
They don't care.
Flowers and animals are smart.
They understand me.
The moon understands me.
People just laugh. And stare.

I think flowers should be president.

Robin
Hampshire HS

Voices in a tunnel
Hollow low
"Come here Johnny
Johnny bring your leg"
Red wing eyelash falling
Drop of ashes
Falling like me

Poet X-9
Hampshire HS

BEFORE THE DREAM

Like water running in a gutter
Like sunlight fading
Like children getting slower
Like buildings coming down
Like bicycles wearing out
Like the underside of aging ships
Like pretzels going soggy
Like fingers getting lean
Like music in one key
Like keys jammed into desk drawers
Like babies waking up
Like dogs on a leash
Like drafts along the floor
Like telephones not ringing
Like cigarettes at night
Like words without meaning
Like getting into bed
Like going off to sleep

Dick Gallup

Japanese Poems for American School Kids? or Why and How to Not Teach Haiku

by William J. Higginson

When the topic of haiku comes up in a conversation with teachers, two responses flash in my mind: Why use Japanese poems in our schools? and, How can haiku be presented to children so as to avoid the pious and sentimental generalities so often poured into the 5-7-5 syllable form? The study of Japanese poetry was the beginning of my own serious training as a writer; I definitely feel it has something to offer Western readers and writers of most any age. And I have wrestled with the problem of presenting haiku to school kids during two years of active work in New Jersey's schools under the aegis of New Jersey State Council on the Arts and the Arts Council of the Morris Area.

I

Why use Japanese poems? Because many Japanese poets manage to remain in the ''child mind'' that sees things as they are, in terms of themselves:

> the nail box:
> every nail
> is bent
>
> Hosai (1) *
> (1885-1926)

There are no metaphors, personifications, or other ''literary devices'' in this poem. A metaphor or similar technique, no matter how apt, would momentarily distract us from the object itself by referring to something *outside* of the here/now experience. Hosai gives us no confusion of focus, only direct seeing of real things. (The Japanese original is no less succinct than this translation.) The Epic Aroma of Thunderous Meters?—replaced, by a subtle onomatopoeia that makes words more like things than like thoughts.

The ''words-as-things'' approach works even when the rhythms take on human concern and metaphor

shows the-human-eye-seeing almost as much as the-thing-seen, like this:

> dadadan dadadan dadadan dadadan dan dan
> dan dan dan dan dah dah dah
>
> night wind licking the Kurashio crawls over the field &.
> three bonfires blaze.
> cra-ra-rackling.
> swinging flames.
> dan dan dan dan
> boys leopardskins round their waists.
> drumsticks carving the wind &.
> dan dan dadadan . . .
>
> from 'hachijo rhapsody'
> *Kusano* Shimpei (2) *
> (1903-)

I sense a directness here unlike much of anything in English after Chaucer until William Carlos Williams rammed us back into life, present, intense. Things not described so much as presented.

The most romantic of early 20th century Japanese poets writes directly from the experience of his senses:

> came to
> a mirror shop
> what a jolt—
> I could've been
> some bum walking by
>
> *Ishikawa* Takuboku (3)
> (1885-1912)

---

* Books are described at the end of the article.

* Many Japanese poets are known by their pen names (e.g., Hōsai). When family names are given, the Japanese usually present them first, but Western publishers are inconsistent. I give all Japanese names in the publishers' order, with family names in italics.

as did the earliest Japanese poets we know:

> The sound
> Of the gourds
> Struck for the pleasure
> Of the courtiers
> Reverberates through the shrine.

> anon. (4)
> (pre-800 A.D.)

Japanese poets have always been keen observers of all nature, including human:

> "What's this for?"
> Says the carpenter
> As he cuts it off.

> anon. (5)
> (18th or 19th century)

as are today's Japanese school children:

DADDY

> Daddy is going to his office.
> I waved my hand "Goodbye."
> Daddy waved his hand too.
> My younger sister said,
> "Goodbye."
> He waved his hand again.
> Mommy said, "Goodbye."
> He didn't wave his hand.
> Why?

> *Kamiko* Yoshiko (6)
> (age 7)

Japanese folk poetry, like that of other peoples, arises from daily life. Perhaps there are not as many ballads as in the West; the affairs of men and women may not achieve epic proportions in Japanese minds as often as they do in the West. But the feelings of the moment, of the only time we ever truly live, now, come directly in poems like this:

> Fog clings
> To the high mountain;
> My eye clings
> To him.

> anon. (7)
> (early 20th century)

Having studied Japanese poetry seriously, I don't want to muddy the considerable distinctions among the various genres. But I think there is an important unity in Japanese poetry, and we'd do well to capitalize on it, rather than dote on the superficial formal characteristics of one poorly understood genre such as haiku. So why use Japanese poems in the classroom? Because they come directly from the experience of the poets, and usually steer clear of the metaphorical cover-up so characteristic of Western poetry. *

Because of this directness and intensity, Japanese poems, at their best (in adequate translations, such as those cited here), can easily be experienced by each reader or hearer for himself. Any response a child (or adult) makes to them cannot be called "wrong," and there is nothing in these poems requiring esoteric explanations. Teachers are freed to help each child find his own understanding of the poem, just as each must find his own understanding of the world, which also requires no esoteric knowledge.

Finally, the Japanese sensibility gives humans a place in nature, not over it. Many Japanese poets write of men, women, and children in much the same way as they write of pine trees, rocks, and factories—seeing directly both the outer and inner life of each. Presenting work that reflects this "child mind" sensibility to our children gives their own sharp observations a family to join in the world, and hopefully will lead them to others.

II

The haiku and its companion genre senryu† demonstrate these unique characteristics of Japanese poetry at their most intense concentration. In the metaphorical thinking, seeing something as having the qualities of something else and using that perception as a *descriptive* technique, seldom appears. Often things and events do illuminate one another, but never one at the expense of the other. To put it in terms perhaps more accessible to Western readers, haiku and senryu depend for their effect primarily

---

* The main exception to this statement is the so-called Court Poetry. Typical of our involvement with the Far East, the most indirect kind of Japanese poetry has got most attention from Western scholars —e.g., Brower and Miner's *Japanese Court Poetry*, wherein a decent discussion of the originals suffers from some of the most linguistically insensitive translating I've seen. Most of Waley's work in Japanese literature is also from this area.

†For clear, accurate definitions of these and related terms see the appendix to *The Haiku Anthology* (10). For present purposes the distinction between haiku and senryu may be oversimplified to the statement that haiku deal with "natural" objects and events, while senryu deal with human foibles. See also reference (5).

upon the single significant image clearly and directly presented, or often upon a striking juxtaposition of two such images. Haiku are almost never philosophical or didactic in intent. They rarely exhibit an author's awareness of a reader who must be proselytized. The best haiku seem to come from a mind clear as a calm mountain spring.

Relatively few translators have successfully captured these characteristics. Most seem to have spent a lot of effort on limiting the reader's understanding of the original to their own limited response, often supplying grammatical connections that subordinate one image to another despite their equal importance in the original, even sometimes constructing similes or metaphors for their translations where none were intended or implied in Japanese.

I have been reluctant to use haiku in schools. The lack of readily available quality translations has given me pause. Also, I have felt the word *haiku* to be so contaminated by the number of sentimental 5-7-5s produced in schools that I did not want to be associated with the term in that environment, though I have edited *Haiku Magazine* for a number of years. And finally, I did not wish to be drawn into discussions of "the haiku *form*," which I consider to be the terminology mainly responsible for many Westerner's poor understanding of haiku. These problems have kept me from presenting haiku to American school children for most of a year, unless cornered by some teacher's or administrator's expectations. When so cornered I have usually fallen into the pedant's last resort, declaiming what a haiku is not.

However, the fortuitous appearance of *The Haiku Anthology* (10) has helped me to find a way of circumventing the bull without being gored on the horns of misunderstood terminology. The following is my diary for the first happy day in my Poets-in-the-Schools career, with added examples from subsequent days.

DIARY OF A HAIKU DAY

Today will be different. I will eschew the *word haiku*, and simply present the haiku itself. By presenting the poems themselves, and helping children to see how they are constructed, I will give them the *experience* of haiku without causing the confusion that using the soiled terminology would bring about. (It is important that I will be using American English originals, not poems in translationese, which is what most of the easily available haiku translations are in.)

First class: Immediately after walking in, I wait for their full attention then explain that I am about to read a number of very short poems. The poems will be so short that if they miss one word, they will miss the whole poem. I also say that they can respond to the poems in any way they want, that there is no correct or incorrect response, and that I will pause at

the end of each poem for them to laugh, cry, or giggle—whatever they want to do. Then I read about thirty-five poems from *The Haiku Anthology*, deliberately choosing those with extremely clear sense-appealing images, some quite traditional, like:

Snow falling
on the empty parking lot:
Christmas Eve . . .

Eric W. Amann

Time after time
caterpillar climbs this broken stem,
then probes beyond.

J. W. Hackett

I deliberately mix in a number that seem quite mysterious, whether through choice of image, juxtaposition, or use of language, and carefully include several with modern, city imagery, such as:

an empty elevator
opens
closes

Jack Cain

Moonlit sleet
In the holes of my
Harmonica

David Lloyd

the old barber
sweeping hair
into the giant bag

James Tipton

an empty wheelchair
rolls
in from the waves

Cor van den Heuvel

I also try to pick a number that rely on senses other than sight, or on more than one sense:

crickets . . .
then
thunder

Larry Wiggin

walking the snow-crust
    not sinking
      sinking

        Anita Virgil

Under ledges
and looking for the coolness
that keeps touching my face.
        Foster Jewell

In all of this, I read very slowly, concentrating on careful enunciation and giving full weight to both punctuation- and line-break-indicated pauses. Leaving space between poems for responses. The reading goes over well, the children laughing, squirming, or wide-eyed at almost every poem. (The thirty-five poems take only seven to ten minutes.)

After reading the poems, I tell the kids that these poems are all made up of "images." Without further explanation, *I ask them to tell me what images are.* Very quickly, as I write their responses on the blackboard, we have the five senses listed, and such words as "in your mind," "thinking about pictures," and "in your imagination" come out. I pounce on this last, immediately writing IMAGINATION across two panels of blackboard in foot-high capitals. Then I say, circling and underlining as I go,

"Imagination is 'I'
           I M A G I N A T I O N

"in the 'country'
           I M A G I *N A T I O N*

"of 'images'!"
           I M A G I *N A T I O N*

The aptness of this mnemonic shocks even me! I go on to ask where images can come from, and after a little prodding, I get them to agree with me that there are basically three sources:

1. the senses — images within the range of *here and now* vision, hearing, touch, etc.

2. the memory — images *stored in the mind*, whether from personal experience or from books, movies, etc.

3. the fantasy — images *invented in the mind*, usually by combining material from the senses and/or the memory.

I also point out that the words *fantasy* and *imagination* are usually confused, but that while *fantasy* refers only to those new images invented in the mind, imagination refers to all images.

All this, and only fifteen minutes have elapsed since the start of the lesson! And more important, each child seems to have been actively following the whole thing, delighting in the poems, more than half of them contributing to the lively discussion, and giving ample evidence of new thought in its quickest and most joyful mode. Important for me to remember that all this discussion, covering topics that could well be the subject of an advanced seminar in some graduate school writing program, arose spontaneously *from the children* and from me in a live atmosphere of curiosity, high energy, and delight. I must keep in mind for the future that the particular details of the discussion, of the terminology, must arise from the children, and that any guiding hand I supply must come from honest interaction with their minds *as equals*, or I will sap the energy from this interchange.

To the writing. To make sure that everyone has a real working knowledge of what an image is, I suggest that we make up a poem that contains two images which connect in some strange way. Asking anyone to call out an image, I get "The Washington Monument," which I put on the board as I wonder where we could possibly go with that. Resorting to the usual last-ditch (it should be the first) technique—i.e., trusting the children to bail me out—I ask for another image to pair with that, one which will 'draw sparks' from it. Given as good as asked, and with a war whoop I present their handiwork to them:

The Washington Monument
The Lincoln Tunnel

Asking the kids what makes this a good poem produces immediate answers like, "They're both presidents' names." "One goes up, the other you look at the inside."

Overjoyed at their understanding, but still wondering if we can cool it a little bit and get a more or less straight haiku-like poem from the class, I ask them for images that are not major landmarks, and momentarily two of the quieter kids respond with:

a desert island
a single flower

At this point I know it's time to shut up and let them write. Most write single images, or image lists, like:

The big eyed owl hooing in the dark.

        Scott Karan

Big skinny frogmen looking for treasure divers.

        Michael Berliner

Ugly scary dangerous monsters
Salty brown crisp pretzels
Big fat hairy canary
. . .
Hot blazing orange Sun
Nice cool flowery Spring
Snuggy white new Pajamas

Ann Marie Morreale

*(from Mrs. Friedman's and Ms.
Lacioppa's fourth grades, Walton
School, Springfield, N.J.)*

With a sense of building success I go on to the next class. Decide to abandon "the haiku" as an objective, simply using the haiku intro as a means of getting into images. This class gets off on whacky, built-up images and lists of same:

Scrumptililious Boo-urple Ice Cream Cone

*Stupid scrumptililious boo-urple chocolate ice cream
    cone*
*A dumb good tasting blue, purple, and chocolate
    striped ice cream cone*
*An ugly great tasting blue, purple and striped ice
    cream cone*
*A drippy scrumpous blue and purple squiggled ice
    cream cone*
*A bad, great delicious ice cream cone with boo-urple
    chocolate jimmies on the cone!*

Heidi Yormark

Blue great terrific hot cold big word,
Blue ugly hot cold terrible muddy alphabet,
*Blue disgusting hot cold ugly alphabet with letters
    missing,*
Blue beautiful wet marvelous alphabet soup.

Jill Jacobs

(from Mrs. Samer's fifth grade)

In the remaining two classes I turn them loose, inviting really weird images, with results like:

Haired purple and green shrivelled prune
Knotted prune
Shrivelled up old lady
Green & brown shrivelled apple
A bowl of gushy rotten fruit

Teddi Lizerman

*A poppy seed elephant with foam
    rubber tusks and a purple with
    pink pokadotted trunk.*
*A south-eastern squirble reminds me
    of a green snake-headed eyeball sucker.*
*A grenapo, stinky, crispy, hairy snake
    eating cold mini ravioli with skin
    from a finger relish on top.*
Bill Koppel
Jono Brown
Andy Dewey

(from Mrs. Aronow's fifth grade)

A man with so much hair you can't see his head
A bag with a head in it

Donna Bain

An old jukebox
A funny record

Ellen B.

An over weight dinosaur
A flattened out archeologist

Buddy Pinkava

Reading a book
Remembering what it was about

John Mann

A cactus plant.
A dark pink flower.

Donna Baltus

*(from Mrs. Larson's and
Ms. Lacioppa's fourth grades)*

As with any lesson plan used frequently, I have deliberately varied my approach somewhat through the day, and of course each class has its own personality to add to the mix. Trying the same basic approach in another school with sixth graders produces work like this:

The tired old doctor
The dusty girl

Barry M.

The sound of a light bulb
when it's off.

> *Robert*

The pointed pyramid
The long belt
Fat boy
The Revolution

> *Jim Taylor*

(from Mrs. Goldstein's class,
Hehnly School, Clark, N.J.)

And I take the same plan to a middle school, where working with seventh and eighth graders produces these:

> *The fire flickering in the distance*
> *consuming*
> *everything in sight.*

> *Mike Giger*

old leather wallet
luxurious apartment

> *Donna Perini*

(from mixed classes, Long
Valley Middle School,
Morris County, N.J.)

Working with the sixth graders in Clark, I decide to turn it into a collaborative writing session. In one class the desks are in traditional rows, so I ask the kids to pair up or make teams of three. In another class they are sitting in groups of four or five, which I ask to work together. This after the usual introduction to haiku as image poems, after giving each child a chance to make one or two short image poems of his own. I ask them to turn their papers over, and put just one image at the top of their papers. Then, "Pass your paper to the person on your right. Now, looking at the image on that paper, try to see it very clearly in your mind. Then put right under it whatever image that brings to mind." After giving them time to get their new image down, I have them pass their papers to their right again, and tell them to do the same thing, concentrating on just the last image on the paper. The trick is to think only of the last image on the list, and put down whatever that image makes you think of (unlike the collaborative story, where each contributor wants to maintain some loose continuity by referring back to the whole story on each round). With the smaller teams I suggest that the papers be passed around the group two or three times. Each child starts his own list, and they finish their own off when it returns to them on the last round by adding the final image to the list they began. Thus in a few minutes a whole class can produce as many collaborative poems as there are children in the class. Later I do the same thing with the seventh and eighth graders in Long Valley. Some examples:

The Attractive Watch

The attractive watch
Mighty Mouse
Little
Piece
War
Death
Ear
Drum
Instrument
Music
Song

> *Bob, Darryl, & Donald*

White snow falling
while stray dogs whimper
jumping
leaping
hopping
wondering

> *Nanci Hilf & others*

A cat sitting on a chair
staring at nothing
being nothing
soundly sleeping
purring silently

> *Becky Mitchel & others*

The Queer Lines

the large frog
a small pond
fish
river
Nile
Egypt
Africa
animals
tiger

cat
small
short
ant

Susan & Ingrid

(from Mrs. Goldstein's
sixth grade, Clark)

clock ticking
grandfather clock
tich toct tick
it stopped
someone wound it up
again

Donna & others

(from Mrs. Greene's
sixth grade, Clark)

a light in darkness
a needle falling in silence
a sound, small but clear
racing through your ears
only to hear the beating
of a heart

Laina Jusko et al.

Holes in an old brick wall
Red bricks with white cement
An old tenement in a newly built-up city
A city under the sun
The desert with one abandoned building
    in the middle
A hole in an expanse of nothing

Mrs. Steffan, Joanne Rice,
Donna Perini, Pat Lane,
and Carolyn Delmonico

a lily in an empty lake
a frog on a lily pad
a frog croaking in the night
a swamp in the pitch black night
a patch of quick sand

Sam Eberhart, Declan Lane,
Tom Dymacek, & James Williams

(mixed seventh & eight grades,
Long Valley Middle School)

One group sits in a large circle; we do whole-class pass-arounds. After the introduction to images each child writes one at the top of his paper. Papers passed to the right, and another image added, same instructions as before, then to the right again, and so on until each paper makes the full round. One of the resultant lists:

Bubbling lava pouring out of a volcano
People running down the streets
With their hair flying in the wind
On a motorcycle
Clock ticking
The paper hanging
Wall paper drapes
Pizza
Brick
A head as hard as a rock
A store washed away
A rock
Pebble
Stone
Dirt
Grass
Trees
Plants
Green slime
King Cong
Mandolins at dusk
Painting on the sky
Rainbow
Collision
Firecrackers in the sky

(Mrs. Bauman's eighth grade,
Long Valley Middle School)

All this may seem pretty far afield from haiku, but in fact the Japanese haiku grew out of the *haikai-no-renga*, or comic linked poem, in which a number of poets would participate in just such an image-association game as these students, often with just such far out results. (An example of traditional Japanese haikai, "The Kite's Feathers", may be found in reference (8), but the images are from medieval Japanese life, and difficult for moderns to fully enjoy.)

Just as there is a slight difference in tone between the mostly traditional Japanese poems quoted in part I of this article and the North American haiku at the beginning of part II, so there is a difference between the productions of adults who see themselves as serious (or comic) poets and children simply taking delight in the images of their own minds. But there is an important unity running through all of this: the unity of vivid, imaginative writing that appeals directly to the senses, and tickles the mind. All this without raising the question that confronts and confounds almost all readers of traditional Western poetry, "What does it mean?" Like life, it is to be felt, not questioned.

A FEW WORDS ON THE BOOKS (check for current prices before ordering):

(1) *thistle/brilliant/morning.* Shiki, Hekigodō, Santōka, Hōsai; translated by William J. Higginson (England: Byways Press, 1973; avail. in U.S. @ $1.50 from From Here Press, Box 2702, Paterson, N.J. 07509). A few poems each by four early 20th-century haiku poets; the translations are accurate; includes many in "experimental forms." Could be used by writers of any age.

(2) *frogs &. others. Kusano* Shimpei; translated by Cid Corman and *Kamaike* Susumu (N.Y.: Grossman, 1969; $8.50, but worth hunting up in libraries). The translations are exquisite, the poems delightful—especially the series of frog poems using onomatopoeia (which had better be rehearsed by anyone intending to read them for an audience). Fun for any age.

(3) *Poems to Eat. Ishikawa* Takuboku; translated by Carl Sesar (Tokyo: Kodansha, 1966; worth $5.00 at your bookstore or from Kodansha International, 10 E. 53rd Street, New York, N.Y. 10022). Extremely romantic poems—try them on 15-17-year-olds—very well translated.

(4) *This Wine of Peace, This Wine of Laughter: A Complete Anthology of Japan's Earliest Songs.* Translated by Donald Philippi (N.Y.: Grossman, 1968; $12.50). Contains all the early poems which did not get into the first Japanese imperial anthology, the *Manyōshū.* Illustrates the full range of the early poetry, from country songs to courtly love poems. Beautifully made book with very good translations. Recommended for fairly sophisticated high schoolers and adults.

(5) *Senryu: Japanese Satirical Verses.* R. H. Blyth (Tokyo: Hokuseido Press, 1949; in U.S. order from bookstores through Japan Publications Trading Co., 1255 Howard Street, San Francisco, CA 94103 or 175 Fifth Ave., NYC 10010—or check libraries; moderately expensive). The shorter and more valuable of two books on the subject by Blyth. Features a 50-page comparison of haiku and senryu, with specific examples, plus many poems with adequate translations and good commentary. Playful, good for any age.

(6) *There Are Two Lives: Poems by Children of Japan.* Edited by Richard Lewis; translated by Haruna *Kimura* (N.Y.: Simon & Schuster, 1970; $4.95). Probably the best of Lewis's dozen or so anthologies. Shows a wide range of work (including a good deal of fantasy) from kids aged 6 to 11. Something good for every mood from fear to playfulness. (One notes rather gleefully that the Japanese seem to have gotten away from their own syllabic straight-jackets; no haiku, tanka, or other set forms in this collection.) I have used this book in adult professional-level writing workshops and would happily recommend it for use with all ages.

(7) *The Silent Firefly: Japanese Songs of Love and Other Things.* Translated by Eric Sackheim (Tokyo: Kodansha, 1963; ordering data same as # 3.) Somewhat rustic short poems, very nicely translated. Something for most anyone, probably best with teens.

(8) *The Penguin Book of Japanese Verse.* Translated by Geoffrey Bownas and Anthony Thwaite (Baltimore: Penguin, 1964; $1.95). The translations are quite good; selections include a fair number of modern poems in free forms. Could be used intelligently at all levels, and definitely the best dollar-value in Japanese poetry that I know.

(9) *Anthology of Modern Japanese Poetry.* Translated by Edith Marcombe Shiffert and Yūki *Sawa* (Tokyo & Vermont: Charles E. Tuttle, 1972; $6.05). One of the few decent books on Japanese poetry among the many bad ones from Tuttle. Translations adequate, and the selection covers a wide range of heavily Western-influenced poems in traditional and free forms. Recommended for advanced high school students, and much here could be of use in middle and grade schools.

(10) Finally, *The Haiku Anthology: English Language Haiku by Contemporary American and Canadian Poets.* Edited by Cor van den Heuvel (Garden City: Doubleday/Anchor, 1974; $2.95). Collects much of the good work by serious poets who have spent some 10 years naturalizing the haiku in English. A number of fine poems, particularly those by Jewell, McClintock, van den Heuvel, Virgil, and Wills, written from settings as diverse as the deserts of the American Southwest and the megalopoli of the North American seaboards. The historical introduction and the definitions of haiku, senryu, haikai, etc., at the back will be helpful to those working with any age level, but remember, this is hardly "kiddy poetry."

How to Teach and Write Adventures, Romances, Mysteries and Horror Stories

by Karen Hubert

How can we provide students with writing ideas that will engage them as much as the books they read, the T.V. and movies they watch, and the games they play after three o'clock? How do we provide students with not just a large enough but a specialized and interesting enough range of writing ideas to insure that they choose out of personal taste and imaginative inclination? Do our students' writing choices (what they choose to write about) fall into patterns and do these patterns provide us with useful information about our students?

We believe that children need to write, and we are so committed to this idea that we purchase books and pamphlets, subscribe to magazines in search of helpful and effective methods that will "work." A writing assignment works when it fully captures the writer's imagination. Put simply, imagination is the set of stories people like to tell themselves whenever an occasion arises for necessary or pleasurable escape. Imaginations are as specialized, or broad, as the individual people they inhabit. A student's imagination, the type(s) of stories he or she likes to tell best, gives the teacher as much information as that person's performance and attitudes in math, reading or sociability. If we wish to learn more about our students in order to provide them with creative writing ideas that will most engage their imaginations, we should observe our students as they visit the school library, as they watch T.V., and movies. Here, we can best observe them as they express themselves by the choices they make for self-entertainment.

At the library one student picks only family sagas, another goes right to the mystery shelf, one busily inspects all the romances, others congregate in the adventure section, while some pick fantasies, ghost stories, westerns. There is also the occasional student who chooses out of a pile composed of many or all of these types of books. This person finds entertainment in almost any story type.

Now, follow individuals in your class to the tele-vision set, to the movies, to the yards or neighborhoods where they play. Notice how your students flick the dial to watch one program instead of another. Out of two nearby movie theaters, one showing a romance, the other a horror story, students will prefer going to one and not the other. In school or after school activities children will choose to play certain roles or sports according to a specific predilection for speed, grace, domesticity or violence.

Your students are expressing themselves all the time in what they read, view, and play. In every instance of self-expression and choice they are ruled by an undercurrent of personal fantasy, by that internal voice of the storyteller living in each one of us. Each student comes into our class carrying a volume of stories all their own. Children like to read or see many versions of the same story in order to re-experience the particular emotions it arouses: adventurousness, bravery, self-pity, feeling unloved, special, winning, or losing. They like to view stories, read them, play them any chance they get. And so would they like to write them if only they were given the introduction, framework and opportunity to do so.

Although children generally recognize that they have free choice of selection within other forms of entertainment, they are not conscious that this same choice is available in the selection of writing ideas and in the process of writing itself. They do not see writing as a form of self-entertainment because it does not match up with their other experiences. "My Life As a Hamster" is somehow too different from Spiderman comics and The Towering Inferno.

Our students fit their writing into forms with which their teachers are well acquainted: book reviews, diaries, fiction, biographies, essays on such subjects as: George Washington Carver, Christmas Vacation, How Sugar Cane Is Harvested, "I Woke Up One Morning as a Pencil." By a remarkably early age children are familiar with almost all the major literary forms that exist. But for the most part they write to entertain us, not themselves. We are not yet providing our students with the variety of literary forms with which they themselves are familiar. These forms, or genres, are legitimate and belong in our classrooms. By offering students the same kinds of choices they face in their other entertainments, teachers can begin to turn writing into self-entertainment.

By the time our students have started school, they have been introduced to every major story "family," or genre: adventure, romance, mystery and horror. Other types of stories such as fantasy, science fiction, westerns may be placed within any or all of these four genres. There are also "hybrid" stories: romance-adventures (remember Errol Flynn?), mystery-horrors, etc. Hybrids are far more common literature than stories that stay within the confines of any one genre. However, the most logical way to begin with your classes in genre is by introducing one at a time.

I began the Genre Project as an attempt to broaden my students' concepts of story, in order to give them a broader choice of writing possibilities. I thought of the various genres as different shaped jello molds into which different flavors and colors might be poured and set. I introduced my students to the various genres and gave them a chance to write in all of them. This allowed them to see what form or forms they liked best, felt most comfortable with and could most naturally fit their voices and their feelings into. I stressed that each genre lent itself best to particular emotions. Certain of my students gravitated to certain forms, and it was always interesting for me to see who traveled easily between the different genres and who got caught in one rather than another.

Imagine Johnny, a chronic fighter, a bully who picks on anyone. Excited by Kung Fu, he takes any opportunity to perform it. He is competitive. He is angry. Now what, based on this general view of Johnny, will we as teachers ask him to write? If we were to design an assignment closest to his heart it might be to describe blow by blow a fight he once saw or was recently engaged in. Chances are, Johnny would do some good writing. But this is just the top of the iceberg. If his fight scene is good, imagine how interesting might be his views concerning the characters who are fighting, or the history of how and why they came to fight. Since Johnny understands the combative spirit so well, why not provide him with the framework in which to write a magnum opus of violence and intrigue? Why not introduce him to the form of an adventure story, or perhaps the murder mystery? He might enjoy creating hard-boiled, indestructable detectives, suspicious characters, lineups, chases, and he may understand feelings of getting caught or catching someone, the nature of suspicion, the logic or illogic behind motives.

Working with genre is one sure way of tailoring writing ideas to individual students' personalities. It provides workable alternatives and variety in the teaching of creative writing. It gives legitimacy to the forms and subjects with which students are already familiar through reading, viewing, playing and fantasizing. It may even provide a little fun and entertainment.

Below I have given a brief description of the special nature of each genre, as well as some practical writing ideas. I hope these serve as an introduction to further speculation and appreciation of story types as well as pleasurable writing experiences for you and your classes.

For further practical methods in teaching genre to students read my book, *Teaching and Writing Popular Fiction: Horror, Adventure, Mystery and Romance in the American Classroom*, from which this article was taken. The book deals with how to introduce each genre to your class, as well as the critical definitions and differences between genres. It focuses on providing teachers with lots of tried and tested suggestions for writing assignments and classroom activities and includes many examples of student writing.

Adventure is the overcoming of an obstacle, or a sequence of them. A force impedes the hero's progress and works against the hero by placing obstacles in his or her path. The force may be human, natural, and even supernatural, as in horror-adventure stories. Heroes must overcome the force(s) that work against them by overcoming their fears and the actual obstacles and dangers that stand in their way. The hero is trying ultimately to get somewhere or something: i.e., to find the treasure, to get a message through to someone, to rescue someone, to get back home, etc.

1. You are climbing a hill. You must get to the top of it! There is something crucial you must do at the top. Time is running out. The hill is so hard to climb. (It may be a sand dune, the sand keeps giving way underneath your feet, or it may be a jagged cliff and you are climbing it without shoes.) The terrain itself is your enemy. It seems to fight you every inch of your climb. Do you make it to the top? Do you slip? What helps or prevents you in your climb.

2. You start out on a perfectly normal trip. (Perhaps to the grocery or to visit a relative, or you are on the subway going to your dentist.) But suddenly something unexpected and unusual happens, and your course is completely changed. You suddenly find that you are on an entirely different trip, traveling a wholly different course than the one you expected to travel.

3. You are trapped in an abandoned building. (How did you get there and why are you there?) It is an old

condemned building in a desolate part of town. Night is coming on and the streets are empty of people. You bang on the windows and shout, but there is no one around to hear you. To make matters worse you were supposed to deliver a very important letter, but now it looks like the letter won't get there. (It might be a matter of life or death.) What is going through your mind? Do you eventually get out?

The horror tale brings us to those dark things that we experience in nightmares, dreadful fantasies and daydreams. In the horror story the hero is engaged in a test of wits and strength with a supernatural or cruel and unreasonable force, human or non-human. This force, or villain, is frightening, and often ugly and disgusting.

l. "It" is coming closer and closer. It terrifies you. You've never seen anything like it. You can't believe that this is happening to you! It's coming closer, it's. . .

(What is it? What does it look like? What is it going to do to you? If it is going to destroy or kill you, invent a special way it has of doing so: i.e., does it have a long tongue with needles all over it that licks you to death?)

2. Choose a part of your body and try to make it frightening, as though it in itself is a monster. Write a description of it that will frighten a reader. Write another description to disgust a reader.

3. Pick a common, often used or familiar house item, plant or animal. It should be something you have used often in your life with ease and comfort. You have never been afraid of it. Slowly, however, or perhaps suddenly, you notice that it has begun to get bigger. At first you thought your eyes were playing tricks on you, but soon it became so big that you cannot help but be frightened by its size and its phenomenal nature. It begins to threaten your life, in subtle or overwhelming ways. Write about what is happening to you in a diary or story form. Try to show the progression of this object from common and familiar to menacing and monstrous, as well as the development of your changing feelings towards it.

Where the adventure and horror story draw upon their hero's brawn, *the mystery story* draws upon the brain. Detectives, or mystery solvers, must outwit a foe by observation and intelligent guesswork. They must have an eye for crumbs and wristhairs, a feel for warm teacups. Their craftiness, their ability to ferret out information and to make decisions on which physical risks may be taken, create the image of a person who can survive on mental faculties alone. For young people the ability to understand motives and outwit others is proof of getting older and smarter. Children like a chance to outfox, outguess; they like to say "I told you so," and "I knew he would do that" because it implies self-sufficiency and independence in the adult world of secrets and mysteries. The mystery genre is particularly rich as a basis for writing ideas.

For the most part mysteries are always concerned with loss—of life, valuable objects or property, information—and with discovery—of clues, witnesses, motive and criminal.

l. Imagine a room in your house. Try to imagine it in very exact detail, all its colors and furniture and ornaments. You have just walked into it. Something is wrong, something just doesn't seem right to you. You look all around. Then you realize that something is missing. What is it? (It can be anything at all in the room.) How did you notice it missing? What did you do after this? Invent a character who stole the object. Describe the character's physical appearance, personal history, personality. What was the motive in taking the object? Was the object important to you? To the thief? Why? You may wish to tell the story of how you discovered the criminal. Invent some clues, and witnesses and suspects if you can. Write from the first person "I," if possible.

2. You did it! You committed the crime! Now write your confession (using "I"). Why did you do it?

3. A crime has been committed. Write an interior monologue (stream of consciousness would be good) of the victim before, during and after the crime. Now write an interior monologue from the viewpoint of the criminal also before, during and after the crime. What are they saying to themselves?

4. You are reviewing a lineup. Who are you looking for and why? You are uncertain of your memory of the face of this criminal. You look into face after face. What do these faces look like? What feelings do they give you? What is going through your mind as you do this? Suddenly you think you see the right face. What are you remembering? How do you know that this is the one?

5. You see a very suspicious man or woman around your home or school—in a neighborhood with which you feel familiar. You decide to follow the character, or chase him if he sees you and runs. Try to be very clear in your description of places around your neighborhood, where he goes or where you hide from him as you watch his movements (alleys, corners, stores, parks). What is he doing? You may or may not decide to chase him. You may or may not catch him.

If you do catch him, what explanation does he give for his very suspicious behavior?

Romances or love stories, are all about people moving closer to one another and moving apart. For some students it may be an impossible genre in which to write, yet it will stimulate others to write moving prose. In a love story one may express loneliness, yearning, attraction, seduction, betrayal, exaltation, fulfillment. In all genres anger and fear may be expressed, but only in romance is the anger and fear related to the closeness and feeling between people. These may be written by both boys and girls. Don't be afraid to try it.

I. What does a kiss feel like?

2. Write a marriage proposal.

3. He or she rejects you. They won't go out with you (or they won't marry you). What reasons does he/she give? What do you say to him/her? Write a monologue from the viewpoint of a rejected lover.

4. What kinds of promises do lovers (boyfriends and girlfriends, fiancés) make to one another? Can you write a list?

5. The day has finally arrived. Your wedding day. Try to picture yourself. How do you look? How are you dressed? Do you feel comfortable? Does anything unusual happen before the ceremony? (An old girlfriend or boyfriend shows up. You receive a gift from "a mysterious admirer" or your fiancé sends you a note. What does it say?) Finally you are walking down the aisle, past people who have come to see you married. You are standing at the altar. What are you thinking? Feeling? Are you experiencing pride? Embarrassment? Regrets? How do you feel after its all over?

6. What is romantic? Write a list. What does a romantic place look like? An unromantic place?

Poetry and Athletics

by Ron Padgett

*I used to play second base in
the little league. One day I
let a ball go between my legs:
I was totally absorbed in looking
at some beautiful cloud formations.
After that I played right field.*
—A contemporary poet

All those years while you were doing calisthenics in phys. ed. class, where was your mind? What did you think about as you jumped up and down, pushed, stretched and groaned?

Between exercises I would blank out mentally. Watch the floor. Count doing push-ups. Or, when the going got tough, agonize in vagueness. I don't recall ever having had an interesting idea during calisthenics. No one ever mentioned the mind; it seemed to be understood that our thoughts would sort of fall into agreement with our bodies, but our bodies, straining and bored, felt disagreeable.

In bed last night, absolutely immobile, I realized all this and wondered if something interesting couldn't have been done with my mind during those calisthenic routines. In school we now urge our students to be creative in their writing, art and dramatics. In improvisational theater a person is supposed to behave the way chosen characters feel and to feel the way the character behaves. Social courtesy requires that we learn to "act" polite when being introduced to a stranger and that the stranger reciprocate. In the classroom our students are discouraged from letting their minds "wander." A dreamy or even sleepy student, snapping back, is sometimes asked, "And where have you been?" The question is, unfortunately, rhetorical. But it is in physical education that the expanse of the mind is most severely limited. At most we are told to concentrate, pay attention to the game, keep our eye on the ball, try hard. The average kid follows these instructions and finds that he still doesn't come out on top, because there are always others who win, the natural athletes gifted with great reflexes and instincts.

Now I was an average kid in athletics, nowhere nearly so bad as some and nowhere nearly so good as others. I remember feeling sorry for the uncoordinated fumblers and relieved that I was not among them. I also remember being impressed by how well certain kids hit the ball or ran or caught. These athletic kids seemed to exert no special effort. Were they riding on pure instinct? Where were those minds? They seemed to be in some zenlike state— wham! a solid line drive into left center. I would love to know what happened in those minds then. It was painfully obvious what was happening in the minds of the fumblers.

The emotional result, when all was done, was hideous: one small group of people excessively triumphant over the rest, a most distasteful early flowering of a socioeconomic system based on competition without sympathy. Not only did the best man win, his personality was placed on a pedestal, while you were left to deal with your "inferiority": two states of mind which encourage social irritation and distort the personality.

Obviously I am beginning to generalize about large social and personal psychologies, and obviously calisthenics cannot be equated with athletics, and obviously football does not equal capitalism, and I have strayed from my theme. I had wanted to suggest that it would be interesting to investigate the mental state of a person acting on reflex, and this happens in school most often in sports and play activity. We do get some idea of how it works from reading the success stories of celebrated sports figures, *as told to* someone. Unless that someone is perceptive, too much is lost in the retelling. Very few professional athletes actually write their own books. One who does is the former basketball player Tom Meschery (*Over the Rim*, poems, McCall, N. Y., out of print, and *Caught in the Pivot*, his diary of a year of unsuccessful coaching, Avon Books, N.Y.) Meschery studied at the Iowa Writers School. But even his work, sensitive and intelligent as it is, tells us not so much about the athlete's instincts in action as his feelings in repose, as in "The Moment of Contemplation":

> We are born by some
> portentous harbinger of time
> from the humdrum hustling of nervousness
> into a moment of full silence:
> a void between relaxation and action.
> This is the moment of athletic mysticism,
> the unexplained second.
> There are some thoughts, few fears,
>   few anxieties.
> Silence tiptoes through the locker room.
>   Stillness—
>   the soft breathing
>   of a child asleep.

Or, to come at it from the other direction, we have the example of the basketball-playing poet Tom Clark:

> INTO
>
>   even the
>   perfect
>   jumpshot
>
>   can't match
>   the perfect
>   pass
>
>   for insight
>   into the
>   mysterious*

This poem reminds us that contemporary poets have increased the possibilities of writing, just as Wordsworth did, writing about the "non poetic" in his time, and William Carlos Williams, writing about the "non poetic" in his. The day is long gone—or it should be—when a child can't write about anything—be it basketball, melancholy, Pikes Peak, acne, working at the store, a fly on the phone book, dying your hair or pulling it out, stars in daytime, whatever—using the language that feels right, not the highfalutin language of what is sometimes passed off as Poetry. It is ungenerous to require a student to write a poem about Spring when he or she would prefer to write about toes, or to insist that the language resemble English poetry when the student lives in, say, Knox-

---

* In *Blue* (Black Sparrow Press, 1974, Los Angeles), p. 79.

ville.

In this case consider the language of athletics. Is it a coincidence that sports fans often resort to "body English" or that graceful athletes are often described as "poetry in motion?" Probably not. I suspect that the use of these terms indicates a relationship between creativity and athletics—the ultimate blend being, I suppose, dance, or gymnastics—a relationship which is positive and benevolent. Where else do we see the word "poetry" used in such a laudatory way? Not in textbooks.

This relationship is further suggested by the colorful language of sports. Baseball, for instance, has generated its own beautiful lingo: "Blue is throwing real smoke tonight. He checks the sign, rocks and deals and, oh, Piniella hits a line shot into left, snared! by Rudi, boy that was a frozen rope. . ." The image of hurled smoke magically transformed into a cold, rigid rope is worthy of Coleridge. I do not mean that sports is just one big wonderful world of creative literacy. Like journalism, advertising and political gibberish, it is plagued by cliché, a device by which the realness of experience is reduced to a known conventional fiction. But I do mean that sports develops a vocabulary similar to poetry in its suppleness, its unexpected imagery and its interest in the mysterious.

I have the suspicion that there is an intimate connection between the instincts of the moving body and the moving mind, in this case between athletics and creative writing. I have hit the tennis ball with the ease, grace and authority I felt in writing certain poems. People will tell you, "It felt right." If it doesn't feel right when you're doing it, and you're honest with yourself, you know it isn't right. It doesn't have the ring of authenticity. Sensitive people "know" when an actor's good: at a certain point a performance takes off in some amazing way. There's a noticeable difference between a child who feels uncomfortable in creative dramatics and the same child who shifts into an understanding of his role, as if he has been assumed, angel-like, into the situation. The child who approaches you with his newly written poem, face beaming, has just done something he knows has "clicked." To my mind these examples are not so far from the kid who can skip rope like a dancer or throw a ball to the precise point you somehow knew he would.

At this point it might seem that I am about to say that creativity—athletic or artistic—depends on instinct and cannot be taught. To an extent this is true, but to another extent it is not. Creativity is a pleasure which can be developed because it is something people have as a birthright. By the time we have been through high school, we have been deprived of much of this birthright: repressive educational and social pressures have tended to make us lose contact with the creative aspects of our personality, and we develop hobbies instead. If we are poor athletes in school, we will probably not pursue athletics in "later life." If we are required to write an essay on alliteration in Alfred Noyes' "The Highwayman," it is not likely we will then feel like writing poetry at home. Our instincts for these pursuits are dulled.

But if we are taught by sympathetic people the pleasures of creativity, we will be more likely to appreciate and develop that part of ourselves. We might not become Henry Aaron or Shakespeare or Billie Jean King or Fritz Lang or Tu Fu or Jane Austen or Nijinsky, but we will become larger versions of ourselves. We will realize more of the potential which we are mysteriously given at birth.

A Few Notes on Revision

by Alan Ziegler

Rarely does a writer publish the first draft of a poem or story. It's been said that "rewriting is writing," and my grad school workshops consisted mostly of revising and refining poems. Yet, as teachers, we are often in the position of asking children to turn out finished poems in twenty-thirty minutes. It often takes a writer twenty-thirty minutes staring at the typewriter, checking to see if the ribbon is all right, making sure the window is open the right amount, patrolling the halls, etc. before he/she can even get the first faltering—and often discarded—words on paper. So, it's always incredible to me what children can turn out in a classroom situation.

Most children are able to travel freely in the land of their imagination, a place where adults often have to struggle to get a visa to. But even so, they usually don't have the experience with writing to be able to get the most out of their poems without help. I try to run around the room as much as possible, helping them "revise" as they write. Some of the general qualities to look for are: clarity of expression, visual content of description, and the use of the concrete rather than the abstract. I compliment them when they do these things well; and when they're not done well, I say something like, "I don't follow that. Maybe you could describe it a little." When there is time during the class, or when you can afford the luxury of a follow-up session, revision can do wonders for a poem.

One aspect of revision is to "get down to the poem," get rid of redundancies and extraneous verbiage. Sometimes a kid will shift from "showing" to "telling" and back again. Usually, the "showing" parts—where the poem speaks for itself—are stronger. Often, a child will "warm-up" for the first couple of lines; they may be introductory and not really part of the poem, which "takes off" a bit down the page. Other times, a child will tail off at the end, sometimes in the form of "And then I realized it was a dream and I was glad to get out of that place," or other times in the form of a little "editorial" which ex-plains the poem in case the reader didn't "get it." Ask if these lines are necessary, if they really add anything.

Another aspect of revision is to help the student expand the dimensions of the poem. Often, a writer will cop-out in a poem and end it prematurely, sometimes out of laziness and sometimes because the student isn't sure where and/or how to take the material. One can respond, "I think you finished the poem too soon, maybe you could do more with it," and possibly suggest directions it could take. I often say—sincerely—"That's terrific, but I'm greedy and I want to know more," and perhaps make a suggestion. One of the nicest moments is when the student thinks for a moment, smiles, and dives back into the writing.

Also, I try to help make the imagery of the poem stronger. If a child writes, "It was a nice house," ask why it was nice. If he/she answers, "Because it had smooth carpets," then we're getting somewhere that helps the reader experience the house. One more step: "Maybe you could tell me what it feels like to walk on the carpet." So then the child might respond, "The carpets are like whipped cream that feed your feet."

Of course, knowing a child aids the critical process. It helps you detect whether a kid should be "pushed" to work harder or needs a lot of positive feedback and has to be brought along slowly. It also might help you know if the material is hard for the kid to handle for emotional or artistic reasons. If you are not the class's regular teacher, consultation with the teacher is crucial.

Giving criticism in "first person" often helps with children sensitive to negativity. "I'm confused, what's going on here?" sounds better than "You're confused and don't tell what's going on very well" (and also might be a more accurate statement).

I don't think you should be too concerned with whether the children are writing "poetry" or "prose." What we're essentially concerned with is the marriage of the imagination and language and the offspring it produces. (I don't think there are any "illegitimate" births.) Yes, there are differences between prose and poetry, but they are becoming fuzzier. Most poets no longer write in rhyme and pre-established meter; there's a lot of very prosy poetry being published, also much prose that reads like poetry. (Prose poems are proliferating in literary magazines.) In dealing with children, we needn't be too concerned with labels and classifications; the basic concern is with tapping the children's imaginations and showing them that language is a good medium for that creative outflow, just as music and visual art are.

One criticism to stay away from usually is: "You're not following directions." Teachers are often very concerned about following instructions, but this can impede the formation of art, which is often predicated on the ability of the writer or painter to get off the track and perhaps on to a more exciting one. Many great pieces of writing have resulted when the writer veered away from what he/she set out to do. And teaching is no different than any other creative art. Keep yourself open to revising your teaching ideas. Maybe a kid will say something that will take the idea in a new direction. Modify, improvise, perhaps discard in favor of something else. The end result might be an exciting collaboration with the children.

The Trapdoor Method

by Tom Veitch

A little over a year ago Ron Padgett invited me to talk to a few of his elementary school classes at P.S. 6l. As I recall that day now, we visited three or four classes of different ages, and I told them some of the things I had learned about writing stories of fantasy or fairy tales. I demonstrated a few of the simple techniques (of imagination) which writers and storytellers have been using for thousands of years.

What follows are my reflections on that same theme, a year later, again at Ron's request.

Children have natural resources of imagination and fantasy which they use constantly in play by themselves or with other children. However in the presence of adults, even adults whom they love, admire, and respect, children find themselves compelled to perform an act which will win the adult's approval. This act of performance has the unfortunate effect of breaking the magic self-involvement of play, in which imagination functions of and for itself, with no ulterior motive.

Performance is not in itself a bad thing. In fact it is the teacher's assigned role to elicit performance from a child, to bring his talent (whatever it may be) into functional relationship to the social group. Parental and teacher approval is the carrot on the end of the stick that draws a child out of his hermetic play world into the world-at-large.

But writing is a specific kind of social and cultural performance which is usually done in solitude, away from the benevolent or malevolent eye of a parental figure. As such it is an opportunity for a person to dwell in his autonomy, to experience "the joys and sorrows of creation" in their own right, with no end in view.

There's a good chance that when a child sits down to write he will be thinking of pleasing the teacher. He will desire that little gold star or smile of appreciation. The need to perform well, in competition with his friends, will again break that spell of play which could make writing a thoroughly useless, thoroughly enjoyable activity.

It's my understanding that the current teaching of "methods and tricks" to young writers is designed to break the mental block of authority and liberate the autonomous play spirit into the large framework of group culture. In other words, "play" will now be "approved behavior," and kids will see that there doesn't have to be a dark dividing line between their secret inner lives and the rest of society.

That's all well and good, but as a man who has been writing for fifteen or twenty years and getting nowhere fast, I know it's not as simple as that. It is my experience that an authority attitude of indulgence toward imagination will attract to itself mainly clowns and tricksters doing witty marvels for an indulgent authority! Again, as before, *performance* will be the key. The old pat on the head routine.

The actual secret of liberation through writing, I believe, is sealed in that self-indulgent world of play which answers no man. A world which receives neither good marks nor bad marks, smiles nor disdain. A world of isolation, if you please, a scary, sad, sometimes mad world, a dangerous world, a happy world, a world of interesting and joyful experience. I go there by myself. Each man goes there by himself, or in the company of the strangers who inhabit that world. There are no parents there, or little brains reading directions. It is a world of monsters. A world of angels. It is a world that children's books would like to capture but seldom really do. Yes, it's the scary crazy world of *fantasies*, and from childhood we have been taught to feel that there is something slightly naughty and suspicous about this world, because it is a world that operates by its own rules and not those of human society!

The "trapdoor method" is a way of entering the invisible and unknown world which is inside you. As I explained to the kids at P.S. 6l, you will meet many unexpected things there, and it is a good idea to go prepared. Take a sword or other weapon with you. A strong horse is a good friend to have there, for he will carry you quickly away when danger threatens. Maybe you'll even want a suit of armor, or to descend in a diving bell or tank to have a look around before you commit yourself to actually entering this world. Maybe you won't want to enter that world at all! You're a poor kid who has the worst nightmares imaginable and you know that over *there*, in that other world, all the nightmares are waiting to gobble you up!

But suppose you've decided you're ready to give it a try. Where are you going to find the door to this unknown land? That's the easy part! Look under your bed. . . . What do you see there? A *trapdoor*, of course! A trapdoor of old wood and iron rivets, with a big iron ring on one end. (If you can't see it, then close your eyes and you *will* see it.)

Now move your bed or crawl under it if there's room, and pull on that iron ring to see if the trapdoor will open. If it doesn't open, if you can't budge it no matter how hard you pull, then brother you are not ready to enter the magic unknown world. If it opens quite easily, then the trapdoor is telling you that it likes you, and it wants you to climb down and have a look around.

We'll suppose that for you the door opens. You peek over the edge of the opening and see a flight of dusty old stone steps descending into darkness. Oh my! It's scary! Well, you can always close the door again and go back to your homework. Or maybe you can get a flashlight and go down those ancient steps for a little look-see.

Let's suppose you're a brave little kid who is looking for adventure. You take your flashlight and you start down some stone steps. Down down down. Down down down. Your safe warm bedroom is far behind you now. All you can see in the beam of your light is stone steps, stone walls, corners that keep turning to the right. And lots of spiderwebs, beetles, and dust. Maybe some dead torches stuck in cracks in the walls. Maybe some old footprints in the dust, of people who went before you.

Well, after walking down these steps for a long time you come to a flat place, maybe a big room, and on the other side of the room there is a window looking out on a beautiful sunlit garden! Now that's really nice! You run across the room towards the window, tripping over an old rusty sword and spurs. Vaguely, all around you in the shadows of the room, you sense the presence of ancient tables and chairs, suits of armor, tapestries, maybe an old King sleeping in an old bed. But you want to see what's in the garden, so you run to the window, which is open, and you look out at the marvelous garden. . . .

I can't tell you what happens next. Because this is the land of fairy tales, where *anything* can happen. This is the place where dreams come from, where you go when you are asleep. This is the strange country that people call "Imagination." They think it belongs to them, but that's not true, they belong to it. When a writer goes there, he or she goes alone or with a friend and goes seeking adventure and the unexpected: like an explorer going into the Brazilian jungle; like an astronaut going to the moon; like Jacques Cousteau going into the deeps of the sea; like a medieval warrior going into the Orient, or an American Indian into a deep dark forest. And as he goes, *he writes down everything he sees and everything that happens to him*. He hardly ever thinks about the fame and wealth he might win if he comes back alive. He's too busy wondering what unexpected marvels he will find next, and what strange creature he will meet around the next corner!

The method I've just described presupposes children are already somewhat in touch with their imagination and just need a simple scenario (the "trapdoor") to trigger the inward journey. But many will perhaps find it difficult to "participate with themselves" in this manner. These young writers need a more complex scenario, a story that's already to the point where they find themselves emotionally involved.

I used the "extended scenario" method with one of the classes at P.S. 6l and found it worked very well. I made up, on the spot, a little fairy tale replete with characters and action, but left it unfinished, breaking off after something exciting and interesting had happened. I left unresolved "problems" that could only be worked out by further imagining. I let the children's imagination find the resolution to these problems.

One could of course take any classic fairy tale and read half of it to the class, then ask them to imagine the continuation. But in this instance, as I say, I constructed a yarn out of stuff that was coming up in my own imagination, so that even I did not know how the story would turn out. There was a sense in the air of events completely hidden and unknown to all of us—imagination was the only key!

As I recall now (dimly), the story was about a princess who had to take care of her sick old father, the King. She was in the habit of going to the woods every morning to gather wild fruit for his breakfast. (I tried to fill out this basic situation with colorful detail and description, in order to excite the image-making faculty in the children.)

The princess used to feel quite sad that she had to take care of the old King while all her friends were out playing games, riding horses, and having exciting adventures. She just wished that *she* could have an adventure!

One day when she was gathering fruits and berries, a strange gypsy boy came out of the woods and greeted her by name. She had no idea who he was, she had never seen him before. But he knew her name! The boy gave her four magic nuts and told her that if she ate them she would be changed into a perfectly happy being! The boy was very handsome and his voice was like enchanting flute music. The princess could not resist taking the nuts and eating them on the spot. And in a flash she was changed into a tree!

She was quite frightened at first, but then she realized how happy and perfect she felt inside. And she knew she was a very beautiful tree, whose branches could touch the sky and whose roots reached deep down into the warm dark earth. In no time at all she forgot her former life as a princess! The little gypsy boy danced around her and sang a song. Then he disappeared into the forest, never to be seen again.

(The above sequence included some *participation imagining*—pretending what we would feel and think if we were trees, wondering if trees can talk to each other, see what's going on around them, etc.)

Of course all this left something essential unresolved: what about the girl's father, who had been left in his sickbed waiting for his breakfast?! And what about the princess herself—was she going to be a tree forever? She had left behind her whole world, a world where she had responsibilities and things to do. The King would probably die if she didn't get back to feed him and take care of him!

The class was called upon to work out this situation. (I had no idea if it even could be worked out!) Of course they came up with many different answers. The continuation began to fall together in bits and pieces until finally we ended the story with a great feeling of satisfaction and relief.

Since at this time I don't clearly recall what the end of the story was, I'll leave it open-ended, so that the reader can take a practice swim in his own fantasy pool.

As you probably know, there are certain elements which are almost standard fare in stories of fantasy and imagination. These "people, objects, and situations" can be used over and over because they strike points of deep recognition inside us. I now list a few of them:

PEOPLE & BEINGS: King, Queen, Prince, Princess, Magician, Warrior, Knight, Dragon, Monster, Troll, Witch, Evil Animals, Helpful Animals, Boy-seeking-his-fortune, Orphan, Tyrant, Tramp, Giant, Pirate, Hunter, Grandmother & Grandfather, the Three Sisters, the Three Brothers, the Trickster (or mischievous animal), the Council of Wise Men, Angels, etc., etc.

OBJECTS: Magic power clings to all sorts of objects—swords, rings, stones, crowns, cups, books, coats, shoes, tables, etc. In addition there are special objects of conveyance: ships, animals, trains, rockets, cars, flying houses, etc. The most important type of object is the *treasure*, which is often the goal of the adventure.

Objects also carry something of the person who owns them. When they are lost the person loses something of himself and must get it back. *Magical plants* also come under the heading of objects, although they are often characters who sing, whisper secret knowledge, etc. In fact the most amazing trait of objects in the world of imagination is that they easily become personified and act like human beings. Every fragment of the interior world may spring to life at any time. Every object has knowledge locked inside it which it is apt to reveal if the right person comes along.

SITUATIONS: The dark forest, the secret cave, the city under the mountain, the dismal swamp, the pit of snakes, the waterless desert, the teeming jungle, the battle, the lost world, the center of the earth, the voyage to another planet, the magic garden, etc. Of course the most important situations will arise because of the involvement of the characters with each other and with things. These situations are the "plot" or storyline that lies hidden and must be found by imagination. Set the stage, sit yourself in the audience or dress yourself up as one of the actors. Take one hero, add a victim imprisoned in a deep cave, throw in a dash of dragon and a pinch of magic ring—poof!—the action starts to unfold before your very eyes!

(We might add that all the archaic images mentioned here have modern equivalents. But the current forms often lack *the air of mystery* that is so important in the world of fantasy.)

Addenda:

Since writing the above I've realized that there is another whole area of fruitful imagination which some children may find more to their taste than the "adventure in the unknown." This other kind of fantasy is "wish fulfillment," and it is closely related to the method of using "I wish" in poems. In these fantasies the child imagines what he would do *if he could do anything he wanted to*, or what he would have *if he could have anything he wanted*, etc. This is a characteristically American kind of imagination, in fact it may be the central fantasy of our civilization. "It just comes naturally." One good way to enter this kind of self-expansive imagining is to pretend you have a house with a large number of rooms, and each room has something special in it, or serves a special purpose. "The perfect house I will build when I grow up." Or: "I am going to have this car with lots of secret rooms in it, maybe even a cellar." Children proceed to describe what goes on in every room, or what possessions or pets they keep there.

Instead of facing the scary unknowns, which are apt to threaten and deflate the ego, we are here indulging in the *opposite* kind of imagination, the filling out of the self-image. I think that both kinds of fantasy are very healthy, and both kinds should be indulged in. They have a way of balancing each other out.

Further notes: Bill and Ron asked if I could mention something about "Active Imagination," which is a technique used in Jungian psychotherapy, similar in some ways to what we have described here. I would refer the reader to Jung's autobiography and also to the indexes of his *Collected Works*, especially pages 495-6 in Volume 14. Briefly, "Active Imagination" is a method of "dreaming awake" which was used by the ancient alchemists and called by them "*Imagination*." Jung found this technique is highly suitable for psychotherapy, especially in the more advanced stages of psychic development. It consists in closing your eyes and recalling an image from a dream or waiting until a new image appears spontaneously to your inner eye. You then "fix" this image in your mind, concentrating as much attention on it as you can. After awhile the image will begin to change, and you must note carefully how it changes, writing a description. After repeated practice, one finds that the images come quite easily, and attention is easily focused on them. Amazing things begin to happen—strange personages walk on the set and address the ego. One must learn to converse with these 'imaginary' beings, asking them questions, etc. Quite literally one forms a dialogue or dialectic with the collective unconscious! Later, usually in collaboration with the analyst, one examines the written record of these experiences and interprets them. The interpretation of the symbolic content of these imaginings is often the most important part of the process. Of course, that's something we don't do at all in "the Trapdoor Method"!

There now follows a story I wrote in 1964 using the methods I have described in this essay. The chief rule I gave myself at that time was that I must let the story unfold entirely from within, I must not try to figure out in advance *anything* that was going to happen. The story is therefore based entirely on events that were taking place somewhere inside me and that I was merely reporting to the reader.

NANA-BANA DOG
(Example of "Trapdoor Method")

Quite joyfully, I rolled naked down the muddy river bank, head over heels, slip-sliding in the mud and grasshoppers, plop splash into the turgid yellow water.

Downstream I noticed the thick darkness slid noiselessly off a sand bar and beneath the surface. Crocodile, I thought.

Unafraid I scampered in the shallows, playing with brother frip-fish and Nana-bana-dog. Nana-bana-dog yelped and tumbled after me, nipping at my feet. I splashed her, pushed her upside down in the water. "Row, wow wow!" she yiped. Then she spotted something and chased it upstream. I paused to breathe deeply the thick afternoon air. My full belly belched. Overhead the sky was green. In the trees little things played and screamed at each other, with each other, against each other.

Fingering my knife, which hung loosely at my bare thigh, I watch the progress of brother crocodile beneath the surface.

Before he could get to me I was clambering up the bank, slipping in the mud. "Come Nana-bana-dog," I yelled. "Come with me you old hound!"

Nana-bana-dog ran pell mell towards me, splashing water head high. She could not see old crocodile. Old crocodile yawned and swallowed water. Enough delay for Nana-bana-dog, who was now at my side, licking my feet and legs.

The village drums made us quicken our pace. Leaves and branches crackled beneath our feet as we ran through the deep path homeward. Overhead the trees made everything dark. High above we could hear the great tree cats purr and growl, even meow. High above we could hear the great Tree Snake make her hissing sound as she slid over rough and smooth bark, looking for food.

"Tonight," I said to Nana-bana-dog, "I will become a man." I looked at her, running beside me. "What will you think of me then, old dog dog? Will you still be my friend when I carry the long spear and silver knife?"

"I will be! I will be!" she barked.

"Where have you been?" momma-momma asked me, wrinkling up her fat old eyes and mouth. "Come in here sun-boy and have something to eat. You must sleep. Tonight you will have no sleep. Tonight you are to become a man."

I followed her into our house. Nana-bana-dog stayed outside. She filled my already bursting belly with Kapyicks and Pardlops and Brownruds. Then she tucked me to sleep in our great bed.

Outside I could hear my younger friends playing in the noon sun, playing with Nana-bana-dog, playing with Freta-moon-girl. Because of this I could not sleep. Because tonight I would become a man I could not sleep.

In the rasping moonlight they carried me before the council of old men. A giant fire was in progress. I looked up at the supreme old man, my grandfather, Turtlefilth, and he looked down with baleful eye at me. Around me the other boys were being held by men, waiting their turns to be brought before the chief.

What sad violence was my indoctrination into the rites of manhood. What frightening myth and savage ceremony was my initiation into the responsibilities of life.

I shook with fear. Be brave, young one, I thought. It was my grandfather who said this, in his mind, and I heard him, in my mind.

"Take him to the tree," my grandfather said.

I was dragged by these two brave bucks out of the circle of light, to a small clearing on the right of my grandfather. There I was bound hand and foot to the giant Gorgoo tree, the tree of the Living Breath. The bucks stepped back as my grandfather came forward to perform the ceremony before the tree. Lightly he kissed me on both cheeks and then reached over my head to touch the sacred Heart of the tree, a strange formation which is found only on this type of tree and only in this part of the world.

Immediately the tree began to quiver. I felt the bark of the tree spread behind me, rubbing hard against my young flesh. The wood gave way, sticky with sap, folding back and in and around, until I was entirely enveloped in the life of the tree, until I was one with the tree, sealed within the very tree itself.

All was silence.

The wood of the tree pressed firmly against my skin, wet with sap, cold with the night blood of the great tree. I could not move. I could not see.

All was silence.

Hours later I awoke to feel the heat of the fires they had built against the tree, the fires that were gradually eating their way toward me, to free me from my life-prison.

The heat grew more intense. The sap began to bubble around me, scorching my skin. My head began to ache with the heat.

At last I heard the hacking of their machetes and knives, heard the wood splinter as it was stripped away from the living tree.

Then I was free, stepping over the ashes and fresh wood and bark, stepping out into the sweet jungle moonlight. I looked down at myself, saw that my skin was now black with the sap-burned designs, the tattoos of manhood. I looked up into the eyes of my grandfather and smiled. The old fellow laughed through his whiskers.

Then we went to the other trees, where other young men lay imprisoned. All through the night we hacked, until our man-tribe stood two hundred strong!

From *Literary Days* (C Press, 1964)

Some Ideas for Teaching Grammar

by Sue Willis, with Karen Hubert and Phillip Lopate

All human beings are born geniuses at grammar. Babies are born speaking no language and yet by the time they start school they can express desires, demands, wishes, and fantasies. An American baby could be taken at birth and raised on a Chinese collective farm, and he would grow up perfectly comfortable in the use of Chinese. Or Arabic, or Hopi. No one teaches us our native language. We discover it for ourselves, and once we have the rudiments we can generate an infinite number of sentences, many of which have never been uttered before. *That* is creativity. Our grammar is also far more complex than we are usually aware. A reader of any of Noam Chomsky's works on transformational grammar quickly discovers that subjects and predicates are just the powdery snow on the tip of the iceberg. Chomsky takes apart sentences and looks for their deep skeleton structures, and tries to discover how we transform an idea into the actual patterns that we speak.

Language is not only structurally complex, it is constantly in flux. If you were transported to England in the year 1000 A.D., you would not understand the language being spoken around you, and yet it would be English. There is a famous long poem written about 1377 A.D. called *Piers Plowman* in which the poet writes, "Truth is best:/ Learn it to these lewd men." "Lewd" meant "ignorant" and "learn" meant "teach" as well as "learn." Everyday we see change at work around us, for better or worse. We see spelling innovations like E-Z Kredit and we hear slang that blossoms and fades so quickly that it is no longer cool to say groovy. The study of language leads one to take all spellings and many rules of grammar with a grain of salt. In spite of all the years of work by grammar teachers, some of my old schoolmates in West Virginia will go to their graves responding to the question "Who is it?" with "Hit's me." They will be understood too. English especially is notorious for its irrational spellings. A single sound in our language rarely has a single spelling. The vowel sound in "eye" for example, can be spelled at least seventeen ways, including "right," "lie," "aye," and "indict." George Bernard Shaw once pointed out that if you take the sound of "gh" in "enough," the "o" from "women" and the "ti" from "nation," then "ghoti" spells the scaley creature who inhabits our oceans and unpolluted rivers. Interestingly, the spelling anomalies of English are often accurate representations of the way the word was pronounced when it first appeared in the language.

Yet in spite of inconsistencies and change, serious users of written language—report writers and college students as well as poets—regard grammar with great respect. Many good writers spend an enormous percent of their time rewriting, and in large part rewriting is the manipulation of grammar. How best to express the thought? We make constant choices; we consider a word against its synonym for the most precise meaning; we check whether our "he" has a well marked antecedent. When an article or book is about to be published, more time is spent in editing, in correcting and making tiny changes in punctuation. Practice in making these choices, these fine distinctions of meaning, is the only way to master grammar.

The Teachers & Writers Collaborative team at P.S. 75 would like to offer a compilation of ideas for helping children generate effective written language. Some of these ideas are essentially editorial techniques which place the teacher in the role of editor to the student's writer. Some are gamelike and aimed at increasing interest in and awareness of how language works. We have also included two outlines of extended approaches to the study of language. Finally, we have a short list of useful books on language topics. All of these ideas are only suggestions; most of them have been tried in "creative" writing workshops, but we don't really see that there is any creative writing as opposed to uncreative writing; rather there is good, interesting writing versus bad, boring writing. If you have any suggestions to add to our list, please let us know.

Suggestions for Teachers Responding to Work Turned in by Students.

1. Use class discussion and/or a class graph. Kids know what things teachers criticize them for. Have the class list its own problems, possibly keep an anonymous all-class graph. Discuss what problems seem most important to communication, and concentrate on those first. For example, the imprecise antecedent in a sentence like "My brother and the man started arguing and then he hit him," could cause serious misunderstanding. Whereas the misspelling in "My brother hit the man to" doesn't really hamper the idea.

2. Instead of marking corrections on papers, try underlining them. Turn students back on their own resources. Ask them to make the correction on or off the paper. Encourage them to identify the *class* of error: Is this a spelling mistake? No apostrophe? Agreement of subject and verb? Unclear antecedent? Wrong pronoun? Change of tense in the middle of a sentence?

3. Have students graph their recurring errors. Is there one area that he always seems to miss? Is he improving.

4. Individualize spelling lessons. (A) Make spelling lists for the student from his own errors. (B) Make spelling lists according to students' interests: from the sports page, from a library book. Are they working with video equipment? Practice "focus" and "lens" and "lenses."

5. Read aloud for puctuation. Try having the student read his work aloud, slowly, and point out to him that there is a correlation between his pauses and the use of commas, between his breathing stops and periods. A particular tone means a question mark. In reading aloud this way a student will often include an omitted word. Maybe he wrote "Loba biting the bad man" but will read aloud "Loba was biting the bad man." Thus you will be able to differentiate between the errors your student makes through carelessness—his thought may be going faster than his hand can write—and those errors he does not understand *how* to correct. This method gives you insight into the particular character of the students' problems.

6. Try dictation too, insisting that the students who are dictating the story or poem to you should tell where they want capitals and commas.

Exercises for Students to Generate Language Awareness

1. Edit free writing. Free writing is a timed period of writing whatever comes flowing through the stream of one's consciousness. For a minute or five or ten write everything on your mind, the only rule being not to lift your pencil to stop and think. If you think nothing then write "nothing nothing nothing" until something else comes. After trying to capture this thinking, do a rewrite of it carefully, correctly, choosing the parts that are most interesting or appropriate, cutting out the rest. Other rewriting ideas would be to punctuate an entire paper for different purposes: as if two people were talking (use of quotation marks); as if the speaker were excited; as if all the material were questions rather than statements.

2. Do a passage in slang. Some children may be aware of what they think is very hip slang; someone else might be able to write in street talk or in a formal preacher jargon. Try writing in dialect, using ethnic accents, or typical mistakes that a person whose native language is, say, Spanish or Yiddish, might make in English. Work with dialects is important because the speaker of a so-called substandard dialect needs to be conscious of how his way of speaking varies from the standard taught in the school. A very important book called *Black English* by J. L. Dillard presents the impressive case for actual deep structural differences between black and standard English.

3. Do translations. For real awareness of how grammar functions, there is nothing like comparing languages. If you know a foreign language, or can pick up a literal translation as near word-for-word as possible, ask students to put the literal translation into normal English. If any students know two languages, put them to work translating paragraphs, poems, stories. This is the nitty-gritty of grammar, its real function, which is to convey meaning.

4. After a lot of editorial work, for fun and practice, give an assignment to write with as many errors as possible. Or better, with one error at a time. First have the students write sentences where the subject don't agree with the verb. . . then hav thum spel evry wurd rong.

5. Experiment with crazy spelling. In the spirit of the write-wrong exercise, give a mock spelling test of nicely phonetic nonsense words: kerplotz, figul, croop. This is a good entry into the irrationality of English spelling. Even though the correct spelling of kerplotz is with a "k," how else might it be spelled? Cerplots? Curplahtz? You can also invent definitions for the words.

6. Have students do research in the various spellings of a single sound like the "eye" sound. How many ways can you find the sound "f" spelled in English? Compare English to a nice phonetic language like Spanish. (But Spanish has its prob-

lems too, such as the identity of the sounds of "v" and "b" when they occur in the middle of a word.) Point out that "night" was once pronounced something like the German "nicht" and "knight" had no silent letters.

7. Explore roots. Have kids go to some good book like *Origins* by Eric Partridge or show them how to use a good dictionary like the *American Heritage Dictionary of the English Language* and find out the history of some words. From what language did we get the word? Did you know that English "black" has a common ancestor with the Spanish word "blanco" which means white?

8. Collect new words, lately invented, like product names (Kleenex) and technical terms (video). Invent some of your own, such as a special word for a feeling of loving all mankind: "humanility." Our word "chortle" was invented by Lewis Carroll for his nonsense poem "Jabberwocky" and has since come into the language as fully acceptable.

9. More experimentation with words, such as nouning. Use a noun as a verb or vice versa. This may seem a little whimsical; how does one, after all, noun? But it is an excellent way to demonstrate that the real difference between parts of speech is function. Can you really substitute one word for another? Can you say "the swam"? Can you ever "very" someone?

10. Try a son of a spelling bee. Many of the preceding suggestions are completely unlike workbook drills. We like them for that reason. Writing time should be saved for the actual writing and rewriting of reports, stories, articles and poems. Grammar might be drilled orally, however, in competitive team games: a homonym bee to practice the differences between too, two and to and they're, there, and their. Why not for that matter spelling bees too? Or use baseball rules: three mistakes for an out, three outs and the other team goes to bat. The pitching team makes up the questions.

Sue Willis's Linguistics and History of Language for Elementary Schools.

This pretentious-sounding course is still in the process of being invented. I am working weekly, trying new exercises and new materials, changing plans to take advantage of the enthusiasms of the students.

Sample Lesson One:

Languages change, and languages and words have families, ancestors and relatives. We talk about human family trees, and we play the old game of gossip in which a phrase is passed in whispers down a line of players. Inevitably the original comes out unrecognizable. So does language as it passes through time. We examine some samples of Anglo-Saxon, English as it was spoken before 1000 A.D. We go back even farther (because the class seems to like cave men) and talk about how people might have invented language. Why they needed it. We write mistranslations from the Anglo-Saxon samples, that is, we make a phoney translation by taking familiar-appearing words and putting them into a poem.

Sample Lesson Two:

We write a group poem on the board about what life might have been like in prehistoric times: It was cold in the caves, etc. Some kids stand up and try to improvise messages to the others without using words or drawings. We make a list of the first words people might have needed. They choose mostly practical noun words—like good, hunt, animal names—and then social interaction words of questioning—like how? and what? We write poems using the list of first words. Some prefer to write about the invention of language and fire, others write prayers to the gods of fire and wind.

Sample Lesson Three:

Two divergent ideas come to me from the last lessons. First, that other direction that language has taken, the written. We improvise again, this time by sketching on the board. I show them a book of Egyptian hieroglyphics that clearly come from drawings, and some samples of the development of our own alphabet: as, the letter "o" was originally an eye. The second direction, from the prayers they wrote last week to the gods, is the matter of sacred and taboo words. We talk about words that you can and cannot say: names of gods, "bad" words. We write monologues using special words for a situation where you were caught doing something you shouldn't, or where you really hated the other person.

Sample Lesson Four:

Some girls bring in the Cyrillic (e.g., Russian) alphabet and put it on the board and sound it out. We discuss more special words, and I read "Jabberwocky," the great Lewis Carrol epic in nonsense, and a little Middle English, from the General Prologue to Chaucer's *Canterbury Tales*. We discuss the question of whether the poem and the Middle English are English or some other language. Are they grammatical? Do they make sense? Then we make up codes, inventing nonsense words to stand for some ordinary thing, then using one ordinary thing to stand for another. I draw a rebus on the board. The rebus is a message in which, for example, a drawing of a tin can stands for the word "can," a drawing of an eye for the word "I." Everyone writes something in a code of their own. Secret codes seem to appeal to the class. Question: are codes a different language?

Sample Lesson Five:

I list sentences and non-sentences on the board like "Jerk surprising the of cat a" which has perfectly normal English words that make no sense at all, and

"Is reading your father this book?" which is understandable but not quite right as English. We talk about the importance of placement of words. We consider ways you could make an important word seem important in the piece of writing. The class thinks mostly of visual ideas like underlining, capitals, illuminating the first letter, etc. I suggest repetition and giving the important word a lot of space on a line to itself in a poem. I read two poems, "The Knee" by Christian Morgenstern and "I've Watched a Dying Eye" by Emily Dickinson in which word order is freely manipulated. We write poems about special or interesting words.

Further lessons will take up word histories: what words did English get from what languages? Which of our words are brand new inventions of the last twenty years? We will make up some fake etymologies and research some real ones. We will write poems using a lot of Latinate words or only short Anglo-Saxon ones. Why do so many languages have almost the same word for father? We will also write monologues in foreign and regional accents and sentences using fancy diction and baby grammar. To tell the truth, we will probably go wherever my studies and the class's interests take us. . . .

Karen Hubert's Voices

This curriculum is a continuing plan for writing and using grammar at the highest level. Karen begins with the differences in thinking, speaking and writing and gradually progresses through longer and more complex writing assignments to full scale monologues, stories and plays, all of which are very dependent on a creative use of grammar. The supposition here is that awareness of how we think, speak, and write, coupled with practice writing, will improve the product. Good writing is always self-conscious.

Just as we use the outer voice to speak, we use the inner voice to write. The "good writer" is one who has a strong and comfortable relationship to his inner voice; that voice which we hear when we think or talk to ourselves. Consider the processes of thinking, speaking, and writing. Like brothers and sisters they have similarities, differences, and dependencies. Helping your students to be more conscious of these processes will help them in their writing.

1. Begin working with this by discussing it. Ask your class, which process is fastest: thinking, writing or speaking. Which is slowest? Which one does a baby do first? Of them all, writing is the slowest, for it requires that the hand follow the mind. It is a common experience for student writers that their hands get tired, that as they come to the end of one sentence or thought, they have already thought of three or four other things to say and have, by the time their sentence is finished on paper, forgotten what they had planned to write next.

2. Ask your students to observe themselves thinking. Ask them to close their eyes. Time them for 30 seconds. Did they think in words? Pictures? Feelings? When they are telling you and the class about it, ask them to be specific, help them. Thinking is not confined to words.

3. Now, ask your students to talk to themselves, silently, for another thirty seconds. Eyes closed. This time they will be using words. You will notice that some of your students can hear these words very easily, others are really much less conscious of them. See if there is any correlation between the latter group and your "poor writers." Ask the other students to talk specifically about the words they heard. Were they talking to themselves or to another person? To you the teacher? Is this an "I" or first person, or is it a second person voice? Loud? Soft? Whiney? Humorous? Sarcastic? Some of your students will be able to answer this. Others will not, but you *will* be giving them something to think about.

4. Try to talk silently to yourself in someone else's voice; i.e., the voice of your mother, your father, teacher, best friend, or maybe the elevator operator's voice. Did you hear it? What did it say? Can you describe it?

5. Talk to yourself, silently, for 15 seconds. Can you remember one word of what you said? Repeat this 15-second exercise. Can you remember a phrase or fragment of what you said? (Rule of the game is that it *must* be said verbatim, exactly as you said it to yourself while you were thinking.) Repeat the thinking exercise. How much of it can you remember and say out loud *exactly as you thought it?* Can you say the whole thing?

6. This whole exercise may be repeated from the beginning, but now what is remembered should be written down, not all at once, but in the same slow stages as before.

7. Try to picture a room in your house, or a corner or a piece of furniture with which you are very familiar. Close your eyes and try to see it. Write down what you have seen.
   (Note: Both thinking and imagining exercises may be excellent diagnostic tools for teachers. They may see what students are bringing to the writing and imagining process, as well as what students are *not* bringing.)

8. What kind of voices do we possess and use? We use different ones in different situations. The voice we use on a job interview may be quite different from the one we use while gossiping with our best friend, or the one we use with a doctor, or when we are returning a sweater to Orbach's. Ask your students to tell you the voices

they use. If they don't understand the question, give them some situations in which the voice is used: when they are arguing, gossiping, feeling depressed, getting 100 on a spelling test. Write all the voices they give you on the board, scattered all over the board rather than in lists to stress the variety that is possible. Discuss this list with your class. This will lead to some interesting discussions if you pick up on some of their responses to the lesson and to the point you are trying to make.

9. Listen to your students during the day or during an hour, and listen for phrases that are powerful and simple and very common, such as: "Let me alone. I don't want to. I told her that. She said so. That wasn't what you told me before. I'm so glad that happened to her. I feel pretty good today," etc. Quietly write these on the board as you hear them. Your students will enjoy this game and find it strange the way the teacher is writing simple things they say on the board, thereby bringing them to the class's attention. Don't announce what you're doing, just keep on doing it. Tell them as they ask that you thought these words were so powerful and such terrific words that you wrote them down. Obviously if you don't really believe this, you shouldn't say it. But *I do* believe it and this *is* what I say. I ask different students to repeat "Let me alone" angrily, sexily, humorously, etc. Can they say it in a flat tone with no expression at all? Can they whisper? Scream it? Sing it? What you are trying to do here is to show all the ways people can control and use their voices, the amazing variety of things they can do with them.

10. Ask your students to say only negative things. (I.e., I don't want to.) Give only orders. Say only wishful things. Horrible, nasty things. Beautiful happy things. Can you do it? Try it in thinking, speaking, and writing.

11. Ask your students one at a time to speak non-stop for 15 seconds or more. Make bets as to whether they can. Try to count the number of words said in a ten second period of time or in a minute. If you could write these words down, how long would your writing be? A page? A paragraph? A whole composition? Students may talk on specific subjects or off the top of their heads. How much of what you said can you remember? If this was written, would it be interesting?

These exercises have been designed to strengthen your students' relationships to their inner and outer voices. Use them as jumping-off spots for your own ideas. Your basic aim here is to familiarize the students with their own voice(s) and words.

A curriculum like Karen's above suggests a systematic painstaking approach to the possibilities of generating writing. A writer constantly makes decisions about person, mood, tense, voice, tone, and style of diction. As I began to write this memorandum, I had to decide if I would be using my formal voice or a conversational one. Would I admit jokes and sentence fragments for emphasis? In reading too, our full comprehension depends on understanding the tone of the writer, his methods and tricks. Exercises like these lead to a creative writing where style and grammar are inseparable from meaning and story.

POSTSCRIPT
Some Reactions to the Grammar Question
by Phillip Lopate

I sense a certain amount of tension around the teaching of grammar. Are we giving kids a strong enough foundation in the rules? Are they becoming expressive but illiterate?

I've even heard a few "backlash" remarks to the effect that Teachers & Writers has been partly responsible for undermining the teaching of grammar by minimizing the importance of spelling and grammar, and discouraging teachers from marking up their students' creative writing compositions.

As a great former President once said, "I want to make one thing perfectly clear...." Teachers & Writers is not anti-grammar. I myself would like to see much more intensive study of language in the classrooms than is presently taking place. I want children to be able to handle language confidently and *correctly*. But to me that means they have to begin to explore language inquisitively, experimentally, like a biological science. Grammar is always in the process of becoming. What disturbs me is when it is taught as a series of dead, received truths. Grammar is too often administered like punishment, like castor oil. And even the recent anxiety about teaching grammar, with which I sympathize, somehow manages to become intertwined with "get tough" rhetoric: "We have to cut out the kidding around; we have to get down to brass tacks, pull out the workbooks."

I confess that I'm against most grammar workbooks. Not because workbooks *per se* are deadly— though they do seem to kill off the urge to investigate, and to reroute the student's mind into a right-wrong binary channel. I would still find them useful tools if they were only accurate! But most of them reflect an attitude toward language which was abandoned fifty years ago as over-simplified and distorted. Workbooks are full of pious false rules, like "There are two kinds of sentences: sentences which tell something and sentences which ask a question," when in fact there are dozens of kinds of sentences, and anyway, doesn't a question also tell something?

This hunger for the old grammar workbook is like one of those law-and-order reflexes that sweep through the schools from time to time. It's a panic response, it's wishful thinking and it ties the instruction of grammar falsely to conservatism.

Grammar is not the property of traditionalists. Grammar is simply there, like the sky, like peaches. Grammar belongs to everyone.

I suspect that an underlying reason for the grammar anxiety is that many teachers are uncertain about their own command of good grammar. They would like to invoke a higher authority—the workbook—and forget their own feelings of inadequacy. I have the exact same guilty conscience about grammar: it's something that never quite goes away, like when I check to see if my fly is zipped up. Grammatical errors have that capacity to make people blush. Then we should be a little more tolerant and realize that we ourselves have some learning to do.

Sometimes I see teachers correcting items on their students' papers that aren't wrong at all. For instance:

"Don't use *And* at the beginning of a sentence." There is nothing grammatically wrong about using And at the beginning of a sentence. We should differentiate more between grammatical errors and stylistic preferences that were drummed into our heads when we were students. Many of these have gone the way of other fashions. Or, writers have won the right to use certain constructions that used to be frowned upon. Take the sentence fragment. Hemingway, Joyce, Faulkner have made the sentence fragment into an effective way of communicating a piece of thought, in an interior monologue, say, or any other context. Consider this imaginary exchange about the exercises listed in this report: "Is this grammar practice or is it creative writing? Both." The word "both" is a legitimate sentence. How are we to convey to our students that they have that right to make a sentence out of one word, if it helps to keep the reader alert? The mark of a good writer is that he has so many ways of taking hold of an idea and pressing it into one syntax or another. Grammar can be an introduction to that variety instead of a constriction of it.

Some Books.
Language Made Plain, by Anthony Burgess (Apollo Editions paperback). A short, entertaining introduction to the study of language.
The Story of Language, by Mario Pei (New American Library paperback). Longer, but also very entertaining. Mr. Pei also has written books specifically on English as well as many other language topics.
Our Own Words, by Mary Helen Dohan (Penguin Books paperback). Origins of words in American English.
Origins, by Eric Partridge (Macmillan, hardcover only). Origins of words.
Polyglot's Lexicon: 1943-1966, by Kenneth Versand (Links Books paperback). A fascinating compilation of new words and meanings that have come into our language between the years 1943 and 1966.
Black English, by J.L. Dillard (Random House Vintage Books paperback). Fascinating case for black English as a separate branch of English with its own rules. Corollary is that standard English should be taught as a second language to many students.
American Heritage Dictionary of the English Language, edited by William Morris (American Heritage). Also available in an inexpensive paperback edition (abridged), edited by Peter Davies (Dell paperback).

The Moment to Write

by Phillip Lopate

It often amazes me, after I have taught a creative writing lesson and handed out paper, that the children write any poems at all. I doubt I could write a good poem in such vulnerable, exposed circumstances. Yet they do write—sometimes fine poems, at gunpoint as it were. Maybe there is nothing so mysterious about this: they are reconciled to the rule of authority which expects production on the spot, in ways that an adult would never dream of demanding of himself.

When I write seriously I need to go off by myself. For me, writing is a solitary and private act. Yet the teaching of creative writing, including in most cases the actual writing, takes place in classrooms with groups as large as forty students. There is this embarrassing contradiction, which can't be wished away, between the mass public character of the classroom and the need that writing imposes for quiet introverted space.

Perhaps it would be useful to draw a distinction between two kinds of writing: writing on assignment (such as daily newspaper columns, ad copy, bureau reports) which must be done by a certain deadline, and another kind of writing (novels, poetry, philosophy) where the demanding agent is less external than internal. I mean absolutely no slight when I say that it is usually easier to do the first kind—and it often is done—in noisy, crowded workplaces. The second seems to require more isolation. The same person can write excellent advertising copy in an office but must go home to work on a novel. When we ask children to pour their hearts out, to write truthfully and authentically in a vivid individual voice, at the same time as requesting that the work be produced on the spot in classrooms, we are essentially asking that the second kind of writing be produced under circumstances devised more for the first kind.

Unpopular as this fact may be, poetry and fiction require withdrawal. So much is this the case that the only really useful advice I could give to someone who wants to be a writer is—*learn to be alone*. People with all the verbal and imaginative sparkle in the world who cannot sit with themselves will never be thorough writers.* Writing is a long seclusion. Out of the walking, out of the brooding, out of the boredom of childhood, the residue of pleasures and the memory of people who left a confusing last impression, out of all that sifting comes congealed thought: literature.

Let us put away for a moment the question of helping children to write and look at the process in adults, to see what can be learned from that more developed model.

Assuming one has agreed to be alone. How does one know when to start writing? This is not so moronic a question as it sounds; in fact, it may be the crucial consideration. How does one tell when the best moment has come to start writing? What are the emotional hints, the weather signals?

The clues may be different in each person, but that doesn't mean they aren't important, or that we shouldn't consider the possibility of teaching people to recognize their own patterns. Though the motivations which induce a person to write may change, an intimate knowledge of one's own working habits allows one to keep writing by adjusting to the changes. Frank O'Hara once said that when he was young he could write poetry only when he felt gloomy or depressed, but later in life he needed to feel good in order to write. This revealing statement suggests a progression from adolescence to maturity. When an adolescent writes poetry, more often than

---

* A case could be made, it's true, for collaborative literary production by several people in the same room, as the French surrealist poets did, but in my opinion very little of the literature produced in this way has any hope of enduring. Current collaborative poetry tends to read as little more than a party stunt, rewarding quickness of repartee and flipness rather than substance.

not he chooses a moment when he is miserable: his writing is part of a vendetta against the world which has cut him off from happiness. Many people who showed promise as adolescent poets fail to pursue the activity because they have made an unconscious mental equation between poetry and gloom. The emotional crisis of their adolescence has passed, and with it the urge to write poems.

They would not think of squandering their happy times on sitting down to write a poem. Most of us during those brief, charmed moments would rather ride the escalator up and down Bloomingdale's Department Store or go for a walk and stare at the lake. A fear persists that any looking inward, or concentrated mental effort of the sort required for poetry-writing, might spoil the happiness. Yet is it necessarily so that introspection destroys happiness? I doubt it. . . . And poetry would be a much more enjoyable business for everyone if the people who wrote it chose to share their thoughts at the peak of their vitality and love of life, rather than at the nadir.

A third state, the one in which most good writing gets done, is neither depression nor joy, but even-temperedness, clarity, calm. The space around you appears considerable. You feel able to extend outward in all directions, and to entertain any threatening thought or speculation with equanimity, as if the issue of your life were somehow already decided. From this vantage point, it is as if you were able to keep thinking beyond the grave, with utter calm. The terrible fatality has happened; you have already died; and now you are able to say a few things cogently.

I find this clear headed state particularly useful for the writing of long prose, where what I want is the feeling of a large block of time in front of me.

With poetry, on the contrary, it doesn't hurt for me to feel a little rushed, upset, physically galvanized. I know something is up when I start hearing an echo, which makes even ordinary thoughts like "I have to pick up the laundry" take on a meaningfulness and a rhythmic certitude that would be laughable at any other time, when I am feeling more skeptical. This sudden conviction that I *know*, that I am walking in the fields of knowledge and everything is very simple, this impression of shadows and depth behind every thought and observation, is partly the work of the echo. But sound-consciousness alone can be a kind of fool's gold, a trick of phonics, unless it is accompanied by feelings in the body. I can tell a poem is arriving by my stomach. A churning in the stomach is the infallible guide; it alone assures me that my emotion will last at least as long as it takes me to set down the first ten lines. I always worry that the feeling will desert me before I come to the end of the poem. If I start with the musical echo alone, it may turn into drivel. So I look for that peculiar synchronization of ear and gut.

Much modern verse, beginning with Whitman, is held together by the poem's ability to generate waves of charged longing, each line making a new oceanic surge and drifting back again to start the next swelling. For me, the center and generator of these waves is the stomach. It may be another organ for a different poet. I am offering my own responses as a guinea pig, only because I am most familiar with them. The crucial thing is that these physiological signals do exist, telling the writer when he or she is ready to get down to business.

There may be long periods of waiting when nothing directly useful is happening: sluggish states filled with mental static, or subvocal complaints whining and quarreling with each other. When I get like that I don't see any point in writing. The work will only come out fractured and sour. I need to feel whole to write. Which means that I have to be patient with myself when I am feeling dispersed, and wait for a better time. *Waiting is half the discipline of writing.*

I am not saying that a writer should sit on his hands and do nothing while these signals are not occurring. On the contrary, he can take notes; he can edit other material—or he can go ahead and fight the mood and hope to bully it around to his way. He can try to stumble on his wholeness in the act of writing; and with a bit of luck he will. Most professional writers get into situations where they have to ignore their feelings, like Flaubert who boasted that he had written comic scenes when he was bored to tears or ready to hang himself. But even the stalwarts, the Stakhanovites, who allot themselves a fixed quota of hours and pages per day, occasionally have to take a day's vacation before approaching a difficult scene, and dally over minor material until they feel their energies have been marshaled for the climax.

I am convinced there is such a thing as *inner ripeness* in writing. One can ignore these signals or follow them, but the ripening process goes on nonetheless. If I choose to obey the voice of resistance, and refrain from writing when I know I do not really feel like it, I'm too tired, or would rather putter, or read a book, or walk the streets, then I find I will be that much more able to pick up the cues of inner readiness. Often, giving into resistance seems to be a way of tricking the urge to write into appearing: so that, after reading a few pages of a thought-provoking book, I will suddenly put it down and go over to my desk. I have indulged myself, I am ready to work now. The feeling is of an immense willingness to begin.

When you have picked the absolutely ripe moment to write, *then most of the technical problems which come up in composition solve themselves*. The transitions flow unforced, the structure has an inevitable logic which reflects the harmony of the writer's mental state. There is no need to wrack your brains for metaphors or comparisons. The image comes of itself. At the moment you have written it down, the next image, the next thought, is there to take its place. In this charmed state, everywhere the mind turns, objects have a slanted, piquant, amusing side; every association leads to an even better. The piece is not so much written as transcribed, as if it were being sung in the ear. Obviously these experiences do not happen very often. But a few are enough to cement a life's vocation. And the memory of these gifts from heaven are what keep many writers going during all the subsequent hours of mundane drudgework.

I cannot leave off this science or pseudo science of picking the best moment to write, without saying something about the rites of preparation for the act of writing.

Hemingway was reported to have sharpened pencils as a trick of getting in the mood. Keats dressed up in his most formal suit before sitting down to compose a poem. Schiller kept a drawer full of rotten apples from which he took a whiff whenever he was running low on inspiration. Others have performed elaborate morning ablutions.* It would not surprise me if another writer stood on his head for ten minutes to stimulate mental circulation. These practices, collected by literary hagiographers, are equally legitimate, equally arbitrary, and equally irrelevant for anyone else. They point to the superstition which surrounds the act of writing: the idiosyncratic ways in which various authors try to ward off distracting ghosts and summon their concentration by ritual acts of repetition. It is not so important for us to know what the ritual is, as it is to understand that apparently the necessity of one is felt. However silly or self-indulgent it may appear to anyone else, we have to respect the way that he has found out for himself what personally suits his nervous system.

A writer watches himself like a horse trainer. He keeps taking his temperature, alternately resting and pushing himself, looking for signs of strength, looking always for that optimum moment to release him for his run. But it would be wrong to get the impression that this vigilance requires painful effort, or self-consciousness; in fact, it operates automatically, as a sixth sense that has always been there but which one becomes aware of eventually through practice.

2.

Looking at the implications of this for our teaching, doesn't it seem neglectful that the poets in the schools teach children the latest forms and techniques

—————————————
* I like to wash the dishes.

of composition, without letting them in on a factor which counts so heavily in their own writing? We writers have wracked our brains searching for new lesson assignments, new materials, games, whole word catalogs to stimulate the imaginations of our students. A writer who has no particular sympathy with concrete poetry, for instance, will teach a lesson on concrete poetry because he doesn't want to deprive his students of this stylistic option. But his own practices, his own acts of preparation, his own voodoo, as it were, he keeps to himself.

Is it because it is impossible to teach another person an awareness of his own timing in the area of creativity? Is it something one must learn for himself? Are these metabolic regulations so exclusive to each person that they have no meaning for anyone else? Or is it rather that inner ripeness is a hard-won secret that the professional is reluctant to part with?

As I see it, nothing could be more valuable to teach young people than this one quality. Be it in sports, art, research, lovemaking, engineering, business—for a person to know when he is at the peak moment to make an exertion is one of the most crucial advantages he can have. Think of the alternative: without that knowledge, these same students will be doomed to following someone else's timetable—passively waiting for authorities to lead, resenting the order when it comes, bridling, sabotaging, but not knowing how to listen to their own energy's voice.

I wish I could propose a curriculum to transmit this quality, which would make a triumphant finish to my article; but at this point in my thinking I am able only to state the problem. Maybe others will now come forward with approaches and clarifications for teaching the moment to write. In the meantime, it would help to consider some of the recent trends in education which may have a bearing on this problem.

Let us look again at the paradox we started with: how do we reconcile the teaching of creative writing or literature, which is mostly done in groups through lessons, and the solitary act of writing? Or, to put it another way: how can we bring the privacy of the child's room at home closer to the classroom and make him able to feel self-absorbed and alone in a good sense, alone with his thoughts?

The architecture of the open classroom is certainly an attempt to create more of an overlap between home and school. Couches, creativity nooks, reading lofts, sactioned hideouts are all part of a healthy tendency to provide the individual child with more latitude in choosing his own place to retreat and work. Some teachers allow the children to stretch out on the floor and to choose their own writing implements from a variety of magic markers, pens, different shapes of paper—thus encouraging a freedom in the writing materials to compensate for the coercion to write. All of these adjustments have a considerateness about them in not expecting everyone to be able to write spontaneously at their school desks. Since professional writers compose under a wide range of sitting, reclining and standing positions, I think there is every good reason to extend that freedom of posture to the classroom writer.

Unfortunately, many open classrooms are so noisy, with lusty hammering, rabbit cries and small group meetings that they have the ambience of a bomb shelter. Also, many of the children are so socially preoccupied with what the other children—the leaders or whoever—are doing, that they have a hard time getting into themselves. The noise and the opportunities for incessant vague wandering and visiting make open classrooms in certain respects less congenial to the private act of writing than the older traditional classrooms.

Another approach seems to be to recreate the thoughtful, contemplative tone of private space in the lesson itself. One teacher who was successful with children's writing told me she instituted a "poetry hour," during which all the children gathered around the couch and talked quietly and then wrote. It was understood by the children that this one hour a week was a sanctuary, a time to talk about subjective impressions, mysteries, things which made them feel uncertain or indefinitely aroused, or simply, things that made them feel. This sort of quiet truce in the school day would be valuable even if it had nothing to do with poetry.

There is also something of the old ghost-story hour about this practice. The teacher's voice and character tone can be instrumental in setting the scene. Just as the storyteller held his listeners spellbound and made their skin crawl, so a good poetry teacher can exert a spell through the timbre of voice, the choice of words, the intensity of her concentration, and lead the students down and down into it. Here we enter the area of performance. The teacher performs in such a way as to create a mood of inner stillness, like a preacher or a flamenco singer. The students respond as if partly in a trance, leaking words on paper. The transition from speech to writing is very gentle, sometimes barely noticeable. I have been present at such hushed states of suggestibility which led to very good, intimate writing by the students. They make me uneasy, perhaps because even though I have sometimes been the instrument to bring them about, I myself would not like the idea of writing so internally on someone else's deep suggestion.

And yet, there are some students who seem to be able to write only in public. Even in college, they prefer to let go to the scratching sound of other pens. So there is really no way of prescribing a "best" set of writing conditions for everyone.

Another writer asked his students to lie down on the floor and begin breathing deeply. The children

"Perhaps the best incentive to creative writing is a classroom atmosphere in which anyone knows he has permission to go off and write at any given time of the day."

were asked to notice, after awhile, if they could visualize something happening in their chests. They were told to think of an image which illustrated the bodily sensation they were going through; keep taking in deep breaths; see if the internal sensations suggested another image; and at the end of the exercise, to write down these images or write a poem or story connecting the images. This exercise derived from Jungian psychotherapy. The writer reported that the stories the children wrote that day were very serious and deep. Nevertheless, he was unable to think of a way of taking this one-time experience further.

There is clearly an important connection between physiology and writing (or all creative processes). But I confess that I would be reluctant to see yoga or sensitivity-awakening exercises taught nationwide to young children as a prelude to creative writing. First, I have apprehensions that the techniques may be misunderstood and misapplied; second, I have doubts that such exercises performed in a group will actually carry over to helping a child become the master of his potential creative energy when he is alone. Somehow, these exercises were never needed during the centuries of great Western literature, art and artisanship. I have a feeling that what made that tradition flourish was something else, the cultivation of the capacity for assigning oneself tasks, *willful labor*.

We hand out the paper, and they write. There is nothing evil in this, except if we fail to supplement it with more understanding of students' inability, sometimes, to write when we tell them to. Perhaps the best incentive to creative writing is a classroom atmosphere in which anyone knows he has permission to go off and write at any given time in the day. Maybe we need to dispense with the whole idea of poetry hours, or at least recognize for once and for all that the urge to create may strike different people at any time. Why should one hour be more "poetic" than the next? We should talk with our students about the times and circumstances in which they feel most comfortable writing, to learn more about the range of individual response in this area.

Most important, I think, is the understanding that writing is not just a set of techniques or skills, it is an act of *giving*. To place your thoughts on paper you have to feel generous. You have to feel in the mood to communicate. And when you feel in that mood, how much better it comes out! Who wouldn't like to give when he is in a benevolent mood? Then generosity becomes the healthy exercise of muscles that cry out to be used. But on the other hand, nothing can make certain people stingier and more tight-lipped than if they feel an admission is being prematurely forced out of them. The same timid person, resentful when pushed into a hasty self-exposure, would be happy to tell the very same thing if only he or she had been allowed to select his own moment. The best we can ask of ourselves as teachers is to learn how to sense that ripening process in each student: to know when an individual is closed and wants to be left alone, and when he or she is ready to take a new step outward. Ripeness is all.

Dream Workshop

by Bill Zavatsky

One afternoon, browsing as I habitually do among the stationery, I stumbled onto a cache of terrific wide-lined notebooks—they were selling for the ridiculous price of fifteen cents apiece—and the next day I toted them in to my P.S. 84 (Manhattan) workshops. We were working in a special room reserved for writing and art activities placed at the disposal of Teachers and Writers Collaborative. Instead of working with entire classes, I'd ask for volunteers and together we'd troop downstairs to the room to write for an hour.

I'd bought the notebooks for a reason. I wanted to do a project, and thought that by having the kids write in the same books each week, it might strengthen our sense of continuity. It worked. Everybody wanted a book (these were fifth and sixth graders), and it solved the problem of having to lug loose sheets of paper around. And the kids enjoyed personalizing the covers of their books with decorative doodles.

The project was Dreams. For a period of about two months, in groups of five or ten or however many wanted to write that day, we would gather to discuss and write them. The dream as material for writing is sure-fire: everyone dreams. I began things by telling one of my dreams, as vividly and dramatically as I could, and urged the kids to tell one of theirs. After we listened with great excitement and a growing sense of identification to the dreamer doing the talking, I urged the kids to write down one dream that they remembered, even if they had just told it to the group.

Before they wrote, however, I talked a little bit about what dreams were like to me. I compared them to a movie. When you go into a dark theater and suddenly the film flashes on the screen, you don't pay much attention to anything going on around you; you find yourself completely wrapped up in the images. Just like a dream. Often our dreams are so real that we have trouble realizing we're "only dreaming." We wake up terrified, sweating, or aglow with

the pleasant scenes and events we have experienced. I urged the kids to write down everything but *everything* they could remember. I tried to convince them that no detail in a dream was unimportant, even if it seemed silly. What people wore, exactly what they said, what their faces looked like, the colors (if they dreamed in color), and how the things in the dream and what happened in the dream made them feel. I insisted that their written dreams be as detailed as they could make them.

Besides writing down dreams, we did a good deal of talking about the phenomenon of dreaming. Rather than impose Freudian or Jungian theories, I let the discussions go where they would. The kids were fascinated with the subject. Did dreams mean anything? Where did they come from? What about dreams you had more than once (the "recurring dream")? Could dreams predict the future (the "prophetic dream")? By letting the discussions sprawl and remain inconclusive, I hoped simply to instigate their interest in dreaming. I wanted them to take the dream seriously and not to dismiss it as the result of too much anchovy pizza and Dr. Pepper. If by focusing serious attention on the dream I could get them to pay attention to their nighttime adventures, that would be enough. Later, they could begin to psychologize.

The children were particularly absorbed in prophetic dreams, and one of the most astonishing "proofs" for dreams as predictions of future events came from a sixth grader, Jackie Santiago:

One night I had a dream that my cousin had gone to a party and got drunk. So her boyfriend had taken her to a room then he got nasty with her. So she didn't know what she was doing. Her boyfriend's mother locked the door so that they could be all alone. They couldn't get out. So the boy said, Don't worry. He kept on getting nasty but my cousin didn't want him to get nasty. So he got very mad because she didn't want to be nasty. Then he told her that the only way they could get out is that she could tie a piece of rope on her waist and try to get out of the window into another. So she said Yes. The color of her dress was white and it was a wedding dress. So since she didn't get nasty he let go of the rope and she fell. She fell from the 11th floor. And when I woke up and went to day camp, everything came out true, everything. But it didn't happen to my cousin, it was to my friend, and it really happened. I felt terrible. When I saw her casket I couldn't even move. I started to cry. And for the rest of the week I saw her in her coffin. I was thinking, "It's my fault. If I hadn't dreamed it, it wouldn't have happened." I couldn't stand it. I didn't eat a thing. She was 16 years old. That's a pretty young age to die at.

Sometimes one of the children felt compelled to offer an explanation for a dream. Here is a remarkable gloss (and dream) by Mary Ryan (5-6th grade):

"I saw a lot of eyes. I remember that one pair of eyes was my cat's. They all started to slowly advance towards me. I screamed. Then I wasn't there: I quickly saw the Periodic Table of Elements flash before my eyes. Curium, hydrogen, and uranium . . . etc. And someone said, 'Uranium,' and I woke up."
Maybe the reason I saw the eyes is because I was studying the Table of Elements and I made a list of them and most of them ended in "ium" and there were a lot of "i" 's.

As expected, the dreams recorded by the students were often formed by their deepest wishes. Jackie Roman, another sixth grader, was always winning beauty contests or being crowned queen in her dreamlife:

One day I was in Hollywood, California, I was supposed to be in a beauty contest. I was against 50 girls. The girls were from 11 years old to 15 years old. First we had to line up and tell the audience our names, how old we are, where do we live, where do we come from. The winner gets a trip to Hawaii and a $10,000 check. I really hoped to win. The girls are from Puerto Rico, Hawaii, Bermuda, England, Miami, Florida, Paris, Rome, France, Dominican Republic. I was picturing myself with a crown on my head, flowers in my hands and a long cape. Since I was a little girl I wished that I would go to Puerto Rico with the money that I won from the contest. I met lots and lots of stars like David Carradine, The Rookies, Bob Barker and many other stars. The judges had to pick 6 finalists to go up front of the stage and answer questions. I was the first one called up, Miss Puerto Rico, and next were Miss Rome, Miss Paris, Miss Dominican Republic and Miss Bermuda. Bob Barker the judge asked me where would I go if I won the $10,000. I told him to Puerto Rico, and then

he asked questions to the other girls. He had to call out one by one, and those who were out were presented with flowers. The the big time came. They called my name and I started crying, all the 49 girls giving me kisses. I was wearing the long cape.

I have stated that we didn't analyze. I was content to use the dream as a writing vehicle. Most of all, I wanted the children to understand that something very deep within them, an experience we are trained to shake off the moment we awaken, a mode that sometimes by its visual nature defies capture with words, was significant enough to be worth the effort. Uppermost in my mind was to impress them that they carried within themselves, day by day and night by night, an inexhaustible source of writing material. Writing about dreams could lead to other realizations about the sources of literature; that their frequent and arduous complaint of "I have nothing to write about" is contradicted by their daily lives.

These young people were not yet ready to accept the appropriate psychological machinery that would enable them to interpret their dreams intelligently. I did, however, take steps when we discussed dreams to combat some of the folk myths surrounding them. For example, the belief that if one dies in a dream, one will die in real life. "Nonsense," I told them, "I've been killed in a thousand dreams, and here I am in front of you. Maybe it isn't so bad to 'die' in a dream." I then proceeded to explain that we "die" many times in our lives, our dearest ideas die, our habits die, friendships die, the ways in which we have always done things die; and so "dying" in a dream could mean "change" or "growth" or simply "movement." I reminded them that plants had to die every year so that they could grow again and bear fruit.

By the seventh or eighth grade I think many students *are* ready to begin understanding that the totality of the dream refers to the dreamer. Recently a student at J.H.S. 141 (Bronx, N.Y.) stopped me and asked if I could help him explain a dream. I recognized him as a now-and-then member of an after-school poetry workshop I was giving, and drew him aside so we could talk privately.

He very much wanted to know what the dream "meant." The special feature of it that disturbed him (an eighth grader) went as follows: He passed by a food freezer in a grocery in his dream and, to his horror, saw that instead of steaks and chops wrapped in plastic, there were human hands and feet. "Why would I dream *that*?" he said, recoiling at his own terrible dream-thoughts. I wondered for a moment. "Well," I told him, "You know that all those lamb chops and packages of hamburger in the supermarket freezers were once parts of living animals. What we do is cut them up into pieces and wrap them in plastic and sell them in stores." Immediately he saw the connection and his face lit up. What had been abstract cuts of meat in his waking life, objects he had taken for granted and consumed, were forced in his dreams to assume their reality as former parts of living animals. His unconscious mind had made this connection, through images, but it was only by discussing these images that we could understand them. The conclusion was inescapable: we kill living things to nourish ourselves. We didn't discuss the morality of it, or how these dream images related to his own life, though we very well could have. What I wanted to show him was one dream mechanism, the combination of different elements in the state of sleep that brings an important realization to light. I decided to leave him with a question that would force him to reflect on his dream in personal terms: "Do you feel in some way, you yourself are being cut up, packaged, and frozen?"

This is precisely the point at which the dreamer steps into the poet's shoes, for much of the history of poetry is composed of images drawn from the unconscious mind and fashioned consciously to link objects, events, and emotional states that seem at variance. When Robert Burns wrote "My luve is like a red, red rose," he was doing nothing less. The poetic metaphor is one of those crystallizations of human consciousness that fuses-together, sometimes grotesquely (packaged meat = packaged hands), sometimes sublimely (human face and form = rose). These crystallizations are always meaningful, whether we accept or refuse what the poetic image (or the dream image) is showing us. This is where poetry lives; this is the "truth of poetry" we were told about in school. It is what Ezra Pound meant when he insisted that poetry "present" images, not comment upon them. Any discussion I and my student could have had about the implications of his dream-image were ancillary to the fact, the *presence*, of the image, just as discussion or interpretation of a poem is "after the fact" of the poem, and completely dependent on what the poem shows us. In using dreams as a writing vehicle, then, and making any interpretation of them a secondary activity, I was pushing my students toward what I consider to be a primary poetic truth: Give us material in poems that is sensual, that we can hear, see, smell, taste, touch. Leave the job of interpretation to the scholars. The first job of a poet is to give, not to explain.

Let me introduce another example of this approach. A twelve year old with whom I have been working on and off for three years in writing workshops told me of a recurring dream she had earlier in her life. Here is the dream, which she made into a poem:

I'm standing on the tracks of a railroad.
An old fashioned train is there.
But the only part I can see is the caboose,

> "Writing about dreams could lead to other realizations about the source of literature; that their frequent and arduous complaint of 'I have nothing to write about' is contradicted by their lives."

Where my father is standing.
My father is holding onto the
Chain which keeps you from falling.
He's staring at me, but having
No expression at all on his face.
I shout "Wait, please come back"
As I run after the train
My arms flying toward him.
But the train doesn't stop.
It turns the curve of the
Mountain and disappears.

The events presented in the poem and the characters in it are presented without interpretative muddle. From the opening line, we can "see" everything clearly. The young author has faithfully transcribed her dream; we are the ones who must decipher its meaning. I now propose to take just such an interpretative excursion through the dream-poem, honing closely to what is *presented*.

The "theme" of the poem is clear: separation and loss, father being pulled away from child, who is powerless to stop him. An irrational force had intervened—the train. (One does not plead with an inanimate object; and while the father "stares" at his child, his face is as expressionless as the movement of the train is unstoppable. The train has "got" the father, and it is as if the emotionless parent were now one of its metal fixtures.) All of the "feeling" in the poem comes from the poet, who tries desperately to stop the progress of the train and bring her father back, her "arms flying." The father is also standing on the caboose, the last car of a train. Everything in the poem speaks of endings that are irreversible; the train "turns the curve of the/ Mountain and disappears."

The chain that the father grasps is one of the key elements in the poem. Chains join things together, but in this poem the chain holds the father back. Perhaps if he let go of the chain "which keeps you from falling," he would fall off the train and the poet could reclaim him; but he doesn't. In fact, he joins himself to the chain, becoming almost another link in it, and by volition holds himself back. He has, if you will, "linked himself" to the inanimate. None of this interpretation, I think, is farfetched. The poem is coherent and whole, like the dream that gave it birth.

When I discussed this poem with the young poet, she told me that her father had died when she was six years old, and that she did not have the dream until after his death, and thence for several years it came regularly. But the poem has already *shown* us that some kind of unalterable rupture has occurred between the poet and her father, a break which has been compared to a train carrying the father away from her. Had she written, "My father died when I was six years old," the poem could be pigeonholed as just another psychological document; or, it would have become a very different kind of poem. Instead, the poet's unconscious mind created these images, from what material is anyone's guess. Perhaps the train image stems from our habit of telling little children that someone who had died has "gone away" or "gone on a long trip" or "passed away"—the same way that the father goes "past" or "passes by" his daughter in the dream. While she was asleep, her mind was doing healing work. The dream was allowing her to express what she felt in a symbolic way, and having done so, to begin to understand it. As one rarely understands a dream immediately, so poets working with the images that are "given to them" are often hard put to explain what their poems mean. The logic of poetic composition resembles the logic of the dream imagery in this respect; the poet works consciously to arrange his images in an order that "feels" right, just as the dream could have "come out" no other way.

This twelve year old's poem shows her, in my opinion, to be remarkably free of any guilt feelings vis-a-vis her father's death. Some force that she was powerless to halt had taken her father from her. At the same time, the loss of a male role model may have serious consequences in the adult life of this young person. (I am here, of course, invoking the Jungian idea of the "animus" or masculine personality element as a necessity in the proper psychological growth of a female child, just as a feminine model or "anima" is necessary to the emotional growth of a male child.) With this remark we are well beyond the sphere of the poem itself and advanced upon other matters I will not pursue here. What is central to the dream, and to the work of poetry, is that we are presented with some vivid event which we must capture on paper without introducing extraneous matter. That is, without blurring the focus of the experience by interpreting it. If anything, my reading of this dream-poem should underscore the importance of the dream experience for each of us. A dream is hardly the "airy nothing" that popular opinion makes it. The dream is as "packed with meaning" as any good poem.

Dreams are important indications of the emotional state of the dreamer. A child who has nothing but terrifying nightmares, or a child whose writing is filled with negative self-images, can perhaps gain a simple therapeutic value from recording his dreams. Some of the terror drains away in the saying of it, and the child who feels his work is worthless may be nudged to a reconsideration when faced with the existence of the piece of writing he has done. The temptation to play psychologist can become overpowering when working with dreams, however, and I successfully resisted it. While the dreams my students recorded often reflected their struggles with the problems of identity and change, I concentrated on the writing. Often when the children presented me with "finished" dreams, and we read them over, I would ask questions designed to add information to their dream-transcript. One girl presented me with a few sketchy sentences; by asking her to describe what she had written in more detail ("What did the man look like? What was his face like? Could you see it in the dream?"), she was able to produce a much stronger piece of writing:

The dream I had was good and again it was bad. So at the first beginning I had run away from home and my mother was looking for me and I was lost in the woods. It was dark and trees were sticking above me and faces with blood coming from them made noises, and came out of the trees. You could follow the trails of blood and hear women screaming. And they could not find me but I had run into a man and he wanted to give me an apple but I would not eat it. He had like white powder on his head and strings growing from his head. His eyes would glow in the dark like a model of King Kong I had, but more clear. So then I turned round and the apple he had looked so good that I looked at it and before I took a bite my mother called me through the woods and my father had run and bounded down on the floor. And my father took me and we hid under the rock and the apple had exploded and the man got killed and I never ran away from home again.

Right when I was beginning to go into another one I woke up and I was glad but I wanted to find out what the other was going to be.

Bridget Crayton

In another dream this elaboration took the form of a footnote which illustrates the process I am describing more clearly:

I had this dream two years ago. It all started like this. I was coming home from school when I looked up at the sky and saw 3 or 4 angels. They were playing an instrument of some kind. I thought that I was seeing things, but no, it was really there. It made me feel different. I crossed the street but it was still above me. Every time I moved it would move the same place. I got home and there it was in my room. That is where I woke up. But every time I had the dream I would wake up in the same part. I think that there's a part that somebody or someone does not want me to see.

The angels had on long white dresses, with wings on the back of the dress. Two of them had blonde hair and I cannot remember what the other two angels hair was. They don't look like someone I know or have seen before. This is all I remember. But this dream means something.

Elizabeth Serrano

"As one rarely understands a dream immediately, so poets working with images that are 'given to them' are often hard put to explain what their poems mean."

To some, this method of pulling more information out of the children might seem cruel or overly literary. By doing it I hoped to make the children recognize that good writing consists of concrete details that have sensual appeal, not in generalizations or abstractions. Bridget's original "man" (a faceless nobody, an abstraction) became a man who "had like white powder on his head and strings growing from his head. His eyes would glow in the dark like a model of King Kong I had, but more clear." Certainly this description has more power to move us than the word "man," as does Elizabeth's footnote description of what the angels in her dream looked like. I think it is important for teachers to recognize that in the search for illuminating details, poetry parts company with the tendency toward generalization and abstraction that forms the warp and woof of American education. When we train our children to think in general terms, we give and take away, and it is poetry's loss. I am not disputing the necessity of the general statement, but for the poet reality exists in a dazzling and often fantastically complicated matrix of thoughts and concrete perceptions. Poetry cuts against the grain of generalized thinking by moving back to the specific detail. If you want your students to be poets, don't sit still for "The man was nice," a statement which tells us absolutely nothing. "The man in the big grey hat who was passing out quarters on Broadway and 116th Street" tells us much, much more.

Now and then the kids ran out of dream steam. When this happened, I urged them to make up dreams, or to write poems that had a dreamlike feeling. Amanda Gandolf made use of a set of vocabulary cards that was lying on the table to string together a zany dream-narrative:

INVENTED DREAM

Once I was a watch with a gold band living in a fire that was inside a gray house. I was owned by a little girl who had a pet owl. The owl's eyes were never in his head but always wandering down the road. She also had a purple bird and a blue-eyed dog with a nose like a radio. Her mother looked like a pig with paper feet.

One day when the girl and her puppy went out to get some balloons for the fire I was living in, they met an orange with a tail coming off the side. When they got home they told me about what they saw. All of a sudden the puppy started to play hill music on his nose radio.

That night when I was playing cards with the front door key, Mr. Owl said, "Horn the head!" That was one of his expressions he said when it was time to go to bed.

The next morning the girl's mother, whose name

was Hill, said, "Jumping elephants, Mr. Watch! It's four o'clock and you still haven't capped your paper feeeeeeet!"

Lucy Rosa wrote a beautiful, shimmery poem using a very few of the same vocabulary cards. The difference between her and Amanda Gandolf's poems shows that, despite the mechanical approach involved, these students had understood that both dreams and poems often don't "make sense," at least on the surface:

FIRE

The fire in winter
was too late
for the summer days.

The fire in the
night in the winter
would cry.

It would cry fire
in the mid-air.
The fire trembled
when it cries
and it wonders
how bright it is.
That's why it cries.
And by mistake
it blows away.

Learning to take dreams seriously by writing them down can be an important method of confronting the irrational. Our daily lives, like our dreams, sometimes defy our attempts at interpretation. Rather than flee from the strange or unknowable, it is to our advantage to find strategies that will allow us to coexist with it. The sun doesn't shine all day, and when darkness falls those who do not know how to live through the night find themselves diminished in their humanity. Dreams are often unpleasant experiences because they show us things about ourselves that we would rather not see—our anger, our terror, our vanity. Once we can stare unflinchingly into the mirror of self the dream holds up, growth and change are possible.

I mentioned earlier that many of my students' dreams seemed to reflect the crises of adolescence through which they were passing. This dream by Elizabeth Solar chronicles the threats to perception young people often contend with, and ends on a positive note:

Around last year I used to have dreams that I couldn't see or at least in my dreams I couldn't see. My eyes would only open halfway. Usually the dream took place in the school P.S. 75. It was dark and the lights always seemed dim.

One time I got lost in the school but still I couldn't see and nobody would help me. Sometimes I cried, other times I would yell Mommy. Nobody ever helped me. Then soon in other dreams I couldn't see either. Then it stopped and now I always see my dreams clearly and I never forget a dream.

Nile Potter wrote dreams of amazing clarity and complexity. Throughout them the theme of face-as-identity-symbol runs like a thread:

One day while I was walking down the street I saw a car hit somebody so I went over to the scene of the accident and I fell down a hole. I kept on going down and down.

When I hit the ground I didn't seem to get the least bit hurt.

I started walking towards the light so I could get out of this weird place. When I reached the light there was an exit but it was covered with glass.

All of a sudden from out of nowhere came a man who looked like nobody because he had no face. I started running from him but every place I went he was there.

I said to him, "O.K., what do you want from me?" He answered, "I just want to see your face." Then his face started to look more and more like mine.

After that he let me go.

When I got outside everybody looked at me and they all had no faces.

Another theme common to these children just entering their teens was the awakening of the sexual instincts, a kind of dream had more often by girls than boys. Brenda Velez's fright, reinforced by her mother's warning not to shake the tree, finds itself beautifully and naturally expressed in that time-worn symbol. Here is her dream:

Last Friday I had a terrible dream. I dreamed that I was on an island. One day I was in a cherry tree and I was shaking it, and down came the cherries. One evening I was shaking it and shaking it. My mother told me not to shake it but I did. My mother told me again to get down and I got down. When I got down the tree kept on shaking and my mother told me to get off and stop shaking. I said to my mother to come out of the house and see what was happening. The tree was shaking itself. My mother told me, "You see Brenda, since you were always shaking the tree, now it's shaking by itself." I got so scared that I tried to wake up. When I woke up I saw the tree in the air shaking by itself. Every time I went to sleep I kept on dreaming about the same thing.

By writing dreams that inner life of each of us, on

"I think it is important for teachers to recognize that in the search for illuminating details, poetry parts company with the tendency towards generalization and abstraction that forms the warp and woof of American education."

which society seems to place so little value, can be rescued and brought to light. A crucial psychic balance can be restored. And in the process of recording their dreams, children will begin to realize that writing isn't something that comes out of books, but out of their own hearts and minds.

A FEW USEFUL BOOKS ON DREAMS

On Dreams, by Sigmund Freud (W.W. Norton paperback). The classic psychoanalytical statement on the mechanism and interpretation of dreams. A short version, slightly updated, of his earlier *The Interpretation of Dreams* (Avon paperback).

Creative Dreaming, by Patricia L. Garfield, Ph.D. (Ballantine Books paperback). I disagree with Dr. Garfield's premise—that we ought to follow the examples of more primitive societies and "program" our dreams consciously to attain our desired ends. What is extremely useful in this book is chapter eight, "How to Keep Your Dream Diary," in which she offers practical methods for capturing dreams before they disappear.

Dreams, by C.G. Jung (Princeton University paperback, selected from Bollingen Series of Jung's *Collected Works*). The core of Jung's writing on the dream.

Memories, Dreams, Reflections, by C.G. Jung (Vintage Books paperback). Jung's autobiography, containing many of his own dreams and his interpretations of them.

Man and His Symbols, edited with an introduction by C.G. Jung (Dell Laurel paperback). In this collection by various disciples of Jung, his own essay "Approaching the Unconscious" furnishes the gist of his attitude towards the dream. Profusely illustrated.

Half the House, by Herbert Kohl (Bantam Books paperback). A fine book that contains an even more remarkable section (pp. 119-129) in which Kohl elaborates the role of dreams in his own psychological growth. Practical, succinct, and highly recommended.

The Art of Poetry

by Kenneth Koch

To write a poem, perfect physical condition
Is desirable but not necessary. Keats wrote
In poor health, as did D.H. Lawrence. A combination
Of disease and old age is an impediment to writing,
   but
Neither is, alone, unless there is arteriosclerosis—that
   is,
Hardening of the arteries—but that we shall count as a
   disease
Accompanying old age and therefore a negative
   condition.
Mental health is certainly not a necessity for the
Creation of poetic beauty, but a degree of it
Would seem to be, except in rare cases. Schizophrenic
   poetry
Tends to be loose, disjointed, uncritical of itself, in
   some ways
Like what is best in our modern practise of the poetic
   art
But unlike it in others, in its lack of concern
For intensity and nuance. A few great poems
By poets supposed to be "mad" are of course known
   to us all,
Such as those of Christopher Smart, but I wonder
   how crazy they were,
These poets who wrote such contraptions of exigent
   art?
As for Blake's being "crazy," that seems to me very
   unlikely.

But what about Wordsworth? Not crazy, I mean, but
   what about his later work, boring
To the point of inanity, almost, and the destructive
   "corrections" he made
To his *Prelude*, as it nosed along, through the
   shallows of art?
He was really terrible after he wrote the *Ode:
Intimations of Immortality from Recollections of
   Early Childhood*, for the most part,
Or so it seems to me. Walt Whitman's "corrections",

too, of the *Leaves of Grass*,
And especially *Song of Myself*, are almost always
   terrible.

Is there some way to ride to old age and to fame and
   acceptance
And pride in oneself and the knowledge society
   approves one
Without getting lousier and lousier and depleted of
   talent? Yes,
Yeats shows it could be. And Sophocles wrote poetry
   until he was a hundred and one,
Or a hundred, anyway,and drank wine and danced all
   night,
But he was an Ancient Greek and so may not help us
   here. On
The other hand, he may. There is, it would seem, a
   sense
In which one must grow and develop, and yet stay
   young—
Not peroxide, not stupid, not transplanting hair to
   look peppy,
But young in one's heart. And for this it is a good
   idea to have some
Friends who write as well as you do, who know what
   you are doing,
And know when you are doing something wrong.
They should have qualities that you can never have,
To keep you continually striving up an impossible hill.
These friends should apply such competition as will
   make you, at times, very uncomfortable.
And you should take care of your physical body as
   well
As of your poetic heart, since consecutive hours of
   advanced concentration
Will be precious to your writing and may not be
   possible
If you are exhausted and ill. Sometimes an abnormal
   or sick state
Will be inspiring, and one can allow oneself a certain

number,
But they should not be the rule. Drinking alcohol is all right
If not in excess, and I would doubt that it would be beneficial
During composition itself. As for marijuana, there are those who
Claim to be able to write well under its influence
But I have yet to see the first evidence for such claims.
Stronger drugs are ludicrously inappropriate, since they destroy judgment
And taste, and make one either like or dislike everything one does,
Or else turn life into a dream. One does not write well in one's sleep.

As for following fashionable literary movements,
It is almost irresistible, and for a while I can see no harm in it,
But the sooner you find your own style the better off you will be.
Then all "movements" fit into it. You have an "exercycle" of your own.
Trying out all kinds of styles and imitating poets you like
And incorporating anything valuable you may find there,
These are sound procedures, and in fact I think even essential
To the perfection of an original style which is yours alone.
An original style may not last more than four years,
Or even three or even two, sometimes on rare occasions one,
And then you must find another. It is conceivable even that a style
For a very exigent poet would be for one work only,
After which it would be exhausted, limping, unable to sustain any wrong or right.
By "exigent" I mean extremely careful, wanting each poem to be a conclusion
Of everything he senses, feels, and knows.
The exigent poet has his satisfactions, which are relatively special,
But that is not the only kind of poet you can be. There is a pleasure in being Venus,
In sending love to everyone, in being Zeus,
In sending thunder to everyone, in being Apollo
And every day sending out light. It is a pleasure to write continually
And well, and that is a special poetic dream
Which you may have or you may not. Not all writers have it
Browning once wrote a poem every day of one year
And found it "didn't work out well". But who knows?
He went on for a year—something must have been

working out.
And why only one poem a day? Why not several? Why not one every hour for eight to ten hours a day?
There seems no reason not to try it if you have the inclination.

Some poets like "saving up" for poems, others like to spend incessantly what they have
In spending, of course, you get more, there is a "bottomless pocket"
Principle involved, since your feelings are changing every instant
And the language has millions of words, and the number of combinations is infinite.
True, one may feel, perhaps Puritanically, that
One person can only have so much to say, and, besides, ten thousand poems per annum
Per person would flood the earth and perhaps eventually the universe,
And one would not want so many poems—so there is a "quota system"
Secretly, or not so secretly, at work. "If I can write one good poem a year,
I am grateful," the noted Poet says, or "six" or "three". Well, maybe for that Poet,
But for you, fellow paddler, and for me, perhaps not. Besides, I think poems
Are esthetecologically harmless and psychodegradable
And never would they choke the spirits of the world. for a poem only affects us
And "exists", really, if it is worth it, and there can't be too many of those.
Writing constantly, in any case, is the poetic dream
Diametrically opposed to the "ultimate distillation"
Dream, which is that of the exigent poet. Just how good a poem should be
Before one releases it, either from one's own work or then into the purview of others,
May be decided by applying the following rules: ask 1) Is it astonishing?
Am I pleased each time I read it? Does it say something I was unaware of
Before I sat down to write it? and 2) Do I stand up from it a better man
Or a wiser, or both? or can the two not be separated? 3) Is it really by me
Or have I stolen it from somewhere else? (This sometimes happens,
Though it is comparatively rare.) 4) Does it reveal something about me
I never want anyone to know? 5) Is it sufficiently "modern"?
(More about this a little later) 6) Is it in my own "voice"?
Along with, of course, the more obvious questions, such as

7) Is there any unwanted awkwardness, cheap effects,
    asking illegitimately for attention,
Show-offiness, cuteness, pseudo-profundity, old hat
    checks,
Unassimilated dream fragments, or other "literary",
    "kiss-me-I'm-poetical" junk?
Is my poem free of this? 8) Does it move smoothly
    and swiftly
From excitement to dream and then come flooding
    reason
With purity and soundness and joy? 9) Is this the
    kind of poem
I would envy in another if he could write; 10)
Would I be happy to go to Heaven with this pinned
    on to my
Angelic jacket as an entrance show? Oh, would I?
    And if you can answer to all these Yes
Except for the 4th one, to which the answer should
    be No
Then you can release it, at least for the time being.
I would look at it again, though, perhaps in two
    hours, then after one or two weeks,
And then a month later, at which time you can
    probably be sure.

To look at a poem again of course causes anxiety
In many cases, but that pain a writer must learn to
    endure.
For without it he will be like a chicken which never
    knows what it is doing
And goes feathering and fluttering through life. When
    one finds the poem
Inadequate, then one must revise, and this can be
    very hard going
Indeed. For the original "inspiration" is not there.
    Some poets never master the
Art of doing this, and remain "minor" or almost
    nothing at all.
Such have my sympathy but not my praise. My
    sympathy because
Such work is difficult, and most persons accomplish
    nothing whatsoever
In the course of their lives; at least these poets are
    writing
"First versions", but they can never win the praise
Of a discerning reader until they take hard-hearted
    Revision to bed
And bend her to their will and create through her
    "second-time-around" poems
Or even "third-time-around" ones. There are several
    ways to win
The favors of this lady. One is unstinting labor, but
    be careful
You do not ruin what is already there by unfeeling
    rewriting
That makes it more "logical" but cuts out its heart.
    Unlike the

Sweet, blonde, breasty beauty, Inspiration, Revision
   is a hard-
To-please, mysterious brunette who is won in strange
   ways.
Sometimes neglecting a poem for several weeks is
   best,
As if you had forgotten you wrote it, and changing it
   then
As swiftly as you can—in that way, you will avoid at
   least dry "re-detailing"
Which is fatal to any art. Sometimes the confidence
   you have from a successful poem
Can help you find for another one the changes you
   want.
Actually, a night's sleep and a new day filled with
   confidence are very desirable,
And, once you get used to the ordinary pains that go
   with revising,
You may grow to like it very much. It gives one the
   strange feeling
That one is "working on" something, as an engineer
   does, or a pilot
When something goes wrong with the plane; whereas
   the inspired first version of a poem
Is more like simply a lightning flash to the heart.
Revising gives one the feeling of being a builder. And
   if it brings pain? Well,
It sometimes does, and women have pain giving birth
   to children
Yet often wish to do so again, and perhaps the grizzly
   bear has pain
Burrowing down into the ground to sleep all winter.
   In writing
The pain is relatively minor. We need not speak of it
   again
Except in the case of the fear that one has "lost one's
   talent",
Which I will go into immediately. This fear
Is a perfectly logical fear for poets to have,
And all of them, from time to time, have it. It is very
   rare
For what one does best and that on which one's
   happiness depends
To so large an extent, to be itself dependent on
   factors
Seemingly beyond one's control. For whence cometh
   Inspiration?
Will she stay in her Bower of Bliss or come to me this
   evening?
Have I gotten too old for her kisses? Will she like that
   boy there rather than me?
Am I a dried-up old hog? Is this then the end of it?
   Haven't I
Lost that sweet easy knack I had last week,
Last month, last year, last decade, which pleased
   everyone
And especially pleased me? I no longer can feel the

warmth of it—
Oh, I have indeed lost it! Etcetera. And when you
   write a new poem
You like, you forget this anguish, and so on till your
   death,
Which you'll be remembered beyond, not for
   "keeping your talent",
But for what you wrote, in spite of your worries and
   fears.

The truth is, I think, that one does not lose one's
   talent,
Although one can misplace it—in attempts to remain
   in the past,
In profitless ventures intended to please those whom
Could one see them clearly one would not wish to
   please,
In opera librettos, or even in one's life
Somewhere. But you can almost always find it,
   perhaps in trying new forms
Or not in form at all but in the (seeming) lack of it—
Write "stream of consciousness". Or, differently
   again, do some translations.
Renounce repeating the successes of the years before.
   Seek
A success of a type undreamed of. Write a poetic
   fishing manual. Try an Art of Love.
Whatever, be on the lookout for what you feared you
   had lost,
The talent you misplaced. The only ways really to
   lose it
Are serious damage to the brain or being so attracted
To something else (such as money, sex, repairing
   expensive engines)
That you forget it completely. In that case, how care
   that it is lost?
In spite of the truth of all this, however, I am aware
That fear of lost talent is a natural part of a poet's
   existence.
So be prepared for it, and do not let it get you down.

Just how much experience a poet should have
To be sure he has enough to be sure he is an adequate
   knower
And feeler and thinker of experience as it exists in
   our time
Is a tough one to answer, and the only sure rule I can
   think of
Is experience as much as you can and write as much
   as you can.
These two can be contradictory. A great many
   experiences are worthless
At least as far as poetry is concerned. Whereas the
   least promising,
Seemingly, will throw a whole epic in one's lap.
   However, that is Sarajevo
And not cause. Probably. I do not know what to tell
   you

That would apply to all cases. I would suggest travel
And learning at least one other language (five or six
Could be a distraction). As for sexuality and other
Sensual pleasures, you must work that out for
  yourself.
You should know the world, men, women, space,
  wind, islands, governments,
The history of art, news of the lost continents, plants,
  evenings,
Mornings, days. But you must also have time to write.
You need environments for your poems and also
  people,
But you also need life, you need to care about these
  things
And these persons, and that is the difficulty, that
What you will find best to write about cannot be
  experienced
Merely as "material". There are some arts one picks
  up
Of "living sideways", and forwards and backwards at
  the same time,
But they often do not work—or do, to one's
  disadvantage:
You feel, "I did not experience that. That cow did
More than I. Or that 'Blue Man' without a thought in
  the world
Beyond existing. He is the one who really exists.
That is true poetry. I am nothing." I suggest waiting a
  few hours
Before coming to such a rash decision and going off
Riding on a camel yourself. For you cannot escape
  your mind
And your strange interest in writing poetry, which
  will make you,
Necessarily, an experiencer and un-experiencer
Of life, at the same time, but you should realize that
  what you do
Is immensely valuable, and difficult, too, in a way
  riding a camel is not,
Though that is valuable too—you two will amaze each
  other,
The Blue Man and you, and that is also a part of life
Which you must catch in your poem. As for how
  much one's poetry
Should "reflect one's experience", I do not think it
  can avoid
Doing that. The naive version of such a concern
Of course is stupid, but if you feel the need to
  "confront"
Something, try it, and see how it goes. To "really find
  your emotions",
Write, and keep working at it. Success in the literary
  world
Is mostly irrelevant but may please you. It is good to
  have a friend
To help you past the monsters on the way. Becoming
  famous will not hurt you

Unless you are foolishly overcaptivated and forget
That this too is merely a part of your "experience"
   For those who make poets famous
In general know nothing about poetry. Remember
   your obligation is to write,
And, in writing, to be serious without being solemn,
   fresh without being cold,
To be inclusive without being asinine, particular
Without being picky, feminine without being
   effeminate,
Masculine without being brutish, human while
   keeping all the animal graces
You had inside the womb, and beast-like without
   being inhuman.
Let your language be delectable always, and fresh and
   true.
Don't be conceited. Let your compassion guide you
And your excitement. And always bring your
   endeavours to their end.

One thing a poem needs is to be complete
In itself and not need others to complement it.
Therefore this poem about writing should be complete
With information about everything concerned in the
   act
Of creating a poem. A work also should not be too
   long.
Each line should give a gathered new sensation
Of "Oh, now I know that, and want to go on!"
"Measure", which decides how long a poem should be
Is difficult, because possible elaboration is endless,
As endless as the desire to write, so the decision to end
A poem is generally arbitrary yet must be made
Except in the following two cases: when one embarks
   on an epic
Confident that it will last all one's life,
Or when one deliberately continues it past hope of
   concluding—
Edmund Spenser and Ezra Pound seem examples
Of one of these cases or the other. And no one knows
   how
The *Faerie Queen* continued (if it did, as one writer
   said,
The last parts destroyed in the sacking of Spenser's
   house
By the crazed but justified Irish, or was it by his
   servants?).
It may be that Spenser never went beyond Book Six
In any serious way, because the thought of ending
   was unpleasant,
Yet his plan for the book, if he wrote on, would
   oblige him to end it. This unlike Pound
Who had no set determined place to cease. Coming to
   a stop
And giving determined form is easiest in drama,
It may be, or in short songs, like *We'll Go
No More a'Roving*, one of Byron's most

Touching poems, an absolute success, the best
Short one, I believe, that Byron wrote. In all these
Cases, then, except for "lifetime" poems there is a
   point one reaches
When one knows that one must come to an end,
And that is the point that must be reached. To reach
   it, however,
One may have to cut out much of what one has
   written along the way,
For the end does not necessarily come of itself
But must be coaxed forth from the material, like a
   blossom.

Anyone who would like to write an epic poem
May wish to have a plot in mind, or at least a
   mood—the
Minimum requirement is a form. Sometimes a stanza,
Like Spenser's, or Ariosto's *ottava rima*, will set the
   poem going
Downhill and uphill and all around experience
And the world in the maddest way imaginable.
   Enough,
In this case, to begin, and to let oneself be carried
By the wind of eight (or, in the case of Spenser, nine)
   loud rhymes.
Sometimes blank verse will tempt the amateur
Of endless writing; sometimes a couplet; sometimes
   "free verse".
"Skeltonics" are hard to sustain over an extended
   period
As are, in English, and in Greek for all I know,
   "Sapphics".
The epic has a clear advantage over any sort of lyric
Poem in being there when you go back to it to
   continue. The
Lyric is fleeting, usually caught in one
Breath or not at all (though see what has been said
   before
About revision—it can be done). The epic one is
   writing, however,
Like a great sheep dog is always there
Wagging and waiting to welcome one into the corner
To be petted and sent forth to fetch a narrative bone.
Oh writing an epic! what a pleasure you are
And what an agony! But the pleasure is greater than
   the agony,
And the achievement is the sweetest thing of all. Men
   raise the problem,
"How can one write an epic in the modern world?"
   One can answer,
"Look around you—tell me how one cannot!" Which
   is more or less what
Juvenal said about Satire, but epic is a form
Our international time-space plan cries out for—or so
   it seems
To one observer. The lyric is a necessity too,
And those you may write either alone

Or in the interstices of your epic poem, like flowers
Crannied in the Great Wall of China as it sweeps
    across the earth.
To write only lyrics is to be sad, perhaps,
Or fidgety, or overexcited, too dependent on
    circumstance—
But there is a way out of that. The lyric must be bent
Into a more operative form, so that
Fragments of being reflect absolutes (see for example
    the verse of
William Carlos Williams or Frank O'Hara), and you
    can go on
Without saying it all every time. If you can master the
    knack of them,
You are a fortunate poet, and a skilled one. You
    should read
A great deal, and be thinking of writing poetry all the
    time.
Total absorption in poetry is one of the finest things
    in existence—
It should not make you feel guilty. Everyone is
    absorbed in something.
The sailor is absorbed in the sea. Poetry is the
    mediation of life.

The epic is particularly appropriate to our contem-
    porary world
Because we are so uncertain of everything and also
    know too much,
A curious and seemingly contradictory condition,
    which the epic salves
By giving us our knowledge and our grasp, with all
    our lack of control as well.
The lyric adjusts to us like a butterfly, then epically
    eludes our grasp.
Poetic drama in our time seems impossible but
    actually exists as
A fabulous possibility just within our reach. To write
    drama
One must conceive of an answerer to what one says,
    as I am now conceiving of you.

As to whether or not you use rhyme and how
    ''modern'' you are
It is something your genius can decide on every
    morning
When you get out of bed. What a clear day! Good
    luck at it!
Though metre is probably, and rhyme too, probably,
    dead
For a while, except in narrative stanzas. You try it
    out.
The pleasure of the easy inflection between metre
    and these easy vocable lines
Is a pleasure, if you are able to have it, you are
    unlikely to renounce.

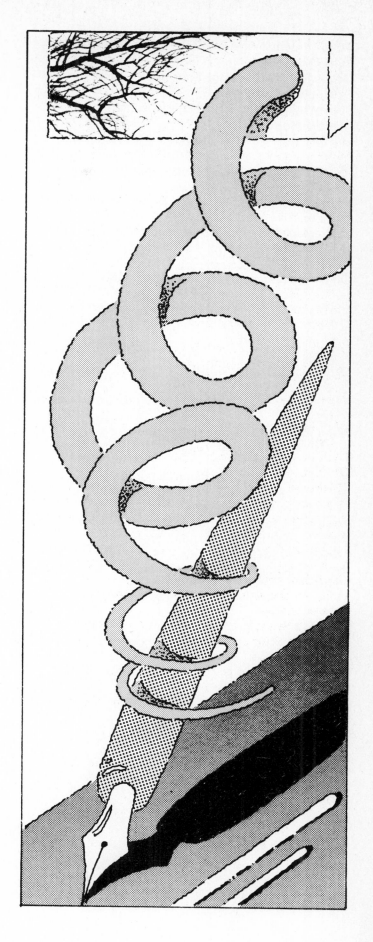

As for "surrealistic" methods and techniques, they have become a
Natural part of writing. Your poetry, if possible, should be extended
Somewhat beyond your experience, while still remaining true to it;
Unconscious material should play a luscious part
In what you write, since without the unconscious part
You know very little; and your plainest statements should be
Even better than plain. A reader should put your work down puzzled,
Distressed, and illuminated, ready to believe
It is curious to be alive. As for your sense of what good you
Do by writing, compared to what good statesmen, doctors,
Flower salesmen, and missionaries do, perhaps you do less
And perhaps more. If you would like to try one of these
Other occupations for a while, try it. I imagine you will find
That poetry does something they do not do, whether it is
More important or not, and if you like poetry, you will like doing that yourself.

Poetry need not be an exclusive occupation.
Some think it should, some think it should not. But you should
Have years for poetry, or at least if not years months
At certain points in your life. Weeks, days, and hours may not suffice.
Almost any amount of time suffices to be a "minor poet"

Once you have mastered a certain amount of the craft
For writing a poem, but I do not see the good of minor poetry,
Like going to the Tour d'Argent to get dinner for your dog,
Or "almost" being friends with someone, or hanging around but not attending a school,
Or being a nurse's aide for the rest of your life after getting a degree in medicine,
What is the point of it? And some may wish to write songs
And use their talent that way. Others may even end up writing ads.
To those of you who are left, when these others have departed,
And you are a strange bunch, I alone address these words.

It is true that good poetry is difficult to write.
Poetry is an escape from anxiety and a source of it as well.
On the whole, it seems to me worthwhile. At the end of a poem
One may be tempted to grow too universal, philosophical, and vague
Or to bring in History, or the Sea, but one should not do that
If one can possibly help it, since it makes
Each thing one writes sound like everything else,
And poetry and life are not like that. Now I have said enough.

From *The Art of Love*, by Kenneth Koch (Random House)

2. Writing Ideas

A. Gimmicks

"Gimmicks"

by Ron Padgett

The word "gimmick" has derogatory connotations. It often suggests something cheap, tricky, fast, without substance, even immoral. There are intelligent people who attack the use of gimmicks or devices in teaching imaginative writing, on the grounds that such devices encourage kids to be thoughtless smart alecks, witty at the expense of substance, satisfied with a glib surface but insensitive to depth of feeling. Such critics usually emphasize the importance of meaning.

Were there a School of Gimmicks, its members might retort that the Defenders of Meaningfulness tend to be boring creeps who confuse self-expression with value, that the most sincere statement of feeling is no better than any other sincere statement, that what makes the difference in creative expression is style. In other words, concern yourself with style, and everything else will take care of itself.

These are two extreme points of view, of course. They sound like rehashings of the old conflict between those who favor Form and those who favor Content in literature. Or those who claim that sex should consist of emotion and those who say it should be pure animal instinct.

The fact is that there is no appreciable difference between a teacher who uses gimmicks with intelligence and one who emphasizes meaning with intelligence. A heartless use of gimmicks will produce worn-out surrealist imitations; a narrow insistence on self-expression will produce baloney.

Self-expression is therapeutic and flashy technique is entertaining, but neither is necessarily good writing. So don't let anyone hornswoggle you into thinking you should teach one to the exclusion or detriment of the other!

FOUND POEMS

The "found poem" or "found object" has thrown some intellectual monkey wrenches into modern literature and few people seem to want to deal with their implications. It is okay to bring a piece of driftwood into a high school art class and declare it a "found sculpture," and it is okay for a Pop artist to paint a Campbell's soup can or incorporate everyday objects into assemblages, but it is not yet acceptable to appropriate, say, a New York Yankees baseball game as an art event or conceptual art work. The notion of originality in art, which became so attractive with the Romantic poets and artists, needs to be reexamined, to see exactly what is meant. Poets such as John Giorno, who has written all his poetry for the past ten or so years using nothing but "found" words, might argue that almost all words are "found" anyway. The subject is too large and probably too boring to be dealt with here.

So, how to proceed in the classroom? Have each kid select a passage from a book, newspaper or conversation, write it down as if it were a poem, give it a title (which they might also find) and read it aloud. If you have a lot of different materials available to the kids, the range of poems will be wider and more interesting. Some will seem quite good, others will flop. You might ask the kids why some "found" poems work better than others.

You might also discuss how context changes words. A paragraph in a news story will change if it is removed from the story and read separate from it. The words are the same, but the different context makes the tone different. Something very sad in a story might be very funny when removed from the story and read to someone who did not know the origin of the piece.

You might feel sorry for a blind person making his way down the street, but if you saw the same person standing before a sunset over the Grand Canyon, you would be astonished and, perhaps, filled with curiosity about this intriguing individual. His context (street, Grand Canyon) has changed the way you feel about him.

Here are two examples of "found" poems by two modern masters of the genre, John Giorno and Charles Reznikoff.

An unemployed
machinist
An unemployed machinist
who travelled
here
who travelled here
from Georgia
from Georgia 10 days ago
10 days ago
and could not find
a job
and could not find a job
walked
into a police station
walked into a police station
yesterday and said
yesterday
and said:

"I'm tired
of being scared
I'm tired of being scared."

JOHN GIORNO
from *Balling Buddha*
(Kulchur Foundation)

Giorno's poem which is probably taken from a newspaper report, gains power by a skillful use of repetition. In the following poem, Charles Reznikoff has also drawn on public documents, in this case from court records of the period 1885-1890, for his long poem *Testimony* (published in paperback by New Directions):

It got to be past ten o'clock at night.
Mr. Stokes read the papers over and over again.
Finally he said: "Don't you think I ought to
    take more time?"

Mr. Siren replied: "You are a businessman, Mr.
    Stokes
and you understand this paper, don't you?"

"Yes."
"And you understand *this* paper, don't you?"
But Mr. Stokes sat there with the pen in in his
    hand and kept hesitating.

Then Mr. Siren said: "Come, Stokes, if you
    understand it, sign it."
"I guess I had better take more time to look it
    over."
"If you put it off,
you will be no nearer tomorrow.
Come on and sign it.
Sign it, Sign it!"

Marcel Duchamp, who was probably the first to raise this art form above the level of the joke, also legitimized the doctoring of the "found" object. He would make small but powerful alterations of the original material. Here, for instance, is a doctored "found" poem (though not by Duchamp):

One of the victims
of that terrible accident
last August 17
was a Bronx woman
whose right leg was
made entirely of diamonds

where the last line is a substitute for the word "severed."

An interesting variation, one which Giorno has explored, is to bring together found material from different sources, placing them one after the other, sometimes in a sort of weave which makes the disparate pieces relate to one another, and to create a new context which has little to do with their original one.

CHALLENGE VERSE

A Penguin book called *Poems from the Sanskrit* (translated with an introduction by John Brough, Baltimore, 1968) tells us how Indian writers would sometimes challenge each other in writing by providing each other with the last line of a poem, asking the friend to write the poem to go before it. The challenge consisted in making the last line so outrageous that it would require mental gymnastics to figure out what might come before. The procedure is more interesting than the one that suggests a given opening line (such as "One day when I was walking home from school. . ."). I gave my sixth graders at P.S. 61 in New York the final line ("And the hippos were boiled in their tanks.") and had them write poems which ended with it. The particular class had a lot of experience in writing poetry, so they had no trouble leading up to this ridiculous conclusion. Examples:

And the elephants turned pink like strawberries.
And the stars came falling by thousands.
And the hippos were boiled in their tanks.

Vivien Tuft

The hippos were there,
just minding their own business,
when suddenly they were boiling.
They felt like a teabag in a teapot.
They tried very hard to get out but failed,
and the hippos were boiled in their tanks.

Jeannie Turner

I then asked kids to make up their own outrageous final line, or to make up one and trade it with a friend, then fill in the poem before. Examples:

There was a fire and my dream caught on fire and then the hippos were boiled in my dreams. There was a fire and my dream caught on fire and then the hippos were boiled in my dream.

Guy Peters

I had a race with a centipede
and it was very fast
but when I won the race
the centipede's feet flew off.

Oscar Marcilla

The square rabbits lay sitting
in the hay (that was burning)

The round salamanders lay changing
to a dim black

And the hippos were boiled
in their tanks.

And the pizza was stuck in the cave
forever.

The spaghetti was steaming hot

the sauce burned my tongue

and the pizza was stuck in the cave
forever.

Tracy Roberts

I dreamed a beautiful dream
that the hippos were drowned in whipped cream.

Miklos Lengyel

The inky paper stinked
and I started to play the violin
My big purple-orange feet hurt in my shoes
and I put my name in a pot of nuts

Lisa Smalley & Tracy Roberts

EXPLOSIONS

Kids seem to like it when things are decimated. A child will patiently build an entire town of blocks for the ultimate pleasure of demolishing it in a single devastating attack. Everyone has lined up dominoes only to watch them topple in chain reaction. Hence, it's a natural to have your kids write about what happens when various things explode. Be sure that they pick some unconventional things for explosions, not just bombs. Examples:

THE NOW EXPLOSIONS

Popcorn explodes like an earthquake
Coffee explodes and smells like firecrackers
Gunpowder explodes and smells like a match
When an oilwell explodes
Whoever got hit by it explodes
An oil tank explodes like a stove
A rocket explodes like a balloon
A garbage can explodes when there's too much
   garbage in it

A notebook explodes when there's too much paper
in it
A black board explodes when there's too many
words on it
A classroom explodes
When there are too many kids in it

—Lorraine Fedison

When we go into the music room
instruments explode

When we hear Rock & Roll
We explode and can't control ourselves

—Jorge Robles

MISTAKES

An entertaining way to teach correct language is to have kids indulge themselves in error, using as many incorrect grammatical forms as they can. The following example, from *The Old Farmer's 1975 Almanac* by Robert B. Thomas, is a little anthology of mistakes:

Each pronoun agrees with their antecedent. Just between you and I, case is important. Verbs has to agree with their subjects. Watch out for irregular verbs which has cropped into our language. Don't use no double negatives. A writer mustn't shift your point of view. When dangling, don't use participles. Join clauses good, like a conjunction should. Don't use a run-on sentence you got to punctuate it. About sentence fragments. In letters themes reports articles and stuff like that we use commas to keep a string of items apart. Don't use commas, which aren't necessary. It's important to use apostrophe's right. Don't abbrev. Check to see if you any words out. In my opinion I think that an author when he is writing shouldn't get into the habit of making use of too many unnecessary words that he does not really need. And, of course, there's that old one: Never use a preposition to end a sentence with. Last but not least, lay off clichés.

You should point out to you kids that mistakes can lead to interesting new discoveries, as with the case of Kenneth Koch's student who wrote "swan of bees" instead of "swarm of bees."

THE BLACKBOARD

It is often surprising for a poet to realize that kids in many classrooms feel that the blackboard is off-limits to them unless they are supposed to be there. The old idea of the grumpy teacher entering the classroom only to find the drawing of an ugly person on the board, with the word "techur" next to it,

suggests that this is a widespread situation: guerrilla attacks on the board must be furtive, and they are almost always political or social, involving control of the media and commentary on social behavior (X loves Y). Sometimes the graffiti are naughty or pornographic. In these cases the board is a reserved precinct which contains "enemy" information (homework assignments, "school" stuff, the date, lesson plans), the enemy being the Teacher as Power Figure, and the weaker person's response is often to strike back when he has the chance. This attempt at self-expression is healthy, although childish. A more civilized and direct form of exchange might take place if the kids were given an area of the board, or given the entire board part of the day (or week). It is not suggested here that students and teacher become indistinguishable, but that the useless exercise of prerogative be abandoned because it is destructive to a healthy relationship.

QUESTION MARKS AND EXCLAMATION POINTS

An interesting experiment you might try with your kids involves changing declarative sentences into questions and exclamations.

In the beginning God created the heavens and the earth!

Do I pledge allegiance to the flag of the United States of America?

Is April the cruellest month?

Did she sing beyond the genius of the sea?

Have I eaten the plums that were in the icebox?

And so on!

I'LL NEVER TELL YOU

Have the kids write a poem beginning "I'll never tell you. . ." It's interesting to see how different kids take this idea. Some will actually tell you things that previously they were shy about saying. Others will toy with you, giving hints of some secret. Some will feel they have some secret that is untellable, even anonymously. This kind of poem will at least introduce the idea that writers withhold as much or more than they say, and that what is left out is often as important as what is put in.

Examples:
I'll never tell you.
I just can't tell you.
I just can't, but can't tell you.

That I hate writing this.

There I just told you.

Ain't I stupid, I just told you.

But then, I can't tell you.
I just can't.
I really can't.

I'll never tell anybody that almost all of
the kids in the class think I'm their friend
but I'm not.

I'll never tell you that you are a duck.

I know a secret!
I know a secret!

  Ha, Ha, Ha
  I'll never tell you. . . . . .
  that. . . . .

I'll never tell you that I have a date
with? 6-1 He He Heh Ha Ha Haw How Ha

Miss Pitts gives me dirty assignments
in muddy classroom. Ha Ha Hee Hee
Haa Ha Ha Ha Haw
That I died in a coma
That I will get married in church
with?

That my new name is?

That I have an excellent personality
And Do Not Read This Letter If you Do

I'll get Hercules and tear gas bombs.

PRONOUN-WHO POEMS

This is a poem that derives purely from an interest
in a particular grammatical form. Have the kids write
lines beginning with pronouns (I, you, he, she, it, we,
they) and with the word "who" in the middle of the
sentence. For instance, "I am the man who wrote this
sentence. You are the person who reads it. He is the
one who saw you reading it. She is the one who asked
what you were doing. It was the sentence who said
just one thing. We are the morons who didn't understand. They are the geniuses who explained it to us."
(Obviously the poem takes a funny jump in the "it"
line.) Some examples from sixth graders:

I am the monster who owns mice.
You are the mouse who is owned by the monster.
He is the chick who is owned by the monster.
She is the mother who owns the monster.
It is the brother who sees the monster often.
We are the family who is full of monsters.
They are the family who owns mice and a chicken.

—Oscar Marcilla

I WHO KNOW

They who call me Vivien don't know my real name.
He, she, me and myself really know.
I who never tell hide behind a black magic curtain
And say to everybody,
"My name is a weird one
And it lies ahead in the never never land in Holland
On a big mountain hidden in the snow."

—Vivien Tuft

WHY & BECAUSE

Have each kid fold his paper across the middle. On
the top half have him write a question beginning with
"Why" and on the bottom half an answer beginning
with "Because."

Any question is okay, but the thing works better if
the kids are encouraged to ask interesting or amazing
questions or questions they've always wondered
about. Naturally many of these questions will be
unanswerable ("Why are there two sexes instead of
three of four?"). In such cases tell the kids that their
Because answers can be guesses, that they needn't
worry about giving the "right" answer to their Why
question.

When everyone's finished, have the kids tear their
papers along the fold, separating Why and Because,
and hand in their Whys first, then their Becauses.
Make a stack of Why questions and another stack of
Because answers. Shuffle each stack separately. Now,
with the stacks side by side, read the question on top
of the Whys and the answer on top of the Becauses.
Continue to read off the new pairs of questions and
answers.

In some cases the results will be utter duds, but
others will make a weird or poetic sense. Ask the kids
how the answers could be considered good ones. Even
the most irrelevant answer can be related to a question.

A variation is for you to think of a Because answer.
Remember it. Ask a kid to ask you a Why question,
and when he does, give your preconceived answer.

Any kind of compound linguistic structure can be
adapted to this process. As much fun as Why &

Because is If You/Be Sure. In the latter the kids give advice, such as "If you come to school/ Be sure to bring your brain," or "If you are a girl/ Be sure to stand up for your rights." Now, just mixing these two examples, we get, "If you come to school, be sure to stand up for your rights" and "If you are a girl, be sure to bring your brain."

Besides strengthening the students' sense of compound sentences and conditional clauses, the If You/Be Sure form alerts them to didacticism in writing. They will be more aware of advice as a form (moral of the story, sermon, etc.).

Both Why & Because and If You/Be Sure are also good for introducing ideas on non sequitur and logical paragraph structuring in expository prose. They are also useful for talking about how some things work and others don't, and to show how we don't have to understand something to have it strike us as funny.

TELEPATHIC POEMS

One teacher suggested a writing idea which we find interesting, though perhaps too bizarre for others. It consists of a sort of experiment in mental telepathy. Here is one way to do it:

Each child chooses or is given a partner. One of them is the "sender," the other is the "receiver." The sender thinks of an image, a line or a sentence and writes it on his paper, so that his partner cannot see it. The sender then concentrates very hard on the thing he has written, either looking into the receiver's eyes, or with eyes closed. The receiver keeps his mind open to receiving the transmission. If something "pops" into his mind, he writes it down, so that the sender can't see it. Then the sender comes up with a second thing to transmit, preferably something that goes with the first he sent, and the receiver writes down what he thinks the second message is, again preferably something to do with the first thing he received. And so on until the participants feel the poem has ended.

Apparently some interesting situations develop: some kids are amazed at how well they receive messages, others find themselves staring into the eyes of one of their classmates for the first time. The situation can extend to discussions which normally do not take place in school. An interested science teacher might coordinate his curriculum to include a study of J.B. Rhine's work (e.g. *The Reach of the Mind*, Morrow, N.Y., $1.95) or Peter Tompkins and Christopher Bird's work (*The Secret Life of Plants*, Avon, $1.95).

It goes without saying that this type of study is not intended to encourage occultism for its own sake, but rather to alert the children to a wider range of possibilities in thinking and writing than they might have hitherto imagined.

I REMEMBER

Many kids who would be thrilled to take a ride in a time machine will also be surprised to learn that they can do just that in one direction, at least. They can take a ride on their memory back into the past. Remembering (or forgetting) is something we do naturally; we just do it. We feel that some people have good memories and others don't, and we leave it at that. The fact is, our memories can be brought to light better if we learn how to do it. I'm not talking about memory systems which teach you to recite the New York phone book. I mean learning to concentrate and keep your attention on things that happened to you. There are books which deal with this subject with far greater authority and intelligence than I can muster, but I forget their titles. Just kidding! One is *The Art of Memory* by Frances Yates (University of Chicago press paperback).

But whether or not you're an expert on the subject of memory, you'll find that by simply training your attention on places, events, people, etc. of the past, your memory will begin to give you more of its dim and hidden treasures, sometimes with such detail, clarity and power that you momentarily have the impression that you have revisited the past.

The artist Joe Brainard invented a new poetic form with his "I Remember" books. He began each thing with "I remember. . ." and wrote down anything that seemed interesting or important, in no particular chronological order. Gradually his memory opened wider. His first book, *I Remember*, was followed by *I Remember More*, and then *More I Remember More*. Here are some examples of his work:

I remember painting "I HATE TED BERRI-GAN" in big black letter all over my white wall.

I remember throwing my eyeglasses into the ocean off the Staten Island Ferry one black night in a fit of drama and depression.

I remember once when I made scratches on my face with my fingernails so people would ask me what happened, and I would say a cat did it, and, of course, they would know that a cat did not do it.

I remember the linoleum floors of my Dayton, Ohio room. A white puffy floral design on dark red.

I remember sack dresses.

I remember when a fish-tail dress I designed was published in "Katy Keene" comics.

Word Combinations

by Regina Beck

I thought that children would enjoy making up poems around words that they themselves had composed. To get the students interested in the idea, I used ''Jabberwocky'' by Lewis Carroll. You can find the entire poem in any edition of *Through the Looking-Glass and What Alice Found There*, but just to refresh our memory here's the first stanza:

'Twas brillig, and the slithy toves
　　Did gyre and gimble in the wabe:
　All mimsy were the borogoves,
　　And the mome raths outgrabe.

I first gave a rather dramatic reading of the poem, and the class had no trouble following the tale; everyone had a copy which I had done up on the rexograph. Then I told them that despite the appearance of words that don't exist in the English language, it is still an understandable poem. In fact, the use of made-up words made it all the more spirited and evocative. ''Frumious,'' which appears in the second stanza, got the point across as well as the two words used to make it up, fuming and furious. (And for Carroll's own explanation of how he coined ''frumious,'' see his preface to *The Hunting of the Snark*, any edition.) The power of that single word was obvious; by splicing together other words it took on a life all its own. The students immediately saw the possibilities of this proposition.

I next handed out a list of about a hundred words, many of whose meanings were unknown to the sixth-graders. I told them that they could combine these or any other words. How they wanted to break up syllables or tack words together was up to them. I suggested that the very sound of the words would let them know when they had hit upon something good.

Some of the new word-creations would be a welcome addition to our often lackluster language. Try: shimoin, funden, oshtamirthogy, pondle, fumblonious, and homoluminous. Or maybe: egalate, jessajaxiply, pozoodal, slitaxi, thirstle, or wherb! Finding homes for these words in poems of their own—the next step in the assignment—was almost as much fun as creating them. The poems the kids wrote ranged from mindboggling to ludicrous.

Once there was a fumblonious tinistic archive.
He had a friendly egalative porteous for a pet.
Harrienlistic was the egalative poreious pet's name.
Harrienlistic like musoino, played on a harmano.
She could sing very loverwaybully.
One suntistic finely day, Harrienlistic was chomting
　　smorgowhichbords
when out of nowhere came a homolunious
　　rudimophond　called Cenlic.
Cenlic said, If you don't give a smorgowhichbord
　　to chomting
I'll chomting you!
So Harrienlistic gared Cenlic a smorgowhichbord to
　　chomting
and they got married all over the smorgowhichbord
　　Harrienlistic owned
by a fumblonious tinistic archive,
who gave Cenlic a homolunious rudimophond.
Don't let anyone ever tell you
an egalative porteous and a homolunious rudimophond
　　don't mix.
They do. I should know.
I'm an egalative poreious homolunious rudimophond!

Lisa Daglian
J.H.S. 141, Bronx, N.Y.

There stood the homoluminous doctor
with his nego
in front of the thirstle wherb
and asked for a pizoodal
The waiter said, I'll look in the funden
He could not find the pizoodal and went back
No more pizoodals, he said angrily
So he egolately pondled out

Kenny Weiss
J.H.S. 141, Bronx, N.Y.

The Most Amazing Thing

by Alan Ziegler

A lot of writing ideas for kids aim to acquaint them with the outskirts of their language and imagination: to have them write incredible things, using their resources to create what the "real world" doesn't offer. This kind of poetry—and this goes for "grown-up" poets (an oxymoron) as well—reveals a lot to us about the way we think and feel and relate to the world: exaggeration often makes a point (as does understatement). But in addition, these fantastic writings can be fun, without questing for "Meaning." (It's like playing with paints: colors and patterns and strange configurations have their reason for being in the act of their creation.)

But much that's in the "real world"—as we perceive it through our senses—is pretty amazing, too. Here the writer's job is distillation, to get at the core of what's amazing and relay it to the reader. The individuality and creativity of this kind of writing lie in how the writer selects what to tell us, and how well it's done.

I wanted to see what children thought was amazing, to get them to take a good look at the world around them and within their memories. To *begin* to get at this, I hooked together an idea that includes both amazing things from the imagination and from reality.

I asked the children (third, fourth, and fifth grades) first to write a short poem about "The Most Amazing Thing I've *Never* Seen." They could make up anything, as fantastic and unlikely as their imaginations allowed. Most of the kids were able to zip right through this (especially the ones who had previously written dream poems). Then, I asked them to write about "The Most Amazing Thing I've *Ever* Seen." The ground rule for this was that it had to be something *real* that they find amazing. I ruled out anything they had seen on television or movies or read about that wasn't "real"—for example, Godzilla wouldn't be allowed, but a lion feeding her children, seen on television, would be.

An extension of this would be to ask the children to write "hero stories," both made-up and real. Chances are that the imagined stories would be "super-hero" stuff, with incredible metahuman feats of strength and courage. But then ask them to tell about some time in their lives when they or someone they knew or saw did something heroic. I would discuss the definition of heroic first, perhaps defining it loosely as something that involves one or more of the following: risk, courage, strength, sacrifice, ingenuity, etc. These real stories would probably be less spectacular, but the writing of them (along with "the most amazing thing I've ever seen") is a step in helping the kids appreciate and communicate about the world around them. Other variations are: "The Most Horrible Thing I've (N)ever Seen," "The Most Beautiful Thing I've (N)ever Seen" and many more. . . .

Here are some samples of "Amazing Things":

THE MOST AMAZING THING I'VE EVER SEEN

The most amazing thing I've never seen was President Ford get in the bathtub and play football and bump into the atomic bomb and blow up the world and the world go down under the ground and find little green monsters that look like string beans with claws.

The most amazing thing I've ever seen was a piece of a tree fly in the air. The boy turned his arm back and let it go. It was about a yard long and 3 inches wide.

> *Jordan Jones*
> *Fourth Grade*
> *P.S. 11, Brooklyn*

The most amazing thing I've never seen was a flying robot. The robot has a skinny neck and it has a round motor and when my friend and I turn it on it started talking to me and her.

The most amazing thing I've ever seen is a walking and moving dummy. It has a dress and it walks and talks. It runs too and me and my friend play with her. Just press the button.

The most amazing thing I've ever seen is the year of 1975 because everybody likes to throw things out the windows and have parties.

The most amazing thing I've ever seen was Darrell fall in love with my godbrother's girlfriend, and he kissed the picture.

Sonia Robinson
Fourth Grade
P.S. 11, Brooklyn

The most amazing thing I've never seen was a man, he was red, black, and green. His nose was as long as a carrot. His feet were as red as blood. His hair is as black as night. His teeth were as green as grass.

The most amazing thing I've ever seen was two peas and a black eye pea. The pea was as soft as a sea. The peas were like mountains in a tree. Do you like peas and a black eye pea. I don't think they are neat.

Robert Willis
Fourth Grade
P.S. 11, Brooklyn

The most amazing thing I've never seen was a stoopacanakatis that grows in South America. A stoopacanakatis is a tree that grows ping-pong balls. My friend picked a ping-pong ball and it turned green.

The most amazing thing I've ever seen was a double ferris wheel. It is bigger than any other kind of ferris wheel I've ever seen. It has different colored lights on it and it is very high. Another amazing thing I've seen was Airport 1975. It was about a stewardess who had to fly a plane.

Lisa Burris
Fourth Grade
P.S. 11, Brooklyn

The most amazing thing I've never seen was a living frog that glows in the dark, but in the daytime he turns brown.

The most amazing thing I've ever seen was Joe Namath run 20 yards.

Thomas Satterthwaite
Fourth Grade
P.S. 11, Brooklyn

THE MOST AMAZING THING I'VE NEVER SEEN

I never saw a rat on a frog kiss a watermelon duck.

I never saw a kid go crazy

I never saw a nice mean man on a lake fork a dear on a roller coaster.

I never saw a mountain sing because when it sings it bounces.

I never saw a flower talk and eat bananas.

I never saw a car that flew in the air and swim to the bottom of the sea and said it's so much fun.

I never saw a birthday cake blow out its own candle.

I've never seen a 6 foot calaccarmeses. A calaccarmeses is a 2foot car, dog, tree and big lip. It used to be 2feet but now it's 6 feet. How did it grow so fast? With a little bit of frog legs, cats tail and snake wood. Isn't that amazing?

THE MOST AMAZING THING I'VE EVER SEEN

I really did see a myna bird talk

I once saw a clown go to town

Once I really saw a pan fry in a stove and the pan had a chicken in it. It was so amazing that the chicken was sizzling.

I really saw a bug crawl into beer

Once I saw a monkey named Sippy. He road on roller skates and jump over a tall stick and played cowboys and indians and road on a tricycle.

The most amazing thing I have ever seen is a 9 year old girl save a 25 year old man. She pushed him out of the way when a car was coming. The man gave the girl $100. She bought herself a bike.

The most amazing thing I've ever seen was a rock fish. If you step on it it will throw out its blade and could kill you. I'm glad it never happened to me and I hope it never will!!

3rd Grade Collaboration
P.S. 11, Brooklyn

THE MOST AMAZING THING I'VE NEVER SEEN

I've never seen a fish with
high heel shoes go shopping
in a nuts and bolts junkyard
that sells little green martians
with pet robots made of
Mr. Anchin's wire sculpture
eating lollipops and
fish eye candy canes at one time

and the four muskateers that's
stuffy not fluffy.

John L.
Atlantic Avenue School
Lynbrook, Long Island

The most amazing thing I've never seen
was an angel
with long brown hair
fluttering in back of her
sliding down a rainbow
with clouds surrounding her.

Jeffrey
Atlantic Avenue School
Lynbrook, Long Island

The most amazing thing I've never seen
was a worm 10 feet tall
driving a car
then he picked up a man
two inches tall
then they went to his friend bird
and he just made a nest in a hole
and boy was it big
it was two inches wide but the bird
was small, 9 foot 10" small
then they ate din lunch break.
They had a vegetable loaf
with tiger lilly sauce and then they went to wake up.

Keith
Atlantic Avenue School
Lynbrook, Long Island

THE MOST AMAZING THING I'VE EVER SEEN

The most amazing thing I've ever seen
was when I fell down the stairs
because I was in the
middle of the air.
My face
was facing
the floor.

Jenny
Atlantic Avenue School
Lynbrook, Long Island

The most amazing thing I've ever seen
was my sister having stitches.

Jean
Atlantic Avenue School
Lynbrook, Long Island

The most amazing thing I've ever seen was my baby
brother naked at 7 months old.

Larry
Atlantic Avenue School
Lynbrook, Long Island

I've seen one thing that amazed me most. It was the
cake my aunt who lives in Italy made with Snoopy
saying Happy Birthday.

John L.
Atlantic Avenue School
Lynbrook, Long Island

The most amazing thing I've ever seen
my brother told me
that he saw a baby
with a body and no arms
and no feet
and one head
and they killed it.

Angela
Atlantic Avenue School
Lynbrook, Long Island

Once I was up in a tree and a car crashed into it and
almost knocked me down. It felt like an earthquake.
Ambulances came for the car that crashed but I was
OK.

Frank
Atlantic Avenue School
Lynbrook, Long Island

The most amazing thing I've ever seen was my sister
going on a diet and sticking to it. Usually you may
find the refrigerator raped because she eats a lot.

The most amazing thing I've never seen was the world
being peaceful. No wars no body getting killed. Gee
wouldn't it be a good thing?

Trenda (5-1)

The most amazing thing I've never seen was my whole
family can fly in the sky and I can fly to school and
my mother be richer than anyone in the whole world.

The most amazing thing I've ever seen was a dog have
puppies and they be scared at first but then when
they get used to us they will want us to pick them up
all the time.

Barbara (5-1)

The most amazing thing I've never seen was a horse get drunk. I never want to see that!

The most amazing thing that I've ever seen was my father do magic. THAT'S WONDERFUL!

Jocelyn (5-1)

The most amazing thing I've never seen is a boy and girl looking like a gorilla swinging on a swing next to me. bow wow one said, how can you say bow wow when I'm a fence to say now now. You little girl you big girl you look just like another girl. Now let's get to the boy. I know this boy he looks so fine he's always drinking wine wine wine wine wine wine. Now this is my boy and girl who look like a gorilla who sat by me.

The most amazing thing I've ever seen is a man getting beat to death with a bat and got hit once in the forehead and then in the back of his head about ten times and then killed. The poor man was 20 years old. I wish that never happened.

Alice (5-1)

Drawings by Glen Baxter

Glen Baxter is a brilliant young English artist and writer whose work can be used with great fun and profit in the classroom. His fantastic drawings can serve as inspirational models for stories, or to encourage kids to give their imaginations free run in their own drawings. They could also be used as examples in a study of the relationship between picture and caption. You might want to explore this area by having the kids bring in picture jokes with their captions (such as those in *The New Yorker*) and then try various captions—or entirely new ones—with various pictures.

Drawings by Glen Baxter (Adventures in Poetry, 437 E. 12th St., New York, N.Y. 10009). Inquire for price.

Fruits of the World in Danger, by Glen Baxter (Gotham Book Mart, 41 W. 47th St., New York, N.Y. 10036). Inquire for price.

The Handy Guide to Amazing People, by Glen Baxter (Gotham Book Mart, same listing as above). Inquire for price.

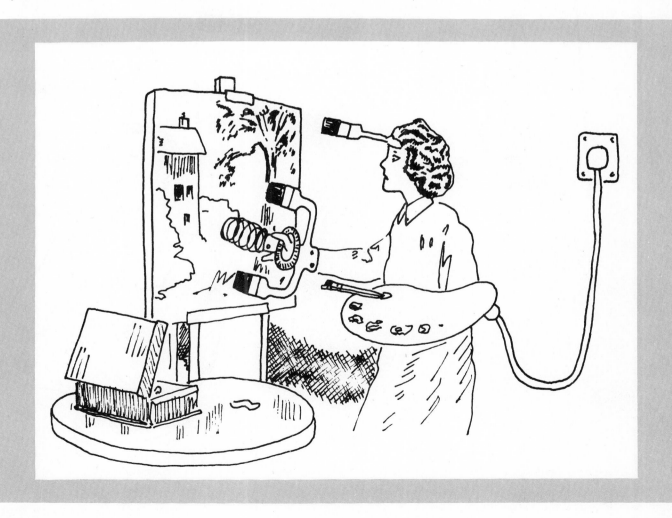

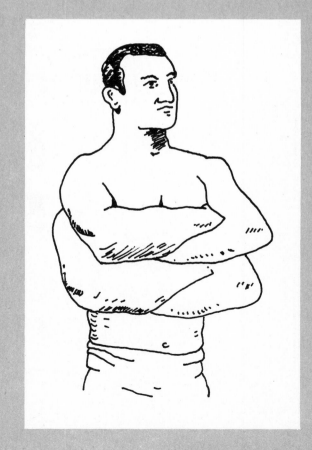

THE MEAL HAD BEEN
OVERSALTED

SHE FAILED
TO UNDERSTAND THE MENU.

THE RESTAURANT SEEMED DESERTED.

THE CLOCK FLEW THROUGH THE ROOM EACH NIGHT AT PRECISELY 7.35.

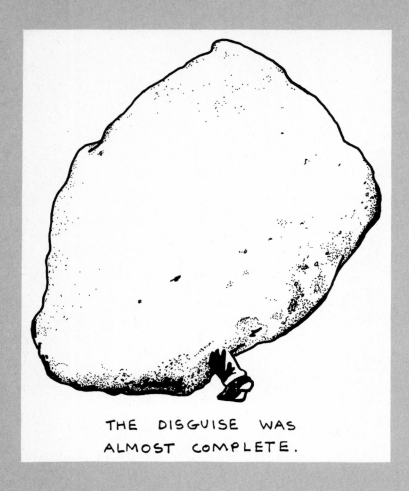

THE DISGUISE WAS
ALMOST COMPLETE.

..... DRIVING THE HIVES THROUGH THE JUNGLE.....

BERTHA WAS EATING THE GLADIOLI

After Magritte
Writing from Painting

by Bill Zavatsky

Though I was happy working with the quietly off beat photographs of Bill Binzen to elicit some interesting writing from children, I was anxious to move into an area that depended less on "trick" photography. I cut up and brought in a copy of *The Americans*, a splendid book of photographs by Robert Frank (Aperture/Grossman, paperback). But when I showed them around, the children in my fifth-sixth grade and sixth grade classes at P.S. 84 flipped through them speedily, without apparent interest. The photographs were either too subtle for the children, too close to their own lives, or I had not found a way to present them properly. Frank's penetrating revelations of the American psyche require some information for their irony to become operative. If you are ten years old and don't really know who General Eisenhower was, or if you can't figure out that the guy hypnotized by the immense luminous jukebox in some western bar somewhere is an American Indian, Frank's work seems a trifle distant. (Later I intend to take some of those splendid photographs and go into them with the children, talking of what I see there, hoping the kids will catch fire.)

Since I couldn't make the more traditional photographs work, I decided to continue working with "pure" visual texts that needed no historical and sociological data to illuminate them. Ballantine Books had just published a full-color paperback selection of the work of one of my favorite artists, the Belgian surrealist René Magritte. I had been saving it, cut up and ready to go, when my experiment with *The Americans* flopped.

Without preamble I took out the reproductions (which were glossy and large) and the students, from the classes of Mr. Philip Seymour and Mr. James Dagress, immediately began to discuss them. Magritte once wrote that his interest as an artist "lay entirely in provoking an emotional shock." [1] I have made it a principle to put something in front of my students that they have probably never seen before, to provoke them. Magritte was forever intent on supplying such occasions. "I painted pictures," he wrote, "in which objects were represented with the appearance they have in reality, in a style objective enough to

The Therapeutist
from *Magritte*, ed. by David Larkin,
Ballantine Books.

ensure that their upsetting effect—which they would reveal themselves capable of provoking owing to certain means utilized—would be experienced in the real world whence the objects had been borrowed." [2] The provocation is *to see*, and to go on seeing once one has looked up from the picture; as I and my students discussed the paintings preparatory to writing from them, I constantly urged them to examine carefully what appeared to be there. This would be the key to what they would write. Why does the man have an apple attached to his nose? Is it that the beautiful red rose is a giant, or that the room it is in is tiny as a hand? How can these men be made of rock; how could that happen? Why does this man have a birdcage for a body? Who are the tiny men in black coats and bowler hats falling in formation out of the sky?

As with the Binzen photographs I had used earlier, I asked the children to "write the story or poem" of the painting they had chosen. Some chose two or three paintings and skipped back and forth between their images. They had recognized motifs in Magritte's work: people and objects of stone; a constant blue sky; doves; and of course the famous man in the black coat and bowler hat—Magritte himself, whom some of the children identified with Charlie Chaplin. Thus a number of the poems and stories published below reflect more than one of Magritte's paintings. I did not supply their title, often startingly beautiful, to the children, but this might prove an exciting experiment. Why did the picture come to have this name? (The huge rose in the room is called "The Wrestlers' Tomb," for example.)

All the Magritte paintings I chose to use were popular with the exception of his overtly *trompe-l'oeil* creations. Paintings of views from windows in front of which are placed easels with paintings of the same views on them eluded the children as much as Robert Frank's photographs did. As the previous sentence illustrates, these paintings nearly defy description! There are always pleasant and exciting exceptions, however, and Guy Marlow's piece proved to be one of them. The two or three other children who were attracted to this theme in Magritte included one talented sixth-grade artist, Francois Monereau.

I encouraged the kids to choose more than one painting if it helped them to write. When a student stalled, I often pointed out incongruities Magritte had woven into the work of art: "How come the sky up there is bright, but near the house and under the trees it's dark and the streetlamp is shining?" He or she would think a moment, and look again. "Why is that happening, humm?" "Oh, yeah! See, it's because in the house there's...." "Write it down!" I'd shout, before the thought vanished in the air. By directing the young writer back to the visual text until he or she had exhausted it, until all the associations had

proliferated and turned into words on paper, I think we were able to write some unique poems and stories which exist independently of the paintings. (And for this reason I told the children not to mention anywhere that they were looking at a picture; if a picture existed in the painting they were using, then it could be mentioned, but only then.)

"In my pictures I showed objects situated where we never find them," wrote Magritte. [3] Like dreams. And so when some of my students complained that they hadn't had any good dreams lately to write down (we had been doing a dream workshop—writing down our dreams and discussing dreams), I handed them Magritte's paintings and asked them to write about them as if they were dreams they remembered from the night before. Jane Shufer's and Nadia Lazansky's writings were composed in this fashion.

In 1961 André Breton quoted Magritte as saying: "My pictures are images. No image can be described validly unless one's thoughts are directed toward its liberation." [4] What we attempted to do by entering the self-referential universe of René Magritte's art was to free those painted images—as words.

Once I dreamt that I was walking through a flat field with mountains in the background but the road just kept on going. Then I came to a big tall bunch of leaves. I stood and looked at them for a while and then they started to form into bird shapes. Just then it started to rain and the leaf birds started to grow more and more. Suddenly they burst from the leaves and flew away. I was so shocked that I woke up.

Nadia Lazansky
P.S. 84, Manhattan

I dreamed that I was on a long terrace. There was a man looking over the rail. Behind him a lady was weaving. She had a lot woven. The part she was working on had me, the man and the terrace. I thought she was weaving a picture of his life. I started to ask but then I was on this mountain that had an eagle's head carved. It was 3-D. Then the sickle moon came and hooked me like a fish. It carried me to where a lot of sheep were and dropped me and I woke up on the floor.

Jane Shufer
P.S. 84, Manhattan

DREAM

One day I had a dream that I was getting up for school. I was putting my sneakers on and my clothes on. I was looking at the mirror. My eyes were bothered by the light. I was all done for school. Then I said to myself, "Let me look in the mirror." And I saw my back in the mirror and not my face. I was scared. I thought it was another person and I touched the mirror to see if it was real, and I said "But it's impossible! It's impossible!"

When my brother saw me looking at the mirror in front of him, he saw my face. I did! I did! But my brother said I was crazy. When my brother went, I saw my back in the mirror again.

Francois Monereau
P.S. 84, Manhattan

There was a man that every time he looked at something he would see a bird. So he looked at an icy mountain. He saw a bird like an eagle of snow. Then he looked at a mountain without any ice, but he still saw a bird; he saw a window painted. He cracked the window but he saw the same thing. He looked at some leaves, so he saw some birds. But when he looked at some birds he saw a dime. So the rest of his life he saw just money.

Guy Marlowe
P.S. 84, Manhattan

From the *Teachers & Writers Collaborative Newsletter* (Vol. 5, No. 3), pp. 54-57.

Notes

[1] *Lifeline*, by René Magritte, in *Surrealists on Art*, edited by Lucy R. Lippard (Prentice-Hall Spectrum paperback, 1972), p. 158.

[2] *Ibid.*, p. 159.

[3] *Ibid.*, p. 159.

[4] René Magritte, by André Breton, in *Surrealism and Painting* (Harper & Row Icon paperback, 1972), p. 269.

Writing Through Photographs

by Bill Zavatsky

Bill Binzen's wonderful book of photographs, *Doubletake* (published by Grossman in paperback), contains color photographs "made by combining two transparencies." Binzen explains:

Sometimes the two halves were taken a stone's throw from each other as with the mannequin's face and the old door (both Lower East Side, N.Y.) . . . sometimes in widely separated places as with the inverted airplanes (New Zealand) and the golf gallery in the train (U.S.A.).

This superimposition of images is, of course, nothing new to photography, although a number of younger photographers, like Binzen, have been recently exploring the possibilities of the photo-collage vigorously. It is a technique as old as literary metaphor ("My mistress' eyes are nothing like the sun"), but its current vogue owes directly to a widening influence-through-practice of the dadaist and surrealist theory of imagery most purely crystallized by the poet Pierre Reverdy:

The image is a pure creation of the spirit. It cannot be born of a comparison, but by two more or less distant realities.

It is a theory which pushes comparison beyond simple likeness and into a third arena in which a new species is generated, a species which is as unlike its parents as much as it mysteriously depends on them.

It is the history of our language and our art, from the kenning ("whale-road" for "sea") to Dali's lobster telephone. It is part and parcel of the cinematic vocabulary: montage, which Eisenstein in part learned from the novel; the dissolve, in which a slowly vanishing image links itself to the fresh, emerging image; and the multiple exposure.

I had worked with photographs before, at the Bedford-Lincoln Neighborhood Museum (MUSE). We were in the habit of grabbing for *Life* and *National Geographic* when the children seemed restless or bored in the past, and this winter we began to encourage them to turn from page to page as they wrote, incorporating anything that struck them

visually into their poems. This transference of visual into verbal vocabulary produced highly successful surrealist poems which drew on everything from advertising to the habits of laboratory octopuses, and produced exciting moments like: "Miss Goolagong fights with a machine gun in the glowing mushroom army."

When I hit upon Bill Binzen's book, it seemed only natural to use it because he had already done the work of uniting disparate images in a single photograph, because they were in color, and because in their mystery and beauty they seemed to lend themselves to a wide range of interpretation.

I purchased a second copy of *Doubletake* and proceeded to cut out and mount the photographs on thick paper to make them look as if I'd just picked them up fresh from my local pharmacy. After using them in one or two classes rather perfunctorily—"Here are some mysterious and exciting photographs and I would like you to make up a story or poem to go with them"—I hit upon a structure that seemed to present the pictures perfectly.

I had been reading Russell Edson's marvelous prose poems to a fifth-grade class, stories in which parents hurl babies at ceilings and argue over damaging the ceilings, in which old men fall in love with themselves before mirrors and propose marriage to themselves, in which houses rear up on their porches when men straddling their roofs cowboyishly holler "Giddyap!" The children followed the poems closely, and our discussion turned to the inanimate, probably when somebody objected, "But houses can't *jump*!" I remarked that most of the things in the world had no mouths, could not talk the way we do, but told us things all the same. How the clock tells us the time. That eggs yodel as they cook—"It's hot! Don't touch!" We began to make a list of things that talked without mouths: the tide, a whirlpool, a sky filled with ominous clouds, the various smells of the flowers, the signals of the changing seasons. I told the children that the French poet Paul Eluard wrote that the poet speaks for the things that have no voice, and then read them Charles Simic's superb poem, "Stone" (from his book, *Dismantling the Silence*, Braziller, paperback):

Go inside a stone
That would be my way.
Let somebody else become a dove
Or gnash with a tiger's tooth.
I am happy to be a stone.

From the outside the stone is a riddle:
No one knows how to answer it.
Yet within, it must be cool and quiet
Even though a cow steps on it full weight,
Even though a child throws it in a river;
The stone sinks, slow, unperturbed
To the river bottom
Where the fishes come to knock on it
And listen.

I have seen sparks fly out
When two stones are rubbed,
So perhaps it is not dark inside after all;
Perhaps there is a moon shining
From somewhere, as though behind a hill—
Just enough light to make out
The strange writings, the star-charts
On the inner walls.

Here Simic penetrates an object and lends his voice to muteness. He answers the stone's riddle with his own imaginary solution. The children were still absorbed, with me. I then told them that I was going to distribute some photographs to them, because although pictures have no mouths, they tell stories anyway. I asked them to be the poets of their photographs, to lend their voices so that the photograph could tell its story. I emphasized that this story was the only story the photograph could have, that what each of them heard the photograph saying to him or her was the *right* story. (It didn't matter what the photograph said to anybody else.) I asked them to look at the pictures very carefully, to really see into them, the way the poet saw inside the stone—and guaranteed that they would be surprised if they did. (Binzen's collection, which also includes black and white photographs, will furnish 32 photographs in color, including the cover, enough for the largest class. I encouraged trade-ins, but insisted that if a trade was made, the child would be "stuck" with his or her second choice.)

I asked them not to begin their writing with useless introductions: "In this picture. . . ." "The man in the picture is. . .," etc. I had it in mind from the beginning that the writings should stand alone, could, without the reader needing to refer to the photograph. Most took the suggestion. And most of the students wrote two and even three stories or poems, rushing up to trade in the picture they had finished with.

"That's the most writing you've done all year," one teacher remarked to a child.

Two kids running in the water with their winter clothes on at the sea shore but there's this tree right in the middle of the water but the water looks like snow and the orange part looks like sand and the water goes up to a certain point and stops and in the water there's this big face the water is pinkish blueish color and the face is pinkish blueish too. and the branches of the tree are going right into the face and one of the kids is walking out into the water the water has really straight lines through it

Michelle Dicesare

Two little girls running into the water the water has wheat in it and right across the middle there's a big line of trees and on the other side of the trees there's snow about 3 feet high and then there's mountains and it's snow capped Looks like the land is all flat till the mountains and the water and the wheat and snow go on for ever and the two little girls are in the middle of no where

Michelle Dicesare

THE DAY THE SUN EXPLODED

*A little girl is rushing home
to tell her mom the sun exploded
The street is full of
colored rays and the cars
gazed in wonder*

Julia Lu

THE NEW YORK BUTTERFLY

*New York City is like a butterfly.
The blue sky are its wings
The outer edge of the wings are
     lined with roses.
Buildings are stripes on the wings.
People are small pokadots.
Then leaving no trace,
It flies away.*

Sharon Breitbart

MYSTERY IN THE DARK

One night there was a shreek it was the moon. The trees said, Why did you do that? You are driving me crazy every night you make a noise. Now stop it. What's wrong. Your pants are too tight? Well if they are loosen them. Come on, please!

What's that? O there's some one in the house! Help!

James Kalinsky

THE LEAVES' LIFE

It starts out in the spring blossoming. It's pretty young and healthy. Then in the summer there's even better weather and it gets to be bigger, beautifuller, stronger. Everything goes fine till fall. Then there's bad winds, wings on frosts. If it hadn't been for the strength it had stored, it would have died right then. By winter it was very weak, and winter was even worse. It knew it was going to die so it produced a seed to take the place of itself. Then it died. Soon after it came dried out and very light. Then a wind picked it up and brought it up to heaven, and there it rests on the clouds.

Bill Belloise

THE WORLD

Birds flying over the ocean
and a paint brush mark. The
brownish sky. The ocean as
a line through the picture.

Paul Kaufman

The shadow of a former beauty who is sad because her hairdresser slipped with a razor and kind of took off her hair. She is standing by a church door praying for a quick recovery of her hair and a win when she sues her hair dresser for hair slaughter on the 5th Amendment. She looks like a person who is about to cry but is sorry for her hairdresser when he has to pay 500 dollars because of the sue.

Jimmy Cifelli

A man is gazing over a lake.
He seems to be flying over the lake.
He has a strong imagination.
He imagines himself on a subway riding over the water.
The subway train is practically invisible
There are some park benches nearby
They look very real on one side.
They even cast a shadow
The other side just blends in with the lake
He imagines a hillside filled with trees
A motorboat speeds around to their owners's delight
But then even the man disappears.

Steven Ignelzi

One day a boy got lost and once found a real ugly thing. It bit him on the finger and he could not get it off. So he brang it home with him. He looked in the mirror and saw that it looked exactly like him. So he called it Cousin It.

Richard Pity

THE MONSTER

There once were two men. They lived in Newfoundland. They went to the seashore. They saw something very weird. It looked like a sea monster. The two men look at it with surprise. The things moved very slowly.

The men throw rocks and stones at the monster. It roared and roared and then started chasing the men. The men ran to the coffee shop. The monster stopped running after them and went back into the bluish green sea. The men came out of the coffee shop and went home.

Susanne Luongo

From the *Teachers & Writers Collaborative Newsletter* (Vol. 4, No. 4, Spring 1973), pp. 60-66.

Participatory Pieces: Getting into Images

by Alan Ziegler

Bill Zavatsky, in using photographs to inspire poems, asks the children to "be the poets of their photographs, to lend their voices to the photographs so that the photograph could tell its story."[1] I used Bill's approach with success, but the next time I used photographs (with 3rd, 4th, and 5th grades) I took it one step further: I asked the students not only to write the story of the photograph, but to become a *part* of that story. They should become a participant in the photograph and write from the *inside-out*. A psychic and artistic leap has to take place in order to truly get inside the photograph; telling the children to enter the photograph has to be done in an exciting, dramatic way. And Gregory Orr's magical poem "The Room" provides the excitement needed. The poem goes:

With crayons and pieces of paper,
   I entered the empty room.
I sat on the floor and drew pictures all day.
One day I held a picture against the bare wall:
it was a window. Climbing through,

I stood on a sloping field
at dusk. As I began walking, night settled.
Far ahead in the valley, I saw the lights
of a village, and always at my back I felt
the white room swallowing what was passed.

from *Burning the Empty Nests* (Harper & Row, 1973)

There was a visible stir in the room as I read "it was a window. Climbing through. . . ." We talked awhile about the poem, how both drawings and poems enable us to "travel." I then distributed photographs and asked the children to "enter" their photographs and spend a few minutes getting the feel of the territory around them. I suggested they "interview" other participants in their photograph to find out what was going on, and perhaps take part themselves, especially if there were no other people around. And then write about their experience. There were a few kids who were stumped, and for them "I

can't get into it" was meant literally. I allowed them to try other photos. Most of the children wrote with energy and interest.

With one class, I took Orr's poem literally. I asked the art teacher to have the children do crayon drawings of "places they had never been to." I asked her to encourage the children to make the places mysterious and exciting. When I came in the next day, I distributed the drawings to the artists and asked them to do what Orr did in his poem: imagine hanging their picture against the wall and climbing into it; then write what happens. In this case, the children collaborated with themselves.

Here are some samples of the poems written to photographs, followed by a further use of this "poetic device":

SAMPLES OF PARTICIPATORY POEMS WRITTEN TO PICTURES

I stepped inside a picture of a circus.
There was a frozen clown and a roaring lion.
The lion roared, "What are you
doing in my circus?"
I said, "I don't know, looking around.
By the way, doesn't that clown
move or talk?"
The lion replied, "Yes he does.
Clown TALK."
The clown moved in a rather queer
way and said, "Ha Ha I am a
laughing clown."
He kept on
saying it as he was pushing the
wagon which the lion was in.
They disappeared in a flash of
purple mist gooey and smelly.
It cleared up and there was
just a white surrounding.
I stepped out and continued my
drawings.

Daurice Fleming, 5th Grade
Atlantic Avenue School
Lynbrook, N.Y.

A MYSTERIOUS MYTH

One day in April I took a walk
to an old shabby house. I went inside
and found nothing at all around,
but pure white walls.
I took my crayons out of my pocket
and drew a beautiful room.
I tried to make a picture
over the fireplace but
the picture frame kept
swallowing my crayons.

Lisa Maggiore, 4th Grade
Atlantic Avenue School
Lynbrook, N.Y.

I saw your big feet
Mine were so small
Your feet were about four feet tall
I thought I was dreaming
But I wasn't
I have to leave now
Too bad I can't see your head
I felt your big toe
I went to the other side
But nothing was there
So I ran home so fast
And I never came back

Philip Ziegler, 5th Grade
Atlantic Avenue School
Lynbrook, N.Y.

THE ENDLESS WALK

One day a man was walking
up an office building!
Why he was doing it I'll
never know.
I asked him why and he said,
"Never mind."
Suddenly, he came to a field of trees
at the top of the building.
But the man was just a shadow.

Kevin Richert, 5th Grade
Atlantic Avenue School
Lynbrook, N.Y.

I crawled into the picture
I walked along the tracks
I kept on walking for three miles
I walked but still no where did I get
Finally I met the sun
I asked directions
He said keep on truckin straight ahead

So I went ahead straight
And there I met a village
The people greeted me fantastically
I asked are you trying
To soften me up?
They answered back yes
For you'll have to stay here
Throughout your life

Michelle Iadanza, 4th Grade
Atlantic Avenue School
Lynbrook, N.Y.

I climbed into my picture and
started to walk. I sat on a leaf
and started to fly in the red, red
sky and spinning and turning
flying higher and higher and
suddenly I started to fall down
down on a soft white
cloud. I saw something flash
by, it was lightning
so I got off as fast as I could.

Kevin Bien, 4th Grade
Atlantic Avenue School
Lynbrook, N.Y.

A FURTHER APPLICATION

One of poetry's appeals is that it is a vehicle for getting inside one's self, a way of discovering and expressing feelings, fears, desires, etc. If poet/teachers were to carry around business cards with mottos, then "self-expression through words" would rank right up there with "have poems will travel."

But writers also delve into others' selves: what is the other person feeling, what is his poem or song or story? Thus the use of characters and personae. "Being in someone else's shoes" may be a cliché but it is the premise for much terrific writing. In addition to literary importance, there is a great deal of human importance to being able to empathize with and appreciate the plights of others. (Of course, we also find out about ourselves when we find out about others. Vicarious experience touches off our own emotions.)

Another aspect of interesting writing is sensitivity to other settings and environments. Writers should be "mobile" and, through words, be able to place readers in various locations.

I was asked to do a day of workshops with junior and senior high school students at Co-op City in the Bronx, New York. The workshops were arranged by

Peter Lerner, curator of The Museum of Migrating People (which is located in Truman High School, where the workshops were held). During my lunch break, Mr. Lerner invited me to visit the museum. On display were photographs, artifacts, and costumes related to the theme of people in transit and turmoil. Immigration was piercingly depicted through photographs, letters, even an Ellis Island bench that had been sat on by thousands of immigrants. Another main theme was the German holocaust of Jews. Included in the exhibit was a bar of soap made from the flesh of a Jew (horrifyingly benign now in its glass showcase) and many photographs.

I was so moved by the museum that on the spur of the moment I abandoned my plans for the afternoon sessions; I decided instead to take the students down to the museum.

I first read the group Gergory Orr's poem, then discussed the work I had done with younger children and photographs. I asked the students to get the feel of the museum, wandering around for awhile. But then to focus on something that was particularly compelling or intriguing (or perhaps seemed so remote and uncommunicative that an effort should be made to get involved with it), and make a "leap" into the image or object. The nature of their involvement "inside" was up to them; I only asked that they keep in touch with their feelings and let or make things happen. With the photographs in the museum, they could join the people depicted or become one of them; with the objects (like the costumes or Ellis Island bench) their involvement might be trickier.

This activity goes beyond the province of a writing workshop. Schools teach kids about immigration and concentration camps and ask them to know facts; but there is more to know—the human side of these phenomena. Even this kind of writing doesn't approach the original experience, but it might get the students one dimension closer.

It was a fruitful session. Just about all the kids—who ranged from fifth to tenth grades—came up with something moving. I think this experience can be applied to other situations: perhaps a classroom session with photographs could first be tried, followed by a trip to a museum, where the students would be asked to write participatory pieces. Naturally, the writing would vary with the museum. An art museum would inspire different writings than a natural history museum. The ultimate experience would be a place like New York City's Metropolitan Museum of Art, with its Dalis, Da Vincis, and mummies.

Notes

[1] See "Writing through Photographs," by Bill Zavatsky, in this book.

"PARTICIPATORY POEMS"

Based on photos and objects in the Museum of Migrating People, by students from Truman High School, I.S. 180, and I.S. 181, the Bronx.

I came upon a rather dull picture in the museum. The background was gray and a few people were standing behind a wired fence. I was going to walk away from the picture since I did not find it pleasurable to the eye but what stopped me was the look in the people's faces behind the fence. It was a look of sorrow and of pain. They seemed to want to call out, help me, please help me. As I ran my eyes over each person, I began to feel the pain they suffered and found myself also behind the fence. Suddenly a feeling of dread came over me. I knew that I would probably remain there forever and could not bear the thought. The man next to me reached out to touch me, to reassure me that I would be all right. In his eyes though, I saw the truth. I knew I would never get out.

As I looked through the fence, I saw another person look at the picture I was in. I wanted to scream out to him, but he walked away. I went into a cold sweat. My head throbbed and my insides seemed to burn.

Joy Klein

(from the picture of the baby in the Jewish concentration camps of the '40s)

After stepping into the picture
I no longer understand
the way I used to.
I don't know what's going on.
I do know something is very wrong.
My home is no longer the warm
happy place it used to be.
It's cold here, and I'm hungry.
No one is feeding me or holding me.
The shades on the window are closed
so it's dark and gloomy.
I am no longer in a soft crib.
I can sense the fear and uneasyness
around me,
and I too am afraid.

Roberta Prescow

THE TRAIN

Their images have been reflected in me as I take them to concentration camps.

Ellen Walker

GOODBYE

You must leave.
        We won't be
           together
But you my child
          you'll be safe
      Go to the new
          country
things will be strange but
          you'll be safe
What more can I say
      I must fight back
              my tears
Go child
     you'll be safe
       Goodbye
          Goodbye
             Child
                Goodbye

Now she's gone.   I feel lost
        I have nothing
      I'm alone
        waiting for death.
     My little girl's gone
        she'll be safe
        I mustn't think
          of myself
But I can't help it
      Oh dear God
        let me
          be with
         her
    let me.

The days have past the
     letters are few
        death is near.

                        Marci Gelb

I am a Polish Holiday traditional costume.
I am worn at festive occasions,
     Even in my country's darkest hour
I only see it in a time of glory.
     People might think that I'm lucky,
        but I'm not.
I don't see all kinds of feelings
     just people showing me off.

                 Gina Mitchel

A NEW LIFE

While floating through the dark
      I came upon a picture
of people, unsure people gazing ahead
      Immigrants, they were.
I, an immigrant of sorts, entered through
      and became as they are, one.
Through gates, past desks went I
past misery and hate,
      forward I went, past
        mountains and stacks.
 High over my head
      I saw a light
Faster I walked, I then began
to run, Faster, past eons of time
      I came upon the light
        A window
My gaze shot forward, began to run
      and stopped
I looked up, and there she was
      proud brave, straight narrow
I knew I was safe.

                Dolita Cathcart

I walk along a hall;
The walls, white, with blood stains,
I find a dying child calling me.
Two men stand over him.
One death and the other a soldier.
He pleads to me to take them away
But I helplessly stand there.
I hope to move one step further.
But something stops me.
I walk along a hall a cry for mercy.

                Sandra Molinas

Struggling as hard as a dying animal,
Not wanting to comply with this
      exhausting pace,
Fighting the heat of the brown and
      coppery sun
Hoping the cool breeze will soothe me.
Waiting for the day when liberation will come.
The whips are cracking day in and day out
Being forced to complete the wall.
The guards, satisfied with their jobs,
Acquiring pleasure from our work.
Oh, one day when I can enjoy work,
Doing what I want, telling
      what I want to be done.

            Michael Merenstein

ME THE SOAP

I went to the museum and I saw
a bar of soap it was made from
human fat. What if I was in
that bar of soap and someone
used it, I would talk and they
wouldn't know who it was
then they'd use me all up
and I'be gone.
When they were making me
it was horrible
they had to cut me up and
take out my fat and they
made a bar of soap.

Gina Pyatt

THE ROMAN ARMOUR

The leather has long lost its shine
and is homeless, yet life still glows in the
beaten bronze, and scratched leather.
It breathes.
It pulsates.
Tales of heroic battle and adventure
remain enveloped in the leather.
One has only to close the eyes
and lightly touch the leather to feel
the vibrating, pulsating history flow
along the veins of the
invisible warrior.

David Levy

ON THE BENCH

I saw them on the bench
I looked towards my mother,
        and she motioned me forward.
We walked through the big gate
There were men standing there
They were dressed alike.
One of them was talking to my
        father, but they could
        not communicate too well.
My father motioned for us to
        go join the others on the
        bench.
One man stopped me
He pinned something onto my collar
It was a number, 18, I'll never forget it.

We were all sitting there.
Except for our numbers, you couldn't
        tell us apart.
We were dressed mostly in farmers clothes.
Compared to the people that live here,
we looked like paupers,
We all had the same look on our faces,
Sad to leave our homeland, but
        happy we had escaped.
We left my brother there
He couldn't get out.
I'll never forget.

Marcy Friedman

Teaching Poetry to Spanish Language Classes When Your Spanish Is Nada

By Sue Willis

Ideally, creative writing for bilingual and primarily Spanish-speaking classes would be taught by Spanish-fluent writers. This is not always possible, and I have found myself trying out various techniques to break the barriers. The person barrier is not so hard; the problem is language subtlety and felt rhythms. What is missing is a myriad of tiny verbal cues: the building blocks of responding well to your students.

I find myself using simplistic writing assignments that I can explain in halting Spanish: I speak first in English for my own ego and for those children who understand, then in Spanish. To read from the wonderful South American, Mexican, and Spanish poets is an obvious first step. Sometimes I enlist good readers from among the children; sometimes I have the teacher read. Often I also read an English translation.

Sometimes I preface such a poem-reading (of Neruda, say, or Jiménez) with a word-listing on the board. The word-listing is a participatory exercise: I ask for a list of colors, or fruits (before reading Neruda's *Oda a la alcachofa* or *Ode to the Artichoke*). Everyone can name a fruit in Spanish and probably English, too. As best as we can, we describe fruits. Then we read the poem, and I give the minimal assignment: write something like a poem, or else write a poem using a fruit in every line. I find enough words in the two languages that are similar: *Describe un poema con frutas; Escriba un poema o un cuento.*

Another technique is group poetry—alternating lines of Spanish and English, according to which language the individual child speaks most easily. Many of the children like to show off their good Spanish and help me spell it correctly on the board. I've done group poems about trips, group poems from word lists. Sometimes I do *listas* with individuals, too. Make a *lista*, I say, of *diez cosas*, ten things—*rojas, pequenos, grandes, terribles,* or *comicas.* Sometimes I hand out slips of paper to individuals with what their *lista* is to be; they trade, argue. Ten things I do every day, ten things I see on my street. *Cinco cosas* for the littler kids.

Nonverbal aids work too: the old standbys of playing music, bringing evocative magazine pictures, asking the kids to close their eyes for one or two minutes and then write what they see *con los ojos cerrados.* Also, *Escriba un sueno,* tell the story of a dream you had. Lists of concrete things, responses to visual and aural stimuli, descriptions of anything (your street, your family, your dress—*tu vestido favorito*), memories. The material isn't so different from assignments with English-speaking kids; the problem is the teacher's, how to say it, and in finding someone to help Spanish that is misspelled. The further problem is how to enjoy and appreciate what is written in Spanish. The whole process is, needless to say, most rewarding when I am trying to learn Spanish and the children are trying to pick up English. Many of the pedagogic benefits are indirect —and for the teacher!

B. Letters and Dialogues

Letters That Can Only Be Sent as Poems

by Alan Ziegler

Many have used letter-writing as a cure for writer's block. Letters take away some of the ambiguity from writing by providing an "audience" to focus on. By helping students find an audience, you are helping them get started on a poem: In "letters that can only be sent as poems" the "recipient" chosen establishes the poem's environment. The recipient can be anyone or thing who couldn't in reality receive the letter. (I've found this limitation makes for more interesting writing.) I've classified these letters into three "audience-groupings": letters to objects (cars, trees, windows, etc.); letters to friends or relatives who have died; and letters to figures from history or literature (Columbus, Adam & Eve, Hunchback of Notre Dame, etc.)

I've had successful letter-writing sessions with groups ranging from third graders through adults.

I start the session by reading the class Richard Brautigan's poem "To England":

There are no postage stamps that send letters
   back to England three centuries ago,
no postage stamps that make letters
travel back until the grave hasn't been dug yet,
and John Donne stands looking out the window,
it is just beginning to rain this April morning,
and the birds are falling into the trees
like chess pieces into an unplayed game,

and John Donne sees the postman coming up
   the street,
the postman walks very carefully because
   his cane
is made of glass.

I tell the class that Richard Brautigan had a strong need to communicate with John Donne (a writer who evidently has meant something to Brautigan). Brautigan can dream about meeting with John Donne, or he can write him a poem, which—like a dream—is a place where anything can happen, there are no rules. Poetry is an outlet for communication when the post office and telephone company are inadequate. Sometimes it's the writing of a letter that's important, even if the letter cannot be sent.

For younger kids (elementary school), I ask them to imagine that they have a "magic stamp" that indeed can send letters back in time "before the grave has been dug." And the "stamp" can also send letters to objects, animals, or even people of the future. Many love to draw their version of the magic stamp, (a nice thing to keep in mind at the end of the class, when some might be restless).

As students finish their letters, ask them to write the letter they might get in return. In these replies, the kids should be sure to answer any questions they have raised in the original. Sometimes, an extended correspondence is begun.

You can devote a session to a particular category (e.g., just letters to objects), or describe the various options and give them a choice. What follows are comments on each of the categories and samples of writings I've gotten in response to this idea.

1) LETTERS TO OBJECTS

As an example of a letter to an object, I often read the class Charles Simic's poem "Stone," which I've adapted so it reads like a letter:

DEAR STONE

I want to go inside you,
    That would be my way.
Let somebody else become a dove
Or gnash with a tiger's tooth.
I would be happy to be a stone like you.

From the outside you are a riddle:
No one knows how to answer you.
But inside you, it must be cool and quiet.
Even though a cow steps on you full weight,
Even though a child throws you in a river;
You sink, slow, unperturbed
    To the river bottom
Where the fishes come to knock on you
And listen.

I have seen sparks fly out
When two stones are rubbed,
So perhaps it is not dark inside you
        after all;
Perhaps there is a moon shining
From somewhere, as though behind a hill—
Just enough light to make out
The strange writings, the star-charts
On the inner walls.

I've found that letters-to-objects are often the most successful. Reading through the samples included with this article, it's striking how many "human" qualities inanimate objects have, especially in our relationships with them. Much is revealed through these writings, especially in the responses from the objects: the window that says, "The only time I move is when someone breaks me," or the car that complains, "What bothers me is when people push on my pedals to make me go faster. Then before you know it they're pressing me to stop."

Theater improvisations can grow out of these letters, or vice versa. The improvisations might be dialogues between the students and the objects that surround us. (In the object category, I include such living things as trees, volcanoes etc.)

2) LETTERS TO FRIENDS OR RELATIVES WHO HAVE DIED

Children are able to write about death with insight, feeling, and sometimes, humor. I think that the older we get, the more uncomfortable a subject death becomes, and one reason is that it tends to get hushed up around kids. An important aspect of psychotherapy is opening up feelings that went unexpressed when we were young; these are often feelings of loss and distance. Giving the children the opportunity to write these letters affords them a chance to express such feelings while they are still close to them. It is not the teacher's position to offer therapeutic interpretations, but rather to give the kid space to feel, express and grow.

3) LETTERS TO FIGURES FROM HISTORY OR LITERATURE

If a student writes to someone like Columbus, you might suggest that he/she describe what America and the world are like now. They could tell Columbus what happened to the country he came across several hundred years ago. The writers would have to keep in mind that Columbus wouldn't know what cars and TVs are, so they would have to exercise their descriptive powers. (Likewise, they could write the letter to the Indians who happened to be here when Columbus made his "discovery.")

DEAR WINDOW

I'm glad I'm not you because people see through you and sometimes they break you and even spit on you and it looks nasty and you seem like you're so cold out there. But the reason I do like you because when it is a cold day and I'm inside the house you warm me up when I close the window and I can put up the shade and you make light come in. And when I don't want light I put down the shade and no light comes in. I like you Mr. Window and if I ever see anyone mess you up I'm going to mess them up. When you receive this letter please write back. I love you window.

from BARBARA SAUNDERS

DEAR BARBARA

You asked me to write you back so I did. Barbara you seem like a nice girl to me. And Barbara what you said it is true. When I warm you up I am out there freezing for you. And I feel very sorry for myself when I am looking down at other kids playing and I don't have anyone to play with me. And also I stay in the same place. The only time I move is when someone breaks me. Barbara you seem like a good friend and I thank you for taking up for me because people hit on me and spit, and also break me and I can't hit them back.

Your Good friend
THE WINDOW

DEAR MR. TREE,

I love to climb you
you are brave with those strong branches
you are like a human to me. .
you can die like me,
I try and stop people from cutting you down.

DEAR KEITH

I love you too
you are strong
you can die
you're even brave like me.
I might stand in one place but you
are still my friend.

TO MIRROR

Do they make faces at you and do a lot of stuff in front of you and how do you like it? People wash you off but other people wash off by themself.

from ANNETTE

TO ANNETTE

They make faces at me and they dance at me. They laugh at me. But I tell them when they have dirt on their face. They see when they wash their face. If I was you I would not like to be a mirror. If you was one you will see what I mean.

from MIRROR

TO MIRROR

People do all that because they are ashamed of other people. And don't want to dance with people. And don't want to make faces at people. They do all that because they are ashamed.

from ANNETTE

TO ANNETTE

I know but if I wasn't a mirror I would dance with people and also dance in the mirror but if I was a person I wouldn't make faces at the mirror. It doesn't hurt me. And I hope that people don't hurt me by breaking me up. Cause it hurts me to be broken and it makes me happy if I don't get broken by nobody.

from MIRROR

by VICKIE

TO A PENCIL

I was born from my mother, you was made from a tree and every time you break your leg, all you have to do is get your leg sharp, but I have to go to the hospital for my leg. You can erase words by your head but I can't.

DEAR VICKIE,

When I was made from a tree all I had to do was get my leg sharp and I will be making a letter for you. Then if I break, all my owner has to do is sharp me again and I be ready to work for my owner. But I have a cousin, his name is pen, but his leg doesn't break he runs out of ink and he does mostly every thing like me.

DEAR PENCIL

What does your cousin do because you didn't tell me enough about him, write back and tell me more about your cousin please.

DEAR VICKIE,

My cousin is made from ink but sometimes he has an eraser on his head too. But when his leg breaks he will die. Sometime he will run out of ink and then he will be sick or gone forever. Sometimes my cousin will mess you up while he is helping you write for you. But I will tell you something he is cool like me. Maybe if you have any time you can write to him.

yours truly once again,
PENCIL

by TRACEY

DEAR CANDY BAR,

I like the way you taste, and love to hear you crunch. I like the way you melt in my mouth, not in my hands. I admire your looks, so nice and neat, but when I get through you're all over my mouth and on my hands, you look terrible. I love you with nuts, mostly almonds. Most of your admirers are children, they gobble you up so fast you can't see who's going to eat you!!

DEAR TRACEY,

When I read your letter I cried because now I know I am loved. It is true that they gobble me up. But now I know I am loved. I AM FINALLY, REALLY LOVED!

by LINDA

TO A TREE,

I like you very much because sometimes we can pick pears and apples and peaches and others. But when winter comes there will be no fun without you. I look out the window and see you freezing cold I cry, and cry to see you get cold and tear apart your branches will fall. But when come Spring there is joy for all.

DEAR LINDA,

I like you too so I know how you will feel if you was a tree you will be cold freezing, bold and your branches will fall and I'll cry and cry like you did to me.

DEAR TREE,

I know how you feel in the winter because I feel the same way at night because I get cold I have to scribble together and I dream about you. Because I be thinking that you don't feel warm and cuddle underneath three or two covers. Write back because I want to know how you and your friends feel about what I wrote.

DEAR LINDA,

I have got your letter, it was a very nice letter. I know I will tell you what happens to me. I do feel cold at night and my branches keep me warm. But still I feel a little breeze here and there and I would like to sleep in a warm nice bed but I am much too big to fit in one.

MORE LETTERS TO OBJECTS

TO A CAR,

I never wrote to a car before but
boy you sure are lucky because
you go very fast and never
get tired when we can't even
go half your speed and always
get tired. You hardly eat, all you
have is gasoline, some water, and
oil and you have eight hearts when
we have one and your eyes
glow up in the night and when
you yell everybody moves
out of the way but when I yell
everybody yells back, and you're
old you're always in and out of the
hospital for minor adjustments when
it takes me months to recover
that is why I wrote to you

Bruce Levinson
Riverdale Junior High, Bronx

Dear Mr. Meal,

You were the best
I ever tasted I wish you would reappear
I'd chew you better I'll save an empty
spot in my stomach for you.

Jordan

Dear Jordan

   I will be there by some
fried chicken and rice. I'll be there
tomorrow. I have a couple
of complaints. Your veins are too big your
heart beats too fast and you're not
growing.

                                        Meal

                        Jordan Jones, 4th Grade
                             P.S. 11, Brooklyn

DEAR MR. VOLCANO,

How do you get so
mad that you explode
into fire & lava? You
get awful mad
why don't you
talk it over with some
hill or mountain? You
destroy hundreds of things
so think before you strike.

   (the volcano answers)

I am the great volcano
I blow my lid because
I feel like it and it's none
of your business so you
think before you write!

                  Dominick Bellusci, 5th Grade
                         Atlantic Avenue School

TO THE YO-YO,

If you can do skin the
cat how come you don't look
like a razor, or rock the
baby can you still
do rock the baby, boy
you don't look like
a rocking chair, there
is something strange.
Last year the butterfly
said to me to stop spinning
me and the butterfly
is even stranger than
I thought and my stomach
spins around like you.
Next year write me a
letter back please.

(the yo-yo answers)

Next year if you buy me please
do not do walk the dog that is the
worst trick. It puts scratches in
me, or drop me.

                                   your friend,
                                   the yo-yo

                        William Lewis, 4th Grade
                            Atlantic Avenue School

LETTERS TO OBJECTS
   by ADULTS (from Eng. 14, at Bronx Community
   College)

BY DENISE WILLIAMS

Dear Kool "Cig,"

   Yeah it's about that time again. I'm sorry but you
know it's a force of habit. Can't you understand?
Damn I know how you must feel when I strike that
match and put that fire to your tongue. Tell me
something? Exactly how does it feel? Do you feel like
your insides are burning up, or what? I know how it
feels to be burned. The pain was so unbearable I
thought my fingers would come off one by one. But
to make matters worse for you, there I'll sit puffing
on you puff after puff, making your flames hotter
and hotter. Then when I've had enough I put you
out. I crush you. That's right I crush you to your
death. But seriously speaking I enjoy your company.
I really do like you. I'm sorry I abuse you. Will you
ever forgive me?

                                   Love, Denise

Dear Denise,

   I'm glad that you like me very much, though the
manufacturers like you better because you spend
your hard-earned money on me. Yea, you do abuse
me to the extreme—but you are abusing yourself
more. I don't know, maybe you don't know the harm
I can cause you. Frankly, I really don't care, because
when you're gone I will still be around, and there will
always be somebody who likes me. I'm sorry to hear
that you burnt your fingers, but think of what you
are doing to your lungs. Look at the ashes in the ash
tray. They're black, right? Who knows, maybe your
lungs will look just like that one day.
   Girl get out of my life. I'm no good for you. I can
only cause you harm. Maybe even your death.

                                   "Kool"

P.S. No this is not a dear John but if this is your thing do it. I've warned you; I'm the heartbreak kid.

BY SHIRLEY FLEMING

Dear Car,

Sometimes I really feel sorry for you. People run into you and don't even apologize. Then to top it off they sometimes leave you in the street in any kind of weather. I know you must be uncomfortable out there. If they take you to the shop you really get the business. They hit you, drill you, open your mouth & start probing with your teeth. Oh if I had a car I would be nice to you. I'd make sure you were bathed once a week, and dry my feet before I got into you. Oh yes I wouldn't throw your arms around so hard either.

Well I guess you don't really mind because you have so many sisters and brothers to keep you company. Tell me, how do you feel with a full stomach? I feel awful. I want to sleep it off. Do you ever feel like you're not hungry & wish people would leave you alone?

Shirley

Dear Concerned Person,

I'm so glad there are people like you. Now in answer to your questions: I feel good with a full stomach, but only when I want to eat. I'm like you, I have feelings too. I do feel like napping at times, but that decision is not up to me.

I feel very useful. People need me. You must know how good it feels to be needed.

What bothers me is when people push on my pedals to make me go faster. Then before you know it they're pressing me to stop.

Above all I could hurt someone and sometimes I do. That really makes me sad.

I have several sisters & brothers all shapes and colors, but we're not very close.

Speaking of my arms, they do hurt at times, because some people don't know how to handle me, but don't let that bother you when I get tired of being misused I simply call everything to a halt. Then my owner starts hurting.

Sincerely,
Sedan

GROUP TWO: LETTERS TO FRIENDS OR RELATIVES WHO HAVE DIED

DEAR TART,

hello. Where are you now
I'm just writing to tell you
that now people shouldn't run
in the street acting like superman
If you were still alive you
would be twelve and have fun
I'm sorry you died the day
you was going to see Coney Island
     for the first time

Judy Donovan
Riverdale Junior High, Bronx

DEAR GREAT GRANDFATHER,

I know I can't see you but I
know that you're dead. And when you
were alive I remember when you got
up every morning and went and
bought a toy for me when I
was little. And I remember when
I always loved you. And I still
remember when you were sitting on
the porch and smoking a
cigar I will never forget
that

Good bye.

Ricky Fusco, 5th Grade
Atlantic Avenue School

DEAR GRANDMOM,

Are you having a good time
Well anyway you are a tin can
Well anyway are you still on the roller derby?
Well, if you are, win every match
Still gambling on invisible horses?
Well John Do is running,
     play him he'll pay $1,000
because he's the only one running

Neil, 4th Grade
P.S. 197, Brooklyn

Dear Great, Great, Grandmother,

I loved you very much. You used to buy me things. Sometimes you get mad at me but then you start laughing and you are happy and I hug you. You make good soul food at our family reunion and we have a lot of soda. I love you very much and I was sad when your husband died.

Love
Your Great Great Grandson,
Thomas Satterthwaite Jr.

Thomas Satterthwaite, 4th Grade
P.S. 11, Brooklyn

GROUP THREE: LETTERS TO FIGURES FROM HISTORY OR LITERATURE

TO ADAM & EVE,

I was wondering how it is
in the Garden of Eden. Is it fun
streaking day and night?
Nowadays it is illegal.
to go around without any clothes on.
And by the way, it is legal to
eat apples without God's permission.

Laurie Vunck, 5th Grade
Atlantic Avenue School

DEAR SIGMUND FREUD,

Most people today
are sick.
We really need you.
I wish you were around.
People always complain
but when you tell
them your problems they
tell you to shut up.

—from Psychiatrist John
Riverdale Junior High

DEAR GREAT, GREAT, GREAT, GREAT, GREAT
A 100 MORE GREATS GRANDFATHER,

we have replaced the horse with the car
replaced the pterodactyl with the bird
and replaced the bird with the airplane.
However, planes and cars make pollution,
pollution is dirt coming from cars and planes.
Horses and pterodactyls did make something like it,
but it helped things grow.

You see from the year 1 to the year 1973
things change.

Paul S., 4th Grade
P.S. 197, Brooklyn

TO MR. BOJANGLES,

I heard all about you, you are real cool.
Jump so high dress up fancy
I heard after 80 years you are still alive
Mr. Bojangles dance
I knew a man Bojangles who lived
in New Orleans and now I give
you this letter.

Michael, 4th Grade
P.S. 197, Brooklyn

POSTSCRIPT

I asked the children to do "Letter Poems," and as I was walking around the room, I came across a girl on the rack of writer's block. She just couldn't come up with a letter. I reminded her that every previous time I had been to the class, she had started out with a blank piece of paper and had ended the period with a poem on the paper. Where did those poems come from? She pointed to her head. So then we have reason to believe that there is another poem hiding out somewhere in the head, don't we? She couldn't fault the logic, and she nodded in agreement, starting to perk up. I suggested that she write her letter to that "poem" and see what's going on. This is the result:

DEAR POEM,

Where are you?
I've been looking
for you all day long
why won't you come
out? What is wrong
with you?
Now what am I
going to do?

(the poem answers)

Here I am inside your head.
I won't come out because
you're thinking too hard
try not to think hard
and then I may come
out.

Lynette Sandio
Atlantic Avenue School, Lynbrook N.Y.

Personalism: Writing a Letter

by David Shapiro

"Criticism by exercise in the style of a given period. As you would not seriously consider a man's knowledge of tennis until he either could make or had made some sort of show in a tournament, so we must assume that until a man can actually control a given set of procedures there must be many elements in them of which he has but an imperfect knowledge."—Ezra Pound

"Personalism has nothing to do with philosophy, it's all art.... To give you a vague idea, one of its minimal aspects is to address itself to one person (other than the poet himself), thus evoking life-giving vulgarity.... While I was writing it I was realising that if I wanted to I could use the telephone instead of writing the poem, and so Personalism was born. It's a very exciting movement which will undoubtedly have lots of adherents."—Frank O' Hara

Arthur Waley once remarked that Chinese poetry celebrated friendship between persons in a way which Western poetry had never attempted. While the West has been involved in the idea of romantic love, and particularly sexual passion, Chinese literature is filled with the beautiful factuality of lesser intimacies, private lives and personal fidelities. While Western literature often is filled with exorbitant praise for an over-esteemed love-object, Oriental literature often succeeds in quietly registering the magnificence of rapports and relations which are filled with the everyday and its business.

Ezra Pound's translation of Rihaku (the Japanese name given to the Chinese poet Li Po), entitled "Exile's Letter," is a magnificent example of using an everyday form—the letter—and reminiscences of everyday occasions, drawn from a vivid past, to create a long and inspiring vehicle for poetry:

EXILE'S LETTER

To So-Kin of Rakuyo, ancient friend, Chancellor
   of Gen.
Now I remember that you built me a special tavern
By the south side of the bridge at Ten-Shin.
With yellow gold and white jewels, we paid for
   songs and laughter
And we were drunk for month on month,
   forgetting the kings and princes.

Intelligent men came drifting in from the sea and
   from the west border,
And with them, and with you especially
There was nothing at cross purpose,
And they made nothing of sea-crossing or of
   mountain-crossing,
If only they could be of that fellowship,
And we all spoke out our hearts and minds, and
   without regret.
And then I was sent off to South Wei,
   smothered in laurel groves,
And you to the north of Raku-hoku,
Till we had nothing but thoughts and memories in
   common.
And then, when separation had come to its worst,
We met, and travelled into Sen-Go,
Through all the thirty-six folds of the turning and
   twisting waters,
Into a valley of the thousand bright flowers,
That was the first valley;
And into ten thousand valleys full of voices and
   pine-winds.
And with silver harness and reins of gold,
Out came the East of Kan foreman and his
   company.
And there came also the 'True man' of Shi-yo to
   meet me,
Playing on a jewelled mouth-organ.
In the storied houses of San-Ko they gave us more
   Sennin music,
Many instruments, like the sound of young
   phoenix broods.
The foreman of Kan Chu, drunk, danced
   because his long sleeves wouldn't keep still
With that music playing,
And I, wrapped in brocade, went to sleep with my
   head on his lap,
And my spirit so high it was all over the heavens,
And before the end of the day we were scattered
   like stars, or rain.
I had to be off to So, far away over the waters,
You back to your river-bridge.
And your father, who was brave as a leopard,
Was governor in Hei-Shu, and put down the
   barbarian rabble.

And one May he had you send for me,
  despite the long distance.
And what with wheels and so on, I won't say it
  wasn't hard going,
Over roads twisted like sheep's guts.
And I was still going, late in the year,
  in the cutting wind from the North,
And thinking how little you cared for the cost,
  and you caring enough to pay it.
And what a reception:
Red jade cups, food well set on a blue jewelled
  table,
And I was drunk, and had no thought of returning.
And you would walk out with me to the western
  corner of the castle,
To the dynastic temple, with water about it clear
  as blue jade,
With boats floating, and the sound of mouth-
  organs and drums,
With ripples like dragon-scales, going glass green on
  the water,
Pleasure lasting, with courtezans, going and coming
  without hindrance,
With the willow flakes falling like snow,
And the vermilioned girls getting drunk about
  sunset,
And the water, a hundred feet deep, reflecting
  green eyebrows
—Eyebrows painted green are a fine sight in young
  moonlight,
Gracefully painted—
And the girls singing back at each other,
Dancing in transparent brocade,
And the wind lifting the song, and interrupting it,
Tossing it up under the clouds.
      And all this comes to an end.
      And is not again to be met with.
I went up to the court for examination,
Tried Layu's luck, offered the Choyo song,
And got no promotion,
      and went back to the East Mountains
      White-headed.
And once again, later, we met at the South
  bridgehead.
And then the crowd broke up, you went north to
  San palace,
And if you ask how I regret that parting:
It is like the flowers falling at Spring's end
      Confused, whirled in a tangle.
What is the use of talking, and there is no end of
  talking,
There is no end of things in the heart.
I call in the boy,
Have him sit on his knees here
      To seal this,

And send it a thousand miles, thinking.

Rihaku (Li Po)
translated by Ezra Pound
in *Translations* (New Directions)

Before we attempt to imitate this wonderful poem, let's look closely at it, in an attempt to find those procedures which Ezra Pound said were the true test of one's competence, in tennis as in poetry. First, we notice that the poet is not embarrassed to address a particular "you" in his poem, and constantly throughout the poem he delights in "naming names," never taking the Fifth Amendment, as it were:
  To So-Kin of Rakuyo, ancient friend, Chancellor
  of Gen
Walt Whitman, our great American poet, loved to catalogue American place-names (Hoboken, Susquehanna, Wichita) and this love of names infects all great Chinese poets. When one recalls that this poem has for its theme the loss of friendship over immense distances, then the peculiar pleasure of naming place-names and personal names becomes more significant. Like Adam in the Garden, one gains dominion over something by "naming it," and when sending a letter over thousands of miles, one wants to be certain of the right address! All good writing has to do with this attitude of addressing things and people properly.

A letter is a good form because it also permits the poet to remind the addressee of many colorful details of their life together. It is not at all in the mawkish tradition of the mere love-teller, but a sensuous reminder of a friendly life lived together in comradery. The poem is filled with color:

  With yellow gold and white jewels, we paid for
    songs and laughter

  Ripples like dragon-scales, going grass green on the
    water

This color is loved by and for itself, but it is always making more vivid some common object or festive detail.

We all love newsy letters, and this colorful vehicle shows the Chinese poet as a good gossip and newsy correspondent. He permits himself, and we must learn to give ourselves equal permission, a sometimes flat recital of the facts:

  And then I was sent off to South Wei
    smothered in laurel groves
  And you to the north of Raku-hoku

Note that this is about as flat as saying, "And then I

took off for Secaucus in New Jersey, where they no longer raise pigs, and you drove off to northern Missouri.'' But, paradoxically, the Chinese poet knows that through this flatness he will attain aesthetic effects and evoke an emotional response from his reader.

Flatness is something one must learn from this poem, as well as sensuous color. Gertrude Stein said one does not need to draw every leaf on the tree. One leaf, as it were, will evoke from the viewer an immense inner sense of dense foliage if it is particularly well-drafted, whereas many fuzzy leaves will evoke nothing in us at all, except perhaps a rather linty rug. Thus, this poem is filled with flat details which evoke a sensuous sense of place and time:

> We met, and travelled into Sen-Go,
> Through all the thirty-six folds of the turning and
> twisting waters

How important that the Chinese poet is willing to number those turns and folds in the water. Not forty-seven, not ten thousand, but exactly thirty-six! There are things said in an epistle which would not fit elsewhere, and the Chinese poet thus uses a letter to a friend to record his everyday defeats and frustrations. How often does a Western poet write about graduate school or his academic failures?:

> I went up to court for examination,
> Tried Layu's luck, offered the Choyo song
> And got no promotion,
> and went back to the East Mountains
> White-headed.

Since Chinese society was based on the mandarin system of academic hierarchies, the Chinese poet was quite properly obsessed with his status and the esteem he would win from success, and we are moved that he records it factually and without obfuscating his failure.

This letter is also filled with brilliant similes. These comparisons are fundamentally drawn from everyday life, though they may seem more exotic to us. Perhaps when you write your imitation, you should draw all comparisons from the room in which you find yourself setting. So that, when the Chinese poet says, ''Many instruments, like the sound of young phoenix broods'' you might think of ''guitars, that sound like air conditioners put on for the middle of July.'' For us, the phoenix broods seem exotic, a bit far-fetched, but for the poet they are proper not because they are poetical but because they are part of the sensuous texture of everyday life, as much as air conditioners and fluorescent lights.

Thus, when the Chinese poet uses nature for his similes you might find yourself nonplussed, sur-rounded as you are—possibly in a classroom—with sleek manufactured objects or dismal commercial products. Don't be embarrassed to put these in, any more than you would be embarrassed to hear the Chinese poet speak forthrightly of his lack of academic success. Rihaku writes:

> And my spirit so high it was all over the heavens,
> And before the end of the day we were scattered
> like stars, or rain.

You might find yourself saying, ''Now we're spread apart like street lights and police cars.'' For us, the world of manufactured objects might appear in a letter as unobtrusively as natural objects appear in the Chinese. Thus for the Latin-American writer Gabriel García Márquez, bananas and other imagery indigenous to the Latin-American countries, are as natural as snow is to the Russian poet Pasternak. You must put your world into your letter, since as Pound says, ''poetry is news that stays news.'' While your Sony cassette or air conditioner may corrode, one can hope that in the poem-letter their existence will be as indestructible as the monuments of which Shakespeare speaks. Let the humble form of the letter lead you into cataloguing the most infinitesimal or seemingly trivial aspects of your life: a friend will care about them, and it is to a friend you are speaking.

> To Susan B., of Boston Massachusetts
> You came to see me, that night
>   at the tool and die shop
> We sat in the defense contractor's office
> and smoked camels and you told me
> how selfish and bound up I was and I told you
> how deceitful and manipulating you were
> and we agreed and mapped out the changes
>   in our lives.
> Then you went to your Long Island friends,
> to Mineola, to Massapequa, to Patchogue.
> I found myself in Cambridge, a vagrant for
> the space of a week, and when I came back
> to New Providence you were gone, and the town
> was empty and anyway I was still a bit
> embarrassed to go knock on your door.
>
> I remember the first time I saw you.
> You were on the stage in New Providence
> High School Auditorium, and you were playing
> the oboe, and two dimples formed themselves
> high on your cheeks under the cheekbone.
> You wrote me one letter this year about
> Boston and your journalism and
>   your fashion modeling.
> I reread it fifteen times and
>   carried it in the
> inside pocket of my tweed coat, but I didn't
> write back until six weeks later,

full of apologies.
And you haven't written back.
I came up to see you. Roman and I froze
for an hour in the Bronx, an hour and a half
in Springfield, two hours in Worcester,
    hitch-hiking
towards your city, and then we froze some more
outside of Berklee School of Music waiting
for John Ellis and Gail to come back from
the Jazz Workshop. And I kept calling all
that night, with no answer, nothing but
your bell which rings twice, fuzzes, stops, and
rings twice again. I woke up the next afternoon.
and called again, but Chris Forsythe answered
and said you wouldn't be back until six.
    I called
at six. No answer. And again and again, up
until past twelve, with nothing but your bell.
And we froze again on the way back, in
Sturbridge, in Waterbury, Conn., on the
Taconic State Parkway, and in Scarsdale.
And you are still in Boston without answering,
looking out your window at the American cars
passing on Commonwealth Avenue.

                              LUC SANTE

Letter-Poems

by Ron Padgett

It's customary for classes to write letters to classmates who are ill or who have moved away. Such an occasion is good for writing a poem about the person and his or her present condition: how it feels to be somewhere else, what it's like there, what the person might be doing, etc. Or you could imagine a classmate anywhere, even though he or she had never left town at all. Eliza Bailey, a sixth grader at P.S. 61, wrote the following poem about her poetry teacher, Ron Padgett, when he had gone out of town for a few weeks:

I Can Imagine It Now

I can imagine Mr. Padgett as a long skinny icicle
    with glasses in Minnesota
I can image Mr. Padgett with his teeth chattering,
    in his summer clothes in Minnesota
I can imagine Mr. Padgett eating ice cubes while
    waiting for a bus and it's 10 below zero in
    Minnesota
I can imagine Mr. Padgett talking to his identical
    twin brother, a gopher, in Minnesota
I can imagine Mr. Padgett screaming over the
    intercom to his twin brother the gopher in
    Minnesota
I can imagine Mr. Padgett imagining what we are
    doing now, in New York

Dialogues: Imitating Plato

by David Shapiro

Lytton: Your book is very clever, but wants dialogue.

Shakespeare: Love's labor lost: will you hear the dialogue that
the two learned men have compil'd in praise of the owl and
the cukoo.

In many of our writing assignments we are striving towards a flexible use of the conversational tone, and what could be more natural than to attain this tone by means of the literal handling of a conversation, that is, a *dialogue*. The eleventh edition of the *Encyclopaedia Britannica* defines the dialogue as "a little drama without a theatre," though there is no reason why one's dialogues cannot have the theatre as their destiny. Also, while our assignment does not emphasize stage directions or any so-called "scene painting," there is good reason to supplement one's dialogue with just such decor and milieu of furniture or landscape. One's dialogue will occur, like those of Ibsen, who was himself first a painter, firmly within a world or an atmosphere, rather than as floating thoughts on a bare page, though that too can have its ghostly charm!

The Greeks used dialogue as a logical form for philosophical investigation and presentation. It has always been a favorite poetical modality for invective and abuse. Here the proverbial straw man of an argument can talk, gesture, and make a fool of himself, with a personal pathos; here, too, one's own argument can become animated and surprising in the context of a party or a walk. Clouds can sing. . . . It is one thing to be presented with an instruction manual on beauty and sex—Johnson and Master's, say; another, to see and listen to Socrates in Plato's *Symposium* as he rises dramatically beyond other guests in his vivid and trance-like orations.

Dialogues, like stairways or windows, have innumerable forms. There may be dialogues with the immortal dead, a common desire on the part of those frequenting mediums and clairvoyants. Walter Savage Landor invented many such beautiful conversations with vanished Renaissance figures. You might think of talking to Helen of Troy, or Babe Ruth, or the Medicis, or Marilyn Monroe. One's prayers are often dialogues with suppressed ghostly or godly speakers; an interesting series of dialogues might be created by having one's "enormous wishes" (the ironic phrase is Juvenal's) answered. Look at Job for one of the most terrifying dialogues of the Old Testament, in which the supernatural Artisan speaks in a series of unanswerable yet beautiful questions, reducing Job to a dramatic self-lacerating phrase.

Dialogues can be obviously witty forms, in which time and character and class and space can be refuted and collapsed. Thus a student may have the joy of seeing conversations between Jefferson and Dr. Seuss, Hitler and Buber, a blade of grass and Leonardo da Vinci, Charon and a ferryboat, as with Alice in Wonderland and the tiger lily who talked. This makes the modern dialogue a wonderful analogue of space-and-time confusions in modern physics, and in this backwater of space, Galileo and Einstein can speak.

A peculiarly moving form is that of a dialogue between a man and a transcendental force. Vladimir Mayakovsky, the great Russian revolutionary poet, wrote a wonderful poem about talking to the sun (see "An Extraordinary Adventure Which Befell Vladimir Mayakovsky in a Summer Cottage" in *The Bedbug and Selected Poetry* by Vladimir Mayakovsky, edited and introduced by Patricia Blake, translated by Max Hayward and George Reavey, Indiana Univ. Press paperback), and his poem in turn was parodied by our own American master, Frank O'Hara, in his "A True Account of Talking to the Sun at Fire Island" (see *The Selected Poems of Frank O'Hara*, edited by Donald Allen, Vintage paperback). Here O'Hara gets advice from the sun dramatically and comically, and a kind of sunny pat on the back. Perhaps you have a secret affinity with a supernatural force that you would like to speak to, and the satirical, friendly dialogue is the fitting vehicle for this desire.

The dialogue can be a very serious form, and has been resorted to on many occasions by those who see truth only in its dramatic, evolving and conflicting shape. The Renaissance soliloquy (one thinks of Hamlet's) was often a "collapsed" dialogue, showing mental conflict as a series of self-directed questions and answers. The plays of Samuel Beckett often resolve themselves into monologues. Thus, one's own thought processes can sometimes best be reproduced in the evolutionary, process oriented, flowing form of dialogue.

How dost foole?
Dost dialogue with thy shadow?
—Shakespeare, *Timon of Athens*

Arguments between the body and the soul were typical of the Renaissance masters, and William Butler Yeats used this form explicitly in "well-crafted" rhyme. Thus, there is no reason to suppose the dialogue must be written in either prose or verse, but it *is* useful to imitate particular models first, such as the Italian dialogues of Torquato Tasso, Galileo, and Galiani. And we are not excluding "monologue" from this chapter, since, as the joke goes, "I'm so confused I call me them," James Joyce's Penelope section from *Ulysses* is a beautiful model of a fluent flowing consciousness, questioning and answering itself to a final *Yes*, an ecstasy of inner dialogue.

Coleridge spoke of "puppet heroines for whom the showman contrives to dialogue without the least skill in ventriloquism." Your task is somewhat similar to the ventriloquist, and like the actor in the story of Pasternak, "Letters from Tula," you must "compel a stranger to speak with your own lips." You might take your family, to begin with, and write a dialogue as a record of a true fight between members and then showing it to those members, ask them where they feel you did or did not catch their true idioms. It is interesting, Chekhov used to say, to have such criticism from seemingly untutored playwrights, for their criticism will be most brutally natural. You may find yourself wanting to use a tape recorder to check what the real cadence of a particular speaker is, and anthropologists such as Margaret Mead have written that there is no more serious instrumentality for the concerned field observer than the tape recorder and photograph, to record visually and verbally the contours of speech and living.

While Plato spoke against the "new naturalism" of Greek art of the later fifth century, he often reverted in his dialogues to the most refreshing naturalism. Here is a chance for you to capture the delightful stammerings of an argument unfolding, the horrors of a limpid stupidity personified, the opaque glimmerings of an obscured inner debate. We do much "mental knitting anyway," as Richardson says in *Pamela*, "Thus foolishly dialogued I with my Heart."

C. Writing from Observation

Observation Writing

by Sue Willis

I. Close your eyes: what do you see on the inside of your eyelids? (Colors, shapes, strange creatures?)

2. With your eyes closed, pretend your mind or your eyes are watching a movie screen. What happens? (Give a slightly longer period of time for this exercise, which is a variety of daydreaming.)

3. Still with your eyes closed, what sounds do you hear? Make everyone be quiet. There will be hall sounds, sounds from outside—a dog, a siren.

4. With eyes open, list everything you see within a five foot radius of you: notice details.

5. Go to an unusual place, station yourself for a period of enforced quiet, and note what you hear, see, perhaps smell. Someplace relatively familiar like a window, or the pane of glass in the classroom door. Better, or more exciting, a darkened auditorium, the boiler room, etc. (I have had kids stationed all over a school building, watching and listening.)

6. The eavesdropping exercise. This is an extension of number 5. Outside the main office, another classroom, the girls' bathroom, etc., record as much conversation as you can. What do people really say to one another?

7. Same exercise as number 6, but move out of school to the park, to the street, to local eateries, etc. Always emphasize the quieting of self in order to pick up all the fascinating information your senses are bringing in.

8. Media influence. If you are lucky enough to have a video unit or a super-eight camera (though you don't need to use film to do this), go out and look through the camera. Then write about what you saw with this instrument. Fresh things will be observed: cracks in sidewalks, leaves become interesting when viewed through the lens.

Slow Motion Descriptive Poetry

by Ron Shapiro

The writing lesson dealing with observing the movement of a person, animal or part of nature evolved from a study of poems which suggested that we might look at a single stationary object from several points of view (William Carlos Williams' "Between Walls" and Wallace Stevens' "Someone Puts a Pineapple Together"). The seventh-grade class that wrote the slow motion poems (given below) had written various other kinds of poems, including those in which comparisons are the main device. And they had written poems about stationary objects.

We started by discussing their previous poems about stationary objects, then went on to examples of people, animals and parts of nature in motion.

I asked the students if they had ever heard of the idea of "poetry in motion." Some were vaguely familiar with the idea, and one gave the example of the movement of a ballet dancer. We concluded that "poetry in motion" concerns the body's movements. I suggested that if we look at the movements of our body *very closely*, we can see how graceful and beautiful these movements *really are*!

I gave an example of watching a film of a person, animal or part of nature in slow motion. Through slow motion film we are able to see anew the beauty and grace of movement, even of rather routine actions.

I showed the students that an ordinary action such as touching the frame of my glasses can be viewed quite differently in slow motion. I lifted my hand very slowly, as if I were conducting a symphony orchestra, and then brought my fingers to the metal frame as if they were being drawn there by a powerful magnet.

The previous evening I had written a slow motion description of a person scratching his face. As in all my poetry lessons, I feel it is most important for me to create an example of my own based on the poetry idea I'm planning to teach. If the teacher is unable or unwilling to follow his own directions, how can he expect the students to write anything worthwhile? Here is my poem:

Twitching his left cheek,
the old man

slowly moves his right forefinger
and lazily lifts it off the brown desk,
as if he were only a marionette
in a puppet show.
Closer,
his finger takes careful aim upon his cheek,
like an unshaven pirate
pointing precisely
where the great treasure is located
on the mysterious looking map.

Through this example I tried to demonstrate the beauty and grace of an old man scratching his cheek.

I also selected three other poems to serve as examples in which the poet observed some kind of movement and recorded it in slow motion, emphasizing each part of the movement:

1. "The Artist" by William Carlos Williams: a description of a man who performs a simple "turn around" on his toes. We discussed how the poet was able to look at this movement in slow motion and create a vivid word picture describing the man's action.

2. "The Base Stealer" by Robert Francis: a description of a baseball player getting ready to steal a base. This was an excellent example because of the vivid comparisons relating to the baserunner. Also, my improvised role of this figure enabled the students to see much more clearly the comparisons in the poem. We discussed how the poet had observed this two-or-three-second movement as graceful and beautiful through slow motion.

3. "Poem" by William Carlos Williams: a slow motion word picture describing a cat taking a step.

To summarize, then, the *Slow Motion Poetry Idea*: choose an action that a person, animal or part of nature performs. Then look *closely* at the movement, using your eyes as a slow motion camera, and *describe very carefully* the action. I also suggested that it might be a good idea to choose a rather routine action to write about.

THE ARTIST

Mr. T
     bareheaded
          in a soiled undershirt
his hair standing out
         on all sides
              stood on his toes
heels together
       arms gracefully
           for the moment
curled above his head.
      Then he whirled about
          bounded
into the air
      and with an entrechat
         perfectly achieved
completed the figure.
      My mother
        taken by surprise
where she sat
      in her invalid's chair
         was left speechless.
Bravo! she cried at last
      and clapped her hands.
        The man's wife
came from the kitchen:
      What goes on here? she said.
        But the show was over.

            William Carlos Williams

COMBING YOUR HAIR

The hand embracing the comb
* moves toward the top of*
*   the head like people*
Standing on an escalator, waiting
* to get to the top.*

Next, the comb in hand, falls to
* the scalp, and starts*
*   gliding through the hair like a*
skier sloping down the side of
* a mountain.*

Eventually, the comb takes a
* round trip over the head to*
*   make the hair soft and*
*   per-fect!*

          Kathy Sinopolis

THE BASE STEALER

Poised between going on and back, pulled
Both ways taut like a tightrope-walker,
Fingertips pointing the opposites,
Now bouncing tiptoe like a dropped ball
Or a kid skipping rope, come on, come on,
Running a scattering of steps sidewise,
How he teeters, skitters, tingles, teases,
Taunts them, hovers like an ecstatic bird,
He's only flirting, crowd him, crowd him,
Delicate, delicate, delicate, delicate—now!

            Robert Francis

As the cat
climbed over
the top of

the jamcloset
first the right
forefoot

carefully
then the hind
stepped down

into the pit of
the empty
flowerpot.

            William Carlos Williams

BIRD LANDING

A bird coming in for a landing,
he twists and turns and
*   gently floats down.*
*   His body comes down and*
*   right before he hits land, he*
*   moves his wings with powerful*
*   upstrokes that move the grass.*
*   Feet forcing themselves outward*
*   seeming as a cushion shock absorber.*
*   The feet touch the ground and*
*   the bird strains like*
*   water against more water,*
*   forcing a whirlpool of motion.*
*   The wings are gently tucked back*
*   as the head moves toward its*
*   contented nest.*

            Stephen Gould

Reportage

by Karen Hubert and Ron Padgett

We so often think of creative writing as fiction writing—storytelling, imaginative accounts of unreal happenings and made-up characters. Here are some suggestions for non-fiction writing aimed at strengthening students' relationships to writing in general as well as producing interesting results.

I.   Ask your students to look all around the classroom and to list everything they see. Ask them to move their eyes quickly, and write quickly. This is an exercise in observation, encouraging students to translate into words anything they see.

2.   Ask your students to look at one thing in the classroom. It should be a simple thing, a table top, a chair, the blackboard. A thing in which one would ordinarily think there is not much to see. Ask them to list everything they see. On a table top a student might see such things as: pen marks, blue, square, rivers, Joey, brown, scrape.

3.   Ask your students to close their eyes and imagine some part of the classroom, the teacher's desk for instance. In this exercise, everyone in the class is attempting, visually, to reconstruct the same thing. Ask them to list what they see, or remember. Any words are allowed: square, white, busy, books, ruler, teacher, plant, lines, circles, awful.

4.   Similar "listing" may be done while looking out the window, or sitting in a corner, or standing on the subway on the way to a class trip. Lists may also be made out of remembered things.

5.   Students may observe, and write accurate observations of: classmates, the principal, the teacher, themselves, a student in another class, a person walking down the street, a school custodian. Emphasis here is on accurate realistic description—reportage, in fact.

6.   Send your students out of the classroom to write down conversations they overhear. Good places to sit and overhear are the general office, the teachers' lounge or lunchroom, the hallway, the library. Students may record entire conversations, or parts of conversations, or just random words. This is an exercise in hearing and recording dialogue. Sometimes the results read like poetry. It also might be worthwhile to have your students tape-record overheard conversations as they write, then later compare their version with the tape.

—Karen Hubert

7.   Another approach to writing about the Here and Now consists of having your students forget completely about the past (even as immediate as a few minutes ago) and not let their minds wander toward the future: to tune in as completely as possible to the immediate present. Demonstrate how "the present" becomes "the past" at the very moment you are saying the words. Have them write poems or prose pieces which concentrate on the here and now. To do so you might have them begin their lines with "I see," "I hear," "I touch," "I feel," "I sense," "I think," "I imagine," etc. Point out how their perceptions of the immediate can be of either external or internal phenomena. (Interesting variations in structure can be worked by having the perceptions begin with externals and move inward, from sight to hearing to touch to sensing generally, and to thinking and feeling.)

8.   Here is a surprisingly difficult writing idea. Bring in a lot of different objects. Line them up at the front of the room and have your students write descriptions of them *without naming them*. It isn't easy to write a good description of a guitar without calling it "a guitar." When you read back the descriptions, see how many kids can guess which is the object being described. From this exercise you might gain a better idea of your class's strong and weak points of perception.

—Ron Padgett

The Tree of Possibilities

by Karen Hubert

Begin a story with one or two sentences; put a character in a setting: *Sue is in the bathtub*. Now think of two or three possible things that could happen next in your story. Each possibility must be different:

1. *She drowned.*
2. *She got out and dried herself off.*
3. *She ate the bar of soap.*

Pick one of these possibilities, and add a sentence or two to it: *She drowned. She's lying there. Her mother and father walk in and pump the water out of her. The next day she is buried.* Think of three things that might happen next. Again, each one must be different:

1. *She came alive again.*
2. *She rotted and turned to bones.*
3. *She found herself in heaven.*

Pick one of these possibilities and add a sentence or two to it: *She would rot in a few days, her bones would lie there as if only her bones had been buried.*

Once again, think of three things that might happen next.

1. *Archaeologists would find them and they would be a great help to history.*
2. *They would stay there and worms would chew them.*
3. *They would turn into a skeleton that haunted people.*

Keep on going for as long as you wish.

"THE HOTEL ROOM"

In a certain hotel room, 209 to be exact, two people were moving in. When they opened the door they shuddered with disgust. There on the wall just barely hanging was a lamp light with a dim light which cast just enough light to put the room in an erie spirit. The shade was tattered on one side, and had a huge coffee stain on the other. The striped wall paper which was supposed to cover the wall was coming off in strips. The stuffing of the couch was coming out, and where it was not, springs were breaking through the upholstery. The window was streaked with an egg and some other unpleasant stuff. Brawled out on the floor were newspaper, evidently left from the last people that were there. The newly-weds ran down the stairs and left.

Gina Dementrius

1. *Gina has dirt in her hand. It's brown dirt.*
2. *Mommy tells Gina to throw it in the wastecan.*
3. *Gina walks to the wastecan. The wastecan is half full.*
4. *Gina looks in and says "yuk" and sees some mold on some bread. The mold is purple.*
5. *There is hair on the mold. Pink hairs.*
6. *On the hair is lice, The lice is orange.*
7. *Gina keeps looking at it. Her eyes are suspicious.*
8. *Finally, Gina says, "He-hello" and the purple mold with the pink hair and the orange lice just sits there in the electric blue garbage can.*
9. *Then Gina gives up and look at something else.*
10. *She looks at some orange peels. The orange peels are brown. They smell like rotten apples.*
11. *On the peel there is an ant. The ant is sick. The ant has a wart on its nose.*
12. *On the wart there is a ameoba, and then the ameoba died because the ant bit the ameoba on the brown and smelly orange peel in the garbage can with the purple mold and the pink hair and the orange lice that Gina was looking at with the brown dirt in her hand.*

David Rebhun

Hubert received a draft notice. He was
1) A strong American who was willing to fight.
2) Scared to go into the army and hated America.

1) Hubert rode to his draft board proud and
3) did not pass his physical
4) passed his physical

2) Hubert was worried to go

    5) so he burned his draft notice and became a conscientious objector
    6) but he went anyway and passed his physical

3) Hubert's pride was hurt and disgraced.
    7) But he pulled himself together and became an ALL AMERICAN CONSTRUCTION MAN.
    8) So he became a rebel

4) Hubert loved army life but when he saw someone spit on the flag he died of disgust.

5) Hubert went to court and did not have to go to the army on the basis of him being a conscientious objector.

6) Hubert was captured by the enemies and told them all he knew. Then he was killed.

7) Yes, Hubert was there when all those good American construction workers rioted those radical students. He was hit over the head with a wrench. He did not die but he became a radical.

8) Yes, Hubert was there when all those nasty American construction workers were there. He got hit over the head with a wrench and became a construction worker.

                      Gina Dementrius

Laurie was in an orphanage and she was about to get adopted by some mean people. So she had to decide what to do.
    1) To run away
    2) To get adopted and then run away from the people.

1) She ran away and met her brother who had now become a millionaire and took her to his house and lived happily ever after.

2) She ran away that night from the people, but their dog bit her on the leg. She had to decide what to do.
    3) To arouse the people.
    4) She could let the dog eat her.

3) She aroused the people and they locked her in her room ever since.

4) She let the dog eat her and was put in the hospital and her brother was her doctor and he took her home and they lived happily ever after.

                      Sue Kennedy

I was going to Palisades when:
1. George Washington fell into the toilet bowl.
2. Abe Lincoln burped.
3. My teacher fainted.
I was astonished. I went back to the car when my dad could not:
1. Start the car
2. Go to get the gas because he broke his leg being a Sunday driver.
3. Use the car.
So I walked through:
1. N.Y.C.
2. The dessert.
3. Alabama.
I was tired.

                      The End

I got up to go to school. I ate breakfast and went to school on the way:
1. Someone was throwing milk out the window
2. My friend burped
3. They were having a snowball fight.
And I fainted.
In school we:
1. Played checkers
2. Played chess
3. Played soccer.
And I won.
When we were coming home I saw:
1. A game of baseball
2. A game of hockey
3. A boy eating popcorn.
And that's what happened:
1. Today
2. Yesterday
3. The day before that.

                      The End

1. Is this the end?
2. This is the end.
3. Is that all?

                      Berny the Great
                      Bernadette Fife

Irving was getting out of prison in 15 days, and it wasn't too soon. He had been arrested for juggling the books of his snowshoe business. All of a sudden he was approached by Masher Sheinbaum who informed him about plans for a break. Will Irving
1) go along
2) figure that he has such a short time left, that He'll tell Scheinbaum to get out
3) tell the warden

1) Irving agreed and slowly walked off with Masher. After a while, he was supplied with a spear. He ran down the corridor with it down his pants leg. He suddenly tripped and the spear thrust up into his stomach. He slowly toppled over and died.

2) Irving murmered "very interesting," and slowly started down the hall. He was ushered back into his cell at the next clang of the bell. When he next woke up the break was all ready started. His door was open and he wandered out into the tear gas filled corridor. All of a sudden, a burst of machine gun fire cut across his side as he toppled forward and died.

3) He rushed into the warden's office and told him all about it. When he got outside a spear hit him in the stomach and he toppled forward and died.

Nayland Blake

Sue is in the bath tub.
1) She could drown
2) She could get out and dry

1) She's laying there. Her mother and father walk in and pump the water out of her. The next day she is buried.
3) She could come alive again
4) She could rot and turn to bones

2) She would stand up, get out, put the towel over her and rub herself dry.
5) She could get towel cloth all over her
6) She could get an infection from rubbing too hard.

3) The next day she would dig herself out of the coffin, and out of the ground, go to her mother and be alive again.
7) She could get hit by a car while going home
8) She could make it home safely and her mother would scream.

4) She would rot in a few days, her bones would lie there like only her bones were buried.
9) Archeologists could find them and they would be a great help to history
10) They could stay there and the worms would chew them. Then they would all be gone.

David Rebhun

From the General to the Specific

by Karen Hubert

Imagine someone in a place, or someone doing something. Like the zoom lens on a camera, or like a microscope, begin to move in closer to see what's happening, and as you do, write about smaller and more specific details.

STARTING A LAWNMOWER

Reaching down, down, down
spreading out my fingers
encircling the string
closing the fingers
pulling back
stretching
opening my fingers
letting go
pulling away
room ! rooom!

Joe Dericco

The old man standing like a
lifeless statue, slowly bent over
like a piece of rubber,
his arms dangling in the air.
His legs are being bent like a
coiled spring. He aimed carefully
reaching for the quarter which lay
on the weather-beaten concrete
sidewalk. His large hands grasped
the quarter. He sprung up like
a growing seed. He dropped it
in his blue-gray pant pocket.

Junji Takeshita

YAWN
Gently opening with a sucking breeze,
Growing in size, growing in sound
It reaches height like a
Cave on a hill,
Closing, closing and a wind coming out.

Ron Jorgenson

A PERSON YELLING

He sits and thinks, should I yell or shouldn't I?
Would people laugh? Would I use any energy?
Do I have bad breath? He thinks and thinks, and
slowly
draws a deep breath and then lets it out. Then
thinks again. Then he takes a deep breath
and YELLS!

Sylett Strickland

THE COMB

The fingers get hold on the comb.
Now slowly the hand moves till at the top.
Now the many plowers will plow the wheat
of honey until it is plowed. It will take many
back & forths. Always starting at the top,
then silently going down.
Till it is neat, the person will not give
up.
The plowers will plow till the
master
thinks it is done.

Rita Sardana

Slowly she brought her finger tip
closer to her
mouth.
As her teeth gnawed and
bit down like
a beaver slowly gnawing on
a tree.
She looked like a lion grabbing
his prey, by
sneaking up and . . . 'gotcha!'

Cindy Logan

Dictation

by Karen Hubert

Some students can't or won't write. They are not ready for the writing process, for reasons which may range from poor skills to a miserable mood on one given day. Dictation is made for such students, and such moods. In dictation, the teacher functions as a secretary taking down the words and sentences of the student. The student speaks, and the teacher writes down as *exactly* as possible what is said. Dictation may be done with one student, a "problem" student, a small group, or an entire class. It is one of the teacher's most valuable tools for expanding students' interests in writing. The thinking and talking processes are faster than the writing process. The hand simply does not move as fast as the thought process (the inner voice) or the spoken voice. Dictation allows students to write as fast as their mouths and minds will let them. They are not hampered by hands, which often make mistakes that must be erased and corrected. Usually students are inspired and encouraged by the sheer length of what they have produced by dictating, something much longer than what they are capable of writing by hand. If executed properly, dictation often leads to further, independent writing by your students.

The process of dictation lends itself to indulgence in language; the students may bathe in their own language, for there are no hand restrictions slowing them down. Sometimes, to get at more richness of student imagination and experience, the teacher taking dictation might ask the student questions. The teacher here is functioning as a reader-audience, and as such has the right to express curiosity. It is best, however, that questions be limited to those concerning detail: What color eyes does X have? How does X feel? What is X wearing? What does the room look like? And so forth.

A key to dictation lies in being able to ask the right question at the right time. The questions should open your student up to the possibilities of further descriptions of character, place, physical expression, emotional state, and even point of view. Ask your students how they feel about what is happening in the story, how their characters feel about what is happening. The teacher ought not press for answers if the student has no interest in giving any. Teachers should also restrain themselves from influencing the direction of the plot (if a story is being dictated). Dictation is a process that yields rich results but requires great control on the part of the teacher, for so powerful is the act of handwriting a story that it is possible and easy to forget that the story belongs to the student. And don't worry, usually your hand *will* move as fast as your student's voice, or almost as fast. Besides, there's no law that says you can't ask the student to slow down a moment, or to wait a second until you finish the last sentence, or even to repeat a phrase for you.

You needn't worry, either, about your student becoming completely dependent upon you to write. You can, in fact, hand the pencil back to the student. Sit with your students as they prepare to write. Let them voice, or compose, sentences one by one and verbally give them to you to "hold." "Hold" the sentence in your memory, or jot it down on paper. Then if in the process of their own writing they forget part of what they composed, they can ask you for it.

Another approach that effects the transition from teacher dictation to student writing is to let your students copy over, in their own hand, some portion (their choice) of the writing you have already taken down. Don't expect to make this transition in a day or even a week. Gear it to the individual student. Use your sensitivity to their readiness to reclaim their pencils, and the degree to which they want to use them.

D. Writing and Literature

New Proverbs

by Alan Ziegler

Every kid has heard—probably to the point of tedium—that "an apple a day keeps the doctor away," or "you can't have your cake and eat it." I discussed proverbs (or "sayings") with the children, asking them for examples of proverbs they had heard; we talked about what they mean, and how they say a lot in a few words (one of the ingredients of good poetry). I mentioned how we've heard some proverbs so many times that we don't even listen to them anymore or think about how their words form a message—just like we don't stop to think that an earring is a "ring for an ear." I said that perhaps it was time to get some new proverbs into the language; but first I would read them some proverbs they had never heard before.

In the early 1790s, William Blake wrote the "Proverbs of Hell," some of which are:

The cut worm forgives the plow.
A fool sees not the same tree that
    a wise man sees.
The bush bee has no time for sorrow.
All wholesome food is caught without a net
    or a trap.
The road to excess leads to the palace of wisdom.
Drive your cart and your plow over the bones
    of the dead.
No bird soars too high, if he soars with
    his own wings.

More than a century later, two young French surrealist poets—Paul Eluard (who edited a magazine called *Proverbe*) and Benjamin Péret—collaborated on 152 proverbs, which Bill Zavatsky translated and published in his magazine *Roy Rogers*. Here are a batch of their surrealist proverbs:

Elephants are contagious.
Sleep that is singing makes the shadows tremble.
Whoever moves disappears.
A crab by any other name won't forget the sea.
Animals don't need stitches.
The sun doesn't shine for anyone.
When the road is done, do it again.
I came, I sat down, I left.
Dance rules over a white forest.
You've read everything but drunk nothing.

I asked the students to work on their own proverbs. I said they could either make sense or be nonsense; if they wanted, they could just write things down off the top of their heads. I explained that sometimes words that seem to come from the "top" of our heads really come from deeper down; and when you think about them for awhile, a meaning comes from them—as in some of the surrealist proverbs.

They had fun and were able to turn out a lot of good stuff in a short time; then they loved hearing what their classmates had done. Writing proverbs gives them a sense that certain combinations of words have particular rhythms to them: certain phrases *sound* like proverbs, with a mysterious, authoritative air to them. Also, it was interesting to see the sense of ethics that emerged from many of them.

Here's the "Book of Proverbs," new sayings by fourth graders at P.S. 11 in Brooklyn:

A magic touch brings happiness.
Love is four letters of magic.
A lady is shady and men go crazy.
Get together parents you never know what may happen.
Junkies are full of junk, winos are full of wine, but
I'm full of pride.
Smell a bull it's nothing but bull.
What you don't have in a page of proverbs.

                                        Lisa

Thou who sleeps away keeps away.
When you jump, you will land with a big fat bump.
If you eat a bloom, you will lose your shoe.
If you are dead, you can go to bed.

                                        Robert

If you talk a lot, you'll get it.
If you have a big mouth, you should sew it up.
Pig is making jig on fig.

                                        Lionel

If you're in the snow, watch your toes.
One who knows the alphabet should try for the numbers.
Whoever disappears moves.
Crabs don't care for Santa Claus.
If you don't have any money, you won't have a honey.
No boat will drown you.
If you can't paint, try to draw.
If you can't fight, take off your shoe.

                                        Jordan

Thou who can't fight, shouldn't start.
He who starts, should get punished.
He who discovers something is rich.
The sword can cut the pen.
If you step on something, it will die.
Love will keep everybody together.
If you don't love animals,
    you don't love your parents.

                                        Kenneth

When you cry, the cat dies—
    when you yell, the sand falls—
when you make the pie, the pan cries.

See a pearl eat the pearl,
    then you will have a marble head.
If you have a toothpick, lick it.
The table and chair had a walk in the park.

                                        Sonia

He who knows nothing, must learn to know.
He who knows how to fight
    mustn't start too much trouble.
A mouse a day, keeps the elephant away.
A mouse needs a house.
He who needs help must ask for it.

                                        Jesse

A skunk a day keeps the people away.
If you are dead, you are a stick.
If you're a crab, you're a crab.

                                        Norman

A trap a day keeps the mouse away.
Money is your only thing to get in trouble with.
Bees and trees go with sunny.

                                        Shawn

When you are dead,
    your skeleton guards your body.
If you don't love your parents,
    you don't love anyone.
If your seed is not planted deep enough,
    the crow will snatch it away.
If you feel happy in your heart,
    the snow will melt.
Fruit keeps a tree growing.

                                        Thomas

And here are some new takes on "An apple a day keeps the doctor away," from fourth- and fifth-graders at Atlantic Avenue School in Lynbrook, New York:

An apple a day with a worm in it
    keeps the doctor coming.

A wax apple a day keeps the doctor in pay.

Chocolate keeps the teeth away.

An onion a day will keep everyone away.

A boat a day keeps the ocean awake.

150

Class "Orchestrations" of Pantoums

by Alan Ziegler

A pantoum is a Malay form of poetry consisting of four-line stanzas; the second and fourth lines of each stanza automatically become the first and third lines of the following stanza. The poem may be ended after any number of stanzas (four is a good length). The last stanza virtually writes itself: its first and third lines are, of course, the second and fourth lines of the preceding stanza; and the last stanza's second and fourth lines are the first and third lines of the *first* stanza (which are the only lines of the poem that have not yet been repeated).

Sounds complicated, but once you get the numbers down it's an easy form to work in; after the first four lines, you have a headstart on each stanza. It makes for a good class collaboration: Ask for a line and write it on the board. Then get three more lines and you're off and running on a pantoum. The role of the teacher is to "orchestrate" the poem: in doing the following pantoums with children, I sometimes combined two lines that were yelled out simultaneously. Other times I would take a suggested line and ask another child to change it a little. I also tried to keep some sense of continuity in the poem (a continuity of images, rather than plot).

Pantoums help establish a sense of "the line"—a grouping of words that has its own space on the page. Let the kids share in making the decisions of which lines should go into the poem, which lines should be modified, and which lines should not be used. It's a good, fun group process.

ATLANTIS

I got off the submarine in Atlantis
The people looked like pens
Moby Dick is the watch-whale
Mermaids sing in the opera

The people looked like pens
A catfish was chasing a dogfish
Mermaids sing in the opera
Aaron Burr and Alexander Hamilton were
dueling with swordfishes

A catfish was chasing a dogfish
The flounders were surfing on sea-boards
Aaron Burr and Alexander Hamilton were
dueling with swordfishes
I was sea-seeing this strange city

The flounders were surfing on sea-boards
I got off the submarine in Atlantis
I was sea-seeing this strange city
Moby Dick is the watch-whale

Grade-4
Atlantic Avenue School
Lynbrook, N.Y.

PANTOUM

I am kneeling on the floor and my pen ran out
The rain came down on me
An instrument that plays by itself
Where am I going?

The rain came down on me
I want to go home
Where am I going?
I got up this morning and brushed my teeth

I want to go home
I seem to be lost
I got up this morning and brushed my teeth
I had a hard day

I seem to be lost
I am kneeling on the floor and my pen ran out
I had a hard day
An instrument that plays by itself

Class Collaboration
Valley Stream Central High School
April 4,1974

Teaching Great Literature to Children, or Willis's Stories from Dante

by Sue Willis

It isn't that I really expect fourth and fifth graders to read *The Divine Comedy*, but I am reading it for the first time and enjoying it tremendously. In the middle of *The Purgatorio*, where it becomes increasingly necessary to consult footnotes and feel scholarly, I began to think back to *The Inferno*. What a terrific adventure story! I decided to tell it to Robin Rubinger's class. Last year I had some success telling *The Canterbury Tales* to some of the same children. Children *like* storytelling. The telling is, of course, a personal style, but some of the passages suggested below I read to the children, and they shushed one another to listen.

I used John Ciardi's good translation of Dante's poem. Ciardi uses rhyme in a very natural, attractive style. On the board I wrote the words Heaven, Purgatory, Hell, also Inferno, Purgatorio, Paradiso. One boy, Derrick, really liked that word "Purgatory" for some reason.

I began with Dante in the dark wood, confronting the beasts of Fraud, Violence, and Incontinence—the Leopard, Lion and She-wolf. Dante is in despair, has lost the one he loves, etc. (you see there is a strong plot to the *Comedy*), and is met by Virgil who was sent, of course, by the lady from heaven, Dante's departed beloved. Before you go up to joy, says Virgil, you have to go down. And down they go.

Abandon Hope, All Ye Who Enter Here. Hell as the place of no hope. "I know where I heard of that before," says Caroline. "My mother has that written on the refrigerator. . . ."

We have a great discussion of issues of the Protestant Reformation: the edge of Hell, the virtuous pagans, and Limbo. Why are they in Hell if they didn't do anything wrong? A lot of indignation. Why can't they walk out like Dante walks out? In Canto III, ll. 61-66 describe the river Acheron and the souls lined up to get into Hell. In Canto V, there is the pathetic story of the lovers, Paolo and Francesca, who were reading a love story and became enflamed and fornicated—"We didn't read anymore that afternoon," says Francesca. Canto VI, ll. 10-20, presents the gluttons and their torturer, Cerberus, with his three heads. Some kids began to recognize certain figures from mythology. There follow various punishments for the violent—rivers of boiling blood, etc. Far

too many punishments, so I chose particularly vivid ones. The wood of the suicides (Canto XIII, ll. 31-43) especially gives a poignant picture: the suicides turned into trees, only speaking when a branch is broken off, and then words of blood flow from the wound.

I stopped there and gave as a writing assignment a trip to heaven or hell, or some ideas of proper punishments for certain sins. A number of children illustrated their writings in colorful detail, for *The Inferno* is a poem filled with colorful, powerful images.

When I came to the class the following week, I brought with me a bad translation that included some illustrations by Gustave Doré, the great nineteenth century French artist. To see what images had stuck, I called for a group-writing of the story so far:

When he broke the tree and the people came
and started talking and blood came pouring out.
The lovers floating around and hugging
The gluttons and the dog
Sea of blood with Hitler
Those trees . . .
Beautiful lady on a boat
That tiger lion and wolf
When he steps on the boat it goes down
and it doesn't for them
Ice cream cone with rings
The angel Virgil
Shivering people
The bees and wasps
Everyone floating
That sign:
ABANDON HOPE ALL YE WHO ENTER HERE

I continued with more readings, more discussion. The plain of burning sand for the violent (Canto XIV, ll. 22-27); Geryon, the monster of Fraud; Dante's spiraling ride down the cliff on his back; the bad priests in holes with fire dancing on their exposed feet; the fortune tellers with their heads wrenched backwards. Canto XXI, especially lines 28-36, shows the grafters in the sticky path and the grotesque clownish demons who caused so much laughter among the kids.

I finished *The Inferno* in this fashion, reading as much as I dared, acting out as much as I wanted, arguing with the children over the unfairness of the practice of damnation. The kids were captured by the brilliance of the images, the vastness of the conception, and were fascinated by the geography—Where is Purgatory? What shape is Hell?

I envision Chaucer and Dante as the answer to the censors and bookburners who don't want salacious twentieth century trash on their school shelves. Revive the exciting, morbid, bloody, sexy, religious classics: Dante, Chaucer, The (gulp!) Bible.

Using There Are Two Lives

by Bill Zavatsky

There Are Two Lives: Poems by Children of Japan, edited by Richard Lewis, translated by Haruna Kimura (Simon and Schuster, New York, 1970, $4.95, hardcover).

To get done with it, I have two complaints about this book. One, it doesn't contain the texts in Japanese. Why complain? Because I've taught in schools with bilingual students who could have read these poems for the class in Japanese, and that would have been quite an experience for all of us. Two, Simon and Schuster's policy of never issuing this—or any of Richard Lewis's other collections of writings by children—in a reasonably priced paperback edition. *There Are Two Lives* has been out for six years. The people at Simon & Schuster should realize that they could be making even more money with a paperback edition. The number of copies that a cheap edition would allow me to *give* away would probably pay for a substantial portion of a first printing!

So much for complaints. This is one of the finest collections of poetry produced by anyone, anytime, ever. Most importantly, it is completely written by children, and sensitively translated. I have been using the book in classrooms since it came out, and the poems in it never fail. Lewis has divided it into six sections—*Family, Play, School, Creatures, Nature,* and *Thoughts*—and the poems range from straight William Carlos Williams-type recordings of daily life to fantasy trips. I have used *There Are Two Lives* in kindergarten classes and with high school juniors. The little kids yell and shout with enlightenment at what their contemporaries have to say to them, and the older students understand the poems immediately. In fact, I have often used one poem to generate forty-minute discussions in "slow" classes. Here it is:

BROTHER

The baby was born.
Every day
when I come home from school
I take care of the baby.
Grandpa says,
"Don't touch it."

I answer him,
"This is my brother."
Grandpa says,
"It's my grandson."
This is our fight.

"Who owns the baby?" That's what I ask the children, and we take off from there into remarkable discussions that revolve around the question, "Who owns you, kid?" In one class we had a subtle argument about the difference between "owns" and "belongs to." If you're a thing, you are owned—like a bicycle. But how do you "belong to" someone? What makes someone belong to you, and vice versa? Parentage? Ah, but do you still "belong to" the daddy who walks out on you? Or do you "belong to" the man across the street who always talks with you and listens to your problems and sometimes takes you to the zoo with his own kids? Does ownership have anything to do with love? What about the mother who yells at a child and always makes him feel awful? Does that child "belong to" her? When your parents get a divorce, who "gets" you? All this, and much much more, has come out of an eleven-line poem written by Ikenaga Tomoymi, who put this down on paper at the age of seven.

Often we just talk about poems. The "Family" section is inexhaustible in this respect. The poems are short enough and clear enough for even the youngest children to grasp after two or three readings, but you'll want to have copies of the texts you're using ready to distribute, for the poems serve as excellent models for free-verse composition. Discussion of the poems can begin, on the earliest level, a basic "analysis" of literary texts. What happens in the poems can be discussed, as well as the words the young Japanese poets have chosen (but don't forget for a minute that you're dealing with a translation!). Students will begin to understand that a very important source of poetry is their own lives, that nothing is too "insignificant" to write about. An important family tug-of-war over who takes care of the baby can make a good poem. "Is there anything that happens in this poem that makes you think of something that happens in your own family?" I ask the kids. "Write about it!" As often happens in discussions, the students will sometimes jump the track and begin introducing ideas that are simply *not* in the poem under consideration. When this happens, we read the poem again. (I usually call on several students to reread the poem during our discussion, and after hearing it as many as ten times, most of the kids have memorized it by the end of the class period.) Repetition has definite benefits, though the memorization-as-a-form-of-punishment routine that was popular in education not so many years ago can only lead to a hate of poetry. For example, I'll never forget how nonplussed I was by the high school junior who laughed and blurted the "Brother" poem out to me one dreary December morning before class started, this from a member of a group of poor readers and writers, and at a moment when I thought that nothing I had done was getting through to them.

Occurrences like this reaffirm one of my most cherished notions, that the poetry best suited for children is poetry *written* by children. "Children's verse" of adult manufacture is usually the worst junk, cutesy-wootsy beyond any decent poet's sitting still. I include the famous Dr. Seuss in this category. I have observed a neighbor's daughter learning, from the pages of *The Cat in the Hat*, that poetry *always* rhymes, is *always* goofy, and *never* has anything to do with real life. Why should she believe me when, in five years, I walk into her classroom, the Visiting Poet, and tell her just the opposite? Parents want to be entertained, too. Why bother to summon the strength and seriousness necessary to read poems from *There Are Two Lives* to a child, when Dr. Seuss is so much fun? "Children's verse" exists for the edification and entertainment of parents. But the whacky situations and the rhymes and pounding meters reverberate in the growing child long after they have served their purpose. They leave the impression that Poetry is a Never-Never Land where real thinking and human feeling are banished.

For the act of writing a poem is a very special kind of thinking, and the best poetry joins intelligent thought to exciting language. Evidently these young Japanese children have been taught to think, since over and over again in their poetry they seem unafraid to confront their daily life or their fantasies. The tendency in our society is to equate poetry with fantasy. That is what the word "imagination" has come to mean when people speak of poetry: "fantasy." But look at this poem, again from the *Family* section of *There Are Two Lives*, called "Supper":

When I was eating supper,
I dropped some food.
My father scolded me and said,
"It's because you were looking
    the other way."
My younger brother said,

"Yes, it's because you were looking
    the other way."
A few minutes later
my father dropped some food, too.
The whole house became dead silent.

                Ashibe Yoshiaki, Age 9

I leave to the reader's imagination the discussions that this poem can provoke. I asked one class of students to write a poem based on this one, about funny things that happen in their own household. One little boy in the fourth grade wrote about how he always had supper alone in his room. Daddy comes home, he wrote, and mommy and daddy like to have supper together, so I have supper every night alone in my room upstairs. "I like to have supper alone in my room," was the last line of the poem. I wish I could quote all of it, but the poem was considered too harmful for the boy's parents to read, and once I made the mistake of turning it over to the authorities, I never saw it again. If this isn't an example of the prevalent attitude toward poetry in our schools—that it is not about real things, that it should not tell the truth—then nothing is. I often think about that little boy, his lonely suppers, and what his parents might have learned about what they were doing to him if they had had the opportunity to read his poem, a poem that was not a protest, not an act of anger, but a simple record of fact.

There are so many remarkable pieces of work in *There Are Two Lives* that it pleases me to give in to another of my favorites, one of which (from the *Play* section) is "The Candle's Light":

I took a bath.
The candle's light on the water
moved like a snake.
When I stirred the water
the light crawled into the water.
I stirred the water again.
Then the snake of the light
curled around my leg.
I put out the candle.
It became completely dark
like the time they showed the movie.

                Nakamura Akinori, Age 8

If this is "play," let us have more of it! The similes in this poem (candle light = snake in water; darkness of bathtub = darkness of movie theater) are those which we traditionally associate with the "imagination," but without the close observation of reality so characteristic of the Japanese intelligence, that "imagination" could not flourish into metaphor. For me this poem called up the magic of early bubble baths, when I pretended that the mounds of crystally froth were icebergs or banks of fog through which I carefully (or tragically) had to navigate my toy boats. Until I read this poem, that important playtime of my childhood remained submerged. Reading poems such as this can resensitize children and adults to their world. Dr. Seuss represents a kind of packaging of the imagination; when the story is over, we can cease being "imaginative." But this kind of poem is open-ended, and can lead its reader anywhere. Most of all, it can lead young readers to realize that the stuff of poetry exists all around them, in their simplest activities, at every given moment.

The more fantastic poems in *There Are Two Lives*, dispersed throughout the book, always focus on something seen a million times. "Lily" begins with observation, journeys deep into the imagination, then brings us back to the world of our senses:

As I watched a lily
it became a cave.

Outside it was white,
inside it was shining.
As I went into the cave
there was a door.
As I opened the door
there was a water pool.
Water of the camellia
tastes good.
What is the taste
of
the lily's water?

Kuriowa Harumi, Age 10

Simplicity, clarity, and an absence of "prettified" literary language (which the most talented kids pick up all too fast and confuse with poetry)—all of these elements characterize the poems in *There Are Two Lives*, which I consider to be the best of all Richard Lewis's anthologies for children. It is nothing less than a rulebook for the poetic art.

Toward an Intelligent Use of Rhyme: A Sketch

by Bill Zavatsky

Poets working in the schools have banished rhyme from the art of poetry—at least for the time being. *Why?* ask the teachers. *How come I can't rhyme?* the students demand. And on the receiving end of this barrage, the poet too eventually asks himself: *Why?*

There are good reasons *why not*. Though most children find it simple (and fun) to rhyme along, most of the poetry they produce when rhyming is markedly inferior to their free-verse efforts. There is an easy answer that explains this. While it is relatively easy to find like-sounding words, most children lack the wherewithal to put them to work. Their rhymed poems generally become vehicles for the cliché, the pre-formed sentiment, the icky (but acceptable) sentimentality: "I will be good/ The way a boy should," etc. Left to his own few resources, the child almost inevitably seizes on whatever hackneyed expressions pour into his mind. After all, it is the making of the rhyme that's important, and all those useless other words that lead up to it seem so much stuffing to fill up the coming surprise. The sweet flavor of the end-words sustains the child's attention at the expense of anything real.

The reason for this attitude is easy to pin down. Most of us regard rhyme as an ornamental device, a cluster of pleasant sounds. For many of us, rhyme *is* poetry; and there can be no poetry without it. Unfortunately some poets have the opposite attitude, and clutch their ears in terror at the faintest hint of rhyme. Both attitudes—Rhyme as Institution and Rhyme as Corniness, Inc.—don't bring us any nearer to an appreciation of the virtues of rhyme and how we can rescue it for intelligent classroom use. I am not going to elaborate a major exegesis of rhyme here; what I intend to do is set a few things straight about its use, and hope that I can pique the interest of both teachers and poets.

Just as the "form" of a poem is a kind of rhyme of structure, so the comparison is a type of rhyme in thought, through which the poet attempts to see the likenesses (the rhyming quality) in different things. When Robert Burns wants to tell us what his girl-friend rhymes with, he compares her to a "red, red rose." Like the comparison, then, rhyme is another weapon in the arsenal of a person who is attempting to see the world as a whole—this time *hearing* it as a source of endless harmony. This hearing, however, is a sensual form of thinking; for though it is like-sounds that draw two words together in rhyme, these words mean—they have a history, a denotation, a connotative response in each of us.

If, for example, I think of the words "red" and "head," I can think of a person with red hair. I can also imagine someone who has been struck a blow that has drawn blood from the head. I could produce two different sets of rhyming lines:

1. The color of her hair was red
   and flamed around her head.

2. Everything he saw turned red
   as blood poured down his head.

This kind of rhyme is known as *direct rhyme*: the words have exactly the same sounds—red/head. But let's say I don't think the rhymes I've come up with are very interesting. Another type of rhyme can help me here, *off-rhyme*. In off-rhyme (sometimes known as *indirect rhyme* or *feminine rhyme*) the words have similar but not exact sounds. My word "red" in this case could rhyme with "reed" or "road" or "rod" or "rid," or I could rhyme it with words of two syllables or more: "carried," "borrowed," etc. I might then get:

1. The color of her hair was red
   as the apple that she carried.

Not great poetry—true. But it will be immediately evident that by using off-rhyme the horizons of thought open to the poem have extended infinitely. There are only so many words that rhyme directly with "red." By introducing off-rhyme, we multiply the possibilities of what can be written about. A good exercise—perhaps done with the aid of any good rhyming dictionary—would be to pick a word like "red" and then write a poem in which it is rhymed, directly or indirectly, for as long as the student can keep it up:

The color of her hair was red
as the apple that she carried

down the old river road.
The apple had been borrowed
from her best friend, Rod
(he was skinny as a reed!)
and she was hoping to get rid
of it etc.

Poems such as this may be extremely artificial, but the point is to achieve a wider understanding of the potentials involved in rhyme.

Emily Dickinson and W.H. Auden mastered the off-rhyme, and for examples of it their works furnish a veritable hornbook. This poem is not one of Dickinson's many masterpieces, but it will furnish a fine example of her subtle off-rhyming:

When Night is almost done—
And Sunrise grows so near
That we can touch the Spaces—
It's time to smooth the Hair—

And get the Dimples ready—
And wonder we could care
For that old—faded Midnight—
That frightened—but an Hour—

In the first stanza, "near" and "Hair" are off-rhymes. The "care" of stanza two rhymes directly with the "Hair" of line four. And in the second stanza, "care" and "Hour" compose another set of off-rhymes.

Another exercise: pick a series of rhymes, direct and indirect (you can use the end-words of any poem you want, or a random list of words). Be sure to avoid corny moon/June rhymes. Make clear to the students that these rhymes must come at the end of each line. They can rhyme the words in couplets (red/head; jump/dump) or by using an ababcdcd-type structure (red/jump/head/dump etc.). This is also a good exercise to develop a sense of the poetic line.

Notes on the Poetic Line

by Bill Zavatsky

A dry topic? Hardly. In most of the poetry workshops I've given, one of the central problems I and the teachers have faced is how to impart a sense of when to stop writing one line of poetry and begin writing the next.

Technically, poets refer to this procedure as "breaking the line." And the point at which the line is broken is called the "line-break." Some of the suggestions below are designed to answer the questions, "Where, and for what reasons, is the poetic line broken?"

I

The problem of the line-break is peculiar to unrhymed or "free" verse. In poetry that is rhymed, the solution is obvious: the line is stopped when one reaches what will become a rhyme-word:

Let us go then, you and I,
When the evening is spread out against the sky

> T.S. Eliot
> "The Love Song of J.
> Alfred Prufrock"

In an unrhymed poetry, the doors of possibility are thrown open; and it is predominantly unrhymed verse that the poets of our time have written. Why rhyme began to be abandoned in poetry after the turn of the century is a complex literary and historical question that cannot be fully developed here, but I would like to suggest one fertile line of thinking about the problem. I do so because many teachers have asked me exactly this question, and have shown themselves to be so ill at ease with unrhymed verse that I have been forced to search for answers.

Rhyme isn't just a pleasant sound device, it is a way of comprehending life. All of us would like our own lives to "rhyme," and when they don't, well, we find ourselves confronted with a situation similar to that felt by a number of poets at the beginning of the century. From Homer through the eighteenth century, most poets owed their bed and board to a patron, usually a member of the nobility; or they were of the nobility themselves (Sir Phillip Sidney), and between wars and court intrigues found diversion in literary composition. In a world ruled by kings who, in the Great Chain of Being, were only one step below God in the system of command, rhyme expressed nothing less than the order and balance of the Universal Will. (Homer doesn't rhyme, of course, and neither does Anglo-Saxon verse; but there is no space here to go into the influence that Continental models had on the growth of English poetry.)

With the rise of the democracies beginning in the eighteenth century, monarchy and rhyme began to be subjected to a series of shocks from which they will never recover. If every man was his own king and each home a castle, it would eventually follow that poetry could be made to serve individual rather than courtly ends. Our own Walt Whitman, who sang the "simple, separate person," was the first poet in history to write in a line that dropped both rhyme and distinct meter. The growth of industrialism, with its attendant middle class, and the development of scientific disciplines in the nineteenth century were instrumental in delivering the *coup de grace* to rhyme as the signal mode of poetic expression. (Remember that Charles Darwin would revolutionize human thought by pitting his theory of evolution against the religious doctrine of direct creation.) The doctrine of "human perfectability" and its handmaiden, Progess, that calmed the tempest of the nineteenth century at its close would spiral into the nightmare of World War I, after which poets (and many who had lived through it) found it impossible to agree with Robert Browning's earlier sentiment that "God's in his heaven—/ All's right with the world." (*Pippa Passes*) The chilling vision at the conclusion of Matthew Arnold's "Dover Beach" seemed to prophesy the twentieth century much more accurately, where the world

Hath really neither joy, nor love, nor light,
Nor certitude, nor peace, nor help for pain;
And we are here as on a darkling plain
Swept with confused alarms of struggle and flight,
Where ignorant armies clash by night.

In the wake of the First World War, the divine order of things that rhyme expressed so perfectly, the sweet sonority of existence at equilibrium, were buried in the same vast sepulchre that was to house the "Death of God." With notable exceptions—Frost, Auden, and Robert Lowell, to name a few—it is the flexibility of "free verse" that has come to serve the new vision of reality that Einstein's theory of relativity has proven even more shot with chance than we care to imagine.

II

Let me emphasize that there is no simple solution to the problem of the line-break. It takes most poets years of intensive study and practice of their art to skillfully break lines. Finally such an artistic decision becomes a matter of second nature, in the same way that a baseball player doesn't have to remember how to hold the bat when he comes to the plate. Line-breaking decisions are also rooted in extremely personal factors—nothing less than how one sees the world, as I have tried to suggest in my little historical aside. Walt Whitman's sweeping line derived from the King James Bible and the Vedic Upanishads.

> A child said, What is the grass? fetching it to me
>   with full hands;
> How could I answer the child? . . . I do not know
>   what it is any more than he.
>
> I guess it must be the flag of my disposition, out of
>   hopeful green stuff woven.
>
> Or I guess it is the handkerchief of the Lord,
> A scented gift and remembrancer designedly
>   dropped,
> Bearing the owner's name someway in the corners,
>   that we may see and remark, and say Whose?

> From *Leaves of Grass*

Song of Myself is quite different from the terse, tense line that the contemporary poet Robert Creeley has developed in his work:

THE SIGN BOARD

The quieter the people are
the slower the time passes

until there is a solitary man
sitting in the figure of silence.

Then scream at him,
come here you idiot it's going to go off.

A face that is no face
but the features, of a face, pasted

on a face until that face
is faceless, answers by

a being nothing there
where there was a man.

> From *For Love, Poems 1950-1960*

Whitman's lines advance across the page, often filling it margin to margin, and (as above) some of them even resemble short paragraphs rather than what we are accustomed to calling lines of poetry.

Having recognized that there is no one poetic line in free verse, no "right way" or "wrong way" to break lines, let me proceed to a general discussion of two sources of the line, and then to a series of exercises and forms that will be useful in developing a sense of line.

III

We might divide the sources of line-break into two categories: body or sound (the muscial quality), and mind or thought (which includes the visual or sculptural sense).

Sound is the first guide in breaking lines. And because sound is allied to breath or phrasing, we are here dealing with the physical (or physiological) aspect of the line-break. Here, one's breath, the pulse of one's own heart, suggests where one line is to end and a new one begin. The rule follows from what is comfortably spoken, what sounds right as a line. When Ezra Pound suggested that poets compose in the sequence of the musical phrase, and not by the beat of the metronome, he must have been thinking along this direction (see his *ABC of Reading*, New Directions paperback). After all, to force our breath and our heartbeat which sometimes fluctuate drastically as they register the ups and downs of our emotional state into a rigid meter is a kind of self-betrayal, unless of course the poet genuinely "feels" that meter. My argument in section I of this essay is precisely that, for the majority of poets writing now, these meters are no longer "felt." Probably the most useful question in determining line length by this method is, Does the line sound as if it should end here? The number of syllables, the tone, the pace of the line as it is written, spoken aloud, or recited internally all contribute to the decision.

Sight is the second criterion. For most poets, the "look" of the line is extremely important. If we can say that the sound of the line involves musical elements, sight suggests visual or sculptural aspects. Does the line "look" right? Does it "seem" too short, or too long? If so, how should it be altered?

Once again I want to emphasize that these decisions are extremely personal and become instinctive after wide reading and practice. The rubrics of "sound" and "sight" that I have set up above are not only open to criticism, they are open to drastic modification. These are, I repeat, rules of thumb only. There are no rules.

IV

Below are some suggestions which should help your students develop a sense of line in poetry without using rhyme. (For a few ideas that can aid in the development of rhyme, see my "Toward an Intelligent Use of Rhyme" in this book.)

1. *Line as complete thought*: Suggest to your students that they end a line when an idea is completed:

   I saw him running down the street

2. *Phrase as line*: Lines can be broken after phrase-units:

   In the night
   when everything is quiet
   I watch the headlights
   of the cars
   moving along the wall
   of my room

3. *Lines that surprise or mislead*: Here the idea is to pull the rug out from under the reader via the line-break:

   I danced all night at the ball
   Bearing factory
       (Example by Ron Padgett)

   I love everybody in the world
   except you

4. *Formula poems*: Poems in which each line begins with the same words—"I remember . . .," "In the middle of the night . . . "

5. *Poems with rules for each line*: Certain requirements, decided upon in advance or made up as the poem progresses, must be fulfilled in each line of the poem. For example, a poem in which each line must contain a) a historical character; b) a tool; c) a color. (See Kenneth Koch's *Wishes, Lies and Dreams*, Vintage Books paperback, for poems written in this fashion.)

6. *The collaborative poem*: Two or more poets take turns writing alternate lines.

7. *The alliterative line*: Used in Anglo-Saxon poetry and by later practitioners such as W.H. Auden, this line generally contains four major accented words or syllables, all of which begin with the same letter:

   The *d*ay of his *d*eath was a *d*ark cold *d*ay
       W.H. Auden, "In Memory of W.B. Yeats"

8. *The pantoum*: A poem with a specific form (i.e., with fixed rules). The pantoum is written in quatrains (stanzas of four lines each). The first step is for the poet to write the first quatrain. After that, almost like a multiplication exercise, the rest of the pantoum practically "writes itself."

   1. Over the river and through the woods
   2. A teenager flew like a dart.
   3. The anxious sky was bluer than blue,
   4. The sun spread the leaves with its hands.

Having just written what is admittedly not the greatest quatrain in the history of poetry, let's move on to stanza two—half of which (believe it or not!) is already written. To make the second stanza, take lines 2 and 4 of stanza one and make them lines 1 and 3 of stanza two. Punctuation can be changed, but not the words in the lines:

   1. A teenager flew like a dart
   2.
   3. The sun spread the leaves with its hands
   4.

To finish stanza two, write two original lines for the empty spaces (lines 2 and 4):

   1. A teenager flew like a dart,
   2. So fast the birds couldn't see.
   3. The sun spread the leaves with its hands.
   4. "Why did you run away?" he cried.

Stanza three is constructed the same way as stanza two. Lines 2 and 4 of stanza two become lines 1 and 3 of the new third stanza, and two new lines must be written to fill in the blanks:

   1. So fast the birds couldn't see,
   2. A girl's arms flashed in the sun.
   3. "Why did you run away?" he cried
   4. To her. He was such a creep.

We'll conclude our masterpiece with stanza four, though by following the rules for stanzas two and three (lines 2 and 4 become 1 and 3) the poem can go on indefinitely. I suggest the four stanza pantoum for beginners because four stanzas won't try your student's patience and turn an enjoyable experiment into a horrible chore, and because four stanzas are enough to grasp the mechanics of the pantoum.

Before we begin—or rather, end—ask yourself which lines in the poem haven't yet come into play. Hint: look at the first stanza. We've used lines 2 and 4 of the first stanza, but haven't touched lines 1 and 3. Let's "fill in the blanks" of the last stanza—then watch the fun!:

   1. A girl's arms flashed in the sun
   2.
   3. To her. He was such a creep.
   4.

Here's the trick. Go back to stanza one, grab lines 1 and 3, and plug them into the last stanza where they best seem to fit:

1. A girl's arms flashed in the sun
2. Over the river and through the woods.
3. To her, he was such a creep.
4. The anxious sky was bluer than blue.

Notice the change in puctuation in line 3. We could also arrange the last stanza as follows:

1. A girl's arm flashed in the sun.
2. The anxious sky was bluer than blue
3. To her. He was such a creep
4. Over the river and through the woods.

There are probably other, stranger effects that might be gained by further alterations of punctuation, but I rest my case. Besides helping the student gain a stronger sense of the line, the pantoum is great fun. Tell your students they're going to write a sixteen line poem by writing only eight lines, and see what happens.

9. *The sestina*: Another formal poem. This time the student writes six original lines. The end-words of these six lines are retained throughout the seven stanza, 39-line poem (the extra three lines use two of these end-words in each line; the seventh stanza of three lines is called the "tailpiece"). For a complete explanation of the sestina (and the pantoum), see *The Book of Forms* by Lewis Turco (Dutton paperbacks). The sestina is too difficult, in my opinion, for younger students, and may give even sixth graders grief. Save it for older students who have already written poetry for awhile.

10. *The haiku*: A three-line poem that should *not* be used as a syllable-counting machine. See Ron Padgett's and William J. Higginson's pieces on the haiku elsewhere in this volume.

V

My final, and perhaps most important, suggestion is to have your students *read poems*. The devices I have just outlined are no substitutes for seeing poems on the page, for the reading and study of them. The white space that often surrounds the poem on a page is no accident. It is a kind of "breathing space" that involves the eye and the mind, as well as the heartbeat. The white space emphasizes the poem as a whole, and the line as a unit. It allows us to focus more clearly, throwing language into a three-dimensional setting where its qualities, the individual shapes and sounds of words, become more apparent and have more power. Poetry is a kind of experience of experience, and it is only by going directly to the work of a poet that we can "feel" him think and feel. As I have suggested in drawing a comparison between the line-lengths of Whitman and Creeley, part of what is to be learned finds itself expressed by the poet's strategy of line-break.

There are various ancillary questions I have no space to tackle here. One of them concerns the capitalization of lines of poetry: should each line be capitalized or not? My answer: don't worry about it! Some poets capitalize every line, some don't, some do both. Tell this to your students, and encourage them to do whatever feels best to them. That, after all is said and done, is the guiding principle behind the line-break, too.

Haiku

By Ron Padgett

Walking down the hallway of Harlem Road Elementary School in Amherst, N.Y., late fall of 1973, I noticed a bulletin board decorated with Haiku, and a cursory glance confirmed my prejudice—and a confirmation was all I really wanted—that this poetic form has become so badly used by poets and teachers that we'll never be able to get the sugar off it. The monopolization of the Haiku by the miniaturized and excessively adorable world of Nature has taken all the snap out of the form and left it with its rather sticky content.

This is the kind of highfalutin generalizations which were going through my mind as I entered my next class to do a poetry session with the kids. Before the session proper I began to tell the kids what I thought about Haiku: they had all written Haiku themselves and it was in my mind to tell them what I thought. I concluded by saying that I have avoided teaching Haiku like the plague, but, bingo! my contrary self added, "So let's do some now." The kids seemed to appreciate the challenge I had just given myself.

I explained that there were Haiku I liked, and what I liked about them was the way they surprised you sometimes at the end. There would be two lines, usually about nature, and then a final line which at first didn't seem to have anything much to do with the first two lines (I suggested that everyone forget about the syllable count, unless they could write Japanese and were feeling traditional about it. I added, smart aleck that I am, that I figured we could all count to 5 or 7 so we could forget that).

I drew two parallel lines across the board: these were the first two lines of the poem. Make them about nature; make them pretty or nice things about nature. Under these I drew a third line. Make this last line a complete surprise, something that has nothing to do with the first two lines.

My extemporaneous examples doubtlessly gave the kids a strong slant down which they slid into their own poems, and I think that a variety of examples at this point would lend a greater variousness to the results.

Here are some selections from the Haiku written during that class period.

Silent are the trees
blowing in the wind
Donald Duck drowning in Lake Erie

Flowers in the garden
They are beautiful
Time for bed

It's raining out
the rivers overflow
and I'm listening to the radio

Poinsettias in the snow;
Raindrops in the courtyard,
And where is the UFO?

Little red roses
popping out of the ground
a car blowing up

Fluffy clouds in the sky
a soft breeze blowing
Daffy is dead

It is summer
The river is flowing
My friend has blond hair.

The sun shines
My mother weeds the garden
I hate school

The bees are acting up
They're stinging
Merry Christmas

Rainy days are here
It's ten feet deep
Tarzan's in the jungle

Bird playing songs in the park
Sun laying on the grass
3 kids in school

The sun shines over the shingled roof,
The river laughs with pleasure,
Mother Nature hates me.

It's snowing outside
It's also raining
Meanwhile Winnie the Pooh's stomping on cookies

The shimmering sun looking over the brown
    shady green woods
Flowers dancing in the cooling breeze
I have a piano lesson

Sunshine across the street.
Rain across the street.
Boy my house is so big

It's raining at the beach
It's snowing in the parking lot
Donald Duck is crying

Tiny drops of dew
    Landing in tulips
Mom is cooking turkey

Big orange oranges
With blossoms gay
I like chocolate covered doughnuts

Birds chirping
A rabbit squeeking
Bugs Bunny getting a polio shot

Rain is falling down
    Slowly and clear
        A frog goes "ribit"

Birds are in the park
Foxes making dens
Children spilling apple sauce

Sunshine in the courtyard
Snow in the garden
Don't miss the bus!

Rabbit's hopping in the grass,
He went in a hole,
You're washing your hair!

Butterflies in the air,
floating in the breeze,
The plane went down instead of up.

Trees swaying in the breeze
Beautiful birds floating in the sky
    Popcorn's great

The flowers are blooming
Spring is here
Santa Claus got stuck in the chimney

Flowers in the yard
Berries on the bush
Batman and Robin just killed a pig

Haiku

    First: five syllables
    Second: seven syllables
    Third: five syllables
        Ron Padgett

'Twas the night before Christmas
And all through the house
The teenagers were having a wild party.

(I think this one is
plagiarized—or a "found"
poem, if you will)

Poetry Is Like

by Alan Ziegler

A good opening (which can also be used in conjunction with "comparisons"): Ask the children to make comparisons with "Poetry," by finishing the phrase "Poetry is like. . ." Get a few verbally and then ask them to write as many as they want in five to ten minutes. Most kids are able to write a whole bunch of them once they are convinced that they can write anything. It lets them know right off that poetry is a wide-open field, and any feeling or experience can be made into a poem. One child said, "Poetry is like a scary story," while another said, "Poetry is like a smooth story." One said, "Poetry is like a flower opening in Spring," while another said, "Poetry is junk." You can take this opportunity to point out that all responses are appropriate; there are no "right" or "wrong" answers. It's also good because you can gauge what prejudices towards poetry the children might have. And they love hearing their lists read aloud; it loosens up any who are shy about reading their work to the class. Here are some other responses:

POETRY IS LIKE:

a dream
a mystery
a color mixed with another one
a brown chocolate door
a feeling you want to come out
a messy desk
combing your hair when you're in a rush
something private
soaking up something in your mind
trying to build a puzzle and solve it
a scary night
a flower opening up at Spring
a dead person
a queer feeling
eating a mayonaise sandwich
a teacher at a student's desk
isn't really like something
poetry really is like everything
music in the air
a world in a head
a broken heart
a poet without poetry
swimming on a rock
a little farm
a hamster running under a bed
a dog on a mountain
a blow of ice cream
a kite
a long train
a song spreading through the air
a rat in the garbage
you and me
nuts
moonshine
power
peas coming out of a can
sound standing in the air
closets opening and closing
seed
new born pain in the neck
playing a game
a scary night
daydreaming
Poetry is like the moon because it floats all over the world. When I see the moon it looks like poetry is written all over his face.

by children from Atlantic Avenue School, Lynbrook, Long Island, 3rd, 4th and 5th grades

3. Drama, Film, Video, Music, Art, and Publication

A. Drama

Today We Improvise

By Dan Cheifetz

It was Mohandas' story but he seemed unable to play the protagonist's role.

Mohandas was in my fifth graders' creative dramatics workshop at P. S. 129 in Harlem. We met Thursday and Friday mornings for an hour and a half or so in a large room set aside by the school for arts and writing activities. A foot-high, 8-foot-square platform served as a makeshift playing area. I had asked the 12 children in the group to think up his or her own story—something that had happened to them, something they had dreamed or daydreamed about . . . any story except one they had seen on TV or at the movies. First, they were to tell the story to the group. Then, taking any role they wished, they were to cast the other parts from among their classmates. Finally, they were to play the story by improvising on its themes and characters.

This was Mohnadas' story, more or less verbatim: "There was this bad boy who was mad all the time. He needed a coat, so he asked his father. His father said no. So he ripped off some money from his father and mother. He bought the coat in a store with the money and then he hid it good. His father found he was missin' money and called the cops. Then when the cops came, his mother found the coat under the bed and told his father that it was the bad boy who took it. Then—I don't know what happened after that—they put him in jail or something. . . ."

"Good story," I said. "Now let's play it. Who do you want to be the bad boy?"

He pointed to himself. Then he picked the rest of the cast. I suggested the first scene be between the father and the boy, to show what their relationship was like.

The boy Mohandas picked for his father was his best friend, Leslie. Leslie was a "joker," and a pretty talented one. I reminded him that this was Mohandas' story, and that he should be sincere in his part and try to play it in the serious spirit of the story. I said it, but I didn't have much hope it would penetrate.

"Your grades are terrible," Leslie said, looking down his nose at Mohandas.

"They ain't so bad," Mohandas said mildly.

"They're disgusting," Leslie said, warming to his power role. "Go to your bed."

And Mohandas obediently exited.

"What do you think?" I asked the group.

"It's boring," said one boy.

A girl said, "He didn't act very mad like he's supposed to."

"He's not a bad boy. He's a *good* boy," said a third child.

"Try it again," I suggested. "You start, Mohandas."

Mohandas said, "I need a coat."

Leslie said, "You don't need nothin'. You're just a

bad boy."

"No, I'm not," Mohandas said, offended but intimidated.

"Go to your bed!" Leslie thundered.

Mohandas looked at me.

"Do I have to do like he says?"

"Do you always do what your parents say?" I asked him.

"Yeah!" he said.

"Never talk back to them?"

"Nah," he said, in a tone which implied I must be crazy to imagine such a thing.

"Well, okay," I said. "But this is your story and you can *pretend*. You're not Mohandas, you're this disobedient boy and you need a coat, and you think you deserve one. Start it again, father."

"Why don't you do better at school, boy?" Leslie said. This time he moved forward and grabbed Mohandas' arm. I started to reiterate my rule against physical action, but I didn't have to. Flinging off Leslie's arm, Mohandas moved four determined steps away and faced around.

"You always say I'm no good!" he said. There was conviction in his voice and good, fierce play-anger.

"Don't you be snotty with me, boy," Leslie came back, mugging and drawing himself up tall.

Mohandas began marching around Leslie in a tightening circle, as if he were stalking him. It was fascinating to watch.

"You don't care about me. You never give me nothin'!"

"I give you food and a bed. I give you this house to live in."

Mohandas stopped. His body arched accusingly toward Leslie.

"You never give me nothin' I want!" he shouted.

Leslie was impressed enough to stop mugging for a moment.

"Well," he said, somewhat lamely. "Your grades are terrible. You—you gotta do better to get something."

"I'm sick of hearin' you tell me what I gotta do all the time!" Mohandas continued his angry march, moving around and around his play father, giving him hell. His sincerity was striking—no "jiving" here. Leslie, his pretend father, had never really gotten out of himself and into his role, but Mohandas had been in his all the way. His story had been about the rebellious, individualistic, angry, needy Mohandas. He had wanted to play that part, to be the "bad boy" of his secret fantasy, but he hadn't known how. I guessed he had had little contact with that other Mohandas. Now I had given him permission to become that boy—with his body, his feelings, his gestures, his imagination, his walk—his whole self.

It is this "whole self" that creative dramatics attempts to mobilize. I am always surprised and moved by the almost magical way this kind of activity can *release* a child, help him reach inside to contact parts of himself that would perhaps never otherwise see the light. In relation to an experience like Mohandas', some might counsel: "Let sleeping dogs lie. Why stir up feelings that are better left alone." But good educators, like good psychologists, know that the repressed energy of anger and rebellion must surface somewhere—and how much better it is to have it do so creatively rather than destructively. The more a child is encouraged to contact what is inside him, the more balanced and satisfied a person he is, and will become. This is not training in rebellion; it is education in experiencing the self.

And of course I am not talking only about playing out repressed roles. Drama encourages the child to discover and project all the inner resources of his personality—his intuitive powers, his special experiences and attitudes toward life, his own particular fantasies and ideas. Only in this way will he come to know himself and become aware of what he is capable of. I would bet that Mohandas had never before told a story about his own inner feelings and needs. Television and other media feed children with other people's fantasies. This was Mohandas' own. I was exhilarated that he could get in touch with a fantasy that was not a romantic adventure or some other escapist version of life, but one of anger, deprivation and inevitable punishment immediately relevant to his own life and world—*and to play it out*.

Mohandas' story also provided the group with the kind of open-ended experience—one without right or wrong, good or bad—that is too rare in education. In a later scene, Mohandas' father discovered the money gone. The police arrived (the cops play important parts in many of the children's stories, functioning as a kind of *fuzz ex machina*). Then the bad boy was found out. Leslie had no mercy on his son:

"Send him to reform school!" he demanded of the cops. The mother agreed.

But at this point, one of the other girls in the group gave out a sympathetic, "Awwww!"

"You have a different idea?" I asked the girl, Deborah.

Deborah nodded emphatically. I suggested she come up and play the mother, to see what would happen then.

The new mother said to the father, "He needed that coat. You mustn't send him to jail."

"He's a thief," insisted Leslie. "He's *gotta* go. Take him away," he said to the cops.

"No!" Deborah protested. "I want a new husband!"

"I'll be the husband," said Sean, a cocky boy with a modified Afro.

"*I'm* the husband!" said Leslie defiantly.

"Well, let's see what Sean will do, just for fun," I

suggested.

Leslie relinquished his place reluctantly and Sean came up.

"You gotta go to jail," said Sean. "When you get out, I'll buy you thirty suits, because I'm rich."

"How about that, Deborah?"

"No," said Deborah.

"Okay, let's try someone else. Let's have another father. And another son, too."

"I want *him* to be the husband," Deborah said, pointing to a bean-stalk-thin boy named Joseph.

"Do you want to, Joseph?"

Joseph came up. For the son I picked a boy who hadn't done or said much to date.

Joseph said, "You take the coat back and I'll buy you a new one if you need it."

Deborah smiled. She was satisfied. But a surprise ending was in store:

"I *won't* take it back!" said the latest rebellious son.

We stopped it there. I said they had proved there are lots of ways to tell a story.

Of course, our workshop had not begun with improvisations. Before this kind of activity is attempted, it is important that children build confidence in themselves as individuals with good ideas of their very own, which are worth sharing with others. The teacher should start with group activities and games that will help the shy ones lose a little of their self-consciousness and the sensitive ones lose their fear of being ridiculed. When everyone does the same activity, it is easier not to feel "on the spot." If the activity is fun, as well, one can lose oneself completely in it. The activities I tried were those I myself felt comfortable with, and enjoyed doing with the children. Creative dramatics has the advantage of being without a "curriculum"—which is relaxing for the teacher as well as the student.

I began the group with "body language." For the first session, I led them into the room without a word, and communicated several things with gestures only. Finger on the lips: be silent. Circular motion with my arms: gather in a circle. Downward motion with my hands: sit down. The children quickly picked up what I was doing.

"This is the way the body talks," I said. "You can get a lot of messages across without one word."

Later, I led them through several group fantasies. They were walking in a desert on a hot day . . . they were thirsty, hot, tired, nothing green in sight . . . ah, but now the skies were getting dark and it was beginning to rain . . . cool, splashing rain on their heads and bodies, "doesn't it feel good?" . . . but now there was so much rain, it was beginning to flood, they had to swim or be drowned . . . and now it was hailing too . . . big hailstones that crashed down on their heads . . . but now the rain and hail were stopping, the sun was coming out . . . the waters draining away . . . they were walking, in mud, very sticky, hard to make progress . . . but now that was drying too and as they walked further they found themselves in a pleasant, grassy meadow. Throwing themselves down on the grass, they rested under the shade of a big tree . . . .

It was an exciting trip for them, creating the world as they went along, imagining a rapid succession of experiences they were familiar with and acting them out.

In another session, I had them imagine each was some kind of seed. Only the person involved knew which kind. They were in the earth in the winter, sleeping in the cold, hard ground. Then, the spring rains came, and the spring sun (I played the sun). The seeds began to stir with life. They sent down roots, sent up shoots. The shoots sought the sun, broke the surface, grew—and bloomed! I went around the room, trying to guess which kinds of plants they were—the children were delighted if I guessed right. And they had all learned something about the cycle of growth in perhaps the best "learning format" there is—the subject and object of learning became one. They had transformed themselves into what they were learning about!

We played several games. These were "creative dramatics" games, but as with many games children make up themselves, they gave the children experience in operating on their own, leading the group for a moment, feeling themselves the object of group attention with a minimum of anxiety because they are contained within the group. I had noticed they had all swarmed to the blackboard when they came in one day, writing or drawing with the chalk, and erasing quickly to write or draw something else. Out of this, I made up a blackboard game, in which the children closed their eyes (no peeking allowed) and one child was chosen to write a hidden word on the blackboard, a word which could be pantomimed. The word-writer chose someone to disclose the word to, and that person was supposed to communicate the word to the class without using words. No guessing was allowed until the player finished the pantomime. The player then chooses one of the upraised hands to guess the word. A variation of the game was to write a "group word" or phrase (a pack of cards, the Jackson Five, macaroni). The writer of the word or phrase became the director of a group of students who then played out the word.

At a later session, I asked them to think of something interesting that had happened to them recently, and to pantomime it. It could be something good or bad, sad, scary or fun, or a dream, if they preferred. The group would then try to guess it. What I got at first almost without exception was media stuff—mad scientists, Bill Cosby and Flip Wilson,

Superman and all his super-colleagues, including the then super-popular Super Fly. Especially Super Fly. Even several girls did him, or, alternately, Shaft.

Some of it was done cleverly. One boy beautifully imitated Bill Cosby's walk and drawl. Harry, the lone Chinese-American boy in the group, who wore glasses, set two chairs a few feet apart. He got up on the platform, looked intently offstage, whipped off his glasses and arranged himself on top of the backs of the chairs, his arms held out in the famous flying-through-space position. Harry was a kind of class mascot, and the children really enjoyed his Superman. Several children did variations of the "mad scientist" bit. One boy swallowed a potion, violently stuck out his tongue, made a face and fell down, writhing.

Most of the children were willing to do something. I assigned everyone a number, so each would have an automatic jumping off point. This takes away the need for a child to make a decision about whether to volunteer or not, which results in a few children doing a lot of things, and the others hanging back.

What they did served to get them on their feet and working. But my suggestion that they do something from their own lives and heads didn't penetrate, at first. Apparently, it just didn't seem possible that anything in their own experience was worth "acting out." And of course, it's easier to mimic someone else than dig into yourself and do something that might get you laughed at.

I asked the boy who had done the "mad scientist" to repeat his work. When he had finished, I asked the group to comment, not on him but on what he had done. One girl said she liked the way he had stuck out his tongue, but that he had done the whole thing "too fast."

I asked the "mad scientist" to close his eyes and think about what changes he might really go through after he took a secret, magic potion. What did it actually feel like to swallow something like that? Afterward, did things happen inside him all at once or little by little? I asked him to do it once more, but this time to show us outside what the scientist was going through inside. Maybe that would make it more interesting.

The boy did it again, but about the same as before. He seemed to be in a *hurry*.

"Take your time," I said. "Take as long as you need. We'll pay attention, don't worry."

When he took the potion again, his eyebrows shot up and his eyes opened wide. He grabbed his throat and opened and closed his mouth with great gasps, like a fish out of water. He got weak in the knees and wobbled spectacularly around the platform. He fell to his knees, then down to hands and knees, then flat out. His audience enjoyed it and he loved their approval. Instead of just "getting it over with," he

"The teacher should start with group activities and games that will help the shy ones lose their fear of being ridiculed."

had been willing to dig into himself to find an understanding of the process of change. Not an easy task. It had taken work, inner work, to show the process to us.

After that, a girl did a dream she had had, and we were off the media bandwagon. She pantomimed being attacked by a gang. She was cornered, thrown into a cell. A guard came in and tried to choke her. She fought him off, but then others rushed in and she went under. As in so much of what these children did, physical violence was a central element. The girl, rather overweight and awkward, but quite self-possessed, played her dream straight. The spirit of nightmare was in it—trapped helplessness, sickening horror. She flailed her arms about wildly when the gang attacked. She used her own hands to show the choking. Her body seemed almost liquid in the scene where she was being overwhelmed. She made us feel it.

In later sessions, the children began working in pairs. Two girls did a pantomime in which they were disputing which TV program to watch. One girl, Morgan, was watching her favorite when her sister, Eve, came in and switched the channel. Morgan angrily switched it back. Eve changed it again, and soon they were waving their arms at each other stalking about angrily. A third character, their mother, entered and threw them both out of the room for arguing. Then she switched on the program *she* wanted to watch—something romantic, because she sighed and gazed yearningly at the set.

In the middle of the confrontation between the sisters, one of them had turned to me with a frustrated air and asked, "Can we *talk*?" I considered and nodded yes. I had myself been feeling frustrated in not hearing the words that were lying in them constricted and unexpressed. After I had given my permission, the words rushed out like a dammed up stream. They had an argument, which quickly got "stuck":

"Get out of my room!"

"No, you get out!"

"No, you—it's my room."

"I won't!" I intervened. I asked them to think of new reasons, different reasons, why each should have her way.

Morgan said, "I know!" She turned to her "sister" and said,

"I've got to watch this program for homework."

Eve was outraged: "This is my room and it's my TV!"

"Well, it's the only TV we got and if I don't watch it tonight, my teacher will hit me and beat me up."

"I don't care. I hope she kills you."

"I'll kill *you* if you don't let me watch."

"Yeah?"

"Yeah!"

But at least they had unstuck themselves and had escalated the conflict to a new level. I sent the mother in at this point.

Clearly, we were out of pantomime and into improvisation. It was difficult for these children to do without words, especially when an issue was joined. They were quite right to demand speech. I had planned to stay longer with body communication, to help them increase their skills in creating physical details and specifics of characterization, before getting into talking. But the natural evolution of things had thrown off my plans and I felt it important to go where they wanted to go.

But first, I tried to clarify what improvisation was—and wasn't.

An improvisation, I said, was not the same as an argument you have with someone you know. First, the person you play may not be you; in fact, it's better if you're pretending to be someone else. You have to know who that someone else is, and what he or she wants. Second, the object is not to "win" the improvisation, as you try to win a game or an argument. You are helping to tell a story, so you have to be aware that your opposite is a partner in storytelling. You should react to what he is saying to you in your own way, but also give him back something he can use to build the story further. Avoid going round and round in the same rut. Instead, try to find new reasons each time for the position you are taking. An improvisation has a conflict. It's a fight and as in any fight, each person is after something different. That's what makes an improvisation go. But do your fighting without pushing or hitting. In fact, physical violence is the only way you can "lose" the game of improvisation.

Of course, a lot of what I said didn't penetrate at first. One has to improvise to find out how to do it. The part about fighting was especially difficult for them to understand. To most children, a fight was a fight . . . how could it be anything else?

Leslie, the boy who played Mohandas' father in the skit about the "bad boy" had particular difficulty with this stricture. In his improvisations, he would usually push or grab his opponent at the crisis. He didn't seem to know any other way to assert his point.

I reminded him, several times: "Don't shove. Don't grab. Talk! Make your point with *words*."

Finally, he began to catch on. He would wave his arms and shout but kept his hands off the person he was playing with. Once in a while he forgot, but slowly he was learning to express his aggressive energies without violence. It encouraged me to believe that improvisation might help children like Leslie to rechannel combative impulses into creative ones.

As time went on, and the more experienced the

children became, the less I had to intervene. They began to understand that an improvisation was not an argument, and not merely a fight, but was based on a relationship that had some tension or conflict in it. Two boys, for example, made up an interesting premise involving a policeman and his friend, a bank teller.

"Here's my money. Put it in the bank. Hey, man, you're in a cage, like a monkey."

"Well, listen, at least I don't go around getting my head shot off, like you."

"Oh, it's not that dangerous. And, anyway, I'm doin' a lot of good to the people."

"Well, you know, I'm not doin' so bad. I've been takin' a little money out of here. You know, once in a while."

"Wow, you better be careful. You could get caught."

"Nah, I don't think so. Don't tell anybody, hear?"

When they had finished, I said I thought it was a good idea. But I questioned whether a bank teller would tell a cop he was stealing. A boy, not one of the improvisers, explained matter-of-factly:

"They're friends."

Some teachers might reject improvisatory activities, partly because they feel *their* students would be uninterested or incapable of engaging in it. But to my mind, we are all born improvisers, and the impulse has important educational significance.

Recently, I watched a small boy waiting by himself outside an apartment hotel. He was standing between two metal struts which helped hold up the hotel canopy. As I watched, he began swinging himself at arm's length in a semi-circle from one of the struts. Then he reached out for the other one and swung himself around on that for a while. Drawing himself back between the struts and then letting go, he fell forward, grabbing the struts just before losing his balance. Tiring of that, he swung arm over arm from one strut to the other, back and forth. Finally, he, braced his feet between the struts, grabbed the metal bars as high up as he could and began to inch his body up the improvised ladder.

The boy didn't especially seem to be having fun. His face was rather expressionlesss. He had probably simply become bored with waiting, the struts were there, and so he improvised ways to keep his body active. Each time he got tired of one movement, he tried something new. (Without realizing it, I was waiting all the while for someone to stop him. Eventually, someone did: the doorman. Possibly he was afraid the child might hurt himself and the hotel would be responsible. But I also think there is something threatening to adults in the way children, like animals, expend so much energy in their unstructured, unconscious play; it doesn't seem to have any *purpose*.)

"But to my mind, we are all born improvisers, and the impulse has important educational significance."

I observed another child, a tiny 2½ year old this time, who could barely walk. Her only toy was a small plastic telephone receiver. At first, the receiver was a vehicle. On her hands and knees, she rushed it along the ground, making a barely audible car sound with her lips. The paw of a dog lay across her car's path. Laughing and talking to the dog, she "hung up" the receiver on his paw. The dog watched her with a dignified air. She took off and replaced the receiver several times, saying "Hello, doggy!" and "Hi, daddy." A few moments later, she was pretending to eat with the receiver. After several tries, she succeeded in keeping a few grains of dirt on the mouthpiece. Her father stopped her only a moment before she put the dirt in her mouth.

She rebelled tearfully against this interruption. But a moment or two later, having discovered a new use for her toy from her eating fantasy, she became absorbed in creating a mound of sand, then another to match it. That protean receiver became whatever she wanted it to be.

An imaginative child can even make do with what, to adults, might seem like nothing at all. A friend of mine, now a successful ceramist and pottery teacher, told me that when she was small, her mother would lock her in a room when the mother went to work. She was left with nothing to play with but some pebbles and a few bottle caps she found. She remembers playing for hours, completely absorbed, transforming the pebbles into soldiers, dancers, Martians; the bottle caps into castles, filling stations, dungeons.

These are expressions of the playful, improvisatory impulse of young, preschool children—the marvelous way they "make up things" as they go along, in which the inner life and its outward expression are in continuous flow, one into the other. But only in recent decades has our educational system come to value this impulse.

In the old "factory model" school (so ably described by Alvin Toffler) children went through school very much as raw material goes through a factory—"processed" to become obedient, efficient workers to tend the machines of the industrial society. In such education, the improvisatory impulse had little use—in fact, it was subversive.

But now we are on the threshold of the post-industrial age, in which machines will perform more and more of the routine, mechanical tasks; man, the intellectual, creative ones. So the need is, to quote Toffler: "for men who can make critical judgments, who can weave their way through novel environments, quick to spot new relationships in a rapidly changing reality. The prime objective of education therefore must be to increase the individual's 'cope-ability'—the speed and economy with which he can adapt to continual change."

In other words, the ability to improvise. So the child's natural impulse to "make things up as he goes along"—rather than his capacity to obey or even his ability to absorb facts (since "facts" change so rapidly)—becomes important to develop, rather than repress, if we are to educate him for the future and not the past.

We seem, however, to be in an era of educational "backlash" in which the surge of innovation of the '60s that has been replaced by a wave of conservative belief that only "basic skills" are important. In this frame, improvisational activity would seem on the surface to be almost frivolous. But, on a deeper level, what could be more "basic" than an activity that helps train a student to think on his feet, that helps him to follow one idea logically and naturally with a related one, that gives him experience in solving problems based on his own experience, his own analysis of a situation, his own sense of the world? That encourages him to try out new roles, new identities, new ideas. Improvisation is not "reading, writing or arithmetic" but it is training in how to think logically and creatively—which may be in the long-run the most vital "basic skill" of all! Improvisation activates both the imaginative and the analytical powers of the mind—and integrates body movement as well—so that the total organism is operating.

It is a good way to give students experience in mind work that is not tied to what is "right" or "true" but that flows around what "could be." It gently detaches children from the "secure" world of facts and accepted concepts and sets their minds adrift to imagine new realities—realities that resonate with the truth found in themselves. As such, students can experience themselves not merely as producers of good behavior or good marks, but as creators of good ideas, their own ideas.

Unquestionably, there is some anxiety about such activity, both for teacher and student. By definition, one doesn't know how an improvisation will end, or how you will get there. But an improvisation has a structure. It starts with certain "givens." First, *characters*—it is good for the teacher to encourage a student, before he begins, to describe himself fully as the character, both physical characteristics and personality traits. Second, *specific motivations*—what the character wants and why. And third, make sure there is something tangible and "playable" at issue, based on the characters and their motivations.

The teacher should try to restrain himself from telling the improvisor what to say, where to go. That way, the improvisor will be encouraged to turn inside himself, to find the "answer" by using his own resources and imagination. That is not to say the teacher shouldn't intervene to break an impasse—as I did, for example, with the two girls disputing over the TV set. It is also up to the teacher to help the improvisors shape a rambling story into a real scene, to help bring latent elements of conflict and meaning out into the open, to point out the differences between cooperatively shaping a story and having an argument. The important thing is for teachers to see themselves not as *directors*, but as catalysts and guides. And it is important that the teacher realize that there is no "right" or "wrong"—"good" or "bad"—in such activity. A child will bring out what is deepest in him only if he feels confident that he will not be "put down" or criticized or graded for it.

There might also be a problem at first in children not taking improvisations seriously. It seems too much like play. Not that children aren't serious about their play. On the contrary, it is what they throw themselves into most seriously. But for too many children today, their educational experiences take away their respect for their playful, improvisational part. Recess is the time for play; a classroom is for work. Children quickly learn to make this adult attitude their own. So at first they might misconstrue improvisational activity as a form of recess, and therefore trivial and unserious. And for this reason, discipline might become a problem.

My own solution to this is to tell students that they are going to combine work and play—they are going to both learn and have fun—and the only way they'll be able to do it is if no one takes advantage of the freedom we're going to have. Of course, no matter what one says, some *will* take advantage of it; there will probably be some disruption as the usual rules are relaxed. But as a rule, once students get interested and involved in the activity, and learn to take the work seriously, the problem begins to solve itself.

But it never becomes an "easy" activity. Because operating in an open-ended atmosphere, in which freedom and structure are in an ever-changing, dynamic relationship, is never easy. But a teacher can take great satisfaction in helping a student learn to believe in himself, which is the result of successful improvisational work. Children are greatly reassured and encouraged when they realize they can "make up stuff" that comes out of themselves, and that this creation is both good in itself and can connect with someone else's work to shape a pleasing whole.

The child who learns how to improvise is also learning to cope with change and flux without anxiety. Improvisation places him in the stream of change. He creates each thing anew. He is no longer being "processed." He *is* process.

From *Learning Magazine.*

Activities

Dan Chiefetz

The following is a list of games, activities and exercises that can be used in the classroom. The list is drawn from many sources, including my own head. I have tried all of them at one time or another, with some degree of success. The purpose of the list is to give the teacher some tangible starting points—a chance to choose one activity or another that connects with his or her own purposes and creative bent. The idea is to acquire experience and therefore confidence enough to begin or go further with *your own program*. One of the pleasures of creative dramatics is that teachers can have the fun of making up their own activities, and the satisfaction of seeing how they work out.

Warm-up activities

1. *Raggedy Ann & Andy*. Stand, and starting with fingers, moving to hands, arms, shoulders, necks, elbows etc. shake down all the moving parts of the body. Pretend you have no bones . . . teacher moves around perhaps helping the children shake loose. Now do a boneless dance like Raggedy Ann or Andy. A fast dance, then a slow-motion dance. Then at a drum beat or other signal, freeze. At the next drum beat, turn into a monster, or animal, or some character the children have been studying.

2. *Snowman*. You're a snowman, the sun is coming up, getting hot, hotter . . . you feel yourself begin to drip, begin to melt, from your head to your toes, slowly melting. Eventually, you melt, crumple, turn into pieces of snow, then a pool of water.

   You could follow this with saying that you're now a seed in the earth, in winter, with the rains coming. What kind of seed are you?

3. *Ship*. You're a ship—what kind of ship are you? Sailboat, schooner, ocean liner, etc. You sail along proudly, freely, the wind behind you, or your engines powerful beneath you. Suddenly, a torpedo strikes (make a sharp sound to dramatize). You feel the torpedo crashing through you, the water entering. You feel yourself sinking . . . slowly sinking, until you go down with a loud gurgle, to the bottom of the sea. You settle slowly at the bottom. You look up . . . what do you see? Later, divers come down to investigate your wreck. What do they find in your hold?

4. *You're a candle*, flickering. Your wax is melting, loosening, running down your sides. Slowly, very slowly, you turn into a gooey pool of wax. Then, perhaps, someone comes along and molds you into another shape. What are you now? Show us with your body.

5. *You're a limp balloon*. Someone begins to blow you up, fatter and fatter and fatter . . . until you pop! Or you're a fat balloon, full of helium, floating over the houses and treetops. You begin to lose air, and slowly come down, ending up as a limp piece of rubber.

Group games

1. *"I am your master!"* (or "I am your magician!") Begin with sitting. Everyone has a number and when your number is called, you are the master. The master announces, "I am your master!" and everyone must rise. The "master" says, "Be a motorcycle" or "Be a baby," and everyone must transform himself or herself into that person or creature or thing.

   The teacher then calls, "Freeze!" and then "Express yourself." At that, the group gets a chance to express their feelings about what the master has done to them, using words or gestures or whatever—without touching the master, of course. One master can stay up for several transformations, then move to the next master. Stop the playing of the game to work on details of expression, with the purpose of developing more accurate observation and self-expression. Thus if the order is "Be a horse!" you can demonstrate (or have someone good at it demonstrate) the actual way a horse gallops or trots—which is unlike the way a child hops or a kangaroo hops.

2. *"I Am Your Magician of the Magic Carpet!"* Similar to "I am your master!" but this time the leader transports the players to another place—a planet, a playground, the bottom of the sea, the top of the Empire State Building—and the travelers must act out being in that specific place. Make sure the magician gives orders that allow specific acting out, not just "Go to England!"

3. *Simon Says.* Similar to the classical game, except that instead of Simon ordering the players to "Put your left hand on your head!" he commands: "Be a sick dog" ... "Change a tire" ... "Play hop scotch" etc.

4. *Blind Man's Walk.* A good exercise to help give children the experience of being responsible—what responsibility really means and feels like. Also, to give them sensory experiences to complement their verbal learning. Get children in pairs—best way for this is to give odd and even numbers to the class members, and then pair odds or evens. One child of the pair is the blind person, the other sighted (use odd and even numbers again). The only rule is "Don't peek!" or you can use blindfolds. The sighted child must take the blind child for a trip around the room, giving him as many experiences as he can with the objects and textures in the room. Make it very clear that the one who can see is responsible for the blind partner, and must keep him safe from all danger. After a time, switch roles.

Process the experience afterwards by asking which role the child liked better, being led or being the leader. How did each experience feel? Were you frightened? Did you trust your partner? How did it feel to be responsible for someone else's safety? Did you enjoy introducing your partner to new experiences? Etc.

A variation on this is to have one pair of blind and sighted children walk through a maze created by other students, in which one student is a burning house, another an airport, another a fruit store, or a tree. The sighted guide talks to his partner, describing the environment and helping him avoid unpleasant things and introducing him to pleasant ones.

Movement activities

1. *Walking.* Begin by having the class walk in a large circle or oval. How does it feel to walk like yourself. Now walk faster than usual, walk in slow-motion, walk as if you're very tiny, as if you're tall, walk fat, tired, happy, etc. Now walk through the desert, the mud, marshmallows. Walk through shaving cream, peanut butter, ice. Walk through water, through the jungle, etc., perhaps ending with everyone in a cool grassy meadow to rest.

2. *Robot and human.* Turn off the lights, lower shades if possible, to create a quiet, dim atmosphere. Tell the group they're dreaming. They're dreaming they're robots. You feel like a robot, which is to say, you don't feel at all. You can move only as a robot moves—back and forward and at right angles, arms and legs stiff, eyes straight ahead. If you hit anything, you move backward in a straight line, etc. Your instructions should be robotlike, toneless, monotonous.
Slowly wake up and discover, slowly, you can begin to be a human again. You can move in a curve; you can turn your head; you can wave your arms, kick your legs. You have feelings again; you can smile, frown, contact others, find friends. Isn't it great to be human again?

Afterward, you can make this into an excercise in drawing body images, having the children draw themselves as a robot and as a human. Or a writing exercise, in which they describe the one or two things they liked best about being a robot and about being human.

3. *Different ways of locomotion.* How many different movements can you use to get from one place to another? Walk. Jump. Slide. Etc. Use combinations of movements: skip and leap, etc.

4. *Different ways of occupying space.* How many different ways can you occupy space. Stand, kneel, lie, etc.

5. *Different routes of locomotion.* Designate two points in the room. How many different routes can you take to get from one point to another? Circular, zig-zag, straight, meander, etc.

6. *Movements and shapes in space.* At each beat of the drum or other signal, make one movement that is different from the one before. You can move a small part of your body—finger tip—or a large part—your leg. Then, using your whole body, make a different shape in space each time the drum beats. Teacher starts with well-spaced beats, then speeds up the rhythm, and varies it.

Word games

1. *Monster Word.* The children write a word on the blackboard or a piece of paper that is the name of a monster they've never heard of. Draw the monster. Describe its life, likes and dislikes, etc. If you want, read what you've written aloud, and answer any questions people may have about your monster. Move as the monster might.

2. *Sentence Game.* Form a circle. One person starts a sentence with a word, and as you go around each person adds one word. Don't use "and," and try not to finish the sentence. Last person ends the sentence.

3. *Story Game.* Create a group story in the same way. First person begins a story with one sentence. The next adds a sentence advancing the story. The rule is, don't end the story until you've been all around the circle. If the story is a good one, you might want to have children act it out.

4. *Nouns & Verbs.* Have children list all the *nouns* they can think of on the blackboard. Next, ask them for *verbs.* List verbs opposite the nouns, letting them fall as they come. Children can make sentences, as funny as possible, using the noun and verb combinations to begin the sentences.

Guided fantasy activities

1. *King and Queen.* You are a king or queen, walking about your throne room, greeting and bowing to other monarchs. You decide to go hunting in the royal forest. You choose your weapon to hunt your favorite game. Then you are transformed into your prey: you are the hunted, trying to escape the hunter. Then you are transformed to the tree or plant you are hiding behind. A storm comes up. You are blown about furiously and are finally knocked to the ground by the storm.

2. *The mountain.* You are climbing a steep mountain. It is very difficult getting to the next pinnacle, and the next. You struggle, and finally you're at the top! You relax, rest . . . and look down at the obstacles you surmounted, then out at the world. What do you see from your height—use your imagination and describe what you see.

(Once, when I did this exercise, one boy said, "I'm falling!" and he did, saying "Squish!" as he landed. The other children followed suit. I followed their lead, remarking on all the dead bodies lying around the mountain, and said that maybe all these bodies can come to life again magically. They can have new lives, any lives they want. Everyone turned into new creatures. I had them describe their "resurrected" selves and it got pretty wild and wonderful!)

3. *The cave.* You find a cave, and inside is something you've always wanted. You go in to get it. Show us by your expression and movements what it is you found in the cave.

4. *Jungle.* You are trekking through a jungle. It's dense and difficult; you have to cut your way through. You go under and over logs, stones, underbrush, etc. You rest from your efforts, and then you slowly feel yourself turning into something in the jungle—an alligator, bird, stone, log, moss, swamp, or native. The teacher or a student can go around, perhaps with a tape recorder, and "interview" the things and creatures in the jungle. Without saying exactly what they are, the children can describe themselves, their lives, habitat, feelings, families, etc.

5. *Journey.* Close your eyes and imagine you are going on a journey—to somewhere you want to go, or hate to go. Decide how you want to go—walk? fly? sail? What preparations must you make? What will you take with you? Show us these things by your movements. Again, close your eyes. Imagine an obstacle in your path. What is it? What's it made of? How big is it? What are you going to do about it? Show us what you do about it.

6. *Balls.* In pairs or in a circle, play with a series of imaginary balls—each person decides what his ball is—tennis ball, beach ball, medicine ball, etc. Show us its size, weight, bouncability, by how you handle it, throw it. The person who catches it, must guess what kind of ball it is, then handle a ball of his own. Other possibilities: skip rope without a rope, throw an imaginary frisbee around, have a tug of war with an imaginary rope.

Nonverbal games, in pairs

1. *The camera.* One child is the camera and the camera operator, the other the star being "shot." The camera can shoot down or up, dolly in, come in for closeups, or pull back for long shots, etc. The star can do anything he or she wants, as long as there is continuous motion to be shot by the camera—dance, ski, orate, etc. Then switch roles.

2. *The mirror.* One child is the mirror, the other the person being mirrored. The mirror must reflect every movement, no matter how small. The per-

son looking in the mirror must move slowly, so the mirror can keep up. Then switch roles.

3. *Gibberish.* Have a conversation in gibberish—language that doesn't mean anything. Express a strong feeling, or tell a story. See if your partner gets anything out of it. Then switch. In a circle, each person tells the next something in gibberish that conveys a feeling or piece of information.

Sample of gibberish: Corg lastogarth frincetance morgid.

4. *The game of pairs.* Children form random pairs, with the teacher or a student as the "caller." Precede each instruction with "Get in the position of. . . ." Any activity that a pair of people can do together is the subject. Examples: "Get in the position of dancing" . . . "Get in the position of playing a game" . . . "Get in the position of building something" . . . "Get in the position of carrying some heavy object in space. . . ." After each instruction, allow time for the activity, but not too much—the idea is to keep them moving and changing position. After a few moments of the activity, call "Freeze!" and they become statues. Then move on to the next, "Get in the position of. . . ." With older children, you can use the "frozen" position as the beginning point for an improvisation; the physical position they are in should suggest the emotional/psychic starting point for the improvisation.

Improvisations and storytelling

1. *Tell a story.* One person begins a story, something he has seen, dreamed or made up—not something from TV or a comic book or movie. As the story unfolds, the storyteller assigns roles to his classmates, including casting trees, elevators, snakes, etc. In some cases, depending on the child doing the telling, you might want him to finish the story before it is acted out—or have someone else finish it if he cannot. Sometimes, you might want to have the characters cast in the roles to take off from the storyteller's premise and begin an improvisation on the theme.
With younger children, you might ask one to start by telling a story he knows—Cinderella, The Three Bears, etc.—and cast as before. Then, instead of asking him to finish the known story, have the characters he has cast improvise the story as they want it to go.

2. *The tap.* Form two groups, lined up opposite each other. One group faces the wall. Each individual in the other group approaches the person opposite, taps him on the shoulder in some expressive way—firmly, softly, heartily, with both hands or one, etc. The person tapped turns about and responds to *the nature of the tap* with a sentence, beginning an improvisation.

3. *The chair.* Place a chair (or a table, or whatever) in front of the room. Say that this is a special chair. Tell the children they will soon form into groups and tell a story about this chair. First they must consider some questions: *Where is this chair?*—on the moon? in a dentist's office? etc. *What's special about it?* Does it turn normal people into monsters? Is it haunted? Then, *who is sitting in the chair?* An astronaut? Magician? *What happened to this chair?* Did it fall apart when a Martian sat in it? *When did it happen?* Last night? In the future? In 1492?

Then form the groups, work with each of them in spinning their stories, try to have each member contribute some element. Then have them play out the stories, and finally, if they wish, have them play out the stories in front of the entire group.

Concentration and observation activities

1. *I see. . .* Form pairs, facing each other. One partner begins by stating one thing that describes what he sees—"I see two brown eyes. . . ." The other partner responds with his own observation . . . "I see curly hair." This goes back and forth, with a statement only of what is actually seen—no comments, or evaluations, etc.—until each has described everything observed.

2. *Echo.* Form pairs or parallel lines of partners. One partner makes a sound, the other tries to reproduce it exactly. Switch, and repeat the activity several times, back and forth, faster and faster. Next, one partner says a short sentence his partner must repeat exactly. Switch, and accelerate the back and forth exchange. Finally, one partner says several related sentences. (i.e., "I saw a dog. He was black and white. He liked me. He licked me.") The partner repeats it back, or you might ask them to give only the *gist* of what was said.

3. *Pass Around.* Pass some simple object around the circle (can, box, eraser). As each person holds it, he makes one statement about it—(i.e., "It's cool" . . . "It's hard" . . . "It has an edge" . . . etc., that does not repeat what has been previously said.

4. *Look and tell*. Place some large object in the front of the room—a chair, table, etc. Say that this is not just a chair, but one particular chair, with specific things about it. Ask them to look at it as if they were Martians just arrived on earth, who had never seen this kind of object before, even though they can speak English. Then go around the circle and ask each child to contribute one thing—as simple as possible—that he observes about this chair, table or whatever it is.

5. *Change and tell*. Form two lines, facing each other. The people in one group are the observers. They are instructed to look carefully at the persons opposite them, who are the observed. The observers then turn around, closing their eyes. Each member of the observed group then changes *one aspect* of his or her appearance—rumple hair, close one eye, untie tie, unbuckle shoe, etc. Observers are then instructed to turn about and see if they can pick out what has been changed. Then, switch roles—observed become observers and vice versa. This can continue, with two aspects, then three, changed, all of which must be discovered.

Some books I have found useful

Barnfield, Gabriel. *Creative Drama in Schools*. New York: Hart Publishing Co., Inc., 1968. $2.95. Though Brother Barnfield teaches secondary school in England, and his book is a little "stiff" in style, it is very rich in ideas—especially regarding movement, the use of music, and comic improvisation—for American teachers. There is a good section on school drama production.

Cheifetz, Dan. *Theatre in My Head*. Boston: Little, Brown, 1972. $2.95. My book is a running account of a children's workshop as it progressed, focusing on the individual children, their special characteristics and problems, and the various activities which helped them learn and grow. Along the way, it gives the teacher many ideas to use and also ways of looking closely at children's psychic and imaginative needs, and trying to fulfill them.

Huizinga, J. *Homo Ludens: A Study of the Play Element in Culture*. Boston: Beacon Press, 1955. Not directly useful in classroom work, but an evocative, fascinating study of the play instinct in men (and women) and its powerful influence on almost every component of culture—poetry, war, politics, even the law. The book concludes with a discussion of the woeful decline of the authentic play element in our own era.

Morgan, Fred. *Here and Now*. New York: Harcourt, Brace, 1968. $4.95. A Gestalt approach to teaching writing, using the senses and immediate experience. A valuable book, not too well-known, with good writing selections and exercises.

McCaslin, Nellie. *Creative Dramatics in the Classroom*. New York: David McKay Co., 1968. $5.25. A kind of overview of the field, with good definitions and an extensive annotated bibliography. Valuable in its discussion of poetry as a jumping off point for creative dramatics.

Schwartz, Dorothy and Aldrich, Dorothy., Eds. *Give Them Roots & Wings*. Washington, D. C.: American Theatre Ass'n., 1972. A guide to drama in the elementary grades, prepared by leaders in the field and edited by the co-chairpersons of a project for the Children's Theatre Association. Published in workbook form, with good dramatic activities and checklists for rating children's growth.

Spolin, Viola. *Improvisation for the Theatre*. Evanston: Northwestern University Press, 1963. This book was not written for use with children, but is valuable to the more experienced teacher because of the richness and variety of the exercises and theater games.

Way, Brian. *Development Through Drama*. New York: Humanities Press, 1967. $3.50. A famous book, and a very solid one, by the originator of the "Brian Way Approach." Way puts major emphasis on developing the whole child, and how creative dramatics helps do this. Way is British, and his approach is directly useful mostly to teachers of older children (as is Barnfield's), yet I think it is a basic book—in terms of both the why and how of this subject—for anyone who wants to dig beneath the surface of theater techniques as a way of education (pun somewhat intended).

Playwriting for the Very Young

by Sue Willis

The beauty of having kids aim their writing at some form of production is that the writing, while valuable in and of itself, also holds the promise of physical involvement and the excitement of a performance, even a little one. With some second and third grade bilingual students I am using the following series of techniques. Some take only a few minutes, others an entire period.

1. *Metamorphosis-monologues*. Kids choose or are assigned an animal or an object, and write a short piece pretending to speak in the voice of that object or creature. One possibility is actually to bring little toys, sea shells, lipsticks, etc. into class and let the kids choose which one they want to be:

LA PALETA

La paleta es rica.
Cada dia me comen más y por eso,
me voy poniendo más flaco y
un dia me voi a morir.

THE LOLLIPOP

The lollipop is rich.
Everyday they eat more of me and
because of this I am getting thinner and
one day I'm going to die.

—Rafael Granado

2. *Dialogue*. Holding their objects like puppets, the participants converse with one another. When it begins to get interesting, the teacher transcribes the dialogue (a tape recorder can be used), then types or prints it up for everyone to read.

3. *Improvisations*. If the objects still hold interest, have the children act out being those things—a flower, a salt shaker. Changing into something else is a good idea—obvious changes such as a caterpillar to butterfly, but also teakettle to steam. Then I will usually move on to something else, animals, for example. I repeat the writing exercise: make up a monologue for an animal. We then improvise being the animals—lions roar, butterflies flutter around. Sometimes the kids begin to chase one another, or if they are timid, I make suggestions—the butterfly goes to the flower; someone be a lion tamer in the circus, etc. Everyone begins wildly to flutter and roar and run around the room.

4. *The story*. Immediately after such action, bring everyone back to the writing table and do one of two things. If most of the group can handle the task of writing, have them write the story of what happened in the improvisation. Everyone writes his or her own version, remembering different details and points of view.

The seals ate the fishes.
The butterfly was on the flower.
The elefante was eating his hay.
The butterfly was going to eat the flower,
but the butterfly could not get to eat
the flower because
the elefante and the seal helped the flower.
And that was the way the butterfly
could not get to eat the flower.
   The End. And I finished the story about
the butterfly the seals and the rabbit
fish elefant.

—Christina Vargas

Alternatively, if I want participation from non-writers or very slow writers, I have the whole group tell the story. Usually one person leads and the others add details or dispute the implications of certain actions, etc.

LOS TIGRES Y EL ELEFANTE Y LA GENTE

Habia un show de tigres hicieron toditos bien entonces le dieron carne. Y estaban bravos y se lo comieron al hombre. Y se escaparon del circo. Entonces la gente se fueron corriendo gritando "¡Ayuda!"
   Entonces un tigre soltó un elefante afuera de la

181

jaula y el elefante destruyó el circo. Y la gente gritaba "¡Vamonos! Vamonos de este Circo Malo! Dame mi cuarto! Vamonos de este circo que no es bueno! Dónde sueltan los animales!"

There was a show of tigers and when they were good they gave them meat. And they got mad and ate the man. And escaped from the circus. Then the people went out running shouting "Help!" Then a tiger let an elephant out of his cage and the elephant destroyed the circus. And the people yelled "Let's get out of here! Let's get out of this Bad Circus! Give me my room! Let's leave this circus that is no good! Where they let the animals loose!"

Freddy Matos, Alexander, Fernando Bautista, Luis Valverde, y Josefine Martinez

5. *The play.* All of this can immediately lead to an interesting subject for a little play. Discuss the possibility of dramatizing the story. Excitement over the prospect is guaranteed, but the children may express a preference for more conventional subject matter. One group of second and third graders found a box with cowboy hats and holsters and decided at once that they wanted to do Cowboys and Indians. Josefine found some pieces of flowing gauze which she attached to her jeans as a tail and declared that she was a horse. So we began again, writing about the characters first, then improvising a little Cowboy and Indian story. Later we wrote up the story they had improvised. The next session I read their story back to them and they wrote more short pieces on their characters and then we improvised with changes and improvements.

6. *Rehearsals.* Most fun for the kids and hardest work for the teacher. We made do with two sessions of rehearsals (it was only a ten-minute skit) and then invited the rest of the class to see it performed. The performance was raggedy, but the response was enthusiastic, mostly on the order of "When is it my turn to make a play?"

7. *Aftermath.* Type up copies of the monologues and the story for the class to read.

THE COWBOYS AND INDIANS
by Josefine Martinez, Luis Valverde, Otto Pueyo, Daniel Aguilera, Maria Castro

Los indios son malos porque ellos creian que los vaqueros mataron a un hombre de ellos. Los indios matan a los vaqueros, y los vaqueros matan a los indios.

The horse:
It's better to die now before the bombs and the world's end.

The sheriff:
It isn't right to kill people, only the enemies.

The Indians:

Luis Valverde

I am an Indian.
I will fight the cowboys.
I threw arrows. I kill the cowboys.

I am hunting a tiger, and I kill
the tiger,
and then I eat the tiger,
and then I went to kill a lion
and the lion bites me but I kill
the lion.

Otto Pueyo

Yo soy un indio. Yo tiro flechas. Mato a los vaqueros.

The Cowboys:

Josefine Martinez

I am a horse. I am on the cowboys' side. The cowboys are going to fight with the Indians. The cowgirl rides on me and she is very heavy. They want to fight us because they thought we killed their master. I am a horse. I like to ride my owner the cowgirl on me and sometimes I ride the sheriff.

Maria Castro

Yo soy vaquera. Matar los indios. Y matar los malos. Los matamos a los indios.

*El canto de la vaquero
Paseo con mi caballo
a donde el agua para bañar*

Daniel Aguilera

I am a cowboy. I am the sheriff.
I shoot bullets. I put the bad
guys in the jail. In the gun store
they sell guns.

I don't like to kill persons because that's against the law. So the people don't have to fight.

THE PLAY

Cowboys and Indians—Vaqueros y Indios

Starring Otto Pueyo as Patchulen; Daniel Aguilera as the lion and the Sheriff; as Josefine Martinez as the horse; Luis Valverde as Big Fox; and Maria Castro as the cowgirl.

Patchulen is hunting and the lion bit him. And he fell on the floor. "I'm going to kill the cowboys!" said Big Fox.

The cowgirl was walking with her horse then Big Fox kills the horse because he thought the cowboys killed Patchulen.

The cowgirl is crawling on the floor. She was telling the sheriff what happened. The sheriff was going to get the Indians. They took Big Fox and they put him in jail.

The cowgirl wants to kill him and the sheriff said no. "If you kill him you have to go to jail or else pay $100."

Patchulen came to the Devil's Island. He was alive—he was not dead.

"Look! Patchulen is not dead!"

They let Big Fox loose, then he got a new horse for the cowgirl.

The End

Patchulen está cazando y el leon lo mordió y él cayó. Big Fox vinó y lo encontró en el piso. El dijó que los vaqueros lo mataron. Big Fox se puso furioso.

La vaquera estaba andando con su caballa entonces Big Fox mató el caballo porque él se creia que los vaqueros mataron a Patchulen.

La vaquera estaba arrastrandose por el piso. Ella estaba diciendo que pasó al sheriff. El sheriff va a coger los hombres malos, y dieron a Big Fox y lo cojieron y lo pusieron en el carcel.

La vaquera lo queria matar y el sheriff dijó que no. El sheriff dice "Si tu lo mata, tu tienes que ir al prision, si tu no quieres ir al prision, tienes que pagar 100 dollares."

Patchulen llegó al pueblo. Estaba viviendo no estaba muerto. "Mira! Patchulen no está muerto!"

Dejarón al indio suelto, entonces él vinó paratras con un caballo nuevo para la vaquera.

Fin

B. Film and Video

Basic Media Projects

by Theresa Mack

"All right, now, everyone in a circle," I shouted, trying to sound calm and in control of things. Thirty fifth and sixth graders crowded into a circle in the corner of the classroom. It was my first day as video teacher at P.S. 75 in Manhattan. "We're going to play a game. Everyone will have a chance to use the camera and the microphone." I handed the mike to the boy on my left, and gave the video camera to the girl sitting across from him. The kids on either side of her started pulling at the camera to look through it. She struggled to hold on and gave one of them a punch. "Just *wait* a minute," I said to the group, sensing their impatience. "You'll all get a turn. We're going to pass the camera and the mike around the circle. Each of you will use the camera to record the person opposite you as he introduces himself and tells us something about himself."

Groans. "This is dumb," someone muttered. But I persisted with my plan. After all, I'd figured it all out ahead of time. The perfect introductory video exercise, I had thought. Everyone will get their hands on the equipment and everyone will appear on the tape. The video ideal. So I persisted.

"I'll go first," I volunteered good-naturedly, thinking the only problem was breaking the ice. I took the microphone from the boy next to me and began. "I'm Teri Mack. I'll be teaching video here this year." I paused, feeling awkward. Who was I talking to, the

kids or that camera pointed at me? "Ahhh . . . I live on 106th St. . . . I just got a new bike that I like to ride in the park." I was embarrassed. This is no way for people to talk to each other, I thought. But still I persisted. "OK, next, pass it on." The camera and microphone started moving slowly around the circle. Some kids giggled and blushed as they introduced themselves; others made smart-assed comments. All the while there were interruptions as someone clung to the camera and the next in line struggled to get it for himself. 'Pass it *on*!" I insisted, as kids panned wildly around the room. "No, stupid," screeched an experienced sixth grader to a kid clicking the camera button wildly, "don't push the button. You just stopped the recording!" The circle had become a small mob of kids fighting over equipment and throwing insults and taunts at each other.

"This is *not* working," I proclaimed. There was a collective sigh of relief, and the struggling died down. "Why *isn't* it working?" They sensed I wasn't playing games anymore, that I really was confused and wanted to hear what they had to say. "You feel stupid saying a sentence about yourself." "I wanted to try out the camera. It's no good if you have to pass it right on." "Nobody wanted to cooperate." "It's just a dumb game." Everyone drifted away from the equipment, and I wandered around the room talking to kids for the rest of the period. I liked the kids and felt sure we would do good work together, but I still felt uncomfortable about my introduction.

Later, I described the morning to a friend. "The kids just weren't up for it. They were too excited, the class atmosphere was too chaotic." "No," he said, "it was a bad idea. Kids don't like pointless games."

I winced. I knew what he said was true, and it hurt to hear it stated so baldly. I decided right then that, rather than spend more time on introductory video exercises, I would immediately begin working on substantive projects with kids.

The next week I entered the classroom diffidently, feeling sure that I'd ruined my image as a respectable adult. But several kids ran up to greet me, and a few pulled at my arm saying they wanted to make videotapes. I felt reassured.

I needn't have worried about having things to do. Before long I was swept along on a wave of video projects proposed by kids or initiated by me or other members of the Teachers & Writers team. After working with kids on several projects, I've come to see my role as a kind of producer/director. I offer guidelines and define parameters that I think will insure the success of a project. I try to react honestly to ideas, to camera work, to interviews, offering my personal standards of quality. At the same time, I struggle to remain open—to expect the unexpected; to take risks with kids on projects that seem outrageous or doomed to failure; to acknowledge that sometimes my standards are substantiated only by convention or habit and can, therefore, be influenced by the creative ways that children use video.

No matter who proposes the initial idea for a project, all projects are active collaborations between the children and adults involved, with the children doing all camera and sound work. Out of the tension of collaboration, we have developed several projects and made many videotapes. Each project described here was, for us, an exciting discovery. Perhaps none of these projects can be duplicated. All were the result of a unique combination of factors—personal relationships, time (or lack of time), imagination and hard work. But hopefully these descriptions will serve as stimuli for the development of your own video projects.

MONOLOGUES & CAMEOS

In small groups, children develop dramatic situations, and each child chooses a character. The children then develop their characters' identities, through poetry or song writing. They should give careful thought to details, such as how the character walks, talks and dresses, what his past was like, what he thinks about when he's alone. Then each child does an improvisational monologue based on his character development, and the monologue is videorecorded. A tripod-mounted camera with little camera movement

is effective. Or turn the camera on and leave the student alone in the room if he wants. Play back the monologue immediately, and allow the student to do it until he is satisfied. Three or four attempts are often necessary to develop a strong, authentic character. A series of such monologues done by related characters may then lead into a skit, which could be loosely scripted or improvisational. The skits will benefit from the monologues, since the dialogue and action will come from each character's well-developed sense of self. This activity can be the material for finished tapes, or an exercise for actors in a more complex or scripted drama.

MONOLOGUES & CAMEOS, I:* The Farmer and His Wife; Smart and Stupid Monsters; The Dressing Room (30 min.)
MONOLOGUES & CAMEOS, II: The President's Kidnappers; Rabbit(20 min.)
(both tapes made by 3rd-4th graders)

VIDEO-VERITE

Video lends itself to a unique type of improvisational, on-location drama. A group of children decides on a dramatic situation and the characters involved. But rather than write a full script, only a loose dramatic structure is defined. This structure may consist of the time and place, and a few key events or interactions. Preparation for the taping should include attention to character development (e.g. through monologues) and a visit to the shooting location to decide on props and use of the space. For the video shooting itself, the actors literally put on their characters and live the chosen time period. With the dramatic structure as a guide, they can freely improvise dialogue and action. A small video crew follows the actors, documenting this live-drama experience. The crew is faced with the challenge of intimate documentation—being careful not to disrupt the subjects, selecting the moments which are most important to record and moving quickly to capture them as effectively as possible. A dual consciousness is required of the actors. They must be totally absorbed in their characters and in each other, while simultaneously being aware of the recording, perhaps cooperating with the video crew in subtle ways. The result can be startling in its realism and in the quality of acting which develops during this process. The tapes may require only some simple editing to finish them off.

HOW TO LIVE WITHOUT A FATHER: one day

---

*All videotapes mentioned in this section were produced at P.S. 75, NYC in the past few years. They are available, on ½" B & W reels, for rent or sale from Teachers & Writers Collaborative.

in the life of a family; a letter arrives from the absent father agreeing to a divorce, and leads to emotional arguments between the mother, grandmother and three daughters. (25 min.; made by 5th-6th grade girls)

VIDEO SOAP OPERA

Using television soap operas as a model, students may write their own soap opera, or perhaps even a series. They might do a spoof of a television show, which deals with love and hate, birth and death. Or they might attempt to deal with an unusual subject (e.g. fighting in the classroom) through this format. Imitation of the camera style and the melodramatic acting used in TV soaps will be important if the take-off is to be successful.

> SHADOWS OF LIFE: The Gilfrey family faces a crisis when the wife starts playing around with the mailman in this half tongue-in-cheek, half-serious Child's Version of a Soap Opera. (15 min.; 4th-5th graders)

VIDEO FEEDBACK AND FILMMAKING

Video has great potential as a self-reflective tool, and meaningful ways to use it will develop out of your relationships with children. We used it as an integral part of a 5th-6th grade class's first filmmaking experience. The class had written a script for a silent movie. Through taping, playback and discussion, we first sensitized ourselves to our body movements and facial expressions, and to how, through careful control, we could convey particular emotions. Then, again with the video equipment, we experimented with camera angles and intercutting, as different kids took turns directing the same scenes. By keeping the TV monitor hooked up on "live feed," the entire class could watch how each shot was set up and executed, and offer suggestions and criticisms. Then we'd review the tape and assess the effectiveness of the different directing styles. This recording and review was also very helpful for the actors' character developments. After a video version of the film script was developed to everyone's satisfaction, a film shooting-script was written based on the videotape, and we moved into film production. As a result of the video preparation, the class was able to shoot the film within a few days.

> THE MAKING OF A MOVIE: Documentary tracing the evolution of "The Love & Hate of Mrs. Jones," through acting workshops, to scene building, to Super 8 editing; includes the "video model" for Super 8 movie and interviews with class members and teacher. (15 min.)
> THE LOVE AND HATE OF MRS. JONES: Mrs. Jones and her lover plan to kill her husband; her

children overhear the plot. (8 min.; Super 8 with musical sound track)

DRAMATIC DOCUMENTARY

There is no clear dividing line between fact and fiction, so when using video consider integrating "drama" and "documentary" formats. The video-verité project described above is one example of this integration. Here are a few other approaches. Students can do video-research (interview someone, or explore a strange place with the camera), and then write a drama based on this information. For example, someone might do an in-depth interview with an old person about his past, then write a drama based on the person's life. The interview and drama could be shown together. Another approach would be to make a tape about an issue of concern, which interweaves a dramatic story line with live action and interviews. A dramatic structure may enable the students to make a more complex statement than if they were restricted to a standard documentary format.

> GRAFFITI IN THE STREETS: Two graffiti artists are caught in the act by a tough cop and thrown in jail. As they sit in their cold cell, they reminisce about the thrills and trials of graffiti writing. Effective use of documentary and interview material for flashback scenes. (20 min., 6th graders)

N-DEPTH INTERVIEW

Video is a good medium for allowing people to talk about themselves. On-the-street or off-the-cuff interviews are easy to get. Instead, try some interviews which go deeper and give a sense of who the person interviewed is. The quality of this kind of interview will depend on the relationship of the interviewer and interviewee, and the interviewer's ability to listen and let the subject talk freely. Have plenty of tape with you when you begin such an interview, and let it roll nonstop; you never know when your subject will relax and talk more personally or engagingly to you. Let your subject see the video playback, and approve the final edit before it's shown publicly. If possible, videotape your subjects in their everyday contexts, doing what they ordinarily do. As a variation, try making a tape that shows a person at work rather than talking about himself. A good source of subjects for these tapes are the people around you everyday whom you may know very little about.

> MALLACHY DONOGHUE: P.S. 75's Chief Custodian relates stories from his past, when he worked in Alaska, and talks about his views on life, as he goes about his daily business. (15 min.; 6th graders)

VIDEO HISTORY

There are many people, now growing old, who have had rich lives and now have a desire to talk about their experiences and insights. Discovering these people and recording their memories can be a full-year project. Possible subjects are the students' own parents and grandparents, or people at a nearby senior citizens home or center. A few possible approaches: Choose a particular time period in living memory (the depression, World War II, immigration in the early 1900s) and talk to several people about their lives during that time. Or do an in-depth interview with one person, allowing him to talk freely about his life. Or explore local history by talking to people who've lived in your area for most of their lives. You may want to videotape particular sections of town the person once knew well, then show the person these visuals while audiorecording his comments on what has changed. Old photographs could be used to supplement a video history, and might be particularly meaningful as part of a family history. Students could tape-record interviews with older family members at home, then use the interviews as voice-over a video recording of family photos. After gathering this kind of oral history, you and your class might do an interesting study comparing the rich oral history of a particular era to the more one-dimensional record in a history textbook.

A 5th-6th grade class at P.S. 75 has established a relationship with a senior citizens residence across from the school. In-depth interviews and video history, as well as collaborative works in drama, creative writing, film and video are developing out of children's relationships with the residents.

DOCUMENTING THE EVERYDAY OVER TIME

An extension of the in-depth interview, this type of project entails selecting some aspect of daily life, perhaps in the school or neighborhood, and recording it several different times. The goal is to capture on tape important aspects of the subject matter—underlying patterns and meanings. Making this kind of tape requires patient and careful observation, both with and without the camera, to illuminate the obvious and draw attention to the often unnoticed phenomena of daily living.

DISCOVERING NEW THINGS IN P.S. 75 LIBRARY: 5th and 6th graders visited the library regularly to record the daily happenings there; the tape shows the library's services and how kids use them. (20 min.)

OPENING DOORS: the video specialist edited the material shot by the students into another version for librarians and administrators, with an informative narration on the nature of an "open library" in an elementary school. (10 min.)

VIDEO PEN PALS

The purpose of this project is for two classes in different parts of the country to develop a relationship with each other through a regular exchange of videotapes. The tapes might begin with each class introducing itself and its school, then showing students' homes, families, neighborhoods, and hangouts. After these initial orientation tapes, subjects might include popular games, chores, local environment and points of interest, religious practices, and opinions on topical issues. When one class receives a tape, it may want to record its reactions to the tapes, and then go on to make a related one of its own to send back. These tapes should be simple in design, with emphasis on the communication process rather than on polished production. In making the tapes, the children involved must look more closely at their own environment and their daily lives as they select what to record about themselves. The tapes they receive will give them a better understanding of the beliefs, concerns, and daily life-style of people in another part of the country. In addition to the videotapes, the classes could exchange detailed area maps, pictures, snapshots, personal letters, and artifacts from their area (e.g. stones, seashells, bus and subway tokens), anything that would add to a sense of what life is like in their area.

A 5th-6th grade class at P.S. 75 is presently participating in such an exchange with a 5th grade class in Charleston, S.C.

CLASS VIDEO SERIES

This is a helpful way to organize the production of a series of videotapes that can involve every child in a class. Begin by choosing a subject of general interest. Life in the neighborhood, life in the school, daydreams and fantasies, workers in your area are some possibilities. Then, after discussing different aspects of the subject, let the kids group together in three's and four's and choose their particular topics. It helps to post a list of all the topics and who's working on what, and keep a public record of the progress of the series. I suggest working with one small group at a time until it finishes its videotape (this will take at least four to six 1½ hr. sessions), although you may have several topics in progress at once. With the topic of each tape already settled on, kids can put their energies into developing their approach and making the tape. The completed series can be edited together with music and titles and is ideal for a gala show for parents, friends and administrators.

THE SIDEWALKS OF THE CITY: How does a

construction worker feel about his work? What goes on inside that noisy ugly factory on 96 St.? What happens to a robber who doesn't read signs? These are some of the subjects covered in this series of charming documentaries on city life, which looks in new ways at the familiar blocks around us.

PART I: Writing on the Wall; Some City Sounds; Geometric Shapes; Cars; The Heart of the Subway. (25 min.)

PART II: Construction; Watch Those Signs!; Old People; Kid Power. (20 min.) (made by 3rd-4th graders)

Video for Kids in Theory and Action

by Theresa Mack

Video is educational because, in the process of making a tape, a child is required to exercise several mental skills. Planning and producing a videotape involves imagination, abstract and concrete problem-solving, concentration, verbal and visual communication, and organization of ideas. Video invites a child to structure reality, through use of a camera and editing, to express his or her particular vision.

Video is conducive to trial and error, to shy tentative self-expression. I've seen a child turn on the video camera and wave it around, and then be thrilled with the immediate playback because it's his own choice of images on the TV screen. That thrill, combined with practice and guidance from a teacher, can lead to a very creative use of the equipment.

But there is one nagging characteristic of videotape-making that threatens to undermine all this. Making a videotape is invariably a chaotic experience. The microphone cable gets hopelessly twisted up with the camera cable, and then someone gets the headset caught in his hair. The camera isn't rolling when the interviewer begins. Someone bumps into the tripod. I lunge to catch the camera and pull out the power plug. Everyone gets so excited that calm cooperation becomes impossible.

So how, in the midst of all this chaos, can you lead a child beyond wild camera-waving to a disciplined and expressive use of the equipment? And how can you take fullest advantage of video's educational potential? I've found that, as a counterbalance to the chaos, it helps to think of a video project in terms of a loose structural outline.

In three years of helping kids make videotapes, no two tapes have ever been alike. However, I have become aware of a structural framework that is inherent in the production of most videotapes. Now I keep this structure in the back of my mind, and refer to it if a project starts falling apart or becomes hopelessly disorganized. The outline helps me to pace a project and to make sure that we give enough thought and time to every aspect of the production. Kids like having a sense of the stages involved and can appreciate that turning on the camera is not the beginning and end of a videotape.

The following "Structural Guidelines" crystallize some of my concerns and considerations as I help children make videotapes. The library documentary was made at P.S. 75 (Manhattan) last year and is one example of how the structure applied. Many tapes do not develop in such linear fashion, but most do contain elements of every stage described.

STRUCTURAL GUIDELINES

1. PINPOINTING THE NATURE OF THE PROJECT AND DEVELOPING AN APPROACH

First there's that mysterious process—the birth of a project. Wherever the project idea comes from—your head, children's heads, or your experience together—everyone who plans to work on it must embrace the idea and commit their energies to it.

After the general idea is agreed upon, allow yourselves plenty of time to talk and plan your approach. Consider every idea, every possible perspective. Brainstorm together. If it's video drama, allow time for character development and attention to dramatic details and camera work. For a documentary, visit the site and look at it through new eyes. Think about what the video camera can capture most effectively. If you plan to record a live event, be aware ahead of time of as many details and discuss what your point of view will be—what mood or information you'll convey through what you select to record.

This is the time to do research or write shooting scripts, to prepare questions for interviews, and to reserve the equipment for the days you plan to shoot.

2. THE VIDEO RECORDING

Although it's useful to teach the basics of the equipment, especially the camera, before you begin your tapings, I always do much of my teaching during an actual shooting session. Kids grasp the principles of good camera work and crew behavior very quickly when they're faced with a real shooting situation.

After teaching the camera basics—how to operate the lens and manipulate the tripod—these are other important principles to stress:

— Be steady (this means muscle coordination and

concentration)
- Don't zoom unless you have a reason
- Don't search with the camera; look away from the camera and use your eyes to find a new shot
- Be conscious of framing, the composition of every shot (most basic—don't cut off heads or have lots of empty wall or ceiling)
- Be conscious of how camera placement limits what you can see with the camera; always consider changing the camera position
- Never stop concentrating; using a camera means making endless decisions.

Sound is also important, so make sure your interviewers know how to handle the mike properly. If you want clear "general" sound, position your external microphone carefully.

The other important aspect of a recording session is the coordination that's necessary among the crew members so that camera and sound begin together, and no one trips over cables and rips the connections. Specific division of labor helps in smoothly setting up the equipment. (Marlene, set up the camera; Janet, clean the machine and thread it; Shirley, hook up the mike and headset.)

Whenever possible, play back the tape immediately and redo what you're not satisfied with. Actors and interviewees also benefit from the playback. If you need more than one shooting session, review the tapes in between sessions so the kids can learn from their work.

3. VIDEO REVIEW

Find a quiet place where the kids can look at their tapes without being interrupted. If the tapes are to be edited, it's especially important for the kids to become familiar with their material. This video review requires the same kind of visual concentration necessary for good camera work. As preparation for writing an editing script, it's very useful to "log" your material. Logging is a process of distilling the main idea from each section and evaluating its content and technical quality. A "section" might be takes in a drama or questions in an interview or different camera angles—whatever division is most useful for you. Write down this information for each segment as well as its location on the tape (you can refer to the VTR's counter for this). Based on your written log, you can decide whether any reshooting is necessary, and then write an editing script. Your editing script is a listing of the desired sections in their appropriate order. The script can also indicate what graphics you want, and whether you want to add narration, music or sound effects at any point.

4. THE EDITING

For most projects, completion of the videotape requires editing it into a polished form. This may be simply assembling your best takes in a video drama, or creating a meaningful structure out of documentary footage. If your project was well conceived and well recorded and if you've done the necessary editing preparations, the editing itself can be the most exhilarating and satisfying part of the production. Although half-inch video editors are not technically perfected—some quality is lost in editing and there may be difficulty in getting clean cuts—this should not discourage you from editing.

A shooting session will always be far richer than the shooting script that guides you. The same holds true for editing. Being familiar with your material and planning your edits is important preparation, but the actual editing itself always involves experimentation and discovery as you actually bring the material together—the pacing, the visual continuity, the variety created through juxtapositions of images or sounds and images. This is the challenge and excitement of editing.

Children are capable of mastering both the mechanical and conceptual aspects of editing. With careful supervision, kids as young as third graders are able to operate the editing system. Some kids become truly engrossed in the project only during the editing stage, when they're involved in the final shaping of the tape.

Try to have all the titles and credits recorded, and music, narration, or sound effects available (on a cassette) so that as you edit, you incorporate all of the finishing touches. What's left for later may never get added at all.

In some cases, because of the time pressures, I am not able to bring the children through the editing process itself. In those instances, I have them do the logging script so that, although I myself do the editing, I can be guided by their choices as much as possible.

5. THE SHOW AND OTHER KINDS OF FOLLOW-UP

After making a videotape, it's very important to show it to people.
- Show it to classes throughout the school; try to have a few kids involved in the project present at these showings to answer questions and see the audience reaction; distribute a catalog of videotapes throughout the school, so classes can request particular tapes; some may even relate to curricula work.
- The kids involved in the project might want to have a special show and party for parents and friends.
- Show tapes at special school events and parent meetings; occasionally set up a monitor in the entrance way or parent's room and run a tape.
- Exchange tapes with other schools using video.

— Arrange a regular program on your local cable station (public access channels).
— If you're lucky enough to have an extra unit simply for playback, keep it set up in the library with tapes accessible, so students can view them when they want to.

THE LIBRARY DOCUMENTARY

P.S. 75 had just opened its new library and since it was used heavily by the kids, I suggested we make a documentary about it. Six fifth- and sixth-graders (mostly very poor readers) were interested, so we got together to talk about it. "Why do kids go to the library?" I asked them. "To return books or take new books out," said Shirley matter-of-factly. They gave me quizzical looks—why was I asking such an obvious question? "I know," I said, "but why else do you go? Why do you like to go to the library?" "To get away from the teacher 'cause she talks too much." "To get some peace and quiet—this class is so noisy!" "To do research." "To sit and think—or daydream." "To meet my friends from other classes."

Michael started drawing a floor plan of the library, and pointed out his favorite "hiding place," where he could sit without the librarian seeing him from her desk. The library was beginning to feel like a place of intrigue and excitement. I stressed that we would try to capture what the library really meant to kids in the school, what they liked and didn't like about it—that we would try to document more than the obvious. By now we were all really excited.

During these conversations there was an undercurrent of constant teasing, poking and pushing among the three boys and the three girls. I decided to avoid this energy-diversion completely by segregating the sexes into two shooting crews. Another asset of the small crews was that each child could be more actively involved during a shooting session.

We checked with the librarian and planned to visit the library every Tuesday or Wednesday morning with the video equipment, for as long as we needed.

Since no one on the library crew was experienced with the video equipment, we spent one morning interviewing each other and learning the basics of the camera. Then we began work in the library. From the start I established a pattern which the kids quickly incorporated: leave the equipment in a corner and wander around the library for a while; try to get a sense of the mood and to notice small centers of activity. Then, when you know what you want to record, come back and we'll set up the equipment.

During every shooting session each child had about a half-hour stretch to use the camera, while the other two monitored sound or handled the mike. The lack of obvious "action" in the library forced the children to look carefully around them. A child quietly reading a book in a corner came to be seen as an important activity. After the first few shooting sessions, when I monitored each kid carefully and pumped them with "camera consciousness-raising," they worked more and more sensitively and deliberately. All of the kids became very conscious of camera placement and framing. Even Shirley, who was the most excitable and whose first camera work was punctuated by jerky random movements, learned to look around her, choose a focus, set up a shot, then leave the camera alone and allow the action to unfold before the camera.

The decisions they made were usually perceptive and often ingenious. One day the boys staged a rendezvous between two friends, who whispered gossip to each other as they searched for a book on the shelf. The librarian, unaware that this was being recorded, demanded loudly that they be quiet or return to class. The boys sheepishly left. The incident was as real as if we'd stumbled upon it and been lucky enough to have recorded it.

The library's atmosphere imposed a valuable discipline on the crews. They had to work smoothly and quietly together. Each time they returned to the library, having reviewed their last tape, they had a more refined sense of what to look for to record.

Every time we filled up a tape (eight altogether), the crew who made it viewed and logged it carefully. The logging was painful at first and I directed it closely. At the end of a segment I'd order, "Stop the machine. Now what was happening there?" The kids would struggle to describe what they'd just seen, to condense all the information into a meaningful general statement. "Everyone's standing around and writing things down and holding their books and talking and waiting to leave the library." "So how would you describe the general activity in that shot?" "Kids are checking out books." "OK. Put that down. Now what about the camera angles. . . . Did that show us something about the library? Was it boring or interesting? . . ." Soon they needed less prompting and began to understand the value of the log. They liked having a written record of what they'd shot, especially as they planned another shooting session.

By the time we were ready to write an editing script, they knew their material in depth and could refer by memory to particularly good shots or interesting moments.

Because there was so much material (four hours) with no inherent structure, I suggested they put each shot on a separate index card (another tedious process which they did carefully after initial prodding) and try organizing shots into categories and shuffling them into various orders. This helped them structure the material into a loose editing script.

(The librarian, who had seen many of the tapes and was very impressed, wanted an edited tape to play for administrators and librarians. Rather than pressure the kids to satisfy her requirements, I agreed to work closely with her to edit a tape. This freed the kids to make all their own editorial decisions.)

The two crews had come together during the final tape review and script writing and thus identified with each other's material, and saw themselves as a group making one tape. When it came time to do the editing, everyone wanted to be involved—especially because it meant a subway ride to the West Village where the editing setup was, and a whole day out of school. Everyone had worked so hard and was so excited about the tape finally being completed, that I gave in and took the entire group to edit. The editing setup was in a loft, and no one was there all day but us, so there was lots of running around, hiding in corners, and teasing and flirtation. The kids discovered a cat hospital upstairs where, as Marlene put it, "They're getting their ovaries removed," so kids took turns running upstairs to croon over the cats. However, they had really prepared well, so I set up a round-robin style of editing.

I would grab two kids and concentrate on involving them in the editing. Then as their interest waned (all the playing around was very distracting), I'd let them go and grab two more to take their place. Because the group worked out an editing structure, the tape didn't suffer too much from this constant change of editors. We managed to edit about half of the tape that day.

The next time I took only three kids, who had showed real interest in the editing. The others moaned "unfair" at first, but then quickly forgot and seemed relieved. We finished the edit at the second session—all but the music and the title, which were chosen later and added frantically at the last minute before the tape's "debut." We called it "Discovering New Things in P.S. 75 Library."

In the meantime, I worked with the librarian, shaping the same raw material into a less exciting but more informative videotape for interested librarians and administrators.

Both versions of the library tape have been shown —to kids, parents, teachers and administrators. The librarian is using her copy to promote the concept of "open" libraries in elementary schools. All the kids graduated except for Janet, who's in sixth grade this year. We're showing the tape to her class and others on request, and Janet proudly sets it up and answers questions about the project.

What I wish I had had the time to do was to be more aware of the influence, if any, that making this videotape had on the kids' reading habits. This would have been especially interesting since all but one of these kids was an "under-achiever" and behind in reading. I often wonder if making the videotape

affected their use of the library. Whether they used it more often or more wisely for reading and research; whether they felt more at home there. This type of follow-up—keeping in touch with how the video project affects other aspects of the students' school experience—is an important thing to do if you have the time.

DEFINITIONS OF CAMERA ANGLES, SHOTS, AND MOVEMENTS

FRAMING—What you see when you look through the camera. What you *frame* tells you what kind of shot you have. "Watch your framing"—make sure that you show in the frame whatever is important to your shot (the top of someone's head; what someone's hands are doing).

ESTABLISHING SHOT—Usually a wide-angle or long shot, it shows you where the film tape takes place, who the characters are, whatever is important for the audience to know as the film/tape starts or a new scene begins.

WIDE-ANGLE (W.A.)—A shot which shows a large area, such as the street or a whole room. It lets you see where the characters are and what they are doing.

LONG SHOT (L.S.)—A shot like a wide-angle, but also showing something from a great distance, such as buildings that are far away from the camera.

MEDIUM SHOT (M.S.)—This shot shows you something particular in your scene, such as a sofa where two people are sitting, or one person sitting in a corner. It brings the audience's attention to something special without getting too close to your subject.

CLOSE-UP (C.U.)—This shot shows an important detail. A kiss, a face, a knife fills up the whole frame. A close-up can really add to the emotion of the scene by showing a wrinkled brow, a clenched fist in a fight, the feet of an approaching murderer.

CUT—A cut is the most common way of moving from shot to shot. It is a sudden change from one shot (such as a medium shot of a man) to another (such as close-up of the man's face). You can make cuts in the camera (as you are shooting) or when you edit.

ZOOM—By moving the zoom (a push button or a ring on the camera lens), you can slowly move "in" from a wide-angle to a close-up, or "out" from a close-up to a wide-angle. Use the zoom *only* when you want to bring special attention to something by changing your framing in this way. A lot of zooming in and out for no good reason will give you a dizzy feeling.

FADE—This is a gentler way of moving from shot to shot. The screen goes soft and dark at the end of one shot, then brightens as another shot begins. A fade can be used to show passing of time, or movement from one place to another in the film, or a change of consciousness—like starting to daydream or falling asleep.

PAN—This involves moving the camera from side to side. A pan is used to follow some particular action—like a person nervously pacing back and forth— or to move from one subject to another when it's important to show the space in between them.

TILT—This means moving the camera up or down. Tilting can be used to slowly show something to the audience, such as beginning on someone's feet and slowly tilting up to show the face.

TRACKING OR DOLLY SHOT—This shot involves moving the camera, for example to follow a person as he walks down the street, or to get closer to your subject (instead of zooming in on him). You can do this shot by hand-holding the camera (if you have a very steady hand) and walking with it; by putting your tripod on wheels (called a dolly); or by using a wagon or wheelchair or car to move the camera operator along.

"BIRD'S-EYE" VIEW—The camera is placed very high so that a shot is taken looking down on something; for instance, a shot from the top of a building might make people look like helpless ants.

"WORM'S-EYE" VIEW—The camera is placed very low so that it looks up at something; this angle might make a person look tall, overpowering, evil.

AN ANNOTATED VIDEO BIBLIOGRAPHY

Chuck Anderson, *The Electronic Journalist* (Praeger, New York, 1973). Based on the author's experience teaching video to high school students, this book has basic technical information and some project ideas. Written as a handbook for high school students.

Kit Laybourne, editor, *Doing the Media* (Center for Understanding Media, 75 Horatio St., New York, N.Y. 10014). This portfolio of media activities and resources is useful for teachers who want to use media in their classrooms but are at a loss as to how to begin or what to do. Includes a section on

video, as well as on film and still photography. Inquire for price.

Phillip Lopate, *Being With Children* (Doubleday, N.Y., 1975). A personal account of working with children in theater, videotape, poetry, and fiction, by the director of the Teachers and Writers project at P.S. 75 in Manhattan.

Phillip Lopate, "Aesthetics of the Portapak," in *Video & Kids* (see entry for *Radical Software* below). A cranky, skeptical look at the problem of quality in ½" Portapak production.

Phillip Lopate, "How to Make Videotapes When You Don't Know the First Thing About It," in Teachers and Writers Collaborative *Newsletter* (Vol. 4, No. 4, Spring 1973). Diaries of a novice getting his feet wet working with kids on their own videotapes. Includes descriptions of making fantasy and documentary tapes.

Ken Marsh, *Independent Video* (Straight Arrow Books, 625 Third St., San Francisco, CA 94107). Paperback. Deals with the physics and electronics of ½" video—information that you don't really need to use video equipment, but would interest the electronically oriented. Lots of fascinating, clear diagrams.

Grayson Mattingly and Welby Smith, *Introducing the Single Camera VTR* (Scribner's, New York, 1973). Hardcover. A very basic manual. Easy to read but uninspiring.

Media & Methods (134 N. 13th St., Philadelphia, PA, 19107). A magazine of film and media teaching. A list of back articles is available which can be ordered individually. Published monthly. Inquire for subscription rates.

Radical Software: A Magazine of Video Technology, "Video & Kids" issue (Vol. II, No. 6, New York, Spring 1974). This issue, edited by the Center for Understanding Media, focusses on ways to work with video and children. Teachers and artists describe their own projects, activities and programs. The magazine is sprinkled with personal philosophies and justifications for using video with kids; it gives lots of suggestions and ideas but with little in-depth description or analysis. Available from Center for Understanding Media, 75 Horatio St., New York, N.Y. 10014. Inquire for price.

Richard Robinson, *The Video Primer* (Links Books, 33 W. 60th St., New York, N.Y. 10023). Paperback. One of the more readable technical manuals, this book gives clear, complete descriptions of how the equipment works and how to use it properly. The author conveys a sense of excitement about the potential of video and exhibits a sound understanding of how it should be used. Also includes valuable appendices: sample shooting schedule and script, where to buy equipment, etc.

Videofreex, *The Spaghetti City Video Manual* (Praeger, New York, 1973). Paperback. A well-organized, clearly written illustrated handbook on the use, repair, and maintenance of ½" video systems.

Peter Weiner, *Making the Media Revolution* (Macmillan, New York, 1973). Hardcover. Begins with rhetoric about how revolutionary ½" video is, yet offers a TV-oriented approach to using it, which misses the point completely.

Sol Worth, "The Uses of Film in Education and Communication," in *Media and Symbols: The Forms of Expression, Communication and Education*, edited by David Olsen (National Society for the Study of Education, University of Chicago Press, Chicago, 1974). Presents sound arguments for the educational value of putting cameras into the hands of children and teaching them to make movies. Relevant for video as well.

SOME EQUIPMENT SUGGESTIONS

EQUIPMENT	RECOMMENDED MODEL	APPROX. PRICE
PORTABLE VIDEO SYSTEM (portapak)	Sony or Panasonic	$1700
External Microphone with cables	electrovoice 635A (very sturdy, good only at close range)	$55
Headset	Must be high impedance (250—*e.g.* Telex)	$10
Tripod	Husky or Vivitar	$55-85
TV Monitor	1 small (*e.g.* Sony 9") *and* (if possible) 1 large (*e.g.* Panasonic 23")	$250 $400
Videotape (plenty of it)	Sony or Scotch	$12 for half-hour

SUPPLIES

BASIC
— video headcleaner and swabs
— screwdriver set (with phillips head)
— AC extension cords
  ALSO
— extra headset and audio cables
— extra batteries, take-up reels
— camera extension cable

If you still have money to spend, consider improving your sound system by buying better microphones, a mike mixer, and an amplifier and speaker (to hook up to large monitor for video shows). Also get some simple light stands, reflectors and bulbs, for shooting in low-light situations. If you can find one, a small body brace would also be useful.

If you have still *more* money to spend, consider buying an editing system. Avoid the expense and restrictions of setting up a studio.

Interview with Anna Heininey

by Theresa Mack

The Williams Residence, a formidable sixteen-story building across the street from P.S. 75 in Manhattan, is a Salvation Army hotel for people over sixty-five. Except for a few residents who are active and come over to the school to work as volunteers, there has never been much contact between the Residence guests and the P.S. 75 students. Sometimes, when you look out the windows at school, you'll see an old person sitting in his window watching the children come and go.

Last fall I decided to start visiting the Williams Residence regularly with a group of children to make videotapes with some of the old people living there. I found ten interested kids from a fifth-sixth grade class, and every Tuesday afternoon during the school year we went across the street to visit, lugging the video equipment with us.

Every one of the kids loved spending those afternoons at the Residence. Their delight was, I think, more than pleasure at getting out of class. The quiet, soft, almost smothering atmosphere of the Residence lounge seemed to comfort them. Making videotapes in this setting, they became the strong, the knowledgeable, the helpful ones. They were in control, yet were still lovingly babied by the old people simply because they were young and small.

Each afternoon began with hugs and kisses, and usually ended with a treat in the coffee shop. While we were there, though, the kids worked hard. One week they would do some videotaping—interviews in the lounge, or activities in the coffee shop or craft room. The following week they would show the unedited videotape on a large TV in the lounge to an audience of fifteen or twenty people.

After a few months, when we'd taped several Residence activities and done lots of two-minute interviews, I began encouraging people to give us more of their time for an interview, to share more about their past. But being interviewed in an in-depth manner didn't appeal to many people. They didn't seem to take to the idea of talking to us in detail about their lives while being videotaped—and who could blame them, really? Many expressed concern that the children would be bored with the past, or upset by hearing the painful experiences they had had during the depression or World War II. The kids, on the other hand, were eager for stories, especially about what it was like growing up sixty or seventy years ago.

There were a few people who understood what we were asking for, and whose personalities made it easier for them to be interviewed. One of these was Anna Heininey—sixty-six years old, outgoing and very active in cultural and community affairs—who invited us up to her apartment one afternoon in March. She greeted us in her native costume, showed us her feather bed and her naturalization papers, and talked to us about her life. Heather, the interviewer, didn't have to coax anything out of Anna. She showed her sensitivity by listening, and only occasionally asking a question which didn't break the flow of Anna's story.

When we showed the interview the next week in the lounge to an unusually large audience, the room was more emotionally charged than it had been for any other video showing. People laughed and sighed along with Anna on TV, and Anna watched herself with a soft smile and tears in her eyes. One woman, clearly impressed with Anna's life story, kept exclaiming throughout the interview, "And it's *true*. It's all true!"

An Interview with Anna Heininey

H: What is your name?

A: My name is Mrs. Anna Heininey.

H: That's a very nice outfit you have on. Where did you get it?

A: Oh, from my hometown in the Black Forest. That's in the southern part of Germany. You like it?

H: Yes. Did you make it?

A: No, no. There's a lady made it. She's eighty-two years old. But the young people don't wear it any more. It's just the old-timers. They wear it to go to church, or in parades and things like that.

H: Why don't they like to wear it in Germany anymore?

A: Oh, the children there, the young people there are just like here now. They wear shorts and they wear all the kind of clothes you wear, you see. This now is getting so old that they started putting it in the museums you know? And only the old-timers wear it yet—because they wore it all their life, that's why.

H: What was your childhood like in Germany?

A: Well, it wasn't too happy because we lost our father in the First War. He got killed in the First War. And my mother was left with four small children, you see. Had two brothers and two little girls. So, she brought us two girls to America. But in Germany we lived on a farm way up in the mountains where it was very cold. And we all slept in feather beds (laughs). But I went to school there until I was fifteen years old, and then my mother—she had to wait two years till it was our turn to immigrate to America. Then we came to America. And then we got to New York and there was no one on the boat to get us, you see? And we were left on the boat with some more people. The next morning they took us to Ellis Island on a small boat. And there we stayed for a whole day. And some people that are there, they're from all over the world and they're there and wait till someone comes to get them. And sometimes nobody does. And they're there three four weeks and then they have to go back to their homeland where they come from, see?
But we were lucky—this man, he couldn't come to get us. He was a friend of ours in our hometown and he had to stand up for us, you see, because my mother was a widow and she had two small children—I was fifteen, my sister was twelve. And if anything happens to us in five years he would be responsible—you see? If we would get sick, you know what I mean, he would be responsible for us. So, he could not come on the boat to get us because he had the flu, see? So he sent his son to Ellis Island to come and get us out. And then he brought us over to Hillside, New Jersey. That's the first place we saw. And in Battery Park, there's the first big buildings we saw. And all we did was look up at those big buildings, you see.

H: It was different, real different. . . .

A: It was—oh yes, how different. And then we stayed at those people's house for about two, three weeks until my mother got a job and I got a

job as a domestic, to live in. I got $25 a month and I got my room and board. And also, my mother did the same and she put my little sister in an institution and we paid for her there, until she got to be sixteen years old, see.
But, ohhh the nicest thing when I first came here was the player piano. You put a roll in there and that thing was rollin' around and the keys was movin' like that, you know. That was the happiest thing for me, you know? I sit there for hours—those people had the player piano, that thing was going for hours, you know (laughs). And a rockin' chair they had, which I never saw. And I kept rockin' and rockin'. And also bananas—I had never had bananas.

H: They don't have bananas in Germany?

A: No, not where I was, didn't have any bananas. The first banana I ate was when I was fifteen years old, see. (sigh) So . . . that was happy. That was in 1926 when I came, when we came, see?

H: Did your brothers stay in Germany?

A: Yes, my brothers stayed there. They were bigger. And afterwards they had to go in the Second War, and they both got killed in the Second War. And my mother stayed here ten years until we got on our feet. And then she went back, see? She wanted to die in her own homeland, of course. My father was there in the cemetery in the hometown, and she wanted to be with him. So after we got on our feet she went back.
Well, lo and behold, I wasn't here long, and I got married quick! When I was seventeen (laughs) to a man who was born in Beirut, Lebanon. That's in the Holy Land, you know, in the Middle East. And we were married thirty-five happy years. . . . Ohhh, he was a good man. I was so lucky. And we had one child—a little girl—and she died in infancy.
So during the depression—we got married in Brooklyn, New York and we were there five years. The depression came and he couldn't get no work nowhere. He used to work in the shipyards. And so he said, I'll go out of town and see if there is anything doing. So he went to Connecticut. He knew somebody there and he got a job in the shipyard which was in Groton, Connecticut—that's by New London, you know, the naval base there. And he got a job three days a week and started to pick up and then he started to get five days and so on.
And we lived up there for forty years. You know where it is, Mystic Seaport and those places up there? You never been there?

H: No.

A: Oh, you should go there some day. Mystic Seaport is great. So we lived there by the Thames River. There was Groton on one side, New London on the other side. And in the meantime, my husband died there and, uh, my sister also died. My sister never married. She was a domestic all her life because she was sickly all her life. And she also died and they both are buried in Connecticut, where I'll also go eventually. That's in Fairfield, Connecticut, see.

And, uh . . . anyway, then I was left alone and it was kind of lonely up there in the country alone, so I says, "Well, now I'll go to 'fun city'. I'll go to New York and I'm going to settle there." Which I did—I made the application here to the Salvation Army, and here I am now two and a half years and I like it very much. . . . I have a nice old age. Have a miserable youth, but I got a nice old age.

From the *Teachers & Writers Collaborative Newsletter* (Vol. 7, No. 3), pp. 2-5.

The Case of Hector Martinez

by Ron Padgett

Two years ago, at the beginning of the school year, I began working with Jean Pitts' mixed fifth and sixth grade class at P.S. 61. I expected good things from this class, partly because of the kids, partly the teacher, and as time went by those expectations were not disappointed. I did notice, though, that one boy never wrote much, if anything. He was well behaved, attentive and friendly, perhaps a trifle nervous or unsure. I was involved in other things in the class and didn't feel I had enough time to give Hector personal treatment, so I opted for what I felt was the next best, to leave him alone, be friendly, not pressure him. I sensed that pressuring him, even in a friendly manner, would backfire, so I simply laid off.

As the year went on there was little apparent change in his attitude about writing poetry, but then near the end of the year, to my surprise, he handed me a rather long and thorough poem. It wasn't a particularly outstanding work, but the effort involved, the degree of self-engagement were laudable, and it made me happy.

Summer came and went. Hector never crossed my mind.

The following fall I found him in Miss Muczyn's mixed fifth and sixth grade class. He was now a sixth grader. He had also been put into the second-best class, demoted, so to speak, from the previous year's top class. While his work had not been bad, Miss Pitts felt that the change might do him good, that rather than being among the lowest students in the best class, he would develop more fully among the highest of the second-best class.

Hector continued to write more frequently in my classes, but somehow the results weren't very exciting as poetry. They sounded more like scenarios, or summaries of stories. Hector began making them into little booklets with his own cover designs, which were bright and clever. At this point I was still too dumb to realize in what direction he might go, but his classroom teacher, Miss Muczyn, was more alert.

One day I walked into the room and found a play in progress, a puppet play written, directed by and starring Hector Martinez. I was amazed at Hector's talent for mimicry: his imitation of the leading character, a girl rabbit courted by various male animals, was at once precise and hilarious. The play was a great success. I got excited about the play, returned the next day with a tape recorder, taped a performance, typed up a playscript (none existed until then: the outline of the play was established and much of the dialogue improvised, so that each performance was different), and encouraged the troupe to give performances in other classrooms, where word had spread. I followed them from class to class, never bored for a moment. I was delighted by what seemed to me Hector's sudden blossoming, and I paid him a lot of attention.

I suggested to him that we could make a movie and his eyes grew as big as silver dollars. He soon came up with the idea of a film called HORRIBLE HERMAN, in which a giant hand ravages the entire earth, growing hair on its flesh and smashing everything that comes in its path. We talked about this idea, trying to figure out how to make it practical. I didn't know much about filmmaking, but I did know that we could make the hand change by stopping the camera, doctoring the hand, shooting a few feet, stopping, doctoring, etc., and at some point one of us came up with the idea of having the hand change colors. We finally rejected the smashing idea because we felt it would be too unrealistic—no one would really believe it if a hand were knocking over toy cars and houses—and too complicated.

I borrowed a good 8 mm camera from Young Film Makers, gathered various props, and set up a shooting area in the art room, where the art teacher, Dale Kars, had laid out boxes of colored chalks and other materials. Hector was excused from his room and we shot HORRIBLE HERMAN that afternoon, a simple 7-minute film which took 3 hours to shoot! We were making constant adjustments so that the hand would appear to be floating in space, disembodied, changing colors and moving about menacingly. We had a wonderful time, and when I went out in the hall and saw that it was 3:15 I said, "Yikes" to myself, wrote a note for Hector to take home to his mother, explaining his lateness, and cleaned up.

Most of the editing was done in the camera—I tried to shoot as much of the film as possible exactly as I wanted it to come out on the screen, in sequence and ready to view. This, of course, requires more planning than one in which the filmmaker is at liberty to cut, rearrange, reshoot, etc.

I had the film developed, did some minor cutting, then showed the film to Hector's class. Some kids loved it, others were disappointed. They had heard it was supposed to be about Horrible Herman, a big monster, and this was just a hand with colors on it moving around. But Hector was ecstatic. He could hardly contain his joy. We showed the film to other classes, with Hector proudly in attendance.

Not too long after that Hector presented me with the entry form for a Young Movie Makers Contest sponsored by the Kodak Company. The grand prize was a trip to Hollywood and a mini-course in filmmaking, or a scholarship for several thousand dollars. Hector was undecided as to which prize he would choose. I told him to mail in the form to receive complete details before we started on a new film (I didn't think HORRIBLE HERMAN was professional enough), so that our new film could conform to any contest rules (length of film, etc.). He neglected to do so, so I did it. It took what seemed like eternity for the rules to come back, by which time I had already decided to go ahead with the new film and to hell with this contest.

Hector's idea for a new film involved karate, the great wave of which was beginning to break over the nation's youth. He had enlisted the aid of several classmates, Ronald Kelly and Tony Nuvoa. These three boys decided they would be Oriental karate experts: two Puerto Ricans and a Black. Immediately everyone realized what a strange Oriental Ronald would make, and when we finished laughing I suggested that art didn't have to follow life all that closely. I had several lengthy conferences and phone conversations with the boys, mostly with Hector, and the story began to take shape.

The new film, later to be called JAPANESE KARATE KILLERS, would be far more involved than HORRIBLE HERMAN. It would require a narrative, with decent acting, a likely setting (not the Lower East Side, where we live, but somewhere such as Chinatown), more elaborate props, more thought as to action shots, slow-motion, choreography, and the sheer logistics of getting the boys, the props, the camera, etc. all down to Chinatown at the right time.

I had to secure the permission of the parents, some of whom asked me to come to their homes and discuss the project. Tony had just come to P.S. 61 and his father, a hard-working bus driver, wanted to be sure his son would be in responsible hands. I had to convince him of my probity. (Little did I suspect that I was legally responsible for the kids the entire day of the shooting—had one of them broken an arm or twisted an ankle, I could have been sued, I am now told.)

At long last I collected the kids early one Saturday, and we climbed into a cab with our collection of props and headed for Chinatown. This was my first experience of working with kids outside of school: I had often seen my students in the street because we all live in the same neighborhood near the school, but I had rarely been in what might be called a social situation with them, such as riding in a taxi.

When we arrived in Chinatown the boys recoiled: there were real people walking around on the street! They felt self-conscious. I did too, frankly. I didn't want people looking at me as I worked the camera. We veered across the street to a modern housing project on the south side of Chinatown. Back between the modern buildings was a secluded terrace, with various walls and benches and flower beds. A few people were sitting or lying there in the sunlight, someone listening to a Mets game. They paid no attention to us. I suggested we start the film here: it would give us confidence, and it was a surprisingly interesting space. We set up and started to shoot. The first take was all wrong, so we repeated. As we were working, a man with a grim expression on his face approached us in an authoritative manner. I sensed that he was a guardian or representative of the property.

"You'll have to clean up this garbage now," was his opening remark.

My most Machiavellian self took control. My blood boiled, but invisibly. I felt that here, now, was a really educational situation. I felt that my reaction to this man would not only set the tone of the afternoon but would teach the kids something basic about getting along in the world.

I could tell the man to kiss my ass. He would then slug me or call the Security Officer on duty, probably the latter. We would be escorted from the premises. Not a good result.

I could yessir him, pick up our things and sulk away. Not a good result.

"Oh, I'm sorry," I answered, "I didn't realize what a mess we're making. I assure you we'll have it cleaned up in no time."

(The "mess" or "garbage" consisted of our props.)

"My name is Ron Padgett and I'm a Special Teacher at P.S. 61 here in Manhattan. These boys have been assigned a special project, to make a school film, and we're here on location. I hope you won't mind if we finish our job: it'll take only 15 or 20 minutes, and I assure you we'll leave the place spic and span." My tone was polite official, reasonable, but not obsequious. I had put the man in the position that if he were to order us off the property, he would be a monster.

"Uhn," he grunted, "but be sure this place is clean when you leave." And he stalked off.

I shot the boys a sly grin and they immediately

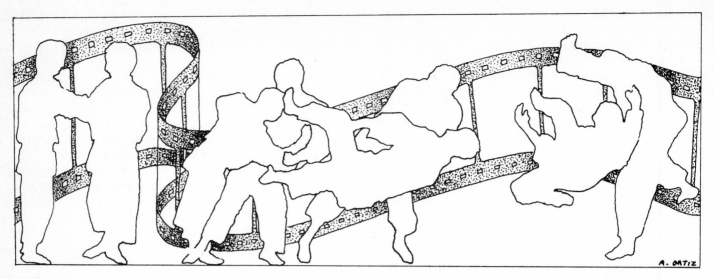

understood what had happened. And we talked about it over lunch.

During the shooting here, a Chinese girl from the neighborhood wandered in. We coaxed her into being in the film, which is what she really wanted. Her name was Laura Louie and she worked fine. All three boys fell in love with her immediately.

Now they had gained in courage and momentum; they were "into" the film. We braved the actual streets of Chinatown, following our outline but incorporating whatever seemed useful or fun: we passed by a knife shop with quite a window display, and it was written into the script, for instance. We went to have lunch, and that was "written in" as part of the film. I worked the camera and made suggestions. The boys did the rest.

It was their first film acting, and I think they did remarkably well. The karate scenes were really beautifully done—a corny way of putting it would be: it was like classical ballet. Hector could be a fine dancer, it seems to me. The fight scenes were surprisingly convincing. They were teaching each other how to act and they were learning about filmmaking, and there were those moments, some too small even to remember, during which they learned other things about simply being alive and growing up.

One too obvious example was in the Chinese restaurant. Tony had never been to one. He had no idea of how to use the chopsticks. Ronald and Hector had more experience in this rather delicate area. Some had a better grasp of what a menu was and how it was arranged. We had some incredible conversations about fortune cookies and the notion of putting words inside of food. None of the boys knew whether or not we should leave a tip, and if so, how much. I explained Basic Tipping. Hector had a twinge of conscience when he realized that he had never left a tip at his local soda fountain.

Time and again small situations developed in which the kids seemed to be learning something basic about just getting along in the world, the kind of thing they learn faster from an outsider than from their parents (this is true of my own son, too). I wish I had taken notes that day, but there wasn't time, and the rush of sensations was too intense to stop and note them or think about them.

We finished the shooting that afternoon. The action went as follows: Ronald makes bets that no one can beat his strong man, played by Tony, who is a hefty kid. A lone fellow, played by Hector, accepts the challenge. Hector and Tony battle. Hector defeats the strong man. Ronald reneges on his offer and takes Hector on. Hector demolishes him too and seizes the money. He flees past the beautiful Chinese girl who has been watching this contest from a safe distance. She waves as he sprints past: he has no time for affairs of the heart.

He disappears into the maze of sights and sounds that is our Chinatown. Strange language, strange signs. He pauses before a knife store, surveys the display, goes in to buy a knife. When he comes out, we might notice two suspicious characters in sunglasses, their faces covered with Band-Aids. These suspicious characters (Tony and Ronald) follow our hero to a Chinese restaurant where he has lunch. He loves his lunch. But the fortune cookie spills out this terrifying message, "You blinded me. I'll get my revenge. Signed, Ronald." As he leaves the restaurant, we might notice two suspicious characters lurking outside, one of them a blind man reading a Chinese newspaper, the other a derelict weaving around in the street. These two individuals follow our hero to a street where they attack him for the final climactic encounter. The two villains attack Hector with swords! In a stunning display of karate and sheer spunk, he completely destroys them, the real coup de grace coming when he plunges his two fingers into the blind man's eye sockets and dislodges the ocular orbs. Ronald grabs his face in agony and, as he lowers his hands, opens them to reveal two incredibly bloody eyeballs!! Then the screen says, "The Bloody End."

I had the film developed, and I did some basic editing at home, then took it to school and played it to the boys' class. It was an instant smash hit. Other classes loved it also. The only class which shied away from it was a timid second grade class: they thought the eyeballs were real. It scared the daylights out of them.

By this time I had realized that no judging committee on earth would award this film first prize: its violence and lack of professionalism left it out of the running, and by this time Hector realized that he was more interested in making films than in winning contests.

As the school year ended, I heard that Young Film Makers, the New York group which had lent me the camera and given me much good advice, had a center for kids on the Lower East Side. I found out the details and gave them to Hector. I told him that he could go to this center and learn more about movie making, and I strongly encouraged him and the other boys to do so, but secretly I thought nothing would come of this.

In the fall Hector called me to ask if he could borrow the print of JAPANESE KARATE KILLERS to show at his new school P.S. 60, a junior high. I said sure and made arrangements to lend him the film—he should have his own copy. I hesitantly inquired about the summer and Young Film Makers. To my surprise he said he had gone, had liked the people, had his own space there all summer and had made five animated films, as well as going on a field trip and working with videotape! I was thrilled to pieces and I still am.

From *Teachers & Writers Collaborative Newsletter* (Vol. 5, No 2) pp. 13-17.

Television for Writing

by Sue Willis

Television is the source of so many images and impressions in the students' lives. They love to recount their TV experiences. "Did you see *Kung Fu* last night?"

1. Write the story of a really good TV program you saw recently. This assignment is more creative than it seems; even rotten shows will sometimes supply the emotional food a person needs. It is often what the person brings to the TV show that gives it value. What a child remembers about a TV program (or a movie) is often far more emotionally authentic than the original.
2. Write a new story or script for your favorite show.
3. Take your two favorite TV (or comics) characters and write a story or script that has them meet and share an adventure. Write directions for the "camera": "First you see a mountain from far away, then you see a helicopter, and then you see close up to the helicopter, and hanging from a rope is. . . "
4. Write an ode (a poem of praise) to your favorite character or program. Or an anti-ode, a hate poem to a program you really hate: "*Soul Train*, they dance so nice; but *American Bandstand*, they dance like they're seasick!"
5. Write some commercials, either parodies or straightforward efforts to sell a product, or, say, to give away some kittens. Give the visual instructions: "First, a shot of a darling kitten looking lonesome. . . ."
6. Write about the experience of watching television. Your own private experience. Where is the TV in your house? Do you watch alone or with your family? Do you eat when you watch TV? How long do you watch TV every day? Does your mind wander when you watch programs? Where does it go? Why does it come back to the TV show?

C. Music

Poems with Music Made by Hand

By Richard Perry

Children love to make music. What better way to examine the concepts of tone and rhythm in writing than to have individual poems and stories set to song?

Some of your children may play instruments. If possible, have them brought in. If you play an instrument, bring it in.

A good beginning: the teacher reads aloud a short piece and follows that reading with a musical interpretation. If the instructor doesn't play then he or she should hum or groan or whistle or beat on a table. By all means, be dramatic.

Instruments can be improvised. Tables can be drums; pencils or rulers, drumsticks. Jars partially filled with paper clips make swell maracas. How about stretched rubber bands, hair combs, jars of the same size containing different amounts of water?

You probably won't have to go to such lengths, however. Check with the school's music teacher. There might be instruments you can borrow. Look around your home. I found in various closets: an old harmonica, a kazoo, bongos, a tambourine and a fluteaphone. Whatever you have, makeshift or genuine, gather them and assign one to each child.

I learned that initially I had to assume more control than I wished; had, in essence, to be a conductor. Otherwise the piece of writing being interpreted became lost in the cacophony. The method I adopted was this:

I had the child who wrote the piece read it aloud, dramatically. I told the musicians to listen carefully, and, when the piece was reread, to attempt to reproduce the sound and the rhythm as the reader presented them. If they had no idea of what to do, they should watch me; I would indicate with hand and body signals.

Rhythm was easy; tone took some time and work. I knew we were on our way to success when the writer interrupted. "The tambourine is too loud," she said. "And the fluteaphone should be like this...." She made a sound that seemed to soar from a spot behind her nose. "You mean like this?" the fluteaphone player replied, and produced a note so close to the original that I got a chill.

As the project evolved, the children proved to be much more perfectionist and harmonic than I expected. They began to see in a practical way that written words have tone and rhythm. An unexpected plus was that each of them became eager to write and have his piece interpreted, and in two weeks I received more material than I'd gotten the previous month.

Song Writing

by Bill Zavatsky

I don't quite remember how we (meaning I, my co-worker Larry Fagin, and the children) began writing songs at our Lincoln-Bedford Neighborhood Museum (MUSE) workshops in Brooklyn. There was an old upright piano in our room, and one day we graduated from using it to supply sound effects to inspire writing ("Write down what the sounds of the music make you think about"), to actual song writing.

We'd cluster around the piano and hammer out whatever flew through the air. All the kids contributed lines which we'd all sing together, stop, then add more words. By the time our song was finished we'd been singing it for maybe half an hour, goodness knows how many times through. Once our "first draft" was finished (that is, a fixed melody and one chorus of lyrics), we'd add more words until time was up or we ran out of steam. Sometimes everything blew up, and we gave up completely. (The kids get quite excited and wild in group collaborations of this sort.) More often than not, though, we finished. But be prepared to tolerate an extra amount of noise and nuttiness if you decide to write songs in your classroom.

Sometimes the songs grew directly out of whatever writing idea Larry and I were trying that day; sometimes they were totally spontaneous and had nothing to do (seemingly) with what was going on in the writing workshop; but usually whatever was bouncing around in the kids' heads crept into our song words.

These songs were collaborations. I supplied the basic chord structures (most of which were anchored in the standard I—mVI—IV—I rock 'n' roll or "Heart and Soul" chord progression), usually working them out from what the kids sang. Our perennial literary "What happens next?" turned into "What comes now? *Sing* it!" Larry would adjust melody lines, suggest refinements of rhyme and so forth, and everybody would keep things moving. (Song writing, incidentally, is an excellent way to "place" rhyme in its most viable contemporary context—the popular song lyric, where it is very much alive—rather than in poetry itself, where for the most part it has become a dead weight.) Instead of notating the songs, we tape-recorded them, and published the lyrics in the poetry collections of the kids' work that MUSE mimeographed for us regularly.

There's no reason why any teacher who can play songs on the guitar or piano or autoharp should leave song writing out of classroom activities. Many of our "hits" were built on songs we all knew well. Our "Alexander's Ragtime Mosquito" was built on "Alexander's Ragtime Band," and our "Calypso Melody" owed its tune to the old favorite, "Sloop John B." Fitting these warhorses with new sets of words can save time (you won't have to make up new tunes) and can turn into marvelous exercises in the art of parody.

Every so often, because the children demanded it, we'd haul out the words (although one of the benefits of our "sing it a million times" approach was that nearly all the kids had memorized the words already) and have a songfest of songs we had written ourselves. What a way to electrify dull school assemblies, holiday pageants, or graduation ceremonies. The graduates compose their own class song! And why not an entire school musical with songs written by P.S. or J.H.S. or H.S. whatever?

Once, our experimentation with singing led us into strange territory, an instance I must relate briefly because of its eclipsed nature. Joey never appeared at MUSE again after his singing "debut" that week.

He was a difficult boy, this Joey. Always disrupting, always climbing under the table, upsetting the chairs, refusing to cooperate at even the minimum level that Larry and I had come to demand in a workshop that provided plenty of opportunities for creation and chaos.

We couldn't get Joey to do any writing by himself. Collaborations, with Larry or me writing the words down, were as far as he would go—and it wasn't very often we could get him to cooperate that much. But one week when several of us were gathered around the piano, we coaxed him into singing. The sounds that issued from his mouth were strange and tortured. For that, they had the pure quality of a choirboy—of an unsullied, almost girlish voice.

Things were particularly relaxed at MUSE that morning, and rather than "write down" song words, we encouraged the kids to improvise songs on the spot. First I would strike a few chords, let the singer hear them, then Larry and I would encourage the kids to *go*, to sing out with whatever the music was calling up within them. It was a logical development of the improvisatory nature of the workshop.

One of the little girls—also not a writer of her own works by her own hand, but a child who had always responded brilliantly in dictation—gave a remarkable performance, singing continuously and, if I remember correctly, managing to throw in a rhyme or two, though we made no insistence on that. When Joey's turn came, he halted but suddenly gave out with astonishing squeaks. The only analogy I can make to his vocalizing is to compare it to some of the more experimental, more dissonant twentieth century

musics. He began to cry out, in song, about his mother, about how he wanted to kill her, over and over again! I hasten to add, for those who will be disturbed by these revelations, that neither I nor my co-worker had encouraged or anticipated this outburst.

I have often thought about that morning and Joey and his singing. I have thought, too, of his crippled mother, who would question us relentlessly about Joey's progress in the workshop. And how we would only smile and answer, "Fine," for the workshop was Joey's and not hers. Joey's attendance at the workshop had always been erratic, and we had no reason to suspect that his mother ever learned of what came to his lips when he sang.

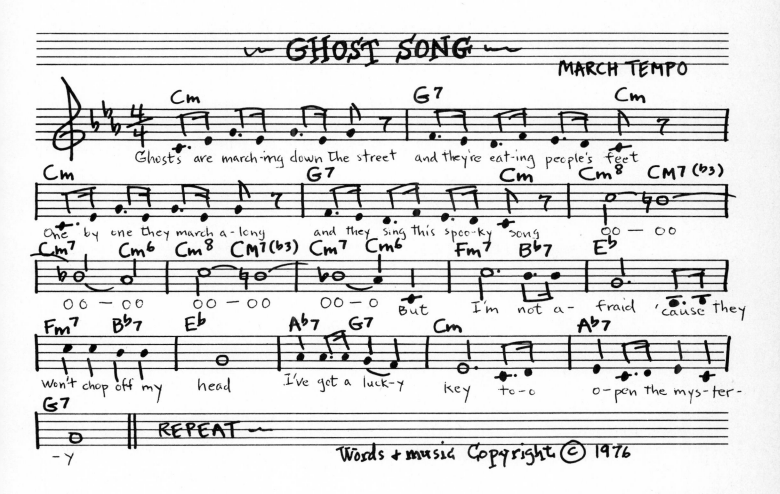

ALEXANDER'S RAGTIME MOSQUITO
[To the tune of Alexander's Ragtime Band]

I like to fly
I like to bite
I just might bite you on the nose

I like to eat
I like to fight
I like to wear blue baby clothes

You can find me in the swamp
Where it's really nice and damp
Making paper airplanes 'neath fluorescent lamps

10 cents will get you to the door—
Smorgasbord!

Come on and fly
Come on and bite
The puppet people in their cars

Come on and play
Come on and say
"I want a ticket to the stars!"

And if you care to hear THE TWELFTH OF NEVER
Played by psychos!

Come on and sing
Come on and swing
The Mosquito Serenade
                    —Pennye and Ruthie Glover

CALYPSO MELODY
[To the tune of "Sloop John B"]

I woke up and brushed my teeth
I cooked french fries and eggs
I put on my pants and dress
over my legs

   I want to go home
   I want to go home
   I feel so crazy
   I want to go home

My mother has gone insane
My father he robbed the train
Then it started to rain
all over my brain

   It happened so slow
   What do you know
   It went over my nose
   and stomped on my toes

I jumped up and down just twice
I was standing on the head of lice
Blood came out and knocked me onto the floor

   I felt like a bean
   I was sent to the Dean
   He smacked my nose
   and stomped on my toes

So I woke up and brushed my teeth
I cooked french fries and eggs
I put on my pants and dress
over my legs

   I want to go home
   I want to go home
   I feel so crazy
   I want to go home
                    —GROUP COLLABORATION

MOBY DICK BOOGIE
[Boogie-woogie shuffle beat]

Don't you know
There's no blues aloud
In the bar on the corner
Of Sky & Cloud

Oh yeah
Oh yeah
Rain's comin' down
Poundin' on the ground
Moby Dick come save me for the second time
   aroun'
Oh yeah

I'm diggin' up the ground
To find the bones
Of Jerry Lee Lewis
And James J. Jones

Oh yeah
Oh yeah
Rain comin' down
Poundin' on the ground
Moby Dick come save me for the third time aroun'
Ohh yeah

Inside the bar
Smokin' a cigar
Thinkin' about the weatherman
Who stole my daddy's car

Oh yeah
Oh yeah
Rain comin' down
Poundin' on the groun'

Moby Dick come save me for the fourth time
  around
Oh yeah

Out on the street
People are asleep
Dreamin' 'bout the movie
That's showin' on their feet

Oh yeah
etc.

Out on the street
People are asleep
Dreamin' 'bout the movie
That was really really groovy

Oh yeah
etc.

—GROUP COLLABORATION

207

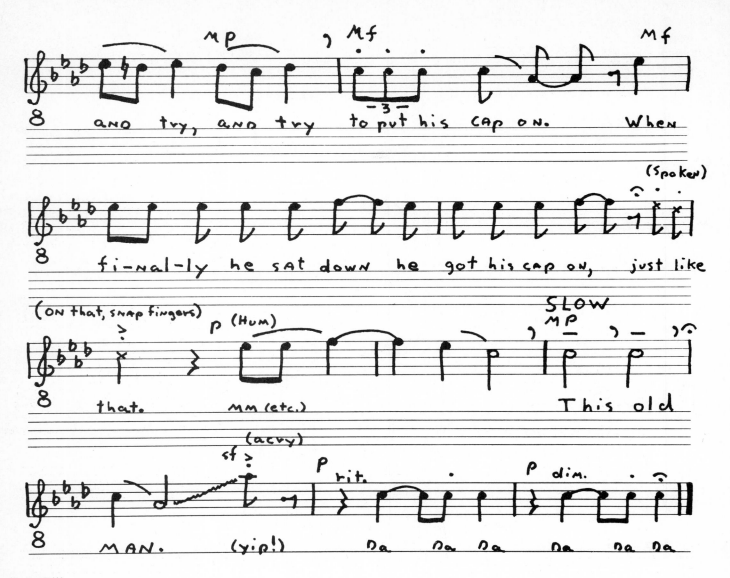

Dear Bill,

We had been doing some writing to music. I tried to have the kids convey the same sense of melody and improvisation with their words that jazz musicians do with their instruments. Anyway, after doing the work with music, fifth-grader Lisa Borris wrote a line in a poem, "And they sang a scary song." So, I asked her to write the lyrics to the "scary song" and she came up with the lyrics to "Haunted, Haunted," which Cliff Safane then set to music. I brought in a tape of Cliff singing "Haunted, Haunted" the following week as a surprise for Lisa. The class gathered around the cassette tape recorder and Lisa's face practically exploded when she heard her own words being sung.

Writing to Music

by Bill Zavatsky and Ron Padgett

There are various ways of using recorded material in the classroom. You can play a record or tape which contains information you wish your students to absorb: what a Chinese folk song sounds like, how William Carlos Williams reads his own poetry, or what English sounds like.

You can also use recorded material, and music in particular, to inspire writing. The name of the game, in the case of music, is response. For instance, you might play the "William Tell Overture" to the kids. What images the music evoked in them, how it made them feel is obviously more important than telling them that it was an example of Romantic music by Giacomo Rossini.

Kenneth Koch discusses techniques for using music for evocative purposes in his *Wishes, Lies and Dreams* (Vintage Books paperback, pp. 224-245). To summarize his approach: he suggests playing a passage of music and discussing it in terms of what it reminds you of. "William Tell" makes everyone think of galloping horses, the Lone Ranger, excitement, etc. But sometimes kids won't see what you're talking about. They'll say, "It makes me think of an orchestra in a big city." What we are looking for is not identification, but an opening up, a direct line from the music to the imagination, where the music will call forth scenes, characters, actions—almost like a silent movie score. Naturally these pictures will be peculiar to the individual, though the kind of music selected (overtly "spooky" stuff, for instance) will have its effect. And lest we forget, it is useful to remember that the word "imagination" means first and foremost the "making of images" in the mind. It is just these images, summoned by music, we are searching for.

The selection of recordings to be played is important. Steer clear of rock 'n' roll and jazz; you'll have the kids bopping around in their seats, and no writing will get done. Most children don't have the habit of listening to symphonic music, so almost any orchestral piece with variations of tempo works well. Igor Stravinsky's *Firebird Suite* and *Le Sacre du printemps* (*The Rite of Spring*), though children may remember them from the soundtrack of Disney's *Fantasia*, are dependable standbys. Piano pieces by Liszt, Debussy (the *Etudes*), and Chopin are alternately powerhouse and dreamy, and the quirky sense of humor in Erik Satie's piano pieces ought to be given a whirl. The symphonies of Charles Ives, our wonderful American composer, can be tried on the students, and for weirdness—music like none you've ever heard before —the electronic music of Karlheinz Stockhausen is highly recommended, particularly *Stimmung, Song of the Youths*, and *Telemusik* (available separately on the Deutsche Grammophon label). Edgard Varèse's futuristic music will set your kids' brains spinning, too, especially the *Poème électronique* (see *The Varèse Album*, Columbia Records). But half the fun of using music for writing is finding the recordings that work best for you. Try anything. If it flops, you can always change the record!

To begin with, tell the students that you're going to play them some music, kinds of music they've maybe never heard before. (Giving the names of the records will slow things up; save that for later.) All of us have had the experience of sitting in a comfortable chair and, as we listened to the phonograph or the radio, creating pictures in our minds to "go with the music." Talk a bit about this with the students, see how many of them have done it.

Next (as the record spins on the turntable, ready for the tonearm), you might ask them to get comfortable in their seats—without falling asleep!—and listen for a while before writing. (Just before setting needle to record, you might switch off the lights to supply a little "atmosphere," an invitation to turn inward toward that mental movie screen where the pictures play all day.) They can close their eyes if it's helpful; they can put their heads on their desks if they want. Encourage them (without saying so) to get in touch with the continual stream of imagery that the music is about to activate.

Before the music starts, though, tell the children that as they listen, as they are drawn into the music, they will begin to see a place—whatever place the music says to see. Emphasize the fact that each of them will find themselves in a different location, that there is no "right or wrong place" to be. As the place becomes clear, things will begin to happen in that place. What? Why, listen to the music and it will tell you; it will show you what is happening! This preparation, or something of your own devising similar to it, is vague enough to get the children thinking without programming them. Without it, some students will flounder around for the whole period, "seeing" nothing. Rather than a place, you might suggest a person. A place seems open-ended enough, however, and can contain people, things, and the action the music hopefully will generate.

Put on the record after telling the kids that they should begin writing as soon as they "see" their place, or as soon as something begins to happen there. Now and then, and especially if the tempo of the music shifts or crescendoes or softens to a whisper, ask the kids "What's happening now? What is changing?" If they can't write down everything, urge them to get down what seems most important. And insist that they write a narrative, not a list (though doing a list might be an interesting experiment later; images could be recorded more quickly that way, and be expanded in a subsequent story or poem). Another good exhortation you can shout over the music now and again is: "What do you see now? What does that remind you of?"—referring to another change in the music, all of which (if done at the proper times and as unobtrusively as possible) will sensitize the children to the dramatic qualities of the piece they are listening to. (Which makes this writing exercise a kind of visceral, nonacademic foray into "music appreciation.")

One piece of music can be played for the entire writing period, but with good timing you can move through several LPs if you wish, playing whatever portions of them appeal to you. You might also try playing short pieces (Satie's *Trois Gymnopédies*, on *Piano Music of Erik Satie*, Vol. 1, Angel Records, and the compositions on Charles Ives's *Calcium Light Night*, Columbia Records, will be useful). That way, the children can follow the music for a few minutes, write like mad, and have a breather. Some of the writing could then be read aloud, and ... on to another writing experiment!

Don't think of these pieces the kids have written as "finished products." Naturally, some will be, but in the majority of cases your students will need time to rewrite them or put them into shape. Written in haste, their papers may in certain cases defy legibility. As a further assignment, ask the kids to recopy or rewrite their musical meanderings, but make sure that they hand in the original.

Most of the students will write directly in prose, but encourage those who can write in poetic lines to do so. If some kids want to rewrite their compositions as poems—fine. But don't insist on any specific form *as they write*. Remember, they're working at top speed, and rules of neatness and legibility that might be observed for other kinds of composition

should go out the window here. A good rule to follow is: "As long as you can figure it out later."

The following poem was written to music by Hyam Kramer, a gifted seventh grader with whom I worked at J.H.S. 141 in the Bronx, N.Y. Hyam follows the leaps of the music with great skill, and isn't afraid to "write crazy" by jotting down whatever pops into his mind as he listens:

Whirling, winding, ouch!
Wow! Hey shut-up!

No, not again!
Hey, stop it!
Good boy!

Johnny Carson isn't my game!
This isn't The Watergate Hearings!
Everything is now understood!

Or is it?

Please don't shatter me
with wows!
Oh, my heart is breaking up
into pieces of broken glass,

Quiet, slow, yes . . .
Now relaxation . . .
Slow, slow, slow . . .

Hark the herald angels . . .
Frankenstein?

Mother Goose lost her touch!
Stop drilling on my egg!

Pop, a chick was hatched!
Slow down, I hear something unusual!
It's coming by faster!
It's . . . It's . . .

Here!

Help, the world is eating itself up!
Now me!
Silence!
Just war, hate, pestilence, dreary . . .

Alacazam!

It's Bozo the . . .
Nothing! Quiet, erupt! OW!

I'm gone, it Zapped!

I found myself in a river boat.
We're now under water!

The mermaids!
Who is it?
From where are you!

It's the King!
He's mysterious
Behind the crowd I can see something!

I hear voices!
It's Johnny Mann's Stand Up & Cheer!

And now it's time for a commercial,
Sing, sing a song . . .
Let's get back to King!

Here he is again!
Johnny! We want more!

You're singing for Bob Crane!
This isn't his network special!
Is Nixon approaching!

Well, if it isn't your wife!
She's telling us something!
She disappeared!

Hey, where is everybody!

They're all back again!
We are running wild!

Now Maude is starring!
But this is The Johnny Mann Show!

Oh no, we aren't on the air any more!

It's the Waltons, or maybe Lassie!
We're in a tough spot!
Mary is caught behind the truck!
It's starting up!
Oh help her before she goes!
Here comes Jim, we can't find Mary!
Help her, he's starting up the engine!
He has the gear in reverse!
 Now he's backing up,
 And . . . And . . .
 No . . . Mary's crunch

Jim, get the hospital guy!
 Hey, the ambulance!
Hurry, Hurry, Hurry!
Get her on the stretcher!
Jim get MaMa!
We must save her!

Now lift her, she isn't breathing!
No pulse!

Hurry ambulance!
 Flat tire!
Will Mary survive?
 Oh, help Jim, help!
 To be continued . . .

And that was our show!
See you next week on . . .

LOVE OF LIFE!

Hyam Kramer
J.H.S. 141, Bronx, N.Y.

Hyam's dizzying, exclamation-punctuated poem reminds, stylistically, of Gertrude Stein, whom he has surely never read. It is also filled with humorous pokes at television, which in a sense, is *all* soap opera with its hyperactive situations and strident reactions: tragedy merges with the game show and the variety hour in a bubble bath of insanity. Most student compositions written to music won't be of this sort, but we include this example to suggest that a teacher must expect the unpredictable. No one knows exactly what kind of fantasies that music will whirl up inside young writers.

WACKO RECORDS

For sheer imaginative joy and the art of parody, records by Spike Jones, the Firesign Theater, Bonzo Dog Band, Monty Python's Flying Circus, and others, can't be beat. Teachers over 40 (and some younger) will recall such immortal classics as Spike Jones' version of "My Old Flame" (as sung by someone portraying Peter Lorre, who grows angry when he can't remember what his "old flame" was called: "What was it??! Betty? Adolph?"). Jones, along with his sidekick Doodles Weaver, created some true comic masterpieces.

In the era of *Mad* magazine and its counter-cultural offspring, the *National Lampoon*, students ought to become acquainted with the madcap mania of Spike Jones. Little kids will love him, and there's no reason why his and other recordings can't form a unit on comedy with the emphasis on parody. Virtually all of Spike's outings were meant to demolish the crooner corn he saw littering the American musical landscape, and in his masterpieces—"Cocktails for Two," "Laura," and "Der Fuehrer's Face"—he attacked without mercy. Jones' records are continually being repackaged and reissued by RCA; the two best are *The Best of Spike Jones and His City Slickers*, and *Spike Jones is Murdering the Classics*. The former LP contains his parodies of popular songs, and the latter his ungentle restructurings of the "William Tell Overture," the "Blue Danube," and others. Playing the originals for your students, then Jones' dadaist cavalry charges, will give them plenty to discuss!

Thanks to educational television, many young Americans will recognize the name of Monty Python, the group of English humorists who manage to swoop from the heights of inspired genius down to the depths of utter drivel on a single LP side. Their material is most appropriate for older high school students, but in fact even grammar school kids watch the Pythons. In any case, screen the records first if "embarassing moments" are not your classroom forte. Two LPs currently on the market: *Monty Python's Previous Record* and *Another Monty Python Record* (both on Charisma Records).

The Bonzo Dog Band was an English rock 'n' roll group composed mostly of art students who produced some agonizingly hilarious songs and stagings. Their records are still on the market, but will no doubt become very difficult to find in a few years. See: *Urban Spaceman* and *Tadpoles* (both on Imperial Records), and *Let's Make Up and Be Friendly* (United Artists Records).

The Firesign Theater is America's answer to England's loonies, a group of mad geniuses whose inspiration (often of a high verbal order) is as zany as it is exciting and, sometimes, completely incomprehensible. At least the early work of the Theater is heavily invested with drug-culture references. Your move. Some of their many recordings (all on Columbia Records) are: *Waiting for the Electrician or Someone Like Him*, *How Can You Be in Two Places at Once When You're Not Anywhere at All*, and *I Think We're All Bozos on This Bus*.

From here, a unit on comedy could study W.C. Fields and the Marx Brothers (via films and filmscripts), analyze a few issues of *Mad*, discuss TV comedy shows, Woody Allen and Mel Brooks movies: there's no end in sight! Except the end of this piece.

D. Art

Bugs: One Insect Leads to Another

by Bob Sievert

It started as an insect project in the Bronx. Debbie Kantor, Assistant Principal at C.S. 232 in the Bronx, introduced me to Wendy Branch, who taught a fourth grade. We discussed ways in which we might work together. I suggested we do a project that would tie in with something the class was doing and help illuminate it with a visual art element. We talked over social studies and science projects. The idea of insects kept circling around, until finally we decided it had to be an insect project.

The project led in unexpected directions. After three weeks it was going so well that I started a second insect project in Selma Benjamin's third grade class at P.S. 84 in Manhattan. In each group there was a different momentum, and each achieved something different. Both groups made fantastic papier-mâché insects. At the end, Wendy's class had made a giant mural; Selma's had produced a film in which the school is menaced by a horde of insects from Mars and the teacher devoured (to the class's delight) before their eyes.

During the week that followed my first talk with Wendy, I had found a book on ants with some pretty good pictures in it. I realized that if I taught ant anatomy, it would serve as an introduction on all insects, since insects seem to me to be variations on the same form. I made a "basic insect drawing" and brought it to Wendy's class.

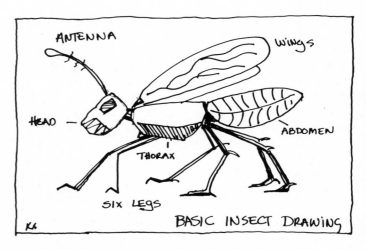

BASIC INSECT DRAWING

At the first session I drew the insect on the board, naming each part as clearly as possible. I explained that millions of different kinds of insects had these parts, although some of them varied greatly: whereas butterflies had large, feathery wings, beetles had hard shell-like wings.

After the ant was drawn, we made a list of insects on the board and tried to sketch them. Butterflies, dragonflies, cockroaches, and bees all had the basic form. After the board was covered with drawings, I passed out paper and crayons and had everyone draw the basic form. Everyone was able to do it (the triumph of teaching form rather than trying to evoke emotion). Each child did a very personal rendition of the drawing, and I let them spend the rest of the period drawing all the insects they could think of. We cut them out and hung them on the wall. It was exciting to see the work, and the class responded with great enthusiasm.

Throughout the first half of the project, pretty much the same format was used. I would come in with some material about insects and explain it with drawings on the board. The class would draw from the board and make up their own drawings about the materials presented. Some of the topics were: insect life cycle, insect homes, social insects, and beetles.

Wendy got mealworms for all the children. They watched them grow and change from larvae to pupae to adult beetles.

I began the second project with Selma's class at P.S. 84 to see if it would meet with equal enthusiasm. A student teacher thought the class needed three-dimensional work, and she and Selma suggested making models. Wendy had also asked about making models, so I thought about it for a while and finally sat up one night playing with wire, papier-mâché, string and plaster and came up with this recipe:

heavy wire, string, wallpaper paste, newspaper, and masking tape = basic insect.

For the first model-building session, an armature is fashioned. Three loops of wire, representing the head, thorax, and abdomen of the insect, are put together. The body loops should be about three inches long. Then three wires are twisted into the joints (one between the head and thorax, two between the thorax and abdomen) for the six legs. Antennae are fastened to the head.

After the wire armature was completed, I had them stuff newspaper into each wire loop, which was then held in place with masking tape. This made a rough model that could be covered with papier-mâché during the second session.

Most students were able to build the armature independently; some needed help. In projects like this, I always give as much support as possible, without doing the work for them.

One girl in Wendy's class had us do as much for her as possible. When we got tired, she took her work into a back corner of the class. With patience she worked on her almost completed version until suddenly, using wild destructive energy, she crushed it shapeless and came screaming across the room holding the mangled form.

"Oh, God, I've killed it. It's dead. I've killed it," she yelled.

Immediately everyone rushed to revive the crumpled bits of wire and string.

In the second model-building session, we took the armature stuffed with wadded newspapers and cov-

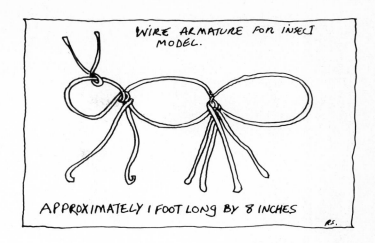

WIRE ARMATURE FOR INSECT MODEL.

APPROXIMATELY 1 FOOT LONG BY 8 INCHES

ered it with two or three layers of papier-mâché. We smeared wallpaper paste on medium-size pieces of newspaper (envelope-size) and fixed them one at a time to the armature. Each leg and antenna was carefully wrapped. After this "rough" coat was on, we began to mold and shape it.

Ricardo, a boy in Wendy's class, revealed himself to be a gifted artist at this point. While most of the children had relied on the basic insect form to convey the image, Ricardo's insect had definition and personality. It was a bright, cheerful praying mantis, with a wonderful sense of form and life. However, at some point Ricardo became frustrated and smashed it. I was shocked.

"Don't you want to fix it?" I asked.

"No. Why do I need that junk!" he said.

It scared me to see him reject his talents so easily.

In the third session, we applied several more coats of papier-mâché, until the dried insects had the feel of stiff cardboard. The coats of mâché became easier and easier to apply. Once it was stiff and dry (after three weeks), we painted the insects in bright colors, and found we had a wonderful series of insects crawling about both classrooms. In Wendy's class we attached clear plastic wings, but the plastic was not heavy enough and the wings never seemed substantial.

Wendy and I were both very happy with the results, and we moved on to working with plant forms for a while—also a good project. I brought in a giant piece of "seamless" photo background paper (9 ft. by 12 ft.) on which we painted a huge mural of insects and flowers.

However, in Selma's class, everybody was still getting off on insects. They hovered about the room in eerie inspiration. They had to be realized more deeply. So we decided to make a movie using the insects. The whole class was to make the film.

I showed them how to make a story board for a film, and Selma assigned them to bring in a story the next day. It was amazing how similar the stories were. In most, the lovely insects were cast in the role of hostile monsters that attack the class and kill poor

DON'T BUG ME! (STORYBOARD BY MS BENJIMANS CLASS)

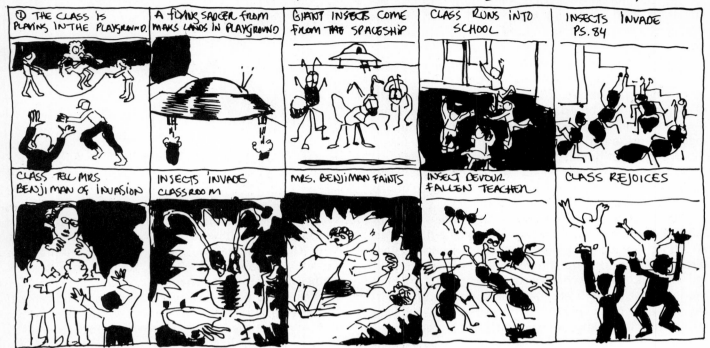

Selma. Every time a story was read with Selma's demise, the class went wild cheering. Selma seemed to enjoy it as much as the children.

I made a story board that was an editorial digest of all the stories. We rehearsed as a group two or three times and finally shot the film on the hottest day of early June. The heat made everybody very business-like and professional. No one wanted to waste energy.

The film was shot with a Super 8 movie camera that Marie Charney, a P.S. 84 corridor teacher, lent us. It had a single-frame device, so that we could film live action scenes, and then, when the insects were supposed to "act," we placed them in position and shot four to six frames. Then we advanced the insects barely an inch and shot a few more frames. The insect shots were hard to control because each child had the responsibility of moving his own insect. I worried a lot about the quality of various shots. The scene in which the insects devour Selma was shot in the classroom under hot lights, an awfully demanding situation, but the class was up to it.

The finished film was a delight. With no editing, we managed a very believable fifty-foot, three-minute horror film. The scenes with the children running in terror juxtaposed with the mechanical scurrying of the insects were perfect. Only in one or two places did the visual line of the film break credibility.

We were all pleased, and at some point during this year, we plan to let the two groups at the two schools see each other's work.

From the *Teachers & Writers Collaborative News-letter* (Vol. 7, No. 2), pp. 32-35.

Paper "Film" Strips

by Barbara Siegel

PAPER "FILM" STRIPS

To make paper filmstrips, take a roll of the widest adding machine tape (4 inches is fine) and cut off a length of paper several feet long for each kid. Also cut up cardboard cylinders into the same number of 4" lengths. Onto each piece of cardboard, glue a length of the paper at one end and roll it up. These will be the filmstrips. For the screens take cardboard boxes or shirt cardboards, paint them black and cut two vertical slits 4 inches long and 4 or 5 inches apart. The kids can slip the paper strip right into the screens and make the drawings, pulling the strip through as the story develops. The dialogue could be put into balloons in each frame or narrated.

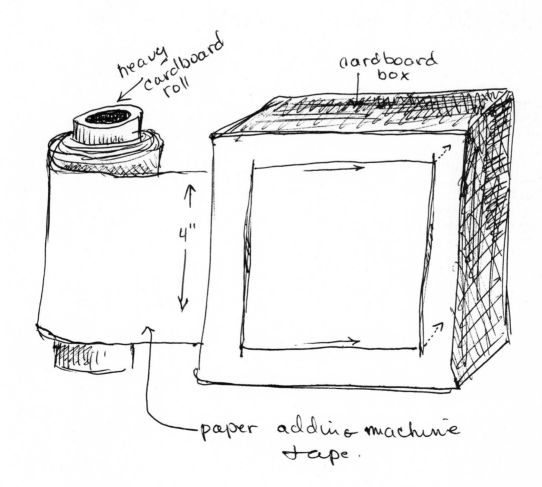

Life-size Theater Dolls

by Barbara Siegel

LIFE-SIZE THEATER DOLLS

Have the kids lie down on large pieces of heavy cardboard and trace around them including the head and hair. Cut out the figures and have each person paint and decorate his own figure so that it represents himself. Openings should be made somewhere near the face so that the children will be able to see out when holding the dolls in front of them. Fasten two dowels or long cardboard cylinders onto the backs of the dolls for holding them. The dolls should be large enough so that when a child is holding it from behind, he won't be seen. Make up plays or stories in which the kids are the characters and the dolls are the actors. After they have acted themselves, they might exchange dolls and take on the character of another person in the class.

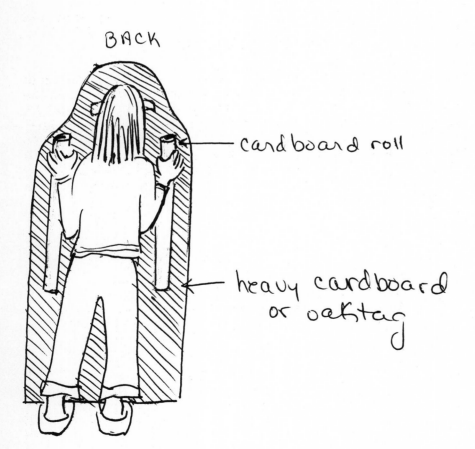

BACK

cardboard roll

heavy cardboard or oaktag

FRONT

New Super Heroes

by Ron Padgett

Have your kids invent new super heroes by changing an object into a human-type creature and drawing a picture of it. For instance, Vase Man, Per Cent Man, Net Man, Button Man, Word Man, Paper Man, Suitcase Man, Line Mouth Man, Pool Man (water) and Pool Man (billiards). Then have them write a poem or story which involves the protagonist. Super Heroes can be female, Super Heroines—Cloud Woman, Baseball Bat Woman, Long Distance Phone Call Woman, etc.

Following examples by Sonja West and Wayne Padgett

SUITCASE MAN GOES ALL AROUND THE WORLD

There once lived a man named Suitcase Man. He went all around the world. A man named Karl Dinsler owned him. He got sick every time he went somewhere. He turned black then blue. Suitcase Man thought the man who owned him was very stupid. He treated him like a suitcase and not like a person. But how could the man do that? Suitcase Man looked like a suitcase. He said, "Darn!" to the man. But the man did not hear. Karl Dinsler did not know that Suitcase Man could talk. He did not know Suitcase Man could talk because he did not hear him.

For one thing, he was always being carried. But one night there was an adventure for Suitcase Man. A man with a long dress with black stars and a white background gave Suitcase Man magic powers. He was very strong. He could do anything. He had a golden gun. He had a gold suit. He lost some weight. Now he could help people. He had cavities. He had grown a mustache and a beard. He had become very rich. Also very sick. He's 2,000,000 years old. He lives on my street. His master lived to be 1,000,000. Me and Wayne got 2,000,000 of his inheritance. We split it 1,000 1,000 each. We bought everything in blue. Some people gave us money. Because we were Suitcase Man's owner. Instead of Suitcase Man, his name turned into Super Suitcase Man. Finally after hard years of work, he died.

by Sonja West

PAPER MAN TO THE RESCUE

Once there was a piece of paper. It got carried to school. Once he got his face written and it looked like two eyes and a nose and a mouth. It blinked. He opened his mouth and it sounded like a blind freak. Then it sounded like Yogi Bear. It flew out the window and went to Jellystone Park and said, "It is time to hibernate," and went into a cave and slept until next year and then Yogi went inside the cave and crumpled the paper.

by Wayne Padgett

suitcase man

paper man

worD man

word

line mouth man

_ _ _ _ _ _ _

percent man

vase man

Pool man

Indian Writing

by Bob Sievert

In the beginning of this school year I approached most of the teachers I work with on the possibility of doing a continuous project that could combine art-work with a larger classroom study. Several suggested a study of the American Indian civilizations. Since I had been reading a lot of American Indian material over the last few years, I was delighted.

I started the projects in two classes, Susan Morton's third-fourth grade class at P.S. 84 (Manhattan) and Katy Washofsky's fifth grade at C.S. 232 (in the Bronx, N.Y.). Later I did work with Pat Parker's fourth-fifth grade and Audrey Reagan's bilingual fifth grade at P.S. 84.

I began by showing pictures of Indian art and reading at random poems and songs from various anthologies. There were several poems with responses that the kids could join in. Everyone loved to do this and we did it often.

Farewell oh friends for I must leave you O friends
Response: A Ye Ha A YE YA HA AYE!

O brothers do not take it to heart that I must go
Response: Ah YE yah Ye Ya YE ah YE Aye!
[Chippewa song]

After looking at pictures of Indian work we talked about how the designs were made up. Then I asked the kids to mark off small spaces on their paper and imagine themselves Indians. I asked them to fill in the spaces. What I got back was several batches of interesting crayon drawings, though they were not particularly Indian in flavor or spirit. I realized that what I wanted in the work was a more accurate understanding of Indian culture and a sense of the spirit that I felt was communicated in the work we had seen.

I began to experiment by using symbols that I found in several books. I came up with a "vocabulary" of about thirty symbols. I drew them on the board and the students copied them into their notebooks. The interest and care with which the students copied the symbols excited me. Many students helped me continue the search for signs.

Next I suggested that they take their basic vocabu-lary and produce drawings that told stories. The work grew even more exciting, for now each student began to organize his work and present situations that showed a sense of Indian life.

Many of the students felt that they understood the content of their work. While at one level the work depended on using an established vocabulary that was limited, a whole new area of exploration emerged: devising places onto which to put the symbols. Several students from Susan Morton's and Katy Washofsky's classes elected to make tepees. The construction of them was fairly simple—two sheets sewn together, out of which a large semicircle was cut to serve as the covering, and seven poles tied together. The symbol designs were carefully worked out. One class painted the tepee and the other did crayon drawings that took perfectly on the sewn sheets. Later in Susan Morton's class, one group worked on costumes and another on wooden implements that were then decorated with symbols. Each tepee told an elaborate tale in which hunting, rain, and battles were the main topics.

Audrey Reagan copied the symbols on a rexograph master, with the names of the symbols in both English and Spanish. Each student was given a copy and we did large chalk drawings using one or two symbols chosen from the sheet. The drawings were not only drawings but visual poems, since they could be spoken as well as seen. For example:

"Thunderbirds over the mountains."
"Two men hunting across the river from three deer"
"Three bears, two deer, hiding in the trees"
"Lightning at sunrise"

Many of the students began to experiment with making narratives, stringing symbols together to tell a story.

I found an Ojibwa chant that I found very moving. In each class I copied it on the board. I explained the meaning of each symbol and then we discussed the poem. The poem was a great success, so we decided to enlarge each of the seven characters and put them up on the wall. I finally began to feel that I was beginning to get something of the culture across.

The work continued to develop as various students began to search out books and tried to interpret the picture writing they found in them. I found an excellent book on American Indian picture writing, and the interest in deciphering the pictographs we found in it continued. As we went forward, it became clear to me that the symbols themselves were responsible for conveying information and understanding of the Indians.

Here are brief descriptions of other projects in this series:

1. *Indian Names*. One student made a list of Indian names he found in various books. He wrote out the names phonetically and in translation.

2. *Totems*. We had several discussions about the idea of animal spirits and their relation to names, tribes, clans and places. We made a list of animals and their qualities—fox: sly, clever teacher; lion: brave, agressive. We made masks and painted a column into a totem pole in one class.

3. *Meetings*. Once the tepees were constructed, the students used them to hold meetings. They assured me they were talking about Indian matters.

OJIBWA CHANT.

I HEAR THE SPIRIT TALKING TO US

I AM GOING TO THE MEDICINE LODGE.

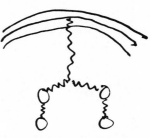

I AM GATHERING MEDICINE SO THAT I MAY LIVE.

I GIVE YOU MEDICINE AND A LODGE

I AM FLYING TO MY HOME

THE SPIRIT HAS DROPPED MEDICINE WHERE WE CAN GET IT.

THE MEDICINE IS IN MY HEART

SYMBOL VOCABULARY

man

horse

rain

turtle

BIRD

rainbow

teepee

sun

mountains

Bear tract

foot prints

GATHER

HEAR

SEE

SPEAK

river

TREE

DEER

TREE in the earth

Buffalo

BEAR

SNAKE

Native Peoples of North and South America: A Short Book List

by Bill Zavatsky, with contributions by Bob Sievert

Indian Tales, by Jaime de Angulo (Hill and Wang paperback, 1953). Marvelous stories suitable for every age level by an anthropologist who lived among California Indians and threw away his textbooks in order to get to know them.

American Indian Prose and Poetry [Earlier title: *The Winged Serpent*], edited by Margaret Astrov (G.P. Putnam's Capricorn Books paperback, 1946). In many ways still the best of these kinds of anthologies, with a luminous introduction by the editor.

Nothing in the Word: Versions of Aztec Poetry, by Stephen Berg (Mushinsha Books/Grossman Publishers paperback, 1972). "These versions," it says here, "are based generally on the Spanish translations of Nahuatl poetry by Angel Maria Garibay K. in his collection *Poesia Nahuatl*." No introduction of value, no notes, etc. *Caveat emptor*.

Beyond the Frontier: Social Process and Cultural Change, edited by Paul Bohannan and Fred Plog ("American Museum Sourcebooks in Anthropology Series," Natural History Press, 1967). Contains one of the most fascinating analyses of the systematic policy of genocide carried out against Native Americans in New England that I have read, "Celt and Indian: Britain's Old World Frontier in Relation to the New," from *The American Indian Frontier* by William Christie MacLeod (published originally in 1928). MacLeod shows convincingly how British policy of extermination of the Scottish clans was applied to the New England tribes. Other essays on Native Americans as well. This collection should be available through Doubleday Anchor Books.

The Spiritual Legacy of the American Indian, by Joseph Epes Brown (Pendle Hill Publications, Pamphlet 135, 1964). A concise sketch of our spiritual debt to the Native American, by the author of *The Sacred Pipe*.

American Indian Mythology, by Cottie Burland (Hamlyn Publishing Group, no date). The best parts of this book are the reproductions of many different styles of Indian art. The text consists of Native American myths told in a rather flat style. [B.S.] This title is out of print, so check your library.

The Maya, by Michael D. Coe ("Ancient Peoples and Places" series, Frederick A. Praeger paperback, 1966). A predominately archaeological tour of Mayan civilization, not for everyone but featuring excellent maps and photographs.

American Indian Poetry: An Anthology of Songs and Chants, edited by George W. Cronyn (Liveright paperback, 1918; reissued in 1973). Stilted Victorian renderings of Native American song-chant. Useful in that it (a) exists and (b) that your students may put these poesies into contemporary American language.

The Indians' Book: Songs and Legends of the American Indians, recorded and edited by Natalie Curtis (Dover Publications paperback, 1923; reissued 1968). A huge five-pound tome valuable primarily for its field notations (i.e. music) of Native American song.

The Sky Clears: Poetry of the American Indians, by A. Grove Day (University of Nebraska Press Bison Book paperback, 1951). A useful collection riddled with stilted translations.

The Conquest of New Spain, by Bernal Diaz, translated from the Spanish with an introduction by J.M. Cohen (Penguin Books paperback, 1963). The eyewitness account of Cortes' destruction of Montezuma's Aztec Empire.

Eskimo Songs and Stories, translated by Edward Field, with illustrations by Kiakshuk and Pudlo (Delacorte Press/Seymour Lawrence, hardcover only, 1973). See the Book Review section for an appraisal of this volume.

The Indian in America's Past edited by Jack D. Forbes (Prentice-Hall Spectrum Book paperback, 1964). A brilliant and powerful collection that documents, from primary and secondary sources, the tragic relationship between the white settlers and the Native American peoples.

The Patriot Chiefs: A Chronicle of American Indian Resistance, by Alvin M. Josephy (Viking Press Compass Book paperback, 1961). Fine studies of Native Americans like King Philip, Tecumseh, Crazy Horse, and others who stood up and fought when their lands and lives were threatened.

The Broken Spears: The Aztec Account of the Conquest of Mexico, edited with an introduction by Migueo Leon-Portilla, translated from Nahuatl into Spanish by Angel Maria Garibay K. and into English by Lysander Kemp. Edited from post-conquest chronicles written by remnants of the Aztec intellectual class, this stunning book is a must for anyone willing to face the psychological impact it bears. Superb illustrations adapted from the original codices.

American Indian Prose and Poetry: We Wait in the Darkness, edited by Gloria Levitas, Frank R. Vivelo, and Jacqueline J. Vivelo (G.P. Putnam's Sons Capricorn Paperback, 1974). See the Book Review section.

Picture Writing of the American Indians, by Garrick Mallery (Dover Publications paperbacks, 1888; reissued 1966). Two Volumes. These volumes are a reprint of all the known Indian writing and pictographs c. 1900, and was originally prepared for the Smithsonian Institute. The text is transcription where possible and contains extensive information on the locations of the signs. The great wealth of the set is the many diagrams, pictures, drawings of petroglyphs and pictographs. It is a visual primer of picture writing. [B.S.]

The Ancient Civilizations of Peru, by J. Alden Mason (Pelican Books paperback, revised edition 1968). A sweeping study of the Inca civilization of Peru that includes an excellent brief history of the Spanish Conquest.

The Ghost-Dance Religion and the Sioux Outbreak of 1890, by James Mooney, edited and abridged with an introduction by Anthony F.C. Wallace ("Classics in Anthropology" series, University of Chicago Press Phoenix Books paperback, 1896; abridgment 1965). An absorbing account of the messianic revival cult that swept through the tribes of the Plains States at the end of the last century.

Two Leggings: The Making of a Crow Warrior, by Peter Nabokov (Thomas Y. Crowell Company Apollo Editions paperback, 1967). The story of "one of the last Crow Indians to abandon the warpath."

Black Elk Speaks: Being the Life Story of a Holy Man of the Oglala Sioux, as told through John G. Neihardt (University of Nebraska Press Bison Book paperback, 1932; reissued 1961). One of the great treasures of American literature, this heartbreaking story should be mandatory reading for every American school child. In fact, for everyone.

Genocide Against the Indians: Its Role in the Rise of U.S. Capitalism, by George Novak (Merit Pamphlet series, Pathfinder Press, 1970). This Marxist analysis of the extermination of Native American tribes and the grabbing of their lands seems less radical and more common-sensical every day.

Savagism and Civilization: A Study of the Indian and the American Mind, by Roy Harvey Pearce (The Johns Hopkins Press, paperback, revised edition 1965). The image of the Native American as reflected in American literature. An invaluable study.

The Autobiography of a Winnebago Indian, by Paul Radin (Dover Publications, 1920; reissued 1963). Fascinating for its early revelations of the peyote ceremony, this little book has achieved the status of classic in its field.

Technicians of the Sacred: A Range of Poetries from Africa, America, Asia & Oceania, edited by Jerome Rothenberg (Doubleday Anchor Books paperback, 1968). Expert versions of primitive poetry from many cultures. Rothenberg, a noted poet himself, commissioned other poets to rewrite earlier translations of texts. The result cannot be considered translation, but the versions produced are miraculous and fresh as a good new book of poems. Many notes and a fine introduction. This volume is essential.

Shaking the Pumpkin: Traditional Poetry of the Indian North Americas, edited with commentaries by Jerome Rothenberg. (Doubleday Anchor Books paperback, 1972). Another magnificent collection edited by Jerome Rothenberg that perhaps suffers slightly from his organization of the material along contemporary *avant garde* lines. Still, the texts in this book are alive, not ethnological museum pieces in the mouths of wooden Indians. Goes right next to *Technicians of the Sacred* on the bookshelf.

Seven Arrows, by Hyemeyohsts Storm (Ballantine Books paperback, no date). This is a long narrative with many stories that document the society, religion, personal growth, and need for visions of the Plains Native Americans. Included are explanations of how inner visions produced symbolic art. Many art illustrations and numerous photographs of Edward S. Curtis, the famous nineteenth century documentarian of Indian life. [B.S.]

Teachings from the American Earth: Indian Religion and Philosophy, edited by Dennis Tedlock and Barbara Tedlock (Liveright paperback, 1975). Jerome Rothenberg's sometime collaborator and his wife have compiled an excellent anthology of essays by various hands that will enrich anyone's studies of Native Americana. Particularly enlightening is Barbara Tedlock's essay "The Clown's Way" for the light it sheds on Black Elk's personal narrative, not to mention recent Hippie and Yippie spiritual tomfoolery.

Indian Sign Language, by William Tomkins (Dover Publications paperback, 1931; reissued 1969). A lovely Boy Scout-type manual of Native American hand-jive. To make an owl, cup your hands and stare through them like binoculars. Utterly delightful!

Disinherited: The Lost Birthright of the American Indian, by Dale Van Every (Avon Books paperback, 1966). The whole sad sordid story of how we stole It from Them.

New England Frontier: Puritans and Indians 1620-1675, by Alden T. Vaughan (Little, Brown and Company paperback, 1965). A superb history of America's first frontier and the expansionist policies it set in unstoppable motion. Another sine qua non.

Realm of the Incas, by Victor Wolfgang von Hagen (New American Library Mentor paperback, revised edition 1961). A fine introduction to ancient Peruvian civilization by an authority in the field.

The Aztec: Man and Tribe, by Victor Wolfgang von Hagen (New American Library Mentor paperback, revised edition 1962). A good introduction to the civilization of ancient Mexico.

Book of the Hopi, by Frank Waters, drawings and source material recorded by Oswald White Bear Fredericks (Ballantine Books paperback, 1963). First disclosures of Hopi myths, significance of religious rituals, and ceremonies. An invaluable "total-view" book with fine illustrations.

The Way: An Anthology of American Indian Literature, edited by Shirley Hill Witt and Stan Steiner (Random House Vintage Book paperback, 1972). A wide-ranging collection that focuses equally on historical material and on the "New Indian."

The Discovery and Conquest of Peru, by Agustin de Zarate, translated with an introduction by J.M. Cohen (Penguin Books paperback, 1968). An abridgement of Zarate's history of the conquest of the Incas, with supplementary material supplied (from contemporary accounts) by the editor-translator.

The Marriage of Heaven and Hell

by Phillip Lopate

I had this grandiose scheme, to build a large screen out of cardboard and have the kids paint a triptych of heaven, earth and hell, as in Bosch's *Garden of Earthly Delights*, and also write poems of a cosmic order. We bought the paints, I made the screen (very proud of that), I read Dante's *Inferno* and Blake's *Songs of Innocence and Experience*, and Rimbaud's *A Season in Hell* to get ideas for the presentation.

Tuesday I came in and a few students—Britt, Gene and Roberto—were hanging around the writing room, so I asked them to lay a white coat of paint over the screen as a base. . . .

Wednesday, I brought the screen into Lois Phifer's room to work with the whole class. . . . I told them I had this idea of doing a heaven and hell mural and held up a monograph on Bosch to show them what a triptych looked like. Then I began talking about hell, first Dante's conception of it, and the idea that each sinner was given a punishment metaphorically appropriate to his sin: the killers were submerged in a bloody lake and shot with arrows if they lifted their heads up too high; the suicides were encased without a body in a tree because they had abused their bodies. . . .

I decided to do a collaboration poem with the class on the subject of how different sinners would get their just deserts. Not a bad idea. It generated some interest and some good lines: "The thief will have his veins stolen by the Devil/ The person who hurt your feelings will have his feelings taken away/ The swindler has all his money wrapped around his nose so he can't breathe/ The hijacker sprouts wings and flies forever. . . ."

We handed out paper, and I asked the kids to write their own conception of a modern heaven and hell.

We also divided up the group into work committees for the mural-painting which would take place in the afternoon. . . .

I gave the muralists a few instructions before starting: to draw it first in pencil, to try to cover the surface with details, thousands of details, and most important, to watch what the person to the left or right was doing and try to link up with them, so that the composition would hang together.

The boys were coming out with a magnificent Hell. Fiery figures like Stan Lee comic-book heroes sprang out of a huge oil refinery; there were staircases and vultures and mysterious hulking monsters. The whole thing had an astonishing flow of action. Everything connected. Heaven was something else again: static cloudlets with happy figures imprisoned inside. Dolores had managed to get in her maternity clothing store. Lilly put in a few kites and apples. I was painting an inch frame around the border with special gold-leaf paint. Christine was the most alert to the possibilites of connecting; she did a yeoman's share of the work. Clearly we were up against the Miltonic problem of Hell upstaging Heaven.

. . . Lois Phifer commented on how intelligently everyone seemed to be working (this was especially true at the Heaven panel, where they made a lot of fine decisions for connecting and jazzing up the place—famous Dead figures floating around, carnivals, a three-dimensional ferris wheel, superhighways with trucks labeled God Industries).*

*Selected from "The Marriage of Heaven and Hell," in *Teachers & Writers Collaborative Newsletter* (Vol. 5, No. 1), pp. 9-12.

E. Publication

Instant Publication

by Ardis Kimzey

In these days of paper shortage and school secretary rebellion (I would rebel, too, if someone asked me to type three hundred children's poems set up on lined paper and inspired by someone who had told them punctuation and spelling didn't matter), I figured I would have to find some way for the kids to have "publication" in case the schools didn't have funds for anthologies. I feel that it is super important for a sharing of work to take place and, in addition, to have some sort of communication about poetry with the kids who did not attend the poetry class.

The best way I've found to do this is to get the principal to designate one well-traveled hall wall as the poetry publication wall and to supply a very large roll of masking tape, lots of colored construction paper, glue, scissors, and several boxes of all different colored felt-tipped pens. At most schools, it is good to prepare in advance. It's amazing how difficult it can sometimes be to get a school to dispense a large roll of masking tape and a few dozen felt-tipped pens. At the last school I was in, I had to sign the masking tape in and out with the school secretary every day.

Let the kids choose anything they write to go on the board. They then pick the color paper they want, cut it in any design that turns them on, copy the poem on it with aforementioned pens, and mask it to the wall to be read and admired (and sometimes lifted) by schoolmates, passing parents, teachers, and other personnel. They may or may not want to put their names on these works of art.

In addition to instant publication, this affords the students an opportunity to take a good look at what they've written and to tidy up or change their work if necessary. Also, it prompts an association with the color and the physical shape of the poem they have written.

LOTS OF COPIES

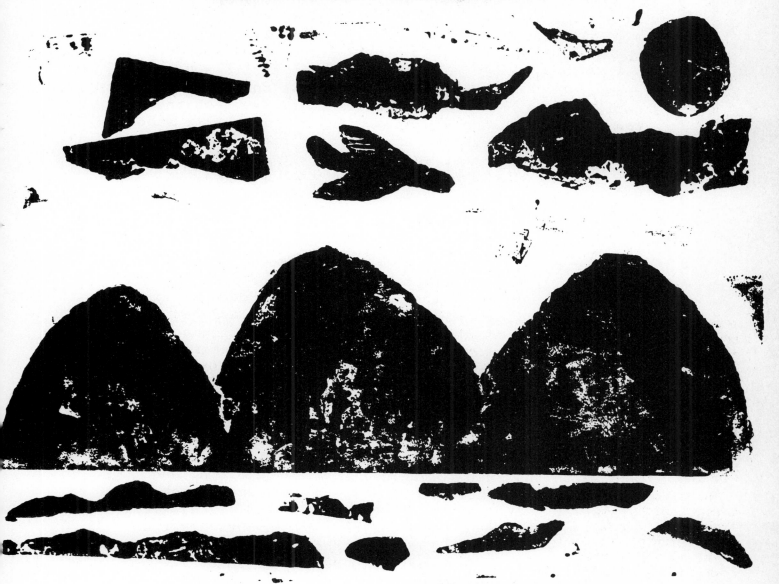

making editions
in school

by Mary Scherbatskoy

LOTS OF COPIES

The purpose of this section is to describe and evaluate
ways of making editions of children's written/art work
in school: books, 'newspapers,' magazines, and reports.
This is not a how-to manual. It will not tell you how
to do linoleum printing or silkscreen, but only give
you an opinion on their usefulness in public school
classrooms. However, as many specific details, appli-
cations, and improvements as possible have been included.
The methods recommended have been used in public schools,
grades 3 to 7, both traditional and 'open' classrooms.
They are for teachers who want the kids' work to come
out looking nice, and who realize that a clean, grown-
up looking presentation is one of the best motivations
for good writing.

An edition is a lot of copies of something. The benefits
of having a lot of copies are several. If you have 35
attractive copies of the kids' work, you can use it for
reading or social studies lessons. The class can study
things that there are no books about by making a book
themselves. You can lend the material to other classes.
Administrators like to have good looking copies from
student editions as a tangible illustration of good
educational programs.

The technical skills acquired in producing an edition
are worth the extra trouble. It is an exciting and
unifying experience for 30 kids to be jointly responsible for a physical product. On the individual level,
technical things provide shelter and encouragement for
the kids who are not famed as 'the artist' or 'the
writer.' The joy of having 40 copies of something you
did all yourselves -- clean, colorful, and legible --
justifies having to learn a few techniques.

art

Kids are very gifted at non-realism: abstraction, surrealism, etc., more by accident than intention. They are also totally unappreciative of it. You must have noticed with what disinterest they stuff all those groovy little potato prints into the wastebasket as you struggle to rescue the ones you thought were artistic; and with what zeal they labor to produce mathematically perfect Batmans and Godzillas, all neatly colored in.

One of your jobs is to help the kids appreciate and develop the things they CAN do in art: surreal creations of color and meaning. Gently steer them away from the things they CAN'T do -- photographic realism -- which result in one or two kids being exalted while the rest moan, like yourself, that they 'can't draw.' One way to do this is through materials. All of the methods recommended here tend to encourage non-realism because of their technical aspects and their unfamiliarity. Also, all of these media have some technical standards; through experience, a child can develop and improve his technique. The trouble with traditional school media (crayons, magic markers, ugly tempera with flabby paintbrushes) is that no matter how hard you work, there is no way to improve. If you've made one crayon drawing, you've made them all. After several years of school paint brushes, it is no wonder the kids give up art and turn to Godzilla.

planning

Planning is the most important part of any project. You have to decide what you are going to do (book, magazine, etc.) and then plan how to do it. Since it will take at least a month to finish any publishing project, I recommend a book or magazine rather than a newspaper. The news will be no longer new (last month's cake sale). Also, since a newspaper is mostly words,

Q is for Queen.

I saw the queen. She wears a crown. She tells the king, "I don't want to be a queen any more. I want to be a boat driver." She sat down in the boat. She wants to drive the boat.
                                            —by Kenneth Yuen.

cardboard print by Bernadette Tow

Teacher, David Liu, 3rd and 4th grade Special English, P.S. 23

it will probably come out ugly. It is better to do a group of stories or reports with clear writing and bright illustrations. Whatever you decide to do, remember it will take extra effort, so the writing and the artwork should be the result of serious work. The subject should be something you (the teacher) want to spend time on: Peoples of the World, Our Neighborhood, Wishes, Lies and Dreams, etc.

Once you have decided what to do, then you have to plan how to do it. Technically, don't try to do a lot of new things at once. Start with what is easiest and most common in your school, and plan to do it well, adding a few improvements. Pick your medium for the artwork, and do it a few times with the kids until the hysteria wears off. Don't be strict about the subject matter during these explorations.

I have found that it is best to do artwork and writing simultaneously, with all kids encouraged to work on both, then to select. The artwork and the writing reinforce and enhance each other. Some kids will do only one, some will do both, in varying quantities. Give the impression that some work is required, and all work is welcomed.

You cannot plan the book until you have all the material in your hands. You must have one copy of each selected print (AND the intact printing block) and a legible copy of the writings. Then decide what the book is going to look like.

The paper size will have to be 8½ by 11, or 8½ by 14, unless your father is a printer. Therefore, your book can look like:

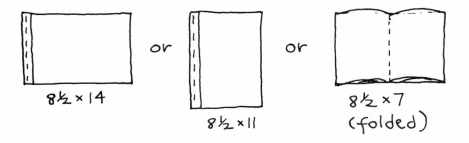

8½×14   or   8½×11   or   8½×7
(folded)

If you are doing cardboard printing, it is best to put the pictures on pages by themselves since cardboard prints are hard to do small. Small linoleum prints can be cut out and pasted into a space in the page. A standard cardboard printed book format looks like this:

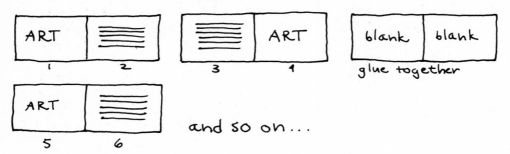

and so on...

You cannot do prints on the back of other prints because everything gets smudgy.

At this point, decide on basic page design. Here are some possible page layouts if you are pasting in the prints:

etc...

These are two-page openings. Use only ONE style per book. Don't make every opening a new and different experience.

This is the time to lay down the law about margins (which see). Make sure that all final writing (on stencils, etc.) keeps the same margins. See that enough space is left in the right places for the art-work. Number the pages as you go. If a whole page is to be devoted to artwork, skip a number. Make a working table of contents so you don't get lost. It is best if only one or two kids do the final copying, in the in-terest of uniformity. The other kids can start on the arduous business of making 30 or more copies of their prints. Trim the prints to cut off the dirt, if necessary. Figure out which page goes on the back of which page. (If you are doing the folded method, you will have already done this. See Bookbinding.)
Send the stencils to be printed. When they come back, glue on the prints (see Glues). Collate. Bind. Read.

(Put this catalogue away and take it out in October. No book project should be started later than spring vacation, or you won't have time to read the product.)

RECOMMENDED METHODS - text

These are the methods which I recommend, after con-sidering ease, effectiveness, time, and cost.

rexograph 3rd grade and up

Rexograph, or spirit duplicator, is the most common school duplicating medium. Rexo stencils will make 50 to 75 copies. Their major advantages are that they are easy to work on and come in colors. They are avail-able not only in regulation purple but also in blue, green, and red. I have heard of orange, brown, and black (very feeble). Their major weakness is that their copies are comparatively faint and blurry. The paper which must be used comes only in white.

It is easy to make one master which prints several colors at once. First, separate the master from the attached ink sheet, and put it face up on a clean piece of paper. Plan the page lightly in pencil, and decide which parts you want to be what color. Or plan in different colored pencils so that you can see what you are doing. Put the master on an ink sheet of the chosen color and go over all the parts you want to be in that color, in the regular way.

Then move the master to a different color ink sheet, and do all those parts and so on. Mistakes can be scraped off the back of the master with a razor blade. The ink sheets (but not the stencils) can be saved and used many times. Don't store them near heat.

This method requires some forethought and planning, but no unfamiliar techniques. It is adequate for passages of text, and even attractive if the color planning is done carefully. However, it is not very good for artwork; the drawings are always confused and indistinct. Use rexo for text only, and paste in artwork in some other medium.

mimeograph 4th grade and up

Mimeograph is the regular big school machine which takes the green (or, sometimes blue) stencils. Typed on with an electric typewriter, they are a good way of doing the text for a book. But mimeo stencils are extremely tricky to write or draw on by hand. They will make several hundred good copies. The ink in the machine is almost always black. Colored inks are available, though changing inks is a very messy business. Paper is available in pastel colors, as well as white. Some of the newer machines from Gestetner and A.B. Dick companies are sophisticated and reliable. There is a machine which electronically makes stencils for the mimeo. Many schools have them. The electrostencil machine makes it possible to do artwork on the mimeo. However, both machines must be working properly, and the person running them must be interested in making good copies. If your school has a Thermofax Secretary copying machine, you can buy special Thermofax stencils and make masters with the copying machine. It is, however, even trickier than the electrostencil machine to make good masters and get good copies from them in this way.

It is more difficult to do electrostencil than rexo. The machine makes a stencil by copying a black and white original which you make. (It will also copy fingerprints, smudges, blobs of glue and coffee rings.) It will not copy photos, colors, grays, or light writing. The Thermofax machine will also not copy black magic marker. You must give it an absolutely clean original on white paper, done in black ball point, or typewriting, or pen and ink (see Materials). It also cannot handle big solid areas, so teach kids to go like this:

 or  or

Originals may be very carefully pasted up on thin papers. (see Pasteup) Mistakes may be covered up with white opaquing (see Materials).

Get the stencils back before they are printed and correct them using stencil correction fluid, as you would on a regular mimeo stencil. Often there will be extra black lines and marks caused by dirt on the original or a small problem with the machine. If there is a huge black area where the original was clean, the stencil maker is out of adjustment. Some color can be added to the mimeo copies with magic markers ... one at a time.

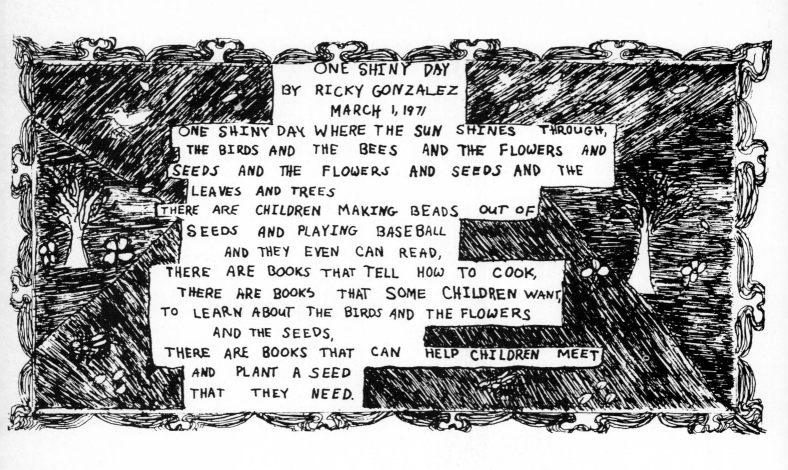

ONE SHINY DAY
BY RICKY GONZALEZ
MARCH 1, 1971
ONE SHINY DAY WHERE THE SUN SHINES THROUGH,
THE BIRDS AND THE BEES AND THE FLOWERS AND
SEEDS AND THE FLOWERS AND SEEDS AND THE
LEAVES AND TREES
THERE ARE CHILDREN MAKING BEADS OUT OF
SEEDS AND PLAYING BASEBALL
AND THEY EVEN CAN READ,
THERE ARE BOOKS THAT TELL HOW TO COOK,
THERE ARE BOOKS THAT SOME CHILDREN WANT,
TO LEARN ABOUT THE BIRDS AND THE FLOWERS
AND THE SEEDS,
THERE ARE BOOKS THAT CAN HELP CHILDREN MEET
AND PLANT A SEED
THAT THEY NEED.

RECOMMENDED METHODS - art

cardboard printing   3rd to 7th grades

Cardboard printing is a simple kind of relief printing,
requiring less equipment and fewer bandaids than linoleum printing. The block is made additively by gluing
cutout shapes of automobile inner tube onto a piece of

238

cardboard, then inking this master and pressing paper
onto it to make a print. The block, if carefully glued,
may last for fifty copies. You can print on almost any
kind of paper. The pieces of cardboard for the blocks
must be slightly smaller than the printing paper. It
is possible to ink different parts of the plate in different colors. Prints tend to be very abstract, with
unintended blobs of ink. You have to help the kids see
the interest in these: -- it looks like clouds -- it
looks like the man is kicking up dust -- it looks like
rain.

cardboard print by Kok Seng Lee, 7th grade
from "Arriving: NYC" published by A.R.T.S. Inc.
teacher, Jane Kasper 7th grade ESL, JHS 65A

Materials: inner tubes, white glue, pieces of cardboard,
scissors, plus the regular printing equipment: water-
based block printing inks, cookie sheets, paper.
A.R.T.S. has published a booklet on cardboard printing
by Nancy Kitchel. You should order it, and try it.
(Copies are 75¢ each from Art Resources for Teachers &
Students, Inc., 32 Market Street, New York, N.Y. 10002.)

linoleum printing
5th grade and up

Many books, full of examples, are available on methods
and materials for linoleum printing. Most of them make
it seem harder than it is. The technique does require
special materials, most of which are reusable, but it
produces as many prints as you care to make. The prints
are clear, detailed, and may have interesting texture
and design. Linoleum cuts look very much like wood
cuts. Almost any kind of paper may be used to print on.

Use only water-based block printing inks. (Order extra
boxes of blades. There is nothing so dangerous as a
dull blade.)

Do not try to cut on asphalt or vinyl tile -- it is
much too hard. Use only the old fashioned 'battleship' linoleum which is thick and soft. Don't bother
buying the expensive blocks mounted on wood. Just
buy battleship from a floor covering store and cut it
into pieces yourself.

To avoid serious bloodshed, construct bench hooks. A
bench hook is a square board about 10 by 10 inches with
pieces of 1 by 2 pine (furring strip) glued and nailed
across the ends on opposite sides. One end hooks on
the edge of the table, the other holds the linoleum
(and stops runaway knives).

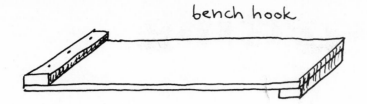

bench hook

NEVER allow a child to hold the linoleum down with his
hand and then cut towards it. He will be seriously
stabbed. Use the bench hook; steady the work with the
fingers kept in back of the knife.

Technically, the only problem with linoleum cutting is
to persuade the kids to cut enough. They tend at first
to do a kind of negative line drawing which is usually
quite ugly. A more interesting picture is achieved by
cutting away a lot, and by texturing.

photography 5th? grade and up

If you or a friend have a darkroom, it is possible to
make 30 or so prints from a couple of negatives, then
paste them onto the pages. But for heaven's sake don't
mess around with polaroid, which is just an expensive
way of making one foggy print which probably can't be
reproduced in any way.

OTHER METHODS

These are methods which are frequently mentioned in
how-to-do-it books, but which I consider to have one
or more serious drawbacks.

typewriting

It is possible to set the kids up with typewriters and carbons, and type out all the copies you need. This has the disadvantage of being very smudgy, and probably of immortalizing a lot of mistakes, as well as erratic design.

photo offset

Photo offset is the tops in the field; it is the way that REAL BOOKS are made. It can reproduce anything, in any color, size, intensity -- FOR A PRICE. You also need to know how to prepare the materials for the printer (basically the same as for electrostencil). However, if you have done several rexo, etc., books with the kids, and you are ready for something new, telephone some quick (kwik) copy places listed in the yellow pages under 'Offset,' and compare prices. The basic rate is for 8½ by 11 or 8½ by 14 inch paper, white paper, minimum 100 copies, usually black ink, extra charge for photographs; 8½ by 11, both sides, is about $6 to $8. Some places will print a colored ink on a certain day at no extra cost. Service is usually one day. Don't be afraid to telephone and ask. There are a lot of these fast service places, and if you plan the job to their requirements, they are pretty cheap. If the shop starts asking a lot of questions you can't answer, you have reached a custom printer, which is out of your class.

The main usefulness of this kind of offset is to make more than a hundred clean, intense copies, with artwork or photos, for a reasonable price. However, even the most reasonable price may be out of your league unless you have some kind of special budget (or two jobs).

proof press

Using a proof press for classroom printing is one of those seductive but unworkable ideas. There are several hundred pieces in a font of type, and in no time at all you will have type in your gerbils, and no 'e's' in the drawer. Briefly, the set-up consists of a heavy frame with a roller, a lot of metal or wooden type and a special drawer to keep it in, separator slugs for between the lines, wooden 'furniture' to go around the edges, a chase to lock it up in and some other things. The purpose is to be able to set up type, lay it on the proof press, and print it by running the roller over it. If all this is done correctly, you will be able to make as many copies as you want of the text; the product will look like real book printing, if the type faces didn't get mixed up.

potato printing

Potato printing, for kids older than 1st grade, is aim-less. A potato is not big enough or strong enough to be a workable material, it won't hold up for 30 copies, and it is the wrong shape for convenient printing. There is little use for the kind of squiggle a potato can produce; one possibility would be to make repeti-tive borders on cards or pages.
However, most children have little use for design per se. Unconsidered use of this kind of medium only sug-gests to the kids that art is a useless, unproductive, and demeaning activity. Let's stamp out potato printing!

silkscreen

Silkscreen is a medium which is always and deservedly raved about, but which is so messy that you would have to be out of your mind to try it in a classroom. It is suitable for not less than 30 or so posters or tee-shirts. Its technical requirements are very complex. The best introductory book on it is:

AN INTRODUCTION TO SCREEN PRINTING
by Anthony Kinsey   Watson - Guptill Pub., NY

NOTES on useful subjects

bookbinding

Real binding is very slow and hard to do. If you are interested in trying it, there are a lot of books on hand bookbinding. Unfortunately, for the classroom, various makeshift methods will have to do. There are lots of methods that teachers usually use: stapling on one edge, punching holes and binding with yarn, or using paper fasteners, etc. Any of these methods will do, and can be strengthened by gluing a piece of cloth or naugahyde like this to cover the staples:

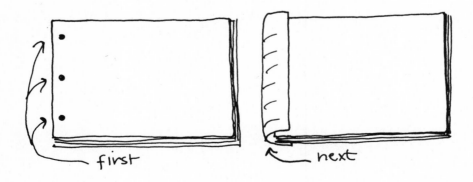

first   next

If you plan to bind your books this way, remember when you decide on the margins that this method uses up nearly one inch of paper on the inside edge of the pages, so you must make allowances.

Another way of making books is by folding the sheets and stapling or sewing -- like this catalogue. It is more elegant, but is more complex to plan since each side of every sheet will have two non-consecutive pages on it. Take this magazine apart and study the page numbers. You have to know before you start EXACTLY how many pages each story, etc. is. Also you need a stapler with a long reach. This method is the first step of real sewn-in-signatures binding. What you make is one signature.

calligraphy

Calligraphy means fancy lettering; everyone wants to do it. To become proficient in several styles takes about three years. The following is a modernized, pasteurized, and homogenized adaptation of the rules of this most painstaking of arts.

Use any edged pen, carpenter's pencil, or marker. 'Edged' means that the writing edge is chisel-shaped rather than pointed, thick in one direction, almost nothing in the other.

Write only between guidelines. The distance between the lines must be not less than three, nor more than seven times the width of the fat part of the writing edge.

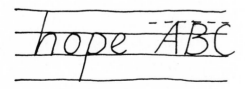

Always keep the pen, etc. pointing in the same direction as you write.
This is called the
pen angle. It doesn't
matter what way you keep
it pointing, but keep it
steady. You have to keep
trying and practicing and trying until your letters
start to look regular and consistent. Just try your
own handwriting style first. Varying the height and
pen angle is what produces different styles of writing.
Do not get bored and try six different styles at once.
(The curse of Edward Johnson and Lloyd J. Reynolds is
on these instructions!)

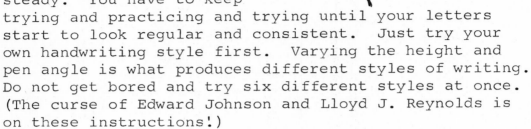

glue

White glue (Elmer's, Sobo, etc. -- all much cheaper in
large sized containers. Buy it by the gallon, which
costs about $6.) is excellent for wood, cardboard, and
cloth. It does not work on non-absorbent materials,
like glass and metal. It always leaves a lump and wrin-
kles paper. However, a TINY drop of it on the corners
of drawings and prints is the usual way of attaching
them to mounts, or other pages. When it dries it is no
longer water-soluble. Thinned with water, it is used
in bookbinding.

Rubber cement, if properly thinned with rubber cement
thinner, is the best glue for paper. It does not lump
or wrinkle paper, and any excess can be rubbed off.
However, after about six months or a year, it will discolor and start to attack the paper or photograph.
Therefore, it is not good to use on anything valuable
or permanent. Rubber cement is also very good on
leather. Scotch tape is not for art. It will discolor
and ruin anything it is stuck on. An emergency medium
only. Forget it.

margins

The first secret of making a page of writing look good is to think about the margins. A margin is the empty part which is usually left around the edges of the page. A page or poster without a margin looks either a) very cheap or b) very modern. One with too much margin looks either a) weak or b) very elegant. As a general rule the top margin should be the smallest, and the bottom by far the biggest; the side margins should be the same as the top, or a little bigger. For an average 8½ by 11 inch page, make the top margin 1 inch, the sides 1½ inches, and the bottom 2 inches. Keep all the pages in the same format, unless you are an experienced designer. If you are totalitarian about the format, the book will look polished; if not, it will look junky, and hard to read. DO NOT try the squished up newspaper format of columns with no margins. It only works if you are a linotypist, not if you are a kid with a magic marker and a ruler.

materials

There are a few special materials which you ought to buy if you are serious about making books with (or without) kids.

Invest $1.25 each in a few of those 12 inch L-shaped metal rulers -- invaluable for getting things straight. T-squares can be used only on the edge of a table.

Sharp scissors! and maybe some single-edged razor blades or X-acto knives.

Gum or kneaded erasers. Do away with smudges and tears!

White glue and rubber cement. Also get a rubber cement eraser.

For electrostencil also get:

Pen and ink -- the old fashioned dip pens (25¢) and points (5¢) and India ink. Most kids become quite excited by this unfamiliar and adult medium.

White opaquing, which is a special thick white paint sold in small jars in art stores for covering up mistakes in the above. Only get one jar for the class; a little goes a long way.

Eyeliner brushes -- tiny, thin, and strong -- for using the opaquing.

pasteup

Pasteup is not an art form but just a way to make designing cleaner and easier. It means to make a page out of pieces pasted together -- like writing a paper in college where you wrote down all your ideas, then made sense out of them using scissors and scoth tape. You can paste up for electrostencil, thermofax, offset, and posters. You can not do it for rexograph. Pasteup is very handy because one kid can do a drawing, the one with the good handwriting can copy the words, and the clean neat one can paste it down so it looks nice. Use rubber cement. MAKE SURE that everything is straight. Another advantage is that you can design the page AFTER the work is done. You can use Prestype (see below) for titles. Mistakes can be cut out with a razor and a correction substituted. Small mistakes can be covered up with white opaquing. Pasteup is a good way to make a few posters, using different colored papers.

transfer lettering

Transfer lettering is like decals, except you don't use
water. You rub gently. Many brand names are available,
but I like Prestype the best.
The lettering comes in many styles and sizes, stuck on
sheets of clear plastic. You lay the sheet down where
you need a letter, rub on it with the back of a ball-
point or paint brush, and Prestype! the letter is stuck
on your page. Kids love transfer lettering. It is
suitable for pasteup, and for making posters and report
covers. It costs about $3 for a 10 x 15" sheet of let-
ters. To make the words come out straight, you must
draw a light guideline on your page which you can see
through the sheet. Be careful erasing around transfer lettering, as it is easy to damage.

assembling

You will have noticed that whenever possible I recommend
doing things piece by piece, then assembling them at
the end. If a product is to look neat and clean, it
must be touched by as few unskilled hands as possible.
Children expecially are prone to panic when they feel
they have made a mistake -- and to do something which
will wipe out the work of 16 other kids along with their
own mistake. If things are done piece by piece, the
damage is minimized, and neatness is promoted. Also many
more kids can work on a project assembled piecemeal, whether
it is a book, a mural, or a stage set.

You may have noticed that this article looks different from the rest of the catalogue - a little bit
homemade. That is because it was done entirely by
the methods described herein: typed copy, Prestype
headings (36 point Cooper Black), handwriting, and
pasted up by me. The only difference is that it was
not mimeographed, but reproduced by photo offset.
This is the way a class project can look.

LOTS OF LUCK!
LOTS OF COPIES!

by Mary Scherbatskoy
ARTS Inc.
32 Market Street NYC

These are the graves of two men from Burma. They were good rich men who were killed by the bad man also from Burma. They were killed because they wanted to build a swimming pool for the poor people of Burma. The bad man wanted to build a bar, so he killed them and took their money. That is it.

story and cardboard print by Patrick Lee, 5th grade

This is a peace symbol because I want peace—
every where, all over the world, especially in
Vietnam. I have a brother there. He is twenty-
something, and the rest of my brothers are
in Arizona and Brooklyn. They came out
already. He's there about three years — he's
supposed to stay there five years. My
father made him go.

story and cardboard print by David Nieves
teacher, Burt Schuman.

4. Studying Society

Archeology of the City

by Sidney Goldfarb

This piece covers a segment of my work under the auspices of Teachers and Writers Collaborative at P.S. 3 in Manhattan begun in February 1973. The work consisted in meeting twice weekly for a period of twenty weeks with twelve fifth grade students in a "seminar" we called "From Cavemen to Cities." The original form of the class was a course I taught in as an Instructor in Humanities at M.I.T. called "Archeology of the City."

We found a bare classroom on the top floor of P.S. 3 and, having utterly no idea what would happen, I and twelve kids began traipsing up there every Tuesday and Thursday morning to consider baboon power structure and the discovery of seeds. The dilemma for me would be how to make things like technological and economic revolutions, relation of art to social and economic context, etc., perceivable in very active and simple terms. My aims in the long run were the same as those in teaching the class in college: first, to give the students some sense of the fact that they were not born yesterday, that they are the inheritors of a long history of man's struggle both to adjust to and change his surroundings and, second, to gain an appreciation for ways of life other than our own, both ancient and contemporary, through discussion of the kinds of human activity that have been lost to us through the steady roll of so-called "progress." Rather than simply "study" ancient man, I had hoped to always have the present contemporary megalopolis as a reference, using the continual juxtaposition, the way African Bushmen court and marry as opposed to the present status of courtship and marriage, for instance, as a way of seeing more deeply into both.

The course was to be divided into three main segments: 1. Cave Men, studying the life of pure hunters, augmented by the study of contemporary hunting tribe, the Bushmen of South West Africa. 2. The beginning of agriculture and the earliest towns. 3. The first cities. I had hoped that this would lead eventually to the development of tools of examination that we might, toward the end of the class, begin applying to our own surroundings, but a misjudgment in time limited that to happening more or less casually along the way rather than in a summary study. I did not have a fixed plan. I did have ideas about what I hoped could be learned and explored, but most of the assignments evolved more or less spontaneously as I got to know the students and what they would be willing to do and capable of doing. Sometimes I would attempt to do things that the classroom teacher would have known to be impossible, at least with the particular students I had to work with. And since I worked alone with them most of the time, when things dissolved into chaos, they dissolved completely. For instance, in an attempt to give the students a sense of how a pre-legal system operates, how small groups of independent tribes might develop *customary* ways of dealing with each other (with the tangential hope that we might be able to identify some of the *customary* ways we had of dealing with each other), I sketched out a little scenario for the class in which one tribe which was in need of marriageable women sent a party to the headman of another tribe with an excess of women to negotiate for a bride. I hoped to use the occasion to show how the delicate balance of small groups could be easily upset unless they could depend on certain aid from other small groups, although there were no laws, codes or even taboos to assure that this would happen. In this instance the group in need would simply shrivel up and die without outside aid. I divided the class into two tribes, and they assigned themselves parts, but once they began they were unable to keep straight faces for any of it and the careful discussion and planning disintegrated into a bedlam I could not break by any rearrangement. Perhaps if the parts had been *written* out beforehand disaster would have been avoided, but then *that* would have removed part of the spontaneity in figuring out what was going to happen themselves. This instance was simply a loss. Other chance occurrences worked quite well. During our discussion of cave life, in fact when we were building papier-maché caves and talking about how we would decorate the insides, I was having a great deal of difficulty explaining to the students what shamans were. At one point we did get off onto an interesting tangent about what psychiatrists were, and from there to considering some of the fearful forces they felt in the world, and from there to imagining some similarity between what we think of as sickness or mental illness and what a stone age man might think of as being inhabited by spirits, but I was unsatisfied with this "parallel" understanding and wanted to find a way to get them to imagine what actually being a shaman was like. The highly secular background of the students I had (most of them had never once been in a church or synagogue) made it almost impossible to refer to experience as a means of stirring interest in religious or even more general "spiritual" feeling. And, of course, there are no "texts" to refer them to. Or so I thought. By chance I had given one of my students a book called *Technicians of the Sacred* (ed. Jerome Rothenberg) and asked him to read the section called 'visions and spells' which included an excerpt from *Black Elk Speaks*, an autobiography of a Sioux medicine man. One day after class I saw him reading one of those comic book form biographies of baseball players, and I asked him if he could make a comic book about a shaman's life complete with illustrations of his visions and other important events. This he did over the weekend on his own time with spectacular results. I could sense that reading Black Elk's own story, having a chance to contemplate that on his own and outside of class, was much more convincing than any *explanation* I could have given as to what shamans do. All that was needed was the form of the comic book to give occasion to his imagination. More often than not this was how fruitful means of study emerged: trying to do something one way, failing, adjusting to the failure, or simply taking advantage of the way in which interest developed in and of itself.

I would like to explain here how just one section of the class worked in detail as a model for the way things worked in general. The "neolithic revolution," the term used by archeologist Gordon Childe to describe the period after the discovery of agriculture somewhere in the sixth or seventh millennium B.C., is a pivotal event comparable in import to the industrial revolution in more recent times. I wanted my students to build neolithic towns as a way of understanding the whole life form of that particular change. Periodically we would meet in our classroom (which became known as our cave), and I would briefly sketch out on the board some of the chronology in man's evolution. There was no attempt to impress on anyone dates or even places particularly, though these were mentioned and some students became interested in that literal aspect of things. What I was interested in was trying to show that from the moment the first chip was flaked from a stone human history changed irrevocably because there was an interposing factor between man and nature, his *tools*. The students were impressed with the fact that men learned to take chips off one side of a stone, and

then learned nothing further for something like 600,000 years, at least from what we know from what has been dug up. And they immediately compared that to how quickly *things* change in the world they live in. After the discovery of tools per se, the domestication of animals and the discovery of agriculture mark, in an economic sense, the next important change in that it now became possible for man to settle, to be free of the whims of the hunt and chance gathering. It also meant, though there is much speculation as to how this happened, the beginnings of diversification in the division of labor on other than a sexual basis, and the development of political and religious hierarchies. The possibility of storage and accumulation, the fact that one man could have more food than he needed for his own consumption, and that he could preserve it, meant that he could trade his surplus for other goods and services. Settling also meant the beginnings of "urban design," the necessity of some plan for maintenance and protection and an orderly relation to the agricultural process upon which the economy of the town was based. I had hoped that all of this would come clear to the students in the *activity* of designing their towns, figuring out not only how things were to be shaped, but who executed the plans and under what authority.

The preparation for building the towns took about four sessions. We had been studying the life of the hunters for about eight weeks previously, focusing on the life of a contemporary African hunting tribe through the use of ethnographic films, readings, cave and tool making projects, and discussions. An inordinate amount of time was spent on this section of the class because I was trying to use it to develop a common language that we could apply to later developments. For instance, after viewing the film, *The Hunters* by John Marshall (available from McGraw-Hill), we spent about three classes discussing the division of roles according to sex that we observed in the movie. Though the movie is deceptive in the sense that it deals with the subject of giraffe hunting, and less so, only tangentially, with the roles of women, it was quite clear to everyone that among these hunters, at least, there were fixed economic roles for men and women. Grossly simplified, this boils down to the men doing the hunting and the women doing the gathering and householding. The girls in the class were outraged by this, or at least some were. Predictably I had not forseen that this subject would turn into a consciousness raising session, but it did, and I rode with it until the subject exhausted itself, for the moment. The question I put to them was, why does this division occur and then, why does it persist? The boys in the class, of course, insisted that the men did the hunting because they were naturally stronger, had more endurance, could run faster, etc. than the women. This was encountered immediately by A. saying, "Bullshit, I can run faster than either you or Ricky!" "Oh, Yeah?" "Yeah." I suspected she was right since she looked pretty fast to me and no challenge race was proposed by the boys. "Well, you might be faster, but we're stronger than you are! Besides, you'd get sick cutting up a giraffe!" We decided to have an Indian Wrestling contest to settle the issue. The boys carried the day but only by a score of 6—3, not enough to prove their point: i.e. if strength was the only issue, certainly those women who are stronger than men should be allowed to hunt. Why doesn't this happen? Various answers: how can you tell who's going to be stronger when they're born? Men are generally stronger than women and it's less confusing to have to choose. I would let all the answers pour out until the name-calling stage. Why do women accept this division? One girl answered that she would rather stay at home anyway, let the men be heroes and get themselves killed by elephants for all she cared. Another said that the men had all the weapons and if the women tried anything the men would kill them. Yeah, but we could secretly practice while the men were hunting and take them by surprise! During the first session I was content to let the discussion go where it would, hoping to use a second session to formalize what we had been talking about.

I'm not sure whether it was a matter of age or the way I went about dealing with the subject, but it was difficult, even with a topic in which everyone was interested, to get them to move from the single assertion or single conception stage to anything more general. They liked to talk and argue about things while there was some intensity of argument like a game or contest going on, but calm discussion, *as a group*, seemed impossible. What I would do was try to remember what their positions were in the arguments, and then, while we were doing something else bring up what they had said and discuss it with them. They were much more open and pliable talking one to one. For instance, hardly anyone was willing to admit they liked anything about Bushman life in class, but one day during lunch one girl told me that after the Bushman movie she couldn't stop thinking about them, about the fact that their life seemed so completely different from hers. She kept asking me if they were living *right now*? *right now*? And I kept telling her that as far as I knew they were still out there in the Kalahari Desert doing the ostrich dance and eating turtles and melons. You mean, well, I always thought that we were the only people in the world. We went into the empty classroom and I turned to the page in the worn atlas that had a map of the world in it, and began telling her off the top of my head about all the different tribes I could think of and where they lived, and then about the differences between different countries. She had seen Nixon and Mao on TV but she hadn't thought about the fact that China was different from the United States except there was a Chinatown with 600,000,000 people in it. Once the differences between Bushman and modern American economy had been actually registered, it was interesting to be able to talk about the differences between the Chinese economy and our own. This conversation about how all the different people on the surface of the earth survive, that there is not simply *one* way of living, that it might even be possible to choose the way you wanted to live, was not what I thought we would be talking about, but it was, till lunchtime ended, and her friends came back.

Reactions and conversations such as this were few and far between, but I think that most of the students understood that the way in which the Bushmen live is the way man lived till about ten thousand years ago, at least economically. And I think they got a *sense* that ten thousand years was only a small part of man's history. Before moving on to towns and the discovery of agriculture, I wanted to see what they had absorbed about the way hunting life works. I asked them as a group if they could name for me every single physical element in the bushman world and what these things came from. This would include not just tools, but apparel, food, musical and religious instruments, shelters, i.e., anything other than the flesh and bone of the Bushmen themselves. Under the heading BUSHMAN I put on the blackboard I also put two subheadings, NATURAL and PROCESSED, so they would get some idea not just of the elements themselves, but also of the means of transformation. This immediately led to a discussion of what a "process" is, and whether the making of a compound, transforming an element by a chemical, could be thought of as a "process" in the same way as chipping a flake from a stone. At last on one side of the board was a list of everything in bushman material life: bone, wood, melons, animal gut (for bow strings), beetle poison (for tipping arrows), gourds (for utensils and musical instruments), straw (for huts), skin (for clothes), stone, etc. Participation was lively. They seemed to enjoy reaching back into their memory of the films they had seen. Often discussions had been chaotic with much boredom and mind-wandering. I don't know if it was simply the pleasure of showing what they had learned that made this discussion so lively, but in a very short time they were able to name everything I could remember. This surprised me because I thought they had been very bored watching a rather slow documentary about Bushmen hunting equipment with a narration intended for college students, but they remembered what they saw. We noted that there was nothing in the "processed" column except a kind of poison the Bushmen extract from a beetle which is heated, evidentially to make it stronger.

To emphasize the specificity of this technology I put the word US on the other side of the board, again with "processed" and "natural" underneath. I then asked them to list every thing they use, eat, are sheltered by, etc., from the time they get up in the morning till the time they go to bed at night. This naturally precipitated a crazy discussion: is toothpaste natural? What is toothpaste anyway? What does the bus run on? Is oil natural? Where does water come from? How is nylon made? What are bricks? Glass? Yogurt? Paper? What are the streets made out of? Do we have anything that's natural? Yes, wood! Milk! Apples! Applesauce! No! Your applesauce has preservatives in it! The board was quickly covered with hundreds of materials and products, many of which required a short discussion of the processes behind them. As often happens there were many more questions that I couldn't answer than I could, a reminder of how little I knew about the world I was trying to explain. Actually, what I didn't know had a good effect on the discussion in this case: it made me more of a participant in a subject we were exploring mutually. Finally we had a board in front of us with some sort of rough comparison between Bushman technology and our own. They drew the obvious conclusions: that Bushman life was much simpler than our own in a material sense, although they had to know much more about the things that they did have. This seemed attractive to them. They were dismayed from the overbalance of the artificial in their lives. Then one student said he would miss the comfort of his bed and blankets, and another said she didn't want to kill animals. Then someone asked her if she didn't eat meat. Whereupon a debate ensued about whether it was better to be Bushman or a New Yorker. As the debate was fizzling I asked them to close their eyes and imagine that they were all going to sleep in a Bushman hut. As their eyes were closed I described what the night was like outside in the African veldt. Then I asked them to open their eyes and come over to the window. There from the fifth floor of P.S. 3 the dozen of us stood for a moment in silent contemplation of the view north up from Hudson Street to the smoky city rising into the clouds.

We came back to our chairs and, redirecting their attention to what we had on the board, I explained that archeology is the means by which we can see from what we dig out of the earth how ways of living have changed from time to time, and how knowledge is accumulated and spread. Previous experience showed me that they had about a thirty to forty-five minute tolerance for pure talk or discussion, so I decided to give them a writing assignment of design-

"....it was difficult, even with a topic in which everyone was interested, to get them to move from the single assertion or single conception stage to anything more general."

ing a town. Referring to the lists of hunting material on the board, I explained to them that the next big change in history began with the domestication of animals. We discussed what domestication was, and I told them about some of the first domesticated animals. I then asked them to write a short story imagining themselves as a hunter discovering how to make some animal dependent on him. Some students balked at the assignment, and while others were writing, I took them aside to talk with them and show them some pictures of fossils of early domesticated animals. What some did writing, others did talking. Then we read the stories aloud and speculated on the likelihood of each. Some of the stories were as usual silly or scatological, and some dealt imaginatively with the problem, but they were all fun to listen to.

The second stage of preparation was as follows. In the next class I explained to them that soon after the domestication of animals man first learned how to plant seeds. We discussed how this might have happened, and what the results in living might have been. I wanted them to see how having something to store would increase the possibility of inventing something to store it in, and how the breadbaking process might eventually lead to an understanding of ceramics, etc. I also wanted them to think about the fact that as a village accumulated stores, it would have to be able to protect those stores from nearby peoples whose harvests had failed or who were not agriculturists. We noted that since hunters consume what is most valuable to them, their meat, on the spot, it would be very hard to steal from them unless you arrived just as they were killing something. But with a settlement, there began to be things to steal that stayed still, and some *system* would have to be devised to protect those things. I also asked them to think a little (although this was to continue to be a difficult subject) about how what a settled farming people would think of as gods would be different from a hunting tribe. I told them that we were going to build some early farming villages, and that they should pay close attention to the discussion so that they would know what they were doing when it came time to build their towns. Rather than talk to them about the "neolithic revolution" I hoped that the actual content of that revolution would become evident as they planned and built their towns. I showed them a book called *Catal Huyuk* by James Mellart, a study of an early farming village in Turkey. They gathered around informally passing the book back and forth as I explained to them what was in the pictures. Since this was the first time they had seen pictures of an actual "dig" I spent some time talking to them about who archeologists were and how they worked. They were fascinated by the fact that digging up the town revealed level after level and began speculating im-

mediately as to why one town had fallen and another built over it. I asked them to pay special attention to any paintings or statues in the pictures and to compare them with some pictures in a book of cave art (*Paleolithic Cave Art*, Ucko & Rosenfeld) we had in our "cave" library. I wanted them to be aware not simply of the permanence of the town, but of the peculiarity of the statues of bulls and fertility goddesses that were found in each of the dwellings. Of course, the term "fertility goddess" would have meant nothing to them, but their attention was certainly aroused by a beautiful photograph of a seated leopard who seemed to have a man's head coming out of her womb. The boys thought this was great, though maybe not so great as the cave painting of a man who had a hand where his prick should have been. The girls were more thoughtful in their contemplation. I also showed them a book called *Technology in the Ancient World* by Henry Hodges, which had pictures of most of the tools related to early agricultural villages and some contemporary photographs of similar tools. In looking at both books I spoke as I could about town design, religion, tools, placing special emphasis, as we looked at the projections of different levels of Catal Huyuk, in getting them to speculate about the people that lived there: How many were there? Were they rich or poor? How can you tell from the houses? Who did what? How was the village protected and governed? What were these ovens used for, and were they used by the whole town? What did they grow? Where did the water come from? What kind of animals did they have? Who or what did they worship and why? Why are these courtyards arranged like this? Having them think about the life of Catal Huyuk by looking at the projections of the remains was intended to prepare them for answering all these questions when they began planning their towns. This was one of the few instances in which I had pretty thoroughly prepared my questions before hand. I even made myself a list of all the possible implications that looking at the pictures might yield and I tried to cover all of them. If I did this aspect of the class over again, I would make it even more like an archeological mystery game, leaving out all but the barest pre-explanations, and trying to get the most mileage out of the joy the students seemed to take in guessing what things were. Usually they came up eventually with the right answers, and their concentration was much greater and they remembered things much longer than when I explained things myself.

I then divided the class into three work groups and asked them to spend the rest of the class making a plan for their town and writing me a description of it under the following headings: population, time in history, location, kinds of food, kinds of tools, climate, government (who's boss?), religion. I reminded them that there was no metal, so they would have to figure out how the whole agricultural process took place using only wood or other "natural" material for tools. The plans themselves caused something of a hitch. In one group, four girls who usually worked together, there was a lot of argument about the design and, although the argument was interesting, it seemed like it might not produce results. So I asked them to make individual plans, so that we could discuss the virtues of each and on that basis try to develop one plan. One of the boys' groups had a different problem. These three boys tended to work well together, but in a kind of fixed one-leader-two followers arrangement. They had quickly decided and approved of T's plan. The followers could see no point in thinking about designing the town themselves since T had already made a plan which was good enough. I tried to coax them into it, pointing out that they always followed T and it was about time they did something on their own, but nothing could change their minds. I decided to make an arbitrary division of labor: T could design the town, but J would have control over everything relating to farming, designing the stable or corrals and fields, etc., and B would have charge of making models of all art and implements, tools, statues or paintings and ceramics. Though this didn't involve all of them in the town design per se, it did serve to integrate them somewhat in the planning and give them some say in the overall shape of the place. A third group of three boys were either too bored by the project or too lazy. No amount of help would get them started. This was disappointing since they were among the brightest students verbally. They simply balked at the assignment. Eventually they did begin work on a village that had terraced farming in the mountains above it, but this required a few weeks of peripheral work with them which drew me away from being able to pay as much attention to the other towns as I wanted.

This was one problem I ran into continually with students who are, in the moduled open classroom atmosphere of P.S. 3, often given choices about doing one thing or another. This seems fine in terms of range of things to do, but it also seems to nurture the habit of opting out once one particular choice has been made if a *specific* assignment doesn't seem like the most interesting thing that's happening at that particular moment. Sometimes I was able to invent alternate assignments, but I often missed the discipline that would force, if I may use that forbidden word, the students into doing what they thought they couldn't do or wouldn't enjoy doing. This was partly a limitation of the "seminar" nature of the class. L, on a certain day, would be willing to involve himself in the class: other days the two hours would be entirely wasted, and he wouldn't go back to the home room for fear that he would be dropped entirely from the class and thus not be able to come to it when he

"Of course, the term 'fertility goddess' would have meant nothing to them, but their attention was certainly aroused by a beautiful photograph of a seated leopard who seemed to have a man's head coming out of her womb."

was in the mood. I think a regular classroom teacher would have an easier time doing these projects more casually and over a longer period of time, getting the projects started and then letting the students work on things when they wanted to. For the three boys who didn't manage to get their plan together, their description was as follows:

Time: 5000 B.C.
Place: Iran
Population: 50
Climate: just like our summer, fall, winter, spring (I allowed this cop out after a fight.)
Animals: dogs, pigs, cattle, sheep
Crops: corn, tomatoes, squash, watermelon
How governed: men vote together
Tools: wooden plows, pottery, wooden yokes, bone drills, bow and arrows, stone axes
Clothing: animal skins and wool
Building materials: mud, straw, wood

They had left out religion, and said they wanted to think about it more. It seemed foolish to insist that they create a religion immediately, so I let it slide. They were able to refer repeatedly to *Technology in the Ancient World* for ideas. There were many questions and conflicts. For instance, archeologically speaking, there might not have existed any wheels, or wells, or irrigation, etc. for the time and place they chose. In discussion with them I would try to point this out just so they would get the "idea" of "economic stages," but usually we compromised and let some unlikely inventions stay unless they were quite obviously from another time like metal spears. I would talk about dates from time to time, but I was not insistent that they remember anything specific. Some students took my mini-lectures seriously and took notes (while others drowsed). The main point in preparation and actual designing of the towns was how life changed with the possibility of preserving food as opposed to what we knew of the instant consumption of the hunters.

For simplicity's sake, I'd like to describe the process of building just one of the towns. Materials and approach could obviously vary. What is important in the building of the towns is to constantly question the student as the town is being built as to every aspect of its nature. If the town starts to go up without protecting walls, you might ask if there aren't other people in the area who might be interested in stealing your stores. Or, if all the houses appear to be absolutely uniform in size, this serves as a basis for asking if everybody is as rich as everybody else, and, if there are differences in wealth, how this happened. This should also lead to talking about how the place is governed and how *that* happened. If the houses are also uniform in shape, you might ask if a farmer and a potter would have exactly the same

kinds of houses, or if there are any religious buildings or at least some houses with more religious objects than others, the home of a priest, for instance. If the town plan appears too geometrical, ask if it's not more likely if the town shape didn't develop more slowly than at a single blow. If the students insist on sticking to their strict geometrical plan, ask them to explain what the power was behind the possibility of implementing such a plan. The aim would be to see how one focus fits together in all its aspects rather than simply reproducing a model that was archeologically correct. My boy students tended to imagine everything governed by a male dominated egalitarian communism. Rather than questioning the likelihood of this happening, in this instance I tried to get them to describe to me exactly how this worked and then question their description. If only the men govern, why do the women accept it? How do you prevent one man from gaining more wealth than others by trading with outsiders? Do you forbid contact with outsiders, or is trading also communal? Communal trading. Great. How does it work? This incidental questioning is really where imaginations come most into play and where this approach in studying early man most differs from fixed kits like "Man, A Course of Study," and other packages. I think it is the most creative and enjoyable way to approach things for both teacher and student. I certainly had fun listening to how these twentieth century city dwellers imagined the early neolithic for themselves.

In the actual building of the town, we first constructed a low platform out of wood for the town itself. In their designs they had decided that the fields were to lie outside the town with a river between the town and the fields, so we had also to construct a low platform for the fields, with a gap in the middle for the irrigation ditch. Once the bases for town and field had been built, I had them cut big pieces of paper to the size of the bases and draw in a projection of their earlier plan to the scale of the base. At first we used regular pottery clay to cover the bases, but by the next day the surfaces had dried and cracked, making our uninhabited site look like it had been hit already by a devastating drought. So we decided to cover the boards with heavy construction paper and build the town itself out of plasticene. The gap for the irrigation ditch was filled with chicken wire so that we could papier mache the water, giving it a different surface than the town and the fields. The river was a board nailed to the bottom of both bases and also covered with chicken wire. Before we actually began to put up the walls, there was a long discussion about whether the houses should have roofs or not. I wanted them to at least know what the roofs were made of and how they were constructed, but they thought it was more important that people could see inside the houses. So we decided to just put up the walls of the houses for the time being. The ideal way to build the town would have been from completely natural materials, i.e., tiny sun-dried bricks, etc., but exigencies of time, materials and concentration made this impossible. I did insist however that the students *know* what the materials were that they were representing. This would often lead to an alteration in design. For instance, in discussing the possibility that the bricks might have been fired rather than sun baked, it would have been necessary to add some firing or kiln area to the town plan. When controversies such as these came up, the students tended to opt for the simplest plan, but I would encourage them to be free in rearrangement just for the sake of seeing how one change could lead to many changes.

At first we all worked together on the town, constructing the outer walls. Plasticene proved a perfect material to work in. If something developed we didn't like, or some better alternative became evident, we had only to pick up what we had done and start over. When J, who had been given charge of agriculture, noticed that the stable area was at the opposite end of the town from the fields, he asked if the stable couldn't be on the other end. Somehow taking the animals across the river to graze appealed to him. He then began thinking about how the stable was to be divided and, as we were working on the stable together, we talked about how the animals were cared for. Needless to say, this conversation between two city slickers about the intricacies of sheep shearing was highly speculative. Another instance of instant design came when I noted that the town had no public space. In typical New York fashion we had forgotten that some area just for common rest and chatting might be desirable. We talked about the possibility of common courtyards for some of the houses or a square or a park. All building stopped for a while as each student rapped about where he hung out and what he liked or didn't like about it. It was interesting to hear about Bleecker Street, Washington Square Park or Tomkins Park from the point of view of ten year olds. This took us on to a discussion of streets as public space, and also stoops, alleys, stores, etc. We were all impressed by the fact that there was hardly any public space in New York except for the parks that you thought of as such. You just take what you can get as you can get it: the street is a ball park until a car comes; the stoop is a park bench till someone throws you off; the newspaper stand is a library until the owner yells, "This ain't no library!" Momentarily we all became fascinated by the fact that in *our* Iran 5000 B.C., we could have things just exactly the way we wanted to have it. We could actually begin thinking about the kind of habitation that was most desirable to us. From all this one of the students suggested that we have a shaded well at the center of the town as a

"This incidental questioning is really where imagination comes most into play and where this approach in studying early man most differs from fixed kits like 'Man, A Course of Study,' and other packages."

convenient place to hang out. This was immediately incorporated. Later someone decided that we should have a guardian statue near the well facing the entrance to the town. These kinds of alterations were to occur again and again as more of the town began to be visible, more questions were asked, and more brainstorms happened. For the teacher, being involved in the building is invaluable. In this type of project the students have a tendency, once they get started, to rush on to get the thing done, achieved. The teacher's participation can slow down the process and take advantage of possibilities as they arise. It is also a very good time to fill out the students' knowledge of the people they were imagining. I would constantly ask questions about who lived in each house and how they were related to one another, who else they were related to in the town, what kind of stature they had in the town. In short, I would try and make them see as much as possible what the everyday life was like of the people they were in fact creating. In the case of this town the students themselves thought of many of the alterations, each one of which took them deeper into the nature of the place they were creating. One mistake I made here was in getting so wrapped up in the town planning and tools that I did not place sufficient emphasis on the people themselves. I should have had all of the people named in the planning description according to age, relations, occupations. We had drawn our own family trees previously, and this would have been an excellent chance to explore the nature of kinship and to speculate about individual biographies. Stories could have been written about the town or the people in it. It would have been useful to have each student write a kind of "Day in the Life" of their favorite person in the town, but I didn't think of any of this until it was too late and we were already studying the Egyptians.

Another aspect of town building which was pretty much unsuccessful, at least in this town, had to do with religion. I had hoped that in looking at the photos of Catal Huyuk and discussing them, the students would become aware of the differences between farming and hunting gods and be able to incorporate these differences into the towns they were building. This was one part of the preparation to which I wish I had given more time. How religious or spiritual life changes relative to economic life should have been a fundamental part of the class right up to considerations of contemporary materialism. It should have been obvious after noting the almost exclusive preoccupation of cave art with animals of the hunt that the presence of fertility goddesses and human forms signaled some kind of spiritual change in this emerging urban people. Either I didn't explain this well enough, or the highly secular point of view of the students made them unreceptive to such changes, or maybe that was just something that couldn't be understood at this level and would have to be reserved for older students. Outside of this one drawback, it seemed to me that the town building experience gave the students a more direct experience of what the early neolithic was actually like than would be possible in academic surroundings.

From *Teachers & Writers Collaborative Newsletter* (Vol. 5, No. 3) pp. 4-15

Egyptian Diary

by Ron Padgett

14 December, 1973

First meeting. Loose and easy. Explained what this "seminar" *wouldn't* be. Kids make a good group. Some special talent: Drew knows about pottery-making and art, Chi Wo speaks and writes Chinese (useful as illustration of picture-languages and hieroglyphics). Kids know random things about Egypt but have little general knowledge. Class period passed quickly. Everyone so happy to be out of classroom situation.

Mr. Bowman would like our group to make some kind of presentation after Xmas vacation. I'd like to, but not just a committee report. Something which would *involve* everyone.

Now I have a lot to do: reading, study, research, big thinking about the group. I told the kids I knew next to nothing about the subject, Egypt, which is one reason I wanted to "teach" it.

Need to get a notebook for each kid, into which they can put anything they want. None of them have ever *taken notes!* They tend to think of knowledge as exterior objects which *others* create.

20 December

Everyone present. I gave kids my phone no. and address and encouraged them to call me if they wanted to talk about Egypt—unlikely, but I want the option to be there.

I started today by explaining that I thought we should start with the basics, and by this I meant the geography and meteorology and flora and fauna—Earth, the Great Mother! The kids took notes in notebooks I had given them. I realized as I talked that while I knew certain things—e.g., that there's a White Nile and a Blue Nile which join to form the Nile—that I knew them only half-way—I didn't know which branch of the Nile was which. What I gave them was some basic geology, using Egypt as my example. It was really interesting talking about Lower and Upper Egypt, which, to common sense, appear to be reversed on the map. It led to a discussion of how people in the other hemisphere—if we could see through the earth—would be upsidedown to us. This led to concepts of up and down and how its relativity is determined by gravity: where we are at the moment. This interested and slightly perplexed the kids and I could see that in most cases it was the first time they had considered this idea. I also talked about the oases—guessing wrongly that the word oasis was of Arabic origin—it's Greek—and about mirages. We tried to guess how mirages worked: were they mental tricks, natural phenomena or a combination of both. To be discussed further when we find out more.

Finally I got to the Nile Delta and was about to explain the origin of that word, Greek △, but got sidetracked, went on to trees and fruit, at which point I took out a large cold orange, a lemon, a lime, some grapes, dates and dried apricots, cut segments and passed them out on paper plates.

The kids were really interested in this and it was nice the way they naturally helped pass things out and see that everyone got their slice.

Two kids had peculiar aversions: Ivory wouldn't touch the apricots nor would Chi Wo—neither had ever tried them.

I wrote other fruits of Egypt on the board: pomegranates, olives, figs, melons, bananas (the banana I brought got smashed in the sack). Soon the room was smelling delicious.

This was the point for me to say that while in Hollywood movies the "average" Egyptian looks tired, thirsty, downtrodden and exhausted by hauling huge blocks of stone and by being lashed by a muscular brute, in fact his life might not have been like that. Then I really socked it to them: "Egyptians weren't storybook characters, they were *real people* just as real as we are. They laughed, went to the bathroom, had their feelings hurt, were eight years old, got spanked, etc."

I started to say that they went to school, a fact I was utterly unable to corroborate, so I stopped short.

Our time was up. Alas! The period whizzes by.

Some kids kept their notebooks, others gave them to me (I peeked—their notes were quite well taken).

Once again I didn't have time to show them the books I had brought along.

Tonight I realized that certain kids in the group were naturally more voluble than others. Bradley, a very bright and very well-informed boy, talks like crazy, frequently (and innocently) interrupts others, while James, also bright, hardly ever opens his mouth. I hope to make them, as well as the others, more aware of their personalities in this situation, to encourage Bradley to listen to what others were saying (and not merely to use their remarks as a springboard for his), and to encourage James to come out of his shell a little to see the advantages of sociability (he's *not* distant or cold, just very quiet.)

Soon I want to start getting them to write, after I've given them a basic vocabulary to work with.

Also I have to make ancient times more real to them by comparing it with their own lives. Compare the Nile to the East River, for instance.

4 January, 1974

Got a letter a parent had written to us, complaining that his kid wasn't in the Egypt group. A reasonable letter, which I hope I answered reasonably tonight.

Drew Bailey absent.

I picked up in my lecture where I left off last time. Talked more about geography, flora and fauna, and Time—Lillian didn't know about B.C. and A.D. Betty Machel dropped in to visit, while I explained anno Domini.

My discussion of specific details led inevitably to generalization—today the main point, I think, was how people had to judge other peoples—either foreign cultures, different races, or peoples distant in time, too much by their own standards: the Chinese are reputed to be inscrutable, the blacks rhythmical, the English "nice," etc. I emphasized how we should explode these "myths" in our study of ancient Egypt—to try to see ancient Egyptian culture on its own terms. It helped me when Lisa mentioned how Mr. Bowman had said that people of the far future will have larger heads, no hair on them, no toes, no nails: these people would look back at pictures of kids at P.S. 61 and say, "How ugly their little heads are, covered with that ugly hair, with hard little things stuck at the end of their fingers," and that this kind of judgment was not only unfair, it was irrelevant and obstructive.

So we did a lot of traveling up and down the time-stick.

I went ahead and discussed pre-dynastic man in Egypt and how anthropologists and historians now tend to think that around 3,200 B.C. an invading race, possibly from Sumer, conquered and unified Lower and Upper Egypt.

We also discussed the possibility of particular kids taking certain aspects of Egyptian life as a specialty to study and research. Brad wants to study hieroglyphics—which he called "hydroglyphics"—don't get me wrong! he's a very bright boy, at ease with terms such as "Java Man" and "Cro-Magnon Man."

Lisa, who to my delight had checked out from the 61 library a book on ancient Egypt, is interested in jewelry, and she's seen the collection at the Met!

I feel a little disappointed that I haven't come up with any writing ideas, but what the hell, this is going well as it is and I see no legitimate reason to try to warp it into a writing class at this stage. It's certainly a pleasure working this way. I look forward to each class.

11 January

Four kids absent today!

I had laid on a table all the books on Egypt I have, and when the kids came in I asked them to take a look. Naturally they loved this haphazard collection of items. Brad brought in two or three library books as well.

Then everyone sat down in our circle of desks and I told them about Herodotus' eye-witness account of later Egypt and his *Histories*, how Greek manuscripts had survived and how I had read the relevant parts (Book 2, mostly) in English.

I then read aloud and commented on those passages in which Herodotus discusses Egyptian customs which he considered odd or peculiar and about which I had similar feelings: women floating down the Nile and *insulting* people on the banks during a certain religious festival . . . how the Egyptians sacrificed the bull (exactly how they flayed it, etc.). . .

All this tied in with my previous discussions of how to relate to the differences of other peoples—cultures—lives—places.

Then I asked each kid to pretend *he* was Herodotus seeing Egypt and to record (i.e., invent) an Egyptian custom which might seem peculiar.

We all wrote some (each in his own notebook) and then read them aloud. They were quite good, some very funny (should copy them out of their notebooks.) I wish all the kids had been there. In fact I must take up the idea again—toward making a little collection of (bogus) *Customs of Ancient Egypt*.

Now here's a "writing idea" which evolved—as they say—out of the material at hand. Perfect example of what I want to do.

In a fit of generosity I told the kids to borrow any of the books they wanted.

In the hall outside the office at 3 Les Bowman asked me how it was going, and I found myself answering him in a manner more free of anxiety than I thought possible.

18 January

School closed by maintenance workers' strike.

Got from Bill Zavatsky and read a terrific "juniors" book, *Mummies* by Georgess McHargue, which the kids would love. Will love.

25 January

I reminded the kids where we had left off—with imitations of Herodotus—and explained what that was (to those kids who had been absent), and I had them write further imitations. To my surprise:

1. Two kids (Ivory and Chi-Wo) had written some at home.

2. Three kids had misplaced their notebooks (they think they're home).

3. I still have no key to the room.

A further gripe: the kids arrive ten or so minutes late from Bowman's, and if they're behind in their work they sometimes arrive even later—as was the case with Chi Wo today.

But we had a good time writing today and reading the "Herodotus" works—though they tended to be a little yucky and gooey (eating snake's blood mixed with frog's eyes, etc.).

I asked them each to write one more at home and to make it less gory—try to make it sound like a *real custom*: to do a forgery not a parody.

Gave the *Mummies* back to Lisa. Asked kids to think about specific areas of Egyptian life to "study" —how to choose? Well, think about what you like to do yourself (e.g., race-cars) and see how Egyptians did similar things (make toys, or play games, or transport them).

I was impatient when Josh started telling us about his trip to the Met over the weekend, and his seeing the Egyptian things, and impatient when Lillian expressed a desire to copy Egyptian paintings, impatient when Bradley asked if he could borrow my Herodotus, etc. I was also a little bothered by Bradley and Drew's distracting the class by their minor misbehavior: I guess I want them to sit there like James (who, to my great surprise, actually asked a question today and did some talking!) I was also less than deliriously happy when Chi Wo exhibited his shyness about being Chinese. When I started talking about languages that originate in pictures, Chinese among them, and wrote a few examples on the board (drew a stick man, then wrote the character for "man," which Chi Wo later confessed to being written backwards), he sort of disowned his knowledge of Chinese, and only slowly could I pry any info loose from him. I decided to go whole hog and asked him to bring in, Friday, a short list of Chinese characters which resemble the thing they designate. Everyone was present today, though Rupert came in

about twenty-five minutes late, and some notebooks had been found but a few still missing: I'll wait until Friday to collect them: I want to copy out their Herodotus imitations, make dittos or something and give them back.

I should have let the class develop more on its own today. I lectured too much (though the matter was interesting).

At the end of the period I opened my giant Oxford U *Egyptian Grammar* and we looked over the hieroglyphics. The one of the spurting penis escaped everyone's attention, but for how long, O Lord?

After school I Xeroxed a section in hieroglyphics from the book, Lesson 2, with glossary attached, to have them translate it first without the glossary and then later with. I also Xeroxed a reduced version of the Rosetta Stone.

I feel angry with myself for missing three journal entries, those of Feb. 1, 8 and 15.

As I remember it, Feb. 1 was a good class, during which I handed out Xerox copies of hieroglyphics from the Oxford *Grammar*, second or third lesson, and had the kids guess at translating them. They did very well and wrote some haunting works. It was during this period that, in response to the question of whether or not I would give them grades, I answered that every teacher gives every kid a grade in his head, but I would give none on paper. I told them that I had written about each of them in my journal. Bradley immediately asked what I had said about him, and I told him. Lisa asked about herself, "What are my strong and weak points?" and I answered her as I had written in my journal. My forthrightness made a tremendous impression on her.

The class of Feb. 8 was, as I remember, a dud. The kids had been given the vocabulary for the hieroglyphics from last class and asked to try to translate it for real at home. I think one kid actually managed to do it and bring it in, and the result was not inspired. They arrived late, showed little concentration, in fact made me lose my interest in even having the class that day. Finally, I informed them that it was up to them to make the class good, and that if they went on like this, I would lose interest and dissolve the class, not in anger, but from boredom.

The class of Feb. 15: I started them off with a blank piece of paper and a pencil and I asked them to answer questions: I was giving them a *test*!! A pop test, yet! In a rather dry, professorial way I asked them about twelve questions covering the basic material so far. Then I had them translate hieroglyphics which I put on the board. Finally I asked them to offer any suggestions for the class, how it was to be conducted, etc.

Interesting, they took the test in utter silence, very seriously, and this seriousness carried over to the translation and suggestions sections. I gave them the answers and they checked and graded their own papers. They did rather well—their big weak point was in their concept of time. They have a terrible time trying to understand what 3,500 BC means (who doesn't?). But generally they did pretty well. In the suggestions part, interestingly, all who took the test (three were absent and one was too late) asked for more seriousness in class, keeping on the subject, and the assignment of special projects. I think there's a grain of sincerity in this, especially with Chi Wo, who has an aversion to wasted time.

At the end of the period I told them that we would begin to study Egyptian religion, art (and architecture) and history, all of which met in the Egyptian tombs. Which we will. But tonight, typing up their prose poems, I realized how good they were, and want to use them tomorrow, to have the kids perfect them, real poems.

Sidelight: Several weeks ago Les told me that Josh would have to be dropped from the group: his attendance and homework were poor. I asked Les for a reprieve, telling him I'd talk to Josh and see what I could do. I went to Josh and told him, "Mr. Bowman says you will be dropped from the Egypt class because your attendance and homework are poor. I'd like to have you in my group, because I like you, and if you want to stay in it, you'll have to come to school on time and do your homework. OK?" This was on Friday.

When I went back to the school to drop off some papers on Monday Les said, "Josh is out. He didn't do his homework over the weekend." I resigned myself to the situation and selected another kid to replace Josh, come Friday.

But on Friday, Les, to my surprise, to my very pleasant surprise, told me that Josh had suddenly started doing everything required of him, and that he could stay in the group. Then Les added, "I'm jealous." (He also showed me some very good writing the kids had done for him).

22 February

Last night I typed up the hieroglyphics guess-translations in the prose form in which they were written, and today I handed them back to their authors asking them to consider them carefully: would they like to add or subtract anything: Would the pieces be better as "poetry," i.e., in lines? I took one of my own translations, read it aloud as prose, then demonstrated on the board various ways in which the words could be arranged, discussing the implications of each arrangement.

The kids spent about twenty minutes rewriting their pieces. Reading them over later, I noticed that some pieces were improved, some worsened, and that some kids showed purpose to their rearrangements, others seemed too random. I typed up the various works, some in both their prose and poetry forms, with the idea of making them into a booklet, along with their descriptions of Strange Egyptian Customs. (Some of these, unfortunately, were lost by the kids.)

Then I mentioned various topics the kids could consider as possible subjects for reports. There was some battling over that perennially favorite topic, mummies, but I tried to straighten things out. Here is how the topics were doled out during this period: Drew (Egyptian writing); Bradley (pyramids & tombs); Lisa (clothes, jewelry & cosmetics); Ivory (religion or mythology—I had to press this on her); Lillian and Rupert (mummies: Rupert wants to build a life-size mummy, and I suggested he also learn how to wrap up a live person to resemble a mummy). James and Chi Wo were absent, and Josh has been barred from the group due to poor performance again at homework.

28 February

Les let me have the kids today as well as tomorrow when I asked him for more time with them.

Since last Friday I have scouted out various bookstores and bought a number of books on Egypt which I hope will help the kids with their research—to supplement whatever reading they do at home or in the school or public library. (Ivory had done a lot of work since last time, and she was ready for further material.)

We went from person to person finding out what they had done on their topic (ugh, which Bradley called a "term paper"), and I made suggestions as to how they might discover new information and how they should read with a pencil in their hand, and what kind of information might help them gather as much material as possible. It was interesting to me that the only person who had started to organize his material in an outline was Drew. I have the feeling that children are not taught well in this respect: they are taught how to make an outline, but it's just another subject to them, without intrinsic merit or use. Like the Dewey decimal system seems to be when you're first required to learn it. I wonder if I can make them see the usefulness of actually organizing data.

In my mind this lack of sense of organization is related to the difficulty kids have in learning to write expository prose, exposition based on a linear and logical progression from point to point in relation to the whole of a subject. In fact, one attack on writing which I hope to make is on expository prose. It occurs to me that if poetry is not taught well as it might be, generally in our schools, then Expository Writing might be taught even less well—and it has none of the attractive selling points of Poetry (Imagination, Creativity, Free Expression, all those Holy of Holies). I don't know how I will go about teaching good straight expository prose writing—it's hard enough to write, let alone teach.

Anyway, I informed Rupert that styrofoam in huge chunks is hard to find, and that foam rubber is too expensive, and I suggested that he make a scale model of a mummy, perhaps a foot long; and also do a series of drawings of the mummy, the mummy wrapped, the mummy case, the outer case, etc., sort of a step-by-step diagram of what the whole arrangement looks like (like peeling the skins off an onion). We voted to elect the Live Mummy: Lillian was elected, and then we realized that mummies is her topic: I then had the great idea of having her deliver her oral report on Mummies, dressed as a mummy! She balked at this at first, then daylight hit her and she liked the idea. She refused to run up and down the hall, however, *en momie*.

Bradley decided he'd like to change his topic slightly to Pyramids and Pharaohs, which I said was fine.

At this point we took all our Egypt books and made a library: with a card for each book, and then I suggested which book might be useful for each person's topic, and they signed for them.

Tomorrow, hopefully, we'll have topics for Chi Wo and James: none of the topics I suggested today (Art; Government; Sports, Games and Fun; Learning and School) appealed to them.

There's been some horsing around these last two sessions: I kept the kids after school a little more until I finished.

1 March

Before classtime I wrote one of James' Strange Egyptian Customs on the board, and on another board the words:
EXPOSITORY WRITING:
to show, demonstrate
(World's Exposition, 1899.)
When the kids arrived I handed out typed copies of the Customs writings they had done. (Josh and James absent, Rupert late). I also gave Bradley a copy of the old test for James, and I gave Chi Wo a copy for himself.

A copy of James' piece is appended to this diary installment, as is the piece in its revised form—Bradley took the paper home accidentally. Anyway, I pointed out how good the ideas were in the piece, but how the writing wasn't so sharp as it might be. It had a lot of loose and rattling words which didn't do anything but get in the way, like extra doorknobs that don't help you open the door. Or like excess fat on an overweight person. I pointed to the first

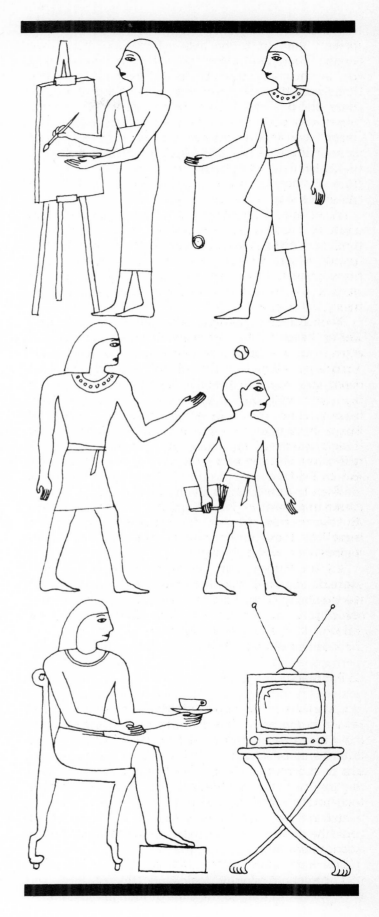

sentence and its "you" . . . who is this you? Isn't the piece supposed to be about Egyptians? Drew suggested we replace "you" with "they," and we were off and running. Both Drew and Bradley understand concision in writing and they understand (and know they understand) the benefit of sharpening or focusing abstractions until they are so specific that they mean exactly what they say. As we went through the piece, dropping out unnecessary words and sharpening others, and rectifying tenses, it was clear to me that the kids in the group were catching on quickly—they had been drilled in this, I'm sure.

After we got through and it seemed as good as it could be, Drew pointed out that it was still too unlikely: the Egyptians wouldn't chop up a cat if the cat were a sacred animal, and he suggested we change it to "bull." He then suggested a title change, and together the class made the title really apply to the work.

I took this opportunity to write the word "then" on the board and point out that they used this word too much and when it wasn't necessary. They tend to start each sentence with *then*, especially when the sentences are sequentially describing a process or action. I suggested that they drop it, for the most part, because the order of the sentences indicate the sequence already. You wouldn't count "one, then two, then three, then four . .," would you? No. It's the same with sentences. The logic of their sequence is just like the logic of numbers, two systems we have developed to help us be civilized.

At this point I asked them to rewrite their Strange Customs works: to read them carefully and to reconsider them the same way we had rewritten James' piece (too bad he was absent).

I went around from kid to kid, seeing how they were doing, making some suggestions. I felt they did a very good job, and that teaching them the basics of expository prose might not be so hard as I had imagined.

I collected the papers and now will type them, perhaps in both their original and revised form.

At this point I launched into a little lecture on expository prose, giving its root meaning, and really got the kids interested by telling them that learning this was important for them because if they learned how to do this kind of writing well, they would have a tremendous advantage over other kids in school for the next ten years. They loved the idea of this! I went on to point out that there was a more basic benefit, one to their mentality, that it would be more organized and yet more flexible, capable of nuance, and that their lives would change for the better. Or some such: I was better in class than I am now home at the typewriter.

I compared sloppy logic and lack of form and precision in writing to the class of mongoloid children at PS 19. These children are, in some cases, unable to identify a triangle, even after lengthy repetitions and identification exercises. This was the far extreme (at first my kids had laughed when I said "mongoloid" but as I continued they grew more sober). I suggested, gently, that there was a little of this chaos in their own writing, and they should try to be more conscious of what they were doing.

"But I like imaginative thinking," said Bradley.

"So do I," I replied, "but when I buy a newspaper with a dollar and get a dime in change, I don't think that's imaginative. I think I'm being shortchanged. I think it's wrong. Or incorrect. It is certainly interesting to give someone ninety cents for the *Post*, and I could dig it, but not unless I were aware of what was going on. In fact you can't appreciate the situation unless you know it's wrong and you just let it go."

I wrote four sentences on the board:

1. I woke up.
2. I put on my clothes.
3. I had breakfast.
4. I went to school.

Boring, but "correct," and in sequence. Now, poetry might state things differently, because poetry offers endless options to the ennui of everyday reality, or what is called everyday reality—I mean the humdrum. For instance, we could make this more "poetic" by scrambling the lines:

I had breakfast.
I went to school.
I put on my clothes.
I woke up.

A case of a sleepwalking kid who went to school in his pyjamas!

So these sentences can be used as examples of "straight prose" or as "poetry." Both kinds are equally "good", but one is sometimes more appropriate for a given situation than another. In some instances they are mixed, in the journalism of Addison and Steele, for instance; or in the prose of Francis Ponge (wherein the poetry has a strong discursive underpinning).

But in the writing of themes, term papers, articles and essays, it is useful to know the rules and regulations of expository prose, and when the kids present their written reports, I want them to have their material, facts, data, information organized so that all the triangles are in the triangle group, the circles in the circle group, etc. and that everything is in logical sequence.

From 1 March class

James' Strange Egyptian Custom, original version and revised (by class)

THE WAY TO GET BAPTIZED

First you have to go to an Egyptian priest. He will go kill a perfect cat, take the foot or hind leg and burn it to a crisp, then put it under the baby and the smoke is supposed to be some blessing. The smoke rises under the baby and blesses it.

THE WAY EGYPTIANS BAPTIZE THEIR BABIES

First they go to an Egyptian priest. He kills a perfect bull, takes the foot or hind leg and burns it to a crisp, then puts it under the baby. The smoke rises under the baby and blesses it.

Today's class was so much better than this written account of it. I felt tremendously exhilarated, because of how good and how relevant and meaningful the class had been, and how it added another dimension to the writing we're doing around our subject, Egypt.

5 March

Today, Tuesday, I found my room taken by the (I think) school psychologist, with the librarian, Mrs. Brown, out (jury duty) and Mr. Bowman absent: it was a clean sweep.

I had wanted to relocate our Egypt library in the regular school library, as a sort of Reserve Shelf for my kids, with the books more accessible than they are locked up in the Art Room all week; but with Mrs. Brown gone, I thought I'd set up such a shelf in Les' room, and I did so, only to have my regular kids advise me that the books would just disappear if I left them there. Mr. Bowman's substitute, a patient and friendly looking fellow, had his hands full: it was a nice warm day and the kids were going wild with that Lower East Side explosive brat energy that starts to surge this time of year.

Anyway, I took my kids out onto the stairs and set up a brief session with them there, during which time I discussed the library idea, told them how good Jon White's *Everyday Life in Ancient Egypt* was and how useful it would be for all of them in their special studies; returned Rupert's Customs works to him and suggested ways in which he might improve them; gave *Ancient Egyptian Mythology* to Ivory after picking it up at the bookstore today; assigned Art to Chi Wo (since he had come up with nothing himself), and asked the kids to see that James please be present sometime! I told them that I would give deadlines for

their research on Friday, that I hadn't decided yet. (In fact I have only the haziest notions of what they're doing in this area, and I realized that I didn't really know why I was having them do it: it had seemed like a thing to do. I had hoped they would have by now shown more spontaneous interest in a particular aspect of our class, but I'm afraid it's turning out to be just another "assignment" to them. Maybe not. Still, I don't feel right about the thing.) In the meantime I took the Egypt books across the hall and left them with Jean Calandra, who agreed to serve as temporary Egypt Librarian. Now it's time for me to start to think about how to introduce Egyptian literature into what I'm doing. That is, poems and stories in translation. *The Literature of Ancient Egypt* ed. Wm. Kelly Simpson is a nice book with some good things and will be useful. What I'd really like to find is *The Love Poems of Ancient Egypt* by Noel Stock and Ezra Pound, a pretty little paperback that used to be in every bookstore and now is in none. Everyone says the only "great" Egyptian literature is in the love poems and I think there might be grist for our mill in them.

I'm also thinking of the way the Egyptians were addicted to invocations, especially at the beginning of their religious texts, and how we might teach the kids the rhetoric of invocation through this, having them write invocations applicable to their own lives. One way to do this is, obviously through comedy (e.g., "O lamp that shines on my desk, with your 100 watts. . . ."). Beyond comedy? Or as Step 2? The idea of sixth graders writing big heavy serious invocations is mind-boggling! Therefore I must do it!

8 March

This was a class period from which I expected something good which did not materialize. The ever-unpopular idea of teaching Love Poems to kids, yep, I gave it the old college try again and sure enough it flopped.

I began by pointing out how boys tend to pick on Lillian, and how this is the way boys at age eleven or twelve express their affection, or at least attention. If you can't be tender toward someone you like, then you tend to attack them. The boys in the group agreed reluctantly. I called to their attention the idea that tenderness is not an acceptable public emotion in USA.

Then I passed on to them the idea, which I got reading, that the most interesting Egyptian literature is in the love poems, and I read selections from them in *The Literature of Ancient Egypt* ed. Wm. Kelly Simpson and from *The Love Poems of Ancient Egypt* trans. Pound and Stock. These poems, which I had been reading at home (where they seemed not only OK in themselves but useful as teaching vehicles or models) sounded really stale or irrelevant in the classroom, and the wave of ennui that swept over the kids intensified my dismay. Added to this was the way two of the girls (Lillian was absent) took offense at my reading the words "breast" and "breasts." They didn't go nuts, but they did seem a little huffy.

Only James seemed to find any merit in the whole thing, and who knows what he was really thinking. I finished the class feeling disappointed and a little bit embarrassed.

13 March

Today I set out various materials in the Art Room (where we meet) and asked the kids to start working on pictures (drawings or whatever) which could enhance their reports oral and/or written, and I asked Chi Wo to design a cover for our collected Egyptian writings, named EGYPT CLASS GREATS by Bradley. There was a mixed reaction to this art-illustration direction, and Ivory stated flatly, "I can't draw." The same old story. So she helped tear strips from the white sheet which will be wound around Lillian to make her a mummy. Rupert was supposed to help bind her, but he couldn't really, it was too intimate, physically, for him to help.

So I set him to drawing mummies, which he did without much real interest: he does the ink drawings very quickly, with his left hand: one drawing was as good as Dubuffet, really an exquisite piece of work. The rest was so-so, perhaps too tossed off.

Josh has been banned from the group again. It's not possible to work with him effectively this way, never knowing if he'll be there or not. Also, James was absent again! It's incredible! Les says he seems to alternate being absent with his twin (?) sister. When he's in my group he seems sincere and interested, but he misses school too much!

Chi Wo, given the cover design assignment, set to work assiduously for the entire period.

Today's class was affected by the handing out of Report Cards: each kid came in with his envelope, which he opened and peeked to see, first, how many U's he had gotten. No U's was considered great. Apparently Les is a tough marker, but not excessively so.

Lillian became very interesting as she was being wrapped up. Her face became rather bemused or preoccupied or dreamy and she said, "My legs and arms are stiff" (from the binding). "It feels awful, I can't bend my arms or legs." I should have had her dictate a poem (perhaps next time) from the mummy's point of view.

14 March

We (Les and his entire class) set out for a half-day field trip to the Met for a guided tour in the Greek and Roman collections. Walk to subway, change trains, walk to Museum, register, leave coats, check lunches, meet tour guide, all very regimented and (I might add) very efficient (too efficient, though I doubt if there's any other way to do it). The tour guide lady was very good: clear, with a good grasp of what the kids would find interesting and how far they could be taken in that interest, with a give-and-take, and she was tough. I mean tough. And firm. No messing around with her. She took us through the Greek vases and to the chariot (Etruscan) pointing out things that were beautifully easy and obvious once you saw them. Nothing arcane or unnecessary. After she dropped us off in the children's section of the basement, some kids bought souvenirs, some came with me for a quick run-through of the Egyptian collections.

It's a good thing I had checked out the collection before; it enabled me to skip the redundant or second-rate. I took a cue from the tour guide and, rather than trying to show the kids everything, I keyed on major works. (The group of kids was mixed, some from my Egyptian class, others from the regular class—a couple of my kids (Ivory and Lisa) got cut off from me and I couldn't invite them to go to the Egyptian wing). First we went to the mummy, which is of course the star piece in the collection, and the kids didn't laugh, either. Mummies turn out to be unfunny. They're all dirty and falling apart. People! Fingernails! From there we went to the jewelry and small household articles room, where I turned them loose and let them roam about (which counterbalanced the utter efficiency of the rest of the visit), then on the scale models of scenes of everyday life, found in tombs, and into the big statuary room at the end (Sekmet et al) and the exhibition on writing (carved hieroglyphics, Rosetta Stone copy!, papyrus plants, paper, quill and reed pens, sarcophogi covered with inscriptions) and, returning, the entryway to a tomb. I would have liked to have allowed the kids time to be a little more meditative, but on the other hand I was pleased by their interest, even those kids not in my group.

We rushed down to the basement to rendezvous with Les and the rest and to buy quickly some souvenirs, have lunch in the lunchroom, and head back downtown. I enjoyed myself enormously and Les seemed to be in a good humor. At one point on the subway he commented on the Test on Egypt I had given my kids. "How'd they do?" he asked. "That test was like one in college, it was hard."

The idea of today's class was to finish and/or improve upon the art work started previously. This included Chi Wo doing the cover for our collection of writings and the other kids making what I called Egyptian good luck message-drawing charms. I had read that mummies were sometimes wrapped with charms in their bandages, charms which would promote the well-being of the deceased in the Other World. I had wanted to have the kids do charms to wrap up with Lillian, but when they got started the charms got bigger and started turning out very nicely, which surprised me. Generally they consisted of words and drawings, some funny, others not. Chi Wo's cover design for the writings booklet was well done, and once again I saw his ability to buckle down and do the job: he sat down and worked straight through with perfect seriousness. The other kids tended to let their attention wander when they finished what they were doing, and at one point I got rather pissed off at Bradley and Rupert and I asked them to return to Les' room: Bradley was visibly upset, partly because it was more Rupert's fault than his. I relented quickly. I didn't want to alienate Bradley completely. He and I get along OK, but there's something unresolved between us. That I dared to criticize him openly? I don't know. Anyway, I don't believe it's a serious rift. As he worked on a paper model of a mastaba (Egyptian tomb, like a pyramid with its top shaved off) which I had bought at the Met yesterday, he read the instructions aloud and mused to himself, "Step A . . . Step 1 B, Step 2 B, . . . " and then he recited, "Two B or not Two A, that is the question mark." I thought this rather funny and asked him to write it on the board. Here is what he wrote there:

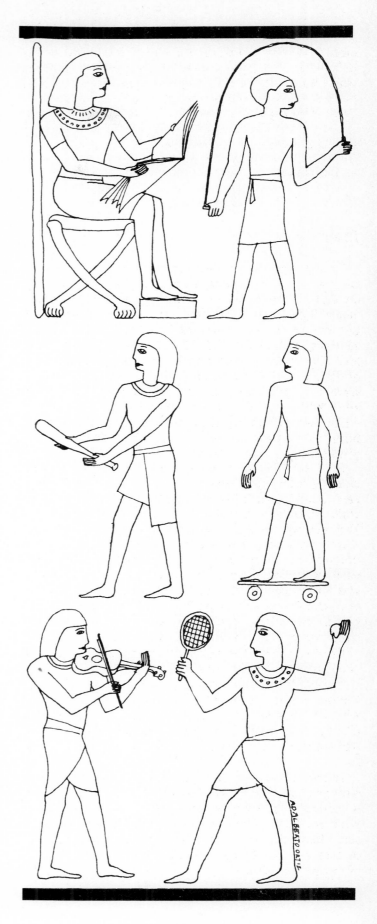

The blobs are splat-marks made by hurled tomatoes.

This was also the day for the kids to hand in their written reports, most of which, at first glance, I found uninspired and disappointing. Drew apologized for his as he handed it in. Lisa had taken ill during the day (because the report was due and she hadn't finished it?) and gone home: she was supposed to have brought extra sheets for making the mummy. Josh has been kicked out again! And even more incredible, James was absent again!! Impossible to work with them.

I'll read the reports carefully soon. I can't face them yet. I feel that I've really let myself down on this one. I can tell they thought of it as a "school report" and nothing else, not a compilation of ideas which might interest them, not an organized system of their knowledge of a subject, not, in short, a sharing. More like a mechanical presentation of facts whose inner life they did not explore in the least. So: does subject matter have to be *fun*, always, for kids to be interested in it? No. Stamp collecting isn't fun. When it's real it's passionate. But this passion I did not communicate to the kids. I flunked.

Still, there was some compensation in how well the message-charms came out. And I stayed after school thirty-five minutes cleaning up the room, just to punish myself!

The pressures of my personal life have kept me from my Egypt class journal, so today'll make up for four lost sessions (one of which was today's).

The session of 20 March is a blank. I can't remember what happened!

22 March: the crystal ball forms an image. During this period I talked about Egyptian Instructional literature. The Egyptians were strong moralists and some of their literature consists of the instructions of various officials, instructions on how to conduct one's moral and social-moral life. We talked about how the conduct of high officials influences a country's morals and morale—the comparisons are blindingly evident.

Then I focused on a particular text, *The Instructions of Amenemope*, and summarized the content and tone of the piece. I read them a chapter from Simpson's *The Literature of Ancient Egypt*. Here is the entire chapter:

The hot-headed man in the temple/Is like a tree grown in a garden;/Suddenly it bears fruit./It reaches its end in the carpentry shop;/It is floated away far from its place,/Or fire is its funeral pyre./The truly temperate man sets himself apart,/He is like a tree grown in a sunlit field,/But it flourishes, it doubles its yield,/It stands before its owner;/Its fruit is something sweet, its shade is pleasant,/And it reaches its end in a garden.

Not terribly exciting poetry, but it does use an interesting device of comparing opposite men to the same object (which has various fates).

I asked the kids to pick a moral fault and describe a person with this fault as being comparable to an object, and to pick the opposite quality and compare it to the same object, but with different results. I know this explanation is confusing; the procedure is simple.

Example:

A liar is like a radiator/That hisses and knocks/And wakes you up in the middle of the night/But never gives off heat./The truthful man is like a radiator/That you never notice:/It comes on automatically/And fills your house with warmth.

The kids wrote some very nice pieces with this structure. These pieces show, I think, how moral the kids really are, or at least their morality or moral firmness is suggested. It's probably the first time I've ever given writing assignments which had this latitude or went specifically into this area. Why? I don't know. Perhaps it's too close to home: our morals are so much a part of us that we do not distinguish them from simple everyday life.

26 March

Today's class was a sort of carry-over from last time. I had intended to read aloud another piece from Simpson, *The Man Who Was Tired Of Life*, because it contains a very good rhetorical section beginning "Behold . . .," in which a disillusioned young man converses with his soul. To lead up to this I had written on the board the hieroglyphics for *ka* (double, image, picture) and *ba* (soul), as well as their transliterations and translations. And I launched into a discussion of how we have various aspects to our "selves." For instance, we have a physical body. Yes, and in that body a special muscle, the heart. But we understand "heart" to mean more than that. A person has a "good heart." Or he is "hard-hearted." This refers to emotions, or a sense of generosity with the emotions.

We also have a brain, in which we locate our intelligence. But intelligence is not the brain. Drew suggested another such area, the Conscience. Which led to definitions of "spirit" and "soul" (laughter here) and "feelings" and "memory." It was a wonderful discussion.

It led to my holding up reproductions from the English Jackdaw portfolio series, *Tutankhaman*, in which King Tut is portrayed going through the experiences of the after-life. I also held up a reproduction of a part of the Papyrus of Ani (from which we derive the so-called *Book Of The Dead*), in which Ani's heart is being weighed. Our discussion had been so interesting that I felt it would be a real come-down to ask the kids to follow the literary model I had intended to give them (the "Behold . . ." section), and so I came up with the idea that each kid write down what they thought would happen to their spirits or souls (*not* their bodies) immediately after they died. The kids set to work and wrote some interesting pieces on what was a difficult subject.

It was a type of educational situation I like, in which the writing emerges from a wider context.

We took a few minutes to discuss the oral reports

which the kids are to give in Bowman's room. I made some useful suggestions.

29 March

Today I started by continuing our discussion of the orals. I spoke with each kid individually, suggesting what each one might do with his material. (Bowman asked us to present them on Wednesday at 2, each report to be limited to three minutes). Each subject has its own possibilities. You shouldn't be so lazy as to present a report on cosmetics in the same way you present one on, say, pyramids (no matter how they are related). You can wear the cosmetics, life-size, you cannot build the Pyramid of Cheops, alas, life-size in the classroom.

After I had done this I turned the class loose. For weeks they have been wanting to rush to the blackboard and write like crazy on it, and I've promised them this chance. (In the regular classroom, almost all blackboard writing has to be purposeful.) So I said, "OK kids, today you can attack the board." With a great rush and roar they grabbed the chalk and ran to the board, where, with glee and abandon they wrote this and that.

Oddly enough, I was surprised to notice that I felt as much a sense of relief as did they: perhaps my sérieux in this class has been a bit burdensome to me too.

Outside the snow (a total surprise today) was swirling and blowing. Drew put a chair on top of a desk, sat in it and stared out the window at the swirling snow. Lisa stayed with me to talk, first about how her apartment had been robbed, and then of other things. I can tell that she really likes and respects me, without adulation.

The other kids were kidding each other with things such as "Lillian loves Frankenstein." Then I noticed they were writing something whose procedure I didn't understand, and they were cracking up. They explained how it worked. First you write someone's first name, such as "Lillian," beneath which you write the first name of someone of the opposite sex, to see, by a special calculation, if they are compatible. They picked "Adolph" (Hitler). (The names must be connected by 'n'). You draw a line, beneath which you list the vowels A E I O U, beneath which you write the numbers 1 2 3 4 5 and draw another line. At this point here's how it looks:

$$
\begin{array}{l}
\text{L i l l i a n} \\
\text{'n'} \\
\underline{\text{A d o l p h}} \\
\\
\text{A E I O U} \\
\underline{\text{1 2 3 4 5}}
\end{array}
$$

Now you count the number of A's in the two names and inscribe the total beneath the number 1. Then the E's and inscribe the total beneath the number 2, etc. for all the vowels. After this you draw a line and total the two rows of numbers, and if the totals have any numbers (such as 1 and 1) side by side, it attests to the compatibility of the two people. Our example will look like this:

$$
\begin{array}{l}
\text{L i l l i a n} \\
\text{'n'} \\
\underline{\text{A d o l p h}} \\
\\
\text{A E I O U} \\
\underline{\text{1 2 3 4 5}} \\
\\
\underline{+\ 2\ 0\ 2\ 1\ 0} \\
\\
\text{3 2 5 6 5}
\end{array}
$$

No matches! Lillian 'n' Adolph do not match.

How about Ivory 'n' Lester? (Les Bowman).

$$
\begin{array}{l}
\text{I v o r y} \\
\text{'n'} \\
\underline{\text{L e s t e r}} \\
\\
\text{A E I O U} \\
\underline{\text{1 2 3 4 5}} \\
\\
\underline{+\ 0\ 2\ 1\ 1\ 0} \\
\\
\text{1 4 4 5 5}
\end{array}
$$

A double match! (44 and 55). The ultimate is of course to have all the numbers add up to the same figure. Bradley found that he and Raquel would not hit it off, but he and Elizabeth (Taylor) had a great future before them.

Before long I was at the board working out various possibilities.

Then, before class was over, I announced that we would meet on Tuesday, and then the orals would be on Wednesday, after which was Easter Vacation—perhaps we should end the class there. Cries of No! No! I said I would continue the class so long as it seemed worthwhile, and if anyone had any ideas for extending the class, I'd gladly listen.

(Some of the other kids in Les' room are still complaining about how they weren't picked for the Egypt class.)

When I arrived last week, or last time, for orals, Lillian (the key to the orals) was absent, so I had to postpone things until today. It was after Easter vacation and I feared that the kids would have forgotten everything. To my surprise they were sharper than I thought they would be.

James was of course absent! He has the worst attendance record of any kid I've ever taught. And Ivory couldn't give her oral unless she read the report she had given me (and which was at my place)—obviously she does not understand what a report is. Not that she can't learn. Her written report was copied straight out of books, and her oral was to have been simply a reading of that paper. (Her "creative" work is quite good, though).

First we went to our room and wrapped Lillian *en momie.* She seemed a little nervous, it was so strange to be wrapped up like that. Then we staggered down the hall, where various kids gaped at us in amazement—who was this mummy?? and Why??

Of course our entrance to Mr. Bowman's classroom was sensational. Les cracked a corny joke which somehow was extremely funny, and the class was in an uproar. When we calmed down Lillian delivered her oral, which described mummification, and then reported on what the Other World was like. I was impressed by her aplomb and her failure to remember several basic facts (namely, that all classes of ancient Egyptians were mummified—not simply the pharaohs and queens and upper crust). But she acquitted herself with honor. I was quite nervous—memories of Oral Report Nerves from my past.

Then Brad and Chi Wo delivered their joint report on the pyramids, and did a wonderful job. Brad has the gift of gab (and can bullshit when he needs to give himself time to think), but he, too, surprised me by telling the class that the pyramids were built by "slaves," a common misconception which I thought we had cleared up. I guess when the chips are down we tend to revert to what we feel we know best, even though it's incorrect. Chi Wo had done some beautiful drawings of the pyramids and tomb structures. Their report was quite proficient—it consisted mostly cf what they had learned, and they had learned it, it was now theirs, and they showed little hesitation about sharing it with the others.

Next, Drew reported on Egyptian language. He had written his oral—he read it aloud. Why? He read nothing which he didn't know already, but he gave the impression that he was simply reading from a piece of paper. He lacks confidence in orals. I wanted Les and the other kids in the class to know that Drew really knew what he was talking about, so I asked Drew some questions which would draw out his natural knowledge of his subject. He showed no hesitation in answering, and answering correctly.

Lisa, whose topic was dress, makeup, style, etc. in A.E., gave her talk totally impromptu: she wasn't really ready, but simply charged into her subject with a measure of confidence. I thought her presentation could have been more organized and therefore comprehensible, but she cannot be faulted for lack of courage or for not knowing something about her subject. (Like the others, though, she surprised me by getting at least one basic fact wrong: she said that Egyptian children and common people wore white linen, when in fact it was well-established in our group that these people went naked quite often.)

As for James, who was absent, and Ivory, who wants to read her report, and Rupert, who was supposed to have helped Lillian (and I doubt if he did), I think it best that these not be worried about. There was something about the whole Oral Report form that bothered me, and we did it mostly because Les asked us to, and we did it OK. Still, we could have done much better. We could have been more thoughtful about our presentation: we should have had more daring and flair, we should have rehabilitated the art of the Oral Report. Maybe next time.

THE GRIFFIN

It has the head of an eagle, a body of a lion, eagle's talons, wings of a condor. It always asks strangers this riddle:

> *What is as smart as a fox*
> *Red like blood*
> *Black like darkness*
> *Dangerous to some*
> *Some are dangerous to it.*

Chi Wo Lui

THE STYNX

The Stynx is made of a brown wooden block head with diamond eyes. His body is made of a huge closet, his feet are made of garbage can covers and his legs are made of toilet paper rolls. It has a machine gun for a tail. Its riddle is: what has a blue cover, a black belt and smells?

James Roa

EGYPTIAN CUSTOMS

During the festival of Bugumbala the people float down the river on boats. When they approach crocodiles they snatch a sandpiper off the crocodile clip the wings, replace it and splash it with water and sail away.

Bradley Torrance

EGYPTIAN CUSTOMS

On New Year's all the women must go out in the desert and look for a cobra's shell. But before she goes she must cover herself with hog mud. She has to bring the cobra shell back home and make it into a coat and turn around three times. That's supposed to bring her good luck.

A sculptor on bad luck Friday must sculpt a special rock into some other form.

To take a bath you have to brush your teeth with ashes and put some bull's blood in the water.

When a king has a party at the end he goes around and puts a piece of cooked bull's meat in each person's mouth.

On New Year's Eve they sacrifice a bull and clean it out. And the king has to do a special dance with the bull's skin.

Lisa Covington

Translations of Hieroglyphics

THE SNAKE

One day the moon was still in the sky, a bird came and talked to the sky god. Then the sky god gave him a dish made of gold. Then the moon went away and so did the god. Then the bird was left alone.

THE SMART BIRD

Bird stepped on water at sunrise. This pea was on his arm and in his eye. Then a lady came with a bird. Then a snake came and sat on the pea and told the lady about the moon. She took her hand and put it on the bird and the bird went in the water.

Lillian Mesen

STRANGENESS OF A SCRIBE AND LIGHTNING

Lightning strikes two birds one at a time. An eye sees it, the eye of a scribe without his glasses. A bird flies over the sky in a half moon. Scribe fights the bird with a shield. And walks in a circle.

Lisa Covington

THE HOT-TEMPERED MAN

The hot-tempered man is like a piece of furniture. It shines like the sun and in the night it twinkles like the stars above. Then soon it gets scratched and has no more use. And is then used for firewood. The cool-tempered man is like a piece of furniture that flickers at the firelight. Its beauty is everlasting. And when its job is done it will die a fabulous death. But its beauty will not die, it will live on forever.

Lisa Covington

A MAN WHO TALKS WITHOUT REASON

A man who talks without reason is like a planet taking its unyielding path around the sun, cold and uncomfortable.

A man who talks with reason is a planet, revolving quietly, slowly, peacefully, warm and comfortable.

Drew Bailey

THE IMPATIENT MAN AND THE THIEF

The impatient man is like a cloud. It releases its rain and withers away. But the patient man is like a cloud, snow white and flourishing in the sky.

The thief is like a raven. He will fly in the sky. Someone will come camping. He will watch their every move. The raven will take a shiny object and replace it with a dead bug. But the honest man is like a raven. He will fly in the sky. Someone will come camping. He will be honest and produce much beauty.

Bradley Torrance

The Afterlife

When I die my spirit would go to another person and use its body to figure out my death. I know my death will have to be unusual. I wouldn't die from any usual thing. I would die from something like a disease that has no cure. After I've solved it I would return to my body. And the other body would return to its spirit. And I would rest there until Judgement Day.

Lisa Covington

I have just died. My spirit has gone to where they weigh good deeds with bad deeds. I wait tensely as they weigh the deeds. I have done many good deeds and a few bad deeds. My spirit will flourish in heaven. I will enjoy eternal life in heaven.

Bradley Torrance

When I die my soul or spirit would be sent to a place where you get a ticket and they would tell me to go to a hotel called the Dead Ringer. I would have to wait there until they called me. I would get a note saying, "You, James Rao, will be named and go in the body of Paul Zigger. There you will live out your life and return here."

James Rao

From the *Teachers & Writers Collaborative Newsletter* (Vol. 7, No. 3), pp. 10-23.

Would You Kill a Porpoise for a Tuna Fish Sandwich?

by Christine Smith

"Oh splendid, a writer in our class!" said Saul Rosenfeld, the fifth-grade teacher whose class I was to work with this year at P.S. 86. Was it my imagination, or were those forced smile-lines playing about his lips? "I was sort of hoping we'd get that funding for Environmental Studies." Realizing I might interpret this as a slight, Rosenfeld apologized. "No need, really, I understand," I said, "And I'd *rather* work with you and the class on something you could all get into and carry over into your other studies. Besides, writing can't come out of a vacuum. . . ." *

It was true that I'd been thinking about animals all summer. . . . Two projects had even come to mind. One, a *Roach Ballet*. I'd already designed the costumes—corrugated cardboard strapped to the children's backs, pro-Keds on all their little feet. The other was to be a radio play, *The Mingled Destinies of Crocodiles and Men*, based on the fate of the nineteenth-century Austrian explorer Ludwig Ritter Von Hohnel at the jaws of killer crocodiles while in search

---

I had meant what I said to Rosenfeld about new and different jumping-off points for writing. As a subject unto itself, "Creative Writing" is often of questionable worth, particularly to children whose home or academic needs staggeringly outweigh their need to comprehend the structural workings of a cinquain. Sure, I've pulled an arbitrary writing idea out of nowhere now and again, relevant to nothing in particular, but, as a writer, I crave a diet of new information and real live people's experiences and perspectives (even if they just come off the six o'clock news) to inspire me. Somehow, I often feel that if I'm asking kids to jump into imaginative writing after sitting in a classroom all day, I am somewhat obligated to bring the outside world in with me, to supplement their stash of ideas. Always with the hope, of course, that when I'm not there, they will have learned to be on guard for potential "material." Writer as perpetual student of life . . .

Anytime a teacher of writing takes into the classroom an idea that he would sit down and write about himself, he is that much more alive and worth listening to . . . a better salesman for his craft . . . .

of Africa's Last Great Lake. When I learned, however, we were to be confined to the classroom for our workshops, I settled on endangered sea mammals—something else that had been swimming around in my head.

Awhile back, I had received in the mail an assortment of educational materials from Zephyros, a learning exchange in San Francisco. Included with these were a booklet from Project Jonah designed to heighten children's awareness of whales and dolphins and a comic explaining the slaughter of porpoises by the tuna industry. Also a full-sized wall poster of a baleen whale. Underneath his streamlined hull were printed statistics on the continued whaling and manufacture of whale goods around the world. The poster has remained on my wall. The horrifying statistics have never left my mind.

I visited the fifth-grade class again, devoted some time to warm-up writing exercises, and showed the booklets to Rosenfeld, who agreed to reproduce the material for the class. The project was launched.

I prepared myself with some notetaking in the sea mammals section of the Museum of Natural History and the reading of two books: *Whales and Dolphins* by Bernard Rockett and *Mind in the Waters* edited by Joan McIntyre of Project Jonah. The latter, which includes everyone from Homer to John Lilly, approaches the subject in much the same way Melville catalogued "everything you wanted to know about whales but were afraid to ask" in the preface and certain chapters of *Moby Dick*, infusing the reader with a sort of whale gestalt. Similarly, I wanted to examine with the class these awesome creatures from a number of angles—mythical and legendary as well as physiologically and ecologically.

Whales were first. An attentive group with cleared desks and folded hands received my opening address. I filled the blackboard with diagrams of different whales—humpbacks, fins, belugas and bottlenoses, rattling off the characteristics of each one. The children came to life with a barrage of questions. On blubber, blowholes, baleen instead of teeth, why whales don't get the bends at 4,000 feet . . . and testimonies of all their personal and vicarious whale adventures. Most of them from T.V. Let's face it.

Whales are neat. Nearly every aspect of their existence comes right out of *Ripley's Believe It Or Not* or *Wrigley's Fun Facts*. But what I hoped to wow them with was the data on the slaughter and possible extinction of these highly evolved, intelligent and gentle beings. And how man is discovering ways to put us on their wavelength again. And most of all, how I really believed that saving them was connected to saving ourselves and the rest of the earth. Thirty pairs of wide eyes told me they were sufficiently wowed. . . .

I had chosen to read aloud a number of selections on whales including an Eskimo poem translated by Edward Field* dealing with human beings' primeval and magic connections to animals, and naturalist Farley Mowat's tragic account of a fin whale trapped in a Newfoundland cove.** The children were amazed that townspeople had felt the right to shoot this creature who did not threaten them in its struggle to return to the ocean.

Then I asked the class to try writing one of two things:

A piece taking the point of view of the whale in her attempts to communicate with her kind outside the cove or with these humans, intent but divided in their efforts to save or destroy her.

---

* MAGIC WORDS

In the very earliest times,
when both people and animals lived on earth,
a person could become an animal if he wanted to
and an animal could become a human being.
Sometimes they were people
and sometimes animals
and there was no difference.
All spoke the same language.

That was the time when words were like magic.
The human mind had mysterious powers.
A word spoken by chance
might have strange consequences.
It would suddenly come alive
and what people wanted to happen could happen.
All you had to do was say it.
Nobody could explain this,
that's the way it was.

> from *Eskimo Songs and Stories*
> translated by poet Edward Field
> Delacorte Press 1973 $5.95

** *A Whale For The Killing*, by Farley Mowat, Penguin Books, paperback, $1.95—story of Mowat's struggle and failure to save a whale.

or:

A letter protesting the killing and manufacturing of whale products to be passed along to the businessmen connected with whaling companies.

Certain members of the class attempted both, and later we included in our mailing to the Children's Crusade, poems, stories and drawings along with the letters.

I had looked forward all week to playing for the class a tape of Judy Collins' arrangement of "Farewell to Tarwathie," an old whaling ditty she sings as a duet with a school of humpback whales. They reacted as I thought they might to the eerie, lonely sounds of the whales calling to one another. As if they, too, were being called. They begged me to play the tape again and again, while they drew pictures to illustrate our "Save the Whales" display for the hall bulletin board.

But this session really belonged to Flipper—the dolphin and the porpoise with minds as large and complex as any man's. I told them of the close kinship between man and dolphin portrayed in Greek mythology and Mediterranean and Polynesian legend, of Apollo turning himself into a dolphin to rule the sea. I recounted the Greek fable of Arion, a rich poet and musician returning to Corinth (after a concert-reading), who, in order to escape his ship's mutineers, jumped on the back of a friendly porpoise and swam away. I briefly explained John Lilly's discoveries of the dolphin's ability to mimic human speech, how porpoises and dolphins "see" with sound, and how, when their group is spread out, they can hear and locate one another from as far as six miles away. Then, finally, the tale of their plight. On hearing that the Navy has applied its knowledge of dolphin sonar to developing underwater torpedos using dolphins as homing devices, and that, in an effort to catch the tuna that follow them, fishing companies are drowning and strangling in their nets almost 100,000 porpoises a year, a few children insisted on writing more protest letters. The others wrote stories, imagining they were porpoises with fins and flukes, sonar clicks, and X-ray vision—water powers we might have if we had not evolved in a different direction, walked on the earth, and used our hands to take up more of our share of it. While the boys and girls wrote, I played for them another tape—Fred Neil's song "The Dolphins":

I've been searching
for the dolphins in the sea
Sometimes I wonder
do they ever think of me?

One little boy, Regi, seemed extraordinarily moved

by our discussions, and was still writing odes to sea mammals weeks later when the rest of the class had moved on to Christmas memories.

In my heart I feel I could have a dolphin of my
  own.
I would care for him, but I know that when the
  sailors
would come, they would try to kill him and I
  would
run to him and try to save him.

Then the dolphin would like me, and I would try
  to explain
to the sailors, "He is not yours to touch," but if
  they
would not listen to me, I would tell my dolphin
and his
friends to take care of themselves.

And I would go back home and think of the sailors
not killing my dolphin and his friends.
                                                    Reginald Gardere

He was not alone in his craving for more of the marine, however, and the inevitable connection to whales and dolphins surfaced a few weeks later from the deep—sharks. These fifth graders could listen for hours to one bloody account after another from the quickly reprinted *Shark!* by Thomas Helm, and of course, *Jaws*, whose committee-written, thrill-a-minute prose I figured was worth trying to imitate just once. If only to gain insight into the "literary" world of millions of copies, twenty-seven printings, movie rights, sequels, and official T-shirts, all stemming from man's hair-trigger fear of what he cannot somehow control.

ADDRESSES

To send protest letters and to receive information on why whales are being killed and how to help them:

International Children's Campaign to Save the Whales & PROJECT JONAH
Box 476
Bolinas, California 94924

For information on Saving the Porpoise Campaign:

FRIENDS OF ANIMALS, INC.
11 West 60th Street
New York, N. Y. 10023

(Send them the unused portion of your tuna fish money and they'll send you a button of the porpoise you're saving)

ANIMAL WELFARE INSTITUTE (better than FRIENDS OF ANIMALS)
P.O. Box 3650
Washington, D.C. 20007

(for information on boycotting, leaflets, posters and an extended reading list)

BOOKS AND TEACHING MATERIALS

A Mind In The Waters, edited by Joan McIntyre (Sierra Club/Scribner Library, paperback) (all profits to Project Jonah)

Whales And Dolphins by Bernard Rockett (Puffin Books paperback)

Net Profit, a comic by Michael Becker and Shelby Simpson, ECOMIX for Project Jonah, address above.

"Mammals at Home in the Sea," a fact sheet prepared by Dr. Sarah Flanders, distributed by the American Museum of Natural History's Dept. of Education, New York, N.Y. 10024

Shark! by Thomas Helm (Collier Books, paperback)

There's A Sound In The Sea compiled by Tamar Griggs, Scrimshaw Press, 1975—collection of children's art and writing on the plight of the whales.

Whales: Their Life In The Sea by Faith McNulty, Harper and Row, 1975—illustrated introduction to the evolution and physiology of whales simple enough for children to understand

Man & Dolphin (Pyramid paper) and *Mind of The Dolphin* by John Lilly (Avon paper)

RECORDS: JUDY COLLINS (including "Farewell to Tarwathie" sung with the Humpback Whales) ELEKTRA EKS75010

SONGS OF THE HUMPBACK WHALES by Dr. Roger S. Payne CAPITOL ST-620—recordings of the actual sounds, much like songs, of humpback whales off the coast of Bermuda

DEAR BUSINESSMEN:

Please don't kill dolphin when you go fish for tuna because they act so much like people. When you get some tuna and dolphin in a net, please go down to the net and get all of them out without cutting any of them.

Because they are getting extinct, and if you keep on killing them, they will all be dead. And if they die, more people will die too, because dolphin save people from drowning.

All you people care about is money. But if you keep killing dolphin, people will not buy your tuna and you will not get any money.

Yours truly,
Diego Mieles

DEAR BUSINESSMEN:

You kill a lot of fish, especially whales. I know that you use them and don't throw them away, but how would you like it if people did that to you, Mack? You and your friends should stop killing so many whales and porpoises, especially the Blue Whale and the Sperm Whale.

I know how many things we can buy like my favorite perfume, my favorite soap, my dog's favorite dogfood, and jewelry (the best thing), but it is not worth it. Please don't kill any more whales. We aren't going to have any more, and it is going to be that whales only exist 'til 1977.

Yours truly,
Betsy Vasilakoppulos

Once I was minding my own business when some man started shooting these pointy things at me and my family. A man shot my youngest son and pulled him in. Then boy, did I turn blue. I started to swim closer to the boat, then, went straight into it. It started to sink. I picked up my son and started home. My wife was disappointed when I told her he was dead. We moved to the Atlantic ocean. When I got there, I started a new life. I never was happy. I always thought about my dead son. Every time I see that boat beneath the sea, I cry. My new baby son uses the bodies for cops and robbers. He picks them up and stands them on the sides of the boat. For a bullet, I use my nose and kill them. Many men have died because they killed my son.

And that's why they call me the blue whale.

Hope Simmons

Reginald Gardere

MY NEIGHBORHOOD DOLPHIN

I'm a whale. I just moved in the neighborhood. A dolphin lives next to me. He is playful.

I don't like him. I think he is looney. But one time I was swimming and I heard shots. I said to myself, "I wonder what's happening?" I went to the top to see what was happening. They shot at me. "Humans!" I screamed. They fired at me again. Something grabbed me. It was the dolphin. He saved my life. The bullet had just missed me by an inch. From that day, whales and dolphin have been friends.

Carlton McCollough

There used to be a whale, but he was a strange whale. When he saw people he would attack by the stomach and open it and eat all the meat inside the stomach, and when finished, he would just leave and walk away.

He would keep on doing it. He would try to destroy the life of mankind and make his own world. For a drink, he would see if people were swimming on the beach, and he would kill them, cut their head open, and drink the blood.

But there was this other whale who was kind, and when he heard of this beast, he went and called his friends and destroyed him. Mankind was saved by this nice whale whose name was Willy the Whale.

Reginald Gardere

From the *Teachers & Writers Collaborative Newsletter* (Vol. 7, No. 3), pp. 42-45.

Holidays, or Beyond Those Bulletin Board Cut-outs

by Bill Zavatsky

Halloween was coming, and I was scratching around for new approaches. In the past I had told my students what Halloween was like for me as a kid, my costumes and my adventures, and asked them to tell a few of the remarkable or frightening things that happened to them on their Halloweens. Then we wrote, usually hanging our reminiscences on lines of poetry beginning with the words, "On Halloween . . . ." Okay, fine, good writing. But when I moved from the elementary to the junior high school level, I wanted to move forward intellectually as well.

A week before Halloween I mentioned that the holiday was coming up, got a few random "I'm going to be a Werewolf!" responses, and was ready to let it go at that. Just a little something to get them thinking that, the following workshop, we'd probably tackle Halloween in writing. Suddenly, an inspiration! I asked the kids (*and* the teacher) if anybody knew how Halloween got to be Halloween. In all my classes, the best answer anybody could come up with was that it was the night before All Saints' Day on November 1, celebrated in the Roman Catholic and Episcopal churches as a holy day.

I wrote the word on the board as we were taught to spell it in (Catholic) grammar school: *Hallowe'en*. Okay, I said. You all know that an apostrophe stands for some letter that's been left out of a word. What's the letter; Everyone knew it was a *v*. Fine. So, if we put the *v* back in: *Halloveven*. (We were already into historical process, in this case how words change through time.) I asked them if they could pick out the two words that made up *Halloveven*. Right: *hallow* and *even*. Nobody knew what they meant. I knew they did. Are there any Catholics or Protestants in this room who know a prayer called "The Lord's Prayer" or the "Our Father"? Hands shot up, and I asked one of the children to say it out loud: "Our Father, who art in heaven, hallowed be Thy Name . . . "—aha! *Hallowed*, I shouted, the past tense of *hallow*. Like in *Halloveven*, right? Everyone had heard the word, if only in the old World War II movies. (One third grade student of mine had memorized the 23rd Psalm because he'd heard it on so many old TV movies, but that's another essay—"Television as an Educative Tool Despite Itself.")

Okay, I said to the kids, What does the word "hallow" mean. "Empty?" No . . . are you telling God that his name is *empty*? I let the kids stumble around (and some kids in a few classes did know what the word meant). But as usual in these cases where Rote is Right, I decided to paraphrase the prayer for them: You're saying to God, "God, you're our father, everybody's father, and you are in heaven, and may your name be holy." So "hallow" means "holy." Some of the more avid readers in the class soon figured out that "even" was short for "evening," because they'd seen it in old poems. What the word "Halloween" meant was "holy evening," or "holy night." It was a holy night because it was the night before an important feast day of the church, All Saints' Day, when Catholics and certain Protestants paid tribute to the people who had made their church history. Fine, a nice lesson in linguistic change, a good textual reading of one word in the English language that almost every American child knows; an important word. But nobody knew anthing more about the origins of the celebration of Halloween.

I went home after school and hauled out the *Encyclopaedia Britannica*. I already knew that Halloween was older than Christianity, but I didn't know where it came from. Listen to this: "Students of folklore believe that the popular customs of Halloween exhibit traces of the Roman harvest festival of Pomona and of Druidism." Well, it turns out that in the religion of the Druids in pre-Christian Ireland and Scotland, the Celtic year ended October 31st, "the even of Samhain, and was celebrated with both religious and agrarian rites. For the Druids, Samhain was both the 'end of summer' and a festival of the dead. The spirits of the departed were believed to visit their kinsmen in search of warmth and good cheer as winter approached. It was also the period for threshing and of food preparation for the winter season." The word "Samhain" itself may mean "summer-end," from *sam* ("summer") and *fuin* ("sunset" or "end"); another authority I checked makes *samani*— mean "assembly," i.e. the gathering of the people to keep the feast.

As I read on, I realized that the impulses that got kids dressing up as witches and ghosts were as old as human history. Winter was on the land, leaves had fallen, trees were skeletons of the beauty they had been. Crops growing in the fields had been cut down to help people get through the winter (I reminded the children that there were no electric lights or TV then), and woe the terrors attendant on a poor harvest with the cold winds and snow coming! I discovered why bonfires and magic witches became associated with Halloween, and why mischief-making has always been an integral part of it, too. (I also learned a few interesting sociological facts: that Halloween only became popular in the U.S. in the late 19th Century, after the large Irish immigrations began in 1840.) History was coming alive for me, things were clicking. Why, for example, did we cut weird faces in pumpkins? What did that mean? When I found out that the carved pumpkin is actually (however we've dressed it up and made it smile) the symbol of a disembodied head, a skull, it sent a shiver through me. A death's head—cut in a living thing. Everything about Halloween was designed to point out one irrefutable fact to our ancestors, and they knew it: Man has but a short time to live on this earth. We all become a scary skeleton sooner or later, and the leering jack o' lantern was only another *memento mori*.

I brought this information and a lot more in to the kids, who positively ate it up. (So did the teachers, I might add.) The children who were Christians were fascinated to find out that religions had existed before Christianity (even though the majority of their classmates were Jewish!), and found it exciting to know that the church had purposely set up the feast day of All Saints to counteract the influence of Samhain, which plain folks wouldn't give up.

If you look up "Easter" in any good encyclopedia, you'll find another fascinating story. Easter is directly associated with the Jewish Passover (Pesach), and in France is called *Pâques*, which is derived from *Pesach*. Our English word "Easter," however, is from the German *Oster*, and (according to the *Encyclopaedia Britannica*) "reveals Christianity's indebtedness to the Teutonic tribes of central Europe." As was the case with Samhain, Christianity incorporated many of the aspects of the Teutonic spring festivals:

That the festival of the resurrection [of Christ] occurred in the spring, that it celebrated the triumph of life over death, made it easy for the church to identify with this occasion the most joyous festival of the Teutons, held in honour of the death of winter, the birth of a new year, and the return of the sun.

The Teutonic peoples called our month of April *Eostur-monath* and dedicated it to Eostre, or Ostara, goddess of the spring.

Some of the customs of the Easter season date not only from the Teutons, but far back into antiquity. In the early days of the church it was forbidden to eat eggs during Lent, the period between Ash Wednesday and Easter Sunday. Hence, eggs were eaten as part of the Easter celebration. The symbolism of the egg, however, dates back to ancient Egypt:

[The] conception of the egg as a symbol of fertility and of renewed life goes back to the ancient Egyptians and Persians, who had also the custom of colouring and eating eggs during their spring festival. This ancient idea of the significance of the egg as a symbol of new life readily became the idea of the egg as a symbol of resurrection, as it came to be interpreted by the Christians.

Our Easter Bunny (originally a hare) also came to us from the same source:

The hare is associated with the moon in the legends of ancient Egypt and other peoples. It belongs to the night, since it comes out only then to feed. It is born with its eyes open and, like the moon, is "the open-eyed watcher of the skies." Through the fact that the Egyptian word for hare, *un*, means also "open" and "period," the hare came to be associated with the idea of periodicity, both lunar and human, and with the beginning of a new life in both the young man and the young woman, and so a symbol of fertility and the renewal of life.

From here it was only a short hop to the egg, and because the hare is an unfamiliar species in the U.S., we settled on the rabbit.

There are many other illuminating insights to be uncovered by attacking the encyclopedia in search of holiday origins and customs. On Easter it was considered unlucky not to wear a new article of clothing. Hence, our annual "Easter Parade," for which we cast off the old and buy up the new. And I remember the tradition of the Easter kiss from my Russian Orthodox grandmother. She would greet us at the door, and as the youngest in my family, I was drilled to greet her with the Russian phrase that means "Christ has risen." "He is risen indeed," she would answer in Russian, then proceed to cover all of us with barrages of kisses.

Like Halloween, the Easter celebration is relatively new to the United States. Our Puritan forefathers scorned the trappings of the Roman Catholics and the Church of England, and only in Virginia and Louisiana was Easter celebrated. The Civil War marked a change of attitude. During that time the Protestant churches began to mark the day with special services in an effort to console families who had lost sons in the struggle.

Why not make an intelligent investigation of holiday origins and customs a part of your classroom's life? The paper pumpkins and Santas and bunnies don't even begin to scratch the surface. Besides library field work in cultural anthropology, students could interview their family members to discover how differently these holidays are celebrated today. What was Halloween like in 1950, 1940, 1930? What customs have disappeared? Which have survived—and why? Is Halloween in danger of becoming extinct? (The stories of apples skewered with razor blades and candy laced with LSD have frightened many a parent I know away from letting their children wander freely through the neighborhoods on the evening of October 31st.)

An upcoming holiday could provide plenty of exciting projects that could take your students from ancient Egypt to the Druids of Ireland to dad's spooky reminiscences. Tell your students your own memories of growing up through the holidays—what you did, where you went, how it has changed. Believe me when I tell you that they will love hearing them, and throwing yourself into the spirit of the quest will spark them on their own researches—and no one can know where they'll end.

Working with Working

by Bill Zavatsky

You've probably heard of, or read, Studs Terkel's marvelous collection of interviews with working people, *Working* (Avon Books paperback). The book spent months at the top of the nonfiction bestseller list a couple of years ago, and with good reason.

Terkel, in the course of his career, has focused on the everyday people whom intellectuals don't seem to give much attention to in their writings, probably because many of them are in flight from their own working-class backgrounds. (In recent years no episode has underscored this split more poignantly than one which occurred during an anti-Vietnam War protest in lower Manhattan when construction workers battled with college students, young people old enough to be their sons and daughters, and who in some cases probably were.) In *Working* our fathers and mothers come to life: spot-welder, barber, airline stewardess, gas meter reader, retired persons, jazz musician, bookbinder, strip miners, cops, and dozens of others representing dozens of professions that are glamorous, sweaty, and even illegal.

Very few poets have written about work. It's hard to glamorize punching out valves or selling fruit. And the idea that poetry doesn't have very much to do with "real life" dies a hard death. David Ignatow, however, has made this subject part and parcel of his writing, as in this poem called "The Paper Cutter":

He slides the cut paper out
from under the raised knife.
His face does not lose interest.
"And now I go to my night job,"
he says cheerfully at five,
wiping his hands upon a rag.
He has stood all day in one spot,
pressing first the left
and then the right button.
"And what are you going to do
with all that money?" I ask.
His shoulders stick out bony.
"I will buy a house
and then I will lie down in it
and not get up all day," he laughs.

The poet Charles Reznikoff also wrote many poems about everyday people, and about events like buying fruit from an old Italian grocer whose son is going to war, or about being asked in a post office to write a letter for a man who cannot read or write. Here is Reznikoff's poem about a familiar city figure:

The elevator man, working long hours
for little—whose work is dull and trivial—
must also greet each passenger
pleasantly:
to be so heroic
he wears a uniform.

William Carlos Williams also wrote a number of poems on "unpoetic" subjects, thereby opening new areas of writing opportunity for American writers. Here is "Proletarian Portrait":

A big young bareheaded woman
in an apron

Her hair slicked back standing
on the street

One stockinged foot toeing
the sidewalk

Her shoe in hand. Looking
intently into it

She pulls out the paper insole
to find the nail

That has been hurting her.

What these three writers share in common is an affection for that most abused and misunderstood— and probably nonexistent—commodity, the Common Man. This passion for everyday experience stems from Walt Whitman, but these three poets do not idealize their subject, though Williams presents his "big young bareheaded woman" more as an object for esthetic contemplation (the real loveliness of the simple human action) than do Ignatow and Reznikoff.

For all the lightness of touch in Ignatow's poem, one can't help taking the lead of the poet's question and wonder about the cheerfulness of this paper cutter who works two jobs. Despite the good humor of his response, it is hard to escape the feeling that this is the portrait of a man on a treadmill, a man who can do nothing but pile up the money. Reznikoff's elevator operator also presents us with a rather depressing look at "the job," though as usual (and like Ignatow) he has seen a human dignity in the hopelessness of it all.

In *Working* Terkel has confronted the joys and wastes of the day-to-day head-on. Recently one of my adult students and I were enthusing about the book, and an idea occurred to me. I suggested that he read the interview found on pages 389-395 of the book with Dolores Dante, a woman who "has been a waitress in the same restaurant for twenty-three years." I had had the good luck to hear a radio broadcast of Terkel's interview with her, the same one transcribed in *Working*, and as I listened to this amazing woman speak of her workaday life every word struck me as sheer poetry, ripe for the picking. "Why don't you write a poem based on the interview, using its words, but selecting what you want to put in," I suggested to Elliot. Here is the poem he wrote:

DOLORES

At work they consider me
a kook. That's okay.
I make a rough road.
I can't keep still. What hurts
has to come out.

If a customer
manufactures soap,
I talk about pollution.
I speak sotto voce,
but if I get heated,
I speak like an Italian.

I can't say, Do you
want coffee? Maybe I'll say,
Are you in the mood for coffee?
Or, The coffee sounds exciting.
I rephrase it. It intoxicates me.
I feel like Mata Hari.

Tips?
It's like a gypsy
holding out a tambourine.
If you like people
you're not thinking tips.

If you get too good,
customers don't say,

Where's the boss?
They ask for Dolores—
it doesn't make a hit.
It's not the customers.
It's injustice. My dad
came from Italy. I think
of his broken English—injoost.

We do have accidents
I spilled a tray once
with steaks for seven—
a giant T-bone all sliced.
When the tray fell
I went with it.
It never made a sound,
dish and all
never made a sound.

I'm almost Oriental
when I serve. I feel like
a ballerina. I go
through a chair
like no one else.
They see how delicate.

At the end of the night,
I'm drained. A waitress
doesn't eat. You handle food,
you don't have time.
Pick at something
in the kitchen—maybe
a piece of bread.

It's nerve-racking.
You don't sit down. You're
on stage, the boss is watching.
Your feet hurt, your body aches.

It builds and builds
and builds in your guts.
'Cause you're tired.
When the night is done
you're tired.
You've had so much,
there's so much going.
You had to get it done.
You want to please. You hope
everyone is pleased.
The night's done,
you've done your act.
The curtains close.

The next morning
it's pleasant again.

ELLIOT FIGMAN

This seems to me to be a fine piece of work. There is no doubt in my mind, however, that any number of poems quite different from each other could be written using the same interview, or monologue, rather, for that is what it really is. In the radio broadcast the voice of Studs Terkel made no appearance, and was undoubtedly edited out.

Using the words of others needs no justification, especially in this context. Terkel himself, by editing his own questions and suggestions out of the interview, has altered it for his own purposes. Why shouldn't a poet continue the job, especially when he has the chance to make an important point: the point being that, as the poet Tristan Tzara said, "Poetry is made in the mouth." Using the interviews in *Working* would not only enable students to face one of the key factors of human existence, but it would force them to really *listen*, with poet's ears, to language in action. Any poet worth his or her salt, in fact, must train themselves to LISTEN, both to their own speech and others'. Using the texts in *Working* could be the starting point of what I sense might be remarkable experiments in, call it if you will, "oral literature." Such experiments will serve to bring students closer to their own real voices.

Once the texts in *Working* are made into poems, why not ask those students who have access to tape recorders to interview their own parents, relatives, friends, and even teachers about the work they do. (Reading some of the interviews done by Terkel will sharpen their reportorial sense too.) They can transcribe the texts *verbatim*, leaving in their own questions, and the responses. Next *a la* Terkel, they can edit out their own words. Finally, they could use the edited text to write poems.

I haven't seen any reviews of *Working* that emphasize the linguistic aspects of the book, but how carefully Studs Terkel and his associates have worked to capture the inflections of American talk! What a monumental tribute to our American language this book is, as well as to the people who keep it vital. The "work" talked about so painfully, so depressingly, so inspiringly in this book is not just manual or intellectual labor, it is the work our language does every second of our lives. *Working* could make a superb textbook for language arts curricula, and though this essay is based on a single case, I see no reason why these techniques shouldn't work with intelligent junior high schoolers, senior high school students, and in adult writing classes. It would also be fun to try one of the shorter monologues with younger children. To a child, nothing is more baffling than what Daddy does all day. Sooner or later, you've got to get a job.

Mid-evil Times

by Sue Willis

My own attitude toward the Middle Ages is less informed than enthusiastic; I have no scholarly qualms about mining the Middle Ages for the hooks that will catch the children's interest; I accept telephones in a dance of death play, and when I tell Chaucer's *Knight's Tale*, I give Queen Hippolyta of the Amazons a touch of women's liberation consciousness. When I tell "The Wife of Bath's Tale" and the class demands an uglier witch, I give her a hunchback and more warts. Phillip Lopate did a class poem by having his group imagine what a time was like that we now call the Dark Ages:

A foggy spooky winter when
Everybody marched around with candles.

Nobody claims it's historically accurate, but on the other hand, the epithet "Dark Ages" has carried an emotional force that has misrepresented the Middle Ages for generations. At the same time I have quite seriously tried on occasion to teach myself Anglo-Saxon, and I have read the *Canterbury Tales* in Middle English. In my initial excitement over this project, I reread all the literary introductions in my textbooks; I picked up Henri Pirenne's *History of Europe* and *The Waning of the Middle Ages* by J. Huizinga. I read *Everyman* plus some lyrics and ballads. I made little charts for myself, to see where Beowulf stood in relation to the Crusades and *The Canterbury Tales*. I had a thoroughly lovely time thinking and reading about the Middle Ages.

Back in the classroom, I found the kids divided in two groups when it came to Medieval Times. First there was the dracula-dragon crowd, then the knights-and-ladies crowd roughly corresponding to the kids' economic classes. That is, kids whose families take them to the Metropolitan Museum thought Knights, and the kids whose families don't, thought monsters. I think someone showed them a picture of Saint George and the dragon. When *I* think of the Middle Ages, I think of dirty fabliaux and the bubonic plague and "Whan that Aprille" and saints' knucklebones and Gregorian chants.

Two of the handful of songs I can chord on the guitar are the medieval ballads "Greensleeves" and "Barbra Allen." The interesting point about the oldest version of the latter is that it specifies the reason Barbra wouldn't fall in love with Sir John Graeme: at a big feast, he toasted all the women present in turn, but not Barbra, and she was deeply insulted. This high seriousness over details of courtesy is intrinsic to the chivalric code. My first lesson was a mixed bag of such comments, plus singing handouts of the Lord's Prayer in Anglo-Saxon, Middle English, Early Modern English (King James Bible) and twentieth century English. The class was impressed with the funny sounding language. I don't think they really believed it was English. Some weeks later, I gave them for fun, and to make them examine the old languages closely, a mistranslation exercise using fragments of Old Spanish, (from *The Cid*). The object of a mistranslation is to write a poem piece inspired by a few lines of a language you don't understand. Many words in foreign languages are reminiscent of words in English. Unusual poems can come out of it. Then, on the first day I asked them to write a short piece from the point of view of a person or thing or animal in the Middle Ages. Nelly and Cynthia were fascinated by the absolute power of queenship; their characters give orders to their servants, who included everyone in sight. Ayala, also playing with power, saw herself as Lady Ayala the official head-chopper-offer. Gretchen wanted to write a horse story; so all traces of the Middle Ages disappeared after the first sentence to be replaced by "a sweet little filly" and a "huge Dapple Gray." Trips to the Cloisters and to the armored division of the Metropolitan brought out the thirst for esoteric facts and words. At the Cloisters at least half the class started searching the rooms for something the art teacher had described: "Is that a triptych? No, I think *that* is." Back in the class room one group of boys painstakingly began making chain mail out of soda can tops: others made books of illustrations of weapons and armor. They perfected and hung on the walls sketches they had made of art objects and architectural details at the Cloisters. Felix Moreno is probably the only nine year old in existence to have drawn in some detail, labelled and grasped the function of the PYX. It may never help him make his way out there on the big bad Street, but he certainly had a wonderful complacent expression when Robin, his teacher, expressed her pleasure in learning something from *him*.

At about this time, I had a small personal revolt against matters of the imagination, and I was full of my readings on Medieval intellectual history and political history. The classroom teachers were not Medievalists at all—I think one of the far reaching values of this project was that they had a good time learning in this unit too. Robin's growing enthusiasm for the Middle Ages included her finding one of those adult coloring books of the beginning of the *Canterbury Tales*, complete with a record in the back of a reading from it. I myself was in a mood for sharing all that good wholesome whole-grain information that I often feel is somehow off-limits for us creative personnel. The challenge is to find ways of explaining simply and entertainingly without condescending. I duplicated world maps and we put dots for Jerusalem and circled Europe. This lesson fell conveniently during the Israel-Egypt/Syria war so I could tie the Crusades with two thousand years of problems among Christians, Jews, and Moslems. We made timelines and wrote a class poem about time. "A hundred years," said Nicky, "That's how long announcements last on the P.A. speaker." One day I wrote analogies on the board to show the point by point allegorical comparisons possible when you look at all of creation in a single hierarchy, with a place for everyone and thing, or in microcosms of that hierarchy. God is at the top with the devil in Hell at the bottom and man somewhere in the middle. Analogically, the King would be at the top, serfs toward the bottom, but the infidels down on a level with the damned. "Why, you could put anything into this way of looking at the world," I said in my excitement. "Even the animal kingdom: here's the lion on the top with the king, and the snake on the bottom with Satan"—but unfortunately my pig came out on the same level as common people, and that brought down the house, and class ended with much guffawing.

At the same time I was doing these lessons with the whole class, I was beginning play-making with them in small groups of seven to ten children. As part of the preparation, I told them the story of the *Everyman* morality play. Everyman, of course is not a given name but a label, and the character is not to be a person, but an emblem. The personages in the poemplay all have names like Death, Goods, and Kin. I spoke of the Medieval interest in death: that people died younger; many children never reached adulthood; an awareness of death was important in religion. In one group we chose a variety of types of characters: robbers, litterbugs, a good woman, a bossy woman, one who talks too much. Each child wrote a sketch from the point of view of his or her character. William wrote, and then read aloud in a deep, gratified voice:

"I am the robber.
I love to rob people. I run
down the street and snatch people's
pocketbooks and run off. And then
she says Help Help and she calls
the police and then I get to my
hideout and count the money."

Then we did improvisations with these characters interacting. In the end, a character named Death came out and took all their hands and we danced in a circle around the room. Shielda and Gwen stayed with me after the others left and wrote the beginning of a connected story using the available characters and some of the actions they had improvised. This narrowing down the organizing minds of an improvised play is usually an essential step. The last half of the play they dictated to me. At our next meeting we extended the dialogue with a tape recorder. As the play progressed more children joined in until there were a total of ten with parts. Kimi came up one day and said, "My mother is an actress and she says this play doesn't sound very Medieval to her, not with all the telephones and police sirens." "Ah," said I, "But the spirit is Medieval." The next day Kimi said her mother still didn't think it was Medieval even in spirit, but she had decided to read *Everyman*. We finally presented the *Dance of Death* on a double bill with Phillip and his class's *A Medieval Play*.

We did our play in front of the main auditorium curtain because it still had some of the feeling of improvisation about; all the characters lined up and introduced themselves; the last one was a pale little blonde girl with green makeup around her eyes and cold cream on her lips, wrapped in a sheet-shroud. "I am the person Death," she said, "I am going to get all of you." The other characters hooted her off the stage and went about their business. The business was quite varied: some farce, some violence: a theft from a rich man's safe is followed by the thieves being mugged and beaten by two robbers. A gun battle ensues in which not only the cops and robbers are killed, but so are the litterbugs. The thieves die from being beaten; the rich man kills himself; a good woman has a heart attack. The stage is maggoty with writhing children happily hamming up their death agonies. Death comes out and begins taking them all by the hand; I step up and say "Thank goodness I'm a teacher and Death can't get me!" but you guessed it, little white death comes right over and does take me. We all join hands and go out wailing into the audience and pick up people and take them around the aisles with us. We thought the play was very edifying.

Meanwhile, in the classroom, I had moved on to telling the stories of the *Canterbury Tales*. I tried to read at least a line or two of the actual Chaucer. The class liked the chivalry in "The Knight's Tale" where two young prisoners-of-war fall in love simultaneously with the fair Emilye. The theme of this tale is related to the theme of another one of our small group's plays that was developing. The importance of the chivalric code to the Middle Ages was a system of rules for war, and to a lesser extent, a system of game-rules for love. In "The Knight's Tale," the two young knights learn to have order in both their hate and their love; instead of hand to hand combat in the forest, they join in a tournament over the beloved. In our play, there is a devil, Curtis, a professional teacher's nemesis who causes war between two castles. He disrupts their ordinary lives with unseemly hair pulling fights between the queens; even at the tournament he turns one of the knights into a dragon. Curtis loves his part; whenever the whole group is fighting and kicking and shoving on the stage he dances and laughs off to one side; this was his own reaction to the commotion and I quickly insisted it be part of the play. For all of his love of big excitement and fighting, Curtis quiets quickly with a hand on his head; he is not a particularly bitter kid; he just delights in noise and action. At the end of the play, when he is foiled, the other characters form a circle around him and have a ritual dance while he squirms on the floor.

The kids seem to have an essential grasp of the value of ceremony: I want to present the plays in the halls, in classrooms, wherever we can pull together an audience. They insist on the auditorium, the magic place where your private dramas are transformed into performances and cheering. Phillip did a lesson on ceremony; he asked his class to write some that might take place today:

Ceremony for Separation

Drink Wine.
Go to court.
Bring in some monks.
Make a giant cake.
Tell everybody what you did when
*   you were*
together.

There is a quality here of sensing the importance of *how* things are done, whether or not the significance of adult acts is grasped. The same Curtis who plays our disruptive Devil-force wrote a ceremony for going to church:

THE CEREMONY OF GOOD CHILDREN GOING TO CHURCH

1. First you have to wash up.

2. Put on your church clothes.
3. Brush your hair.
4. Put on your coat.
5. Walk to church.
6. Sit on the back seats.
7. Pray.
8. Mom says "don't" laugh or play
*   in "church".*
9. Go home.

Phillip and I and the teachers too felt the need for some sort of formal event that would pull together and heighten the meaning of all this Medieval inspired activity. We had projected some sort of Medieval festival for later in the year, but Halloween seemed a good time for something to happen. One of the analogical sets that throws some light on the Middle Ages for me is the Procession::Crusade::Pilgrimage:: the Progress of Life. Thus the Crusades were journeys for God, fun and profit—adventure and religion. All human estates could go, poor foot soldiers and kings. The pilgrims who tell the *Canterbury Tales* too have a religious object although some would like to be healed by the saint's relics for their pains; others are taking a vacation. Each day of one's life is a sort of pilgrimage too. On religious occasions the relics of a well-loved saint would be carried about in procession for the edification of the people. The crowd would join in hoping for miracles of healing, to see the action, to see how everyone was dressed for the festive occasion. This was the nature of the Medieval Procession we planned for Halloween. There were Halloween costumes to show off, there was a school to be impressed with our audacity, and then there was this nameless compulsion to celebrate.

Phillip came for the procession as an infidel, a Turk. I came as a leper-beggar. The classes lined up for the procession at opposite ends of the hall. I had a stocking over my face with eye holes cut out so that my features were mauled; there was a sign around my neck: Leper, Unclean! I had an alms cup, and quasimodo style, I frightened little children who had come out for a trip to the bathroom. We had one sword resplendent in aluminum foil. We had one gauntlet of soda pop top chain mail. We had a count dracula and a devil, and girls in long dresses with high cone hats. We had ghosts. Leading the procession were three monks in black hooded cloaks. One carried a cassette with Gregorian chants playing; a second carried a box three pretty girls made the day before, covered with gold paper and with the shape of a cross cut out of the top. Inside lay hairs and fingernails: relics of the saint. Led by the lame leper, we started down the hall chanting, Gobb-el, Gobb-el, Gobb-el, Gobb-el. Our chant rose above the modal music. "Hey," Gretchen whispered to me. "It sounds like "Holey-God, Hole-y God.' " We walked slowly with more dignity than I had expected, all a little awed by the power of our chant and appearance. I can't say exactly what we looked like because my eye holes kept slipping out of place; I know I saw the other procession coming toward us with a silvery knight clanking in front and Phil towering over the kids: the teachers never even knew I was there because my face was masked and several of the fifth graders are taller than I am. I became hoarse quickly from leading the Gobb-el Gobb-el. The dark monks pressed at me from behind; faces popped out of classrooms; teachers herded them back. Secretaries in the office lifted their hands from their typewriters and swiveled their heads as little as possible to follow our progression around the office; in the basement, in the District III offices, a perfectly sane looking adult male pulled his sports coat over his head and ducked into a doorway. When we passed, he jumped out and wiggled his fingers at us.

We spilled out onto West End Avenue, but our energy dissipated in the light. A few housekeepers stopped rolling their shopping carts to look at us; some of the alcoholics on 96th Street lowered their pint bottles. It was over. The leper had come without shoes; there were holes in her stockings. In the Middle Ages, the end of the journey was the saint's tomb or the Holy City, or Heaven. For us, it was a return to the ordinary school day, to the green halls, to being more or less orderly—our devils temporarily repressed. For a little while, though, the Public School had been transformed by strange rituals, alive with chanting and peopled with citizens of a past world, an inner world.

"For a little while, though, the public school had been transformed by strange rituals, alive with chanting and peopled with citizens of a past world, an inner world."

A MEDIEVAL PLAY

ANNOUNCER: *We have a play about the Middle Ages in which we turn back the years and the centuries to the time of kings and queens and cats.*

              (The King and Queen are sitting on their thrones. Cat comes on.)

CAT: *I'm the smallest*
              I want milk
              Give me some sleep

KING: *Nice, nice, little cat.*

CAT: *Meow. When are you going to give me some milk?*

QUEEN: *What a nice cat. What is your name?*

289

CAT:	Samantha.
	(The Messenger comes in.)
MESSENGER:	I got a telegram and it's good news. The Queen is pregnant.
QUEEN:	I'm having a baby! Spread it all around the kingdom.
KING:	Why don't we get married?
QUEEN:	We have to figure out who's going to be the flower girl, who's going to be the ring boy.
	(They dance around).

SCENE TWO—THE WEDDING

MINISTER:	Do you promise to lead this woman to your arms forever and forever? Please take care of whom you love in testimonial honor. You shall long live both a happy life. Now I pronounce you man and wife.
BABY:	Googoo Mama Geegee
	(Everyone dances. An Angel flies in.)
ANGEL:	Bad news! Bad news! The devil is coming.
	(The Devil appears. Everyone screams.)
DEVIL:	I come only for your baby to cook and eat.
CAT:	No! No! No! (Everyone runs away except the Angel and the cat who try to protect the Baby. The Devil carries the baby off to his house.)
DEVIL:	(After putting baby in pot)
	Tani bani Make this cook as fast as I want To be ready at dawn time.
	(The Devil starts to sprinkle pepper and hot sauce in the pot.)
DEVIL:	I better go out and get some more hot pepper.
	(He leaves. The King and Queen rush in and save the baby. They take her back to the Palace.)

SCENE THREE—THE PALACE

	(Everyone is crying because they think the baby is dying.)
QUEEN:	Oh, my poor baby. What can I do?
KING:	(Calls) Angel, angel, come and help our baby.
	(The Angel flies in and circles around the Baby.)
ANGEL:	Spirits of light Side of bay I am so depressed That I must obey
	From the Devil's eye I must thee save From the Devil's greedy Mouth and teeth
	(The baby wakes up and runs away.)
ANGEL:	She's gone.
	(Everyone starts looking for her. Finally the Devil comes in again, holding the baby.)
DEVIL:	I've found the baby. She was in the woods, all lost and crying and screaming.
KING AND QUEEN:	Oh, Angel, turn the Devil into our son. Because he has saved our daughter and he has told the truth of what has happened to her.

(The Angel puts a crown on the Devil's head.)

THE END

by   *Wanda Lewis*   *Valentina Medina*
      Trellan Smith   *Jewell Wade*
      Jennefer Kardeman *Wendy Rojas*
      Melissa Werbell   *PS 75 Manhattan*

THE DARK AGES

In the Dark Ages the sun blacked out
And the moon blocked the sun
People were going around in dark felt suits
A foggy spooky winter when
Everybody marched around with candles.
Wolves went Awoooooh—
Bats flew through the air like haunted quails
Ghosts rattled their chains.
A war was fought with fire and cap guns
And water pistols that shot electricity,
That burned their felt suits.
They are fighting over a gold key
That opened the door to light,
That was kept inside a cover
Inside a cloud
In a place where they had never been
Inside of heaven.
A white place, white as snow
Bleary and foggy white ghosts
White as flowers in heaven.

Class Poem
October 11—After Cloisters trip
P.S. 75 Manhattan

5. Handle With Tender Loving Care

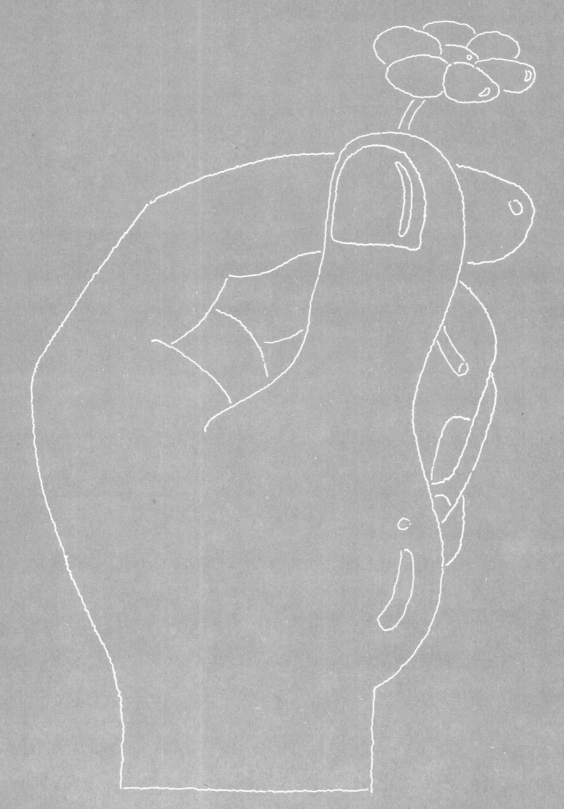

Handle with Tender Loving Care

by Bill Zavatsky

Despite the counseling services, the specialists in "discipline problems," the peripatetic experts who work with students who have problems of perception, and a host of other aides and consultants, the average teacher knows full well that he or she is not merely a skilled instructor in an academic ivory tower. More often than wished for, the teacher is pushed into as many roles as the psychological makeups of the students demand.

For many children the struggle to learn initially means a ferocious and confusing battle with the self. Be he poet or be she painter, the artist who walks naively into a classroom brimming with "creative ideas," ready to save the world through Art, is usually in for the shock of his life. Like the teacher, but often even more ill-equipped for the job, the artist finds himself pulled apart by the emotional currents crashing through the classroom. In my first year of working in a public elementary school in a Teachers and Writers Collaborative project, my habit of bringing my typewriter into class (the better to catch the kids' poems hot from their lips) ended one afternoon with me stalking out in a fury. I had cajoled, I had warned, I had even been pushed to threaten, but when the little fingers and invisible fists of the entire third grade flew past my face, yanked my hair, wheedled up between my typing fingers to slam the space bar and bat the keys and send the carriage crunching, I holstered my machine, told the children I was angry, and stormed out the door. Enough grace was left me to pause outside and apologize to the astonished teacher. "I'm sorry," I told her. "I suppose you want to do this about forty-five times a week; but I just can't take it any more!"

There do exist residencies for artists and writers in schools where Class Control is the byword. But I feel so humiliated, so out of character when after some delirious uproar the teacher dresses down the offenders, that I've come (though my goat is still there for the getting) to prefer Chaos, Incorporated to "If you continue to behave this way, our Poet will *not* come again!"

Naturally both the classroom teacher and the visiting artist are there to accomplish something educational. (Ron Padgett speaks perceptively in this volume of the teacher = business-as-usual, poet = entrance-of-outside-world-into-classroom equations in his "Inside School and Out.") Roughly, the attitude of the average student towards both of these grown-ups who "want something" might be pigeonholed thusly: "I have to give her what she wants; when I'm in the mood, I'll give more" for the classroom teacher; and to the artist: "This person is asking me to do things I have never done before. What do I do?" All schoolwork demands the expenditure of energy, but often the poet seems to be demanding much more. Art opens doors to unknown rooms; this can provoke plenty of anxiety.

Jeannine Dobbs, a poet working in a " 'home for children with problems in living,' " found herself in trouble when she pushed for more from a young girl name Lena. When asked to describe two of her teachers in writing, she replied: "Why should I. . . . They're standing right over there. You can see for yourself." Lena then stormed out of the room. Reflecting on this experience, which acquired a "nearly disastrous" reputation for her at the center, Ms. Dobbs wrote:

> The problem with positive reinforcement is that teachers must take the time, the pains, to find out what is good about a piece of work. It is much easier to be general than specific. And we are so accustomed to looking for faults; faults are easier to find. I began to give more support to my students during the process of writing and less attention to their product. I began to sit beside them while they were writing and to talk to them in a general way about the subjects they had chosen. I began to write with them and to talk about my own writing—its pleasures and its frustrations. I began to respond to their work in pleasant sounding but more non-committal OK's and Mm-Hmms. They began to prefer the classroom to the crisis room [at the center]. Finally even Lena came back. She and the others began showing me their writing with pleasure once more rather than with apprehension. The pay-off came when Alan sent word by way of [the English teacher] that he had completed a poem that he would like me to look at in order to help him improve it. I was being granted the privilege of criticizing. [1]

Without really knowing Lena, Ms. Dobbs was on unsure ground when she made her request for more.

And the facile doctrine of "positive reinforcement" that her employers had urged on her proved useless and even antagonistic. Only by allowing herself to be more fully human, by responding feelingly to the needs of the children as human beings (and in fact to her own needs as a person and an artist) was she able ultimately to work effectively. Many of us have experienced in school that famous well-intentioned but premature criticism which turned us away forever from poetry, music, or art. Perhaps my most pleasant memory of elementary school is of those periods when large creamy pieces of drawing paper were passed out, and the teacher left us alone to draw and color freely. Just watching those big rough sheets float down the aisle warmed something in me that I would later associate with the word "imagination." I also remember the terrors of music class, when boys with cracky, changing voices were forced to produce tones suitable to girls. Only in degree is Ms. Dobbs' description of working in a center for "children with problems" different from many school situations:

> The violence of Lena's reaction is not unusual at Hilltop. Many of these children are there because they've been told all their lives by teachers and by parents that they are dumb or bad or both. Surprisingly, considering their apprehensions, children at Hilltop were often more eager to show their work, to read it aloud, to distribute it to anyone who would pay attention to it, than other students in my experience have been. The Lenas of this world believe that their work is good. They may expect to hear that it is not, but secretly they believe that it is good and want to hear that it is. Of course, we are all this way. We don't want anyone messing around in our ideas and in our expressions of our ideas.

Uppermost in Ms. Dobbs' mind was the need to create a secure environment where her students could trust her to let them be who they were. "What is taught must be secondary, if, in fact, it ever enters into the matter at all," she writes. It has been my experience, too, that the work produced by children may be of far less value than the "permission to be" that creative doing offers, and which the example of the artist supports. In my own education, I have a much firmer and more affectionate memory of those few teachers who expressed a passion and intelligence for what they taught, than for the substance of their teaching. Content-wise, my sophomore year in high school is a virtual blank; yet I have a vivid recollection of my teacher, a man who by his encouragement set me on the road toward being a writer. His generosity lent a kind of blessing to my efforts that opened a growing space within me, a space I could never have discovered on my own.

Working with severely handicapped children, Barbara Merkel came to conclusions that parallel those of Jeannine Dobbs. Most of her students "can't write

very easily at all. Some have no coordination in their hands and/or legs." To help them express themselves, she has worked guerilla fashion, even copying down snatches of conversation and making them into "books" for the children, while at the same time combatting the understandable mania for perfection that obsesses them. [2]

What follows is her account of one student's "breakthrough" in writing, and a selection of his stories:

> Mark has cerebral palsy, and for him it means that he doesn't breathe properly and so speaking is very hard. He also finds it difficult to write. His head is teeming with words, ideas, and punctuation. He seems drunk on it sometimes. He is reading somewhere on a second grade level; his main passion is cars. In the following stories all the punctuation is his. He told me exactly how to write everything. And when he didn't get understood, he would try to write it on the board.
>
> I want to begin with one he actually physically wrote himself not because I think it's one of his best, but because you'll see that he is ready to learn about syllables:

DANNY AND ME

*Danny and I went to the park. Danny sees
    a fly! We ran! D-
anny sees a-
nother fly! We run to to Danny's car. I say: "Danny, go get your gun quick!"
"I won't" said Danny stoutly.*

The end.

A BEAN

One day I planted the bean. It was a navy bean and I had to be very careful not to run over it with my car. My car is a MUSTANG and I wash it every day, because kids throw tarryrocks and dirt at it. So dirty that I have to even wash the hubcaps and inside the car, and take out the mats.

The end

Mark

MY CAR AND TRUCK

This is a story about a boy named Mark. Mark liked cars and trucks. He wished he had a car and a truck and one day his wish came true. A beautiful Chevrolet car was waiting for him. "Yippee!" said Mark, jumping into the Chevrolet. The seats were comfortable. Mark had a safety belt. He put it on. Then he started the motor and put it in reverse. It had automatic transmission. Then Mark put it in drive and he went as fast as the speed limit. There was a license plate on the front and back of Mark's car. Then Mark got a truck with manual transmission. Mark said to himself, "I must get a garage because I don't want the rain to dirty up my car and truck. I am very worried." He said, "How am I going to do this Hmm. Hmm. Let me think." He thought and thought. At last he said, "Aha!" Now I know what to do. I'll go to Mr. Kimberly and I'll get a garage. Aha! I'll buy it."

(end of Chapter 1)

Mark

MR. KIMBERLY AND MARK

Mark said to Mr. Kimberly, "I would like to buy a garage for my car."
"Very well," said Mr. K.
"Oh goody, goody," cried Mark.
"So, how much does it cost?"
"See that garage over there," * said Mr. K.
"What garage?" said Mark.
"Over there," said Mr. K.
"Oh, I see what you mean," said Mark. Mark said excitedly, "I did not know that you had a garage that cost $1."

Well Mark had the garage in a sec. He paid Mr. K. $1 and walked home. He put the garage in his front yard where he parked his car and truck.

A few days later it was time for the garage to be checked. Mark called up Mr. K. on the phone. Ding-a-ling went the phone over at Kimberly's garage.

"Hi," said Mark. "It is time for my garage to be checked."
"It is not November 23rd."
"I'm probably wrong," said Mark. He looked at his calendar. "I am wrong!"
"Look here," said Mr. Kimberly. "I can't have this."
"Well then," said Mark. "I am sorry. I really am, but I have to hang up because I have to eat dinner. Good-by."

Mark went in to his kitchen to cook his dinner. He ate it. He had biscuits and pancakes and a glass of cocoa.

"Oh my, wasn't it good," said Mark. "I'll have to go to Kimberly's garage and I have to change

---

*(He wouldn't let me put a question mark here.)

clothes." So he did. Then he got into his truck. His back-up lights turned on and he first went to the Volkswagon shop because his truck battery was going down. When he got there he lifted the hood up. He looked at the battery then he went towards a Volkswagon bus. His truck was a VW truck. "There was not a battery," cried Mark. "They should put a battery in," he sputtered. A VW man asked him, "What are you doing?" "Oh," said Mark, "I am looking for a battery but I can't find one."

"Oh," said the man. "I see where one is." And he did put the battery in.

The end

Mark

David Fletcher has likewise emphasized process over product in his therapeutic work in a drug rehabilitation community school. His classes do writing based on "minimally structured events," one of which was derived from Otto Rank's concept of the birth trauma [3]:

The event began with my explaining about birth in Rank's opinion as a shocking transition from a snug, protected and secure environment into a world of demands, compromises and self support. The students grasped immediately, and began free relating from Rank's theory. When they first left home, when they broke off with a lover, and when they quit drugs became later versions or analogies to the birth transition. Traumatic transition was familiar turf to them; they term it "changes."

Fletcher notes that nearly all of his students come from ghetto backgrounds, and are "rooted in an oral, not a written, tradition." As we have seen in Jeannine Dobbs' work with "disturbed" children, and in Barbara Merkel's with "handicapped" ones, the teacher must be ready to meet the situation with flexibility and imagination. Mr. Fletcher thus encouraged his students to "rap" into a tape recorder rather than write. More skilled students acted as "scribes" for the nonreaders, putting their "raps" into written form. The willingness of these teachers to jettison traditional "me talk—you listen" classroom roles is something every teacher in a "regular" classroom can learn from.

The day my mother open
    her legs
    and scream
and all that blood came
    out
when the doctor
    pull my big head out

and spank on my
       blackass
the world heard my big
       loud mouth
and when I open my eye
       I saw the light

I know my mother was glad
       I came out
       like I was kickin' her
I knew I was gonna be
the baddest mother
       on this face of the
       earth

                    Rosalie Richardson

Oh its so warm and comfortable
I feel so safe and good
I never want to leave this home
But what's happening?
       I am slipping down, I am falling, oh
I don't want to leave. I am being squeezed.
Oh, it's so tight it hurts. What's happen-
ing to me? Something is grabbing me now.
It's pulling me. Please leave me alone;
I don't want to leave. It's so light what
happened to the darkness. I am scared,
I am cold, please put me back. Now they
they're hitting me and I am going to scream
till they stop. Now there are a lot of
hands on me doing so many things. Why
don't they leave me alone. Always these
fucking changes!

                         Frank Locastro

"Birth Trauma Jive"

       To my limited knowledge of the day I was
born, it was quite hectic. First of all I remember
the way I accidentally slipped out of my Mother's
love. As I was preparing to enter civilization, I
position myself for the "Great Escape". Being that
it was so slippery, I instantly felt slick. My Mother
always enjoyed winter mornings, therefore I was
somewhat cool. And sometimes my Mother use to
tell people that she want to have a gossip column
in the Daily News, so therefore I talk a lot of shit.
       So as I now look back, I used to always lean
against things, and even until today I always seem
to sit with a gangster lean. Now in after effect,
what I am is just a jazzy, jazzy dude.

                         James Landrum

One of the dangers for a "regular" classroom
teacher who deals with "normal" children all day, lies
in marking the students and teachers we have just
discussed as "special cases." Perhaps few of us have
encountered a Lena in our teaching experience, but
almost all of us have been puzzled, exasperated, or
angered by the Wanda that Phillip Lopate has written
about. When the director of his school's reading clinic
reported "at the very least a problem with mental
focusing," Lopate was quick "not to want to acquire
an attitude toward Wanda that would turn her into a
'case' and let myself off the hook." [4] I quote from
his article at length because, in its carefulness and
psychological insight, Lopate unfolds his own changes
of attitude and his student's responses to them:

       In one of my classes is a girl named Wanda who was
       clearly having her difficulties. On my first visit I noticed she
       had a scowling, puzzled expression, moved about in a
       disoriented way and clung to Miss Lowy like a baby,
       whining in a peculiar gruff voice that was hard to decipher.
       She was the target of certain "sophisticated" children who
       made fun of her whenever she showed discomfit.
       There are children who win you over by their irresistibly
       charming looks—and Wanda was not one of them, though I
       later saw she had her share of appeal and cuteness in the
       right circumstance. Then there are children who attract you
       by their vulnerability, and this was Wanda.
       I decided to work with her in creative writing and
       discovered, as I suspected, that writing anything longer than
       three words was a torture for her. Reading was an equally
       grim business. She was far behind the class in reading, and
       had learned all the wheedling and distracting devices that a
       slow reader so often develops to draw attention away from
       her inadequacy.
       The first time we did a play I made sure Wanda was in it.
       Wanda got to play the King, a very dignified, desirable role
       which she managed with a surprisingly royal air. Once the
       play script had been xeroxed, I took her aside and had her
       read from it. This was good practice, and showed her that
       reading had a function aside from embarrassing her. I don't
       think she was reading, though, so much as taking wild
       guesses from memory. Some of her guesses were way off
       the mark, like pronouncing six words where there were
       only three.

Wanda managed her part well in performance, and
Lopate decided—as a sure way to build her self-con-
fidence—to put her into other dramatic productions:

       When we began the monologues video project, I asked
       her to pick a character that she wanted to play. She decided
       to be a witch. I took her aside and asked her to think of a
       short speech that a witch might say. Since she had trouble
       writing it, I let her dictate the speech to me and then had
       her recopy it in her own hand. the speech went:

       I am the witch
       And I will make you disappear
       Because I don't like people making fun of me
       And if you laugh at me

I will laugh right back
And you better not mess with me
Because I will disappear you.

It was clear where this speech was coming from. I thought Wanda had chosen wisely, in taking a role that would give her power and the wherewithal to strike back at those who ridiculed her. Nevertheless, she let herself in for an inevitable bump: when it was announced that Wanda would play the witch several smart-alecky boys doubled over with laughter. "She's already a witch!"

The monologues video project was designed by Lopate and the Teachers & Writers team at P.S. 75 as a method of teaching characterization. Rather than "rush into a role," the childern were encouraged to improvise—alone—for five or ten minutes before a camera. In this way they could enter the character they were going to play and learn what the character thought, dreamt, and what his motivations and past were. When each actor had found the "center" of the character, the production could move forward:

When it came time for Wanda's monologue, I sensed that she could not improvise very much about the past life and secret thoughts of the witch. Witches are fantasy figures, they have no biographies. So I asked her to repeat the speech she had written and continue with anything witchy that came into her mind. We placed her inside the Writing Room Closet, which became the Witch's House, and the shot began with the closet door opening mysteriously and Wanda looking into the camera. She said her lines in a tentative, soft voice I had never heard her use, and that would have been more fitting for a ballerina; then she smiled at me and shrugged. She kept looking for instructions from the people behind the camera. I let her stumble on a bit more, wanting her to try to find the answer inside herself. The second time I told her to ignore the lines, just keep repeating "I am the witch I am the witch!" until she started to feel she was really turning into a witch. I thought a chant might help her find the proper mood. "Just keep saying it in different ways, until you find the right way." Take two. She opened the closet door, repeating the cry a number of times, getting better and more menacing, then flashed us that charming, apologetic smile. "I don't know what else to say." One of her classmates said, "That was good, Wanda." I assured her that it was too, but that maybe we could even make it better.

It struck me that Wanda did not have a very developed self to begin with, and of course it was not going to be easy for her to get inside someone else's skin when she was largely unaware of her own person. This time I asked her to add hand motions. I was aiming for a ritualistic, gut theater approach to the witch, something that would depend not on verbal definition but on vocal timbre and hypnotic movement. Once more she was put inside the closet. She was extremely good-natured, didn't mind doing it again and again; in fact she seemed to enjoy the attention. The camera started; she began clawing the air in a quite extraordinary way. Added to this was a fierce scary growl. Then she lost it. She shrugged at her classmates appealingly.

For the fourth and final take I sent everyone out of the room, including myself, leaving only Wanda and the cameraman (a boy named Jose) behind. I told Wanda we were all going to stand outside the door for five minutes and she was to roar and growl loud enough so that we could hear her through the door. Remember, I said, it's pretty noisy in the hallway so you'd better be loud.

When we came back and reviewed the tape it was wonderful.

What energy! She had found the demon.

The next scenes of the video-play found Wanda "relaxed and self-possessed," writes Lopate.

The kind of care and attention that Phillip Lopate gave to Wanda becomes less and less possible for teachers charged with large classes and extracurricular duties. Yet his method, and those of the other artists presented here, can perhaps impress busy teachers with the importance of this "individual attention." Lopate met with one of his third graders, Bernard Shepard, every Tuesday morning in a storage closet for a month. Bernard felt the need for this kind of privacy, and Phillip followed his directions to the letter, "reduced to a mechanical, but happy scribe. I felt privileged," he writes, "to be in communication which was so pure and clear." Bernard dictated the poems, and Lopate wrote them down. Here are some of them[5] :

PLAYING HOUSE WITH MY SISTER

I like to be with my sister
Very much
With my sister I play
We eat chocolate bars every time
We go over to Andy's
And we see the rainbow
It's up in the sky
High in the sky
Then it starts to rain
The rainbow goes away.

HOW TO MAKE A RAINBOW

I will make a rainbow on a picture
I will put it on a film
Then I will point the film projector
     up to the sky
Everybody will look at the rainbow.

I'M ALONE

I like to be alone, alone every day
I scratch my head when I'm alone
I scratch my head
And I play
I scratch my head and think

I remember everything
My grandmother I saw her be buried
It took a long time
Then I remember my grandfather
When I was a little baby he used to diaper me
And he would always buy me stuffed animals
Then I remember my father
He used to murder me every day
When I told lies.

                                    Bernard Shepherd

Poet David Shapiro enjoyed a similar relationship with Wendy van den Heuvel, a ten year old who had the advantage of private poetry lessons with him over the course of nearly a year. [6]

NOW

Now the stars are gleaming
  Like boats shining
In the river of rootbeer
And I am dancing to the music it makes
My room feels green
Because I am as green as the morning sun
The squirrels go to sleep with their nuts
The deer go to sleep with their fawns
Under the tree of happiness
And I will not go to sleepanymore
Because of the boats shining in the river
And I will not go to sleep
Because I hear my mother crying,
  White sails.

                                    Wendy Van den Heuvel

With this kind of teaching arrangement, we arrive at the opposite end of a spectrum that ranges from institutional care to writing lessons at home. I must again refer the reader to Ron Padgett's "Inside School and Out" (elsewhere in this book). At this point the issues he raises in that essay merge with my concerns. One important conclusion that we can draw from the work of all these teachers, in whatever context they may be working, is their attempt to bring writing back to everyday life by responding to the human situations of their students. If the experience of art (either in the doing of it or in the appreciation) can be said to sensitize us to our world, to "make us more fully human," then it follows that the teaching of writing or theater must be carried forth in ways that are equally "humane." Students can't be slugged over the head with poetry, humiliated when they fail as beginning actors or actresses, or be made to feel worthless if their drawings don't come out right.

About two years ago I began to get telephone calls from former students of mine who had graduated from the school where I had worked for Teachers and Writers, or who had no poetry workshops to attend at a children's museum where I had given them because the program had been withdrawn. "Well you see," I tried to explain, "I *like* having my Saturday mornings free"; or, "It's too bad there aren't any writing programs in your school. I don't see any way I could go there and teach; it just isn't possible." But the kids persisted, pestered, and after six months, naturally, I cracked. "All right," I told them, "Come to my apartment on Saturday mornings at 10:30, and we'll see what happens."

They came. For the past year and a half I think I've looked forward to the workshop more than they have. I'm going to leave the full story for a later telling, though. In a sense, we've personalized education completely. The kids and I interact as friends, and they show up because they want to. No bells ring, the loudspeaker doesn't croak some idiotic message, and the problem of discipline doesn't exist. Sometimes we just sit around and talk. More often than not, though, the kids are impatient to write, and restless with me for enjoying myself so much. The workshop supplies plenty of "tender loving care" not only for the kids, but for their "teacher" as well. Their "handicap," their "problem," their "trauma" is that they are almost too talented. I am a little older and wiser, if not more talented, and so I have become their weekend resource.

I wish I could always leave my regular in-school jobs with the same warm glow that Saturday morning guarantees me.

NOTES

[1] "Teaching Writing to Emotionally Disturbed Children," in *Teachers & Writers Collaborative Newsletter* (Vol. 6, No. 1), pp. 22-25.

[2] "Creative Writing with Severely Handicapped Children," in *Teachers & Writers Collaborative Newsletter* (vol. 4, No. 4), pp. 127-132.

[3] "Birth Trauma," in *Teachers & Writers Collaborative Newsletter* (Vol. 6, No. 1), pp. 46-48.

[4] "Working with Wanda," in *Teachers & Writers Collaborative Newsletter* (Vol. 5, No. 3), pp. 19-21.

[5] "A Book About Rainbows," in *Teachers & Writers Collaborative Newsletter* (Vol. 4, No. 1), pp. 20-21.

[6] "The Classes of David Shapiro," in *Teachers & Writers Collaborative Newsletter* (Vol. 4, No. 4), pp. 151-152.

Notes on a Health Class

by Aaron Fogel

The New York public school system provides for what it calls "special education" or "health" classes, for brain-damaged, crippled, or otherwise sick children, who are thought to be incompatible with regular classes. I worked with one of the three health classes at a Manhattan elementary school, two afternoons a week throughout 1973-74. In the fall when I first walked into the class, I expected special children. Now that I've been there awhile, the motives for keeping these students in separate classes are not too clear to me—or at least the rational motives aren't. There are obvious details that give impulse to the decision—difficulties getting up stairs, reading levels, hyperactivity. But when these are weighed without preassumption, I think the choice that has been made (what other voice to use than the passive?) to set these ones apart tells more about the limits of the concept of the classroom than it does about the students who've been excluded. My own experience, however, is only at one school. I didn't make any attempt to tour health classes, and don't intend to. What I want to write about, then, is just one year spent in one place, completely in the dark about administrative intentions and superviews.

I came in as poetry teacher and left without any defined role. By the end we had done some writing, some reading, an overambitious puppet show project, a little magazine which was half pictures, some tapes of "trials" trying to resolve conflicts between members of the class. But the best moments (as has been the case with my other classes at the school) are often just physical play without any fantasy trapping: throwing a volleyball around the room or going outside to play baseball. P.S. 216 seems to me an extraordinarily cramped, neat place. Many people in the community think of that as its virtue. To me it seems sad. The children brighten whenever they can move, one of those metamorphoses for which there's no picture but the dead coming alive. In my experience the children in the health classes and the children to whom they refer with O'Neill-like pathos as "upstairs," are exactly the same in this respect: both need to go outdoors and play, and neither gets enough.

But the "health" class students get much less even than the regulars. When I first came to the class, they had a new teacher who worked throughout the year to change the notion of the health class as "special." He changed the name, and simply called the class by its room number, like the regular classes in the school. He worked against a years-long tradition of restriction set up by the teacher of the middle level "health" class, whose manner toward her children at times approached the kind of things Dickens is always accused of exaggerating and never does. And he worked to take the class outside, something previously forbidden. But the schedule for the "health" children, who were mostly between 12 and 14, called for an hour in "cot room" with the two younger health classes. The two sets of blinds, yellow and black, came down. And for an hour, after early lunch, which they ate separate from their peers, the health classes are supposed to sleep. Sleep perhaps the younger kids did. The diversions of the children in the eldest class were more wide awake, and consisted largely of boys and girls edging cots next to each other and committing the happy crime of "feeling culo," as they loved to put it, and laughing. The trial which we recorded in the beginning of the year concerned the accusation by one member of the class that two of the others were engaging in feeling culo. Pretty obviously, he was jealous and envious, and his accusations were real, shrill, and oratorically moralistic. "You shouldn't do that!" he kept screaming. The culprits and the rest of the class were having a terrific time with the story, and there were gradual teasing admissions of the facts. These in turn led to reminiscences about their romances when they were ten, hilarious and beautiful.

After lunch the regular students went outside and played on the block near the school, a long sloping hill down which they like to charge. It wasn't till late in the year that the new teacher managed to get his class outside as well. At times they were shy and inactive, a good half of them clinging around the teacher. When I arrived during lunch hour, they'd cling around me a lot. They were afraid, partly because of the conditioning. There was some ostracism and jeering from some of the kids, but there was also some integration. There was no reason for the kids not to be outside. This year, there's a new teacher again, and the kids are not going out after lunch. The disappointment and depression is intense.

At the beginning of the year they wrote some poems by dictation about the "cot-room" issue. "Why should we lay down? We don't need cots. Cots are for kids, not for me. I get enough sleep at home, when I be home."

Maybe it isn't impossible, but certainly it's pointless to teach poetry to people who are physically depressed. Those who wrote best in the class were those who were most visibly abnormal—that is, they were wild. There were a couple of boys who were fairly outside the range of social understanding—they did strange things that showed a lack of awareness of other people. These two were very productive within that depressed space, because I think somehow they didn't let it cramp their style. One wrote a "novel." One did endless pictures. On the other hand, there were two girls who were super close and spent all day talking to each other. They were both mildly crippled, and not brain-damaged at all. The class depressed and quieted them enormously, and if my observations of the year were accurate, they did very little work for the main teacher and virtually none for me. The class was intolerable for them, even though the teacher was excellent. Their activity and productivity were almost completely zeroed by their social receptiveness. They stopped doing because they could sit. (The same thing applies perhaps to the whole culture. Egomaniacs function well in institutions which tend to make the people who are aware of others quiet and resistant.) No one could fully provide them with the kind of joyous physical environment which would have been necessary if they were to produce something beautiful. They disliked their own writings because there was too little good about the world that they had to say: they didn't want to be phony and "make up beautiful things"—so, one gets the impression, they just stopped thinking and tried to limit their seeing to when it was necessary for self-protection.

So, for example, one of the young women wrote a piece at the beginning of the year which began, "The Ghetto is a place where blacks grow up hard," and went on to say simply and eloquently that anybody who hadn't experienced it couldn't understand it just by reading about it. That was the only thing she wrote all year. I told her that it was good. At the end of the year we put it in the class magazine as her piece. But she didn't believe it was good and she wanted simply to read the books I brought in—books of poems, books of anything. So I brought in a lot of books. And she read them.

If this sounds like approval of her resignation, I don't mean it to be. The problem was, however, that poems simply do not give anybody the kind of

physical exhilaration that everyone needs. The kids who were totally self-involved could write novels about themselves and horses or paint vast murals about themselves and animals. They were working something out which was already in their own terms: dream images from inside. The others were much happier writing love letters to real people—whether they really had anything going or not—and then hiding them. I saw some of the letters but I wouldn't ask to hand them round. The "trial" on tape was a big success because it brought love or love play—the main issue—into the community in a form that was hilarious and that dealt with the problem of slanders among them. We did other tapes, none as good.

When we went outside to play ball for the first time in the spring I was astonished by the change. They were different people. Big laughs, loads of talk and unmalicious laughter, clear happiness. I thought, why not do this every day? I came home thinking about the afternoon outside.

This year they don't go outside any more. The teacher's a woman who wouldn't play with them. So one afternoon we were in gym—there were only five kids present—and I played baseball with them. Enormous fun. Bad tempers. One of the boys, Kelly (the accuser in the tape) is a terrible loser, and had two very good hits caught on a fly by a kid who never should have been able to catch them. The second time he was caught out this way, I fell on the floor of the gym laughing at the sheer unfairness of it. Kelly, who was always griping and grouching and was about to go into a tantrum of sore-losing, saw the joke, started laughing, and also fell on the floor and rolled around. That's the only way I know how to teach in this school—by the occasional physical uproariousness.

The same need for a physical breach in the cramped neatness exists "upstairs." It's no different. My best lessons there involved things like taking ten kids out of a class and running around with a ridiculous plastic flute we found, playing unplanned notes in their ears, and having them write poems on the board while I did so. They wrote some of their simplest, prettiest poems. They nudged each other for space on the board: the weaklings ended up writing thin poems with short lines, because they couldn't get much board space. No doubt that's where short lines come from. Other times I let them run around like mad, undisciplined. I'd get infuriated with them. Then I'd let them do it. What did it matter? But they wrote a lot of good poetry in between, on and off, here and there. So I have a grind to axe.

Downstairs, if I'd run around playing a plastic flute, it wouldn't have worked. They'd have shrunk away. Because *I* would be monopolizing physical space that they had no access to, that had been effectively beaten out of them—*not* because they're crippled or spastic—that doesn't stop them from moving. What stops them is the drugs, the image, the cots, the black blinds, the lack of gym, the lack of outside, the different schedule, the absence of sufficient physical activity.

I introduced a puppetry project which turned out to be a fizzle. The teacher had been the art teacher in the school, then a fifth grade teacher, and now was moving on to special education. Not knowing enough about time and the river, I chose a particularly fancy way of making puppets—by casting in plaster from originals they'd made, and then producing the finished product in plastic wood. The whole physical process of making the puppets was all right. I had some difficulty at first explaining what casting was all about, and of course it had to be seen. I wanted them to see casting and duplication because it had left a magical impression on me in childhood. They were tentative, and a bit repelled by the gooky materials involved: vaseline, oily clay, plaster, and worst of all plastic wood with its almost intolerable smell. Intoxicating. Dangerous. They made their own puppet heads in several sessions. Then they worked along on the process of casting, as apprentices work with masters—helping, never supervising. The finished products (after about four months) were really snazzy painted costumed puppets which were simply too immense and proper for them to handle with ease. We did a couple of lessons on the gestures of puppets, and I tried to teach them how to render emotion. I tried to show them about exaggeration. Some of them got the idea and enjoyed themselves. Others were bored and resistant. We improvised a few little plays. We had an immense puppet stage which they'd helped build, which sat at the back of the room, with its curtains, and became another closet to hide in and play secret games. But before we got to the point of really putting on a play, we had a new thing going, which was a rexograph in the room. With that we made up pictures and put together the magazine. Then the term was over. I suppose the experiences of casting and building brought some pleasure, and I don't regret it. But I think the disappointment of the project is a lesson.

Another good physical scene: there I am, coming in week after week, time after time, the poetry man. They joke about me and my poems. He wants poems. Then one day we get a typewriter for the class. I can do 80. Till now I've been taking down poems and stories by hand. I've been reading them poems. Not much of an impression. But now they dictate to me their stories and I'm typing away fast as they can talk. Impressed! Wow! they said. This guy really knows something about words. They were joking, not naive—but they were seeing something go. And they worked.

A remarkable capacity to sum up their major experience concisely, so suddenly you've nothing to say. Connie writes about her thoughts at home: "I sit in my room all night and dream about lovebirds, singing in the night. They're at it all the time, you go up and ring the doorbell, and they have a sign that says, Do Not Disturb! Lovebirds at Business! Attorney At Law! For Lovebirds Only!"

Or Elliot, who distrusted with good reason all the time. He wrote a small novel called, "Me The Pinto Horse." The relationship between horse and master goes through ups and downs of affection and hatred. Here's the peripety:

"Then his master tricked him and said nicely to him, you have to do some work for me. Then the horse felt good, because he thought his master liked him then. And the master said, you have to pull this wagon, it's very light, you don't have to worry. And then he hid all the heavy rocks under the cover of the wagon so the horse wouldn't know it. And then the horse had a feeling that he was tricking him. The master saddled the horse up and then he started pulling the wagon. Then the horse said, O my god, what's the matter I can't pull this thing. And the master said, I tricked you, huh? And then he whipped him and told him to go faster and faster. Then the horse got so angry, and so mean, he pulled it so fast, it was going at least forty miles an hour one horse pulling it. Suddenly he fell. He passed out. A horse can't pass out, can it? Then the master got down off his buggy, and then he felt the horse's heart. The horse whispered to him, I'm gonna get you back one way or another for giving me a heart attack.

"The spirit of the horse rose and started dancing. A horse can't dance, but the spirit of a horse can dance. It had one leg; three heads, one at the end one at the front and one at the middle.

"Then the master got frightened. He took a 210 year old gun, and shot the spirit. The horse vomited. The master died because he couldn't stand the stink of the vomit."

Is this a recollection and rewrite of a book he was reading? I don't know. I don't think it matters. Most of this was not dictated, but written out by Elliot by hand, while he kept asking me how to spell this and that. A very physical and emphatic story.

From *Teachers & Writers Collaborative Newsletter* (Vol. 6, No. 2), pp. 36-39.

Teaching Poetry to Blind Kids

by Ron Padgett and Dick Gallup

PADGETT: Wasn't there a school in Romney (W. Va.) for deaf, dumb and blind kids?

GALLUP: Deaf and blind. I taught blind kids, but I didn't work with the deaf. The administrators told me that the deaf kids were too hard to work with. Apparently being deaf was a worse disability than being blind. For one thing you have to learn to talk. So I worked with blind high school kids, a junior class and a senior class of college-bound kids—they called them "the college-bound"—about twelve to fifteen kids. And they weren't all blind: some of them just had glasses about three inches thick. They were legally blind. Others were stone-blind. So I didn't know what the hell to do. But they were all smart kids, and it was OK, for one thing they were great listeners, so I read them a lot of poems. Partly because I knew these poems weren't going to be transcribed into Braille. And they reacted very well to them.

PADGETT: Did you have them do any writing?

GALLUP: Yes.

PADGETT: Was it any different?

GALLUP: Yes, there were several differences. Let's see: one is that there was a lot of self-pity. They feel sorry for themselves because they're blind, but they fight against it. They know that self-pity isn't good for them, but on the other hand they get very depressed, and they try to help each other out of depressions. They're very supportive. Another thing is that the smarter ones tend to be verbose: they use too many words rather than too few.

One thing I found very interesting is that kids who had been blind a long time would try to write about visual stuff but not using visual imagery, because they couldn't see, so that all their images would be tactile or aural. One kid wrote a poem about the sun coming up in the morning and going down in the evening. And the basic images were tactile. It was a very interesting piece of writing.

Other than that, their emotional lives tend to be a little bit stilted, due to the fact that they live in these dormitories and it's hard for them to break out of the situation. It's hard to sneak out and see your girl friend when you're blind. So they felt lonely in that way.

Anyway, I worked with them four or five weeks. Some of them typed up the works and some of them would read the Braille aloud to the class. They showed little hesitancy in reading their work to the class, because—remember—they are supportive. The class would respond not by gesturing but by saying something, the only way they could communicate. So there was a lot of "ooh" and "aah." And they tended to be very clear about what they liked and didn't like.

The two things I did which were different were to read a lot of poems, and to put in words everything I wanted to express. I stopped gesturing. And I counted on their remembering what I said to them, because most of them have superior memories. It would have been interesting to work with them for a whole year, to explore their different sense of imagery.

THE SUN

First comes the false dawn with a graying in the east, creating nothing but a hazy gloom.

Then the sun starts fingering its way above the horizon, slowly but steadily sweeping away the cloak of darkness, revealing whatever there is to see.

It glides first into the open spaces where there is no obstacle to defy it, then filters tiny pathways in the forests, causing dancing lights whenever the wind moves the leaves.

As the day progresses, it beats down upon the earth, some places with a kind hand, but in others with an intensity as though it were mad at the world, and wanted to destroy it.

The evening comes, and with it the sun seems to tire of its task. It tiptoes over the horizon again replacing the cloak of darkness.

Leroy Richards

Writing in First Grade

by Anne Martin

Introduction

It seems to be widely assumed that first grade merely performs the function of teaching technical skills which can then be applied later on in creative effort. There is also the unspoken assumption that very young children have not yet developed the drive and intensity to work at written communication beyond a very cute, stereotyped sort that can usually be found tacked up on bulletin boards. The consequence of these assumptions is that most first grades concentrate on reading and "skills," relying heavily on commercially prepared materials, and that writing is a subsidiary subject consisting mostly of handwriting practice and answering questions about reading.

This approach to primary teaching leads to a lot of the damage that T & W is so much concerned with undoing, and it's time that these assumptions were directly confronted. My own experience convinces me that first graders are not only well able to make a start on learning to express themselves powerfully through the written word, but that furthermore, if they are not helped to do this, they may build up fears and dislike of the whole writing process, which may remain with them throughout their lives (unless of course they are lucky enough to be released by T & W or some other source). It seems to me we should concentrate more on giving young children a good start with writing in their primary years, so that they can grow steadily in their sophisticated use of written language, rather than resigning ourselves to undoing the damage of mechanical "skill teaching" later on. The *Newsletter* has had many discussions about the need for using tricks, props, or gimmicks to stimulate writing, because the children were so reluctant and afraid to write, due to their previous school experience. Instead, it might be more worthwhile to put the emphasis on reaching children and teachers at the primary level. Then it might be easier to dispense with the artificial devices for getting around children's inhibitions about writing at the higher grade levels.

On the first day of the term, when I asked my new first-graders what they would like to do during the year, one little girl said, "My mother and my sister want me to learn to read, but I don't want to read. I just want to learn how to write." It's obvious why writing should have such appeal to most young children—it's active, it uses tools closely allied to art work (magic markers in color are particularly prized), and it's considered an especially grown-up thing to do and generally evokes praise from other people. Of course, to a very young child "writing" doesn't necessarily mean stories and poems. It might just mean filling pages with letters, numbers, printed names, or words copied from TV, signs, or books. I see my task in teaching writing to very young children as the attempt to make clear the connection between the child's pleasure in manipulating language orally and his pleasure in doodling on a piece of paper. In other words, I hope that gradually each child will realize that he can use letters and words to capture thoughts and experiences, that he can be playful, serious, or factual in his writing, and, most importantly, that he can learn to do this independently, in his own style.

When you consider the tremendous range of knowledge necessary in order to transcribe thoughts onto paper—the sounds of letters, the shapes and sizes of letters, the physical control of a writing tool, the order of letters in a word, the order of words in a sentence, the (often irregular) spelling of every word, the staggering amount of technical know-how before you even begin to struggle with the ordinary difficulty of self-expression—it seems a miracle that six-year olds can begin to master these during a year at school. And yet, towards the end of the year, most of my first graders can write a couple of sentences, quite a few can write creditable stories, poems, or descriptions, and some advanced writers can easily dash off pages of whatever they feel like writing. It is the growing sense of accomplishment that makes teaching writing to first graders such a gratifying task, even though it's a long struggle before the children can actually produce interesting writing. Not only is it a challenge to help children gain a minimum of ease with mechanics in order to free them to write, but it's an even greater challenge to keep them eager to work at a task that is so fraught with difficulties and so slow to show dramatic results.

If writing becomes a natural part of everyday classroom life from the first day on, before the children have learned to know letters or sounds or reading, then it isn't as likely to seem so formidable later on. In order to create written communication without the frustration of mechanics, I encourage the children to dictate stories, both individually and as a group. Although I use dictation much more during the first part of the year, I continue using it even after the children have learned to write, as a way of recording complicated thoughts more quickly or of involving the whole group in making up a poem or story together. Sometimes group dictations come up spontaneously, and I just grab a piece of paper and write them down. The following examples from two different classes just happened to bubble up, the first as a reaction to a factual book about dinosaurs, and the second during a sweltering September afternoon in a stuffy classroom.

SOME DINOSAUR THOUGHTS

Get that dinosaur out of that picture, and put him
  on a scale.
He's ripping our book, he's ripping it up,
So put him on a scale.

So we put him on a scale,
And he broke the scale.
Oh, no! He broke the scale!

Let's put him in the zoo,
Or put him in jail,
Or tell his mother to keep him home.

(The dinosaur's saying, "Boo hoo.")

HOT WEATHER THOUGHTS

When it's hot it makes you want to. . .
Go in swimming,
Jump into freezing water,
Turn on a fan,
Turn on the air-conditioning and lie on the bed,
Go to sleep,
Have a popsicle,
Eat ice cream,
Eat ice cubes to make you cold,
Eat watermelon,
Put ice cubes on your head.
Get in a freezer (then you'll be freezed
  and turn into ice cubes),
Jump out the window and fly down,
  and the air would make you cool,
You could land in the snow,
Go in the snow and put your head in it.

Take a piece of paper and fold it
  and put water in it,
  And then put water on your face
    whenever you get hot.
Get on your bunk bed and drink miles and miles
  down the road.

More often, a group dictation may be a deliberate effort to describe something familiar in a new way. I often start by suggesting a nature topic, such as rain, snow, or wind, on a day when the children have just experienced some rough weather. Sometimes I ask them to describe it to someone who may never have seen it, and this may evoke some interesting comparisons. Or sometimes I ask them to imagine that they are the ocean or a leaf or some other inanimate object, and that they tell me what they see, hear, and feel. I usually give them a little while (sometimes overnight) to think about it, and then try to choose a time when the children are alert and relaxed. Mostly I get so many contributions from so many sides at once, that I have to slow the gallop enough to be able to scribble things down. Afterwards, I sometimes change the order of the children's ideas to help put them into a kind of loose sequence, but I never change any words or grammatical constructions or add anything myself. The children love to have the whole thing read back to them, and they gleefully identify each person's contributions. The result (which I then duplicate and give to all the children) may read something like this:

SNOW

Snow makes things look white and bumpy,
And it falls on roofs and tree branches.
It's like a white ceiling, but it's soft.
You can make a snowman,
And you can have a snowball fight,
And go sledding, and skiing, and skating.
It's water when it's cold and turned to ice.
It makes places colder.

Snow falls from the sky in little flakes
That are soft like feathers,
But they're cold.
They are like little stars that have holes
  in them,
And they're pretty.
They are like drops of milk
Or an angel's tears.

Snow is like when God is trying to figure out
What to put in the whole wide world.
He puts snow for the children to play in,
And for the winter, so that it could be different
From summer, spring, and fall.

It's so that when Santa flies and gives children
    presents,
He could bring his sled on the white snow.
It's to make the city and towns and country look
    pretty.

Snow doesn't make any noise.
It's quiet, like you're not talking
And there's no T. V. or radios or records.
Or when you go to bed and nobody is up.
Snow is like little pieces of cloud
That broke off and fell on the ground,
And nobody knew
Because they couldn't hear it.

After working with many kindergarten and first-grade classes, I have noticed that while individual children differ tremendously within a class, each new group begins to develop a kind of class character based on the interaction of the various components of the group. Not only do some groups tend to be more volatile, or particularly artistic, or sociable, but they may develop quite specific tendencies of thought and temperament. This emerges very clearly in the kind of writing that they do, both by dictation and in their own writing. The group that made up the dinosaur thoughts was a bunch of very bright individualists who somehow seemed to be unusually aware of language and interested in symbolic thought. They requested some sessions to work on a group poem, and they went at it with great seriousness and critical awareness, rejecting some contributions and praising others. The following poem was one on which they worked like this, including the sequence of ideas (which most first graders are not very concerned about) and the result is a more polished, if also more self-conscious, product.

RAIN

Rain is like little pieces of crystal
Falling from big rock clouds in the sky.
When it's raining hard, it's mad at the flowers
And makes them weep.
It hits you and wants to get you wet.

Rain is like seeds dropping down on the ground.
The flowers are bending over, the grass is dry.
The hedges are dying.
Rain is tears dripping from weeping clouds.

Perhaps the clouds are sad
Because it's cold in the sky.
Perhaps they want to come down to the earth,
Or go in a house to wash the dishes,
    or make a shower.

Or maybe it's too hot in the sky
And the sun is shining too hard,
Making a golden rainbow
Like a backward smile
Or a painted frown.

Perhaps one reason why this group became so particularly interested in writing poetry was that Jonathan happened to be a member of the class. Jonathan was one of the rare type of gifted children who understood immediately every suggestion touched upon in class, and then would go home and work out ramifications for hours on his own, just for his own pleasure. He always knew what he wanted to learn in school so that he could go on and explore things in depth by himself afterwards. Along with his unusual intellectual capacities, he was a modest, friendly, humorous child, and he was respected and loved by all the other children. Although writing poetry was only one of his many interests, Jonathan responded to our class discussions of poetry by starting a notebook of original poems and stories. Here is one of the poems he brought to school:

I wish I could ride
With all the other horses.
And no horse would say, "Ha ha ha."
And they wouldn't kick sand at me.

And I could go with them
And pick berries and milkweed and thorns,
And go out in the desert
And out on big plains
Where I could run for miles
And where the sun is red.
But I am too little to go.

But although Jonathan's writing undoubtedly sparked up the class, almost all the children seemed to share an affinity to poetic thought. When I asked them to think about the night and dictate individual poems to me, timid, dependent little Christine (the youngest in the class, not even six yet) came up with this poem:

The night is dark and long,
The night is damp.
And the cars are like little giants
Coming up the road.
And the cats miaow in the night,
But I don't pay any attention
So they go to sleep.
And I think that the night is long.
Only that I think when I go to sleep
That things are dark and short.

Peter's poem about the night included the line, "The light of the moon shouts over the world." And Robby's had the haunting phrase, "But in the winters of the night. . ." Even the cliché subjects, such as springtime (during May) brought some surprises. I especially liked the one that Chris wrote because of its (I.T.A. inspired?) pseudo middle English spelling.

SPRING IS HIRE

I luve the spring
With butrfliys flutring abote
And flowrs bloming up
And plants groing
Bees in the ar fliing to flowr to flowr.
I luve the bees thay give you good huny.

In sharp contrast to these poets were my children in last year's first grade, a very sweet, friendly, academic group. When I read poetry to this class, the children listened politely, and some of them even enjoyed some of the poems, but they were clearly not fired up by my reading. When I tried to evoke discussions of poetic symbols, the children again politely, but very firmly, made it clear that they were not interested in metaphor. On the other hand, if I started to read a factual book about nature or Indians, they would fervently beg me to read "just a little more" even if it was lunchtime. These children were extremely sensible, literal, down-to-earth types, and the kind of writing they enjoyed doing most were diary-type personal "news" or nature descriptions. Thus, examining things on the nature table, they wrote descriptions such as the following: "Daffodils are all yellow inside, and their inside has black little spots, and they have yellow petals outside." Or, "This shell looks like a tornado and sounds like the ocean." Or, "The coral looks like it has the chicken pox and big bumps. It's weird."

When we had a family of baby mice, the children observed their growth and wrote notes on their progress every few days. Right after the baby mice were born, Gigi wrote, "The baby mice are cute and pink. They are the smallest babies that I have seen. Their eyes are closed. They drink milk from their mother." A few days later, Andrea wrote, "The babies are pink. The class thinks that one of the mice crawled into the jar by itself and then I saw them drinking from their mother. I don't like the mice because they scare me sometimes. They remind me of bats." Some days after that, Anda observed, "The little mice are white and they are runny and I am surprised." On our last official observation, Julie wrote, "The mice are much bigger. They have more of fur. Their ears are like their mommy's ears. They eat what their mommy eats." All the children enjoyed the observations and writing about the mice,

"After working with many kindergarten and first grade classes, I have noticed that while individual children differ tremendously within a class, each new group begins to develop a kind of class character based on the interaction of various components of the group."

and they each had a mouse book to take home.

After the first months of school, I gave each child a writing notebook, covered with bright colored paper and the child's name. Every week I asked the children to write their news in their notebooks, but many children began to make more frequent entries of their own. One of Stephen's entries read, "I went to a parade and I got a cork gun, and my cousins took the gun away from me, and I was mad!!!" After a trip to New York, Susie wrote, "I was on the Empire State Building. The cars were so little they looked like toys. The people looked like ants because they were so little, and the building was higher than all the skyscrapers." Lisa wrote, "Now I have another loose tooth, and it is on top of my mouth." The children liked to read these items aloud to the class, and there was often a lively follow-up discussion among the children. Once the discussion about an incident became so heated and prolonged that after 15 minutes or so some of the members of the class said they were sick of hearing about that subject, and I invited the participants to finish their talk out in the hall, which they did, returning to the room with a look of peaceful satisfaction on their faces.

While most groups of children don't exhibit such extreme definite characteristics as the two groups I just mentioned, there always is a great deal of variation in outlook and interests even in children as young as first graders. I think it's important for a teacher to expose children from the very beginning to a great variety of types of writing, so that when they've had a chance to try out stories, fairy tales, news, poetry, description, factual material, jokes, riddles, etc. they can pursue the kind of writing that is most akin to their own styles of thought. By "expose" I mean both reading examples of each and asking all the children to try to write some. That may seem like asking quite a bit of first graders, but it's amazing how well they rise to the challenge. Sometimes it is the children who seem least ready to do academic work who produce the most interesting and original writing. Time after time I have been surprised by children who were termed "immature," who couldn't or wouldn't quiet down or listen, the ones who were always hiding under a table or being singled out by specialty teachers as uncooperative, and who (sometimes to their own amazement) showed great aptitude and pleasure in dictating and writing. It was only after trying many kinds of writing that Dougie could decide he wanted to write a natural history book about dragonflies, or that Susie and Emily could write the script of a play, or that Elizabeth could write pages of romantic fairy stories, or that Johannes could painstakingly write a blow by blow account of his family's camping trip.

If it is important to introduce an unlimited variety of writing styles and types, it is even more important to accept each child's writing on its own terms. Young children are usually eager to please the teacher, and they are apt to produce what they know will be well received. If a teacher has a preference for one type or style, the children (if they like her) will probably try to fit themselves into that mold, whether it's Dick and Jane or Haiku. Since I take writing seriously, so do the children, but I try to guard against expecting or preferring any particular form or style. I do lay down the ground rules that there has to be some effort involved and that the writing should be reasonably genuine. This still permits individual children to interpret assignments rather freely, and it leads to some oddball writing that might otherwise never show up within a classroom. Six-year-old humor tends to be somewhat eccentric anyway, and for adults the humor lies partly in its very incomprehensibility. When I asked the children to write about something they love and something they hate, Greg came up with this:

I hate Mom to turn out me
And kiss the light.
I love Mom to turn out the light
And kiss me goodnight.

Joe, a quiet, deadpan little fellow sidled up to me with this:

I am a lollipop.
If you can read this
Scratch my ear.
O.K. I will scratch your ear.
If you can't read this
Tell someone to read my story.

When I ask the children to describe a member of their family, I usually get a great variety of responses. If the children are assured that I am soliciting neither pious sentiments of devotion nor defiant denunciations, they can feel free to write either or neither. Here are some comments on mothers and siblings. All of these were written by happy, more or less well adjusted middle-class children. Five year old Haig wrote:

I like my mother when she gives me a lot of presents, and sometimes she goes and tells daddy to play with me.

Another five-year-old wrote:

My mother is always mad at me when I do something that is an accident. I am always mad. I wish I could give Mom a spank and shout at her. When she is nice to me I am nice to her.

Karen, who loves animals, wrote:

I like my mother best because she feeds my cat. My mother is the best in the world.

A bright, precocious second grader described her mother:

She screams at me almost every time I sit down to read. She also screams at me whenever I am a little slow in dressing. She hardly ever stops screaming at me. I can not think of one time that she has been nice to me.

As for brothers and sisters:

My brother does not share and he is not polite.

My sister wears slobbery slippers and she wears a crummy coat. My sister rides her slobbery bike all the time and she says "blah blah blah" to everybody all the time.

My sister is so funny when she pulls my hair. I laugh and laugh.

My brother fights with me. He has glasses on. He's mean to me and my Mom too. I hate my brother. He's dumb. Golly I wish he was not in my family.

My little sister does not eat much. She likes everybody and she shares her stuff. She gets mad when people don't share with her. Sometimes she looks very pretty.

The most enigmatic and original comment about a family member was Todd's single line description: *"My mother looks like a peeled potato."*

When I say that I ask a great deal of first graders, I mean that I ask a lot potentially. The first independent writing efforts of such young children are bound to be stilted and way below their actual language ability. By the time they get one word written down, they have usually forgotten the end of a projected sentence, and it comes out all wrong. Yet the children are usually proud of these first meager efforts because they know they have written something all by themselves. They seem to be able to accept quite realistically the gap between their present writing ability and their potential in the future. It is my job to keep taking each child a little further each time, so that gradually the gap between the faltering first steps and the possibility of a rich, varied use of written language becomes perceptibly smaller.

Alison, an artistic, creative child, wrote her first independent story on Halloween: "This bat flew up above the devil house." By spring time she was writing poems like this one about the ocean:

Waves are me.
In the night and in the day
I splash on rocks.
And when I go down,
I go down the crevices.
I go quietly
And swiftly.

Jeff, whose Halloween story consisted of "A ghost went out on Halloween and scared all the people," a few months later was writing:

I like trees because they give us shelter.
And they give us food. And they give us shade.
And I like trees because you can climb them.
And they make the world look green.

And:

I want to be a dog
So I can bark
In the thunder and lightning.
And I can run fast
As a shooting star.

Looking over my years as a teacher of young children, I would be inclined to agree with the little girl who felt that writing should have a higher priority in first grade than reading. In order to write well, a child has to learn reading anyway, since writing involves all the same—and more—skills than reading. And while reading can be a passive, sometimes even meaningless, experience, writing by its very nature has to actively involve the child in all his complexities of thinking and feeling. If writing (including dictation) takes place in kindergarten and first grade as an important means of self-expression, along with art, music, dance, crafts, and drama, children are much more likely to become literate, and perhaps more in touch with themselves, very early in their school lives. And teachers of first-grade children will have something more to look forward to than the dull routine of workbooks and exercises. Whatever the teacher manuals say about specific "skill teaching," I think that even in first grade the broad skill of writing takes precedence over the peculiar aims of textbook lessons, and that moreover it provides one more channel of a close and continuing communication between a teacher and the children in a class.

From the *Teachers & Writers Collaborative Newsletter* (Vol. 4, No. 4, Spring 1973), pp. 139-150.

Concentration's Hope: Introducing Jonathan Rosenstein

by Larry Fagin

MY FACE

I am a good poet
& when I die
my face will be put
on apple sauce jars.

Most likely. He was either ten or eleven when he wrote that. I get his age and the years mixed up, never having kept track, but he must be at least fifteen by now. I first encountered him on a visit to Ron Padgett's Saturday writing workshop for kids at MUSE back in 1968. He reminded me of an introspective Jerry Lewis. We tried a poem. He was in love with pens and notebooks at the time. "Are you smart?" I asked. He shrugged. "Write about how smart you are."

BRAINS

Brains are human
They're smarter than we are
They force us to think something
They force us to think that we're animals
We are not we with brains
We are more we

The brain is its sleek tan finish
The nails of a chair are really brains

At this point his Bic pen ran out of ink. Ron loaned him his Rapidograph. Jonathan had never seen one—love at first sight! He finished the poem:

The pen
The ink of a pen is its blood
The pen is beautiful when you throw it
*   into the sky*

Other poems on the same theme (writing materials):

THE FEEL OF A NEW NOTEBOOK

The feel of a new notebook

You tear one page out and feel terrible
I just feel sad 'cause you got to make up
*   all that paper*
'Cause it's brand new—a bother
It's new and just new
And you gotta write
It's the first page
And you see all those pages to write up
If you had feeling, you'd just write the way
*   you feel*

THE FEEL OF A PENCIL & PEN

A pencil feels tight and sticky
A pencil is a good thing to write with
It feels very sensitive too

If you had a pen it would be
*   more attractive*
And you'd know where you were going
(If a teenager had a psychedelic pen,
*   for example)*
It makes you pay more attention
Like you don't spoil a good thing

There was also a near obsession with perfection and "concentration," possibly reflecting my own approach to constructing poems with smooth surfaces. (One title was THE UNIMPERFECT IS REALLY PERFECT.)

WE DON'T REBEL

We like to make peace
because of concentration.
Concentration—
a good idea.

PEACE LEADS TO CONCENTRATION

The moon might be our goal
but I don't think so.

PRUNE PIT

The spine
of the text
is imperfect.

SWEATER

Put on your sweater
& concentrate
on the good life.

CONCENTRATION

A sweat
Sometimes a joy
Sometimes a beastly howl

PLEASURE

Pleasure
is
amazing.

It is a perfect dark blue platinum wall.

And, combining the two themes:

GOOD PEN

Prosperous, always at your side
Concentration's hope
Always writes
* In concentration*

Eventually I took over Ron's workshop. Jonathan and I hit it off well: two nervous Jewish boys not quite sure of themselves in their roles—poet and teacher. Sure, he reminded me of myself at his age, so a degree of personal interest, perhaps narcissistic, was inevitable. He came to MUSE on Saturdays for most of three years, during which time he wrote seventy-five to a hundred poems and prose pieces (not counting collaborations with other kids). It wasn't always easy to "get" Jonathan to write. Sometimes I gave him titles—several at once (LOVE OR MONEY, POPCORN, THE GIFT, etc.) and gave him his choice. Some he accepted, others were rejected for reasons of his own. Titles also frequently came from what was going on in the room, where the atmosphere ranged from contemplative to zany. Objects and ideas were scrambled and passed back and forth between us and the kids. Old *National Geographics*, comic books, pet mice or frogs, carried-in food, cameras—anything was fair game and supplied ideas for poems or ended up in them. I never figured out how Jonathan's mind worked and, frankly, never wanted to know. I

thought it might spoil the magic to poke around for "motivation." Also, there just wasn't enough time to devote to on-the-spot analysis.

Looking back on how we worked, I'm sure I must have encouraged his interest in poetic forms that were close to the ones I was writing in at the time, or acquainted him with some of the work which had been an inspiration to me, such as the short poems of Charles Reznikoff, William Carlos Williams, and Robert Creeley. We paid a lot of attention to how poets broke their lines, uses of repetition, and most importantly, avoiding redundancy. Jonathan had no trouble with clichés—his thinking was simply too fresh and original to fall into that trap. His images came from God-knows-where, to my amazement and delight. Talking wheat germ and policemen whisk-brooms, hearts like drains, green corpuscles, sweet-and-sour heat, and sandwiches of noses between eyes, were irresistible. I wonder now, after five years, if *he* would have any idea of their origin. Often, with only the slightest encouragement or lead-in, left to his own devices, Jonathan would come up with gnarled, mani-acal, mysterious prose poems, written like a drunken driver. This one was triggered by Bill Zavatsky ran-domly banging away on an old piano shoehorned into the corner of our workshop room:

IN GREEN

Somebody playing cards with a green pencil, post office, a salamander going to the cellar, vitamin C off-key, milk & cookies, drugs, no—the sheriff just got shot in the head—now ernest hemingway can step in—creepy music, a bigotted neighborhood, someone got hit by a car, Iberia Airlines music, a haunted house at 3 o'clock, a bear, more creepy, tv music, russian music, sweaty hands.

He would also "knit" a poem together, one line leading to the next—an intuitive technique used by many poets. In this example, one kind of bowl leads to another. The title is obscure but fascinating:

CHARM

At the Rose Bowl a girl stood up & said "Can I have a bowl of Campbell's soup?" "Wha-at?" said the handsome colored man as the football flew into his arms. The crowd went diagonally forward & the sun struck all the clouds in the sky.

It is remarkable that almost all of Jonathan's poems were written "under the gun"—within a fifty-minute period. He could dash off several brilliant short poems in a few minutes and then spend the rest of the hour being bored or belaboring an unsuccessful longer piece. When and if he hit a dead spot in a poem I would prompt. "What *kind* of heart?" I would ask, if he got stuck on the word *heart*. Or "what color/flavor/fabric/shape" or "how does it smell" or "what is it doing" or "what's wrong with it." He would rarely follow the "assignments" or themes I gave out to the other kids, but would take it his own way—either a fanciful variation or something entirely different. One day, deciding there had been a surplus of frivolity in the writing we were doing, I suggested that the kids write about something sad, either real or imaginary. Jonathan's poem is a reaction to the assignment, complete with a fake epigram:

ART NEWS

"The armed forces are forcing us to write a sad poem."

I'm really killing you with my corny jokes
said the wheat germ.
I wanted to tell you about
my friend Sherm
but I'm too nervous
(he's a sportscaster, too)
tho he can take a joke.
Sherm is on the 10th floor.
(Forget I ever said that.)
It's possible to write a sad poem
but this isn't it.

One Saturday morning he and his friend Nathaniel Coleman read some of my shorter poems and I encouraged them to mimic them. Here, under their pseudonym "Nathohn Colenstein," are the parodies:

mine	theirs
Gravity	Light
pulls	shines
me	on
down	life
so	so
hard	hard
I	you
can	can't
only	even
say	see
my	your
name.	foot.
*	*
When a tree falls	If the frog jumps
on your head,	into your mouth,
it says yes	will it croak
or no.	or live?

A balloon	A volkswagen
is going up	is gliding uptown
filled with problems	filled with hair
*	*
I walk	I talk
you walk	you talk
we walk	we talk
through	out
each	the
other	mike
into	into
our	the
selves	sky

Jonathan is interested in photography, as evidenced in:

4 NEGATIVES OF HOUSTON

These old buildings are backed
by millionaires.
Their shapes are so strong
when you close your eyes
you can still see them
sticking into a polaroid sky.

It's unlikely that Jonathan would have produced the same volume and quality of work in a schoolroom situation. MUSE provided a unique environment with plenty of individual attention available from such enthusiastic poets as Bill Zavatsky, Ron Padgett, David Shapiro, and Dick Gallup. Significantly, attendance was voluntary, so the kids were there because they wanted to be. In Jonathan's case, I saw a golden opportunity to help bring out a strange, hot-house talent, and jumped at the chance, sometimes spending the whole hour working with him while Zavatsky and the rest of the kids were producing masterpieces of their own. We found this an effective way of working, though at the time it was purely intuitive and spontaneous—I giving special attention to individual children, Bill dealing with a group. This did not prevent us from switching roles, however.

There was very little development in Jonathan's work. It was a matter of putting his not-so-latent genius to the test. He had originally come to MUSE "ready to write," as Padgett observed. But he seemed to be able to take it or leave it and was generally unimpressed with his own talent. Most likely he has written little since leaving Brooklyn for Houston. He might become a filmmaker or photographer and never write again, but who can tell about a kid with such a rare sophisticated ability?

DON'T ERASE THE INK

Don't erase the ink.
Do you really think
it would make a difference?
A small difference. You would see
a silver filter floating
north over the paper.

POPCORN

Mad at my heart
like a clogged-up
drain. If it stops
we'll have to use mops.

COFFEE SERVICE

The old lad
christened the cup

"Coffee"

& poured it
for his poor self.

FRAGILE

You'll never know how fragile
the useless thought is
in the ballerina's brain
on the dusty stage.

CANTO ANTELOPE

antelope
eating cantaloupe
in an envelope

THE GIFT

It was not a real gift
but it still had a trace
of rainbow around the edges.
It was for me but I gave it
to you because I thought
it would wake you up
from a dream of gold needles.

HEH-HEH

A fat adult sits
on a hotel bed
with a glass of whisky
& a deck of cards.
"Heh-heh," he says,
"I'm lonely." I,
Jonathan, personally
think this is funny.
Sorry about that.

The minute you see
something to howl about
you hit the ceiling
with your green corpuscles

FRENCH HOSTESSES

They are very clean
They serve
delicious chopped lamb
bore you to death

OLD WORLD POEM

Think about abstraction—
Too way out.
There was a lady
Who practiced cello
Every day
Way out
On a mountain field
Just a few notes were pencilled in
On wood
The rest were metallic
Oldies but goodies
Gliding in and out of the trees

3 INVENTORS

Edmund Cragston—inventor of the gimmick.
Jerry Weinstein—inventor of the cherry-red card game.
Velazquez—inventor of the dark house.

ADVENTURES IN POETRY published SELECTED
POEMS by Jonathan Rosenstein in April, 1975 $2.00
from: ADVENTURES IN POETRY, 437 East 12th
St., New York, N.Y. 10009.

POEM

Wavering away
in the heat
Is it sour?
Is it sweet?
If I told you
it was bitter
you'd probably walk
on two feet
like most people
in the street

AS USUAL

You could stare
right
into someone's eyes
& they wouldn't even
know it. Not human
In the park
they are going
into life
with a detainer.

INSPIRATION PLANT

Don't leap at me
about to fall down
                to   inspire me.
                    Plant yourself
in the nose of my mind.
(But I shouldn't be greedy)
So long for the time
not being.

6. Inside School and Out

Inside School and Out

by Ron Padgett

A reading teacher described the case of a high school student who showed little reading ability. [1] In fact at the age of 16 he was still classified as a nonreader. The teacher had him look at a sentence and repeat it with her: "Mom and Dad met Tom." He repeated the words mechanically, his eyes moving about the room at random. She asked him to repeat the sentence faster and faster. He did so, but with the same lack of intonation and comprehension, until finally he reached a verbal speed which was equal to his normal speaking pace—his face changed. It understood, it came into focus, it became him the way he was outside of learning situations. "Mom and dad?" he asked. "What are *they* doing in school?"

The fact that he had momentarily imagined the characters in the sentence to be his own mother and father did not obviate the fact that now for the first time he had at least perceived the words as meaningful. They reminded him of real things, things which affect him.

It is interesting how often children associate the meaningful with life outside the school and the meaningless with life inside the school. Their attitude has several sources: one's time is less structured and more subject to chance outside the school; people tend to behave more formally in the social context of school than they do in the private context of home; written and learning materials are usually less entertaining at school than at home (comic books vs. readers; movies vs. educational films; rock music vs. choral singing, etc.). It is safe to assume that what people enjoy personally is more positively meaningful to them than that which they do not enjoy.

This is partly why experienced poets and artists are often greeted with cheers when they enter a classroom—they bring that out-of-school pleasure with them. They make the children feel not quite so much in school anymore. This in turn partly accounts for the sudden zest children feel in writing poetry under these conditions. Sometimes without even being aware of it, poets bring the out-of-school world into the learning situation, or, if you prefer, they take the kids out of the school. What follows are excerpts from poets' diary accounts of their teaching experiences which (often unconsciously) illustrate this tendency.

Poet Allan Appel [2] points out the difference between spoken and written words and goes on to say that he has seen many teachers alienate entire classes in the name of correctness:

Fact is I like the way boys and girls . . . communicate with each other. But it is different from how we do it, those of us who teach and write and are prejudiced to words. Reality is that the parents of the students, and therefore the students too, are cops and sanitation men, construction workers and plumbers. They are people who cannot always find the words to express the nuance of how they feel about one another and that is partly why, I think, there is a lot of touching, physical touching among them—a pat on the ass, the shoulder, the grabbing of the arm by the elbow and the step toward the face, in order to communicate in gestures what another man who has more words can express in an earnest verbal formulation. These people will say it with actions. And that is why the classroom always seems such a strained place too, I think. Out on the campus where the girls and boys are lolling around, sitting in close quarters on the benches, and sometimes in the early morning in the hall outside the classroom door, they are touching, standing, gesturing, and doing the communicating with a few words and a lot of gestures. The class is an alien place to start with, where a different language, formal written English, is spoken, or so it sometimes seems. . . . I sometimes feel like a foreign language teacher.

Phillip Lopate has written persuasively [3] about how the world outside the classroom—and by "classroom" I mean a conventionalized state of mind as much as the physical space in which these conventions are honored—is sometimes quickly captured and subdued when it does manage to get inside:

Some teachers did make the effort to connect the feelings and intuitions of children with every part of the learning process. But in most cases attention to the interior life tended to be reserved for special occasions, held ready as a treat or a favor. The ghettoization of sensitivity is exemplified by the teacher who asked me at a conference how she could "set up a creativity corner." When I said with wonder that I didn't understand why she would want to restrict her students' creativity to one small corner of the room, she answered peevishly: "You know what I mean." She was right: I did know what she meant. But I didn't want to.

Instead of viewing human creativity as the source of strength out of which all learning flows, the average public school sees it as something to put on bulletin boards or in assembly programs. This is true of Creative Writing, which seems destined to be cut off from the rest of the curriculum in spite of the efforts of Ashton-Warner and Herb Kohl and a hundred others to show the organic connection between personal writing and academic skills. Even the name, "creative" writing, implies that it is an afterthought, something extraneous and in addition to "regular" writing—oh, very worthwhile of course, one wouldn't dream of eliminating it—but this very sense of its being worthwhile, this very tolerance which disguises condescension is the Kiss of Death. Poetry we won't even talk about: what could be more "worthwhile," more elevated, more isolated from the meat and potatoes subjects?

Poetry is the exclamation point one gives to the well-apportioned classroom, the classroom "that has everything." Two sticks of poetry on the walls will do, one in front, one in back: like religious scrolls.

How often have I had to battle that iconic reverence for verse, as something fine and mushy that doesn't mean much but to which one still pays lip service, before I could get poetry and myself taken seriously? Until people see poetry as springing from all of life, they will isolate it in a creativity corner and treat it like a mascot.

Further along Lopate says:

One reason why poetry should have a place in the curriculum is that it is able to turn to use those mysterious, grotesque, creepy, crepuscular, iridescent experiences which the child generally feels he had better leave outside the school door, but which obsess him and rob his attention. The teacher who would like his or her students to write deeply must first persuade the class that these emotions are not only allowed in literature, they are recommended. How to get a child to go beyond the product that one knows is facile and shallow for him—spiritually beneath him? Maybe he was taught to write superficially by an earlier teacher; who knows? It seems pointless to fix the blame of the original sin when he first learned to deceive and hide behind written words. Most children (like most adults) are afraid to know what is going on inside them. Sooner or later they would have discovered the knack of literary evasion.

I became more aware of the in-school and out-of-school dichotomy several years ago when I worked on a film project with some kids from P.S. 61 on a Saturday afternoon, and in an article [4] I emphasized

... how valuable this type of experience had been for me, valuable because it was removed from the typical school environment, with its restrictions, its tacit demands on standard behavior, its very schoolness. I've had wonderful teaching experiences in schools, but none which equalled this one qualitatively. The making of this film turned out to be the most valuable single teaching experience I've ever had, because it was a more complete experience: the children and I were friends working together on something which gave us mutual pleasure, instruction and satisfaction, in a "real-life" situation, and there was a way to give this pleasure to others, by showing the film.

On a recent teaching jaunt out of town I heard several teachers express a strong desire to work with some of their kids on Saturdays. Apparently their school system discourages or forbids this because of insurance regulations. I don't really know the facts. I do know that while most teachers take a well-deserved rest on the weekend, some have special interests they would pursue on these days, and they should be permitted to do so.

But it's not just weekends I'm talking about: I'm talking about the quality of the experience, a quality which I'd like to have every time I teach, no matter when, no matter where.

A yearning for the meaningful and the real is not limited to the children who feel trapped in school. Sometimes their teachers feel even more harassed than they do—and here I must pause to say that while some teachers fit the image of the middle-class, conformist, vaguely personable young lady who has a teaching degree and little else, there are many others who are genuine, enthusiastic, independent and sympathetic people. It is this latter type who must deal with the baloney of school. The following poem is an example in which its extremeness makes it memorable. [5]

The Teacher's Loneliness Poem

Will you listen if I say what it is that's loneliest . . .
—sitting in a room corner, white walls, on the floor, dirty
   hair & crying—after someone walked out the door.
—Gerard's lower lip trembling with those soft eyes just
   melting.
—looking at faces in a faculty meeting & wondering what all
   these people are mouthing about.
—tense kids at 2:00 P.M. with one hour to go & no energy
   left.
 & you shrink smaller & smaller into GETTING ANGRY.
Yeah—it really stinks—where's the support—get yourself
      together—Fuck you man. It's hard to get out of bed
      in the morning sometimes—when it's very very cold &
      you pretty much know that your car isn't going to
      start
 &   you think about the pile of crap on your desk that
      needs to be corrected & those reading scores that
      other teachers keep talking about—& how Eric isn't
      learning to read because he thinks there's something
      bad about putting a cat in a freezer & where's
      Bobby's father.
& you do try to work it out with those you love—patient
   talking, understanding, listening & listening & it's hard
   to grab yourself when you don't listen to yourself very
   well—
—walking down the hall at 7:45 A.M.—before there are any
   voices in the School—knowing that your supervisor is
   coming to see if you're 'fit to work with children.'
—well—why doesn't Arthur call & say "Hey Cand—let's run
away in the truck. Let's go camping in Canada for the rest
   of our lives."

—But it's the worst loneliness to sit around waiting for that to happen.

—Candy Nattland
2nd grade teacher

If you can't get the outside in, go out yourself. The old term "field trip" reminds us that there was a day when it was more common for children to leave the classroom and go out into a field. Today it usually means boarding a bus to drive to a performance or a museum, an urban pastoral. Regardless, it still strikes pleasure in the hearts of those heading for the "field."

Poet Bill Zavatsky found one spring that he was simply unable to remain inside the classroom and so he turned a class trip to nearby Central Park into a poetry field trip. His students took notes on the way and rewrote them at home that night. Bill took Jane Shufer's work as an example and discussed it in a piece which has as its basis the dichotomy we have been discussing. His article [6] by going far afield, is perhaps the fitting conclusion to the present piece.

A WALK IN THE PARK

pink flowers nesting on
bare limbs. a green and pink mist,
a living mist. yellow on the
ground. now white helps the mist.
old houses rise above the mist.
a white petal carpet on the ground.
a flower, white, I found it.
tinged pale pink, on outside
petals only. inside snow white.
two more. pink, Mrs. Berl
dropped one. the reservoir is colored
plastic, always moving. a pale flower
is losing its petals. pretty cherry
flowers. Judy S. gave me a white
one. people on horses, so nice.
Mrs. Alpert says this is great.
a lovely bridge, an almost
gothic pattern. yum! I don't see
any water under bridge. green
mist again with pink, snow white
and pale pink. Old houses seen
through it. A flame red coat
against the green. a big flat
rock, long imbedded in the
ground, bigger than 2 or 3
people. robin-red-breast?

A PARK POEM

A green and pink mist fills the air
A
*   soft white fog joins it.*
There
*   is a green and yellow carpet on the ground.*

The
*   yellow vanishes and white takes its place.*
A
*   flower lies on the path.*
It
*   is white as snow at heart, but*
Pale
*   pink tinges the outside. Judy's*
Gift,
*   as white as she is sweet.*
A
*   Gothic bridge, all green. The*
Mist
*   rises once again, accompanied by*
Fog.
*   A bright spot of color flashes.*
I
*   sit on an imbedded rock, 9 x 2 1/2 perhaps.*
A
*   bird, I see a touch of orange,*
A
*   robin? If so, then spring is really here.*

Jane Shufer

Jane has a clear idea of what constitutes poetry for her. It's highly instructive to note what she fails to include in her "finished poem," what material enlivens her "notes" and how they differ from the poem proper. Immediately there are several lovely phrases in the notes which Jane rejects for the poem: "pink flowers nesting," "a living mist" (really a superb phrase), "white helps the mist." What becomes clear is that Jane is giving up a lot of verbs/verbals ("nesting," "living," "helps"—all of them *action* words) in favor of a more static vision in her poem. Clearly the activity, the doingness of the walk, transferred itself immediately to her notes, but for some reason (which undoubtedly is her sense of esthetics, of what should make up a poem) it is rejected in the finished product. This is, I feel, a real loss: what is active and aggressive becomes static and "poeticized." The seeming "confusion" of the first nine lines, with their sentence fragments, is much more energetic and vivid—actually communicating the curves and twists and interpenetrating juxtapositions of real flowers on real trees—than the finished poem, where the activity is much more refined, much "smoother" ("fills," "joins," "vanishes"). Jane obviously believes that there is no room in her poem for this ruggedness, this "confusion" of vision; that indeed, a poem is a smoothed-down object, as if experience were something to be flattened out by a steam iron on a mental ironing board. In fact, what Jane does in her finished poem is to abstract, rather than retain the powerful concrete scenes she has noted down. One of the differences that struck me immediately on reading the two versions was that two people and two illuminating actions had disappeared from the final text: Mrs. Berl's dropping of the flower, and Mrs. Alpert's enlivening colloquial remark, "This is great." Judy's simple act of giving, so clearly noted in the notebook, has been prettified, poeticized; and while the comparison between the whiteness of the flower and the sweetness of Judy is highly sophisticated, it is also clichéd. Other interesting observations are also dropped: the reservoir "colored plastic, always moving," and the beautifully observant and colloquial "people on horses, so nice." The exclamatory "yum!"—another indication of individuality and personality—is also lost, along with the remarkably observed "flame red coat/against the green," which is abstracted completely as "A bright spot of color flashes." It is also interesting to note that the vivid and personal rock "bigger than 2 or 3 people" is completely flattened into a mere geometrical construction, "9 x 2 1/2 perhaps." And finally, Jane sacrifices the beautiful Emily Dickinson-type question in her notes, "robin-red-breast?"—a question which creates a living presence with a minimum of words—for two lines of cliché: the corny old saw about spring being here at last etc. Obviously, a poem *must* end with some kind of moral; the final triumph of abstraction is moralism.

Jane's conception of poetry, it seems to me, drifts away from the "rawness" of observation into a "cooked" atmosphere where smoothness and cliché dominate. Jane is a reader, and it is clear that the tendency toward "literariness" pushes her toward a highly finished product that shoehorns reality out of it. People are erased and mist, the mist of the literary, the poetic subject, floods in.

I read the poems and spoke to Jane as clearly as I could about these transformations. I tried to impress her with the fact that there were two kinds of poetries: one that comes out of books, out of fantasy, out of one's "head," and another that came from keeping a sharp lookout on things in the world. She said, "Well, that's the kind of poetry *you* like, isn't it? The kind that comes out of your head, the kind that's crazy?" I told her yes, that until recently I had pretty much thought that the fantasy kind of poetry was the best, but that I was now trying to *see* things, to really look at them, and to write about them the way that they were. I told her that both kinds of poetry were equally important, and that a good poet had to learn how to do them both well. I think she followed me, and that the talk was an important experience for both of us.

It seems to me that this distinction, between fantasy, between "made-up stuff" and the "real world," is crucial. This is what all the ecology talk about "integrity of the object" is about. There are times when it is simply, well, not *wrong* to distort the tree or the rock, but ... simply *inaccurate*, irresponsible to the demands of the tree or the rock. (It's important when explaining this not to fall into the same moralistic pit oneself; the tree possesses no morality, it is simply a thing with roots and leaves.) I've just finished reading *Spring & All* by William Carlos Williams, a book in which he tackles just this problem.

Let me point out what is genuinely good in Jane's second poem. First, Jane has absolutely transformed her material, worked with it and on it. Whatever objections I may have to her sense of poetry, of what is poetic, she proves beyond a doubt that she has handled the material she has collected in a wholly artistic way—a remarkable achievement for anyone, let alone a fifth grader! If Jane has "suppressed" what I think are energetic, truly beautiful, and significant elements in her notebook entry, she has introduced other elements for the purpose of unity, notably the "mist," which permeates and touches-together everything in her second, "finished" poem. She has striven for and achieved a delicacy that is only suggested in the notebook poem. Rather than giving us process, she has given us the activity of landscape; her poem is quite "painterly." Perhaps she has "erased" most of the people in her notebook entry to concentrate more upon what she has decided is the real subject of her second poem, the landscape

of the park (a highly selective portion of it). Regardless of what objections I have to Jane's equation of Judy's sweetness and the whiteness of the flower, she has succeeded—and I think quite brilliantly—in making Judy and her gift like another element in the landscape; that is, Judy and her gift are floral, the park is like a giant, white, lovely flower; indeed, the entire landscape/poem is like an enormous, delicate blossom that contains splashes of color on its "petals": a Gothic bridge, "A bright spot of color," a rock, a bird, etc. This is an extraordinary metaphor: park as flower. Judy obviously by her sweetness is more flower-like to Jane than her teachers; a fact which is clinched by her gift of a flower.

Also, rather than baldly stating, "tree ... tree ... tree," as most of the other kids did, Jane chose to "Impressionize" her park; the trees and their green and pink leaves become "mist" rather than just tree-parts; the fallen petals are not just castaway elements, but part of a fabric, a carpet-weave. The first several Impressionist lines of her poem suddenly clarify: *A/flower lies on the path*. Jane clearly knows what she's doing; she wants an Impressionist atmosphere, creates it beautifully in her opening lines, then, Wham! presents us with a vivid 3-D flower! The dreamy experience of the opening suddenly jumps into reality, which is described in detail, then compared to a living/loved human presence, her friend Judy. The remainder of the poem, with its return to object and landscape (still and imaginative landscape folded in mist), cushions and surrounds the main experience of the poem: the flower-gift and its giver. Finally, like the sudden appearance of the flower on the path, a robin materializes which like Judy and her gift, seems to call for a bit of interpretation: "If so, then spring is really here." While I am still not convinced by the truism, it appears to me to be a satisfactory way of ending the poem. Perhaps a better ending would have been simply for Jane to return to the question of her notebook poem: "robin-red-breast?" Thus a cliché would have been avoided, and a sense of expectancy (stemming from the appearance of the flower in the path) might have been created. But perhaps this device is a bit too sophisticated; and as is, Jane has found a good solution, which at least has tradition and Spring to back it up! I want to talk to Jane about these things, and I want to backtrack and praise *both* of the poems. I want to talk with her about why she chose certain elements in her notes, and introduced others in her finished poem. Finally, in my opinion, both poems stand on their feet brilliantly, but I am interested in knowing (if she can tell me, and she may be unable to; art is itself and not an essay on why it was written, otherwise there would be only explanation and no poem) what conscious choices she was making as she sifted through the material.

Further Suggestions:

1. Take another "poetry walk," this time *without* notebooks. The assignment would be to return to the classroom and write about it, or to write it at night and bring it in the next day.

2. Take a walk *with* pencils and notebooks, but ask the students to pick just one thing they've seen and write about it as fully as they can. This could be done without writing materials, too. The idea being *focus*.

3. As Williams writes, it is both impossible and unnecessary to "count every flake of truth that falls." What is important is detail, the observation of detail, which is always personal;

somebody saying, "I like your shirt," or "You've cut your hair!" Such observations are always indications of personality and of individuality, and are essential to poetry. Thus, it would be more important for a kid to write about that big rock covered with orange spraypaint insignias than to try to encompass Central Park in a composition. Maybe shorter walks would do it.

NOTES

[1] See "Imagery and Comprehension" by Rose Ortiz in this book.

[2] "Open Admissions Journal," in *Teachers & Writers Collaborative Newsletter* (Vol. 5, No. 3), pp. 50-53.

[3] "Getting at the Feelings," in *Teachers & Writers Collaborative Newsletter* (Vol. 5, No. 2), pp. 4-12.

[4] "The Case of Hector Martinez," in *Teachers & Writers Collaborative Newsletter* (Vol. 5, No. 2), pp. 13-17.

[5] In *Teachers & Writers Collaborative Newsletter* (Vol. 5, No. 1), p. 51.

[6] "Two Kinds of Poetries," in *Teachers & Writers Collaborative Newsletter* (Vol. 5, No. 1), pp. 5-8.

After the Poet Goes Home

by Bill Zavatsky

Probably all writers or artists who give their all working an a school arts program find themselves, at one time or another, wondering what if anything happens when they pack up and leave. Do students and teachers remember? Has anything gotten through to them? And that darkest of all thoughts, Was this a complete waste of my energy? All of us have high secret hopes for that proverbial "seed" of instruction that may or may not take root and flourish. In the end, like any teacher, we've done our best, we've tried to "plant" something intangible, some flicker of newness, some dawning apprehension that may be extinguished by time or TV.

Ron Padgett has reported two experiences of activities generated by his visits to schools. The first is a fine Lies Poem written not by students but by a fourth grade teacher with whom he worked, Mrs. Bisset of Capon Bridge School, Capon Bridge, West Virginia. The poem was written in the spring of 1974:

LITTLE-KNOWN FACTS

Garson Mongold needs new sneakers because turtles and
    snails outrun him every day.
Mark Meadows has a plant that will grow girls.
Julie Shelley pressed a button and her head pulled her hair
    in.
B.C. Baker has planted forty acres of chocolate eggs instead
    of beans.
Cindy Wolford has answers written on the inside of her
    glasses in invisible ink.
Ribbie Lovett is really a mad-scientist.
Pat Moore works nights in a gum-drop factory.
David Shanholtz has blue hair and blonde eyes.
David Boyce's glasses are movie projectors, and he can show
    movies whenever he wants.
Mary Bradfield has a pet bear named Ralph.
Peggy Kerns has a cherry jaw tooth that has never lost one
    speck of its flavor.
Janet Bailes is just so bubbly because she eats two cakes of
    soap a day.
Carol Sirbaugh can cross her eyes so hard she can see herself
    without using a mirror.
Marcelle Strother's horse runs so fast she has to wear a
    crash helmet when riding.
Terry Davis is working on a way to make rocks that can not
    break windows.
Stacy McKee is really a shadow. Mrs. McKee keeps the real,
noisy Stacy home.
David Smith is a zoo-keeper in real life.
Tina Heishman and her horse can float like feathers through
    the air.
Sarah Richards crocheted all the spider webs on Cooper
    Mountain.
Garry Eaton gets his energy by eating Cocoa Krispies and
    gunpowder.
Erma Kerns is quiet because the cat *had* really got her
    tongue.
Ricky Fitzwater's insides are a 442 engine with a 13 to 1
    compression ratio.
Marilyn Himelwright cuts holes in the sky every day to get
    the blue for her eyes.
Wayne Morelana is a 8 ton Mack truck at night.
Tammy Daugherty   horse has a tail so long it sweeps out
    its own stable once a week.
Kim Hall makes pillows for a sheik in Arabia.
Steve Mantz is a 42 year old midget.
Judy LaFollette has grown a plant that will eat all the
    "dumb brothers" in the world.
Terri Braithwaite's earrings are transistor radios.
Bonnie Linger's glasses are periscopes.
Pam Heare smiles so much because her magic lunchbox
    only lets good things in it. It spits out sandwiches.
Denise Thorne can fly when she spreads her silver wings.
The maple tree in Julie Cooper's backyard grows
    bubblegum balls.
Tammy Moreland has dimples that twinkle in the dark.
Kent Orndorff's new lamb has orange, green, and
    white-striped wool.
Lisa Shanholtz has rosy cheeks that are colored with pink
    sun rays and apple blossoms.
James Jordan's flowers are made of dreams that he spun
    into yarn.
Before she was married, Mrs. Bisset's last name was
    Frankenstein.

MRS. BISSET
4th Grade Teacher
Capon Ridge School
Capon Ridge, West Virginia

Mrs. Bisset's poem, each line of which begins with the name of one of her students, is no doubt filled with class in-jokes, but manages to bring the spirit of each kid across in an affectionate way: "Stacy McKee is really a shadow. Mrs. McKee keeps the real, noisy Stacy home." The poem concludes with a charming bit of self-directed kidding on Mrs. Bisset's part ("Before she was married, Mrs. Bisset's last name was Frankenstein."), although it could have been added by a student! I can see it hanging there on the bulletin board, and as the class files out the class clown adds that final touch.

Cheryl Schmandt sat in on one of Padgett's classes in a New Jersey school; her own class wasn't on his schedule. She took one of his lessons back to her own class—but let's let her tell the story:

IMAGINE ME

The impetus for this collection was my visit to a fourth grade poetry workshop led by Mr. Ron Padgett. I enjoyed the relationship he tried to create with the class. I believe we both feel that children are reservoirs of untapped creativity with all the candor and freedom of speech available to man.

The following paragraphs will set the scene found in our fifth grade open-space classroom.

The informality of sitting on the carpeted floor with an Anthony Newley album playing softly in the background, created the mood I intended. The children were aware that it was time for creative writing this particular period because the music was their clue to bring a pencil and paper to a secluded section of the room. This partiuclar group enjoys this time together every day because we share each other's thoughts in writing and sometimes through illustrations—they may also bring in any record albums that have music they enjoy.

I initiated this particular lesson by saying, "Imagine me gentle as a hand waving a sad good-bye" (I demonstrated silently), "or a swaying tulip in a spring breeze," "a baby breathing during an afternoon nap," "or snowflakes resting on a windowsill." The children agreed with silent nods. The next step was to have them each share their imaginings—they chose to imagine themselves hot—"Imagine me hot as a cup of boiling cocoa," another said, "Imagine me hot as fondue oil ready for meat." I nodded in agreement. Their ideas ran rampant—some suggested cold things, tiny things, etc. Tiny things seemed easy for them to relate to—different ones called out, "Imagine me as tiny as a tear in a puppy's eye," "Imagine me an eyelash," "Imagine me a baby's fingernail."

I wrote each of their "Imagine me" feelings on large chart paper, and at the end of the period I hung the chart on the chalkboard for the children to read and enjoy.

To my surprise it was the group's idea to continue our "Imagine Me" feelings the next day. This enthusiasm continued for a week—we then had a collection of eight charts. Encouraging them to use colorful words to describe the objects or people was easy—possibly the most palatable lesson on parts of speech they'll ever devour. A few children are budding artists and simply spilled over with enthusiasm to illustrate the group effort.

The final draft was copied on ditto masters to make copies for Christmas or Chanukah gifts to parents, a donation to the school library, and an addition to each classroom.

To crack the dam that holds back

A child's reservoir of words and feelings
Takes a concentrated force known only to
Those who will truly listen

Cheryl Schmandt

Ms. Schmandt's children produced excellent poems, and like Mrs. Bisset she herself found the pull of poetry irresistible. One of the responses that pops up in the wake of a poet's visit to a school is poetry, and not only poetry written by students.

Perhaps the greatest thrill any teacher can have is to hear from a former student eager to continue writing. Alan Ziegler relates just such an incident:

I got a call at the end of August from Mike Eisenberg, one of my students at Valley Stream Central High School (N.Y.)—he said he had been writing all these poems late at night and he didn't know what was going on in them, and they kind of scared him because they sort of "wrote themselves." He came to see me to talk about it. I assured him that was how poets often worked—when they're really cooking.

Here is one of the poems Mike had written:

THE HUNTERS OF THE WORLD

The hunters of the world
have gathered in an underground tavern;
At the sign of the red eagle.

Above them,
    the mountains
        (angry blisters of solid pus,)
            flowed freely over
Tuesday's garbage,
and Monday's newspapers;
Pricked by a gaseous pin.

Men on Pluto invented the wheel.
The ocean parroted
        the sound of the wind on wood,
    and a curious noise escaped
        the sun as
            water
                took the place of
                    centuries;
at the sign of the red eagle.

Mike Eisenberg
Valley Stream (N.Y.)
Central High School

My own contacts with former students come through the mail, over the telephone, and in person. There's something extremely precious in them for me, and I try to be as diligent and prompt as I can in answering mail or lending my ear. One of my correspondents is a twelve year old whose class I never visited, but whose teacher brought her to me as a "talented poet." We spent a few of my lunch hours working together during my stay at the school, and evidently something "took."

Another student of mine, from whom I've just had two letters (each with poems enclosed for me to "criticize") has just entered college. She was part of the Culture Cabal of bright kids at a Long Island high school where I worked a couple of years ago, and has started to write marvelous poems. Another member of that same clique, Matthew Arnold, has kept in touch and sent me about a hundred short poems over the past two years:

*I never type
I never write outside of my bedroom.
I hate to advise people advice that I should be
    following
It's hard to get started again
after all this time, I still don't know all of it
It is inconceivable to me that no one in camp
    knows of Marcel Duchamp.
My feet are wet and the rest itches.
Do people die when you don't pay attention to
    them?
I am always cutting my hands over something.*

*

*The Martian counter-parts
of all my friends are having fun
without me.*

*

*I want to get dressed-up
in a very fancy suit
and go out to a nice wine and cheese place,
with a very pretty girl.
No two ways about it.
That is what I want to do.
It probably won't happen, though.
Mainly because I don't exist.*

*

*Getting out of the shower
with an infected scalp,
turning on the radio and hearing the Cowsills
is my life.*

These poems are funny and poignant, the outpourings of a gifted, self-conscious teenager (Matt is about fifteen now) who is very aware of what joins and separates him from the world around him.

The former students of mine who began coming to my apartment on Saturday mornings for poetry workshops a year and a half ago make a very special case. (See my article "Handle With Tender Loving Care" in this book.) Most of them are girls, and some of them I've known for almost six years. For them, I am not only the poetry teacher, I am closer to a big brother, an alternative father. One of the girls, now fifteen and quite sophisticated, calls me at least twice a week to gossip and get advice. I fully expect writing to play a role in their lives when they're fully grown, but I don't push. The pleasure of watching them grow up, of having their confidence and affection and being able to return mine, is what every teacher dreams of. Without it, without the daily contact of the school brought into my after-school life and personalized, there would be something missing in teaching. Some vague suspicion that I was being less human, more of an education machine, than I want or have to be.

Imagine me Rough

Imagine me day-old grey-whiskers
Shaved by a piece of sandpaper.
Imagine me dry chapped lips
Being scraped with a steel brush.
Imagine me a dog sitting on a rockpile—
"Ruff—Ruff!" (joke)
Imagine myself.

Imagine Me Soft

Imagine me a pink flower petal
Blinking at the sun's rays.
Imagine me a baby's breath
During an afternoon nap.
Imagine my squishy mashed potatoes
Running with fresh butter.
Imagine me a puppy's tummy
Quivering with love.
Imagine me a white cotton puff
Just right to treat a hurt.
Imagine me a favorite stuffed animal
cuddled by a sick child.

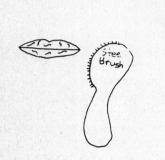

Imagine Me Dark

Imagine me a black cat
Creeping through a sewer pipe at night.
Imagine me an Old basement
Without window.

Imagine me a dusty bat
Soaring through a cave.
Imagine myself.

Imagine Me Noisy

Imagine me a stick of dynamite
Exploding in a 747 jet.
Imagine me a cattle stampede
Charging on New York City during morning rush
hour.
Imagine me a thunder bolt
Striking a moving tank.
Imagine me a world of chatterboxes
All shouting at the same time.
Imagine myself.

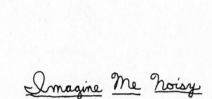

324

7. Reviews of Books and Recordings

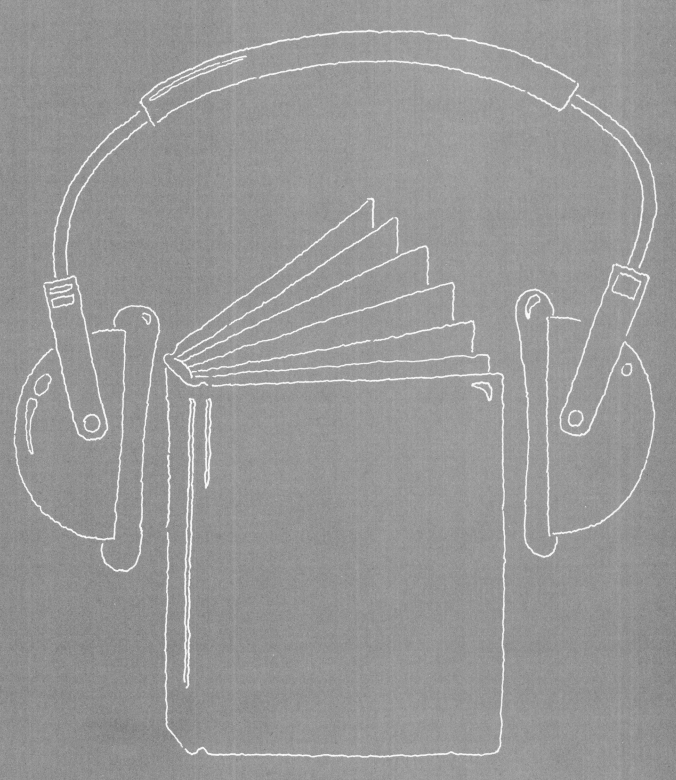

Recordings

CAJUN SONGS FROM LOUISIANA, recorded by I. Bonstein (Folkways Ethnic Library FE 4438). $8.95.
LOUISIANA CAJUN MUSIC, Vol. 2 (Old Timey 108 and 109, Arhoolie Records). No price listed.

There are several good LPs of Cajun music available, among them *Cajun Songs from Louisiana* and *Louisiana Cajun Music* (a four-record series). I prefer Volume 2 of the latter because the singing is more beautiful, but you have to hand it to the Folkways people: again they have issued remote material that is well presented (their descriptive notes can save you several trips to the encyclopedia).

Folkways, with their tremendous catalogue, has become a national resource, one which could be used to help draw children out of their provinciality. For instance, if you played some Cajun songs, a cut by jazz musician Ornette Coleman, Indian healing songs, Appalachian ballads, Leadbelly, John Cage, Pentecostal glossalia "singing," etc., one after the other without identification, your kids would probably be surprised to learn that all were recorded in the continental United States. And it might take some of the glitter off the heavily packaged pop music which too often leads people to neglect the music they can hear in their own backyards, and other people's. (R.P.)

THE FIRE PLUME: LEGENDS OF THE AMERICAN INDIANS read by Jay Silverheels (Caedmon TC 1451), edited by John Bierhost, $6.98.

The four stories on this record were among those collected and presumably translated by the pioneer ethnographer Henry Rowe Schoolcraft in the early nineteenth century. The occasional awkwardness of the English can be irritating, but it can also be charming in a kitschy way. ("Indian learn English from Latin teacher.")
Nostalgia figures in a big way too, for the stories are narrated by none other than Tonto, and if you were a fan of the Lone Ranger radio show you will find yourself irresistibly drawn to the voice of Jay Silverheels. It is a beautiful voice. But it is a voice that reads as if the comma did not exist, and worse, as if the material seems unfamiliar from line to line. (Alas, the Spanish word "tonto" does mean "fool, dolt, ignoramus.")
Even with all these faults, the record holds its own. You appreciate the genuineness of Schoolcraft's work. You sense the Indian originals burning behind the English. You feel the mythic power of two of the stories ("The Fire Plume" and "The Red Swan"). And you have that beautifully sonorous voice echoing in the room. (R.P.)

ORIGINS AND MEANINGS: PRIMITIVE AND ARCHAIC POETRY (Broadside Records BR 651).
FROM A SHAMAN'S NOTEBOOK: PRIMITIVE AND ARCHAIC POETRY (Broadside Records BR 652).

Both arranged by Jerome Rothenberg, with David Antin, Jackson MacLow and Rochelle Owens, both distributed by Folkways Records.

Jerome Rothenberg, with a host of fellow poets, has done primitive and archaic poetry (and us!) a tremendous service by reworking scholarly translations of texts from all over the world, so that these texts can shine free of the generally terrible English that made them previously unreadable.
Rothenberg's two big anthologies, TECHNICIANS OF THE SACRED and SHAKING THE PUMPKIN, are now well known and easily available in paperback editions (Doubleday). These two records are not simply readings of material from those volumes, they are interesting performances by poets who have years of experience in reading poetry aloud. They bring with this experience a genuine interest in and knowledge of the material.
Placed side by side, the diverse poetry (from the American Indians, the Maoris, the Eskimos, the ancient Egyptians, the Aztecs, the Pygmys, etc.) is seen to have a lot in common. The idea is not to blur distinctions, but to demonstrate how song makers on the earth have sought to translate the magic of life into words.
Rothenberg and Company have brought us this

magic on these two beautiful records. (R.P.)

HEALING SONGS OF THE AMERICAN INDIANS,
recorded on location by Dr. Frances Densmore
(Folkways, FE 4251).

Dr. Densmore began to record American Indian
music in 1907. Some of the material on this wonderful album dates from the following year. Recording
techniques were crude in those days, so that what we
hear has a distant quality, as if we were hearing it
broadcast from an empty soup can. Folkways has not
doctored the material, so it has a remarkably real
sound: Indian men singing songs to heal their brothers. Hollywood visions of Indian life vanish before
this onslaught of reality. How terrific to be able to
hear these songs! And how surprising to learn that the
"hiya hiya hiya" type of chant actually meant something in the original language! The album is accompanied by an informative booklet. (R.P.)

WAR WHOOPS AND MEDICINE SONGS, (Collected
and edited by Charles Hofmann (Folkways FE
4381).

The album does not tell us, but I'd guess these
recordings were made in the late forties. Like the
HEALING SONGS, this is not music for the cocktail
hour, although it is certainly likeable. Much of the
singing on this album is tribal, such as the SONG OF
WELCOME, FRIENDSHIP SONG, RIDING SONG,
MOCASSIN GAME SONG, LOVE SONG, etc. Not so
hostile or pugnacious as the attractive title suggests.
Some of the material (such as FRIEND'S SONG)
sounds like Irish or Scottish folk tunes—just an old
man singing alone. Classes studying tribes such as
Black Elk's Oglala Sioux would be particularly interested in selections from that tribe (recorded, of
course, after Black Elk's heyday). (R.P.)

WASHO—PEYOTE SONGS: SONGS OF THE
AMERICAN NATIVE CHURCH, recorded by War-
ren d'Azevedo (Folkways FE 4384).
THE KIOWA PEYOTE MEETING, recorded and
edited by Harry Smith (Folkways FE 4601), 3
discs.

Mr. d'Azevedo's recording was made at a peyote
ceremony; Mr. Smith's were not. There isn't a noticeable difference, not to me anyway. They are beautiful
documents, charged with presence. The historical,
religious, psychological and artistic material associated with the peyote ritual is vast. There are many
ways the interested teacher might use these fine
recordings. (R.P.)

The Chinese Language for Beginners by Lee Cooper
(Turttle, ppbk., Rutland, Vt.).
You Can Write Chinese by Kurt Wiese (Viking ppbk.).
About Chinese by Richard Newnham (Penguin).

CHINESE POEMS OF THE TANG AND SUNG
DYNASTIES read by Lo Kung-Yaun in Northern
Chinese, Peking dialect (Folkways Records).
CHINESE FOLK AND ART SONGS sung by Wonona
W. Chang, Anna Mi Lee, pianist (Spoken Arts
Records).

The first two books might be found in the children's books area of your bookstore: they are merci-
fully elementary. They are both pleasant books which
teach some very basic Chinese without giving you the
impression that it's an incredibly difficult language.
They emphasize written Chinese, especially words
derived from pictures. Yes, the Chinese character for
"man" looks like a stick figure of a man. These would
be useful books for the creative classroom, not only
for the kids, but for the teacher who might like to
sneak a look at them.

For those teachers whose appetites are then whet-
ted for deeper stuff, there is Richard Newnham's
About Chinese. This is a pleasantly written book for
those who wish to learn something about Chinese
without necessarily studying the language.

It strikes the American ear as oddly pedestrian, Lo
Kung-Yaun's readings of Chinese poetry. Here are
beautiful and sensitive poems by the likes of Li Po
and Wang Wei. We expect them to be read with
expression, and I suppose they are, but to me it
sounds as if a grocery list were being read. Which
shows how much I know about it! Most of us haven't
attended too many Chinese poetry readings. Records
such as this can give us some idea of what those
poems sound like. And the booklet which accompanies this (and all) Folkways Records includes an
introduction, the Chinese texts, their romanizations,
and translations (by Lo Kung-Yaun and Ralph
Knight).

The art songs on CHINESE FOLK AND ART
SONGS are fairly recent, so recent as to suggest that
they might have been influenced by modern Euro-
pean composers such as Satie and Poulenc. The folk
songs derive from "traditional" sources, but even
these sound Westernized, perhaps because of the
performers' classical music backgrounds. It's a little
like an opera singer doing "O Susanna!" Folk songs
accompanied by piano sound classicalized. I guess I'm
too much of a purist: I like to hear folk songs sung by
folks. (R.P.)

1, 2, 3, AND A ZING ZING ZING (STREET GAMES AND SONGS OF THE CHILDREN OF NEW YORK CITY), Folkways FC 7003.
TONY SCHWARTZ RECORDS THE SOUNDS OF CHILDREN, Folkways FH 5583.
MUSIC IN THE STREETS, Folkways FD 5581.
NUEVA YORK (A TAPE DOCUMENTARY OF PUERTO RICAN NEW YORKERS), Folkways.

These are four of Schwartz's documentary records available on Folkways Records. His records remind me of William Carlos Williams's poetry in the way they present the everyday as something beautiful. Just as Williams immortalized a red wheelbarrow, Schwartz gives us the sound of kids chanting as they skip rope, something which sounds as beautiful as it really is. It makes you want to grab your tape recorder and rush out into the streets.

New York is, of course, particularly rich in sound, so rich that most of its inhabitants have learned to screen out the unnecessary. This can lead to a kind of mental deafness: passersby ignore the street musician who turns out to have been the Reverend Gary Davis. A lone saxophonist walking down the white line in the middle of 57th Street would be regarded as a lunatic to be avoided—Tony Schwartz tapes him. Puerto Rican people who arrive in New York are interviewed not because they are in trouble with the law, but because they are interesting "ordinary" people. The rich, elusive world of children's game songs and rhymes is usually limited to the kids' private world, a world they are slow to open up to adults. Schwartz's records reminded me how funny this world is. If I remember the weird songs I used to make up with friends, or spicy rhymes that floated through the school: this was a folk poetry which in my case went by like clouds.

With these records the possibilities for a good teacher are endless: documentary, historical, scientific, dramatic. Tony Schwartz is a genius who makes us realize that these possibilities are ours. (R.P.)

UNDERSTANDING AND APPRECIATION OF POETRY, prepared by Morris Schreiber (Folkways FL 9120).

This record is a disaster, mitigated only by its ludicrousness. If you are in a good mood you will roll on the floor as you listen to Mr. Schreiber explain Poetry, at least during side one; it is unlikely you will wish to continue your sadistic (or masochistic) fun by listening to side two. But if you are in a bad mood, you will tear the record from the turntable and smash it into as many pieces as possible, for here is a record that presents poetry in its most unattractive light: Poetry the uplifted and uplifting, Poetry the expression of the sensitive soul, Poetry that uses rhythm as its life-blood and rhyme as its muscle, Poetry that expresses Man's inexpressible yearning for the inexpressible, etc. Mr. Schreiber's introduction to poetry, spiced with quotations from Christina Rossetti, John Masefield, Alfred Noyes, John Greenleaf Whittier, to name a few, is enough to drive the sensible student right up the wall. You might want to have a copy of this record as a museum piece, though, because it's a distorted, almost insane point of view which is rapidly disappearing. (R.P.)

A HISTORY OF THE ENGLISH LANGUAGE, A Discourse with Illustrative Passages, by Diane Bornstein, read by J.B. Bessinger, Jr. (Caedmon Records, TC 3008, 3 discs).
BEOWULF, CAEDMON'S HYMN AND OTHER OLD ENGLISH POEMS read in Old English by J.B. Bessinger, Jr. (Caedmon TC 1161).
KEMP MALONE ON OLD ENGLISH POETRY (Caedmon TC 1424).
SOUNDS AND SWEET AIRS—SONGS FROM SHAKESPEARE sung and read by Christopher Casson, Barbara McCaughey and Pamela Mant (Spoken Arts Records, SA 900).

The boxed three-record set A HISTORY OF THE ENGLISH LANGUAGE is a resource which every English teacher should have access to, whether or not the course of study involves the history of the English language. The material on these records takes us on a chronological trip through our language, from the earliest extant English writing (the "Song of Caedmon") to an essay by Thomas Jefferson on instruction in Anglo-Saxon. Each selection from the literature is preceded by a brief statement which locates the selection in history. The presentation is cogent and clear. It is really fascinating to listen to these records straight through: you can hardly understand a word of the "Song of Caedmon," but gradually, as you listen to each succeeding band, the language becomes recognizable, until—voila!—you realize that you understand everything. It is as if you were watching a movie out of focus. It is blurry. The projector is slowly brought into focus, and there on the screen you see it is yourself.

The language in school is usually modern. The textbooks are now conscientiously updated, so that many kids these days do not even have the chance to hate Longfellow and Tennyson. I remember that my first experience with an older form of English came with a reading of Macbeth in the tenth grade. It seemed so odd that people would speak that way, but I enjoyed playing the game and figuring out what it meant. Most of my classmates gagged on it. Generally the sheer remoteness of the language made it hard to read Shakespeare. It seems that had we some acquaintance with Old and Middle English, then Shakespeare would have made more sense to us.

Don't misunderstand me. I don't mean that third graders would sit through these selections without growing distracted. Still, there is so much material on these records that one can pick and choose. They are accompanied by a book which gives the texts. (Here in fact is the only deficient component of this package: the texts do not necessarily start and end with those on the record, so one must race forward and backward in the written text until the spoken words have been located. You'll have to annotate your own copy of the book.)

BEOWULF, CAEDMON'S HYMN AND OTHER OLD ENGLISH POEMS is essentially a repetition of the first disc of the HISTORY set, with extended readings from BEOWULF. It is recommended for those who are interested in the Old English only.

KEMP MALONE ON OLD ENGLISH POETRY is a nice record by a genuinely authoritative scholar. It begins as a lecture and gradually becomes a reading of texts or oral anthology, with less and less commentary. It's true that most students wouldn't like to sit for long periods listening to Old English poetry, because they can't understand it and it sounds so heavy, but it's a well-done record which, in the hands of a sensitive teacher, would prove useful in the classroom.

SOUNDS AND SWEET AIRS is a real charmer. It consists of songs and sonnets by Shakespeare, some read and some sung, with musical accompaniment (harp and recorder). The music is taken from folk tunes, Elizabethan composers such as Campion, Dowland and Forde, and later composers such as Arne and Purcell, arranged by Christopher Casson. The performers sing and play so sweetly and naturally that you find yourself actually enjoying it! This record could be used as a complement to a reading of Shakespeare or a study of Elizabethan England, or simply as examples of how composers have set words to music. This isn't so dumb as it sounds, especially when you have Thomas Campion setting Shakespeare. A lot of kids are interested in music these days; and while few of them would take to Schubert's songs right away, there's no reason why a curriculum, starting with say *Tommy* by The Who and working back to Elizabethan song, couldn't be worked out. We should not allow our children's tastes to be formed solely by the music "industry." (R.P.)

STREET AND GANGLAND RHYTHMS, collected and edited by E. Richard Sorenson (Folkways FD 5589, $6.98).

Mr. Sorenson recorded six 11-to-12-year-old black kids (all boys) at a "training school," in fact an institution for New York juvenile delinquents. None of the kids had any musical training or instruction, other than what they had learned on the street. It seems to me that such neighborhood musical groups are less common than they were ten years ago, when one would hear street-corner jam sessions more often (how often depending on your race and what neighborhoods you had the nerve to stroll through).

These kids do some improvised percussion numbers, some rhythm numbers with nonsense syllables sung or interjected, others with take-offs on jukebox favorites such as "Bo Diddley," and rhythmic dramatic improvisations based on real-life experiences (fist- and knife-fighting, shining shoes, getting shaken down, being in the training school, etc.). Some of these improvisations are hair-raising in their violence. One wonders if anyone has thought of getting such kids interested in theater, where they might bring their sheer energy under control. Otherwise it seems likely that the energy will control them right into prison.

This record is too powerful to be merely entertaining, but it could be used sociologically to educate kids about certain facts of life, or artistically to inspire them toward improvisation based on their own experience. (R.P.)

THE CAEDMON TREASURY OF MODERN POETS (Caedmon TC 2006, 2 discs).
T.S. ELIOT READING POEMS AND CHORUSES (Caedmon TC 1045).
FOUR QUARTETS READ BY T.S. ELIOT (Caedmon TC 1403).

T.S. Eliot might not be your cup of tea, and you might object to the selection of poets in the *Caedmon Treasury*, but at least we are given the poetry read by the people who wrote it. Some of them are better readers than others, but all are preferable, in my opinion, to actors who tend to ham up the texts, to elucidate the texts with proper enunciation and dramatic timing. This usually results in a good performance that has little to do with the text. I prefer Ezra Pound's quavering old voice, W.H. Auden's matter-of-factness, Wallace Stevens' stately groan, Richard Eberhart's almost hilarious, but beautiful prissiness. I am thrilled to hear William Carlos Williams's voice; I would not like to have it replaced by the voice of Ed Begley.

THE CAEDMON TREASURY includes readings by Eliot, Yeats, Auden, Edith Sitwell, the ever rip-roaring Dylan Thomas, Louis MacNeice, Robert Graves, Gertrude Stein, E.E. Cummings, Marianne Moore, William Empson, Stephen Spender, Conrad Aiken, Frost, Williams, Stevens, Eberhart, Pound and Richard Wilbur. I can't say that I wouldn't put together a very different selection, but I also can't say I don't like this one. For one thing, it's been around a long time. A lot of young poets, myself included, first came into contact with the real voices of the "masters" through this record. I never hear Eberhart read the *Groundhog* without being thrilled. I never hear Pound read without thinking of Yeats, his early mentor—their reading styles are similar. If you are to have an oral anthology of early twentieth century poetry, get this one.

The Eliot records are beautiful. Again, I do not like all his poetry equally, but I can't imagine anyone reading it better than he does. (If your school has a small budget, stick to the TREASURY (which does include *The Waste Land* complete). (R.P.)

Literary Recordings: A Checklist of the Archive of Recorded Poetry and Literature in the Library of Congress, compiled by the General Reference and Bibliography Division, Reference Department, Library of Congress (Washington, D.C., 1966), paperback, 190 pp. Order from the Superintendent of Documents, U.S. Government Printing Office, Washington, D.C. 20402.

This treasure-trove of recorded American poetry and related materials housed at the Library of Congress is one of America's secret weapons. Catalogued through June 1965 and unfortunately now out-of-print (but available in public libraries everywhere), practically every American poet of note that one could think of speaks out here on tape and disc.

Even a partial list would have to mention, in alphabetical order, the voices of: A.R. Ammons, W.H. Auden, John Berryman, Elizabeth Bishop, Robert Bly, Gwendolyn Brooks, Cid Corman, Gregory Corso, Robert Creeley, E.E. Cummings, James Dickey, Owen Dodson, Alan Dugan, Robert Duncan, Richard Eberhart, T.S. Eliot, Allen Ginsberg, Paul Goodman, John Hollander, Langston Hughes, David Ignatow, Randall Jarrell, Robinson Jeffers, LeRoi Jones (Imamu Amiri Baraka), Galway Kinnell, Kenneth Koch, Stanley Kunitz, Denise Levertov, John Logan, Robert Lowell, Walter Lowenfels, Edgar Lee Masters, W.S. Merwin, Marianne Moore, Ogden Nash, Kenneth Patchen, Sylvia Plath, John Crowe Ransom, Kenneth Rexroth, Adrienne Rich, Theodore Roethke, Muriel Rukeyser, Carl Sandburg, Delmore Schwartz, Anne Sexton, Karl Shapiro, William Stafford, Wallace Stevens, Allen Tate, Diane Wakoski, Philip Whalen, Richard Wilbur, William Carlos Williams, Yvor Winters, James Wright, and Louis Zukofsky.

There are literally dozens more—and some strange items of historical interest as well. For example, William Jennings Bryan doing his hit single, "Cross of Gold"; Robert Browning intoning the first four lines of "How They Brought the Good News from Ghent to Aix"; and 28 poets each reading Shakespeare's sonnet, "When in disgrace with fortune and men's eyes"! (The latter were recorded between 1938 and 1941 at the City College of New York, and were no doubt used to drive freshmen English students wild.)

And can you guess who the most recorded poet in (official) American literary history is? Carl Sandburg? Nope. Merrill Moore? Close. Give up? It's—of course —Robert Frost, whose recordings take up a full five pages in the catalogue. Part of the real pleasure of this book lies in ferreting out one's favorites, and anyone who loves poetry will be tickled pink by his or her own discoveries. A signal but not surprising omission is Ezra Pound, and as we await the forgiveness of history, see the other listings for commercially available recordings of Pound reading his poetry.

These recordings are available on LPs, on 78 RPM discs, and on tape. The catalogue gives precise instructions on how to obtain copies. This collection provides schools, libraries, and individuals with an unparalleled opportunity to build their own "live" poetry archive for just plain exciting listening and classroom use. And for those of you who want a copy of their own, my spies in the Library of Congress tell me that a revised edition of LITERARY RECORDINGS listing poets through 1975 should be available by the end of 1976. (B.Z.)

CLASSICS OF AMERICAN POETRY FOR THE ELEMENTARY CURRICULUM. Read by Eddie Albert, Ed Begley, Helen Gahagan Douglas, Robert Frost, Julie Harris, Hal Holbrook, Eartha Kitt, Frederick O'Neal, Brock Peters, Vincent Price, Basil Rathbone, Carl Sandburg. (Caedmon TC 2041). Two records.
CLASSICS OF ENGLISH POETRY FOR THE ELEMENTARY CURRICULUM. Read by Jeremy Brett, Katharine Cornell, Ronald Fraser, George Grizzard, Boris Karloff, James Mason, Frederick O'Neal, Ralph Richardson, Cyril Ritchard. (Caedmon TC 1301).

I switched on the turntable, prepared to hate these records. The fact is, however, that these chestnuts are useful. Great poems?—Baloney! Poems to use in the teaching of poetry-writing?—Salami! But as cultural exhibits poems like "Paul Revere's Ride" and "Gunga Din" can furnish superb grist for class discussion, and I would suggest to teachers that rather than presenting these works as "great poetry," they be mulled over for what they now are: crystallizations of very specific needs and responses that have become documents of American and British consciousness. They reflect with great precision the didactic burden that, until the twentieth century, poetry carried—often with genius in its service. These poems teach us to be brave, struggle through, grit our teeth, carry the flag, carry the ball, straighten up, fly right, volunteer for active duty, and in general to run the gamut of citizenship that has overwhelmed the process of education in our public schools. If you doubt that for a moment, listen to "Barbara Frietchie" or "The Charge of the Light Brigade." Oh, of course, a small room has been kept lighted for those occasional cranky individuals like Emily Dickinson and Edgar Allan Poe who now and then pass through the American landscape, but even Walt Whitman stands reduced to his costume of stars and stripes in *Classics of American Poetry*. Reverie, after all, does not build railroads ("John Henry"), win battles, or especially inspire the industry that farmed the land ("The Man with the Hoe"). But when the human lodges itself exclusively in that part of the psyche that responds to patriotic fervor only to scoff at private revelation, great areas of spiritual possibility die. John Henry and the famous "Village Smithy" of Longfellow's poem represent an ideal of the Industrial Revolution, for example—man as machine. Yes, the Blacksmith is permitted a tear or two at Sunday services when he thinks of his departed wife, but in the final stanzas of the poem the hammer returns. Feelings, when all is said and done, are a damp hanky, sissy stuff amidst the real getting and spending job of life, and ought to be able to be jammed back into one's pocket:

> Toiling,—rejoicing,—sorrowing,
>   Onward through life he goes;
> Each morning sees some task begin,
>   Each evening sees it close;
> Something attempted, something done,
>   Has earned a night's repose.
>
> Thanks, thanks to thee, my worthy friend,
>   For the lesson thou hast taught!
> Thus at the flaming forge of life
>   Our fortunes must be wrought;
> Thus on its sounding anvil shaped
>   Each burning deed and thought.

It is the image of the muscular smith that dominates the poem; everybody remembers the description of the first stanza, which utterly overwhelms the two stanzas given over, out of eight, to the feeling life. Here, then, is a portrait of the Good Life circa 1840, when black men wore chains perhaps forged by Longfellow's industrious smith, and the U.S. Government had embarked upon a campaign of systematic extermination of the American Indian tribes east of the Mississippi. And John Henry never makes it out of his song alive.

As documents, therefore, and not as specimens of great poetry, these chestnuts are of incalculable importance. Each of them shaped our lives, for the people and attitudes in them were held up to us as models of civilization for a hundred years. In the reading of them the actors on these recordings have

themselves a field day. Perfectly understandable, for today these poems must be acted. They must be bitten and gnarled and crooned out because they are precisely performances in a museum of attitudes which have in great part outlived their usefulness for us. For those of us who believe that human spiritual life as expressed in poetry can never be frozen in suits of armor, in bloody shakos, or in unquestioning salutes.

As to the role of these poems in the "Elementary Curriculum," as the titles of these albums suggest, I say No. In the first place, most grammar school students won't understand half of the words in them, and the real impact these poems will have on those in the early years of education will be to convince them that poetry must be rhymed with a heavy beat. It will not be matter that impresses young listeners here, but music—although I am certain that the content of these poems would have its insidious effect. Play them for your students and poetry will lodge in their brains forever as ta-BOOM ta-BOOM and life-strife. Let Dr. Seuss do his idiotic work in the homes, but leave rhyme and meter for high school, when it can be properly handled. Very few poets now at work tailor their poems to a rhyme and a beat, and my experience has been that most of the battles a teacher of poetry-writing has to fight in the schools takes place exactly in this arena. "But that isn't a poem!" screams the talented fifteen year old, "It doesn't rhyme, it doesn't scan,—it doesn't *sound* like a poem!" These recordings clearly exhibit what poetry *did* sound like, but not what it sounds like now. Poetry, if indeed it is to *be* poetry, follows the pulse of contemporary life, and our daily experience of the world has shown us for some time that our lives can no longer be tied neatly in the pleasant bow of the rhymed couplet. Take a look at the headlines on today's paper if you don't believe it! For hundreds of years rhyme and meter coalesced in living demonstration of the fact that God was in his heaven and all was right with the world. The horrors of World War I blew that to pieces, and the Nazi extermination camps supplied the *coup de grace*. In our time, and well before it, poetry has moved towards the human speaking voice in all its complexity and richness, towards the way people really talk. Today's poets cleave to that voice, purifying and heightening it in thousands of individual ways, realizing the hope that Wordsworth expressed in his Preface to the *Lyrical Ballads* (1849): "I answer that the language of such Poetry as is here recommended is, as far as possible, a selection of the language really spoken by men." While Wordsworth was dreaming of a new poetic diction, in America Walt Whitman was making it come true, and in the *Leaves of Grass* that he wrote, set type for, and paid out of his own pocket to print in 1855, our real literary Declaration of Independence was set forth for all future American poets to sign. By offering us these chestnuts as real poems fit for elementary school children, these recordings ask us to refuse to enter our own century and our own unique patterns of speech.

So keep these records aside for high school students. Discuss the poems as museum pieces, not as life lived now. If you must give your students rhyme and meter, give them Keats and Shelley and Shakespeare and the host of great poets whose works line the shelves of any respectable library. The poems on these recordings are, for the most part, entertainment, and at worst, unadulterated jingoism. There may be, though, another way to use them. From my own grammar and high school days I remember hilarious parodies of "Paul Revere's Ride," "A Visit from St. Nicholas," and other poems. One began:

'Twas the night before Christmas
    And all through the house,
Not a creature was stirring,
    Not even a louse.

The teacher was hung
    Near a package from CARE,
In hopes that the garbageman
    Soon would be there.

And on and on into the night. *Mad* magazine has specialized in these kinds of sendups for years, and most kids are more than familiar with them. But even before *Mad* parodied these "classics" (first with visuals and then with actual rewrites), kids were busy combatting the corn dumped on them by the school anthologies. I suggest, then, that a few of these poems be dittoed up specially for the purpose of parody—an activity that will embrace the natural tendency kids have for "making fun." You can first discuss the notion of parody, read a few examples of the genre (why not use *Mad*?), distribute copies of the poems, and let the class go to town. Reading the finished products should be a hilarious, and instructive, experience. For the sad fact is that so many of the poems on these recordings that were jammed down our throats in school fall easy prey to being stood on their heads, and that is something that has made them suspect all along. (B.Z.)

SMALL VOICE, BIG VOICE, songs and commentary by Dick Lourie & Jed (Folkways Records FC 7547, $6.98).

Dick Lourie is a poet who has worked for years as Poet-in-Residence in elementary and secondary schools. On this record he sings and plays songs he wrote for kids ages three through nine, and he's helped by a kid named Jed. Most of them invite us to

join in with verses of our own, or to write our own lyrics entirely. They are simple, sweet songs, in the tradition of Woody Guthrie's children's songs, and they remind us that the pleasures of singing need not be complicated, that we can sing about anything we want so long as we know we can do it with love. In the printed brochure which accompanies the record Lourie tells us how he feels about his songs and suggests ways they can be used by the listener, inside the classroom or out. (R.P.)

TREASURY OF 100 MODERN AMERICAN POETS. Produced by Arthur Luce Klein and edited by Paul Kresh (Spoken Arts). Package: $117.00; $6.50 per disc.

Volume I: Edgar Lee Masters, James Weldon Johnson, Gertrude Stein, Robert Frost, Carl Sandburg.
Volume II: Wallace Stevens, Witter Bynner, Max Eastman, William Carlos Williams, Louis Untermeyer.
Volume III: Ezra Pound, William Rose Benet, John Hall Wheelock, H.D. (Hilda Doolittle).
Volume XVII: John Ashbery, James Wright, Peter Davison, Donald Hall, Anne Sexton, Adrienne Rich.

The scope and inclusiveness of this series, which is a kind of Noah's Ark of American Poetry, is staggering: 18 records, 464 poems. To review the whole package would involve me in a "review" of American Poetry in the Twentieth Century—no thanks! No one will love all of these poets, and as in any anthology—in print or on vinyl—the listener will have to pick and choose among his or her favorites, with one eye toward classroom presentation. Some of the originals from which these recordings have been taken are old and scratchy and should not be approached without the text at the students' disposal, others are studio-recorded and bright as icicles. Spoken Arts has supplied short and generally excellent biographies of the authors listing their books and various achievements. A teacher will find these useful. In fact, I would recommend that these—and all—library recordings be used in two ways: first, for a "raw" listening to the work, without the printed text; second, listening to the poets read their poems as the students follow the published work line by line. The first listening will acclimatize the ear to poetry-hearing, the second will reinforce the first: poetry is primarily a print medium.

Of the recordings listed above, I particularly enjoyed the squeaky Venusian midwest voice of Edgar Lee Masters, James Weldon Johnson's booming oratorical shout, and the toughness of Robert Frost's delivery, so unlike the sweet, doddering old man who squinted over the smoking podium at John F. Kennedy's inauguration. And how slow and boring Wallace Stevens is! And how friendly, natural, and passionate a reader William Carlos Williams, before the strokes that cracked his voice (listen to *William Carlos Williams Reads His Poetry*, Caedmon TC 1047, for a later, startling contrast, though the beauty of the poetry is never eroded). Ezra Pound's throat rattles with phlegm, and the silence that was to engulf him in later years seems at times a syllable away; and yet the three *Cantos* he reads (# 3, # 49—and not *Canto 38* as the album lists—and # 106) have a dazzling beauty, like troves of gold and bronze. The younger poets on Volume XVII provide various pleasures—John Ashbery's crisp renderings; James Wright's beautiful and mysterious poem, "Rain"; Anne Sexton's hard elegiacs; and the careful weight Adrienne Rich extends to each word.

Other records in this series contain readings by Eliot, Ransom, Roethke, Bishop, Patchen, Jarrell, Berryman, Levertov, Plath, and dozens of others. To all this I add my one meek complaint: the dates when the poets recorded their works should have been listed. (B.Z.)

WISHES, LIES AND DREAMS: TEACHING CHIL-
    DREN TO WRITE POETRY, with Kenneth Koch
    and students from P.S. 61 in New York City.
    Directed by Natalie Slohm, presented by Arthur
    Luce Klein (Spoken Arts SA 1101).

I don't know any better introduction to poetry on records than this one. Its first advantage is that many of the students (from grades one through six at P.S. 61 in Manhattan) who wrote the poems, read them; or have them read by their classmates. The readers— Lynn Bonner, Fontessa Moore, Jeff Morley, Marion Mackles, Mayra Morales, and Markus Niebanck—do a spendid job, and never ham things up. Structuring the readings, which were generated by poetry writing classes given at the school by Koch, are his succinct and pleasant explanations of what is to follow. (The texts, of course, are available in his *Wishes, Lies, and Dreams*, published in paperback by Vintage Books.)

Koch (and his producers at Spoken Arts) have had the good sense to put in big and small poems—which should give elementary school listeners the idea that even one good line is worth writing down. Whether one chooses to adopt the *Wishes, Lies, and Dreams* approach or not, this record is a definite "turn on," for, rather than the gushy theatrical approach of actors-reading-for-children, or adults-writing-for-children, we have here the Real Thing. (B.Z.)

MIRACLES: POEMS WRITTEN BY CHILDREN,
    collected by Richard Lewis. Read by Julie Harris
    and Roddy McDowall (Caedmon TV 1227).

Written by children, but not *read* by them. And that is the overriding fault of this collection—the

actor's approach to poetry. Though I find Julie Harris' readings generally inoffensive (though, expectedly, marred by overdramatization), Roddy McDowall is intolerable. His voice, with its "cultivated" semi-English accent, throws many of the poems completely out of joint, making him sound like all those funny teachers we laughed at in school, and passing that fussiness on to poetry itself, which hardly ever outlives these associations.

Like *Wishes, Lies, and Dreams*, the texts of these poems—some of them beautiful pieces of work—are available in *Miracles* (Simon & Schuster, hardcover only), a book too famous to need further comment here. (B.Z.)

TOUGH POEMS FOR TOUGH PEOPLE, edited by
    Florence Howe. Read by Ruby Dee, Ossie Davis,
    and Henry Braun (Caedmon TC 1396).

Henry Braun's positively unctuous rendering of a Lou Lipsitz poem starts this record off on a huge wrong foot, but the majority of this collection ("the choices of high school and college students in Mississippi, Chicago, and Baltimore," the liner notes tell us) is in the hands of two superb actors—Ruby Dee and Ossie Davis. Mr. Davis generally reads with dignity and restraint, and gives an excellent interpretatation of Etheridge Knight's powerful poem, "The Idea of Ancestry." Ms. Dee, however, ranges between hissing overdramatization ("We Real Cool" by Gwendolyn Brooks) and clarity (Adrienne Rich's "In the Evening"). Once again, however, poetry finds itself at the mercy of the actor, someone who seems to feel that visual absence must be made up for by interpretative hokum. Oh, for the simple voices of poets, who surprisingly seem to have much more a sense of proportion about how their own work should sound. (B.Z.)

PROMISES . . . TO BE KEPT: YOUNG POETS-TO-
    BE READ FROM THEIR WORKS, selected and
    edited by Susan Sherman. Directed by Paul Kresh.
    Presented by Arthur Luce Klein (Spoken Arts SA
    1099).

The cover of this LP just about sums it up: a Victorian little girl (staff in one hand, Red Riding Hood basket in the other) emerging from a Victorian wood in a Victorian engraving. Hearing these thirteen-year-olds read their Victorian poems in 1975 makes one wonder why Ezra Pound and T.S. Eliot ever bothered to fight their battles for literary modernism. This record is *that* retrograde. Oh sure, in the 74 poems included, a few sound like real kids reading real poems, but 95 percent of them are straight out of the Wispy Cloud School of Children's Verse—about as edible as a overdecorated party cake a hundred years old. With no introductory commentary, I played several of these poems for a group of young friends of mine, all poets, all between the ages of 11 and 13, all of the female sex. They couldn't help miming the poems spontaneously in "Oh golly gee!" gesturings, and when we discussed the poems afterwards the comments ranged from "spoiled brat poetry" to "sickeningly pretty." This record is not without its uses however. It ought to be played for kids to show them exactly all the things poetry *shouldn't* be. (B.Z.)

POETRY-IN-THE-ROUND: A POETRY WORK-SHOP, narration and poems by George Abbe (Folkways Records, FI 9164).

This recording is nearly fifteen years old, and, in all kindness, may have been an important departure when it was released. George Abbe's methodology is (or was): Read one of your own poems to kids and have them write down their interpretation of it. The matter of this presentation may be found on Side 1, which contains Abbe's rather startling conception of poetry's usefulness:

The importance of music and painting in the treatment of the mentally ill has universal acceptance. The therapeutic value of poetry, for everybody, deserves similar recognition. Of all the arts, it may have the greatest power to probe and release subconscious conflict.

Much of the best poetry from earliest times has been subconsciously, not consciously, written. Poets have expressed themselves *under compulsion* to relieve inner tension.

That is, "All poets are crazy, and if you read their work you'll feel better." What follows—Abbe's reading of one of his rather mediocre poems and numerous responses to it from grammar and high school students—has got to be one of the most courageous acts or one of the biggest ego trips on record. My responses to his approach are perhaps best expressed in the interpretation voiced by one sixth grader:

The animals knew they were in God's world, and they hushed so they could be sure that they were not doing wrong. The people on the sidewalk were small. They were not as big as God, but they were very kind. . . .

That's a beautiful summary of the colonialized intelligence this method fosters. The grown up poet (God) is nice enough to allow the little animals (kids) into his world (the classroom, or the poem, or the fact of being "taken seriously" by a grown up), and of course for this privilege good kids keep their mouths shut "so they could be sure that they were not doing

wrong." Though small (not as big as the God-poet), they were "very kind," probably because, like all colonized peoples, they had little choice.(B.Z.)

SOUNDS AND ULTRA-SOUNDS OF THE BOTTLE-NOSE DOLPHIN, recorded and edited by John C. Lilly, M.D. (Folkways FX 6132, $6.98).
SONGS OF THE HUMPBACK WHALE (Capitol ST-620, $5.98).
BIRD SONG AND BIRD BEHAVIOR, by Donald J. Borrer (Dover lp 22779-0, includes 32 pp. booklet, $3).

SOUNDS AND ULTRA-SOUNDS is fascinating. On it John Lilly sets out some basic material derived from his research on sound communication between dolphins and vocal exchanges between humans and dolphins, the same material presented in his books *Man and Dolphin* (Pyramid Books) and *The Mind of the Dolphin* (Avon). He introduces recorded segments from lab tapes in which dolphins communicate with each other (one incredible band features them set against a background of snapping shrimp), others in which dolphins mimic human sounds. Lilly's presentation is clear, the sounds of the dolphins chillingly intelligent. This record would be marvelous for any science class, but it could also be used to stimulate classroom discussions of language and to help kids see the world from an underwater point of view.

It might well be used as a lead-in to SONGS OF THE HUMPBACK WHALE, where the whale sounds are independently produced and more extended than those of the dolphins on the Lilly record, hence more available for guess-translation.

Donald Borrer's BIRD SONG AND BIRD BEHAVIOR is a pretty and interesting record, and a steal at $3. Sometimes it's unintentionally funny when it veers close to self-parody, as in the case of "a Carolina wren with rather loud truck noise in the background." The next band, though, repeats the material with the truck noise filtered out—it was educational! Actually it's a very likeable record, partly because birds usually make such nice sounds. The added interest of considering these nice sounds to be forms of communication can lead us to other areas, such as guess-translation. Recorded bird calls don't lend themselves to this very well, because they are usually so brief that kids naturally imagine the birds to be saying things such as, "Hi," or "It's a nice day."

I suppose one could easily go overboard with this type of material—as I suspect someone has done in producing the beautifully recherché SOUNDS OF NORTH AMERICAN FROGS (Folkways)—but the idea that the earth is populated by creatures which "speak their language" (hence are less alien to us than we might have thought) is one which could help develop the idea in children that different languages and species are to be respected, not dismissed. (R.P.)

BIBLIOGRAPHY OF SPANISH LANGUAGE RECORDINGS

by Julio Marzán

(Note: Since it would be impossible to comment on the value of each poem for classroom use, the teacher should be forewarned that the following brief recordings are largely best suited for an advanced group of students, although a careful examination might help the teacher make his or her own judgment.)

ANTOLOGIA ORAL; POESIA HISPANOAMERICANA DEL SIGLO XX/ORAL ANTHOLOGY; SPANISH-AMERICAN POETRY OF THE 20th CENTURY. Recorded by Octavio Corvalan. Folkways Records FL 9926.
The lists of poets aside, the selection of poems ranges from the good to the rhetorical to the corny. Mr. Corvalan's voice is not engaging and at times monotonous. Texts and translations included.

GOLDEN TREASURY OF MODERN SPANISH VERSE READ BY EUGENIO FLORIT. Spoken Arts SA913.
A fine selection of Spanish poets of the generation of '98, the era of Juan Ramon Jimenez (generation of 1925), and the postwar generation. Mr. Florit reads well. Spanish texts included.

THE GOLDEN TREASURY OF SPANISH AMERICAN VERSE READ BY MANUEL DURAN. Spoken Arts SA839.
A foolproof selection of Spanish-American masterpieces from colonial times to Modernism. A praiseworthy choice read with controlled enthusiasm by Mr. Duran. Spanish texts and commentaries.

JUAN RAMON JIMENEZ READING HIS POETRY IN SPANISH. Caedmon TC1079.
A good selection, although Mr. Jimenez did not excel as a reader. The reading, however, is adequate. No texts.

PABLO NERUDA READING HIS POETRY. (In Spanish). Caedmon TC 1215.
Good sound quality and Neruda's resounding delivery. One of the highlights: the entire *Heights of Macchu Picchu*. No texts.

POEMS OF FREDERICO GARCIA LORCA. Read in Spanish by Jorge Juan Rodriguez. Folkways FL 9580.
A broad selection of Lorca's best poems in a two-record album. Read well, although at times a bit histrionically, by Jorge Juan Rodriguez. Spanish texts and biographical data.

Books

Selected Poems, Kenneth Patchen (New Directions, N.Y., $1.50, 145 pp.).

SELECTED POEMS OF KENNETH PATCHEN READ BY KENNETH PATCHEN (Folkways Records, N.Y., 12'' lp record, $6.98).

KENNETH PATCHEN READS WITH JAZZ IN CANADA, with the Alan Neil Quartet (Folkways Records, N.Y. 12'' lp, $6.98).

The haunting tone, mysterious atmosphere, undercurrent of bitterness which explodes in anger, the surprising, almost otherworldly sweetness, these are typical of Patchen's writing, qualities which make his work accessible to sensitive high school kids. Poems such as "Do the Dead Know What Time It Is?," "The Reason for Skylarks," "She knows it's raining. .," "I Feel Drunk All the Time," "The Origin of Baseball," "For Whose Adornment," "The State of the Nation," "The Murder of Two Men by a Young Kid Wearing Lemon-colored Gloves," "The Lute in the Attic," "The Oranges Bears," plus any of the last 15 poems in the book would be good ones to present to students and let them take it from there.

These last 15 poems are from Patchen's *Because It Is,* an absolutely delightful collection of "nonsense" poems with drawings by Patchen. No age limit on these.

Patchen's reading manner is brooding and powerful; he's not one of your anemic types. The strength of his personality comes through his voice and surrounds you. The reading with jazz was a nice try, but eventually it gets tiresome. The Folkways SELECTED POEMS record makes a nice complement to the New Directions book. (R.P.)

Rose, Where Did You Get That Red: Teaching Great Poetry to Children, by Kenneth Koch (Random House hardcover, $7.95, Vintage ppbk., $2.45, 360 pp.).

Kenneth Koch has followed *Wishes, Lies & Dreams*, his exemplary volume on teaching poetry writing to children, with another exemplary volume, this one on teaching great poetry to children. He gives us ten lessons, in which poems by the "masters" are discussed and imitated by kids. Specifically, poems by Blake, Herrick, Donne, Shakespeare, Whitman,

Stevens, Williams, Lorca, Ashbery and Rimbaud are discussed in ways that make them as accessible as they really are, and kids are shown how they can write poems inspired by these models.

Let's face it: Koch is a master himself, both as poet and teacher. He has the breathtaking ability to go straight to the heart of what is beautiful and pleasureable in poetry. With Blake's poem "The Tyger," for example, he first points out that the speaker in the poem is questioning a mysterious tiger. "Tiger, how did you get the way you are?" Most poetry teachers would get bogged down in Symbolism, or reluctantly pass by the poem as too "difficult" for "children."

When *Wishes, Lies & Dreams* appeared, teachers loved it, but some asked, "How about teaching adult poetry to children?" In some cases they meant Walter de la Mare, Longfellow, Alfred Noyes, etc. But in others they meant, "How do I teach really good adult poetry to kids?" This book provides a wonderful methodology for doing that. It also includes lots of poems by kids inspired by the models, as well as further models and a curious selection of poems by kids in Swaziland, poems written after reading *Wishes, Lies & Dreams*. (R.P.)

Pedagogy of the Oppressed, by Paulo Freire, translated from the Portugese by Myra Bergman Ramos (The Seabury Press, N.Y., 1970), $2.95 ppbk., 186 pp.).

Paulo Freire, a Brazilian leftist champion of the Third World, has written a book that is both a philosphical and passionate critique of education in a large sense of the word. Working with the impoverished, "oppressed" peasants of Brazil, he came to see education not as a process by which people are filled up with facts, but as one by which a person becomes able to examine his situation critically in a dialogical encounter with the world. More specifically, he discusses how curricula can be developed from the real-life situations of those in the process of being educated, rather than imposing on them an irrelevant system of facts.

Although as a leftist, he is sure to be viewed with suspicion by many, his real passion is for human sympathy, social benevolence and intellectual clarity. Thus, while he deplores capitalistic oppression, he is equally against a revolution based on propaganda and violence, which in his view is just another system imposed on a helpless people. He is such a sane humanitarian that his views will doubtless be unwelcome among the governments of the Left or the Right.

I should add, in this simplistic summary, that his writing is repetitive and somewhat abstract, but while one yearns for less repetition and more detailed examples, one is all the while glowing with the warmth of conscience and intellect that emanates from the pages of his book. If you come home every day tired from school, you will probably not have the energy to read this book quickly. If you sometimes wonder why you go to school at all, this is a book you'll enjoy reading slowly. (R.P.)

Poets in the Schools, the Connecticut Commission on the Arts Poetry Program (1972-1973), written and edited mostly by Kathleen Meagher, supervised by Richard Place, and published by the Connecticut Commission on the Arts, 340 Capitol Ave., Hartford, Conn. 06106.

Most state arts councils publish an annual report similar to those published by corporations for their stockholders. In some cases these reports amount to little more than gestures toward good public relations, assuring the legislator and taxpayer that it was a great year for us all and that their public money was well spent. The Connecituct Arts Commission, on the other hand, is establishing an honorable tradition for itself in presenting lengthy, personal and diverse reports which give us a pretty good idea of how they work, from administrator through artist to student. Occasionally their reports contain information which is surprising in light of the fact that it is being issued by a state agency. (R.P.)

American Indian Prose and Poetry: We Wait in the Darkness, edited and introduced by Gloria Levitas, Frank Robert Vivelo, and Jacqueline J. Vivelo (G.P. Putnam's Sons/Capricorn Books, New York, 1974), paperback.

This collection is yet another culling from existent books and monographs on American Indian life and "letters," but is worthy to stand beside Margot Astrov's *American Indian Prose and Poetry (The Winged Serpent)* as one of the best anthologies of the subject. Arranged by geographical area and, within that, by tribe, the book boasts an intelligent introduction and an extensive bibliography, including sections on written works by American Indians, and on American Indian periodicals. The editors have steered clear of selections marred by the verbal Victorianisms of ethnological field workers, and this anthology can be picked over for classroom use. (B.Z.)

Eskimo Songs and Stories, collected by Knud Rasmussen, selected and translated by Edward Field, with illustrations by Kiakshuk and Pudlo (Delacorte Press/Seymour Lawrence, New York, 1973), $4.95, hardcover only.

Collected by Danish explorer Knud Rasmussen on his Fifth Thule Expedition through Arctic, these Netsilik Eskimo poems have been beautifully reworked (*not* "translated from the original language") by poet Edward Field into a language that escapes the translatese in which most "primitive poetry" often finds itself cast. Their language is simple and ice-bright, and for that catches the nobility of these "people of the seal" whom Rasmussen sought out because of their remoteness from then-contemporary civilization (1921-24). Though this is a "children's book," these poems can be appreciated by anyone, and would light up any curriculum of Native American studies. A special treat are the prints of two Eskimo artists, Kiakshuk and Pudlo, which work hand in hand with the poems. This book includes a few helpful pages of introduction, biographies of the two artists, and brief bibliography of suggested reading. It's a crying shame there's no inexpensive paperback edition of the book. (B.Z.)

Printing It: A Guide to Graphic Techniques for the Impecunious, by Clifford Burke, illustrations by Chuck Miller (Wingbow Press, San Francisco), paperback. Available from Bookpeople, 2940 Seventh St., Berkeley, CA 94710.

This is an important book not only for anyone who has never "printed it," and who wants to, but also for those experienced in turning out magazines or books who want to sharpen up their basics. Burke, one of the West Coast's legendary geniuses of the printerly craft, has put his hard-won knowledge between covers. He tells all: from the offset printing process and how it is done, through design, paste-up, mechanicals, paper, binding, layout—you name it. There's none of the snobbishness—"Oh, you know what I'm talking about" (so I don't have to explain it clearly)—that often besets other how-to-do-it books of this sort: Burke is clear and decisive, will tell you which pencils are best. This book should be read from cover to cover, it's that chock-full of info. An indispensible guide for anyone who's decided they want to memorialize their students' writing in a form more palatable than the school rexo machine, but who has to do it on a budget. (B.Z.)

The Voice That Is Great Within Us: American Poetry of the Twentieth Century. Edited by Hayden

Carruth (Bantam, N.Y., 1970), $1.95 ppbk. 722 pp.

Two dollars for over seven hundred pages of *anything* is hard to beat these days. Carruth's catholicity of taste and the extent of his homework—reading the entire published work of these 136 poets, for instance—are thoroughly commendable. While most poets would have made very different selections, there's no question that this book would be a nice one to have available for really interested students (high school, or if a few naughty words don't bother you, junior high). (R.P.)

The Haiku Anthology, edited with an introduction by Cor van den Heuvel (Doubleday Anchor Books, Garden City, New York, 1974), $2.95 ppbk, 278 pp.

The Haiku Anthology gives us some very good poems, as well as the very good feeling that there are talented and serious poets working well in a form which too often is regarded as a diminutive, simple, instant form of poetic candy. It also gives us the welcome idea that haiku is not a fixed form: it is one which grows with time. Includes a bibliography and an interesting appendix in which the term *haiku* is defined, along with its look-alikes *hokku, haiki* and *senryu*. Good for any grade level. (R.P.)

Mind Games by Robert Masters and Jean Houston (Delta), $2.75, 246 pp.

Subtitled *The Guide to Inner Space*, this book, by the authors of *The Varieties of Psychedelic Experience*, is not to be confused with *The Varieties of Religious Experience* or with the work of sexual therapists Masters and Johnson, though it all seems to be reverberating inside the same big cultural drum.

Mind Games lays out a series of meditational exercises which are designed to deepen and/or enlarge one's idea of human inner space. Some of the exercises sound like Teachers & Writers poetry assignments (cf. "Visionary Anthropology, the exploration and study of imaginal worlds" and Richard Murphy's *imaginary Worlds*, or the very first exericse in the book, which follows the same procedure as Tom Veitch's "Trapdoor Method" described in the present publication). Much of the material in *Mind Games* could be adapted to classroom use, provided that it's done with tact and good sense. Generally it's interesting to see ways of using the mind which were exclusively Eastern now being presented to the West in purely Western terms. Unfortunately the book is written in a droning, mechanical style which precludes even a suggestion of humor, so that while the content is fascinating, it leaves one feeling a little glum, as if you had just spent the last several hours conversing in a monotone. (R.P.)

The Norton Anthology of Modern Poetry, edited by Richard Ellman and Robert O'Clair (Norton), $9.95 paperback. 456 pp.

Do you remember the old Jackie Gleason Show and the character Art Carney played in "The Honeymooners"? He played Norton, the sewer worker. At long last a book we have all been waiting for and needing so desperately, *The Norton Anthology of Modern Poetry*.

Seriously, though, you might be amazed to learn that "modern poetry" means you were not modern if you wrote in a language other than English, because all the poets in this book did. No Apollinaire, no Neruda, no Mayakovsky, no Leopardi, etc. Hence the title is distorted, as is the preposterous back cover note which states that "this is needed for a college course in modern American and British poetry." My suggestion, then, is to tear off the front and back covers.

Inside the covers we are given generous selections from the work of 148 poets, from Walt Whitman (b. 1819) to James Tate (b. 1943), with detailed biographical and critical notes, indices, suggested further reading, a preface, and an introduction. A massive job!

Poets such as myself, reviewing anthologies of poetry, tend to be persnickety. I deplore certain omissions (*e.g.* Charles Reznikoff, F.T. Prince, John Wheelwright, Kenneth Patchen, Lorine Niedecker, Philip Whalen, George Oppen, John Wieners, Edwin Denby, Jack Spicer, Reed Whittemore, Helen Adam, David Schubert, Ian Hamilton Finlay, Jack Kerouac, for starters). I climb the walls with rage on seeing hundreds of little footnote numbers growing like carbuncles on the poems. I pound on my desk when I find incorrect factual material (*e.g.* Ted Berrigan does not currently teach at the University of Iowa; Dick Gallup was not born in 1942). I groan when I'm told that "excellent poems are still being written." But I also appreciate the tremendous scholarly intelligence and labor that goes into making such a massive and minutely detailed book, and, unlike some others, I welcome a new poetry anthology. Although the present one is unsuitable for little kids, it would be nice to see it in high school libraries. (R.P.)

Math, Writing & Games in the Open Classroom, by Herbert R. Kohl (A New York Review Book). Paperback 252 pp.

Herb Kohl has become a young old master of open education. The author of *36 Children, The Open Classroom*, and *Reading, How to* has come through once again with a book on education that is at once readable, intelligent, sincere, inventive, practical and sympathetic! Quite a tall order to fill, but Kohl does it.

In this book he reports on his investigations into teaching writing and math in ways that were interesting for his students. But he has gone beyond, say, the use of word games, into games themselves. For me this is the heart of the book, where he demonstrates how, through playing traditional games and inventing new ones, children can be led to a sense of their own intelligence. Kohl relates how he, his students and his own children revised traditional games, such as checkers and chess, and how they invented entirely new ones. (Diagrams are included.)

The idea, roughly stated, was not only to encourage inventiveness, but to suggest to the children that they had the power to participate actively in their environment, that they were not victims of circumstance who must passively accept whatever is given them. You see young people hitting the trail, building their own houses, living in the woods: books such as Kohl's will encourage them to be as bold and free and happy with their intellects. (R.P.)

The Ant's Forefoot, the poetry journal edited by poet-teacher David Rosenberg, has received a special grant to publish issues devoted to children's writing. David will devote issues 13 to 16 to this project, which will present poems by Larry Fagin, Ron Padgett and Rosenberg himself, alongside the work of three kid poets (Jonathan Rosenstein, Wayne Padgett and Turan Wright) who have been writing for at least a year with the adult poet. It is hoped that the four issues will illuminate the cross-fertilization that takes place when adults show kids how writing can become art.

Subscriptions for the 4 issues are $8.00 postpaid. Address orders and/or manuscripts to David Rosenberg, 29 St. Marks Pl., New York, N.Y. 10003.

General Anthologies (Laura Gilpin)

Naked Poetry: Recent American Poetry in Open Forms, edited by Stephen Berg and Robert Mezey, (Bobbs-Merrill Co., Inc., 1969), $2.95.

A good place to begin if you're feeling confused about what's happened to poetry since Robert Frost. The emphasis here is on free verse or "open" forms and, within that context, covers a broad spectrum of different styles and voices. The nineteen poets included here are so well represented that the reader has a sense of them not only as poets but as people. Also includes photographs of the poets and essays by most of them on using the "open" form. *Naked Poetry, Volume II* is expected to be out soon and if it's anything like Vol. I, it should be a welcomed addition to the anthology market.

The New American Poetry, edited by Donald Allen, (Grove Press, Inc., 1960), $2.95.

A short course in the history of American poetry from 1945-1960. The poets are arranged in the groups or schools that each was identified with, including the Black Mountain Poets, San Francisco Renaissance, Beat Generation, and the New York School. Also includes a section of essays by some of the poets. Although some important poets were left out because they were never associated with a particular School, this is one of the few anthologies that actually traces the course of how poetry became what it is today.

Contemporary American Poetry, Revised and Enlarged Edition, edited by Donald Hall, (Penguin Books, 1972), $2.25.

Includes fairly good selections of all the better known poets, although it leaves out many good but lesser known ones. The poets are listed chronologically by year of birth. The younger poets are not well represented, but the ground that is covered, is covered well.

The Voice That Is Great Within Us: American Poetry of the Twentieth Century, edited by Hayden Carruth, (Bantam Books, 1970), $1.95.

Also listed chronologically, this anthology begins much earlier than the Hall anthology (going back to Robert Frost) and also includes many lesser known poets that are too often overlooked. But because of the huge number of poets included, the selections tend to be sketchy, often relying on only two or three poems to represent each poet. Considering that it covers sixty years of American poetry (for only $1.95), it's well worth the price.

The Contemporary American Poets: American Poetry Since 1940, edited by Mark Strand, (Meridian Books, 1969), $3.95.

The emphasis here is on younger poets, listed alphabetically. A reliable anthology, giving a sense of where poetry is going rather than where it's come from.

The American Poetry Anthology, edited by Daniel Halpern, Equinox Books, (Avon, 1975), $5.95.

Brand new and so up-to-date that many of the poets are still relatively unknown. Everyone in it is under forty, which includes some of the best poets writing today who have emerged only within the last few years. A very good picture of what's happening today.

Women's Anthologies

No More Masks! An Anthology of Poems by Women, edited by Florence Howe and Ellen Bass, (Doubleday Anchor Books, 1973), $3.95.

A history of women as poets arranged chronologically from Amy Lowell to young poets writing today. One of the few women's anthologies that doesn't push for a particular point of view other than that of women saying what they have to say. A very good anthology showing the range and variation throughout the century of poetry by women.

Rising Tides: Twentieth Century American Women Poets, edited by Laura Chester and Sharon Barba, (Washington Square Press, 1973), $1.95.

A history of women's ideas rather than a history of women's poetry. Being feminist in its point of view, it leaves out some important poets making it somewhat incomplete as a collection of women's writing. But it does include many of the younger relatively unknown poets whose work isn't included in many anthologies. Also includes photographs of each poet.

We Become New: Poems by Contemporary American Women, edited by Lucille Iverson and Kathryn Ruby, (Bantam Books, 1975), $2.25.

An interesting collection of women poets, both known and unknown, who write from a feminist point of view. Arranged neither chronologically nor alphabetically but in what the editors call "a musical arrangement," which creates a very strong effect by the end.

Black Anthologies (Comments by Wesley Brown)

Black Poets, edited by Dudley Randall, (Bantam Books, 1971), $1.65.

A very comprehensive anthology including poets from the eighteenth century to the present.

Soulscript, edited by June Jordan, (Doubleday, 1970), $1.75.

Natural Process, edited by Ted Wilentz and Tom Weatherly, (Hill and Wang, 1970), $1.95.

Two good anthologies of black poets of the sixties and seventies, including many young, relatively unknown poets.

SPANISH LANGUAGE POETRY IN TRANSLATION: AN ANNOTATED BIBLIOGRAPHY OF BILINGUAL EDITIONS.
by Julio Marzán

The following is a list of Spanish language bilingual poetry books briefly reviewed for their general merit as translations and for their usefulness to teachers. Teachers with some knowledge of Spanish should keep in mind that books not highly rated for their translations may be quite valuable because of their selections. Oftentimes bilingual books provide a "selected works" of a poet at a much lower price than one would pay at a foreign language book store.

Benson, Rachel, *Nine Latin American Poets*. Las Americas Publishing Co., New York, 1968. Cloth, no price.

The nine poets in this volume are: José Gorostiza (Mexico), Vicente Huidobro (Chile), Pablo Neruda (Chile), Luis Palés Matos (Puerto Rico), Octavio Paz (Mexico), Carlos Pellicer (Mexico), Alfonsina Storni (Argentina), César Vallejo (Perú), Xavier Villaurrutia (Mexico). All these writers appear in different more recent anthologies, but this collection presents a good introduction to their work in one volume. (Las Americas Books are not well distributed; teachers may request price from publisher at 152 E. 23rd St., N.Y. 10010.)

Bishop, Elizabeth and Emanuel Brasil, ed., *An Anthology of 20th Century Brazilian Poetry*. Wesleyan University Press, Middletown, Conn., 1972. Cloth and Paper.

Fourteen contemporary Brazilian poets admirably translated by 16 American poets. This book was sponsored by the Academy of American Poets. Something in the Brazilian voice makes this poetry appealing and would serve very well in the classroom. Highly recommended.

Caracciolo-Trejo, Enrique, ed., *The Penguin Book of Latin American Verse*. Penguin, Baltimore, 1971, 150pp.

A collection of leading late nineteenth century and early twentieth century poets. Each poem is accompanied by a *prose* translation which might make this anthology more useful for a Spanish (language) class.

Guillén, Nicolás, *Patria o Muerte: The Great Zoo and Other Poems*, trans. & ed. by Robert Márquez. Monthly Review Press, New York, 1972, 233pp.

Guillén, Nicolás. *Man-Making Words: Selected Poems*

of N. Guillén, trans. & ed. by Robert Márquez and David Arthur MacMurray. University of Mass. Press, 1972, 214pp.

Cuba's national poet excellently translated. The poetry ranges from Guillén's personal experience as a mulatto in the New World to poems about the contemporary social and political history, all seen through the eyes of a revolutionary consciousness. Their biting wit and engaging rhythms are lost in translation.

Hays, H.R., ed., *Spanish American Poets*. Beacon Press, Boston, 1972, 336pp.

Originally published in 1943, this anthology includes poems by Neruda, Vallejo and Borges available elsewhere. The other nine may not be as familiar although all appear in later collections or anthologies. Some of Nicolás Guillén's best early Afro-Antillean poems not found in the Guillén anthologies are superbly translated in this collection, as are the poems of Huidobro and Rohka (Chile), Carrera Andrade (Ecuador), Lopez (Colombia), and Velarde and Gorotiza (Mexico).

Bly, Robert, Ed., *Lorca and Jiménez*. The Seventies Press/Beacon, Boston, 1973, 193 pp.

Considering the fact that Lorca's poetry has been translated equally well elsewhere, and that Jiménez is not the kind of poet recommended for the classroom (light, though not lightheaded, an ethereal poetry that sounds very old-fashioned in translation) this book evokes little enthusiasm.

Bly, Robert, ed., *Neruda and Vallejo*. The Seventies Press/Beacon, Boston, 1971, 265 pp.

A solid selection of poems by the two great poets of Latin American literature commendably translated by James Wright, John Knoepfle, and Robert Bly.

Matilla, Alfredo and Ivan Silen, ed., *The Puerto Rican Poets; Los Poetas Puertorriquenos*. Bantam, New York, 1972, 238 pp. Out of print.

Twenty poets, from the post-Modernist period to the present, mostly writers who write in Spanish with two who write in English. With few exceptions, a poor selection poorly translated.

Mistral, Gabriela, *Selected Poems of Gabriela Mistral*, trans. & ed. by Doris Dana. John Hopkins University Press, Baltimore, 1971, 235pp. Cloth and Paper.

Powerful and human poems by the Chilean Nobel

Laureate perfectly suited for classroom use. Translations very fine.

Neruda, Pablo, *Elementary Odes*, trans. by Carlos Lozano. Las Americas Pub., New York, 1961, 155pp.

Well translated book of odes that the teacher will find useful because of their variety, wit and imagination.

Neruda, Pablo, *Five Decades: Poems (1925-1970)*, ed. & trans. by Ben Belitt. Grove Press, New York, 1974.

Combines three other Ben Belitt editions, *Selected Poems, New Decade (1958-1967)*, and *New Poems* (1968-1970). Good selection of Neruda's work, but the translations are often far from faithful.

Neruda, Pablo, *The Heights of Machu Picchu*, trans. by Nathaniel Tarn. Noonday, New York, 1967, 71 pp.

Entire 12-part poem extracted from *Residence on Earth*, well translated and published in book form. Original can be found (with respective translations) in *Five Decades* and *Residence on Earth*; the attraction here is the translation. A major contemporary work which would prove difficult for the average student.

Neruda, Pablo, *Residence on Earth*, trans. by Donald Walsh. New Directions, New York, 1973, 359 pp.

Existential fatalism and Surrealist technique characterize this book which has become Neruda's most celebrated in the United States. Smooth translations. Recommended for the classroom.

Parra, Nicanor, *Poems and Anti-Poems*, ed. by Miller Williams. New Directions, New York, 1967, 149 pp.

Parra is a Chilean poet. "Anti-poetry" here means anti-lyrical or anti-devices; a cool medium that yields good biting satire and black humor not without musicality of speech. Well-translated by a list of poet-translators; especially good for the urban classroom.

Parra, Nicanor, *Emergency Poems*, ed. and trans. by Miller Williams. New Directions, New York, 1972.

Parra's later poetry, angrier and more socially committed but less effective as poetry and not representative of the poet's present ideological position. Musicality of speech reduced to a lot of talk.

Paz, Octavio, *Configurations*, trans. by a list of poets, New Directions. New York, 1971, 198 pp.

Mysticism and metaphysics characterize the work of

this Mexican poet. Important poetry and well translated, but perhaps rough-going for the average student.

Strand, Mark, ed., *New Poetry of Mexico*. Dutton, New York, 1970, 224 pp.

A bilingual edition of the works of 24 contemporary Mexican poets selected from a larger anthology *Poesia en movimiento* edited in Spanish by Octavio Paz and four other younger poets. Much consideration is given to the English-language reader's taste in poetry, a factor which does make the bilingual edition an aesthetic success. The teacher should be warned that much of the poetry thrives in a metaphysical air which might make the anthology more suitable for the advanced student.

Tarn, Nathaniel, ed., *Con Cuba: Anthology of Cuban Poetry of the Last Sixty Years*. Grossman Publishers, New York, 1969, 144 pp.

Emphasis is given to the poetic response to the Cuban Revolution. Many of the poets were relatively young at the time they appear in this anthology, especially conscious of opening poetry to a broader spectrum of society than the literary. The result is a poetry accessible to the student.

Vallejo, Cesar, *Poemas Humanos, Human Poems*, translated by Clayton Eshleman. Grove Press, New York, 1968, 326 pp.

Strong, engrossing poems by the great Peruvian poet. At times, perhaps, a bit difficult for the average student but definitely required reading. Translations quite good.

Vallejo, Cesar, *Spain, Take This Cup From Me*, trans. by Clayton Eshleman. Grove Press, New York, 1974.

Vallejo's last volume. Stirring poems of the Spanish Civil War.

T&W At Work

Being with Children, by Phillip Lopate (Bantam Books). $1.95

From the moment he walked through the doors of "P.S. 90" to set up an arts program, Phillip Lopate realized that the attractive status of "artist" he carried with him had to be ground down into the very atoms that compose the daily life of a school. He knew he had to get closer, hang out, become one of the crowd at the coffee machine, abolish his specialness so he could work usefully rather than scaring people away with the laurel-crown of the *noli me tangere* poet. To do this he advanced with gentleness, understanding, and *chutzpah*, finding out the secret school hiding places only kids (and weary teachers) know, listening with commiseration and humor to the hip chatter of frustrated teachers, sizing up the principal and making friends. Most of all, he went to the children, to bring them what he knew, to listen to what they wanted.

Lopate writes his adventures in the style of the novel. (Chapter III, "The Big Show," is a novella-in-disguise about the staging of "West Side Story" at the school.) Immediately this focus brings the school community to life, pulling us inside the kids and the teachers as well as inside the author himself. How refreshing to witness a man who is the hero of his own daily round, doing what he knows how to do, giving his energies to the point of exhaustion, listening patiently, giving advice, getting angry, withdrawing to cool off. *Being with Children* is a brilliantly written book, and aside from the real wisdom it contains, the reader will delight in its "hidden" short stories, essays, nitty gritty instructional writing, and lively diary entries. As writing, *how* the book tells us becomes as important as *what* it tells us.

What Lopate carried into "P.S. 90" was not a bag of artsy tricks, but the quality of *humanitas* that seems more pressed out of our educational systems each day. That is, "humanness," "humanity,"—that wonderful Latin noun which suggests what it means to be human. Lopate's absorption in human relationship is a hallmark of his *humanitas*, and while it manifests itself throughout the book, the "Seven Lessons" section stresses it concretely: "Going Mad" (the absence of relationship); "Walking Around" (looking at people and things with the senses); "Eavesdropping" (listening in to the heart of another's uncensored self); "Portraits" (what we choose to depict, we are); and "The History of a Friendship" (how relationships grow and wane, the eternal subject of most great writing). But without its handmaiden, the quality of compassion, a relationship can be exploitative, brutal. If Lopate finds himself preoccupied with the problems of human relationships, he is kind, and knows how to stretch out a hand to the child who won't come forth from her "Land of Polka Dots" where nothing of the real is allowed in the cotton candy atmosphere; because to live is to feel, and to feel is to open oneself to the possibility of hurt. Yet, he knows when to give up, when to leave the resisting child alone, though it pains him to do so.

Lopate is a superb teacher and *Being with Children* is an essential book not merely because it is brimming with practical ideas for the classroom, which it is; it is important because Lopate never forgets that he is teaching human beings, not just poetry writing or filmmaking.

Bill Zavatsky

Contributors' Notes

REGINA BECK has two books of poems; *Headlines* (No Books) and *Looking at the Sun* (Telephone). Her poetry has appeared in *The World*, *Telephone*, *The Harris Review*, among other places. She was a teacher for Poets in the Schools for the past two years.

DAN CHEIFETZ . . . author of *Theatre in My Head* (Little, Brown), about children's improvisational theatre. He has led Teachers & Writers workshops in creative dramatics and related arts in Harlem and Queens public schools, and has trained teachers to use creative techniques in the classroom at CCNY, Lehman College and at several public and private schools.

LARRY FAGIN, poet and editor/publisher of *Adventures in Poetry* magazine and books, has worked in poet-in-the-schools programs throughout the U.S. since 1968, including a long association with writing workshops at the Brooklyn Children's Museum. A collection of his poems, *I'll Be Seeing You*, will appear late this year from Full Court Press.

AARON FOGEL, b. 1947 published his first book of poems, *Chain Hearings*, with Inwood/Horizon Press in 1976. He was a Kellett Fellow and holds degrees from Columbia and Cambridge.

SIDNEY GOLDFARB's two books of poetry, *Speech, For Instance*, and *Messages* were both published by Farrar, Straus and Giroux. He has taught at MIT and Harvard. He is currently teaching at the University of Colorado.

WILLIAM J. HIGGINSON, editor/publisher of From Here Press and *Haiku Magazine*, has poems, prose, and translations from Chinese and Japanese in *Center*, *The End*, *Small Press Review*, *Sun*, *The Ardis Anthology of New American Poetry*, and *The Haiku Anthology*. He has worked in Indiana, New Jersey, and Pennsylvania PITS Programs.

KAREN HUBERT is the author of *Teaching and Writing Popular Fiction in the American Classroom* (Teachers & Writers). Some of her articles and stories have appeared in *Learning*, *Sun*, *Nitty-Gritty*, and *Outerbridge*. She teaches writing for Teachers & Writers Collaborative, The Lincoln Center Program for Arts In the Schools and The New School for Social Research.

ARDIS KIMZEY is a poet, freelance reviewer and teacher. She is the former coordinator of the North Carolina Poetry in the Schools Program, and a member of the editorial staff of *The Southern Poetry Review*.

KENNETH KOCH is well known for his education books *Wishes, Lies and Dreams* (Vintage) and *Rose, Where Did You Get That Red* (Vintage). He has published several volumes of poetry including *Thank You and Other Poems* (Grove Press), *The Art of Love* (Vintage), and the forthcoming epic poem, *The Duplications* (Random House).

PHILLIP LOPATE is the author of *Being With Children*, a book about his teaching methods, published by Doubleday and Bantam Paperback. He has also written two books of poetry, *The Daily Round* and *The Eyes Don't Always Want to Stay Open*, both published by Sun Press. His articles and stories have appeared in *The American Review*. The *New York Times*, *The Paris Review*, and *The Best American Short Stories of 1974*. He generally teaches at P.S. 75 in Manhattan for Teachers & Writers Collaborative.

LEWIS MACADAMS latest book is a long poem, called *News From Niman Farm* (Tumbouctou Press, distributed by Serendipity in Berkeley). Kulchur Press will publish a new book of poems in the Spring of 1977. MacAdams is the director of the Poetry Center at San Francisco State University, which administers The Poetry in the Schools Program for the State of California.

THERESA MACK teaches video and film at P.S. 75. She has produced several videotapes and films, run community media centers, and presently teaches video for the Graduate Program at the New School for Social Research.

ANNE MARTIN is currently a fourth grade teacher at the Lawrence School, Brookline, Mass. She previously taught in New York City, London, and Amherst, Mass. She has published articles in *Elementary English*, *Teachers & Writers Collaborative Magazine*, and the *Harvard Educational Review*.

JULIO MARZAN presently teaches at Fordham University and has recently received a N.Y. State Creative Arts in Public Service (CAPS) Fellowship for Poetry, 1976-77.

ROSE KATZ ORTIZ coordinates the Reading, Writing and Study Skills Center at The College of Staten Island. She studied with and worked for Dr. Caleb Gattegno. She has taught beginning and remedial reading in elementary and secondary schools as well as in college.

RON PADGETT has published ten books, poetry, prose and translation, the most recent of which are *Toujours l'amour* (poetry, Sun Press, N.Y.) and *The Poems of A.O. Barnabooth* by Valery Larbaud (translated with Bill Zavatsky, Mushinsha Ltd., Tokyo). He has been associated with Teachers & Writers Collaborative since 1968.

RICHARD PERRY teaches at Pratt Institute. His first novel *Changes* was published by Bobbs-Merrill.

MARY SCHERBATSKOY is co-director of ARTS Inc. for 6 years. ARTS Inc. is a resource and development project in Arts in Education, with special attention to Chinese and Puerto Rican cultures, working in the public elementary schools of the Chinatown area of New York City. ARTS Inc. also publishes materials on these cultures.

DAVID SHAPIRO has published four books of poetry and has been nominated for the National Book Award. He has taught poetry to children since 1964 and is an Assistant Professor of English at Columbia University. A new book of poetry, *Lateness*, will be published by Overlook/Viking Press.

RON SHAPIRO has worked with Ron Padgett when he was a Poet-In-Residence in the Newark School District in Delaware (Spring 1975). He spent nearly nine months traveling through India and has a deep interest in Eastern religions. He was co-editor of *Cosmic Feelings*, an anthology of creative writing by junior high school students. He is currently teaching English at Conrad Senior High School in Wilmington, Delaware.

BARBARA SIEGEL is an artist living and working in New York City. She recently had a show of paintings and drawings at Briarcliff College. Her work is in the permanent collection of the Newark Museum. She teaches at P.S. 11 in Brooklyn.

BOB SIEVERT is an artist, teacher, and writer. He has been showing his paintings in New York at the Green Mountain Gallery for the last five years. He teaches regularly at P.S. 84 Manhattan and C.S. 152 in the Bronx. He is a regular art critic for *Womanart*

Magazine and the *Staten Island Advance*. His writing on teaching has appeared in *Teachers and Writers Magazine* and in *Learning Magazine*.

CHRISTINE SMITH's poems have appeared in a number of magazines including *Some* and *Clown War*. A book of her poetry is forthcoming from Konglomerati Press. Former director of an alternative school in Florida, she teaches writing at P.S. 152 in the Bronx and has recently completed work on a Teachers & Writers research grant from the National Institute of Education studying the effects of creative writing programs on children's literacy.

TOM VEITCH is the author of *Death College & Other Poems* (Big Sky Books, Bolinas, CA.) and *The Luis Armed Story* (Full Court Press, NYC). Tom was educated at Columbia College in New York City and wrote his first novel in 1962. From 1965 to 1968 he was a cloistered Benedictine monk in Weston, Vermont. Since that time he has lived and worked in San Francisco. He has written six novels, a screenplay, edited a magazine (*Tom Veitch Magazine*), been a printer, and scripted underground comicbooks. In 1973 he received the Big Table Award for Poetry. He spent three years in Jungian analysis, and has done extensive research in dream symbolism and archetypal images.

MEREDITH SUE WILLIS has taught story-writing, drama improvization, poetry, comics, film editing, exercises for the aged, swimming and Sunday School. Her fiction has appeared in *Story Quarterly*, *Mademoiselle*, *Epoch*, and *Minnesota Review*.

BILL ZAVATSKY has taught workshops for Teachers and Writers since January of 1971, first at P.S. 84 in Manhattan and currently at J.H.S. 141 in the Bronx, N.Y. He is the author of *Theories of Rain and Other Poems* (SUN) and the director of SUN, which publishes volumes of poetry and SUN magazine. In 1976 he was the winner of a CAPS Fellowship from the New York State Council on the Arts. Besides co-editing *The Whole Word Catalogue 2* with Ron Padgett, he and Ron have also co-translated *The Poems of A.O. Barnabooth* by Valery Larbaud, due out this year from Mushinsha Ltd.

ALAN ZIEGLER, a member of Teachers & Writers Collaborative since 1974, also conducts writing workshops for Poets-in-the-Schools and Poets and Writers, Inc. He has taught at the college level and worked as a journalist. His poetry and prose have been published in such places as *Paris Review*, *American Poetry Review*, *Poetry Now*, *The Village Voice*, and the *Ardis Anthology of New American Poetry*. He is co-editor of *Some* and Release Press, and his books of poetry include *Planning Escape*.

Index

ACKNOWLEDGMENTS

"The Art of Poetry" from *The Art of Love* by Kenneth Koch. Copyright © 1972, 1974, 1975 by Kenneth Koch. Reprinted by permission of Random House, Inc.

"Daddy," "Brother," "Supper," "The Candle's Light," and "Lily" from *There Are Two Lives: Poems by Children of Japan* compiled by Richard Lewis and translated by Haruna Kimura. Copyright © 1970 by Richard Lewis and Haruna Kimura. Reprinted by permission of Simon & Schuster, Inc.

"The Base Stealer" from *The Orb Weaver* by Robert Francis. Copyright © 1948 by Robert Francis. Reprinted by permission of Wesleyan University Press.

"To England" from *The Pill Versus the Springhill Mine Disaster* by Richard Brautigan. Copyright © 1968 by Richard Brautigan. Reprinted by permission of Delacorte Press/Seymour Lawrence.

"The Room" from *Burning the Empty Nests* by Gregory Orr. Copyright © 1973 by Gregory Orr. Reprinted by permission of Harper & Row, Publishers.

"Fog clings. . ." from *The Silent Firefly* translated by Eric Sackheim. Copyright © in Japan 1963 by Kodansha International, Ltd. Reprinted by permission of Kodansha International.

"came to a mirror shop. . ." from *Takuboku: Poems to Eat* translated by Carl Sesar. Copyright © in Japan 1966 by Kodansha International, Ltd. Reprinted by permission of Kodansha International.

"The Sign Board" from *For Love, Poems 1950-1960* by Robert Creeley. Copyright © 1962 by Robert Creeley. Reprinted by permission of Charles Scribner's Sons.

"Into" from *Blue* by Tom Clark. Copyright © 1974 by Tom Clark. Reprinted by permission of The Black Sparrow Press.

"An Unemployed Machinist" from *Balling Buddha* by John Giorno. Copyright © 1970 by John Giorno. Reprinted by permission of The Kulchur Foundation and the author.

"The Moment of Contemplation" from *Over the Rim* by Tom Meschery. Copyright © by Tom Meschery. Reprinted by permission of the author.

"Exile's Letter" from *Personae* by Ezra Pound. Copyright © 1926 by Ezra Pound. Reprinted by permission of New Directions Publishing Corporation.

"Property" from *Testimony: The United States 1885-1890* by Charles Reznikoff. Copyright © 1965 by Charles Reznikoff. Reprinted by permission of New Directions Publishing Corporation.

"Proletarian Portrait," "Poem (As the cat. . .)," "This is Just to Say," and "The Red Wheelbarrow" from *Collected Earlier Poems* by William Carlos Williams. Copyright © 1938 by New Directions Publishing Corporation. Reprinted by permission of New Directions Publishing Corporation.

"The Artist" from *Pictures from Brueghel and Other Poems* by William Carlos Williams. Copyright © 1954 by William Carlos Williams. Reprinted by permission of New Directions Publishing Corporation.

"The elevator man, working long hours" in *By the Waters of Manhattan* by Charles Reznikoff. Copyright © 1941 by Charles Reznikoff. Reprinted by permission of New Directions Publishing Corporation.

"To Susan B., of Boston Massachusetts" by Luc Sante. Reprinted by permission of the author.

"Stone" from *Dismantling the Silence* by Charles Simic. Copyright © 1971 by Charles Simic. Reprinted by permission of George Braziller, Inc.

"The new janitor is Puerto Rican" in *By the Well of Living & Seeing: New & Selected Poems 1918-1973* by Charles Reznikoff. Reprinted by permission of Marie Syrkin and The Black Sparrow Press.

"The Paper Cutter" by David Ignatow. Copyright © 1961 by David Ignatow. Reprinted from *Say Pardon* by permission of Wesleyan University Press.

"Magic Words" translated by Edward Field in *Songs and Stories of the Netsilik Eskimoes*, part of *Man: A Course of Study* developed by EDC school and society programs under a grant from the National Science Foundation. Text copyright © 1967, 1968 by Education Development Center, Inc. Used with permission.

TEACHERS & WRITERS COLLABORATIVE PUBLICATIONS

THE WHOLE WORD CATALOG (72 pages) is a practical collection of assignments for stimulating student writing, designed for both elementary and secondary students. Activities designed as catalysts for classroom exercises include: personal writing, collective novels, diagram stories, fables, spoof and parodies, and language games. It also contains an annotated bibliography.

IMAGINARY WORLDS (110 pages) originated from Richard Murphy's desire to find themes of sufficient breadth and interest to allow sustained, independent writing by students. Children invented their own Utopias of time and place, invented their own religions, new ways of fighting wars, different schools. They produced a great deal of extraordinary writing, much of it reprinted in the book.

A DAY DREAM I HAD AT NIGHT (120 pages) is a collection of oral literature from children who were not learning to read well or write competently or feel any sense of satisfaction in school. The author, Roger Landrum, working in collaboration with two elementary school teachers, made class readers out of the children's own work.

FIVE TALES OF ADVENTURE (119 pages) is a new collection of short novels written by children at a Manhattan elementary school. The stories cover a wide range of styles and interests—a family mystery, an urban satire, a Himalayan adventure, a sci-fi spoof, and a tale of murder and retribution.

BEING WITH CHILDREN, a book by Phillip Lopate, whose articles have appeared regularly in our magazine, is based on his work as project coordinator for Teachers & Writers Collaborative at P.S. 75 in Manhattan. Herb Kohl writes: "There is no other book that I know that combines the personal and the practical so well. . . ." *Being With Children* is published by Doubleday at $7.95. It is available through Teachers & Writers Collaborative for $7.00.

TEACHING AND WRITING POPULAR FICTION: HORROR, ADVENTURE, MYSTERY AND ROMANCE IN THE AMERICAN CLASSROOM by Karen Hubert (236 pages). A new step-by-step guide on using the different literary genres to help students to write, based on the author's intensive workshops conducted for Teachers & Writers in elementary and secondary schools. Ms. Hubert explores the psychological necessities of each genre and discusses the various ways of tailoring each one to individual students. Includes hundreds of "recipes" to be used as story starters, with an anthology of student work to show the exciting results possible.

TEACHERS & WRITERS Magazine, issued three times a year, draws together the experience and ideas of the writers and other artists who conduct T & W workshops in schools and community groups. A typical issue contains excerpts from the detailed work diaries and articles of the artists, along with the works of the students and outside contributions.

 Teachers&Writers   186 West 4th Street, New York, New York 10014